HELLENISTIC CULTURE AND SOCIET

General Editors: Anthony W. Bulloch, Eri
and Andrew F. Stewart

I. *Alexander to Actium: The Historical* -sc,
by Peter Green

II. *Hellenism in the East: The Interaction of Greek and Non-Greek Civilizations from Syria to Central Asia after Alexander*, edited by Amélie Kuhrt and Susan Sherwin-White

III. *The Question of "Eclecticism": Studies in Later Greek Philosophy*, edited by J. M. Dillon and A. A. Long

IV. *Antigonos the One-Eyed and the Creation of the Hellenistic State*, by Richard A. Billows

V. *A History of Macedonia*, by R. Malcolm Errington, translated by Catherine Errington

VI. *Attic Letter-Cutters of 229 to 86 B.C.*, by Stephen V. Tracy

VII. *The Vanished Library: A Wonder of the Ancient World*, by Luciano Canfora

VIII. *Hellenistic Philosophy of Mind*, by Julia Annas

IX. *Hellenistic History and Culture*, edited by Peter Green

X. *The Best of the Argonauts: The Redefinition of the Epic Hero in Book One of Apollonius' Argonautica*, by James J. Clauss

XI. *Faces of Power: Alexander's Image and Hellenistic Politics*, by Andrew Stewart

XII. *Images and Ideologies: Self-definition in the Hellenistic World*, edited by A. W. Bulloch, E. S. Gruen, A. A. Long, and A. Stewart

XIII. *From Samarkhand to Sardis: A New Approach to the Seleucid Empire*, by Susan Sherwin-White and Amélie Kuhrt

XIV. *Regionalism and Change in the Economy of Independent Delos, 314–167 B.C.*, by Gary Reger

XV. *Hegemony to Empire: The Development of the Roman Imperium in the East from 148 to 62 B.C.*, by Robert Kallet-Marx

XVI. *Moral Vision in the Histories of Polybius*, by Arthur M. Eckstein

XVII. *The Hellenistic Settlements in Europe, The Islands, and Asia Minor*, by Getzel M. Cohen

XVIII. *Interstate Arbitrations in the Greek World, 337–90 B.C.*, by Sheila L. Ager

XIX. *Theocritus's Urban Mimes: Mobility, Gender, and Patronage*, by Joan B. Burton

XX. *Athenian Democracy in Transition: Attic Letter Cutters of 340 to 290 B.C.*, by Stephen V. Tracy

XXI. *Pseudo-Hecataeus, "On the Jews": Legitimizing the Jewish Diaspora*, by Bezalel Bar-Kochva

XXII. *Asylia: Territorial Inviolability in the Hellenistic World*, by Kent J. Rigsby

XXIII. *The Cynics: The Cynic Movement in Antiquity and Its Legacy*, R. Bracht Branham and Marie-Odile Goulet-Cazé, editors

XXIV. *The Politics of Plunder: Aitolians and their* Koinon *in the Early Hellenistic Era, 279–217 B.C.*, by Joseph B. Scholten

XXV. *The Argonautika* by Apollonios Rhodios, translated, with introduction, commentary, and glossary, by Peter Green

XXVI. *Hellenistic Constructs: Culture, History, and Historiography*, edited by Paul Cartledge, Peter Garnsey, and Erich Gruen

XXVII. *Josephus' Interpretation of the Bible*, by Louis H. Feldman

XXVIII. *Poetic Garlands: Hellenistic Epigrams in Context*, by Kathryn J. Gutzwiller

Antigonos the One-Eyed
and the Creation of the Hellenistic State

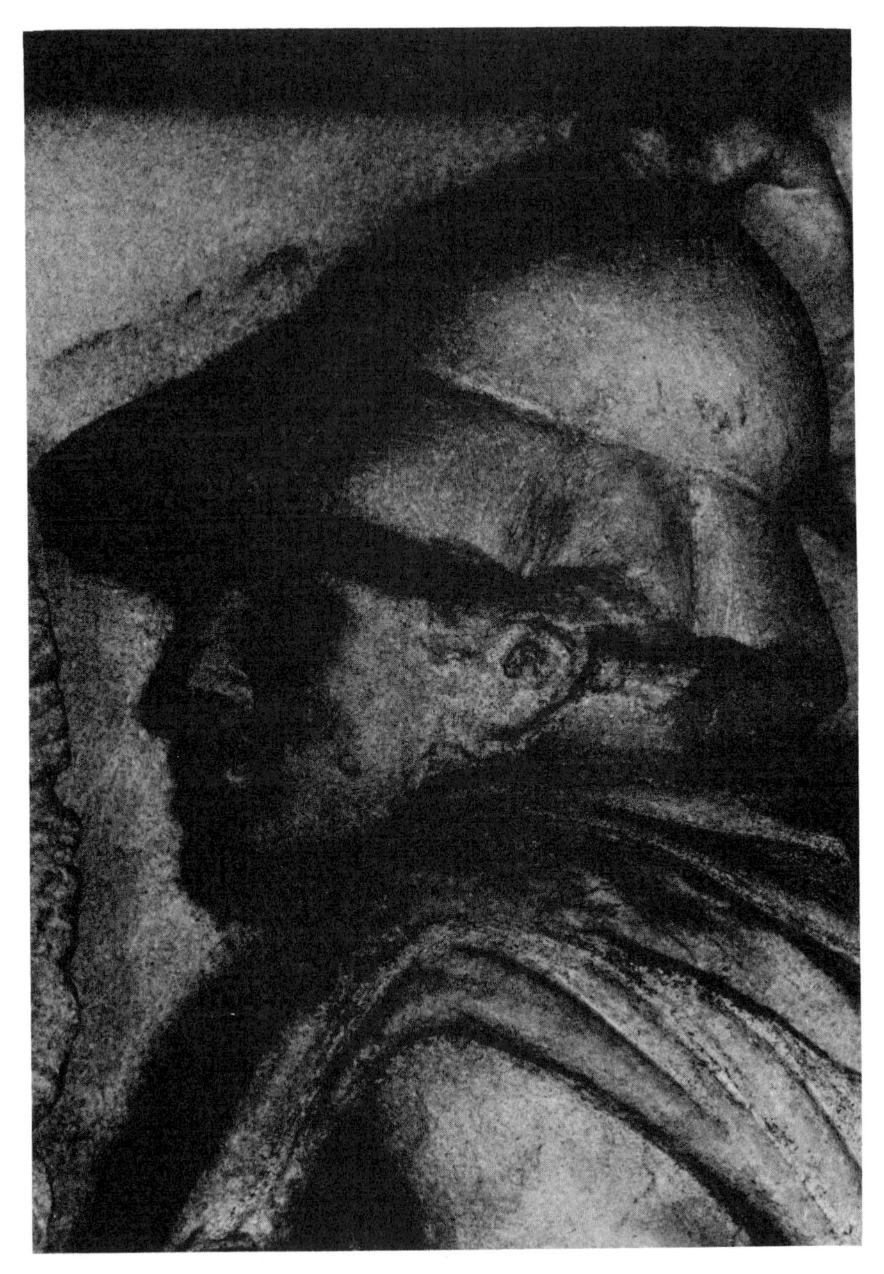

A Macedonian Horseman depicted on the "Alexander Sarcophagus" in the Archaeological Museum, Istanbul. Possibly intended to be Antigonos Monophthalmos. (Photo by Herr Dieter Johannes, courtesy of Professor V. von Graeve.)

Antigonos the One-Eyed and the Creation of the Hellenistic State

Richard A. Billows

UNIVERSITY OF CALIFORNIA PRESS

BERKELEY LOS ANGELES LONDON

University of California Press
Berkeley and Los Angeles, California
University of California Press, Ltd.
London, England
©1990 by
The Regents of the University of California
First Paperback Printing 1997

Library of Congress Cataloging-in-Publication Data

Billows, Richard A.
Antigonos the One-eyed and the creation of the Hellenistic state / Richard A. Billows
p. cm.—(Hellenistic culture and society ; 4)
Bibliography: p.
Includes index.
ISBN 0-520-20880-3 (alk. paper)
1. Antigonus I, King of Macedonia, 382–301 B.C. 2. Macedonia—History—Diadochi, 323–276 B.C. 3. Greece—History—Macedonian Hegemony, 323–281 B.C. 4. Macedonia—Kings and rulers—Bibliography. I. Title. II. Series.
DF235.48A57B55 1990
938'.108'0924—dc19
[B] 89-4677
CIP

Printed in the United States of America

1 2 3 4 5 6 7 8 9

The paper used in this publication meets the minimum requirements of American National Standard for Information Sciences—Permanence of Paper for Printed Library Materials, ANSI Z39.48-1984. ♾

This work is dedicated to Ann,
en dit werk is ook gewijd aan Oom Max en Tante Frans.

History has many cunning passages, contrived corridors
And issues, deceives with whispering ambitions,
Guides us by vanities. Think now
She gives when our attention is distracted
And what she gives, gives with such supple confusions
That the giving famishes the craving. Gives too late
What's not believed in, or if still believed,
In memory only, reconsidered passion. Gives too soon
Into weak hands, what's thought can be dispensed with
Till the refusal propagates a fear.

T. S. Eliot, *Gerontion*

Contents

List of Illustrations

List of Abbreviations

Note: Abbreviated titles of books cited in the Bibliography are given in parentheses there following the relevant entries. Abbreviations used for most epigraphic, papyrological, and cuneiform sources will be found in the List of Sources.

ABSA	*Annual of the British School at Athens.*
AC	*L'Antiquité classique.*
AClass	*Acta classica.*
AE	*Archaiologikē ephēmeris.*
AIV	*Atti dell'istituto veneto di scienze, lettere, ed arte.*
AJA	*American Journal of Archaeology.*
AJPh	*American Journal of Philology.*
AM	*Mitteilungen des Deutschen Archäologischen Instituts, Athenische Abteilung.*
AncSoc	*Ancient Society.*
AncW	*Ancient World.*
Arch. Mak.	*Archaia Makedonia* (Ancient Macedonia). Papers of the international symposia at Thessaloniki on pre-Byzantine Macedon.
ASAA	*Annuario della scuola di archeologia in Atene.*
AUMLA	*Journal of the Australasian Universities Language and Literature Association.*
AUT	*Annali delle università toscane.*
BCH	*Bulletin de correspondence hellénique.*
BEFAR	*Bulletin des Ecoles françaises d'Athènes et de Rome.*

BN	*Beiträge zur Namenforschung.*
CA	*Classical Antiquity.*
CAH	*Cambridge Ancient History.*
CE	*Chronique d'Egypte.*
CPh	*Classical Philology.*
CQ	*Classical Quarterly.*
CR	*Classical Review.*
CRAI	*Comptes rendus de l'Académie des Inscriptions et Belles-Lettres.*
FGrH	*Fragmente der griechischen Historiker* (F. Jacoby, editor).
G & R	*Greece and Rome.*
GGM	*Geographici Graeci minores* (E. Miller, editor).
GRBS	*Greek, Roman, and Byzantine Studies.*
HSCPh	*Harvard Studies in Classical Philology.*
IG	*Inscriptiones Graecae.*
JClPh	*Jahrbuch für classische Philologie.*
JHS	*Journal of Hellenic Studies.*
JÖAI	*Jahreshefte des Österreichischen Archäologischen Instituts.*
MH	*Museum Helveticum.*
Misc. Acad. Berol.	*Miscellanea Academica Berolinensia.*
NC	*Numismatic Chronicle.*
OGIS	*Orientis Graeci inscriptiones selectae* (W. Dittenberger, editor).
OLP	*Orientalia Lovaniensia periodica.*
PACA	*Proceedings of the African Classical Association.*
PCPhS	*Proceedings of the Cambridge Philological Society.*
PP	*La parola del passato.*
PSI	*Publicazioni della società italiana per la ricerca dei papiri greci e latini in Egitto* (G. Vitelli, M. Norsa et al., editors).
RAss	*Revue d'Assyriologie.*
RBPh	*Revue Belge de philologie et d'histoire.*
RdA	*Rivista di archeologia.*
RE	*Paulys Real-Encyclopädie der classischen Altertumswissenschaft.*
REA	*Revue des études anciennes.*
REG	*Revue des études grecques.*
RFIC	*Rivista di filologia e d'istruzione classica.*
RhM	*Rheinisches Museum für Philologie.*

RIN	*Rivista italiana di numismatica.*
RN	*Revue numismatique.*
RPAA	*Rendiconti della pontificia academia di archeologia.*
RPh	*Revue de philologie.*
SDAW	*Sitzungsberichte des Deutschen Akademie der Wissenschaften zu Berlin.*
SEG	*Supplementum epigraphicum Graecum.*
SIFC	*Studi italiani di filologia classica.*
Syll.	*Sylloge inscriptionum Graecarum* (3d ed., W. Dittenberger, editor).
TAPhA	*Transactions and Proceedings of the American Philological Association.*
VSWG	*Vierteljahresschrift für Sozial- und Wirtschaftsgeschichte.*
ZPE	*Zeitschrift für Papyrologie und Epigraphik.*

Preface

This book, a revised and reorganized version of my Ph.D. dissertation, completed for the University of California at Berkeley in 1985, is in large part a biography. In writing it I have had to face the problem I imagine all biographers face: that they come to like or dislike their subject, with consequent danger to objectivity. It will be obvious to the reader that I rather like and admire my subject, Antigonos Monophthalmos, but I hope that this has not colored my treatment of him here: I have certainly tried to remain objective.

A feature of this book that the reader needs to be warned about in advance is the spelling of Greek names. It used to be the custom to latinize the spelling of Greek names in English—for example, Cassander for Kassandros, Antipater for Antipatros, and so on—but I see no reason to perpetuate this curious habit. Instead, I adhere to Greek spelling of Greek personal and geographic names, but not entirely consistently. Some names of people and places are so familiar in their latinized form that it seems to me excessively pedantic to change them back to Greek spelling. Thus I refer throughout this work to Athens rather than Athenai, Thebes rather than Thebai, Cyprus rather than Kypros, and so forth; likewise I retain the latinized spelling for Alexander the Great, Philip of Macedon, and Ptolemy of Egypt. This has the added advantage of distinguishing these three famous men from all other bearers of the very common names Alexandros, Philippos, and Ptolemaios in my text. I should further mention that, while I have tried to use all relevant scholarly literature up to 1985, works appearing after that date have necessarily been used only very selectively.

It is a pleasure here to acknowledge the help, advice, and support of many scholars and friends who have been of incalculable aid in the production of this book. In the first place there are my Ph.D. advisers, Raphael Sealey, Ronald Stroud, and Erich Gruen, who with extraordinary patience read and gave their comments on the inordinately long first version. Erich Gruen above all has been an indefatigable source of scholarly criticism, useful advice, and friendly support, not only during the Ph.D. phase of the work but during subsequent revisions with a view to publication. Christian Habicht, while visiting Berkeley as a Sather Professor in 1982, was of immense help in initiating me into the mysteries of Greek epigraphy, and subsequently very kindly read and commented on large portions of the manuscript, to my great advantage. I should also mention with gratitude the Regents of the University of California for making available a travel fellowship which enabled me to visit Turkey and Greece when I was doing research for this book in 1983; the staff of the British School at Athens for their hospitality; and Mrs. Molizani of the Epigraphical Museum at Athens for allowing me to examine several inscriptions there. Furthermore, fellow students at Berkeley also contributed in numerous discussions of early Hellenistic history both in and out of the classroom: in particular Joe Scholten, Brady Kiesling, and my wife, Ann Kuttner.

Since moving to Columbia University I have received support and encouragement from a variety of sources: the Center for Research in the Social Sciences at Columbia provided a stipend enabling me to visit Greece again in 1986 to clear up some loose ends of research; my colleague William Harris has been uniformly helpful and supportive; and Roger Bagnall very kindly read through an earlier version of this book and provided numerous helpful comments. Columbia University's generosity in the matter of faculty research funds has greatly helped me to defray the costs of preparing this work. For all of this I am deeply grateful.

In the process of consideration for publication by the University of California Press, the book was read by Peter Green and August Frugé. Their criticisms were an invaluable guide in the reorganization of what was in some respects a verbose and diffuse dissertation into a much tighter and more carefully structured work. Finally, the staff of the University of California Press, especially the acquisitions editor for Classics, Doris Kretschmer, production editor Mary Lamprech, and copyeditor Peter Dreyer, and the reader of the Press's Editorial Committee, Buchanan Sharp, have been helpful in more ways than I can easily set out here.

Needless to say I have often disagreed with the various readers and other helpers whom I have identified above, and stubbornly insisted on doing things my own way; but I do thank all of them for their efforts and assure them that, however recalcitrant I may have been at times, I am well aware that without the input of all of them, this book, whatever its flaws and merits, would have been very much inferior to its present state.

Introduction

Antigonos Monophthalmos (the One-Eyed), the greatest of Alexander the Great's successors (the Diadochoi), is not so well known a figure as to need no introduction—certainly not as well known as he ought to be. In modern times, as in ancient, he has been overshadowed by his contemporaries Philip II and Alexander the Great, whose achievements have captured the imagination much more than have those of Antigonos. The reason for this is not far to seek: Antigonos ended his life in defeat, and so is regarded merely as an interesting failure. But he was responsible for important and lasting achievements in spite of his final defeat, which entitle him to more careful historical scrutiny than he has yet been accorded.[1]

Antigonos was an exact contemporary of Philip II of Macedon, but outlived that king by thirty-five years and enjoyed his greatest and most prominent period after the death of Philip's son, Alexander, in 323. From 320, when he was sixty-two, until his death aged eighty-one at the battle of Ipsos in 301, Antigonos dominated the eastern Mediterranean region and rose from private station to make himself and his descendants kings. In so doing, he established an administrative system and structure in western Asia that formed the basis for the

1. In the past twenty or so years a number of works about Antigonos have been published, but none can claim to be a full and thorough biographical treatment: Wehrli's *Antigone et Démétrios* is quite full on Demetrios, but sketchy on Antigonos, especially before 320; Briant's *Antigone le Borgne* only deals with Antigonos's career down to 320, stopping just when things begin to get interesting. Admittedly partial treatments of Antigonos's career in monograph form are Engel's *Untersuchungen zum Machtaufstieg des Antigonos I Monophthalmos* and Müller's *Antigonos Monophthalmos und das "Jahr der Könige."*

later Seleukid Empire. There are therefore two themes to be covered in this book: the life and activities of Antigonos Monophthalmos (part 1); and the creation, in large part due to Antigonos's efforts, of a new state system from the wreck of the Persian Empire conquered by Alexander—Hellenistic monarchy, the political milieu of Hellenistic civilization (part 2).

Though the writing of history from a biographical viewpoint is nowadays rather discredited in some circles, to ancient historiographers it seemed a self-evident truism that great leaders were directly and personally responsible for the course of historical events. Consequently our literary sources for the ancient world are written from the viewpoint of what may be called the "great leader theory of history": we have a great deal of information about the political, military, and cultural leaders of the ancient world, but very little about social and economic conditions except what can be gathered from incidental remarks in the sources and from non-literary evidence (that is, archaeological, epigraphical, and numismatic evidence).

Antigonos dominates the literary sources for the period 323–301, towering like a colossus in the narratives of this period: he is the central character in the narrative of Diodoros of Sicily, our best and fullest surviving source, and he plays a major role likewise in Plutarch's biographies of his enemy Eumenes and his son Demetrios, as well as in book 4 of Polyainos's *Strategemata*.[2] To some extent this prominence is no doubt due to the fact that the most important and influential primary historian of the period was Antigonos's officer Hieronymos of Kardia, but it is clear that Antigonos was in fact the leading figure of the period, who more than any other leader shaped the course of events in the decades after Alexander's death.[3]

Since the ancient historian must necessarily use ancient historiography as a major source of information, it is inevitable that many works of ancient history should be strongly oriented towards the leading men of antiquity; and since an exaggerated respect for "great men" was an important feature of the ancient world, the biographical tendency of much work on ancient history should not be considered regrettable. Indeed, in the ancient world, with rather static social and

2. On the extant sources and their relative importance, see app. 1, pp. 341–52.

3. For Hieronymos and the other lost primary sources, see app. 1, pp. 329–40. For modern recognition of Antigonos's dominance of the period 323–301, see, e.g., Will, *Histoire politique*, 1:45–83, "L'Epoque d'Antigonos le Borgne"; Jouguet, *Macedonian Imperialism and the Hellenisation of the East*, pt. 2, chap. 2, "Antigonos"; now also Will in the *Cambridge Ancient History*, 2d ed., 7.1, chap. 2.2, "The Period of Antigonus Monophthalmus (321–301)."

economic conditions and societies dominated by small elites, great individuals did have a more profound impact than in today's mass societies. The absence of an in-depth treatment of Antigonos has long been noted as a major gap in scholarship on the Diadoch period.[4] This absence is the more unfortunate in that it has allowed a wrong perception of Antigonos and his role in the developments of the late fourth century to be perpetuated, a perception based on hindsight value judgments in the ancient sources rather than on the factual information they purvey. It is well known that Hellenistic historiography was influenced by tragic drama, and Antigonos has certainly suffered from this: "Pride goeth before a fall," and since Antigonos fell at the end of his life, he must have been guilty of hubris.

The ancient sources mostly portray Antigonos as an arrogant man of overweening ambition, driven by a fixed dream of ruling all of Alexander's empire, and intolerant of any rivals or peers; and this is also the standard view of Antigonos to be found in modern scholarship.[5] In fact, some scholars have even gone so far in the notion of Antigonos as an emulator of Alexander as to describe him as being "of the school of Alexander."[6] This is absurd. If Antigonos was of anyone's "school," it was that of Philip, the great leader and reformer under whom he lived and served for twenty-three years during his early manhood (from the ages of twenty-three to forty-six), rising ultimately to an important position in the state. He was for a few years—336–333—a senior adviser of Alexander, but was left behind by Alexander to govern part of Asia Minor and so played no role in Alexander's romantic (but foolhardy) exploits in the far east. Far from emulating Alexander, Antigonos never showed any interest in the eastern regions of the Persian Empire that so fascinated Alexander, but concentrated his ambitions instead on the eastern Mediterranean lands, on which Philip's great general Parmenion is said to have advised Alexander to base his empire.[7] In this Antigonos showed

---

4. Thus, e.g., Ehrenberg, *Greek State,* 2d ed., p. 278: "On Antigonos I much has been written, though there is still no comprehensive work"; and cf. the reiteration of this point by Seibert, *Zeitalter der Diadochen,* p. 196.

5. For the standard view of Antigonos as obsessed with ruling the entire empire of Alexander, it will be sufficient to refer to Will in the *CAH* (cited in n. 3 above) restating a view already expressed in his *Histoire politique.*

6. Thus Tarn, *Hellenistic Military and Naval Developments,* p. 34; cf. also Devine, *AncW* 12, nos. 3/4 (1985):75–86.

7. Arrian (*Anab.* II 25,1–2) reports that when Dareios offered to cede Asia west of the Euphrates to Alexander in return for peace, Parmenion urged acceptance. Some scholars believe Parmenion's advice reflects the aims Philip had in mind in planning to invade Asia (e.g., Ellis, *Philip II and Macedonian Imperialism,* pp. 227–34).

sound strategic sense, for under ancient conditions of communications, it was obviously unrealistic for a power drawing its strength from the Balkans to attempt long-term domination of regions as distant as Baktria and India, and the attempt to do so was more likely to prove a drain on power and resources than a boost to them.

Instead of accepting the sources' judgments of Antigonos at face value, it is necessary to scrutinize the evidence carefully and seek to understand the basis for such judgments. Analysis of the course of events shows that Antigonos's aims and ambitions changed and developed during the years 323–301;[8] that at least as late as 311 he was ready and willing to accept peers as independent rulers of parts of the Macedonian Empire, confining his own interest to western Asia and Greece; and that he never entertained serious ambitions to rule the far east. The charges in the sources of Antigonos's arrogance and overweening ambition derive in large part from the propaganda of his enemies and from retrojection from his last years, when he did, in a burst of embittered aggressiveness, seek to eliminate his rivals.[9] It needs to be recognized that the sources in fact have an obsession with the idea of the Diadoch period as a scramble for supreme power over all of Alexander's empire, an aim attributed to Kassandros and Ptolemy as well as Antigonos, and which is obviously a product of hindsight review of the conflicts of the period.[10] A recently published papyrus fragment indicates that this view of the period was already

8. This was pointed out by Cloché, "Remarques sur les étapes de l'ambition d'Antigone Ier jusqu'en 316 av. J.-C."

9. Note that the charges of arrogance against Antigonos at Diod. XVIII 52,4; XIX 56,2; and XX 106,3 in each case report the views of his enemies (Arrhidaios, Seleukos, and Kassandros respectively). This is not to say that Antigonos was not at times harsh and arrogant: he was. But it was only his enemies who made this his main characteristic, though they were themselves really no better: see Ptolemy's seizure of Laomedon's satrapy of Syria in 319 (Diod. XVIII 43, 1–2; Appian *Syr.* 52); Lysimachos's relations with Seuthes (Diod. XVIII 14,2–4; XIX 73,8–9) and later with Kassandros's son Antipatros (Justin XVI 2,4); and Seleukos's conquest of the upper satrapies between 307 and 302, involving hostilities with satraps such as Stasanor of Baktria (Justin XV 4,12; Schober, *Gesch. Babyloniens*, pp. 148–51). See, too, n. 27 below.

10. Diod. XVIII 49,2 reports that Kassandros aimed at supreme power; Diod. XX 37,3–4 has Ptolemy aiming at supreme power by marriage to Alexander's sister Kleopatra, and accuses Kassandros, Lysimachos, Antigonos, and "in general all the leaders who were important after Alexander's death" of seeking the same. Plut. *Dem.* 15,3 says that it was universally accepted that it was supreme power that was at stake at the battle of Salamis between Ptolemy and Demetrios in 306. This last was falsified by the event, and the idea no doubt derives from Antigonos's assumption of the kingship as a result of Demetrios's victory. The hindsight nature of this obsession with supreme power is further shown by the premature attribution of such ambition to Antigonos as early as 323 (Plut. *Eum.* 3,3), when he was merely satrap of Phrygia.

prevalent by the second century B.C., and that the attribution of excessive ambition to Antigonos is probably at least in part due to inimical Rhodian evaluations influenced by (and glorifying) Rhodes's successful war against Antigonos in 305/4.[11]

Besides being the first comprehensive treatment of the leader who dominated the last two decades of the fourth century, therefore, my work is a fundamental reappraisal of the aims and significance of Antigonos's activities. In further pursuance of this, part 2 of this book focuses for the first time on his contribution to the process of state building which began to develop the procedures and institutions characteristic of the Hellenistic monarchies, and of the Seleukid Empire especially.[12] Antigonos, as the first of the Diadochoi to take the royal title, had a decisive impact on the form and nature of Hellenistic kingship. He was also the leader who established respect for the local autonomy of the Greek *poleis* as a guiding principle, and so determined the outline of relations between the ruling powers of the Mediterranean world and the Greek city-states throughout the Hellenistic period. Though the evidence is not as full as one might wish, careful analysis shows beyond reasonable doubt that Antigonos established a comprehensive administrative structure in west Asia (especially Asia Minor and Syria/Palestine) which was taken over and completed by Seleukos and his successors, and thus formed the basis of the Seleukid administration in Asia, a fact largely ignored by modern scholarship on the administration of the Seleukid Empire.[13]

Again, an overestimation of the importance of Alexander lies behind the underestimation of Antigonos. Alexander's empire is seen as the direct forerunner of the Seleukid Empire, and the intervening twenty-year rule of Antigonos is skipped over except insofar as he is seen as a continuator of Alexander's aims. But Alexander, for all his romantic career of conquest, was essentially a destroyer, not a crea-

---

11. See app. 1, "Addendum," and chap. 4 n. 44 below on this.

12. Cf. the urging of Ehrenberg, *Greek State,* p. 141 that "we must not overlook the fact that, between the empire of Alexander and the final establishment of the states of his heirs stood, in point of time, the ephemeral but powerful and important empires of Lysimachus and, above all, of Antigonus Monophthalmus. They formed at once a bridge and a zone of division."

13. Antigonos is scarcely mentioned, e.g., in Bikerman's *Institutions des Séleucides* and Musti's "Lo stato dei Seleucidi" (now available in revised form in *CAH,* 7.1, chap. 6). For his pioneering role on the form of Hellenistic monarchy, see Müller, *Antigonos Monophthalmos;* for his decisive influence on the nature of relations between rulers and Greek *poleis,* see chap. 6 below.

tor. The work of his great father, Philip, gave Alexander an opportunity that he seized with both hands, namely to destroy the old politico-cultural balance of power between the Hellenic world and the Persian Empire. By conquering the Persian Empire, Alexander destroyed a balance that had existed for nearly two centuries and created an opportunity to bring forth something new in its place. This he did not live to exploit, and it may be doubted whether Alexander—the quintessential military man—would have known how to exploit it.[14] It fell to the Diadochoi, especially Antigonos and Seleukos, to try to make something of the opportunity won by Alexander, and what emerged from their efforts is what we call the Hellenistic monarchy and Hellenistic civilization. As to influences on Antigonos's administrative work, more to the point than Alexander is Antigonos's service under his contemporary Philip, a great reforming administrator, and his service for twelve years between 333 and 321 as a satrap in Phrygia, functioning essentially under the Persian system of administration.[15] In other words, the sources of ideas and inspiration for Antigonos's work are more likely to have been the methods and practices of Philip, and of the Persian Achaemenids, than of the brilliant, but unstable, Alexander.

Though centered on the career and work of one man, this book is only in part a biography. Part 1 is a politico-military biography of Antigonos, but also an account of the political and military events of the Diadoch period in general. Part 2, though still focussed on Antigonos, is an account of the creation and running of an administrative system. The appendices deal with the sources for the period generally (appendix 1) and with the forces and aides who helped Antigonos achieve his aims (appendices 2 and 3). The reader will not find any attempt to delve into personality, psychological motivations, and the like, which are normally features of biographies. There are good reasons for this. In the first place it was not my aim to write a book of that sort, and one may doubt generally the validity of any attempt by a twentieth-century historian to reconstruct the personality and mindset of people who lived over two thousand years ago.[16]

14. For the view of Alexander adopted here see, e.g., the works of Badian listed in the Bibliography.

15. For this see pp. 46–47 below.

16. The biographies of Alexander the Great and Antigonos Gonatas by W. W. Tarn illustrate the excesses such attempts can lead to. Though they are in many respects excellent books, Tarn's post-Victorian principles made it necessary for him to maintain, against all the evidence, that Alexander did not have homosexual affairs, for example, and was not given to heavy drinking bouts.

In the second place, the sort of evidence we have for Antigonos is not conducive to a psychological approach: we have politico-military narrative and inscriptions; we do not have a biography by Plutarch, which might have provided the sort of anecdotes useful to a more conventional biographical venture (if Plutarch had written such a work and it had survived).

Nevertheless, some brief remarks on Antigonos's appearance and character traits as they emerge from the sources we do have are in order here to introduce the man Antigonos, the more so in view of a recent attempt to explain Antigonos's ultimate defeat and "failure" by psychological analysis which is one-sided and inappropriate.[17] Antigonos was an exceptionally large man. His son Demetrios is described as being of "heroic stature" (Plut. *Dem.* 2,2; Diod. XIX 81,4; XX 92,2–3), meaning no doubt that he was six feet or more tall, but Antigonos was taller even than Demetrios and was big as well as tall—in extreme old age he became rather immobile because of his great size and weight (Plut. *Dem.* 2,2; 19,3). This huge man was made even more formidable in appearance by the fact that he was one-eyed, having lost an eye in battle at some time, possibly at the siege of Perinthos in 340 (see pp. 27–29 below). To his soldiers, the stature and scarred visage of Antigonos must have been impressive, and he evidently understood the psychological benefits of this, for he was in the habit while on campaign of striding about making jokes and laughing in a booming voice to instill confidence in his men (Plut. *Eum.* 15,2; *Dem.* 28,4).

It is a pity that, though a considerable number of portraits and statues of Antigonos are known to have been created during his lifetime, no securely attributable likeness of him has survived.[18] There is, however, an ancient work of art which *may* show us a

17. Hornblower, *Hieronymus of Cardia,* pp. 211–23, makes harshness and arrogance Antigonos's leading characteristics, and suggests that they made him blind to the needs and feelings of others, causing him to drive recklessly to disaster, like such psychologically blind and disastrous British generals as Sir Redvers Buller (1839–1908) and Sir Charles Townshend (1861–1924). But how in this case are we to explain Antigonos's brilliant successes from 320 to 311? The absurdity of such analysis and such comparisons is too obvious to require further argument.

18. We know of statues of Antigonos at Skepsis (*OGIS*, no. 6, lines 21–22), at Rhodes (Diod. XX 93,6), at Athens (Diod. XX 46,2), at Olympia (Paus. VI 11,1; *Syll.*, nos. 349–51), on Delos (*IG* XI. 4, 566 and 1036), and at Delphi (Paus. X 10,2); and there were very probably statues elsewhere—for example, at Samos: see *SEG,* 1, no. 362, mentioning a festival of Antigoneia that suggests a cult and hence a cult statue. In addition, there were paintings of Antigonos by Apelles (Pliny *NH* XXXV 90 and 96; Strabo XIV 657) and Protogenes (Pliny *NH* XXXV 106).

contemporary portrait: it has been suggested that one of the Macedonian horsemen depicted on the famous "Alexander Sarcophagus" in the Archaeological Museum at Istanbul could be Antigonos. One of the long relief panels on this sarcophagus depicts a battle between Macedonians and Persians, and at the right and left edges of the scene are two Macedonian horsemen charging into the fray, each in the act of killing a Persian cavalryman with his spear. The Macedonian horseman on the left is Alexander the Great, in a depiction clearly drawing on the head of Herakles with a lion-scalp helmet and Alexander's features shown on Alexander's coinage. The horseman on the right, who is given equal billing (as it were) with Alexander, has been identified as Antigonos Monophthalmos; and though this suggestion has met with a mixed reception, I think it must be correct.[19] If so, we get a glimpse here of the face of Antigonos. This horseman has a mature face, with prominent cheekbones and chin. The nose is fairly long and fine, and the cheeks are slightly hollow, suggesting that a portrait of some individual was aimed at.[20] Of course, even granted that this horseman is intended to depict Antigonos, one cannot

---

19. Charbonneaux, *Rev. des Arts* 2 (1952):219–23, made the suggestion; Wehrli, *Antigone et Démétrios*, and (tentatively) Hölscher, *Griechische Historienbilder des 5. und 4. Jahrhunderte v. Chr.*, pp. 189–90 n. 1183, agree with it. Against the identification see, above all, Graeve, *Alexandersarkophag*, p. 135, whose own suggestion of Perdikkas is, however, unconvincing (see Hölscher, loc. cit.). The sarcophagus was found in the royal tomb of Sidon in Phoenicia and was evidently the coffin of a Sidonian king of the time of Alexander and the Diadochoi (see Graeve for all questions of style, date, and so on). This monarch is generally believed to be Abdalonymos, who was placed on the throne by Alexander in 332 (Graeve, pp. 123–25). The identity of the horseman must be decided on the basis of historical significance in connection with Abdalonymos and Sidon: the depiction of Alexander and other Macedonian leaders is clearly the result of their relations with Abdalonymos. As ruler of Syria/Palestine from 314 to 301, Antigonos was Abdalonymos's political master, if the latter was still alive (see app. 3, no. 129). Alexander is shown fighting without breastplate or sword, another horseman (Hephaistion?) also lacks a cuirass, and one of the infantrymen is depicted heroically nude. The horseman identified as Antigonos wears full Macedonian battledress, which may indicate that this person—unlike Alexander and Hephaistion—was alive at the time of creation (i.e., that the lack of armor for Alexander and Hephaistion is because of their status as "heroized" dead). If correct this would exclude identification of the right horseman as Parmenion, Perdikkas, or Krateros (all have been suggested; all were dead by 320), and increase the likelihood that this horseman is Antigonos. A final and in my view clinching argument is that unlike those of the other horsemen, the head of the one on the right is depicted in strict profile, even turned in a little towards the back wall of the frieze; and we know that it was precisely Antigonos who liked to be depicted in profile, thus hiding the unsightly scar of his missing eye (see, e.g., Pliny *NH* XXXV 90).

20. Hölscher argues that the heads (other than Alexander's) are not portraits (*Griechische Historienbilder*, p. 190), as does Smith in *Hellenistic Royal Portraits*, p. 63 (taking a very skeptical position). But in fact the unusual features of the rider on the right at least—deep-set eyes, prominent cheekbones, hollow cheeks, and jutting chin—show that this was indeed intended to be a portrait of someone.

assume that the face is a true, realistic likeness. The sculptor has evidently been at pains to present this horseman as one kind of archetype of a military man of fierce energy and willpower. Nevertheless, it is reasonable to assume that in looking at this Macedonian cavalryman, we get some idea of what Antigonos actually looked like (see frontispiece).[21]

An attractive feature of Antigonos's character is that he was very much a family man. He married his wife, Stratonike, when he was in his early forties, and remained married to her for the rest of his life, so far as we know never even having affairs with other women, in sharp contradistinction to many contemporaries.[22] As dynast and king he gave advancement to various nephews and to his half-brother Marsyas (see app. 3, nos. 33, 67, 100, and 111). He brought up his younger son Philippos with care and strictness (see app. 3, no. 92). In particular, there was a genuine devotion between Antigonos and his son Demetrios, which seems to have served as a model in his family in later generations (see Plut. *Dem.* 3,1–4). Plutarch reports that there was such trust between father and son that Demetrios was allowed free access to Antigonos even with weapons in his hand, and that Antigonos was so proud of this trust (unusual among the powerful in his day) that he called it to the attention of certain ambassadors from his rival dynasts, regarding it as one of the securest props of his power. Elsewhere Plutarch records further anecdotes indicating the affection between Antigonos and Demetrios. Though Antigonos himself disapproved of indulgence in "wine, women and song," he was tolerant of Demetrios's weakness for these pursuits: when Demetrios once greeted him with a particularly fond embrace, Antigonos laughed and said, "One would think you were kissing Lamia"

21. Hafner, *RdA* 4 (1980):17–25, proposes that a painting found in a villa at Boscoreale near Pompeii, and now kept in the Museum at Naples, depicts Antigonos Monophthalmos and his wife Stratonike. His arguments are utterly unconvincing, however, involving as they do the rejection of the tradition that Antigonos was one-eyed! To this end, Hafner tries to argue away some of the evidence, but he simply ignores the most clear and definite statements of Antigonos's disfigurement, Pliny *NH* XXXV 90, Plut. *Sert.* 1, 4, and Plut. *Mor.* 11b–c.

22. Ptolemy repudiated his wife Eurydike and his son by her in favor of his mistress Berenike and a new family of children. Lysimachos married at least three times, the last two—Amestris and Arsinoë—overlapping, and aquiesced in the murder of his eldest son, Agathokles, so that Arsinoë's children might claim the succession. Kassandros seems to have married Alexander's half-sister Thessalonike by force. Demetrios had a host of wives and mistresses, by many of whom he produced offspring (see for all this, e.g., *RE sub nom.*). Though we have a good number of anecdotes about Antigonos, and the anecdotal sources were very keen on sexual scandal, no evidence links Antigonos to other women, except erroneously in Athenaios (XIII 578a–b): the story in fact concerns Antigonos's grandson, Antigonos Gonatas (see app. 3, no. 86).

(Demetrios's mistress: Plut. *Dem.* 19,4); on another occasion when Demetrios had been partying hard, he excused his absence from business affairs on grounds of an illness, and Antigonos joked, "So I heard, but did you catch it from Thasos or Chios?" (famous wine-producing islands: Plut. ibid.).[23]

These anecdotes also illustrate another trait that must have helped Antigonos win friends and inspire loyalty in his subordinates, namely his sense of humor. Plutarch, especially, records a number of excellent witticisms of Antigonos's, which besides a good sense of humor, display a good degree of learning and culture. Antigonos was able to remember and adapt on the spur of the moment a line of Euripides (Plut. *Dem.* 14,2–3), and could twit a young pupil of the rhetorician/historian Anaximenes for his lack of knowledge of the subject on which he had presumed to give a speech (*Apophth. Ant.* 13 at Plut. *Mor.* 182d–e).[24] He could even joke about his deformity, remarking when he received a despatch written in particularly large letters, "Even a blind man can read this" (Plut. *Mor.* 633c), though he was otherwise rather sensitive about his scarred face and missing eye: the famous artist Apelles for this reason painted him in profile so that only his good side was visible in the portrait (Pliny *NH* XXXV 90).

The main impression we get of Antigonos during the years 323–310 (when he was in his sixties and early seventies) is one of immense physical and mental vigor and energy. The campaigns he undertook in these years would have taxed the energy of most much younger men, and Antigonos did not spare himself during these campaigns, taking a personal part in the battles and sharing in the work and hardships of his soldiers (Diod. XIX 26,6–7; 30,7–10; 42,4–6; Seneca *De ira* III 22,3). This physical and mental energy may be considered his outstanding characteristic, making him the successful general, statesman, and administrator that he was. The ancients already recognized this: Diodoros called him the most active or effective (πρακτικώτατος) of the Macedonian leaders, and described him as outstanding in daring and intelligence (XVIII 23,3–4); Plu-

23. Another amusing instance of this humorous tolerance is Plutarch's story (*Dem.* 19,5) that Antigonos visited Demetrios once when he was supposed to be sick and met a beautiful girl just leaving his son's room. Antigonos went in, sat down, and took Demetrios's hand. Demetrios then said that the fever had already left him, and Antigonos replied, "Indeed, my boy. I just met it at the door as it was going."

24. Other witticisms or examples of Antigonos's sense of humor are recorded by Plut. *Dem.* 23,4; 28,2–4; *Eum.* 15,2; and *Apophth. Ant.* 1, 5, 10, and 11 at Plut. *Mor.* 182a–d. Though one cannot be sure that these anecdotes actually preserve Antigonos's own words, it does seem that he was noted for his humor and wit.

tarch used him as a classic example of a robust and powerful old man (*Mor.* 791e). But more even than his vigor or energy, the ancient sources characterize Antigonos by the love of power (*philarchia*) in the pursuit of which he displayed his energy and daring. His pride and his love of power are repeatedly noted by the sources (e.g., Diod. XVIII 50,1; XXI 1,1; Plut. *Dem.* 28,2; Aelian *VH* XII 16), and the criticism is expressed that this led him at times to be harsh and arrogant (Plut. *Dem.* 28,2). Some modern scholars have seized on this aspect of Antigonos and made harshness and arrogance his leading characteristics, blaming them for what they consider his ultimate failure—though, to be sure, in this they are merely following Plutarch's judgment at *Dem.* 28,2.[25] However, this is a simplistic and inaccurate view both of Antigonos's character and of the sources: Antigonos was a complex man, and the sources make a variety of pronouncements and judgments on his character and disposition, depending on the occasion they comment on.

There is no doubt that Antigonos was at times ruthless and even harsh, but being occasionally harsh and ruthless was inherent in the career of command he followed and the times in which he lived, and mostly when Antigonos was ruthless it was a matter of policy rather than of personal spite.[26] The other Diadochoi were no better than Antigonos in this respect: it was not by being mild and tolerant that the Macedonians had conquered a great empire, and it was not by mildness and tolerance that the dynasts who succeeded Alexander secured parts of that empire as private domains. At least Antigonos displayed no such horrific cruelty as Lysimachos.[27] The fact is that

25. See, e.g., Hornblower, *Hieronymus of Cardia,* pp. 211–23.

26. Examples are Antigonos's ruthless treatment of would-be deserters in Egypt, which was intended to give pause to any other soldiers who had ideas of defecting and thus damaging his military position (Diod. XX 75,2–3); further, the execution of Peithon Krateua in 315 (Diod. XIX 46,1–4) and the order for Alexander's sister to be murdered in 309/8 (Diod. XX 37,3–6): Antigonos could not afford to leave Peithon to make trouble for him in the east or contemplate with equanimity the prospect of Kleopatra marrying his rival Ptolemy.

27. Lysimachos inflicted a horrifyingly cruel punishment on a friend for a jest at the expense of his wife Arsinoë (Athenaios XIV 616c; Seneca *De ira* III 27,2–4; Plut. *Mor.* 606b). Kassandros murdered a friend and benefactor on the merest suspicion of excessive ambition (Diod. XIX 105,2–3; XX 28,1–3). Ptolemy was a cruel tyrant to the Jews of Jerusalem (Josephus *Contra Apionem* I 210; cf. Appian *Syr.* 50) and treacherously murdered his ally Polemaios in 309/8 (Diod. XX 27,3). Likewise the "plausible and insinuating" Eumenes (Plut. *Eum.* 11,2) was ruthless towards the traitor Apollonides (Diod. XVIII 40,7–8; Plut. *Eum.* 9,1–2) and towards Sibyrtios for supporting his rival Peukestas (Diod. XIX 23,4). Even Seleukos, of whom the sources have very little to relate that is adverse, apparently joined Antigenes in the murder of Perdikkas (Nepos *Eum.* 5,1), who had promoted him to the highest cavalry command in the empire (Diod. XVIII 3,4).

Antigonos lived in a ruthless age, and actually had a reputation for being relatively mild and forgiving, especially towards the end of his life: he behaved kindly (φιλανθρώπως) to captured enemy soldiers (Diod. XVIII 45,4), and to his own men (Diod. XIX 20,1); when he captured a number of enemy leaders at the battle of Kretopolis in 319, he merely imprisoned them (Diod. XVIII 45,3; XIX 16,1–5) rather than killing them, and he later took one of them—Dokimos—into his service (Diod. XIX 75,3; XX 107,4); Seneca's pamphlet concerning the evil effects of anger cites Antigonos as a shining example of a king who controlled his temper and refrained from punishing insults (*De ira* III 22,2–3); and Plutarch reports that mildness and gentleness characterized his rule towards the end of his life (*Mor.* 182b = *Apophth. Ant.* 3). In general Antigonos's posthumous reputation, unlike those of Lysimachos and Kassandros, was fairly good (see, for example, Plut. *Phok.* 29,1), especially for such a proud and ambitious man.

Basically, the picture of Antigonos in the sources is inconsistent: he was harsh and kind, arrogant and mild, haughty yet just, grasping and generous. Nor is this in my opinion in any way an unrealistic picture: the characteristics displayed by Antigonos depend on the circumstances of any particular occasion, and the truth is that he was neither especially harsh nor especially kind, but capable of displaying either trait as the occasion arose; and so with the rest of these good and bad qualities attributed to him. The keys to his personality are, I believe, ambition and intelligence. Ambition caused him to seem harsh and arrogant to those who stood in his way, while intelligence caused him to be just, and even at times kind and generous, to his friends and subordinates, and mild towards defeated foes who were willing to give up opposition and join him, since he understood that lasting power must be based upon loyalty and good repute, which can only be won by showing justice and generosity. This is really as much as can plausibly be said about Antigonos's character. Perhaps I should emphasize that while I reject those interpretations which depict Antigonos as a man fatally flawed and brought to ruin by excessive arrogance—a notion with obvious roots in ancient tragedy—this in no way means that I wish to whitewash Antigonos. To portray him as a bundle of virtues with scarcely a flaw or vice would be even more unjustified than is the hubristic view of him. But the sources primarily concern themselves with Antigonos's deeds, not his character; and his deeds likewise form the main subject matter of this book.

Part I

Antigonos's Life and Career

I

The Early Years

ANTIGONOS'S BACKGROUND AND YOUTH (382–359 B.C.)

Antigonos Monophthalmos was born about 382 B.C., as we know from his reported age of eighty-one at his death in 301.[1] He was therefore an almost exact coeval of King Philip II, also born in 383 or 382,[2] whom he outlived however by some thirty-five years. Antigonos's father was named Philippos; his mother's name is unknown. The family's social standing is disputed, some authorities claiming that Antigonos came from peasant or yeoman stock, others that his family was linked to the Macedonian royal house.[3] Neither of these claims can be proved, and both seem unlikely. Since the few definite

1. Hieronymos of Kardia in *FGrH,* no. 154 F 8 = [Loukianos] *Makrobioi* 11. Cf. also Appian *Syr.* 55: Antigonos died *ὑπὲρ ὀγδοήκοντα ἔτη γεγονότι*; Plut. *Dem.* 19: in 306 Antigonos was "almost eighty" (*μικρὸν ἀπολείποντα γεγονὼς ἔτη ὀγδοήκοντα*). Porphyrios in *FGrH,* no. 260 F 32 makes Antigonos eighty-six at his death, no doubt an error.

2. See Justin IX 8,1 and Pausanias VIII 7,6 and cf. Griffith's comment in Hammond and Griffith, *History of Macedonia,* 2:204 and n. 3.

3. The name of Antigonos's father is recorded by, for example, Plut. *Dem.* 2,1, Hieronymos (loc. cit. n. 1 above), Arrian *Anab.* I 29,3, and many other sources. Tarn supposes that the family was of "yeoman farmer" stock (*Antigonos Gonatas,* p. 5 and n. 2); Edson, *HSCPh* 45 (1934): 213–46, argues that Antigonos's family was connected with the Argead royal house. The evidence is: Aelian *VH* XII 43 says that Antigonos was a peasant (*αὐτουργὸς ἦν*); Diod. XXI 1 says that Antigonos rose from private station to high power and kingship (*Ἀντίγονος ὁ βασιλεὺς ἐξ ἰδιώτου γενόμενος δυνάστης*); Polybios V 10,10 says that Antigonos's descendant Philippos V of Macedon was a *συγγενὴς Ἀλεξάνδρου καὶ Φιλίππου* or rather that he wished to appear such. None of this has much value: Aelian's statement is from a list of some twenty-one mostly untrue defamations of famous men and is worthless; Diodoros's statement is literally true, but tells us only that Antigonos was not of royal descent; and since all the successor dynasties—Lagids, Seleukids and Antigonids—claimed kinship with the Argead house, Polybios's statement proves nothing either. Cf. on this the discussion of Briant, *Antigone le Borgne,* pp. 19–25.

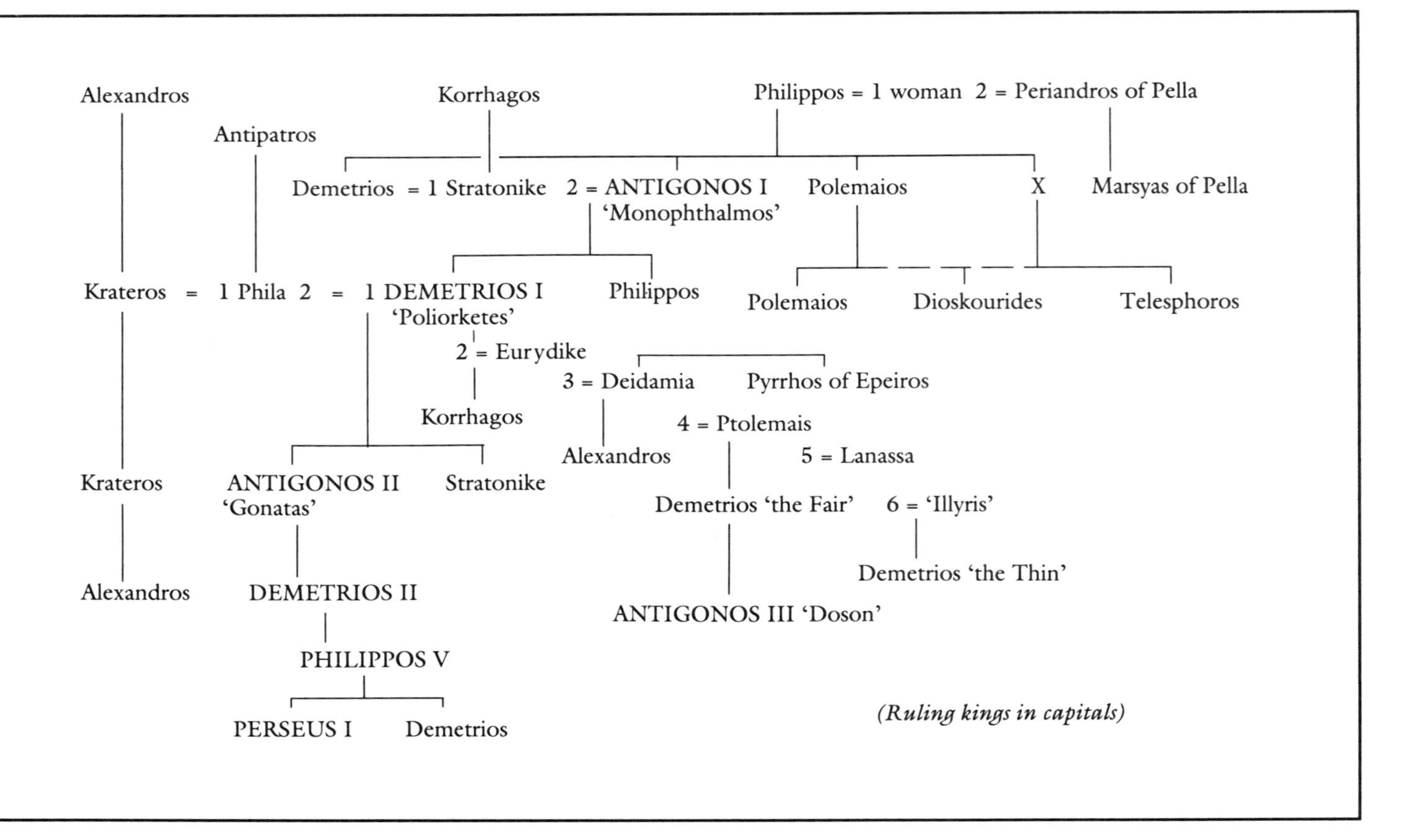

Figure 1. The Family of Antigonos Monophthalmos

statements about Antigonos's social background are unreliable, only indirect arguments can be used to determine his family's social standing. Three facts lead to the conclusion that in all probability the family was socially prominent and from the Macedonian nobility.

In the first place, Antigonos's mother was widowed in early middle age and made a second marriage to an important noble from Pella, the capital, showing that she must have been of noble birth herself: only wealth, noble birth, and important connections can have overcome the defect of middle age in persuading an important noble to marry her.[4] Hence in all likelihood her first husband, Philippos, would have come from the nobility too. Secondly, Antigonos's wife, Stratonike, seems to have belonged to a noble family, perhaps related to the royal house,[5] which suggests again that Antigonos was a noble. Thirdly, Antigonos and at least one of his brothers made successful careers as officers and administrators under Philip and Alexander, again suggestive of noble status.[6]

Antigonos had two brothers named Demetrios and Polemaios, the former probably the oldest of the three, and at least one other sibling (see fig. 1 for a family tree).[7] With his parents and three siblings, he grew up in a noble milieu, probably in lowland Mace-

---

4. Antigonos had a brother named Marsyas whose father was not Philippos but Periandros of Pella, thus a uterine half-brother (see app. 3, no. 67 below). This Marsyas was enrolled by King Philip II as a foster-brother (*syntrophos*) of his son Alexander (the Great), showing that Marsyas was some twenty-four or more years younger than Antigonos, and that his father must have been an important noble.

5. Stratonike is a name attested only once before in Macedonian history, when it was borne by a sister of King Perdikkas II (Thuc. II 101,6), which suggested to Edson, *HSCPh* 45 (1934):228, that Antigonos's wife had royal blood; conceivably Philippos V's claim to *syngeneia* with the Argead house can be seen as a further evidence of this (Polybios V 10,10). Stratonike's father was named Korrhagos, a name otherwise attested at this period only as borne by a general and a *hetairos* of Alexander the Great (Berve, *Alexanderreich* [henceforth cited simply as "Berve"], vol. 2, nos. 444, 445), who in view of the relative rarity of the name (Holleaux, *Etudes d'épigr.*, 2:81; H. Seyrig, *RN*, 6th ser., 5 [1963]:31 n. 1) may be connections of Antigonos's father-in-law, again suggesting noble status. The name was retained in the Antigonid family: Antigonos's son Demetrios named one of his sons Korrhagos (Plut. *Dem.* 53,4). Briant's claim (*Antigone le Borgne*, p. 24 n. 3) that Plut. *Dem.* 2,1 calls the elder Korrhagos a king is erroneous.

6. For the career of Antigonos's brother Polemaios, see app. 3, no. 99. Not all top officers were necessarily nobles, but apart from Erigyios under Alexander (Berve, vol. 2, no. 302), I believe, no commander of the top level can be proved to have been of non-noble origin, whereas noble status can be demonstrated for many of the top officers (e.g., Parmenion, Leonnatos, Perdikkas, Kalas) and was, I believe, normal.

7. For Demetrios, see Plut. *Dem.* 2,1; for Polemaios, see app. 3, no. 99; for the existence of at least one other sibling, see my argument concerning Antigonos's nephew Telesphoros in app. 3, no. 111.

donia around the capital of Pella.[8] Nothing specific is known of his youth, but what it would have been like can be gathered from the nature of Macedonian society, especially upper-class society, at the time.

Macedon was a region which had lagged behind the rest of the Greek world socially, economically, and culturally, failing to develop the *polis* or city-state institutions characteristic of the most advanced regions of Greece, but remaining instead a tribal society ruled by kings and dominated by a land-owning aristocracy.[9] Indeed, there is some question as to whether Macedon should at this time be counted as part of the Greek world at all, for it has been doubted whether the Macedonians were a Greek-speaking people, on the basis of a few passages in ancient sources that appear to speak of a Macedonian "language."[10] These passages can equally well be understood to refer to a Macedonian "dialect," however, and though it cannot at present be formally proved that the Macedonians were Hellenic in race and language, I think it highly likely that they were, for three reasons: the overwhelming majority of personal names known to have been used by Macedonians were good Greek names; the names of the months in the Macedonian calendar were basically Greek in form; and the religion of the Macedonians was largely the same as that of the Greeks, with Zeus, Herakles, and Dionysos being particularly prominent.[11]

---

8. Edson, *HSCPh* 45 (1934):213–46, argues that Antigonos's family was from Beroia, but unconvincingly; cf. Lévêque, *Pyrrhos,* pp. 156–57. Since Antigonos's half-brother Marsyas was from Pella (see app. 3, no. 67), it is reasonable to think that Antigonos may have been too; in addition, Antigonos seems to have later founded a colony in Syria named Pella (see p. 299 below), suggesting again that this may have been his home town (cf. Seleukos's foundation of colonies named after his home town, Europos).

9. On early Macedon, see, e.g., Edson, *Arch. Mak.* 1 (1970):17–44; Hammond in Hammond and Griffith, *History of Macedonia* 2, pt. 1: 3–200; Errington, *Gesch. Makedoniens,* chaps. 1 and 6.

10. E.g., Plut. *Alex.* 51,4; Plut. *Eum.*14,1; Curtius VI 10,23; 11,4. A few non-Greek Macedonian words are also preserved by ancient lexicographers, e.g., *peligan,* elder; *gotan,* pig.

11. On the Macedonian dialect, see Hoffman *Die Makedonen;* Kalleris, *Les Anciens Macédoniens,* vol. 1; Hammond and Griffith (op. cit. n. 9 above), pp. 39–54; and cf. now the judgment of Errington, *Gesch. Makedoniens,* p. 13: "Dass die Makedonen . . . einen griechischen Dialekt sprachen und Namen griechischer Art trugen darf heute als gesichert gelten. Der makedonische Dialekt benutzte zwar viel lehnwörter aus den Sprachen der illyrischen und thrakischen Nachbarn." For the Greek character of the Macedonian calendar and religion, see Edson *Arch. Mak.* 1 (1970):23–24; Hammond and Griffith loc. cit. The cult of Zeus was prominent at Dion, at Beroia there was a cult of Herakles Kynagidas, and the Bacchic rites of Macedon (admittedly influenced by the Thracian Sabazios) are famous for inspiring Euripides' play *The Bacchae.*

The Macedonians, then, were probably a Greek people (though certainly with an admixture of Illyrians and Thracians) akin in language and culture to their neighbors to the south and west, the Thessalians and Epeirots.[12] Like the Epeirots, they were divided into several tribes and ruled over by a tribal monarchy. The main division in Macedon was between the lowland Macedonians, living in the plains of Pieria, Bottiaia, and the Amphaxitis, and the highland Macedonians, who were themselves divided into a number of "cantons": from south to north, Tymphaia, Elimiotis, Orestis, Eordaia, Lynkos, and Pelagonia (see map 1). The kings came from a royal family known as the Argeadai, who claimed descent from Herakles, but the Argead house was rooted in lower Macedon and the cantons of upper Macedon had dynastic families of their own who frequently claimed to rule as independent kings over their own regions.[13]

Like the Thessalians, the Macedonians never developed beyond the aristocratic form of society typical of early Greece and probably depicted in Homer's epics.[14] The Homeric appearance of certain elements of Macedonian society has been widely noted; the chief of these elements is the so-called *hetaireia,* an institution which bound together the king and the nobility: it was the privilege and duty of the nobles to attend the king as his *hetairoi* (companions) both in war and peace, as cavalry fighters and officers, or as councillors and boon companions.[15] That this institution was deeply rooted in Macedon is shown by the existence of a religious festival named the Hetairidia, and it is clear that the *hetairoi* formed a noble class of major importance in the state. Although as chief priest, chief judge, commander in chief, and political leader, the king embodied the state, he was constrained in practice to function in consultation with his *hetairoi.* Thus the chief organ of state policy was the *synedrion* or council of the

12. For the similarity of Macedonians and Epeirots, see Strabo VII 449 and IX 612, who says in the former passage that some people simply included Epeiros in Macedonia because "the inhabitants have about the same hair styling, the same speech, costume and so on"; cf. Hammond and Griffith (op. cit. n. 9), pp. 39–54, also noting similarities with the Thessalians.

13. For the independant rulers of upland Macedonian tribes, see Thuc. II 80 and 99; IV 79 and 124–25; Aristotle *Pol.* 1311b13; and cf. generally on the Macedonian regions Hammond and Griffith (op. cit. n. 9), pp. 14–54; Edson (op. cit. n. 9), pp. 18–22, 25–30; Errington, *Gesch. Makedoniens,* pp. 12–17.

14. That Homer's epics depicted a genuine phase of Greek society at some time in the Geometric period has been most persuasively argued by M. I. Finley, *The World of Odysseus* (rev. ed., New York, 1978); cf. also O. Murray, *Early Greece* (Stanford, 1983), pp. 38–68.

15. See Edson (op. cit. n. 9), pp. 22–23; Errington, *Gesch. Makedoniens,* pp. 198–99; Stagakis, "Institutional Aspects of the Hetairos Relation"; id., *Arch. Mak.* 1 (1970):86–102.

king and his friends, in which the king took the lead and made the decisions, but would find it hard to decide against a consensus of his nobles.[16] In particular, actions against the lives of leading members of the *hetairos* class could normally be risked by a king only with strong backing from his friends, and at times the king might prefer to hand over the decision on a capital charge against a great noble to the *synedrion* of his friends.[17]

The basis of the social and economic standing of the *hetairos* class was clearly landed wealth: Theopompos tells us that the 800 *hetairoi* of Philip II, for example, owned as much land as the 10,000 wealthiest men of the rest of Greece put together (*FGrH*, no. 115 F 225b). Being proprietors of great estates gave them an inherited status within their regions, and hence in the kingdom as a whole. In particular, like the Thessalian nobility, the Macedonian *hetairoi* raised horses on their estates, and provided the cavalry forces of the Macedonian state, riding in to support the king in time of war, each noble with a mounted following of his own.[18] Since Macedon before the time of Philip II had no significant infantry force, but relied almost exclusively on cavalry for its defense, their domination of the cavalry gave the Macedonian nobility great political influence. This was especially true when a weak king was on the throne, when factions of nobles often coalesced around other members of the royal house claiming the throne and reduced the state to near anarchy.[19]

It was as a member of this powerful and wealthy *hetairos* class that Antigonos almost certainly grew up. He is specifically recorded to have been a *hetairos* of Alexander, and the historian Justin makes Antigonos's son Demetrios claim in a speech to a gathering of

16. For the festival of Hetairidia, see Athenaios XIII 527d; for the *synedrion* of *hetairoi*, see Berve, 1:33–35, and for the influence of the *hetairoi*, cf., e.g., Arrian *Anab.* I 25,4–5 and IV 11,1–12,2, where Alexander has to bow to the disapproval of his Companions on his plan to introduce the practice of *proskynēsis* at court.

17. See on this, and on Macedonian kingship and its relations with the aristocracy generally, Errington, *Chiron* 8 (1978):77–133, esp. 89–91.

18. Thus Thuc. I 61 records the Macedonian nobles Philippos and Pausanias in the time of King Perdikkas II having a following of 600 cavalrymen; cf. Schachermeyr, *Alexander in Babylon*, p. 24: "Jeder Paladin [i.e., high Macedonian officer] hatte seine Verwandten und seine vertrauten Genossen (*philoi*)."

19. Thucydides (I 57–61; II 98–101; IV 124) and Xenophon (*Hell.* V 2,38–3,9) describe Macedonian campaigns in the late fifth and early fourth centuries that make it clear that the Macedonians had no significant heavy infantry force, but relied almost exclusively on heavy cavalry; see further Griffith in Hammond and Griffith, *History of Macedonia*, 2:405–6, and app. 3, pp. 705–13; and cf. now R. Develin, *Historia* 34 (1985):493–96, and Errington, *Gesch. Makedoniens*, pp. 212–18. For the disruption caused by aristocratic factions, see, e.g., Thuc. I 60–61, and cf. Errington, pp. 11–17, 33–42.

Macedonians that his father had been a *socius* (= *hetairos*?) of Philip II throughout that king's reign.[20] Though the sources here are unreliable, and though both Philip and Alexander added men to their *hetairoi* from outside the old noble class, the facts I have noted above about the status of Antigonos's mother and wife make it extremely probable that Antigonos enjoyed *hetairos* status as a member of the nobility. Growing up as a member of this class entailed in the first place wealth and privilege, and in the second place an education in which the ability to ride, fight, and hunt played a major role. For example, though the upper class in Macedon had adopted the Greek habit of reclining at their meals, it was a rule that young men had to sit at the table until they had achieved the feat of killing a wild boar without using a hunting net;[21] and Aristotle (*Pol.* 1324b) reports that a Macedonian who had never killed an enemy had to wear a halter instead of a belt.

While retaining strong resemblances to the old Homeric warrior aristocracy, however, the Macedonian nobility was nevertheless in touch with mainstream Greek culture in Antigonos's day: under King Archelaos (*regn.* 413–399) some of the leading men of Greek literature and arts had even spent considerable time in Macedon.[22] It is certain that Antigonos received a thorough education in Greek culture. Later in life he was able to rebuke a sophist giving a speech at his court with a line from Euripides and to persuade his son to a useful marriage alliance by a punning adaptation of another line from Euripides.[23] We can assume that a familiarity with Euripides' plays was not the limit of Antigonos's literary education; Homer, at least, would have formed part of his early reading, and in general it is probable that his education would have encompassed the normal smattering of tragic and lyric poetry, rhetoric, and philosophy that formed the basis of any upper-class Greek's education.

---

20. Aelian *VH* XIV 47a includes Antigonos in a list of *hetairoi* of Alexander, which seems reliable with respect to the other men named; Justin XVII 1,12 makes Antigonos a "*socius Philippi et Alexandri*" and, though Justin is unreliable (see app. 1, pp. 348–51) and is here reporting possibly fictitious or tendentious words of Demetrios Poliorketes, the claim itself is credible.

21. See Edson (op. cit. n. 9), p. 23.

22. The tragic poets Euripides and Agathon and the painter Zeuxis, among others, spent time in Macedon: see Hammond in Hammond and Griffith, *History of Macedonia,* 2:149 n. 1 for sources.

23. Plut. *Mor.* 182e (= *Apophth. Ant.* 13) records Antigonos quoting Euripides' *Iphigeneia among the Taurians* 787 to rebuke an orator; Plut. *Dem.* 14 has him persuading his son Demetrios to marry Phila by a punning adaptation of Euripides' *Phoinissai* 396.

Antigonos grew up, then, as a member of a wealthy and privileged class, trained in Greek culture and in the martial pusuits of a warrior aristocracy. As a young man of the *hetairos* class, he belonged to a powerful and wealthy caste, who consorted with their king with a freedom of speech (*parrhēsia*) and access unthinkable in the rigidly hierarchical Persian court or the sycophantic courts of the Greek tyrants. If one is right in supposing that his family came from the region around Pella, there is even a good chance that Antigonos would have been a playfellow when growing up of his exact coeval Philip, who was at that time merely the third son of King Amyntas III, with no particular prospect of coming to the throne.

Though Antigonos's youth was probably, then, marked by privilege and exalted social and economic standing, it would not have been without anxieties and insecurity, for the period of Antigonos's youth coincided with one of the most difficult phases in Macedonian history. For though the fourteen-year reign of King Archelaos had brought growth and stability to Macedon, his assassination in 399 ushered in a forty-year period of strife, during which the kingship was disputed between a large number of rival claimants, the highland cantons became more or less independent of the Argead dynasty, and the country became a battlefield of foreign interests, with armed interventions by Olynthos, Sparta, Thebes, Athens, and the Illyrians.[24] Philip's father, Amyntas, came to the throne in 393 and ruled for twenty-four years, but his reign was a troubled one, with several interruptions caused by an incursion of the Illyrians just after he came to the throne, and his temporary ejection in favor of a rival—Argaios—around 385–383 B.C.[25] In addition, Amyntas had trouble in the latter part of his reign with the Chalkidian League of Olynthos, and with renewed pressure from the Illyrians under their ruler Bardylis, who forced Amyntas to pay tribute in order to secure peace.[26]

The death of Amyntas in 370/69 did not improve matters. By his wife Eurydike, Amyntas left three sons—Alexandros, Perdikkas, and Philip—of whom the oldest succeeded as King Alexandros II. The assassination of Jason of Pherai about this time had removed one potential threat to Macedon, and the youthful Alexandros was emboldened to intervene in Thessaly at the invitation of the Aleuadai clan of Larissa. This intervention had two disastrous consequences: it

24. On this period of Macedonian history see, e.g., Geyer, *Makedonien bis zur Thronbesteigung Philipps II*, pp. 105–39; Errington, *Gesch. Makedoniens*, pp. 33–43.

25. Thus J. R. Ellis, *Makedonika* 8 (1969):1–9.

26. On Amyntas's problems with Olynthos, see Xenophon *Hellenika* V 2,12–3,9; for Amyntas's tribute to the Illyrians, Diod. XVI 2,2.

brought Thebans north under Pelopidas to interfere in Thessalian and Macedonian affairs, and it enabled a powerful noble connected with the royal house, one Ptolemaios of Aloros, to raise a rebellion in the young king's absence. Pelopidas was appealed to by both sides in this civil war, and entered Macedon as arbitrator. He ostensibly reconciled the two enemies and made a treaty with Alexandros, extracting from him thirty hostages for his future good behavior, including his youngest brother, Philip, who was thus brought to live in Thebes for three years. However, shortly after Pelopidas had left Macedon, Ptolemaios rebelled again, assassinating King Alexandros at a festival in 368 or 367 and assuming power in Macedon as regent for Alexandros's brother and heir, Perdikkas.[27]

Ptolemaios's rule was not prosperous: he was immediately challenged by one Pausanias, a member of the royal house, who now claimed the throne and succeeded in raising a large force and occupying much of southern Macedon; only timely help from the Athenians under Iphikrates enabled Ptolemaios to see off this challenge. Next Pelopidas the Theban invaded Macedon with a force of mercenaries, an invasion Ptolemaios could only deal with by bribery and the handing over of more hostages. Finally in 365, after three wretched years of power, Ptolemaios succumbed to a plot organized against him by the young King Perdikkas, who had reached the age of eighteen or nineteen and naturally wished to rule.[28] Perdikkas III's rule was hardly more successful than that of Ptolemaios. He seems to have had good relations with Thebes and secured the release of his brother Philip, but he suffered significant reverses in hostilities against the Athenian generals Timotheos (in 365–362) and Kallisthenes (in 362), and then had to deal with a war against Bardylis the Illyrian, by whom he was disastrously defeated in a great battle in 359, in which he and 4,000 of his men were killed.[29] It must have been about this

27. For these events, in addition to Geyer, *Makedonien,* pp. 105–39, and Errington, *Gesch. Makedoniens,* pp. 33–43, see, for example, *RE* s.v. Alexandros, no. 9 [Kaerst]; s.v. Pelopidas [Reincke]; s.v. Ptolemaios, no. 4 [Volkmann].

28. Perdikkas III's age at his accession is not precisely known; see the cautious statement of F. Geyer in *RE* s.v. Perdikkas, no. 3: Perdikkas was in 365 "schon erwachsen."

29. For Philip's stay as hostage in Thebes, see Diodoros XV 67,4; Plut. *Pelopidas* 26, showing that it was Philip's brother Alexandros II who gave him as hostage; the date of his release is unsure: A. Aymard, *REA* 66 (1954):15–36, argues that Philip had already returned to Macedon in 367; certainly Philip was back in Macedon under Perdikkas III (Athenaios XI 506e–f: a fragment from Karystios of Pergamon). For Timotheos's campaign, see Demosthenes XXII 149–51; Isokrates XV (the *Antidosis*) 107–8, 112–13; and Deinarchos I 14. For that of Kallisthenes, see Aischines II 30. For Perdikkas III's disastrous defeat by the Illyrians, with the loss of 4,000 lives, see Diod. XVI 2,4–5.

time that Antigonos's father, Philippos, died, and one is tempted to conjecture that he may have died in this very battle, which would thus have touched Antigonos closely.[30] Though Perdikkas had an infant son, Amyntas, the situation for Macedon was desperate and clearly called for a man on the throne, and it was hence Perdikkas's 23- or 24-year-old brother Philip who succeeded to the kingship.

THE REIGN OF PHILIP (359–336 B.C.)

Philip II ruled Macedon from 359 until his assassination in 336, a period which coincided with Antigonos's early manhood, from roughly his twenty-third to his forty-sixth year of age. During that period Philip and his associates transformed Macedon from an unimportant backwater and a state on the verge of dissolution into the dominant power in the Greek world and most potent military power in the eastern Mediterranean, in the process reforming almost every aspect of Macedonian society. Apart from inherent probability, two pieces of evidence suggest that Antigonos played a significant role in this: first there is the passage of Justin in which Antigonos is said to have been an associate of Philip throughout his reign (Justin XVII 1, 12); secondly, there is the fact that when in 334 Alexander crossed to Asia with an army that in men and officers was clearly that trained and organized by Philip, Antigonos held one of the most important commands, an eminence he must already have achieved under Philip.[31]

Unfortunately, due in large part no doubt to the loss of the primary sources on Philip's reign, especially Theopompos, we know almost nothing of Antigonos's life and career under Philip. The only men who emerge as major aides of Philip in the relatively scanty surviving sources are Parmenion and Antipatros, who were nearly twenty years older than Philip and Antigonos, and who, as loyal and experienced officers and the heads of great Macedonian families,

30. By her second marriage Antigonos's mother produced a son, Marsyas (see app. 3, no. 67), who as a *syntrophos* of Alexander (born 356) must have been born in 356 or conceivably up to a year or so earlier. Hence the second marriage must have occurred in 358/57 at the latest, and seems likely to have occurred about that time. Thus the death of Philippos, the first husband, seems likely to have occurred a little earlier, about 360.

31. Cf. Errington's statement that "üblich gewesen sein dürfte (wie bei Alexander dem Grossen oder Philipp V. in den ersten Jahren), dass ein neuer König zunächst Berater seines Vorgängers einfach übernahm" (*Gesch. Makedoniens*, p. 198).

became Philip's right-hand men.[32] Nevertheless, the story of Antigonos's life in this period is certainly told in outline at least by the events of Philip's reign. In particular, it must have been during these years that Antigonos's views and ideas were developed and fixed, and in this respect it would be hard to overestimate the importance for Antigonos's development as an officer, administrator, and leader of men of Philip's career, which in its extraordinary successes provided the model for much of Antigonos's activity later in life as a ruler in Asia. A brief outline of Philip's reign is therefore in order, with emphasis on his reforms and on events concerning or involving Antigonos.[33]

The situation that faced Philip at his accession was far from rosy: the Illyrians had occupied a large portion of Macedon in the northwest; the Paionians were raiding and plundering in the north; from the east an army of Thracians threatened to invade to install as king a rival Argead, Pausanias; in the south another rival Argead—Argaios—arrived with substantial Athenian aid to back his claim to the throne; and in Macedon itself Philip had three half-brothers, of whom the eldest, Archelaos, disputed Philip's right to the throne.[34] These threats Philip dispelled with what (in our very inadequate sources) appears deceptive ease, by an astute mixture of diplomacy, bribery, and force. The Illyrians and Thracians were bought off, the Paionians were induced by promises to cease hostilities, Argaios was defeated in battle and captured, and Philip's half-brothers were either killed (Archelaos) or chased from Macedon. Late in the year a swift and bold campaign chastised the Paionians, and in the next year an equally bold campaign against the Illyrians ended in a decisive victory and the recovery of upper Macedon. Philip allied himself with the Aleuadai of

32. On Parmenion as Philip's chief military aide, see Plut. *Mor.* 177c (= *Apophth. Phil.* 2), and cf. Parmenion's independent victory over the Illyrians in 356 (Plut. *Alex.* 3,8); for Antipatros as aide to Philip, see Plut. *Mor.* 179b (= *Apophth. Phil.* 27), and his frequent use as ambassador by Philip (Demosthenes XIX 69 [346]; Justin IX 4,5, and Hypereides F 80 B1 [338]); and cf. Berve, vol. 2, nos. 606 (Parmenion) and 94 (Antipatros), and *RE sub nom.*

33. This brief account of Philip's career is based essentially on Ellis, *Philip II and Macedonian Imperialism,* especially as concerns the chronology of Philip's reign, for which see ibid., pp. 14–20. Other recent studies of Philip are Cawkwell, *Philip of Macedon;* Griffith in Hammond and Griffith, *History of Macedonia,* 2, pt. 2:203–726, which is in my opinion the best biography; and Wirth, *Gesch. Makedoniens I.*

34. For the general situation in Macedon at Philip's accession, see Diod. XVI 2,5–6; for Philip's three half-brothers—Archelaos, Menelaos, and Arrhidaios—see Justin VII 4,5, and for the oldest of the three, Archelaos, cf. Theopompos in *FGrH,* no. 115 F 29. J. R. Ellis, *Historia* 22 (1973):250–54, redates Archelaos's attempt on the throne to 356, perhaps rightly, though his arguments are not conclusive.

Thessaly and the royal house of Epeiros, marrying both the Larissan Philinna and Olympias, the niece of the Molossian king, Arybbas. At about this time, too, the marriage of Antigonos's mother to her second husband, Periandros of Pella, must have occurred, for their son Marsyas was a coeval and *syntrophos* (foster-brother) of Philip and Olympias's son Alexander (born 356).[35] Antigonos's stepfather was thus an important connection for him, tying him closer to the king.

In the next years Philip definitively occupied Amphipolis, a strategic city on the river Strymon, and extended and consolidated Macedonian power along the north Aegean coast. In 356 he founded Philippoi in the region of Mt. Pangaion, well to the east of the Strymon, and in 354 he captured Methone at the head of the Thermaic Gulf and Abdera and Maroneia on the Thracian coast. He also intervened in the Third Sacred War, in 352 assuming the title of *archōn* of Thessaly.[36] During 351 Philip campaigned extensively in Thrace, during 350 in Paionia and perhaps Illyria, and in 349–48 he operated against the Chalkidian League, a war culminating in the fall of Olynthos and the annexation of the Chalkidike by Macedon. In 346, an epochal year for Philip, the Thracian king Kersebleptes was decisively defeated and subordinated to Macedon; the Athenians were persuaded to accept Philip's successes (many of which had been at the expense of Athenian influence) and agreed to the so-called Peace of Philokrates; and Philip crowned the year by intervening once more as Apollo's champion in the Third Sacred War, bringing that war to an end and gaining representation in the Amphiktyonic League, which controlled the Delphic Oracle.[37]

The year 345 saw Philip in the field against Pleuratos of Illyria, and in the next year he put down revolts in Thessaly and reorganized the government of Thessaly. In 342 he replaced Arybbas as king of Epeiros with Alexandros, his own brother-in-law, and then once more invaded Thrace, a war which ended in 341 with the removal of the Thracian kings Teres and Kersebleptes from their thrones and the annexation of most of Thrace. The next two years were disappoint-

---

35. Philinna was, despite the statements of Plut. *Alex.* 77,7, Ptolemaios *apud* Athenaios XIII 578a, and Justin IX 8,2 and XIII 2,11, almost certainly not of lowly birth or indeed a dancer (Ptolemaios) or prostitute (thus Justin): see the remarks of J. H. Kroll, *RE* s.v. Philinna; she was perhaps rather a member of the Aleuad clan, with whom Philip allied himself at this time (Diod. XVI 14,2). For the remarriage of Antigonos's mother at this time (ca. 358/57), see n. 30 above.

36. For Philip's title, "*archōn* of Thessaly," which was for life, see Ellis, *Philip II,* pp. 83–84 and n. 103.

37. Philip was given the two Amphiktyonic Council seats of Phokis in perpetuity for himself and his descendants: Diod. XVI 60,1.

ing, with Philip suffering setbacks in the failed sieges of Perinthos and Byzantion, and a near disastrous campaign against the Triballians, in which he was badly wounded.[38] There is some evidence suggesting that Antigonos may have played an important role in the siege of Perinthos, and that it may have been the occasion on which he lost an eye, thereby earning his nickname "One-Eyed".

A story in Plutarch (*Alex.* 70) tells how an officer of Alexander named Antigenes the One-Eyed (Ἀντιγένης ὁ Ἑτερόφθαλμος) defrauded the king of some money and was found out and punished, but subsequently pardoned by the king in view of his distinguished military record, mentioning in particular heroic service at the siege of Perinthos. Tarn asserted long ago (*Alexander the Great,* 2: 314 n. 1) that this was a case of corruption in the MSS or other error, and that one should understand "Antigonos the One-Eyed." It is certainly the case that the names "Antigonos" and "Antigenes" are frequently confused in our sources,[39] that Antigenes (who really existed) is never otherwise referred to as one-eyed, and that it seems inherently improbable that the two men in Alexander's army referred to as *heterophthalmos* should happen to have names so similar as to be regularly confused in our sources. As if to confirm the matter, we read in two other passages in Plutarch (*Mor.* 180f–181a = *Apophth. Alex.* 21; *Mor.* 339c–d = *De fort. Alex.* 7) that Antigenes (not qualified in the former passage, in the latter called "Pellēnaios") was indeed nearly disgraced under Alexander, but it was to do with a love affair with a woman named Telesippa, and there is no mention of the siege of Perinthos or loss of an eye.[40]

However, matters are not so simple. The story of the money fraud and demotion cannot refer to Antigonos, who was not at Alexander's court at the time (324), being rather satrap of Phrygia, and who was never demoted; indeed, Plutarch tells this same story of

38. Philip nearly died of his wound from the Triballian campaign, and his forces suffered heavy losses in it (Justin IX 3,1–3): conceivably Antigonos's brother Demetrios died there (see n. 43 below).

39. Some examples are Diod. XVIII 39,6: "Antigonōi" for "Antigenei" in the MSS; *Heidelberger Epitome* (*FGrH,* no. 155) 1,4: "Antigonōi" for "Antigenei"; Nepos *Eum.* 5,1 and 7,1: "Antigonus" instead of "Antigenes." Corruption of names and even the meaningless substitution of one name for another (e.g., at Diod. XVIII 12,1: "Philōtan" for "Leonnaton") is all too common in the sources.

40. The epithet *heterophthalmos* is well-attested for Antigonos (see, e.g., Plut. *Mor.* 11b; *Sert.* 1; Aelian *VH* XII 43); it is nowhere used of Antigenes other than at Plut. *Alex.* 70, and nothing else known about Antigenes suggests that he was one-eyed. To make things even more confusing, Plut. *Alex.* 49,9–10 tells the Telesippa story with reference to one Eurylochos of Aigai. However, I take it that it was really Antigenes who got into trouble over Telesippa, and that Plutarch has confused him at *Alex.* 70 with Antigonos.

money fraud, including a much shortened version of loss of an eye at Perinthos, in his *De fort. Alex.* (= *Mor.* 339b) of a man named Atarrhias, son of Deinomenes. Obviously we are faced with considerable confusion here, but not beyond hope of sorting out. For as it happens, we know that Atarrhias really was the hero of a siege: at the siege of Halikarnassos by Alexander in 334 he stood heroically against a sortie when many younger men ignominiously fled (Curt. V 2,5; VIII 1,36). Perhaps the original anecdote had Atarrhias being forgiven by Alexander because of his heroism at Halikarnassos, but there existed a rival version attributing the money fraud to Antigonos, and saying that he only escaped punishment because of the memory of his courage when he lost an eye at Perinthos. This would come from some source hostile to Antigonos, the same perhaps as the source claiming that he was originally just a peasant farmer (Douris of Samos is an obvious possibility), and Plutarch has then thoroughly confused the two versions.[41] This is, of course, only one of several possible solutions to the muddle of these anecdotes, and indeed such anecdotes are in themselves by no means of indisputable historicity. However, my solution does have one great advantage: Antigonos certainly campaigned under Philip and lost an eye during one of his campaigns; the Perinthos story thus fits Antigonos better than we *know* it to fit anyone else.

If my conjecture is correct, then, we learn from Plutarch's anecdote the occasion of Antigonos's loss of his eye, and something of his service under Philip besides. Plutarch's story reads: "When he [sc., Antigonos] was still young, when Philip was besieging Perinthos, though a catapult bolt struck him in the eye, he did not submit to those wishing to extract the bolt or retreat until he had driven back the enemy and shut them behind their wall." It is clear from this that the wound occurred during a sortie of the Perinthians, which Antigonos repelled at the head of a body of Macedonian troops. Now the first half of the siege of Perinthos, when Philip sat down before the city with his whole army and subjected the place to a systematic

41. There is another source suggesting that Atarrhias fell into disfavor under Alexander: Aelian *VH* XIV 47a: [Alexander] *Ἀταρρίου ἐδεδίει τὸ ἄτακτον*. On the sources for Antigonos, see app. 1, pp. 329–40. There seems to have been a "hero literature" about some of Alexander's officers, one strand of which was devoted to showing their Achilles' heels, from which the anecdotes in question here derive. Curtius V 2,5 preserves a list of Alexander's heroes who were supposedly crowned at Sittakene for their heroism which includes Atarrhias, Antigenes, and Antigonos, as well as other famous men of mixed reputations like Alexandros the Lynkestian and Amyntas (Arrhabaiou?).

assault day and night, sending his troops in in relays, is described at considerable length by Diodoros (XVI 74–76) and there seems to be no possibility here of such a sortie, the Perinthians being confined to a desperate defensive. Subsequently, however, Philip moved on with half of his army to besiege Byzantion, and of the remainder of the siege of Perinthos our sources tell us next to nothing, not even who was left in charge. It was presumably at this stage of the siege that the Perinthian sortie took place, and it may well be that the Antigonos who felt bound to repel this sortie was the general left in charge of the siege, or at least of a substantial body of troops among those left to prosecute the siege.[42]

About this time, too, the death of Antigonos's brother Demetrios must have occurred, for Antigonos married his widow, Stratonike, and produced by her his oldest son, Demetrios (born ca. 337/36), soon enough for speculation to arise that the younger Demetrios was in fact the son of Antigonos's late brother, after whom he was named.[43] Conceivably Demetrios was killed at Perinthos or Byzantion, or in the Triballian campaign, in which Philip suffered heavy losses (see n. 38 above).

In the autumn of 339 the Amphiktyonic League declared a Sacred War against Amphissa and elected Philip as *hēgemōn*. This led to Philip's war against Thebes and Athens, which culminated in 338 with his decisive victory at Chaironeia and the establishment of a treaty of common peace (what might be called the "Hellenic Treaty Organization"), with Philip as organizer and leader, at Korinth in the spring of 337. War was declared on Persia, and Philip, now at the height of his power, was to head the Hellenic crusade in Asia. Since Antigonos was the leader of the force of 7,000 hoplites provided by this Hellenic alliance when Alexander crossed into Asia in 334 (Arrian *Anab.* I 29,3) it is possible that he could already have been involved

42. Hamilton, *Plutarch "Alexander,"* p. 196, doubts that Antigonos could have been called a *neos* in 340 (aged about forty-two), but Plutarch actually says ἔτι δὲ νέος ὢν—"being *still* young then," which would apply to Antigonos as against his age fifteen years later. Kassandros, for example, is called a *neos* at Diod. XVIII 48,5 in 319 B.C., when he was about thirty-six (born ca. 355, as we can deduce from Hegesandros *apud* Athenaios I 18a). The concepts "old" and "young" were relative in antiquity, as now. It is noteworthy that Antigonos was surrounded by men who "wished to draw out the dart," and that he seems to have felt responsible for dealing with the Perinthian sortie: evidently he was in some sort of command position. Ellis, *Philip II,* p. 178, suggests that Parmenion was left in charge of the siege of Perinthos, which is possible but unattested. If he is right, Antigonos would have been one of Parmenion's lieutenants during this phase of the siege.

43. See Plut. *Dem.* 2 for this; Demetrios's birth date of ca. 337/36 follows from Plut. *Dem.* 52, stating that he died in his fifty-fifth year, which is known to have occurred in 283 B.C..

with organizing this alliance under Philip, for in 334 Alexander had not yet had the time or achieved the standing to alter Philip's arrangements substantially. Before starting the war with Persia, Philip conducted one more campaign in Illyria, against a chieftain named Pleurias. Then in 336 he sent his most trusted general, Parmenion, into Asia Minor with an advance force to prepare a bridgehead for the main army. However, before he could conduct this crossing, Philip was assassinated at Aigai during the festivities of the marriage of his daughter, Kleopatra, to King Alexandros of Epeiros, a marriage no doubt intended to secure his rear during his absence in Asia.[44]

Two things stand out clearly about these impressive achievements: Philip certainly did not manage all of this alone, and he could not have done all of this with the weak, unorganized, and disunited country, nobility, and army of Macedon in the early fourth century. To deal with the latter point first, Philip II is known to have been one of the most successful reformers in history. His reforming activity touched most aspects of Macedonian life and created the strong, unified Macedon which alone could fulfill his ambitious plans of conquest, though his successful military activity was itself a necessary precondition for his being able to carry out effective reforms. The successes he attained in handling the crises of 359 were thus vital, and the reforms he carried out in the military sphere were the earliest and most necessary of his reforms. Significantly, perhaps, Philip had spent three years of his youth in Thebes, then the greatest military power in Greece and the home of a group of innovative military thinkers. Even if Philip did not himself come into contact with the great Epaminondas and Pelopidas (as he certainly may have done), he is known to have lodged as a hostage at the house of Pammenes, who was of the circle of the two great men and a fine general in his own right.[45] There is every reason to suppose that the military innovations of the Thebans, and indeed of the great Athenian *condottieri* Iphikrates and Chabrias, influenced Philip.

However that may be, the tenor and much of the detail of Philip's military reforms is tolerably well preserved.[46] As to the cavalry, they

---

44. For the "Hellenic Treaty Organization," see pp. 192–94 below. On the family events in Philip's last years, see the interesting and convincing discussion of Ellis, *Philip II*, pp. 209–27.

45. Plut. *Pelopidas* 26, and see *RE* s.v. Pammenes, no. 1 [Lenschau] for the career of Pammenes. Though Philip was only an adolescent of fifteen or sixteen at the time of his Theban sojourn, this does not mean he could not have picked up some ideas on warfare while there; cf. the precocity of Alexander at sixteen (Plut. *Alex*. 9,1).

46. See, e.g., Griffith's accounts in Hammond and Griffith, *History of Macedonia*, 2: 405–49, and in "Philip as a General and the Macedonian Army."

were excellent already and needed not so much to be reformed as to be increased in number: at the time of Philip's campaign against Bardylis in 358 he had 600 cavalry; at the time of his death in 336 the number of the Macedonian cavalry was apparently around 3,500.[47] This increase was due in part to Philip's assertion of his sovereignty over the upper Macedonian regions and addition of their cavalry levies to his army; in part to the importation of numerous Greeks and others, who were settled on conquered lands and added to the *hetairoi;* and in part, no doubt, to Philip's greatly improved revenues, which would have enabled him to provide cavalry equipment to men who were otherwise suitable for cavalry service but lacked the means to equip themselves. And after 352, as *archōn* of Thessaly, Philip could in addition to his Macedonians call out the Thessalian cavalry, who were in no way inferior to the Macedonian cavalry in quality.[48]

Philip's reform of the Macedonian infantry was much more thoroughgoing. As recorded by Diodoros (XVI 3,1–6, placing Philip's entire infantry reform in his first year as king—no doubt an exaggeration) it was Philip who created the Macedonian infantry phalanx: *πρῶτος συνεστήσατο τὴν Μακεδονικὴν φάλαγγα.* This means that he was the first man to form up the Macedonian infantry for close-order fighting as heavy infantry. Before his time the Macedonians had had no heavy infantry worth speaking of, except a few Greek hoplites—mercenary or metic. The problem was the expense of the equipment—helmet, cuirass, greaves, and large shield (*hoplon*)—which few Macedonians could afford. Philip got around this by creating (perhaps in part after the model of Iphikrates' mercenary infantry) a new type of heavy infantryman, without the expensive cuirass and *hoplon,* and in some cases perhaps lacking greaves, but compensated for this lack of defensive armor by the issue of a new pike, the *sarissa.* This pike was some thirteen feet long and required both hands to manipulate; when used by a mass of men in close formation, it produced a formidable array of serried points that was virtually invulnerable to frontal assault. As defensive armor the pike-

47. Diod. XVI 4,3 (campaign against Bardylis); Diod. XVII 17,4–5 says that in 334 Alexander took 1,800 Companion cavalry with him to Asia and left 1,500 cavalry with Antipatros in Europe; in addition there was probably some Macedonian cavalry already in Asia under Kalas (this advance force was a mixed one of mercenaries and Macedonians: Diod. XVII 7,10), so that a total of some 3,500 seems reasonable.

48. Alexander took 1,800 Thessalian cavalry with him to Asia (Diod. XVII 17,4); they fought in all of Alexander's major battles down to Gaugamela, and later distinguished themselves fighting on the Greek side in the Lamian War (Diod. XVIII 12,3–4; 15,2–4: 2,000 Thessalian cavalry were responsible for the Greek victory over Leonnatos).

men had helmets, small shields strapped to the left arm (*aspides*), no doubt some sort of padded jerkin, and, in most cases, greaves.[49]

In addition to thus creating a truly formidable Macedonian infantry force (numbering 10,000 in 358, and some 24,000 by the end of Philip's reign), Philip apparently adopted from Sparta and Thebes the notion of using a special corps d'élite to decide his battles. He established a special infantry guard called the *pezetairoi* (Foot Companions), selected from the Macedonian infantry as the biggest, strongest, and fittest.[50] In his first major battle—that against Bardylis in 358—we read of Philip using "the best of the Macedonians" (i.e., presumably the *pezetairoi*) on the right wing to break open the Illyrian infantry square, allowing the cavalry to exploit the break to take the Illyrians in flank and rear. Unfortunately our sources on Philip's battles are too brief to illustrate his further use of the *pezetairoi* (though Demosthenes *Ol.* II 17 attests to their reputation for excellence, and a snippet preserved by the Etymologicon Magnum seems to show them in action in Illyria), but their excellence and the kind of use made of them is well demonstrated under Alexander (when their name had been changed to *hypaspistai*) and under the Diadochoi (when they were known as the *argyraspides*).[51] The reasoning behind Philip's creation of this unit is clear enough: besides the historic lessons on the value of even a small corps d'élite provided by the Spartiates and the Theban Sacred Band, there is the fact that the training of a whole army to use new equipment and tactics requires a lot of time; by picking out his best infantrymen for special training and special use in battle, Philip eased the transition of the mass of the infantry into their new role by not requiring too much of them all at once.

---

49. On the equipment of the Macedonian infantry, see Griffith, *PCPhS* 4 (1956/57):3–10.

50. For the number of the Macedonian heavy infantry, see Diod. XVI 4,3 (10,000 in the campaign against Bardylis) and XVII 17,4–5 (Alexander took 12,000 Macedonian infantry to Asia, and left 12,000 in Europe with Antipatros). For the *pezetairoi,* see Griffith in Hammond and Griffith, *History of Macedonia,* 2:414–18, and ibid., app. 3, pp. 705–13.

51. Diod. XVI 3,5–7 describes Philip's battle against Bardylis, and cf. Diod. XVI 86,1 where Philip at the battle of Chaironeia leads "the selected infantry." Both the *aristous* at the Bardylis battle and the *epilektous* of Chaironeia were infantry (the former is shown by Philip's separate instructions to his cavalry: Diod. XVI 3,5; the latter is proved by Polyainos IV 2,2, which has Philip in command of infantry at Chaironeia). It makes sense to equate these "best" and "selected" infantry with Theopompos's *pezetairoi*. The *Etymologicon Magnum* preserves the snippet: "He [sc., Philip] invaded Illyria taking the Macedonians called *pezetairoi* with him, these being selected men." This must refer to one of Philip's Illyrian campaigns in 345 (against Pleuratos) or 337 (against Pleurias). For the later name changes of this unit, see chap. 3 n. 25 below.

Indeed, Philip's reforms in military matters went far beyond the mere externals of equipment and formation. In training, in tactics, and in strategy Philip fostered a new professionalism of approach that made his army more than a match for any other that might be brought against him. He boosted the morale of his men by instituting a system of rewards and promotions for good service; he taught his men their job by leading them on arduous route marches and training exercises; he adopted the Theban principle of concentrating his main attack with his best troops on one particular part of the enemy's formation, using victory at that point as a lever to win overall victory; and he was a pioneer in the use of combined arms, using infantry and cavalry in concert to achieve victory on the field of battle, and instituting the thorough and vigorous pursuit of the broken enemy by the cavalry to make his victories decisive.[52] He was the first to arrange the Macedonian heavy cavalry in wedge formation for their charge, which enabled them better to exploit gaps in enemy ranks and made them more responsive to their leader, who rode at the apex of the wedge. In terms of strategy, he was an exponent of the rapid strike—often campaigning in as many as three widely separated theaters in one season—and extended the campaigning season to nine or ten months of the year, instead of the six or so previously customary; he combined the achievement of strategic surprise by means of rapid movement with the rigorous application of the newest techniques and instruments of siegecraft, creating a siege train which enabled him to capture cities like Amphipolis, Potidaia, and Pydna in quite brief sieges, so that his operations did not bog down in the face of fortifications.[53]

Philip's reforming zeal was not limited to military matters. In the social field, he increased his control over the nobility by three main expedients: he instituted the so-called "Page system," whereby the children of the nobility were trained at his court in personal attendance upon himself, being themselves thereby inculcated with loyalty to his person and simultaneously acting as hostages for the loyalty of their parents; he diluted the power of the old Macedonian nobility by

52. For Philip's training exercises and route marches, see Diod. XVI 3,1–2 and Polyainos IV 2,10; for his battlefield tactics and use of combined arms, see Griffith, "Philip as a General and the Macedonian Army."

53. That Philip introduced the wedge formation for the Macedonian cavalry is attested by Aelian *Taktika* 18,4 and Arrian *Taktika* 16,6. For Philip's strategy and his lengthening of the campaign season, see Griffith, "Philip as a General and the Macedonian Army"; for his siege train, see Griffith in Hammond and Griffith, *History of Macedonia* 2:444–49.

bringing into Macedon large numbers of Greeks and other foreigners, whom he admitted to his *hetaireia* and granted estates on conquered land, building thus a large body of *hetairoi* bound entirely to himself; and by granting the Macedonian nobles themselves large estates on conquered land, which they held at his pleasure, he bound them to his interest.[54] As to the rest of society, too, by a policy of population transplants he diminished ethnic resistance to Argead suzerainty and made the transplanted people dependent on himself; and his foundation of new cities in conquered territory (Philippoi and Philippopolis are the best known, but there were others in Thrace, Thessaly, and elsewhere) helped secure his conquests, while at the same time moving dissatisfied elements out of Macedon proper and binding them to his support in their new homes.[55] With regard to the economy, finally, a settled internal peace provided the precondition for economic growth, and Philip evidently promoted improved agriculture, while a regular system of taxation and the exploitation of the Pangaion mines set the state finances on a solid footing.[56]

The effect of all of this reforming activity was to unify the country, strengthen Philip's position as head of state, and create the opportunity for Macedon to become a great power. The establishment of the regular heavy infantry ensured the primacy within the state of Philip, its creator and leader: no aristocratic faction could hope to prevail in warfare against the *pezetairoi* and the rest of the infantry phalanx. Only foreign military aid could do that, so that it is no surprise under Philip and Alexander to find dissident Macedonians living in Olynthos, Athens, or the Persian Empire.[57] Within Macedon opposition could be expressed only by competing for Philip's

54. That Philip instituted the "Page system" is shown by Arrian *Anab.* IV 13,1 and Aelian *VH* XIV 48; for his introduction of Greeks and "other foreigners" into the *hetairoi,* see Theopompos in *FGrH,* no. 115 F 224, 225a, and 225b; for his granting of estates, see, for example, *Syll.*, no. 322 (estate in Chalkidike granted by Philip to Polemokrates, father of Koinos), and [Demosthenes] VII 39–41.

55. For Philip's population transplants and city foundations, see Ellis, *Makedonika* 9 (1969):9–17, and Hammond in Hammond and Griffith, *History of Macedonia* 2:660–62.

56. See Hammond (loc. cit. n. 55), pp. 647–74.

57. E.g., Philip's half-brothers Menelaos and Arrhidaios took refuge at Olynthos (Justin VIII 3,10); one Menelaos of Pelagonia was in Philip's reign an Athenian citizen and helped Athens against Macedon (*RE* s.v. Menelaos no. 5 [Geyer]), though he had already left Macedon before Philip's time; several enemies of Alexander fled to Persia, for example, Amyntas Antiochou (Berve, vol. 2, no. 58) and Neoptolemos Arrhabaiou (Berve, vol. 2, no. 547). Of course Macedonians fled to foreign states before Philip's time too; but under Philip a dissident had no option but to live abroad: one could not maintain oneself in Macedon as Philippos and Derdas had in the time of Perdikkas II (Thuc. I 57; 59; 61).

ear, or, failing that, attempting assassination; by and large, however, most nobles profited from the new dispensation and supported it, the more so because Philip, though he had made the kingship akin to a tyranny,[58] was a genial and generous leader who knew how to inspire genuine loyalty and popularity. For the rest, the mixing up of the population by transplants and common service in the army largely overcame the old tribal disunity of Macedon, while the imperialistic (and highly successful) foreign policy created a buoyant feeling of Macedonian superiority and provided an outlet for Macedonian aggression. It was also doubtless easier for Philip to pursue the consciously Hellenizing policy that was characteristic of his rule, as it was of those earlier strong Macedonian kings Alexandros I and Archelaos, from a position of superior strength vis-à-vis the Greek world.[59]

Again it must be stressed that this was not all the work of one man: Philip was clearly the head of a group of reform-minded Macedonians, who helped him put the state in order. The work of Parmenion as Philip's chief military aide and Antipatros as a trusted administrative and diplomatic agent, as well as a military officer, is well enough known not to need elaboration. Antigonos was clearly also involved: his importance at Philip's court in this period is shown by the friendships he established with Antipatros and Eumenes, the head of Philip's chancery, or secretarial staff.[60] It cannot be too strongly emphasized that the training and experience Antigonos received as an aide in this extraordinary state-building activity under Philip must have been the most important influence on his own career as a ruler and state-builder after the death of Alexander.

---

58. The parallel between the Macedonian kingship under Philip and Alexander and the early Greek tyrannies is worth noting: like the early Greek tyrants, Philip established his power by invoking a new military class of organized heavy infantry against the old military aristocracy. Demosthenes and Theopompos paint Philip's court like that of a Greek tyrant, full of flatterers and sycophants (e.g., Dem. *Ol.* 2. 17–20; Theopompos in *FGrH,* no. 115 F 224, 225a, 225b). The difference is that Philip was a legitimate monarch, who preferred to coopt the aristocracy rather than weed them out, having the advantage of living in a strongly monarchical society.

59. Alexandros I's epithet "Philhellene" speaks for itself (Harpokration s.v. Alexandros); for Archelaos, see above n. 22; Philip had his son educated by Aristotle and admitted large numbers of Greeks to his *hetairoi.*

60. For Antigonos's friendship with Antipatros, see Diod. XVIII 23,3; 54,4; for his friendship with Eumenes, see Diod. XVIII 41,6; XIX 44,2; Plut. *Eum.* 10,3. Eumenes came from an upper-class Kardian family, and his father was a guest-friend of Philip's: Plut. *Eum.* 1,2 and cf. Hornblower, *Hieronymus of Cardia,* pp. 8–9; he spent seven years at Philip's court (Nepos *Eum.* 1,6), and the reliance later placed on him by Olympias shows his position was a prominent one (Diod. XVIII 58,2–4; Plut. *Eum.* 13,1). That these friendships of Antigonos's date from Philip's reign is evident from the fact that during Alexander's reign he was separated from these men as satrap of Phrygia.

THE REIGN OF ALEXANDER (336–323 B.C.)

It is under Alexander that Antigonos finally emerges fully into the historical sources, and though he was not one of the most prominent officers of Alexander, still a good deal is known of him during Alexander's reign. The composition of the army with which Alexander crossed into Asia is given by Diodoros (XVII 17,3–4) as 12,000 Macedonian infantry, 7,000 allied Greek infantry, and 5,000 mercenaries; 7,000 Balkan light infantry and 1,000 archers and Agrianian javelin men; 1,800 Macedonian cavalry under Philotas, 1,800 Thessalian cavalry led by Kalas, 600 Greek cavalry under Erigyios and 900 Thracians and Paionians under Kassandros.[61] The commander of the 7,000 allied Greek infantry was Antigonos Monophthalmos, thereby one of the major figures in the expeditionary force (see Arrian *Anab.* I 29,3, recording that when Antigonos was made satrap of Phrygia in early 333, Balakros was appointed to command the Greek allied infantry *in his place*). Unfortunately this is the only mention in Arrian of any posts held under Alexander by Antigonos, and Arrian records no deeds of Antigonos whatsoever. The reason for this was seen long ago already by Tarn: Arrian's chief source for military matters was Ptolemy, the later king of Egypt, and "Ptolemy was not going to relate the *acta* of one who had been his most bitter enemy [i.e., Antigonos]."[62] Nevertheless, some of Antigonos's deeds are recorded in other sources, and more can be recovered by careful analysis of Arrian.

In the first place, Antigonos must have taken part in the battle of the Granikos in 334. Closely following Arrian's account, one finds that Alexander, after visiting Ilion, "came to Arisbe, where his whole force had encamped after crossing the Hellespont" (*Anab.* I 12,6), whence he then set out with his army, marching past Perkote and Lampsakos to Hermotos. He was heading eastward along the Hel-

---

61. For a review of modern scholarship on Alexander, see Seibert, *Alexander der Grosse*. The Greek cavalry was in fact led by Philippos Menelaou at the crossing into Asia (Arrian *Anab.* I 14,2: the battle order at the Granikos), and taken over by Erigyios before Gaugamela (Arrian *Anab.* III 11,10); whether Kassandros really crossed with Alexander to Asia has been doubted by many scholars (e.g., Berve, vol. 2, no. 414), but see now Adams "Cassander: The Policy of Coalition," pp. 44–50, defending Diodoros's statement; also id., *AncW* 2, no. 4 (1979):111–15.

62. Tarn, *Alexander,* 2: 110, not without a little exaggeration of the enmity between Ptolemy and Antigonos; cf. Diod. XIX 64,8 and 85,3. For further modern suggestions of bias by Ptolemy, see Errington, *CQ*, n.s., 19 (1969):233–42, arguing for bias against Perdikkas and Aristonous; Bosworth, *Entretiens Hardt* 22 (1975):1–33.

lespont, and sent scouts ahead under Amyntas Arrhabaiou (*Anab.* I 12,7). The Persians were encamped with a large force near Zeleia, east of the Granikos, and Alexander evidently had some inkling of this, for (*Anab.* I 13,1): "Alexander was advancing to the river Granikos with his force all ready for battle, after drawing up his hoplites in two lines [διπλῆν μὲν τὴν φάλαγγα τῶν ὁπλιτῶν τάξας], with the cavalry on the wings, and ordering the baggage train to follow behind. The advance reconnoitering party was under the command of Hegelochos, with the lancers as cavalry, and 500 light infantry." It must be strongly emphasized here that according to Arrian's narrative the *entire* army advanced thus, ready for battle, towards the Granikos, except for a small detachment sent to occupy Priapos.

Arrian, however, makes no mention whatever in his account of the actual battle at the Granikos of the allied Greek infantry, the Greek mercenary infantry, or most of the Balkan light infantry—and most modern authorities follow him in this, despite the fact that it is generally recognized that Arrian's account of the battle is highly unsatisfactory. Unfortunately, Arrian's is the only account we have to go by, for Diodoros's seems completely wrong and Plutarch's is essentially a briefer and more rhetorical version of Arrian's.[63] But since the entire army advanced towards the Granikos, it must be assumed that the allied and mercenary Greek hoplites were present; in fact it was pointed out long since by Judeich that Arrian's phrase διπλῆν μὲν τὴν φάλαγγα τῶν ὁπλιτῶν τάξας clearly implies the presence of the Greek hoplites, in that it speaks of a "double phalanx," and that this is repeated at the battle of Gaugamela, where it is universally accepted that it was the Greek hoplites who formed the rear echelon of this "double phalanx."[64]

63. On the errors of Diodoros and the inadequacies of Arrian, whose account concentrates on the person of Alexander to the exclusion of what is happening in the rest of the battle, see Badian, *Arch. Mak.* 2 (1977):271–93. The problems surrounding the battle of the Granikos are now carefully reviewed by Bosworth, *Historical Comm.*, 1:107–27; he prefers Diodoros's account to that of Arrian, wrongly in my opinion, but otherwise gives many valuable insights.

64. See Judeich, *Klio* 8 (1908):372–97. For Alexander's double phalanx and the role of the Greek allies at the battle of Gaugamela, see further Marsden, *Campaign of Gaugamela*, pp. 65–67. Given the undoubted significance of the διπλῆν φάλαγγα at Gaugamela, there is every reason to take it in the same sense in Arrian's description of the Granikos battle, *contra* Badian (loc. cit. n. 63), who rejects Judeich's theory in a footnote, without argument (p. 283 n. 41); Nikolitsis, *Battle of the Granicus*, pp. 20–24, also rejects Judeich's theory, but his alternative theory as to the whereabouts of the Greek allied and mercenary infantry is based on altering Arrian's text so as to have the Greek infantry deployed in the front line, which is not acceptable. Bosworth, *Historical Comm.*, 1:119, describes Judeich's view as "the most popular and cogent view" and accepts it as correct.

Furthermore, Arrian gives the number of the Persian infantry as 20,000 (*Anab.* I 14,4), and though he is obviously wrong in stating that these were all Greek mercenaries, the number itself is credible enough.[65] Arrian also states (*Anab.* I 13,3) that the Macedonians outnumbered the Persians in infantry: 12,000 Macedonians would not give Alexander's army numerical superiority, but 12,000 Macedonians plus 12,000 Greeks plus 7,000 Balkan infantry does. Hence the Greeks were indeed present at the Granikos, and we must understand that when Alexander advanced with a διπλῆν φάλαγγα, this means a phalanx drawn up in two columns: one of 12,000 Macedonians, and the other made up of the 12,000 Greek hoplites. At *Anab.* I 13,2 we read that when the advance scouts rode back to inform Alexander that the Persians were drawn up for battle on the far bank of the Granikos, he "formed the whole army for battle." By this we must understand that the troops deployed from column into line, the Macedonians forming the front line and the Greek heavy infantry deploying into line behind them, creating the "double phalanx."[66] Thus Antigonos must have been present at the battle of the Granikos in his position of general of the 7,000 Greek allies, whom he would have commanded in this battle. Arrian simply ignores this fact, listing in his account of the battle at I 14,1–3 only the Macedonian troops and their officers, and concentrating his account of the fighting on the person of Alexander.

After this victorious battle, Alexander marched south towards the Aegean coast, secured control of Sardis, and from there set out for Ephesos. At the same time, he sent a force under Kalas, whom he had made satrap of Hellespontine Phrygia, and Alexandros the Lynkestian to take over "Memnon's land," which was apparently in the Troad.[67] This force consisted of "the Peloponnesians and many of the other allies except the Argives, for these were left in Sardis to garrison

65. Badian (loc. cit. n. 63) points out that the Persian satraps in Asia Minor cannot have had as many as 20,000 Greek mercenaries; however, with a few thousand Greeks and a large number of Asian light infantry, they may have had a total of some 20,000 infantry altogether.

66. Since Arrian *Anab.* I 13,1–2 clearly implies two evolutions in Alexander's army—he drew it up with a "double phalanx," marched to the Granikos, and then arranged it ready for battle—evidently Alexander marched his army forward in the formation he expected to give battle in, but in column rather than line. At the river the two columns of infantry deployed into line one behind the other, the Macedonians in front (Arrian I 14,2–3). Nikolitsis's view (*Battle of the Granicus*, pp. 14–15) that the army marched some 4–7 km. towards the Granikos in full *line* of battle is thus disproved by Arrian's text, and in any case impossible: such a march would cause the greatest difficulties in keeping formation as soon as any obstacle or unevenness of the ground occurred, as was bound to happen on a march this long.

67. See Polyainos IV 3,15; Strabo XIII 587.

the citadel" (*Anab.* I 17,8). Some modern commentators have assumed this to refer to all of the Greek allies, and either suppose that Antigonos must have accompanied this expedition as a subordinate of Kalas and Alexandros, or else wonder about the nature of his command when his troops were here sent into action under the orders of others.[68] However, Arrian does not say that all of the Greek allies were sent; the Peloponnesians were sent, and by this Arrian presumably means the infantry, for he excepts the Argives, who (being stationed as a garrison at Sardis) were certainly infantry.[69] As to the "many of the other allies," since Alexandros was at this time commander of the Thessalian cavalry, their identity may easily be guessed.

In short, the expedition sent to the Troad consisted of the Peloponnesian infantry (except the Argives), the Thessalian cavalry, and perhaps some (but certainly not all) of the other allied Greek troops. The commanders were Kalas, in whose satrapy the Troad lay, and Alexandros, who led the Thessalian cavalry. It would have been otiose to send Antigonos as well, and in fact he is known to have accompanied Alexander south from Ephesos, presumably in command of the remaining Greek allies (i.e., those from Athens and central Greece). For while Alexander hurried from Ephesos to Miletos, he sent out expeditions to take over other Greek cities: Parmenion with 5,000 infantry and 200 cavalry to Magnesia and Tralleis; Alkimachos, son of Agathokles, with an equal force to the Ionian and Aiolian communities north of Ephesos; and Antigonos to Priene. Parmenion's expedition and that of Alkimachos are recorded by Arrian (*Anab.* I 18,1–2); Antigonos's mission is passed over and is known to us only from an inscription.[70] Despite the silence of Ptolemy/Arrian, however, there is no reason to suppose that Antigonos's job at Priene (a more important city at that date than Magnesia or Tralleis, controlling as it did Cape Mykale and having in its territory the Panionion) was in any essential way different from the tasks of

68. U. Koehler, *SDAW,* 1898, p. 126, supposes that Antigonos went with Kalas and Alexandros as a subordinate; Briant, *Antigone le Borgne,* pp. 34–41, shows that Antigonos did not do so, but concludes from this that Antigonos's post as *stratēgos* of the allies was in military terms a "commandement fictif."

69. The text of Arrian here (*Anab.* I 17,8) actually seems to suggest that the Argives were excepted from the "other allies," but as the Argives obviously *were* Peloponnesians, it is clear that Arrian is here speaking loosely and that the meaning is simply that Kalas and Alexandros were sent "leading the Peloponnesians (and many of the other allies) except the Argives."

70. Hiller von Gaertringen, *I. Priene,* no. 2 (= Tod, *GHI,* no. 186); for the date and significance of this inscription, see, e.g., Briant, *Antigone le Borgne,* p. 35 n. 3 and pp. 37–39.

Parmenion and Alkimachos, and like them Antigonos would have had a substantial force with him, presumably the Greek allies who had not gone with Kalas to the Troad.[71]

From Miletos Alexander proceeded to Halikarnassos, where the Persian generals Orontobates and Memnon had collected a large force to hold the city and block his progress. After some very heavy fighting, however, Halikarnassos fell to Alexander, the siege apparently not taking more than a week or two (Arrian *Anab.* I 20,4–23,8). Since the Greek allies were present at the siege (id. I 24,3) one assumes that Antigonos, too, took part. When the siege was over, Alexander sent Parmenion with the Greek allies, part of the Companion Cavalry, the Thessalian cavalry, and the baggage train to Sardis, with orders to winter there and proceed along the Royal Road to Phrygia in the spring. Alexander himself, with most of the rest of the army (a party of newlyweds had been sent home to Macedon for the winter), conducted a winter campaign in Lykia, Pamphylia, Pisidia, and Phrygia (id. I 24,3–29,4). It has been disputed whether Antigonos accompanied Parmenion to Sardis or Alexander on his winter campaign.[72] A third possibility is that he may have gone with the newlyweds to Macedon for the winter, for he had left his wife, married about 338, with a 2-year-old child and probably pregnant with his second son, Philippos (see app. 3 below, no. 92). In this case he may have been with his wife for Philippos's birth and have returned to Alexander at Kelainai in Phrygia in early spring.

Antigonos also took part in Alexander's war councils during the campaign of 334/33 in Asia Minor, dispensing advice on its conduct. The sources tend to create the impression that Alexander decided everything quite alone during his *anabasis,* only now and then taking time to forcefully reject advice offered him by Parmenion, and there is an understandable tendency on the part of modern writers on Alexander to follow the ancient sources in at least the first part of that impression. Fortunately, there are a number of passages in the sources that supply a corrective, showing that Alexander consulted *hetairoi*

71. Arrian's statement that Kalas took the Peloponnesian infantry, except the Argives, and many others (certainly including cavalry) seems to imply that the majority of the non-Peloponnesian infantry did not go with Kalas. Though the precise numbers sent by various Greek states are not known, presumably the contributions of Attica, Boiotia, and the rest of Central Greece to the 7,000 allied infantry must have at least equaled the contributions of the Peloponnesian states (especially as Sparta was not included among the latter). Hence a force of several thousand is likely, and in any case Antigonos's force should be at least roughly comparable to the forces of Parmenion and Alkimachos.

72. Briant, *Antigone le Borgne,* pp. 35–37, 42–43, argues that Antigonos accompanied Alexander; Bosworth, *Historical Comm.,* 1:174, that he did not; given the silence of the sources neither view can be established.

and officers before deciding and took their views into account. A classic instance of this is the war council described by Arrian (*Anab.* III 9,3–4) before the battle of Gaugamela: "Alexander . . . sighted the enemy; he stopped his phalanx, and calling together the *hetairoi* and generals and *ilarchoi* [cavalry officers] and the leaders of the allies and the mercenaries, he held a council [ἐβουλεύετο]." What is more, Alexander took the advice of this council, which was to remain where he was and carefully survey the plain of Gaugamela for any traps before advancing to battle. We may be sure that similar councils would have been held in Asia Minor, and that Antigonos would have taken a prominent part in them, for he was both a *hetairos* and a general, and in the latter capacity was the superior of "the leaders of the allies," who, we have seen, were also present at these war councils.[73]

Clearly, then, Antigonos played a prominent role during the first stage of Alexander's *anabasis* in 334/33 B.C. With his appointment as satrap of greater Phrygia in early spring of 333, however, his position vis-à-vis Alexander underwent a great change, for he could no longer make any contribution to the overall direction of the war, and was deprived of direct contact with the king (always important in a personal monarchy such as Macedon was). Nevertheless, the post of satrap of greater Phrygia was an important one, and in appointing Antigonos to this post, Alexander displayed great confidence in his abilities. For when Alexander joined Parmenion at Gordion and hurried from there along the west bank of the Halys and over the Taurus Mountains into Kilikia, he left behind him in Asia Minor a vast territory that was in large part only nominally "conquered," and that was certainly not pacified. To be sure the Hellespontine region, Lydia, Karia, and Lykia/Pamphylia were fairly securely held, but Pisidia and Phrygia had been merely traversed by Alexander, and Paphlagonia and Kappadokia had been almost entirely bypassed, after receipt of a formal act of surrender.[74] Surveillance of these critical

73. Other councils of Alexander are attested—for example, before Issos (Arrian *Anab.* II 7,3), at Tyre (*Anab.* II 16,8), and at the Hyphasis in India (*Anab.* V 25,2); cf. on the "*Offiziersrat,*" Berve, 1:211–12.

74. Alexander traversed Pisidia without stopping to capture Termessos (Arrian *Anab.* I 28,2), and in Phrygia did not wait to receive the surrender of Kelainai (see Briant, *Antigone le Borgne*, pp. 46, 101–8, but note that his use of Seneca *De ira* III 22, 4–5 is unwarranted, for this anecdote certainly refers to Antigonos Gonatas, not Monophthalmos). Alexander bypassed Paphlagonia, but received a formal act of submission and assigned the region to Kalas's satrapy (Arrian *Anab.* II 4,1; Curtius III 1,22); he never crossed the river Halys or invaded Kappadokia (Appian *Mithrid.* 8 = Hieronymos *FGrH,* no. 154 F 3), though according to Arrian *Anab.* II 4,2 he did march against Kappadokia as far as the Halys and receive the formal surrender of much of the region beyond that river, sending Sabiktas as satrap.

regions would fall to Antigonos, whose satrapy of greater Phrygia made up the heart of western Asia Minor, bordering on Paphlagonia in the north, Kappadokia in the east, and Pisidia in the south. All the great roads of Asia Minor passed through the satrapy, and it would take a good man to pacify the region and keep the roads open (see map 2).

When Alexander left Phrygia, he left behind him an enemy garrison still in occupation of the important citadel of Kelainai. From the accounts of Arrian (*Anab.* I 29,1–3) and Curtius (III 1,6–8), which are mutually complementary, we learn that the citadel of Kelainai was held by a garrison of 1,000 Karians and 100 Greeks, and that owing to the strength of the position and determined resistance of the garrison, Alexander did not care to press the siege. Instead, an agreement was reached whereby the garrison was to surrender if no aid from the Persians were to reach it within sixty days (thus Curtius). Alexander remained there for ten days, presumably resting his troops after the arduous winter campaign, and then pressed on to Gordion, leaving Antigonos 1,500 mercenaries to maintain the siege (thus Arrian). Since no help arrived within the alloted time, the garrison yielded to Antigonos, who doubtless enrolled them in his own service and took full possession of his new capital.[75] The surrender of the garrison must have occurred about the beginning of May 333, and it seems that with the main resistance to his control thus ended, and new troops made available to him by the same act, Antigonos sent on his 1,500 mercenaries to join Alexander for the major battle that was about to be fought between the Macedonians and Dareios's great Persian army, the battle of Issos.[76]

The battle of Issos was unusual in that the two armies concerned bypassed each other, so that they fought facing *towards* their own territories. As a result, when the Persians were defeated, most of the fugitives fled north into Asia Minor, which Alexander had just conquered. Alexander turned away from the battle to continue his

75. The major discrepancy between Arrian and Curtius at this point is that Curtius (III 1,9) has Alexander receive an Athenian embassy while at Kelainai, whereas Arrian says he received this embassy at Gordion (*Anab.* I 29,5), irrelevant to present purposes. Curtius's statement that the troops at Kelainai surrendered on the appointed day "to the king" ("ad praestitutam diem permisere se regi") need not imply Alexander's actual presence to receive the act of surrender.

76. Alexander reached Gordion at the beginning of spring 333; the surrender of the garrison at Kelainai was set for about fifty days later, which points to about the beginning of May. Curtius IV 1,35 remarks that Antigonos forwarded his troops to Alexander before Issos ("quamquam plerosque militum ex praesidiis ad regem dimiserat").

advance south towards Phoenicia, while behind him a considerable Persian force was built up during the winter of 333/32 in Kilikia, Kappadokia, and Paphlagonia by the fugitives from Issos.[77] The strategic situation that resulted from this is of a peculiar interest: while Alexander was engaged in securing Syria and Palestine (and in particular with the long and difficult siege of Tyre), Dareios was busy gathering a new army in Mesopotamia, the Persian fleet was engaged in a major offensive in the Aegean, and a large Persian force was gathering in eastern Asia Minor for an attempt to reconquer western Asia Minor and link up with the fleet on the Aegean coast.[78] If this had succeeded, Alexander would have been cut off from Macedon and would have had little choice but to break off his operations at Tyre and hurry north to try to restore the situation before Dareios could come west and catch him between two fires. Many commanders would have been diverted from their plans by such a threat; Alexander, with typical coolness, pressed ahead with the siege of Tyre, trusting in his man on the spot in Asia Minor to deal with the situation. That man was Antigonos.

Our only source on the Persian counterattack in Asia Minor in early 332 is Curtius IV 1,34–35, and it is worth giving here in full:

> The generals of Darius who escaped from the battle at Issos attempted to recapture Lydia with the entire force that had accompanied them in their flight and with the youth of Cappadocia and Paphlagonia, which they had levied. Antigonus, Alexander's general, was in charge of Lydia; even though he had previously sent most of the soldiers from his garrisons to the king, he nevertheless brought out his men to battle in his disdain for the barbarians. Here again the fortune of the two sides was the same: in three battles in different regions, the Persians were repulsed.

Brief as this account is, it is full of interest for the historian of Antigonos. In the first place, there is the fact that Curtius gives the recapture of *Lydia* as the Persians' aim, and says that Antigonos was in charge of Lydia (*Lydiae praeerat*). Tarn, the first to see the importance of this information (*Alexander the Great,* 2:110–11) simply assumes that "Lydia" is an error for "Phrygia" in both places; Burn,

77. Curtius IV 1,34: "Darei praetores, qui proelio apud Isson superfuerant cum omni manu, quae fugientes secuta erat." It has been conjectured that the Persian chiliarch Nabarzanes could have been at the head of these "*Darei praetores*" (see, e.g., Briant, *Antigone le Borgne,* p. 55 n. 10).

78. See the excellent exposition by Burn, *JHS* 72 (1952):81–84.

whose analysis of this passage is more thorough, holds that it really was the Persian aim to recapture Lydia in order to link up with the Persian fleet on the Ionian coast, but agrees with Tarn that the second mention of Lydia is an error for Phrygia, Antigonos's satrapy;[79] and Briant has put forward a hypothesis according to which Curtius has here quite consciously and correctly spoken of Lydia in both places, referring thereby to the old Lydian Empire, consisting of everything west of the river Halys. On this theory Antigonos was given a temporary supreme command over all of western Asia Minor in order to deal with this emergency, which threatened the entire Macedonian position, in Asia Minor and beyond.[80]

Briant's hypothesis stretches the evidence too far, though it is true that in the aftermath of this Persian counterattack, we find the satraps Antigonos, Kalas, and Balakros campaigning jointly to mop up pockets of Persian resistance (Curtius IV 5,13). In any case, with the Persians temporarily taking over Kilikia (Balakros's satrapy) and Paphlagonia (part of Kalas's satrapy) again, these two satraps would have had every cause to throw in their forces together with those of Antigonos.[81] As there were three battles in different regions, and also three great routes westward through Asia Minor, it seems likely that the Persians launched a three-pronged assault along these three routes: the Royal Road in the north, running from northern Kappadokia via Ankyra and Pessinos to Sardis; the central route, running via the later Laodikea Katakekaumene and Philomelion to Synnada, where it joined the Royal Road; and the southern, or Pisidian, route, running up from Kilikia via Laranda and Ikonion to Kelainai (see map 2). All three routes pass through Phrygia in order to reach the coast, which was the cause of the strategic importance of this satrapy. It is not known what forces Antigonos had at his disposal. Possibly the 1,100 mercenaries of the ex-Persian garrison of Kelainai, no doubt some hastily levied Phrygians and Pisidians, and perhaps some reinforcements from Balakros and Kalas.[82] It has also been suggested by Burn

79. Ibid., p.82, a suggestion which makes excellent sense.

80. Briant, *Antigone le Borgne,* pp. 63–66; his suggestion is certainly very tempting, though it has been subjected to vigorous criticism by Goukowsky, *RPh* 49 (1975): 265 n. 7. Most probably Burn's view of Curtius's text is correct, but this need not invalidate Briant's hypothesis of Antigonos assuming overall command in Asia Minor, which seems to me to make sense in view of the strategic situation.

81. Curtius IV 5,13 speaks of Balakros later recapturing *Miletos;* if correct, this implies he had been entirely ousted from Kilikia.

82. Curtius IV 12,11 reports substantial Phrygian forces in Dareios's army at Gaugamela, presumably levied by the satrap Atizyes in 334 and taken to Dareios before Alexander arrived in Phrygia; hence Antigonos probably could not recruit very heavily in Phrygia.

that a force of 4,000 mercenaries under Kleandros who joined Alexander at Sidon in 332 may have come through Asia Minor and been commandeered by Antigonos in this emergency.[83] At any rate, Antigonos's forces were clearly much inferior to the Persian forces, yet in a masterly demonstration of the advantage of interior lines, he met each of the three Persian forces separately and thus defeated the counterattacking Persians in detail. Alexander's faith in Antigonos was justified.

While Antigonos was defeating this Persian counterattack, Alexander's relentless assault on Tyre was causing defections in the Persian fleet, and a Macedonian fleet appearing in the Aegean managed to drive off the remains of it. Alexander was thus freed from worry about his rear, and was able (after the capture of Tyre) to move on to Egypt, and then across into inner Asia for the final showdown with Dareios. Meanwhile, back in Asia Minor Antigonos and the other satraps went over to the offensive, Kalas seeking to conquer Paphlagonia and Antigonos conquering Lykaonia (Curtius IV 5,13). The success of Antigonos in annexing Lykaonia was of great importance to Alexander's communications, for Kappadokia remained unconquered throughout Alexander's life, and hence the Royal Road was closed to him. By securing Lykaonia, however, Antigonos was able to open the southern route, which led directly across Asia Minor from Ephesos via Kelainai and Ikonion to the Kilikian Gates; with the securing of full control of the sea by the Macedonian fleet, this route must have become a major link in Alexander's communications to Macedon, as well as being his only direct land link to his satrapies in Asia Minor.[84] And Antigonos's brilliant successes are highlighted by the failures of some of Alexander's other satraps: Kalas of Hellespontine Phrygia failed to impose his authority on Paphlagonia and Bithynia and fell in battle against the Bithynian dynast Bas; Balakros of Kilikia died in a fruitless attempt to impose his authority on the Isaurians in the mountains of eastern Pisidia.[85]

83. Burn, *JHS* 72 (1952):83, referring to Arrian *Anab.* II 20,5—though I am afraid that Curtius IV 3,11 makes it all too probable that Kleandros and his mercenaries arrived in Phoenicia by sea.

84. See on the importance of this route, e.g., Tarn, *Alexander,* 2:110, 171–80; Schachermeyr, *Alexander in Babylon,* pp. 193, 261; Briant, *Antigone le Borgne,* pp. 51, 77–79.

85. For Balakros's death in battle against the Isaurians, see Diodoros XVIII 22,1. That Kalas did not succeed in conquering Paphlagonia appears from its independence shortly after Alexander's death (cf. Berve, vol. 2, no. 397); for his defeat by Bas, see Memnon in *FGrH,* no. 434 F 1 12,4; that Kalas was killed by Bas is a common conjecture, based on the fact that at Alexander's death one Demarchos was satrap of Hellespontine Phrygia instead of Kalas (Arrian *Met' Alex.* 1,6), though Badian, *JHS* 81 (1961):18, argues that Kalas was deposed (and killed?) by Alexander as a relative of the disgraced Harpalos.

Perhaps as a result of his successes, Antigonos seems in 330 to have been put in charge of Lykia and Pamphylia in addition to Phrygia. This is not directly attested, but in that year the satrap of Lykia and Pamphylia, Nearchos, joined Alexander in the east and stayed with him thenceforth; as no successor to Nearchos is mentioned and Antigonos was confirmed in command of Phrygia, Lykia, and Pamphylia at the Babylon conference after Alexander's death, it is generally accepted that he received Lykia and Pamphylia already in 330. At the same time, he must have been charged with oversight of western Pisidia, from Termessos to Lake Troglitis, since this mountainous region lay exactly between greater Phrygia and Lykia/Pamphylia.[86] As the satrap, then, of greater Phrygia, Lykaonia, western Pisidia, Pamphylia, and Lykia, Antigonos was in command of some two-thirds of the Macedonian-held portion of Asia Minor, greatly overshadowing the other Macedonian satraps in this region.

How did Antigonos rule this satrapy? We do not know, but the sources do not support the idea that Alexander was any sort of reformer in administrative matters, or indeed that he had any particular interest in administration. During his conquest of Asia, he retained the Persian satrapial system, simply replacing the Persian satraps with his own nominees or (after Gaugamela) sometimes accepting the fealty of the incumbent satrap and leaving him in place (though in such cases often depriving the Persian satrap of military power and putting that in the hands of a Greek or Macedonian officer).[87] As far as one can tell, the satraps appointed by Alexander were left to run their satrapies as best they could, which must have been in accordance with the established Persian system in most cases. Alexander, chasing his dream ever eastward, had no time to regulate a new system of administration; indeed, from the point of view of his campaigning requirements, it made sense simply to continue the Persian system under new management.[88] Most likely, therefore, Antigonos ruled as satrap essentially according to the Persian system of administration,

86. See map 2; for Antigonos as satrap of Lykia/Pamphylia from 330 on see, for example, Berve, 1:256–57.

87. See Julien, *Verwaltung der Satrapien*, pp. 53–61, on the duties and rights of the satraps, including the depriving of Persian satraps of military command, and pp. 9–53 on the retention of the Persian satrapies by Alexander.

88. Though he may have somewhat altered the financial organization in the interest of efficient forwarding to him of funds: Julien, *Verwaltung der Satrapien*, pp. 60–78; Berve, 1:280–81, 306–17; more generally on Alexander's financial arrangements, see Badian, *G & R* 12 (1965):168–69.

an experience which must have been invaluable to him later when he began to set up an administrative system in his own empire.

An activity of Alexander's of some interest to the historian of Antigonos is his founding of new Hellenic cities in Asia, in which he was imitated by his successors, Antigonos and Seleukos. The major accounts of Alexander as city founder are those of Tarn (vol. 2, app. 8, of his *Alexander the Great*), and Tscherikower (*Die hellenistischen Städtegründungen,* esp. at pp. 138–54), though both are at times overly keen to accept as factual the legends that many cities later concocted to claim the great Alexander as their founder. Apart from Alexandria in Egypt (which Alexander certainly formally founded, though the actual work was done by Kleomenes and Ptolemy), no city seems to have been founded by Alexander west of the Tigris.[89] At least fourteen Alexandrias are attested in inner Asia, but no convincing explanation of how so many full-scale Greek *poleis* were populated by Alexander without using up the greater part of his available manpower seems to be forthcoming, however. Most probably many were merely a result of the imposition of Alexander's name and a Greco-Macedonian garrison on native communities. Alexander's reputation as a great city founder and, in that respect, a Hellenizer of the east has been considerably exaggerated, then, though he clearly made a considerable beginning to the settlement of a Hellenic population in Asia.

It is possible that Antigonos may have played a minor role in Alexander's colonization policy. In 319 we hear of a city in western Pisidia named Kretopolis, evidently a colony of Cretan mercenaries (Diod. XVIII 44,2; 47,4). Its foundation probably occurred during the reign of Alexander, and it may hence have been founded by Antigonos as satrap.[90] Noteworthy in addition is Antigonos's long rule over his satrapy, retaining Alexander's full confidence till the end. No other satrap of Alexander was retained in power by that monarch for as long as Antigonos was, and it has been shown by Badian, in an article on Alexander's "reign of terror" after his return from India in 325, that Antigonos was all but unique in his retention of the king's trust.[91]

---

89. Excepting Alexandropolis in Thrace, which was founded in Philip's lifetime. The reason, no doubt, was that there were already plenty of cities in western Asia and that region was fairly securely held by the Macedonians; Alexander's cities in eastern Asia would have been in large part glorified garrisons, securing control over the vast, semi-barbarous Iranian lands.

90. This was suggested by Briant, *Antigone le Borgne,* p. 78 and n. 6.

91. Badian, *JHS* 81 (1961):16–43.

It must be admitted, all the same, that the further Alexander progressed into Asia, and the more his victories and conquests piled up, so Antigonos's position tended to shrink in importance. For while he was settled for ten long years at Kelainai, perhaps even bringing his wife and sons over from Macedon to join him there,[92] other men of a younger generation were making their mark in the king's entourage and rising to the top positions in Alexander's empire: such men as Hephaistion, Krateros, Perdikkas, and Ptolemy. Nevertheless, Antigonos's position when Alexander died was a strong one. He was the key Macedonian commander in Asia Minor, at the head of a huge satrapy, much of which he had himself conquered. He alone, besides Antipatros, had won entirely independent victories over major enemy forces during Alexander's reign, and he was one of the few major personages left from Philip's time.[93] Consequently, he moved rapidly in the years after Alexander's death from being a peripheral figure to becoming, in the words of Plutarch (*Dem.* 3), "the oldest and greatest of the successors of Alexander."

---

92. Philippos is sometimes thought to have been born at Kelainai ca. 332 (thus, e.g., Berve, vol. 2, no. 776), but see my remarks at app. 3, no 92. Demetrios was certainly in Kelainai in 321 (Diod. XVIII 23,4), and there is no reason to doubt the common conjecture that Antigonos had his family with him during the peaceful years at Kelainai.

93. Antipatros had defeated the attempt of the Spartan king Agis III to expel the Macedonians from Greece (see Berve, vol. 2, no. 94 for sources and details). While Antigonos's victories obviously could not carry the prestige of Antipatros's defeat of Sparta, none of Alexander's other officers, like Krateros, Perdikkas, and Ptolemy, could boast of similar independent victories. He was also the oldest of Alexander's top-level officers in 323—except again for Antipatros—which gave him considerable prestige; cf. the fact that Polyperchon's prestige after Antipatros's death was based on being "almost the oldest of those who had campaigned with Alexander" (Diod. XVIII 48,4).

2

Antigonos's Rise to Power

The death of Alexander the Great in June 323, at the age of only thirty-three, was one of those unforeseeable events that alter the course of history in an apparently haphazard fashion. Few people were more profoundly affected by this event than Antigonos Monophthalmos, aged about fifty-nine at this time. Had Alexander lived to be fifty or sixty—by no means a particularly long life compared to his contemporaries—Antigonos could have looked forward at best only to more years as peaceful administrator of his satrapy in Asia Minor, and he would have been to us only a historical footnote. Instead, the death of Alexander opened a whole new career and field of action to Antigonos, in which for nearly twenty years he dominated the Near Eastern world and established his claim to the attention of historians by his contributions to the process which created the world of the Hellenistic monarchies, the political milieu of Greek culture for the next two centuries. We must investigate how it was that Antigonos was able to rise from relatively obscure satrap to dominant ruler.

THE CRISIS AFTER ALEXANDER'S DEATH (323–320 B.C.)

Alexander's death left the Macedonians in a very difficult position. The ruthlessness of Philip and Alexander towards possible rivals for the throne, and Alexander's refusal to marry early and beget children, meant that there was no obvious and competent successor to the kingship. The Argead family was reduced to Alexander's mentally defective brother Arrhidaios, his yet unborn son Alexandros,

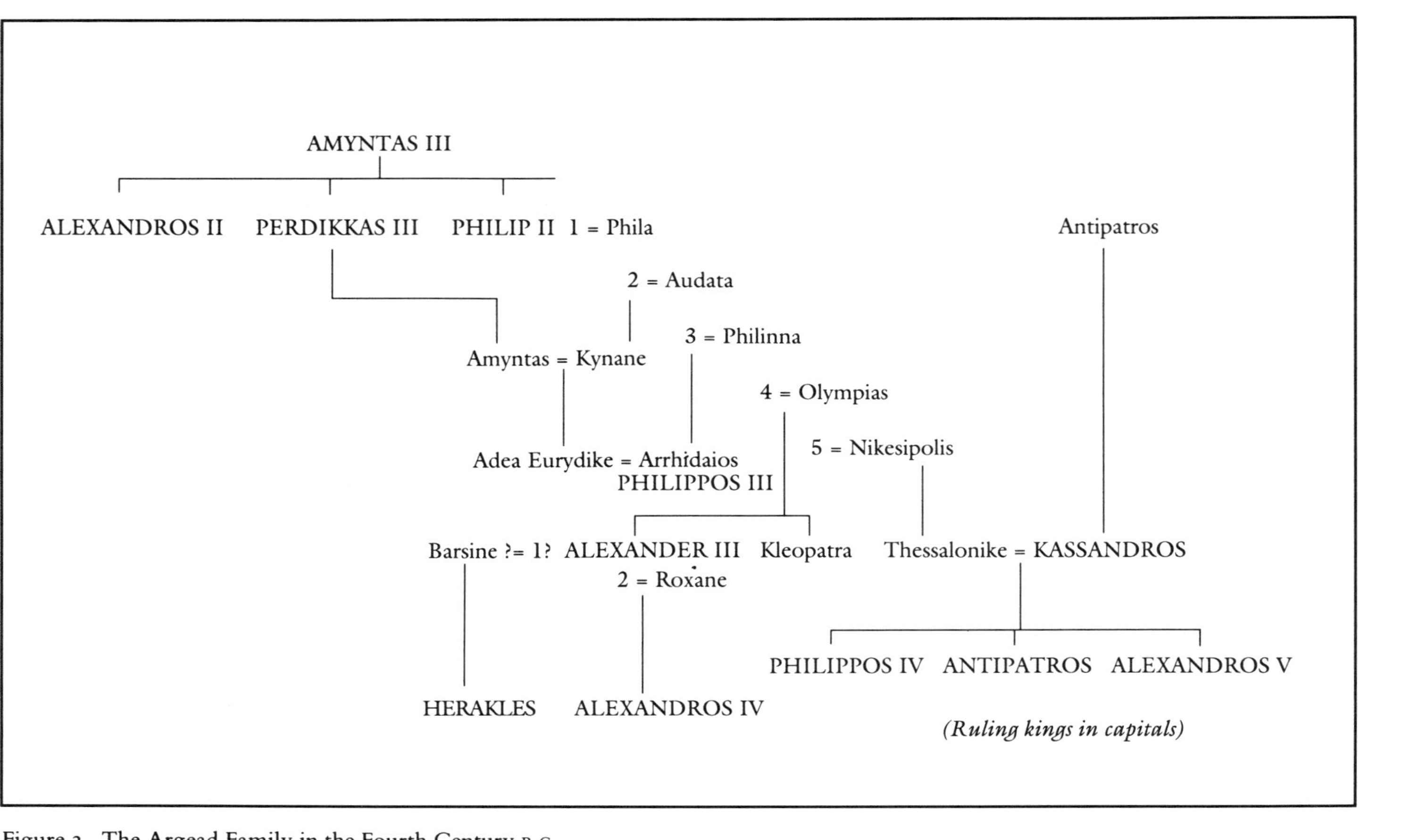

Figure 2. The Argead Family in the Fourth Century B.C.

and his reputed illegitimate son Herakles, a mere child; and the women of the family, most importantly Alexander's mother Olympias, his sister Kleopatra, and his half-sisters Thessalonike and Kynane, with the latter's daughter by Alexander's cousin, Amyntas Perdikka, Adea Eurydike (see fig. 2 for a family tree). The males were thus incapable of ruling, and the women, though possessing great influence through the royal aura a connection with them would confer, were not eligible to rule in their own right. The problem of who was to succeed and how power was to be exercised was therefore acute, and the situation was exacerbated by the nature of the Macedonian state.

Macedon had only recently been unified; fifty years before Alexander's death it had been a hotbed of warring regions and factions, and it still possessed no clear and tested institutional or constitutional mechanisms or precedents to deal with the situation that had arisen.[1] The nobility had a tradition of factional strife, and the administrative and military institutions created by Philip were too new to command automatic loyalty; in any case, the current situation had not been envisioned when they were set up.[2] If there had been a competent man of Argead blood, his succession to the throne would probably not have been disputed; or if at least all of the major Macedonian leaders and armies had been gathered in one spot, it is possible (though perhaps not likely) that a generally agreed upon and lasting solution could have been found to the crisis of the succession and the problem of the exercise of power until such time as a competent king should appear (i.e., until Alexander's son had grown up). As it was, the situation in 323 aroused the competitive instincts of the major leaders and was a fine recipe for conflict.

One must, however, avoid the temptation to regard the conflicts which ultimately arose among the Macedonian chiefs as inevitable from the start, and to read them into the gathering at Babylon. To compete for posts of honor and influence is one thing; civil war is quite another. The Macedonians did come to civil war, and quite soon; but at the Babylon conference it was neither clear nor inevitable

---

1. On early Macedon, see pp. 18–24 above; and for the lack of a constitution or institutions by which the state could have functioned in this crisis and resolved the problems in an orderly fashion, see Errington, *Chiron* 8 (1978):77–133; id., *Arch. Mak.* 3 (1983):89–101; id., *Gesch. Makedoniens,* chaps. 1 and 6.

2. On the role of the nobility in the state, see Errington, *Chiron* 8 (1978):99–105, and cf. this article in general for an excellent analysis of Macedonian royal successions and in particular the present one. On Philip's reforms, see pp. 30–35 above.

that this would be the outcome. The leading officers present in Babylon came together when Alexander's death was known to discuss the situation.[3] It was clear that someone was going to have to exercise power on behalf of the Argead raised to the throne, and there was naturally rivalry for the post or posts of power. The lead in the discussions was taken by Alexander's *sōmatophylakes* (personal staff officers), and of them Perdikkas was in the strongest position, having been in effect Alexander's chief lieutenant during the last months of his reign, and having been given the seal of state by the dying king (Curt. X 5,4; 6,4–5). For him Alexander could hardly have died at a better time. Men like Philotas and Hephaistion, who would have overshadowed him before, were long dead, and his most important living rivals were far from Babylon and hence in a poor position to compete for influence: Krateros was in Kilikia, on his way to Macedon with an army of veterans; Antipatros was in Macedon, and soon had his hands full with a Greek rebellion; and Antigonos was in Phrygia.

Had Antigonos been in Babylon, it is quite possible that his age and experience, and the prestige of his connection with Philip and his victories in Asia Minor, could have enabled him to move at once to a position at the center of the stage. Some historians have wondered why Antigonos (and for that matter Krateros) did not hurry to Babylon to take part in the conferences of the leaders.[4] The answer lies in the slowness of communications and the rapidity of events. Accustomed as we are to virtually instantaneous communications, we need to remember that it must have taken many days for news of Alexander's sudden demise to reach Kilikia, Phrygia, and Macedon, whereas it is clear from Curtius's lengthy account (X 6,1–10,9) that it took little more than a week for the Macedonians in Babylon to settle the royal succession and the powers and posts of the leading officers, with Perdikkas coming out on top. Nevertheless, he did not obtain power without facing a challenge or making concessions to other leaders. Following closely the accounts given by Curtius (X 6,1–10,9), Arrian (*Met' Alex.* 1,1–8), Diodoros (XVIII 2,1–3,5), and

3. Our fullest source is Curtius X 6,1–10,9, who, though often summarily dismissed by modern scholars, is in fact our best source for the initial confusion at Babylon in the first week after Alexander's death, deriving ultimately from a well-informed contemporary source, whether Kleitarchos (so Schachermeyr, *Alexander in Babylon,* pp. 92–104) or Hieronymos (thus, e.g., Errington, *JHS* 90 [1970]:72–75).

4. So, e.g., Briant, *Antigone le Borgne,* pp. 126–32: Antigonos decided that to go to Babylon would do his prospects no good; but see on this (and in general on Briant's book) the criticism of Goukowsky's review in *RPh,* 3d ser., 49 (1975):263–77.

Justin (XIII 2,4), it seems that three factions quickly coalesced at Babylon:

1. The faction of Perdikkas himself, which included his fellow *sōmatophylax* Aristonous, an eloquent proponent of primacy for Perdikkas (Curt. X 6,16–18; Arrian 24,6); two leaders of *pezetairoi* battalions, Perdikkas's brother, Alketas, and his brother-in-law, Attalos (see, e.g., Berve, vol. 2, nos. 45, 181), along with Attalos's brother, Polemon (Arrian 1,25; 24,1); the distinguished officer Seleukos (see Diod. XVIII 3,4: Perdikkas appointed Seleukos his own successor as leader of the Companion cavalry); several less prominent, but still noteworthy, figures such as Medeios of Larissa (Arrian 24,6), Dokimos (Arrian 24,3–5), and Philoxenos (Arrian 24,2); and, perhaps most notable and famous, Eumenes of Kardia.

2. A faction centered, it seems, on three great *sōmatophylakes:* Ptolemy, Peithon Krateua, and Leonnatos. Ptolemy reportedly proposed setting up a ruling council to forestall Perdikkas' being made sole regent (Curt. X 6, 13–16), and when Aristonous successfully opposed this and proposed Perdikkas as regent, Peithon made a counterproposal that there should be a joint regency of Perdikkas and Leonnatos, while Krateros and Antipatros were to govern Europe jointly (Curt. X 7,8–9; Justin XIII 2). These three, then, championed the idea of collegiality, and the rights of the absent leaders, and another *sōmatophylax,* Lysimachos, may have been associated with them.[5] This group concurred with the faction of Perdikkas, however, that the succession crisis should be settled by the Macedonian nobles alone, and that a decision on the next king should be postponed until the birth of Roxane's child by Alexander, which was to be king if it was a boy.

3. A faction led by the *pezetairos* officer Meleagros, who objected to being shut out of the power broking. Meleagros persuaded the Macedonian infantry to back the candidacy of Arrhidaios as king, emphasizing the fact that he was the son of Philip and a true Macedonian, and giving him the name Philippos to symbolize this. Meleagros, naturally, expected to wield actual power in Arrhidaios's name (Curt. X 6,20–8,10; also Arrian 1,2 and Diod. XVIII 2,3).

5. The connecting link between Ptolemy, Peithon, and Leonnatos, whom I have identified as a faction, is that all three are attested as opposing *sole* authority for Perdikkas; that Lysimachos may have been associated with them is a hypothesis based on his siding with Ptolemy and Antipatros against Perdikkas in 320 (see Arrian *Met' Alex.* 1,45).

The Macedonian soldiery played an important part in the succession crisis. There can be no doubt about the genuine loyalty of the mass of ordinary Macedonians to the Argead house, which is amply evidenced, as we shall see below. At Babylon the infantry demonstrated their political strength, supporting the right of Arrhidaios to the throne despite the opposition of most of the important leaders, who had the backing of the cavalry.[6] The infantry evidently felt themselves strong, given their long service and many conquests, and though civil war threatened for a few days, the now united factions of Perdikkas and Leonnatos et al. were forced to compromise.

Under this compromise Arrhidaios was to reign as King Philippos III and Roxane's child was to be co-king and successor if it should turn out to be a boy, as of course it did: Alexandros IV.[7] The show of strength by the Macedonian soldiery did not miss its effect: the most successful Macedonian leaders were subsequently careful to consult their armies on crucial policy decisions (as indeed Alexander himself had been wont to do from time to time) so as to make sure that they retained the support of their men.[8] The leaders also made a point of emphasizing their loyalty to the Argead kings.[9] Besides being kept informed of events and sometimes even consulted on important points, and being reassured as to their leader's fundamental loyalty to the kings, the soldiers naturally wished in their own self-interest to feel that their leader was capable and would lead them well, and that they would be properly paid for their services. Beyond this the troops seem not to have concerned themselves much with the rights and wrongs of the leaders in their various disputes with one another: it must have been as hard for them then as it is for us now to distinguish how true the claims to represent the best interests of the kings put forward by the rival leaders were.

Undoubtedly the greatest gainer at the Babylon conference was Perdikkas: he was appointed chiliarch of the kings, a post which

6. For the cavalry siding with the nobility against the infantry, see Curtius X 8,1–13; Diod. XVIII 2,3; Justin XIII 3,6–10. Of course much of the cavalry would have been made up of retainers of the nobles: see chap. 1 above at n. 18.

7. On the co-rulership of Alexandros IV with Philippos III, see Habicht, "Literarische und epigraphische Überlieferung."

8. So, for example, Antigonos on the occasion of his Tyre proclamation (Diod. XIX 61,1–3) and at his proclamation as king (Plut. *Dem.* 18,1) where the *plēthos* which saluted him as king would certainly have included much of his standing army.

9. Instances are Ptolemy at Pelousion in 320 (Arrian *Met' Alex.* 1,29), Eumenes at Nora and throughout his subsequent career (Plut. *Eum.* 12,2; 13,3), Antigonos at Tyre (Diod. XIX 61,1–4), and the four dynasts who signed the peace of 311 (Diod. XIX 105,1).

entailed authority over the entire empire (thus Arrian *Met' Alex.* 1,3: ἐπιτροπὴ τῆς ξυμπάσης βασιλείας). The strength of Perdikkas's position was thus enormous. He was to run the empire on behalf of the kings, all other Macedonian leaders being subordinated to him. The soldiery accepted this by acquiescing in the purging of the army (Arrian 1,4; Diod. XVIII 4,7; Curt. X 9,9–19); the leaders in effect accepted it by accepting satrapial and military appointments from Perdikkas. Though he had in the initial compromise accepted Meleagros as his *hyparchos* (second-in-command), Perdikkas promptly further strengthened his position by eliminating him. The distribution of satrapies, too, seems to have been managed in such a way as to enhance the power of Perdikkas's faction. Of his main supporters, only Eumenes was to receive a satrapy, the important one of Kappadokia and Paphlagonia, which was to be conquered for him by Leonnatos and Antigonos. In the main Perdikkas apparently preferred to keep his supporters with him to help him establish full control of the central state machinery (such as it was). Most of the satrapies were simply confirmed to the incumbent satraps, no doubt as the easiest system and that least likely to give offense.[10] The rival leaders were, however, granted satrapies as a way of appeasing them, but each with a twist.

Ptolemy was given Egypt as his satrapy, but the incumbent satrap Kleomenes was appointed *hyparchos,* perhaps to keep an eye on Ptolemy (Arrian 1,5). Leonnatos received Hellespontine Phrygia, but Paphlagonia (which had belonged to this satrapy under Alexander: Arrian *Anab.* II 4,1; Curt. III 1,22) was separated and given to Eumenes (Arrian *Met' Alex.* 1,5), for whom Leonnatos was ordered to conquer it (Plut. *Eum.* 3,2). Peithon Krateua received Media, but the northern third or so was sliced off from this satrapy and given to Perdikkas's father-in-law, Atropates (see Diod. XVIII 3,1 and 3,3, with Strabo XI 522–23), and when Perdikkas sent Peithon to counter the revolt of the Greek colonists in the upper satrapies, he gave the troops special orders meant to prevent Peithon from profiting from this command (Diod. XVIII 7,3–9). Finally Lysimachos (on whom see n. 5 above) was given in Thrace a satrapy which he would have to conquer himself before being able to rule (Arrian 1,10; Diod. XVIII 14,2–4), and which was furthermore subject to the supreme authority of Antipatros (Arrian 1,3). The consensus implied in the acceptance of

10. The sources on division of satrapies are Arrian *Met' Alex.* 1,5–8; Curtius X 10,1–6; Diodoros XVIII 3,1–5; Dexippos in *FGrH,* no. 100 F 8,1–6; Justin XIII 4,9–25.

these posts endowed Perdikkas with an air of legitimacy, which was much strengthened by the fact that his orders were issued in the name of the kings, whose legitimacy was unquestioned. However, problems remained: Ptolemy, Peithon, and Leonnatos were still only superficially reconciled to the primacy of Perdikkas; Antipatros, Krateros, and Antigonos had to be induced to accept that primacy.

Antipatros and Krateros were both in strong positions, commanding independent armies of Macedonians and having a prestige at least equal to that of Perdikkas. The latter would need to reach a modus vivendi with them, for they were too powerful and well respected to be pushed aside and he knew it. At Babylon the first steps towards such a modus were taken by the confirmation of Antipatros in charge of the European part of the empire, the acknowledgement also of certain rights of Krateros in that sphere, and the creation for Krateros of the vague, but evidently honorable, title of *prostatēs,* which promised him a role in the running of the empire without as yet defining what that role would be.[11] Antipatros and Krateros very sensibly made a common front in Europe, and enhanced their prestige in Macedonian eyes by defeating the Greek rebellion. They cemented their alliance by the marriage of Krateros to Antipatros's daughter Phila. When a request came from Perdikkas for the hand of another daughter, Nikaia, it looked as if a triumvirate might emerge to run the Macedonian empire, and Antipatros took the appropriate steps in that direction by accepting Perdikkas's proposal for a marriage alliance.[12]

The position of Antigonos in all of this was an ambiguous one. He had his authority over Phrygia, Lykaonia, Lykia, Pamphylia, and western Pisidia confirmed at Babylon, and so had no formal grounds for complaint; and yet he found that Perdikkas and Krateros, much younger men, whom ten years earlier he would have regarded as subordinates, were now to represent the central authority he had to obey. This must have been somewhat galling to a man of Antigonos's

---

11. Despite the many attempts made to explain Krateros's position, no agreement has been or seems likely to be reached. In fact Krateros's position was left deliberately vague by the Macedonian power brokers at Babylon: though absent, Krateros was too powerful and influential to be ignored. Ptolemy, Leonnatos, and Peithon, who would have preferred Perdikkas to have a colleague, may have hoped that the *prostasia* would enable Krateros to assume that role. Perdikkas doubtless hoped that Krateros would become embroiled in a dispute over precedence with Antipatros in Europe. The most that can safely be said of the power or authority attached to the *prostasia* is that it seems to have been intended as a guardianship specifically of the interests of Philippos Arrhidaios.

12. See Diod. XVIII 18,7 (Krateros and Phila); Arrian *Met' Alex.* 1,21; Diod. XVIII 23,1–3; and Justin XIII 6 (Perdikkas and Nikaia).

pride, especially when he was then ordered by Perdikkas to join with Leonnatos in conquering Kappadokia and Paphlagonia as a satrapy for Eumenes (Plut. *Eum.* 3,2). For there was a certain edge to this order that was not likely to escape Antigonos's attention: as satrap of Kappadokia and Paphlagonia, Eumenes would hold a satrapy more or less equivalent in size and potential to Antigonos's own, and one strategically located on the Royal Road from Mesopotamia; and Eumenes would be directly beholden to Perdikkas for this satrapy in a way that Antigonos was not for his. The thought may well have crossed Antigonos's mind that Perdikkas in some sense intended Eumenes to be a counterweight to himself, and contemplation of the details of the Babylonian settlement would have strengthened this notion.

It is clear that Perdikkas and his faction dominated the proceedings at Babylon and, while not able to pass over the claims to advancement of other leaders, were able to put restraints on the authority of rival nobles. This would not have escaped Antigonos's notice, and it looks as if Perdikkas extended the proverbial carrot and stick to Antigonos: the carrot was the retention of the whole of his satrapy; the stick was the command to establish Eumenes, whose rule in Kappadokia and Paphlagonia would make him as much a counter to potential trouble from Antigonos as from Leonnatos. Seen in this light, Antigonos's failure to act on Perdikkas's orders comes as no surprise (Plut. *Eum.* 3,3). Antigonos may have felt that in the absence of himself and other leading Macedonians like Antipatros, Krateros, Polyperchon, and Kleitos (the latter two were in Kilikia with Krateros at the time: Arrian *Anab.* VII 12,4; Justin XII 12,8), the decisions taken at Babylon were not fully valid. However, not too much should be made of Plutarch's statement that Antigonos ignored Perdikkas's orders concerning Eumenes, for as it turned out he could almost certainly not have done much about those orders anyway. Antigonos was supposed to cooperate in this matter with Leonnatos, to whom a substantial force had been entrusted by Perdikkas for the purpose.[13] However, instead of using this force to install Eumenes in

13. Plut. *Eum.* 3,2–3: Leonnatos and Antigonos were to conduct Eumenes into Kappadokia with a great force (χειρὶ μεγάληι) and make him satrap; Leonnatos came down from the upper country into Phrygia to undertake the campaign for Eumenes. Evidently Leonnatos brought a major force with him from Babylonia with which to campaign in Kappadokia, since when he went instead to aid Antipatros, he invaded Thessaly with an army of 20,000 infantry and 1,500 cavalry after enlisting additional troops in Macedon (Diod. XVIII 14,4–5); as Antipatros had already recruited heavily in Macedon the previous year (Diod. XVIII 12,2), one can hardly assume that more than half of Leonnatos's army in Thessaly were new Macedonian recruits.

his satrapy, Leonnatos crossed over into Europe towards the end of 323 to go to the aid of Antipatros in Thessaly, and eventually died in battle against the Greeks in northern Thessaly.[14] In the absence of this force, there was little that Antigonos could do against the massive force built up over the years by Ariarathes of Kappadokia (30,000 infantry and 15,000 cavalry according to Diod. XVIII 16,2), and in any case Eumenes had fled back to Perdikkas on learning of Leonnatos's plans (Plut. *Eum.* 3,3–6).

In 322, accordingly, Perdikkas himself came down into Asia Minor with the royal army and conquered Kappadokia and Paphlagonia, beating Ariarathes in two battles (Arrian *Met' Alex.* 1, 11). Evidently this campaign took some time, and having conquered the area, Perdikkas stayed on to see the place regulated and a proper Macedonian administration set up (Diod. XVIII 16,3; Plut. *Eum.* 3, 7). About the same time that Perdikkas entered Kappadokia, Krateros left Kilikia to go to the aid of Antipatros against the Greeks (Diod. XVIII 16,4–5). Antipatros and Krateros defeated the Greeks and obliged them to come to terms; Athens was forced to surrender unconditionally and received a garrison in October of 322 (Plut. *Phok.* 28,1), and the question of Samos was referred to Perdikkas, who restored the Samians to their home at the end of 322 (Diod. XVIII 18,6–9). Next spring Perdikkas came down from Kappadokia to eastern Pisidia to conquer the Larandians and Isaurians, in which he was successful (Diod. XVIII 22,1–8).

Having done this, Perdikkas decided to humble Antigonos, and summoned him to stand trial (Arrian *Met' Alex.* 1,20) on charges characterized by Diodoros (XVIII 23,4) as "false slanders and unjust accusations." The precise charges brought against Antigonos by Perdikkas are not preserved in any source, though it is commonly asserted in modern works that Antigonos was specifically charged with disobeying Perdikkas's legitimate order, as chiliarch of the empire, to help Eumenes conquer Kappadokia.[15] It is possible, per-

14. Diod. XVIII 14,4–15,4; Plut. *Eum.* 3,3–5. According to Plutarch, Leonnatos had received a marriage offer from Alexander's sister Kleopatra and entertained grandiose and far-reaching schemes of personal aggrandizement. Whatever truth there may be in this, it all came to nothing, as Leonnatos died in battle at the end of 323.

15. E.g., by Müller, *Antigonos Monophthalmos,* 19–20, erroneously citing the separation of Paphlagonia from Phrygia as a possible reason for Antigonos's refusal: Paphlagonia had formerly been part of *Hellespontine* Phrygia and so was never under Antigonos's authority; and by Wehrli, *Antigone et Démétrios,* p. 33. See in general on this the detailed and cautious examination of Engel, *Untersuchungen,* pp. 5–10; and cf. the fact that though Eumenes is reported to have accused Leonnatos vehemently before Perdikkas (Plut. *Eum.* 3,5–6), he is not recorded to have uttered a word against Antigonos.

haps even probable, that this formed part of Perdikkas's accusation against Antigonos, but it is nowhere attested to be so, and it is worth remembering that nearly two years elapsed between Antigonos's "disobedience" in late 323 and Perdikkas's accusations in summer 321.

However that may be, Antigonos gave out that he was ready to face Perdikkas's charges, but secretly made preparations to flee Asia (Diod. XVIII 23,4). Apparently while communications concerning this proposed trial were going on, Antipatros's son, Iolaos, conducting his sister Nikaia to Perdikkas to be his bride, and Alexander's sister Kleopatra, who also wished to marry Perdikkas, arrived in Asia Minor (Arrian *Met' Alex.* 1,21; cf. Diod. XVIII 23,1–3). Since Perdikkas had himself asked for the hand of Nikaia (Diod. XVIII 23,1; Justin XIII 6), he could not now decide to marry Kleopatra instead without giving grave provocation to Antipatros and, though Eumenes advised him to take this chance, he followed the advice of his brother Alketas and married Nikaia (Arrian 1,21). Kleopatra, however, stayed in Asia Minor, and Antigonos evidently knew of her presence.[16] At about this same time another of Alexander's sisters appeared in Asia Minor, namely, Kynane, the widow of Amyntas Perdikka, bringing her daughter Adea Eurydike to be married to Philippos Arrhidaios; Perdikkas was opposed to this marriage, however, and sent his brother Alketas to arrest the women. A fracas ensued in which, whether by design or not, Kynane was killed. This caused a mutiny of the Macedonian troops, and Perdikkas was forced after all to permit the marriage of Eurydike and Philippos Arrhidaios (Arrian, 1,22–23; Polyainos VIII 60; Diod. XIX 52,5).

With Perdikkas in difficulty over the Kynane affair, Antigonos saw that his opportunity had come and made his escape to Europe, taking his family and friends with him and sailing from Asia Minor in Athenian ships (Diod. XVIII 23,4), perhaps with the collusion of Menandros, satrap of Lydia (see app. 3, no. 71). At any rate, Antigonos arrived in Europe late in 321 and joined Antipatros and Krateros, who had spent the year attempting to subdue the Aitolians

16. Kleopatra set up residence at Sardis (Arrian 1,26; 25,2–6; Plut. *Eum.* 8,4), a fact of which Antigonos in Phrygia could scarcely have been unaware. According to Diod. XVIII 23,3 Antigonos learned of intrigues going on between Perdikkas and Kleopatra with a view to eventual marriage. It seems likely that Diodoros is anticipating, due to his extreme compression, the later proposal of marriage by Perdikkas to Kleopatra, which Antigonos learned about when he returned to Asia early in 320 (Arrian 1,26; 25,1–3). But Antigonos must have heard something of the debate at Perdikkas's headquarters as to whether Perdikkas should marry Nikaia or Kleopatra (Arrian 1,21), and he was able to make capital out of this when reporting to Antipatros and Krateros.

and were wintering in Aitolia in the hope of breaking Aitolian resistance (Diod. XVIII 24,1–25,2).[17] They were greatly taken aback by Antigonos's complaints at his treatment by Perdikkas and hints of what Perdikkas intended to do to others, all backed up by a highly dramatic account of the murder of Kynane as proof of Perdikkas's autocratic intentions (Arrian 1,24). Up to this time Antipatros's relations with Perdikkas had been entirely correct: he had referred the problem of Samos to Perdikkas and accepted the chiliarch as his son-in-law, and he had also attempted to prevent Kynane from crossing to Asia with her matrimonial schemes (Polyainos VIII 60); no doubt he had hoped to arrange a peaceful settlement between his two sons-in-law, Perdikkas and Krateros (see Diod. XVIII 18,7). However, the news now brought by his old friend Antigonos made him very suspicious of Perdikkas, and evidently Krateros was also inclined to take a dim view of Perdikkas's actions. The two generals held a council at which it was decided to grant terms to the Aitolians and return to Macedon to make preparations for possible conflict with Perdikkas. Negotiations were already in train with Ptolemy (Diod. XVIII 14,2; 25,3–5), who also became a son-in-law of Antipatros (Pausanias I 6,8) and was likewise becoming embroiled in hostilities with Perdikkas.

After his successes in Kappadokia and eastern Pisidia and the flight of Antigonos, Perdikkas's position seemed very strong, but there were some unsettling factors. One of these was that in the course of 322/21 Ptolemy had on his own initiative added Kyrene to his satrapy by conquest (Marmor Parium, sec. 10; Arrian 1,17–19), and was furthermore building up a substantial army of mercenaries with a treasure of 8,000 talents inherited from his *hyparchos* Kleomenes, whom he had evidently murdered (Diod. XVIII 14,1–2; 21,6–9; 28,3–6).[18] Another was the fact that Antigonos had found refuge with Antipatros and Krateros, who had a large and victorious Macedonian army and might well be considerably disturbed by Perdikkas's proceedings with regard to Kynane. Perdikkas evidently decided to have the body of Alexander brought up from Babylon and taken to be

17. The chronology of events given here is established by Errington, *JHS* 90 (1970):49–77, and Schober, *Gesch. Babyloniens*, pp. 46–73. Though the campaign in Aitolia is often placed in late 322, Diod. XVIII 16,4–19,1 shows that Antipatros and Krateros returned to Macedon for winter 322/21 and Diod. XVIII 24,1–25,4 clearly depicts a long campaign, filling the campaigning season of 321 and lasting into the early winter.

18. Ptolemy's murder of Kleomenes is recorded by Pausanias I 6,3, but without a clear date; it probably occurred in 321 and was one of the reasons for Perdikkas's decision to go to war with Ptolemy, for he had himself appointed Kleomenes *hyparchos* and Ptolemy's murder of the man was thus an overt flouting of his authority; see further Seibert, *Ptolemaios' I*, p. 112.

buried, not in Egypt, but at Aigai in Macedon; and to this end he sent his brothers-in-law Attalos and Polemon with a force to Syria to meet the funeral cortege, perhaps calculating that if he were to march to Macedon in full state with the body of Alexander, Antipatros and Krateros would not venture to oppose him militarily.[19] However, Ptolemy came to Syria with an army and, by arrangement with Arrhidaios, the man in charge of Alexander's funeral cortege, carried the body off to Egypt despite all that Attalos and Polemon could do (Arrian 1,25; 24,1; Diod. XVIII 28,3).

Perdikkas meanwhile held a council of war at his winter quarters in Pisidia (i.e., in the winter of 321/20) to decide what to do about Ptolemy and Antigonos and their allies (Diod. XVIII 25,6). It was decided not to move towards Macedon, possibly because it was not yet clear what, if anything, Antipatros and Krateros would do, though rumors of warlike preparations must presumably have reached Perdikkas. At any rate, he decided to marry Kleopatra after all, which portended a break with Antipatros, and to chastise Ptolemy while holding off possible European enemies by defending the crossing of the Hellespont (Diod. XVIII 29,1–3, and cf. Arrian 1,26). Perdikkas had three substantial forces in Asia Minor, which were to combine to defend that region: there was an army, including a body of Macedonian infantry, under Neoptolemos in Armenia; there was a sizeable force in Kappadokia, including over 6,000 Kappadokian cavalry recruited and trained by Eumenes; and there was an army apparently in western Pisidia under Perdikkas's brother Alketas, probably sent out to occupy Antigonos's satrapy after his flight.[20]

19. Diod. XVIII 3,5 and 28,2–6 states that Alexander was to be buried in Egypt, but shows strong traces of Ptolemaic propaganda here; Arrian 1,25 shows that Perdikkas at any rate did not intend this; and Paus. I 6,3 says that Alexander was to be buried at Aigai. It may be that Perdikkas planned to escort Alexander's body to Macedon with his army, which would certainly have embarrassed Antipatros and Krateros.

20. The precise position of Neoptolemos is unclear: he was not named satrap of Armenia at Babylon, for Armenia was outside Alexander's empire, remaining under the control of its Persian satrap, Orontes: see Arrian *Anab.* III 8,5 (331 B.C.) and Diod. XIX 23,3 (317/16 B.C.). Since Plut. *Eum.* 4,1 and 5,1 has Neoptolemos in charge of a Macedonian force in Armenia in 321, one must assume that Perdikkas had sent him there to subdue the region (thus already Beloch, *GG,* 4.1:313). For Eumenes' Kappadokian cavalry, see Plut. *Eum.* 4,2–3. For Alketas and his army, see Diod. XVIII 29,2; 41,7, and 44,1; Justin XIII 6,15; Plut. *Eum.* 5,2; Arrian *Met' Alex.* 1,41–42; and Appian *Syr.* 52. Since Alketas appears to have been primarily active in western Pisidia (which was part of Antigonos's satrapy) and Karia (which went over to Antigonos early in 320), it seems he was probably sent to occupy Antigonos's satrapy in 321 and interfered with Antigonos's activities in western Asia Minor in 320 (Diod. XVIII 46 for Alketas's activities in western Pisidia, especially Termessos; for his presence in Karia, see Appian and Arrian loc.cit.).

Eumenes was named to command these forces, and Neoptolemos and Alketas were ordered to cooperate with him in the defense of Asia Minor. Eumenes was instructed to proceed to the Hellespontine region to prevent a crossing, while a part of the royal fleet was dispatched under Kleitos to sail to the Hellespont and help Eumenes to hold the strait; Eumenes was also entrusted with the delicate task of negotiating Perdikkas's wedding with Kleopatra.[21]

Perdikkas himself, after receiving news from Attalos and Polemon, set out from Pisidia early in 320 and crossed the Taurus passes into Kilikia. There he deposed the satrap Philotas, who was considered too friendly to Krateros, and replaced him with Philoxenos; he also sent Dokimos to take over from Archon as satrap of Babylon (Arrian 24,2–5). Hearing further that Ptolemy had made an alliance with the kings of Cyprus, he sent an expeditionary force under the command of Aristonous to that island (Arrian 24,6). He himself proceeded with the royal army via Damascus to Egypt, and the greater part of the royal fleet sailed down the coast with him under Attalos.[22] Eumenes meanwhile marched north from Pisidia on his way to the Hellespont; his route would lie through Kelainai and Synnada, where he could expect to be joined by his forces from Kappadokia and by Neoptolemos and his troops from Armenia traveling down the Royal Road. From Synnada he must have diverged westward with a small bodyguard to visit Kleopatra at Sardis, but he nearly had an unexpected meeting of a different kind there.

Arrian informs us (1,26; 25,1–2) that Antigonos returned to Asia Minor with a small force before Antipatros and Krateros had definitely decided on war with Perdikkas. Antigonos, we are told, had with him 3,000 soldiers on ten Athenian ships (perhaps the same ships with which he had fled from Asia a few months before?), and he landed with them in Karia, where the satrap Asandros immediately went over to him, an example quickly followed by Menandros in Lydia and by the Ionian cities, led by Ephesos (Arrian 25,1–4). The

21. Only Justin XIII 6,16 mentions the dispatch of Kleitos with a fleet, but his presence in Asia Minor and on Perdikkas's side is attested by an inscription from Ephesos (published by Keil, *JÖAI* 16, no. 1 [1913], no. II N), which honors him together with Perdikkas's brother Alketas. On Kleitos at this time, see further Briant, *Antigone le Borgne*, pp. 212–15; Hauben, *Vlootbevelhebberschap*, pp. 46–47; and id., *AncSoc* 8 (1977):102–4. For Eumenes' task with respect to Kleopatra, see Arrian 1,26.

22. The mission of Attalos in command of the royal fleet appears from Diod. XVIII 37,3–4, where Attalos is at Pelousion commanding the fleet at the time of Perdikkas's assassination.

ease and rapidity of these successes naturally leads one to speculate that Antigonos had some sort of understanding with Asandros and Menandros from before his flight, for otherwise a landing with just 3,000 troops would have been a most risky undertaking.[23]

Having gained the adherence of Karia, Ionia, and Lydia, Antigonos was in a strong position on the western coast of Asia Minor, and Menandros also brought him important news. Eumenes was in Sardis with gifts for Kleopatra from Perdikkas, who now wished to marry her and repudiate Nikaia. Antigonos immediately set out to try to capture him, but Kleopatra learned of Antigonos's presence in time to warn Eumenes, who fled along the Royal Road back to Phrygia. Arriving in Sardis too late to catch Eumenes, Antigonos sent word of Perdikkas's new matrimonial plans to Antipatros and Krateros, who interpreted this as a sure sign of Perdikkas's overweening ambition and were thereby spurred to set out for the Hellespont with their army to cross over into Asia (Arrian *Met' Alex.* 1,26 and 25,2–6).[24]

---

23. So Fontana, *Le lotte,* p. 169 n. 6; though rejected by Briant (*Antigone le Borgne,* p. 208 n. 3) as "*erronée*" (without any argument), I think it is very likely to be true: Menandros and Asandros had for a number of years been Antigonos's neighbors in Asia Minor, and Menandros subsequently took service under Antigonos (see app. 3, no. 71). Briant's view of Antigonos's subordinate status and activities in the First Diadoch War is vitiated by the fact that he fails to notice that Arrian 1,26 and 25,1–8 together clearly place Antigonos's arrival in Asia Minor *before* the departure of Antipatros and Krateros from Macedon, not *after* their crossing of the Hellespont, as Briant insists. At *Met' Alex.* 1,26 Arrian states that Menandros told Antigonos that Eumenes was in Sardis to propose marriage to Kleopatra on behalf of Perdikkas, and that Antigonos communicated this news to Antipatros and Krateros who *thereupon* set out for the Hellespont from Macedon; and 25,1–8 shows that Antigonos was already in Asia when Eumenes was at Sardis and Menandros brought news of Eumenes' presence there and purpose to Antigonos.

24. The order of events given here is controversial; on Briant's view see n. 23 above, and cf. Hauben, *AncSoc* 8 (1977):93–95, showing that Briant is wrong—indeed, Briant's entire chapter 4, discussing the First Diadoch War, is unhinged by this error. However, Hauben believes Eumenes was at Sardis *before* Perdikkas's war council in Pisidia, and that this was held when Eumenes fled back there to report Antigonos's arrival. This idea is based solely on Justin's statement (XIII 6,14) that at Perdikkas's war council Eumenes received "Paphlagonia et Caria et Lycia et Phrygia": if Karia was given to Eumenes, it must be because Asandros had already gone over to Antigonos; *Lycia* is emended to *Lydia* and it is stated that the satrapies of Antigonos, Asandros, and Menandros were given to Eumenes by Perdikkas. However, Justin's authority is insufficient to warrant such conclusions; and he does not in any case state that Asandros was deprived of Karia—far less that Menandros was deprived of Lydia, which in fact had already been given by Perdikkas to Kleopatra earlier (Arrian 25,2). Justin's garbled statement means simply that Eumenes was given paramount authority over the regions mentioned, and is equivalent to Nepos's notice of a command (*Eum.* 3,2) "inter Taurum montem . . . atque Hellespontem" given to Eumenes by Perdikkas. Thus it seems Asandros and Menandros (then *stratēgos* of Lydia under Kleopatra) were placed under Eumenes' overall command, further explaining their defection to Antigonos.

Conflict between Perdikkas and Antigonos or Ptolemy could be represented as simply the chastisement of recalcitrant satraps by the central government, but conflict between Perdikkas and Antipatros and Krateros clearly meant civil war. A triumvirate of Perdikkas, Krateros, and Antipatros thus failed to come about. Mutual suspicion between Antipatros and Krateros in Europe and Perdikkas in Asia was, perhaps, inevitable, but it might have been overcome had it not been for the activities of other leaders like Ptolemy, Eumenes, and Antigonos, not to mention Olympias, who was strongly opposed to Antipatros's power in Macedon and encouraged her daughter Kleopatra to seek a marriage alliance with Perdikkas to win him as an ally against Antipatros (Arrian 1,21). To further their own ends all of these people fostered and exacerbated the tensions between Antipatros and Krateros on the one hand and Perdikkas on the other, tensions that now led to open conflict and civil war.

THE FIRST DIADOCH WAR (320–319 B.C.)

The chronicler of the Marmor Parium reports the beginning of this war with Antigonos's crossing to Asia (*FGrH* no. 239b sec. 11), and certainly Antigonos's defamation of Perdikkas and Eumenes' urging of Perdikkas to marry Kleopatra were two of the factors most responsible for the war. It is appropriate, therefore, and prophetic for the history of the next five years, that the incident which touched off the conflict should have involved these two men opposing each other at Sardis. However, the war was more than a conflict of these men, its real nature being a challenge to the settlement of Babylon by three men who had not been at that conference—Antipatros, Krateros, and Antigonos—and one who had been on the losing side there: Ptolemy. At issue was control of the Macedonian Empire, and the question of whether any man was to be permitted to ally himself so closely to the royal family as to raise himself definitely above all his peers, as Perdikkas was seeking to do.

With Antipatros and Krateros moving to invade Asia Minor and Antigonos successfully established on the western coast, the Perdikkan cause there was in immediate disarray. If Eumenes were to move to deal with Antigonos, he would leave the Hellespont unguarded and would run the risk of affording Antipatros and Krateros the chance to cross into Asia; yet if he marched on to the Hellespont, he left a not inconsiderable enemy force in his rear. However, even with whatever troops Karia and Lydia could muster, Antigonos's force would hardly be a match for Eumenes and Neoptolemos, and to the latter two Krateros and Antipatros still represented the greatest danger, so Eumenes marched on from Synnada up to the Hellespont and marshalled his forces there (Diod. XVIII 29,3). In this Eumenes may further have calculated that Alketas, who had refused to serve under him against Krateros and Antipatros (Plut. *Eum.* 5,2), would nevertheless check Antigonos with his troops in western Pisidia. At any rate Eumenes positioned himself and his army at the Hellespont, and presumably Kleitos with his ships was by now patrolling the narrows there, for without a fleet it would not be possible for Eumenes to prevent the enemy from crossing.[25]

However, when Antipatros and Krateros reached the Hellespont, they sent an embassy to those guarding the crossing (i.e., Kleitos and his ships) and caused them to change sides, so that they were able to ferry their army across without difficulty (Arrian 1,26).[26] They likewise sent embassies to Eumenes and Neoptolemos inviting them to change sides; and Neoptolemos, who no doubt resented having Eumenes placed over him, was all too ready to comply (Arrian 1,26; Diod. XVIII 29,4; Plut. *Eum.* 5,2–5). Hence when Eumenes finally came into military action, it was against his own ally Neoptolemos, whom he defeated, capturing all his force except 300 cavalry, with whom Neoptolemos fled to Antipatros (Diod. XVIII 29,4–6; Arrian 1,27; Plut. *Eum.* 5,2–3).

After this bitter victory, and facing superior forces with an army that had just been engaged in internecine warfare, Eumenes evidently retired from the Hellespontine region, for scarcely ten days later Krateros and Neoptolemos with part of the army from Europe came up with him and a second battle was fought "near Kappadokia" (Diod. XVIII 37,1; Plut. *Eum.* 8,1). Eumenes was once again victori-

25. An ancient army could not guard a strait dozens of miles long, and hence could only prevent an enemy landing if it had advance notice of where the landing would occur. Eumenes must have encamped his army at some convenient site near the Hellespont and relied on Kleitos's ships patrolling the straits to spot the enemy army when it reached the Hellespont and send him word, while preventing Antipatros and Krateros from transporting their men across.

26. Obviously those guarding *ton poron* (the strait, or crossing) must have been the naval forces in the first place. Once these had gone over to Antipatros and Krateros, the latter could cross at will, landing well away from wherever Eumenes and his army chanced to be. Briant, *Antigone le Borgne*, pp. 192–202, and Hauben, *AncSoc* 8 (1977):108, erroneously assume that it was Eumenes' *army* that was corrupted by this embassy, whereas Arrian 1,26 shows that it was only after crossing that Antipatros and Krateros sent the embassies to Eumenes and Neoptolemos that caused Eumenes difficulties with his army.

ous, owing both of these victories to his excellent cavalry, and both Krateros and Neoptolemos fell in this battle, fought around the beginning of May 320. Most of Krateros's army escaped, however, and rejoined Antipatros, who was marching with the rest of the European army to Kilikia in pursuit of Perdikkas.[27] For it had been agreed at a *synedrion* held after the arrival of Neoptolemos that the latter should accompany Krateros with part of the army in pursuit of Eumenes, while Antipatros hurried on south with the rest (Diod. XVIII 29,6). It is nowhere recorded whether or not Antigonos took part in this *synedrion,* and the role he played in the remainder of this campaign is preserved only in the form of Arrian's information that he was subsequently in Cyprus (*Met' Alex.* 1,30). It seems, then, that while in Lydia/Karia, Antigonos received word of the expeditionary force Perdikkas had sent to Cyprus under Aristonous, and of the hostilities there, and decided to do something about it. For Cyprus was an important source of naval strength and could be either a useful link in Perdikkas's communications in his campaign against Egypt or an invaluable base from which to harry Perdikkas's communications and assault his fleet in rear if the anti-Perdikkan forces there should prevail.

In my view Antigonos probably was present at the *synedrion* near the Hellespont and moved against Cyprus as part of a concerted plan of campaign agreed upon at that meeting. Some hint of this may be preserved by Memnon (*FGrH,* no. 434 F 2,3–6), who reports that Dionysios, tyrant of Herakleia Pontika, an enemy of Perdikkas and allied by marriage to Krateros, at some date fought under Antigonos in Cyprus. I suggest that Dionysios probably joined Antipatros and Krateros at the Hellespont and was instructed at the *synedrion* there to sail to Cyprus with Antigonos.[28] The allied strategy thus had three

27. Thus Diod. XVIII 32,2–33,1 and cf. Bartoletti, *PSI,* 12, no. 1284, with further restorations and analysis by Wirth, *Klio* 46 (1965):283–88. Briant, *Antigone le Borgne,* p. 223 n. 13, and A. B. Bosworth, *GRBS* 19 (1978):227–37, suggest that *PSI,* 12, no. 1284 refers to the battle between Eumenes and Neoptolemos, which seems possible, though I do not find their arguments convincing.

28. J. Kaerst, *RE* s.v. Dionysios, no. 66, suggests that Dionysios's service with Antigonos in Cyprus occurred in 306, when Antigonos's son Demetrios captured the island from Ptolemy; but Dionysios in fact died in 306/5 (Diod. XX 77,1) and not, it seems, in Cyprus; see Burstein, *Outpost of Hellenism,* pp. 77–78, who (following Droysen) suggests that for "Kupron" in Memnon's text one should read "Turon," and that Dionysios aided Antigonos against Tyre in 314. But as Memnon records that Dionysios was an enemy of Perdikkas and that he married Krateros's ex-wife Amestris with Krateros's approval, and since we know that Antigonos fought on Cyprus in 320 against Perdikkan forces, there is no need to emend Memnon's text.

parts, with Krateros attacking Eumenes, Antipatros pursuing Perdikkas in the direction of Egypt, and Antigonos sailing down with a flotilla of Athenian and Herakleote ships to take charge of the anti-Perdikkan operations in Cyprus. Indeed, it is possible that Kleitos and his fleet were also placed under Antigonos's command for this operation, though this cannot be proved.[29]

Meanwhile Perdikkas had already reached Egypt some time before, but he was utterly unable to make any headway against Ptolemy's spirited defense along the Pelousiac branch of the Nile: so unsuccessful were his operations that discontent flared in his army and a conspiracy set on foot by a number of his highest officers, led by Peithon Krateua, resulted in his being assassinated in his tent by Seleukos and Antigenes (Arrian 1,28 and 35; Diod. XVIII 33,1–36,5; Nepos *Eum.* 5,1) just two days before news of Eumenes' victory over Krateros arrived in Egypt (Plut. *Eum.* 8,2). Peithon and his confederates lost no time in making peace with Ptolemy. A great meeting was held at which Ptolemy, no doubt fearing a possible falling-out with Antigonos and Antipatros, declined to take the regency, instead nominating Peithon and Arrhidaios, the man who had conducted Alexander's body to Egypt. When news of Krateros's death and defeat came in, the Macedonians sentenced Eumenes, Alketas, and fifty other leading Perdikkans to death, beginning with a slaughter of pro-Perdikkans in the camp in Egypt (Arrian 1,29–30; Diod. XVIII 36,6–37,2). The royal army then set out under Peithon and Arrhidaios to return to Syria (Diod. XVIII 39,1).

It is not clear whether the appointment of Peithon and Arrhidaios as joint regents was intended to be permanent or only temporary.[30]

---

29. *OGIS,* no. 4, an inscription from Hekatonnesos near the Troad honoring one Thersippos, records (lines 14–16) that Kleitos campaigned off Cyprus, but appears to date this after Triparadeisos (see Dittenberger's commentary ad loc.). However, if the inscription does not adhere strictly to chronological order in what it reports, it could be hypothesized that Kleitos in fact went to Cyprus with/under Antigonos in early 320. However, it is more probable that the inscription refers to an otherwise unknown campaign by Kleitos either late in 320 or perhaps in 319, possibly connected with the havoc caused in the waters between Cyprus and Lykia/Karia by Attalos in 320 (Arrian 1,39).

30. Diod. XVIII 36,6–7 does not seem to regard the posts of Peithon and Arrhidaios as temporary, nor is there any suggestion of it at XVIII 39,2, where Diodoros records their resignation and the election of Antipatros in their place. However, Arrian *Met' Alex.* 1,30–31 says that Arrhidaios and Peithon were appointed *ἐν τῶι τέως*, and that when challenged by Eurydike, they did not resign, but asserted their authority over all affairs *ἕως Ἀντίγονος καὶ Ἀντίπατρος παραγένωνται*. Arrian then seems to have regarded the appointment of Peithon and Arrhidaios as temporary, and his account seems slightly preferable, as Diodoros here shows signs of excessive abbreviation.

However, it was obvious that any new arrangement for ordering the empire would have to take into account the views of Antipatros and Antigonos and their followers, and accordingly messages were sent to Antipatros and Antigonos to come to meet the royal army (Arrian 1,30). While the army marched north, the young Queen Eurydike, wife of Philippos Arrhidaios, began to assert her right to rule in her husband's name. Peithon and Arrhidaios had great difficulty in dealing with this, as Eurydike evidently enjoyed a great deal of popularity among the troops (Arrian 1,31; Diod. XVIII 39,1–2). It seems likely, too, that there was some revulsion of feeling among the troops in favor of the Perdikkan cause, for one of Eurydike's main helpers was Perdikkas's brother-in-law Attalos (Arrian 1,33).[31] Peithon and Arrhidaios, however, asserted that nothing should be decided until Antigonos and Antipatros arrived, and the army encamped at Triparadeisos in north Syria to await them (Arrian 1,31; Diod. XVIII 39,1–3).

Antipatros came down from Kilikia to Triparadeisos, and Antigonos—arriving from Cyprus—encamped with him (Polyainos IV 6,4; Arrian 1,33). Antigonos had evidently been victorious in Cyprus: of the four Perdikkan commanders on Cyprus (Arrian 24,6), Medeios is subsequently found serving with Antigonos (e.g., Diod. XIX 69,3; 75,3), while Sosigenes joined Eumenes (Polyainos IV 6,9) and Aristonous is next heard of serving with Olympias in Macedon (Diod. XIX 35,4; 50,3–51,1). Antipatros and Antigonos were the men of the hour: with the death of Krateros and the decision of Ptolemy to remain in Egypt, these two remained of the quadrumvirate which had successfully challenged the settlement at Babylon, and to them would obviously fall the leading role in establishing a new settlement at Triparadeisos. Antipatros, in particular, the former right-hand man of Philip and viceroy of Europe for Alexander, and the victorious general of two wars against the Greeks, had prestige and *auctoritas* that no other Macedonian could match. Antigonos, however, having conducted successful independent operations during the recent fighting, was next to Antipatros in more than just age and experience—the death of Krateros having been providential for his future ambitions. In Arrian's account of the lead-up to the Triparadeisos conference (*Met' Alex.* 1,30–31) Antipatros and Antigonos are named together as the men on whom all waited—Antigonos even being named first.

31. That the Attalos who was Eurydike's helper in her intrigues was the same as Perdikkas's brother-in-law is shown by Arrian 1,39.

Antipatros was careful to keep his and Antigonos's forces encamped separately, divided by a river from the royal army, in which Eurydike had by no means ceased to stir up discontent (Arrian 1,33). Antipatros decided to cross to the royal camp and address the soldiery, who were demanding arrears of pay (Arrian 1,32; Polyainos IV 6,4). But when he tried to explain that he did not have enough money to pay them immediately, promising to pay them later from the royal treasuries, the impatient soldiery rioted and began to stone him. Antigonos, who had remained behind in Antipatros's camp, saw his friend's danger and charged across the bridge between the two camps into the midst of the tumult with a body of cavalry, overawing the soldiers into making way for him (Polyainos IV 6,4). While he held the soldiers' attention, holding forth with explanations and promises and aided in this by Seleukos (Arrian 1,33), the cavalry surrounded the aged Antipatros and escorted him back to the safety of his own camp (Polyainos IV 6,4). From there Antipatros summoned the officers of the royal army to him and, bereft of their leaders, the soldiers submitted to his authority (Arrian 1,33). Eurydike was brought to heel by threats (Diod. XVIII 39,4), and her helper Attalos was again forced to flee (Arrian 1,39).

At the conference that was now held, the settlement of Babylon was revised in favor of those who had led the opposition to Perdikkas. Since almost all of the great leaders were present or at least (as, for example, in the case of Ptolemy) represented at Triparadeisos,[32] and as the kings were present and virtually all of the Macedonian army gathered at this one spot, the legitimacy of this conference's dispositions for the running of the empire was indisputable. The most important decisions of the conference were the appointment of Antipatros to the regency with full powers and the elevation of Antigonos to a position which made him in effect the overseer or viceroy of Asia. He was given charge of the kings, and a large army—the former army of Perdikkas—was put at his disposal (Arrian 1,38), while Antipatros's son Kassandros was attached to him as his chiliarch of cavalry (i.e., effectively his second-in-command). The implication appears to be that Antigonos was intended to become Antipatros's successor: though this is nowhere explicitly stated, it is obvious that if Antipa-

32. At this time Antipatros was Ptolemy's friend and (presumably) father-in-law (Paus. I 6,8—though the exact date of Ptolemy's marriage to Antipatros's daughter Eurydike is not known); and Ptolemy's good friend Arrhidaios was also present at the conference (Diod. XVIII 28,2–3; 36,6; 39,1–4).

tros had died while Antigonos had physical charge of the kings, no one else could have become regent but he.[33]

The full details of the new satrapial appointments need not concern us here (Diod. XVIII 39,5–6; Arrian 1,34–37). Suffice it to say that Ptolemy was confirmed in his satrapy and Peithon as satrap of Media; that Antigonos's former satrapies were restored to him; that Seleukos, Antigenes, Kleitos, and Arrhidaios were rewarded for turning against Perdikkas by receiving the satrapies of Babylonia, Susiane, Lydia, and Hellespontine Phrygia respectively; and that Kappadokia was assigned to one Nikanor. Four *sōmatophylakes* were appointed for Philippos Arrhidaios, the selections clearly being intended to honor and please great nobles: Lysimachos's brother Autodikos was one, and Peukestas's brother Amyntas another, while the third was Alexandros, the son of Polyperchon;[34] the fourth, Ptolemaios, son of Ptolemaios (Arrian *Met' Alex.* 1,38), was doubtless Antigonos's nephew of that name.[35] Antipatros—well over seventy years old and with only a few years left to live—intended to return to Macedon.

Eumenes was still at large with a victorious army in Asia Minor, however, and had reoccupied Hellespontine Phrygia (he raided the royal studs around Mount Ida in the Troad: Plut. *Eum.* 8,3) and Lydia, where he hoped to give battle against Antipatros on the Sardean plain, but was dissuaded by Kleopatra (Plut. *Eum.* 8,4; Arrian 1,40). In addition, Alketas still had a considerable force in Pisidia, and was joined there by other Perdikkans: Dokimos fleeing from Babylonia, Polemon, and Attalos, who had gathered 10,000 foot and 800 horse, with which he first campaigned in Karia and made an abortive attack on Rhodes (Arrian 1,39–42; Plut. *Eum.* 8,4). Antigonos demanded the job of dealing with these Perdikkan remnants, and thus bringing the war to a close, and was granted it (Arrian 1,38).

The precise nature of Antigonos's position at this time requires some clarification, for it is often suggested that his broad powers over Asia were to last only for the duration of the war against the ex-

33. Suggestive also is the fact that Antipatros appointed his son Kassandros to be Antigonos's chiliarch (Arrian *Met' Alex.* 1,38 and 42), the same position as that given Kassandros under Antipatros's actual successor, Polyperchon (Diod. XVIII 48,4–5).

34. All three of these young men were close relatives of powerful Macedonian nobles who played a major role in the empire at the time of Triparadeisos: the satraps of Thrace (Lysimachos) and Persia (Peukestas) and Antipatros's deputy in Macedon, Polyperchon (see Diod. XVIII 38,1–6 for Polyperchon's defeat of a rebellion by the Thessalians and Aitolians, allied with Perdikkas).

35. See for this app. 3, no. 100.

Perdikkans.[36] However, neither of the two sources we have for this states that Antigonos's office was temporally limited. Diodoros XVIII 39,7 says, "He [sc. Antipatros] appointed as general of the royal army Antigonos, to whom was assigned the task of warring down Eumenes and Alketas"; Arrian *Met' Alex.* 1,38 states, "He appointed Antigonos leader of the army formerly under Perdikkas, and assigning him the care and guarding of the kings, he handed over to him at the same time, at his own request, the war to be waged against Eumenes." The implication, especially of the more detailed Arrian, is clearly that Antigonos's main task was to head the royal army and look after the kings, having a watching brief over Asia, and being (as I have suggested above) thus marked out as Antipatros's eventual successor. The war against Eumenes and Alketas was an additional task, which Antigonos himself demanded, and which fell to him naturally given his military command.

Though Antigonos's position was modified by Antipatros a few months later, it is significant that as originally conceived at Triparadeisos, there was no clear time limit to his power, which in fact seems to have been expected to continue beyond Antipatros's death. The alliance between Antipatros and Antigonos hereby implied was further strengthened by the marriage of Antigonos's son Demetrios to Antipatros's daughter Phila, the widow of Krateros. The fact that this was a marriage of policy is emphasized by Plutarch's description of Demetrios's reluctance to marry the considerably older Phila (Plut. *Dem.* 14,2–3).[37] This being settled, the camp at Triparadeisos was broken up, and the various parties to the conference went on their way: some to their satrapies; Antipatros and Antigonos and their armies into Asia Minor. Since Perdikkas had been assassinated in May 320, the Triparadeisos conference must have ended before the end of July—time enough still for a campaign in Asia Minor. Certainly Eumenes at first thought of fighting a battle near Sardis, but he was persuaded to withdraw into Phrygia, where he vainly attempted to form an alliance with Alketas and Attalos (Arrian 1,41–42; Plut. *Eum.* 8,4).

The maneuvering in Asia Minor in the second half of 320 would be of considerable interest, but we can no longer follow the details of it, since Diodoros passes over it in silence and Photios's epitome of Arrian is so brief. However, as Antipatros and Antigonos must have

---

36. Thus, e.g., Bengtson, *Strategie,* 1:96–8; Wehrli, *Antigone et Démétrios,* pp. 34–35; and, with reservations, Engel, *Untersuchungen,* pp. 13–21.

37. For the date of this marriage (mid 320), see app. 3, no. 10.

taken one of the great roads through Phrygia from Kilikia, while Eumenes was falling back on Kelainai from Lydia, and Alketas was established in Pisidia, the military situation was certainly a complex one. Since Antipatros and Antigonos eventually reached Sardis, and Eumenes avoided them by retreating to Kelainai, they must have marched from Kilikia via Lake Tatta to Ankyra and then down the Royal Road to Sardis (see map 2). Arrived there, Antipatros had an interview with Kleopatra and then moved off towards Macedon (Arrian 1,40); meanwhile Antigonos did not venture to come to grips with Eumenes, but did send Asandros to fight Alketas and Attalos, who had presumably united their forces in Karia (Asandros's satrapy: Arrian 1,37) and succeeded in defeating Asandros (Arrian 1,41).[38] Most likely Antigonos's reluctance to do battle with Eumenes was due to the uncertain allegiance of his army, for he was leading the men who had been Perdikkas's army, an unruly lot and of uncertain loyalty.[39]

Kassandros then began to agitate against Antigonos, accusing him no doubt of failure to prosecute the war against Eumenes with sufficient vigor. Though Antipatros ordered his son to obey Antigonos, Kassandros went to see his father in Phrygia (Hellespontine Phrygia, without doubt) and succeeded in planting suspicions against Antigonos in Antipatros's mind, so that Antigonos had to come to Hellespontine Phrygia to defend himself (Arrian 1,42). The result was that a new arrangement was reached, whereby Antipatros was to take the kings home with him to Macedon, while Antigonos received from Antipatros's own Macedonian army a contingent of 8,500 infantry, a large body of Companion cavalry, and seventy elephants (Arrian 1,43).[40] That this involved an exchange of troops appears

---

38. Arrian's text actually names Antipatros at 1,41 as the man who did not dare to come to grips with Eumenes and sent Asandros down to fight Alketas and Attalos. However, it was realized by Grimmig, *Arrians Diadochengeschichte,* 103, that this is an error for Antigonos, to whom the war against Eumenes and Alketas had been entrusted.

39. Though it was apparently Perdikkas's army which condemned Eumenes, Alketas, Attalos, and their friends to death (Diod. XVIII 37,2–3; Plut. *Eum.* 8,2), the army was fickle, and many of the soldiers had subsequently supported the intrigues of Attalos and Eurydike in Syria (Arrian 1,33; Diod. XVIII 39,2–4). There was much indiscipline in this army, which had already shown itself rebellious in Babylon in 323, in 321 over the murder of Kynane (Arrian 1,23), and in 320 against Perdikkas in Egypt and Antipatros at Triparadeisos.

40. The text of Photios's epitome of Arrian says Antigonos received 8,500 Macedonian infantry καὶ ἱππέας τῶν ἑταίρων ἴσους. This is obviously an error, for the Companion cavalry never numbered anywhere near 8,500, nor did Antigonos ever afterwards control so many of them: for example, at the battle of Paraitakene in 316, he fielded some 8,000 of the Macedonian infantry he had received from Antipatros (the rest presumably having perished in earlier campaigns) and 1,000 Companion cavalry (Diod. XIX 29,3–4). One should perhaps replace *isous* in Photios's text with *chilious.*

from the fact that Arrian says (1,44) that on the way to cross the Hellespont, the army with Antipatros rebelled *again* demanding money: at Triparadeisos it was the royal army that had rebelled seeking money, not that of Antipatros, and hence there must have been a large element at least of the royal army with Antipatros when he set out to return at last to Macedon. Antigonos with his large new body of reliable troops set out to begin operations against Eumenes, while Antipatros promised to pay his rebellious troops at Abydos, but there tricked them and crossed over with the kings at the end of 320 to join Lysimachos in Thrace, the disgruntled troops perforce following after him (Arrian 1,44–45).

Antigonos remained in Asia as *stratēgos* over the Asian part of the empire (Diod. XVIII 40,1); presumably his position was equivalent to that held by Antipatros in Europe during Alexander's reign.[41] Again the question occurs of whether Antigonos's power in Asia was given any temporal limits under this new dispensation, which clearly involved a diminution in his authority and future prospects with the removal of the kings from his control. There is a lacuna in Diodoros's text at this point, the events of the second half of 320 being omitted between XVIII 39,7 and 40,1; in Arrian's text (*Met' Alex.* 1,42–43) there is no sign of any temporal limit. Such a limit is nevertheless thought to be implied by many scholars (see n. 36 above) on the basis of Diodoros's statement at the beginning of XVIII 40,1 that Antigonos was ἐπὶ τῆς Ἀσίας ἀποδεδειγμένος στρατηγὸς διαπολεμήσων πρὸς Εὐμένη—appointed general over Asia with the task of warring down Eumenes. Though this phrase can be taken to imply a limit, Diodoros is here switching his narrative from Antipatros to Antigonos, and the phrase is surely meant simply to introduce the description of the war that follows. In other words, the phrase διαπολεμήσων πρὸς Εὐμένη merely indicates the task facing Antigonos and the matter to be narrated, rather than the terms of Antigonos's appointment as *stratēgos*. The position and the army that went with it were not merely intended for the war against the remaining Perdikkans, but to be in general those of the representative and

41. So Bengtson, *Strategie*, 1:100–106. The criticism of Engel, *Untersuchungen*, pp. 21–28, seems in part justified: Bengtson argues that as *stratēgos* of Asia, Antigonos's powers had been extended, which is clearly wrong. Once the kings and a large part of the old army of Perdikkas were taken over by Antipatros, Antigonos was clearly no longer the στρατηγὸς τῆς βασιλικῆς δυνάμεως; thus Diodoros's statement (XVIII 40,1) that at the beginning of 319 Antigonos was στρατηγὸς τῆς Ἀσίας must be accepted as accurate. In general Antigonos's position is very well characterized by Appian *Syr.* 53: ἐπίσκοπος δ᾽ εἶναι τῆς ὅλης Ἀσίας ἐξ Ἀντιπάτρου περῶντος ἐς τὴν Εὐρώπην ἀπολελειμμένος.

executive of the royal power in Asia; and Antigonos would obviously continue to hold this position until such time as the kings (i.e., the regent, Antipatros) decided otherwise.

It is not certain precisely what troops Antigonos had at his disposal besides those Macedonians granted him by Antipatros in Hellespontine Phrygia: definitely a part of the old royal army, and doubtless a number of mercenaries and Asiatic levies.[42] He faced formidable opposition: Alketas and Attalos had a large army fresh from victory over Asandros; and in Phrygia Eumenes had enriched his army and strengthened its loyalty to himself by allowing the troops to plunder the prosperous villages and estates around Kelainai (Plut. *Eum.* 8,5; and cf. Arrian 1,41). However, the failure of Eumenes and Alketas to reach an agreement for common action (Arrian 1,41; Plut. *Eum.* 8,4) greatly facilitated Antigonos's task, giving him the chance to defeat his enemies in detail. Plutarch states that Eumenes wintered at Kelainai, but this must be an error, for Diodoros reports that Eumenes was in Kappadokia when the winter drew to an end (XVIII 40,1), and Polyainos IV 6,6 shows that Antigonos himself wintered in Phrygia near the Kappadokian border. The failure of his talks with Alketas and the approach of Antigonos evidently caused Eumenes to withdraw to Kappadokia with his army for the winter; Antigonos was thus able to push forward with his army into a position between Alketas and Eumenes, where he wintered in southeastern Phrygia. He was thus running the risk of being taken between two fires, but buying by this risk an opportunity to defeat his two enemies one by one in the spring.

Curiously, both Antigonos and Eumenes suffered defections during the winter of 320/19. In Eumenes' case, an officer named Perdikkas rebelled with 3,000 foot and 500 horse, but Eumenes' friend Phoinix of Tenedos quickly dealt with the problem (Diod. XVIII 40,2–4); the revolt was no doubt a result of Antigonos's propaganda, for during the winter he sent offers of substantial rewards to anyone who would betray Eumenes (Plut. *Eum.* 8,6; Justin XIV 1,9). Antigonos meanwhile had to deal with a rebellion by an officer named Olkias

42. That Antigonos was left part of the old royal army in 320 appears from Polyainos IV 6,6, reporting that 3,000 Macedonians rebelled against Antigonos in early 319 and he was forced to send them home to Macedon, yet in 316 he still had 8,000 of the 8,500 Macedonians given him by Antipatros in 320 (Diod. XIX 29,3). Clearly the 3,000 rebels of 319 were former members of Perdikkas's army, which is confirmed by the fact that they threatened to join Perdikkas's brother, Alketas. At the battle of Orkynia in early 319, Antigonos had 5,000 non-Macedonian infantry, evidently Asians and/or Greek mercenaries: Diod. XVIII 40,7.

with 3,000 Macedonian infantry. These were evidently men still left him from the old royal army (see above n. 42), and though Antigonos was able to capture them by a trick with the aid of a loyal officer named Leonidas, he was forced to allow them to go home to Macedon, a substantial loss to his army at this critical time. At least he had prevented them from joining and reinforcing Alketas, as seems to have been their intention, but they had damaged his cause by their insubordination, and by plundering Lykaonia and southeastern Phrygia (Polyainos IV 6,6). Antigonos had decided to deal with Eumenes first at the beginning of the spring, but he needed to leave a substantial force to watch Alketas and guard his rear. With this and the loss of 3,000 Macedonian infantry, Antigonos was only able to lead 10,000 foot (half of them Macedonians), 2,000 cavalry, and thirty elephants against Eumenes in Kappadokia, who had some 20,000 foot and 5,000 horse.[43]

In spite of having only half the troop strength that Eumenes could field, however, Antigonos adopted a bold, attacking strategy. Eumenes was encamped in a plain well suited to cavalry fighting (Diod. XVIII 40,6), near a place called Orkynia (Plut. *Eum.* 9,2). Clearly Eumenes hoped to decide this battle with his excellent cavalry, as he had the battles against Neoptolemos and Krateros. Antigonos camped on some hills overlooking the plain on which Eumenes was encamped. Thus Antigonos could give or refuse battle at will. Diodoros tells us that unbeknownst to Eumenes, Antigonos got in touch with his cavalry officer Apollonides, who was willing to change sides (Diod. XVIII 40,5–8; Plut. *Eum.* 9,2), but what no modern scholar seems yet to have noticed is that there is an alternative (or perhaps rather complementary) account of this battle at Polyainos IV 6,19:

> Antigonos, having fewer soldiers, was camped over against the enemy under Eumenes. As there was a frequent exchange of heralds going on, he arranged that when the herald arrived, a soldier should come running

43. The figures are given by Diod. XVIII 40,7. Engel (*MH* 28 [1971]:227–31) expresses surprise at the small number of troops led by Antigonos at this battle. However, he fails to notice Antigonos's loss of 3,000 Macedonians, recorded by Polyainos IV 6,6, and naively takes at face value the statement at Arrian 1,43 that Antigonos had 8,500 Companion cavalry (on this see n. 40 above). Engel correctly hypothesizes that Antigonos must have detached troops to watch Alketas and Attalos, who were probably in Karia: Attalos is attested there in 320 by Arrian 1,39, and at Appian *Syr.* 52 we learn that Laomedon of Syria, ejected from his satrapy by Ptolemy (no doubt early in 319, see Diod. XVIII 43,1–2), fled to Alketas in Karia. Since Antigonos had only 5,000 Macedonians at Orkynia, presumably the other 3,500 were detached to watch Alketas, doubtless with a substantial force of Asians and mercenaries.

> up breathing hard and covered with dust and announce: "The allies are here." Hearing this Antigonos jumped up joyfully; dismissing the heralds, he led his army out of their palisade on the next day, having drawn up his phalanx twice as long as usual. The enemy, having heard from the heralds of the presence of his allies and seeing the length of his phalanx (which thus had only a contemptible depth), were afraid to join battle and took to flight.

Of the known battles between Antigonos and Eumenes, this account can only refer to the battle of Orkynia in 319, for this is the one battle between Antigonos and Eumenes in which the former had a significantly smaller army.[44] We learn then that Antigonos and Eumenes were encamped opposite each other at Orkynia for several days while negotiations of some sort went on, and that Antigonos's victory was as much due to a clever stratagem whereby he tricked the enemy into thinking he had twice as much infantry as he in fact had, as to the prearranged treachery during the battle of Apollonides and his cavalry. Thus Antigonos succeeded in negating Eumenes' superiority in cavalry by tampering with the loyalty of the cavalry officers and overcame Eumenes' superiority in infantry by means of a simple, but clever, stratagem.[45] In this way Eumenes' army was put to flight; and, not content with this, Antigonos also managed to capture Eumenes' baggage (Diod. XVIII 40,8), a feat which appears to be described in another paragraph of Polyainos (IV 6,12), according to which Antigonos, looking down from the hillside on which he was drawing up his army at Eumenes' array on the plain, decided to send

44. The other three known battles between Antigonos and Eumenes were at the river Kopratas in early 316, a victory for Eumenes; the battle of Paraitakene in mid 316, a drawn battle; and the battle of Gabiene in winter 316/15, which Antigonos won, but not by the trick described here. There is no room in the fairly full account that we have of the hostilities between Antigonos and Eumenes in books XVIII and XIX of Diodoros and in Plutarch's *Life of Eumenes* to slot in an unmentioned battle. The only scholar who seems to have discussed Polyainos IV 6,19 is Melber ("Über die Quellen und den Wert der Strategemen Sammlung Polyäns," p. 625), who summarily dismisses it as derived from an anecdotal source and hence worthless, mainly because it stands outside the group of stratagems at Poly. IV 6,4–16, which are shown by parallels with Diodoros to be derived from Hieronymos of Kardia. This is an inadequate reason for dismissing perfectly plausible evidence.

45. The similarities between Diod. XVIII 40,6–8 and Poly. IV 6,19 must be stressed: in Diodoros the army of Antigonos is only half as big as Eumenes', while in Polyainos he has far fewer troops than Eumenes; in both Antigonos is encamped in a strong position; and in both he wins an overwhelming victory. Furthermore, the information of Polyainos that the two armies were encamped near each other for some time while heralds went to and fro explains how Antigonos managed to get in touch with Eumenes' officer Apollonides to arrange the treachery recorded by Diodoros.

part of his rearguard on horseback to capture Eumenes' baggage.[46] There were thus three elements to Antigonos's battle tactics, and the result was a brilliant victory, in which his small army slew about 8,000 of the enemy (Diod. XVIII 40,8) and most of the rest went over to him (Diod. XVIII 41,1).

Eumenes, having been completely outgeneraled in this battle, nevertheless showed his mettle in the aftermath. Escaping with a substantial body of troops, he captured and killed the traitor Apollonides, evaded the pursuit of Antigonos's forces, and doubled back to the battlefield, where he buried his dead (Plut. *Eum.* 9,2). He then nearly captured Antigonos's baggage train under Menandros (see app. 3, no. 71). Eventually, however, Antigonos caught up with Eumenes, who was forced to take refuge in a stronghold called Nora with his closest followers, some 600–700 in number (Diod. XVIII 41,1–3; Plut. *Eum.* 10,1). There Antigonos invested him closely, but the fort was well stocked and virtually impregnable; a parley was held, Antigonos sending his nephew Polemaios into Nora as a hostage for Eumenes' safe return, but Eumenes' surrender terms were such that Antigonos thought it best to refer them to Antipatros. He accordingly established guards around Nora with strong siege fortifications (Diod. XVIII 41,5–7; Plut. *Eum.* 10,2–4). Subsequently Eumenes sent an embassy under Hieronymos of Kardia to Antipatros, perhaps accompanied on Antigonos's behalf by Aristodemos of Miletos.[47]

Meanwhile Antigonos himself with most of his army marched away to deal with Attalos and Alketas, who had moved into Pisidia with a large army, perhaps totaling some 20,000 men. The time was

46. That Polyainos IV 6,12 must refer to the battle of Orkynia escapes notice by Melber (op.cit. n. 44, pp. 623–24), who assumes it to be a doublet of Polyainos IV 6,13 on the battle of Gabiene. But this battle was fought on a wide sandy plain with no hills! However, Diod. XVIII 40,6–8 on the battle of Orkynia coincides neatly with Polyainos IV 6,12: in both Antigonos is on a hill loking down on Eumenes' position in a plain, and in both Antigonos captures Eumenes' *aposkeuē*. Polyainos's stratagem simply supplies the means by which Antigonos achieved this.

47. Diodoros says at XVIII 41,7 that Antigonos referred the decision on Eumenes' demands to Antipatros, and at 42,1 that afterwards Eumenes sent envoys headed by Hieronymos of Kardia to Antipatros. For the possibility that Aristodemos accompanied him as Antigonos's representative, see app. 3, no. 16. The interpretation put on Antigonos's parley with Eumenes by Diodoros (XVIII 41,5, and cf. 39,7), who posits a plan by Antigonos to form a coalition with Eumenes against Antipatros and the kings, is no doubt an anticipation of later events. In fact, Antigonos most likely sought to avoid a difficult siege by offering Eumenes lenient terms, but found him intransigent: Diod. XVIII 41,6–7.

presumably about the middle of summer (of 319); Alketas clearly expected Antigonos to come against him, for he had encamped with his army in a pass (so Polyainos IV 6,7), where he hoped to be able to withstand Antigonos's superior force. For Antigonos by now had some 40,000 infantry and 7,000 cavalry (Diod. XVIII 45,1), which indicates that besides enrolling the survivors of Eumenes' army he must have undertaken further recruitment of Asiatics and mercenaries.[48] The campaign against Alketas is described at length by Diodoros (XVIII 44–45), and more briefly by Polyainos (IV 6,7), whose accounts are complementary and derived from the same source.[49] Antigonos obviously had good intelligence of Alketas's whereabouts and plans; his problem was to get the better of a strong force posted in a place where it would be hard to make superior numbers tell. He decided to enlist the element of surprise, and in a march of close to 300 miles (2,500 stades: Diod. XVIII 44,2) in seven days and nights, he reached Kretopolis in Pisidia, near which Alketas was encamped.[50] Though Diodoros says that Antigonos accomplished this astounding march (about forty miles per day) with his entire army, it seems likely that in fact it would have been a mobile elite force only that marched

---

48. Antigonos had 10,000 infantry and 2,000 cavalry at the battle of Orkynia, and at least another 3,500 Macedonian infantry (see n. 43 above). Eumenes had 20,000 foot and 5,000 horse at Orkynia, of whom about 8,000 were slain in the battle (Diod. XVIII 40,7–8), 600 went with Eumenes to Nora (Diod. XVIII 41,3), and a further 2,000 were found wandering about Kappadokia after Eumenes' escape from Nora (Diod. XVIII 53,6–7). The rest Antigonos enrolled in his army (Diod. XVIII 41,1; 41,4; 50,1), and these must have numbered about 14,000. Adding these to his previous forces, one comes to a total of about 29,500, and even allowing that in early 319 Antigonos had other troops besides the 3,500 Macedonians on detached service, one can see that some further recruiting must have been done to reach 47,000.

49. See Engel, *Historia* 21 (1972):501–7, showing conclusively that Diodoros and Polyainos are in harmony on this event, though they highlight different aspects. Their source is clearly Hieronymos.

50. Alketas and Attalos were probably still in Karia in early 319 (see n. 43 above). Diod. XVIII 41,7 states that after dealing with Eumenes, Antigonos heard that Alketas and Attalos were advancing against him (MSS *poreuomenous;* Rhodoman, Dindorf, and Fischer emend to *epiporeuomenous*), and decided to march forth to deal with them. Diod. XVIII 44,1–2 says that Antigonos set out from Kappadokia and marched towards Pisidia, covering 2,500 *stades* (roughly 290 miles) and reaching Kretopolis, near which Alketas was encamped; Polyainos IV 6,7 says that Alketas was encamped ἐν αὐλῶνι Πισιδικῶι—in a pass in Pisidia. Ramsay, *JHS* 43 (1923):1–10, hypothesizes that "αὐλῶνι Πισιδικῶι" is a proper name referring to a pass near the later Antioch of Pisidia; he objects to Diodoros's placing the battle near Kretopolis, which he contends was much further than 300 miles from Kappadokia. Though Ramsay is right to say that the battle could not have taken place at the head of the Klimax pass, where some have placed it, I see no reason why it could not have occurred in a pass to the north or east of Kretopolis, towards Milyas or Selge. The distance mentioned by Diodoros seems about right for a march from southwestern Kappadokia past Laranda and Lake Troglitis to the area of Kretopolis (see map 2).

so quickly, with the rest of the army following more slowly.[51] In any case, the rapidity of his approach was such that the enemy were taken completely by surprise: the first warning they had that Antigonos was anywhere in their vicinity came from the trumpeting of his elephants (thus Polyainos) as his troops occupied some hills overlooking Alketas's position (so Diod. XVIII 44,2).

Alketas and Attalos were now in the gravest of difficulties: with their army totally unprepared, they faced assault in front along the pass, and in flank from the hills overlooking the pass. Leaving Attalos and Dokimos to draw up their phalanx as quickly as possible, Alketas took the cavalry (Diod. XVIII 44,3), or the peltasts according to Polyainos—perhaps in fact a mixed force of both—and launched a violent assault on Antigonos's troops on the ridge, trying desperately to dislodge them. A stubborn battle ensued, but meantime Antigonos charged with 6,000 horse into the pass, threatening to cut off Alketas from his phalanx; at this Alketas was forced back from the ridge and barely managed to get back to his phalanx, with the loss of most of his men (Diod. XVIII 44,4–5). But Antigonos's cavalry assault had occurred with such paralyzing swiftness that Attalos did not have time to get all of his men armed and drawn up for battle (so Polyainos, and cf. Diod. XVIII 45,2). Hence no real battle occurred; the enemy simply surrendered to Antigonos. Alketas managed to escape with a guard of Pisidians, who were particularly loyal to him, and made his way to the almost impregnable city of Termessos; his colleagues Attalos, Dokimos, and Polemon were captured by Antigonos, along with the rest of the army of close to 16,000 foot and 900 horse (Diod. XVIII 45,1–4).

Thus in two brilliant campaigns in the course of one season Antigonos annihilated the remnants of the Perdikkan faction. The two enemy armies had been killed, scattered, or enrolled in Antigonos's own army; Eumenes was locked up at Nora with his last loyalists; Attalos, Dokimos, and Polemon were captives. Only Alketas remained, a fugitive at Termessos, and as soon as the army of the Perdikkans had been rounded up, reassured, and enrolled in the victorious army, Antigonos set out in pursuit of him to put the finishing touch to his campaign. Alketas enjoyed the goodwill of the

51. It has been convincingly argued by Engels in his book *Alexander the Great and the Logistics of the Macedonian Army* that ordinary forces could not exceed a pace of about 20–25 miles per day for more than a day or two at a stretch, and that only elite forces of cavalry and mobile infantry could perform the sort of extraordinary march here attributed to Antigonos's army.

young men of Termessos, who were prepared to defend him, 6,000 in number. The older generation, however, had no desire to see their territory ravaged and face a siege and possible sack for the sake of a foreigner; accordingly they opened negotiations with Antigonos and arranged to hand over Alketas to him when the young men were away fighting. When Alketas learned this he committed suicide rather than be handed over to Antigonos alive; it was thus his corpse which was surrendered to Antigonos, who threw it out unburied (Diod. XVIII 45,5–47, 3). In this way the city which had successfully defied Alexander (Arrian *Anab.* I 27,5–28,2) bowed to the victorious Antigonos.

After spending three days in the territory of Termessos, Antigonos marched back over the Klimax Pass to Kretopolis on his way to Phrygia. At Kretopolis he was met by Aristodemos of Miletos with the news that Antipatros had died and before his death had nominated Polyperchon to replace him as regent of the kings (Diod. XVIII 47,4). This news caused Antigonos to review his position. As general of Asia he now stood at the head of armed forces totaling 60,000 infantry, 10,000 cavalry, and seventy elephants; there was no power in Asia to match him (Diod. XVIII 50,1–3). He marched to Kelainai, his capital, and went into winter quarters (see Diod. XVIII 52,1: Antigonos was at Kelainai at the beginning of spring 318); while there he interviewed Hieronymos of Kardia, Eumenes' envoy to Macedon, now on his way back, and sent him to Eumenes with an offer to forget the past and become allies (Diod. XVIII 50,4; Plut. *Eum.* 12,1). He also held a council of his friends to discuss plans for the future (Diod. XVIII 50, 5).[52] The First Diadoch War was thus at an end, but the death of Antipatros promised plenty of new conflicts, for neither Antigonos nor Antipatros's son Kassandros was inclined to accept Polyperchon as regent of the empire.

---

52. One may doubt whether Antigonos at this time entertained the far-reaching plans Diodoros attributes to him here: according to Diodoros, at this meeting Antigonos outlined a plan to go through Asia replacing the existing satraps with his own friends. Antigonos did in fact do something like this in 318–15, but only as a result of his war with Eumenes: Antigonos's decision to march into inner Asia is explicitly connected with Eumenes' march up-country (Diod. XVIII 73,2 and XIX 15,6). The plans attributed to Antigonos in winter 319/18 are probably the product of Diodoros's hindsight.

3

The Establishment of Antigonos's Rule over Asia

Antigonos's position at the beginning of 318 was a strong one, but in some respects uncertain. He was *stratēgos* of Asia with a great army at his back, but his continued authority depended on his relations with the new regent, Polyperchon, to whom he was not in fact disposed to defer (Diod. XVIII 50,2—with some exaggeration, no doubt). In effect, Antipatros's death enabled Antigonos to bring about a change in the nature of his post. He did not accept the succession of Polyperchon to the regency, and Polyperchon in return sought to depose him and replace him as *stratēgos* of Asia by Eumenes (see n. 4 below). On what grounds Antigonos repudiated Polyperchon's authority we are not told, but doubtless he would have argued that Polyperchon's appointment had not been agreed upon by a general council of the Macedonian leaders and armies and denied that Antipatros had the authority simply to nominate a successor to his post. At any rate by refusing to accept Polyperchon's regency, Antigonos essentially claimed the right to be *stratēgos* of Asia until Alexandros IV reached adulthood, for with Antipatros dead, he clearly recognized no authority over himself except the kings, and with Philippos III retarded, the royal authority was ineffective as long as Alexandros IV was a minor.

In the absence of clear-cut Macedonian institutions and constitutional procedures, the legitimacy or otherwise of Antigonos's position between 319 and 311 cannot be established. The legitimacy of power is ultimately a matter of acceptance by those over whom it is exercised, and by this criterion Antigonos's position was both legitimate and illegitimate: legitimate, because his army and officers continued to accept his authority, as did a number of the satraps of Asia (for example, Nikanor of Kappadokia, and, for a while at least, Seleukos and Peithon Krateua); illegitimate because a number of the leaders and forces in Asia acknowledged the rival authority vested in Eumenes by Polyperchon in the name of the kings, and because other Macedonian leaders denied Antigonos's right to rule Asia. This phase of his life, therefore, consisted of a protracted struggle to force acceptance of his rule in Asia. But though it proved necessary to resort to arms to establish his power, Antigonos continued to legitimize his authority by the agreement of Triparadeisos: see his statement at Tyre in 314, calling himself "the duly appointed *stratēgos*" (*τῶι καθεσταμένωι στρατηγῶι*: Diod. XIX 61,3).

THE SECOND DIADOCH WAR (318–315 B.C.)

Antigonos was not the only Macedonian leader who took stock of his position in the light of Antipatros's death, and the first person to make a move was apparently Arrhidaios, the satrap of Hellespontine Phrygia. Antigonos was still at his winter quarters in Kelainai when he heard of an attack by Arrhidaios on the allied city of Kyzikos (Diod. XVIII 51,1–7; Marmor Parium in *FGrH,* no. 239 b, sec. 12). He chose to interpret this as tantamount to rebellion against his authority in Asia[1] and immediately set out for Kyzikos with a picked force of 20,000 foot and 3,000 horse. Though he arrived too late to assist Kyzikos, which had already repulsed the attack, he decided to punish Arrhidaios, ordering him to vacate his satrapy, select a city as his residence, and keep quiet there (Diod. XVIII 52,1–3).

Arrhidaios declined to obey these orders and prepared for war with Antigonos, seeing to his garrisons and sending a sizeable force to march into Kappadokia to Nora to try to relieve Eumenes from his siege and make an ally of him. In this he miscalculated, for Antigonos had already reached an agreement with Eumenes and released him from Nora, as we shall see. Antigonos sent a force to campaign against Arrhidaios, which succeeded in ejecting him from his satrapy and shutting him up with the remnants of his troops in the city of

1. Antigonos evidently still claimed by the authority vested in him at Triparadeisos to be able to repress rebellious satraps in Asia (cf. Diod. XVIII 52,3).

Kios (Diod. XVIII 52,4–5 and 72,2). Antigonos himself invaded Lydia, whose satrap, Kleitos, had already anticipated an attack by Antigonos and had, after establishing garrisons in the more important cities, sailed off to Macedon to accuse Antigonos to Polyperchon. In Kleitos's absence, Antigonos marched on Ephesos, which he took at the first assault with the aid of confederates in the city. While he was there a flotilla carrying six hundred talents of silver to Macedon under the command of Aischylos of Rhodes sailed into the harbor. This money Antigonos at once seized, with the justification that he needed it to pay his mercenaries, though he must have known that this portended an open rupture with Polyperchon.[2] Antigonos then spent the rest of the spring and early summer capturing the other cities of Lydia and establishing his control in that satrapy (Diod. XVIII 52, 5–8).

Meanwhile, as noted above, Antigonos had released Eumenes from the siege of Nora. According to Plutarch (*Eum.* 12,1–2), this came about as a direct result of the negotiations Antigonos had conducted with Hieronymos of Kardia late in 319. Antigonos had proposed an agreement for common action and had given Hieronymos an oath for Eumenes to swear before Antigonos's representatives at Nora, binding himself to be well-disposed towards Antigonos and have the same friends and enemies (Plut. *Eum.* 12,2). However, before swearing the oath Eumenes altered it to refer rather to Olympias and the kings. Antigonos's officers were satisfied with this, and Eumenes obtained his freedom.[3] He remained in Kappadokia for a time, gathering forces and supplies (2,000 men according to Diod. XVIII 53,5–7; Plut. *Eum.* 12,3 reports 1,000 cavalry). However, Eumenes realized perfectly well that Antigonos was not likely to accept the changed oath he had sworn, in which he had not bound himself to Antigonos's cause, and he therefore prepared to flee. His problem was to find a likely place of refuge, and this was provided by the arrival of letters from Polyperchon asking him to resume the fight against Antigonos in Asia and promising him funds and support from

2. Aischylos probably remained with Antigonos, for a diplomat of this name in Antigonos's service is mentioned in the letter from Antigonos to the Skepsians: *OGIS*, no. 5, lines 5, 48 (311 B.C.), and this is probably the same man; see further app. 3, no. 4.

3. Actually, the oath Antigonos submitted for Eumenes to swear had mentioned the kings at the beginning (Plut. *Eum.* 12,2), but thereafter evidently made reference only to Antigonos as the representative of the kings. Eumenes changed the whole emphasis, adding Olympias's name to that of the kings at the head and swearing to have the same friends and enemies as they.

the royal treasure and forces in Kilikia (Diod. XVIII 57,3–4; 58,1; Plut. *Eum.* 13,1–2).[4]

Antigonos was furious when he heard what had transpired at Nora, for he was virtually in a position of open war with Polyperchon, who controlled the kings and was angling for the support of Olympias, so that Eumenes' revised oath was as likely to make him Antigonos's enemy as his friend.[5] In Macedon Antipatros's son Kassandros, enraged at not having been made his father's successor, had lost no time in beginning to undermine Polyperchon (Diod. XVIII 49,1–3). He now fled to Asia to beg for aid from Antigonos, who was happy to support a venture that would stir up trouble for Polyperchon and keep him too busy to interfere in Asia (Diod. XVIII 54,2–4). Kassandros's strength lay in the loyalty to himself of the Macedonian garrison commanders and Greek tyrants and oligarchs placed in control of Greece by Antipatros. Polyperchon's opening moves, therefore, were to invite Alexander's mother, Olympias, to return to Macedon from Epeiros to help raise her grandson Alexandros IV (Diod. XVIII 49,4), no doubt hoping to use her prestige and charisma to boost his own authority; to begin a propaganda campaign in Greece, quickly backed up by military force;[6] and to send out letters and orders to enable Eumenes to stir up trouble for Antigonos in Asia (Diod. XVIII 55,1–57,4). Thus the battle lines were drawn: against a coalition of Kassandros, Antigonos, Ptolemy, and (no doubt) Lysimachos,[7] were ranged Polyperchon, Eumenes, and

---

4. Eumenes also received a letter/letters from Olympias, seeking his support and advice (Diod. XVIII 58,2–3; Plut. *Eum.* 13,1). His precise position or title is not entirely clear: Plut. *Eum.* 13,1 calls him commander of the forces in Kappadokia with a brief to make war upon Antigonos and to use for that purpose the royal funds at Kyinda and the aid of the Silver Shields; Diod. XVIII 57,3–4 describes him as restored to his satrapy and all former prerogatives (*dōreas*) in Asia, with a brief to receive an army and money to fight against Antigonos; while at XIX 58,1 Diodoros calls him *stratēgos autokratōr* over all of Asia. It is generally supposed that in effect Polyperchon deposed Antigonos and put Eumenes in his place (thus Bengtson, *Strategie,* 1:109–10, 119–23; Engel, *Untersuchungen,* p. 41).

5. Depending on Eumenes' interpretation of the oath: Antigonos always claimed publicly to be on the side of the legitimate Argead kings; but by swearing his oath to Olympias and the kings, Eumenes had given himself the right to oppose Antigonos if he judged Antigonos to be acting against the interests of the kings.

6. Polyperchon sent the Greeks an edict in the kings' names ending the policy of Antipatros after the Lamian War and implicitly acknowledging Greek autonomy (Diod. XVIII 55,2–56,8; 64,3). Early in 318 Polyperchon's son Alexandros appeared in Greece with an army to give force to this edict (Diod. XVIII 65,3–5; Plut. *Phokion* 33,1); and later Polyperchon himself came down to Greece with an army, bringing the kings with him (Diod. XVIII 66,1–3; 68,1–72,1; Plut. *Phokion* 33,4–7).

7. That Lysimachos was a member of the coalition against Polyperchon can be deduced from Diod. XVIII 72,9: Lysimachos's troops arrest and kill Polyperchon's admiral Kleitos; and

Kleitos. Antigonos quickly despatched an army under Menandros to take over Kappadokia and arrest Eumenes, but it arrived three days after Eumenes had left the region, and after briefly giving chase returned to Kappadokia to secure control there (Diod. XVIII 59,1–2).

Eumenes made good his escape with 2,000 foot and 500 cavalry over the Taurus range into Kilikia, where he was met by the generals Antigenes and Teutamos and the Macedonian Silver Shields (Diod. XVIII 59,1–3).[8] Eumenes secured control over these men by playing on their loyalty to, and superstitious awe of, Alexander: he stated that he had had a dream in which Alexander had appeared and offered them all his aid if they would set up a tent and throne for him and there sacrifice to him and conduct their councils (Diod. XVIII 60,1–62,3; Polyainos IV 8,2; Plut. *Eum.* 13,2–4). With the letters of Polyperchon and Olympias to back him up, Eumenes was able to dominate these councils. He set about using the royal treasure at Kyinda to recruit an army of mercenaries, and was able rapidly to gather a force of 10,000 infantry and 2,000 cavalry to add to his own troops and the Macedonians of Antigenes and Teutamos (Diod. XVIII 61,4–5), despite attempted interference by Ptolemy, who had just conquered Syria and Palestine (Appian *Syr.* 52 and Diod. XVIII 43; 62,1–2).

Antigonos quickly learned of Eumenes' activities, but did not at once intervene against him directly, being no doubt still tied up with affairs in northwestern Asia Minor. He did, however, send a group of thirty Macedonians led by Philotas, probably the former satrap of

XIX 56,4: in 315 Antigonos writes to his allies Ptolemy, Kassandros, and Lysimachos. On Ptolemy, see also Diod. XVIII 49,3; 54,3; 55,2.

8. Antigenes was satrap of Susiane (Arrian *Met' Alex.* 1,35; Diod. XVIII 39,6), commander of the 3,000 *argyraspides* (Silver Shields), and had been ordered to convoy part of the royal treasure from Susa to Kyinda in Kilikia for forwarding to Macedon (Arrian 1,38, calling the Silver Shields the "3,000 most rebellious of the Macedonians"; on Kyinda as a staging post for the transfer of royal treasure at this time, cf. Simpson, *Historia* 6 [1957]:503–4). Teutamos's position is less clear: he is often described as co-commander of the Silver Shields (e.g., at Diod. XVIII 59,3; Plut. *Eum.* 13,2), though elsewhere Antigenes is named as sole commander (Arrian 1,35 and 38; Diod. XIX 12,1–13,2; 15,2; 21,1; 41,1; 44,1). But Eumenes later had another elite Macedonian unit 3,000 men strong, the *hypaspistai:* they appear next to the Silver Shields at the battles of Paraitakene and Gabiene (Diod. XIX 28,1 and 40,3), the former passage specifying that these *two* units were led by Antigenes and Teutamos. Probably Teutamos in fact led the *hypaspistai,* who are confused, equated, or lumped together with the Silver Shields except in Diodoros's descriptions—presumably drawn direct from Hieronymos—of Eumenes' battle order at Paraitakene and Gabiene. These *hypaspistai* are probably the men who suffered heavily under Perdikkas in Egypt (Diod. XVIII 33,6–34,5) and were sent from Triparadeisos to garrison the treasury of Kyinda, for Diod. XVIII 58,1 and 62,2 mentions generals and a garrison there, separate from Antigenes and the Silver Shields.

Kilikia,[9] to attempt to disturb the loyalty to Eumenes of the Silver Shields. In this Philotas was very nearly successful, but Eumenes was apprised of the wavering of his most important Macedonian troops in time to intervene and improve his position (Diod. XVIII 62,3–63,5). The subsequent fate of Philotas is not recorded.

Eumenes now decided to move out of Kilikia. In spring 317 he marched into Phoenicia, which Ptolemy seems not to have attempted to defend, and began to raise a naval force on behalf of Polyperchon, who wished to win command of the sea (Diod. XVIII 63,6).

Polyperchon had spent the year 318/17 trying to secure control over Greece, but had met with two serious reverses.[10] His declaration concerning Greek autonomy had brought him immediate popularity in Athens, but Kassandros's loyal friend Nikanor, the leader of the Macedonian garrison, managed to secure Mounychia and Peiraieus and hold them until Kassandros arrived with reinforcements of thirty-five ships and 4,000 soldiers, given him by Antigonos (Diod. XVIII 64,1–68,1; Plut. *Phokion* 31–33). Not only was Polyperchon unable to dislodge Kassandros here, but in a full-scale assault on Megalopolis, which was also loyal to Kassandros, he suffered considerable losses without managing to gain any advantage (Diod. XVIII 68,2–72,1). He then decided that it was essential to gain full command of the sea to cut off any further aid to his enemies from Antigonos. Accordingly, he sent out Kleitos with a large fleet at the beginning of summer 317 to occupy the Hellespont with the aid of the remnants of Arrhidaios's forces, which were holed up in Kios, and to defeat any naval force Antigonos might have raised (Diod. XVIII 72,2–3).

It seems that Antigonos had spent the autumn and winter of 318 in western Asia Minor, consolidating his position and gathering a fleet. In 317 Kassandros sent back to Asia under the command of Nikanor the 35 ships lent him by Antigonos, and with these Antigonos was able to send 130 ships to do battle against Kleitos in the Hellespont.[11] He placed the entire fleet under the command of Nikanor, while he himself marched to the Hellespont with an army. Kleitos was in the Propontis with a fleet probably slightly larger than that of Nikanor. The two fleets met in battle near Byzantion, and Kleitos won a victory in which some 70 of Nikanor's ships were

9. See app. 3, no. 95.

10. For the chronology of Polyperchon's actions in Greece and the related activities of Kassandros, Kleitos, and Antigonos, see Williams, *Hermes* 112 (1984):300–305.

11. Diod. XVIII 72,3 speaks of "more than a hundred"; Polyainos IV 6,8 says 130. Engel, *Klio* 55 (1973):141–45, casts doubt on Polyainos's numbers, but see n. 12 below.

captured, sunk, or disabled, the remnants managing to escape to Chalkedon, where they were joined by Antigonos and the army.[12] Antigonos, far from being dismayed at this loss, laid plans to restore the situation that very night. He ordered the remaining 60 ships of the fleet to be readied for renewed action, and assigned to them as marines many of his strongest soldiers to make sure that the ships would fight. Meanwhile he got the Byzantines to send transports and ferry across his archers, slingers, and javelin men to the European shore, where Kleitos's victorious force was encamped. At dawn all was ready and, when the enemy were still asleep or barely awake, Antigonos launched a double assault by land and sea on the enemy camp. Confident in his victory, Kleitos was taken completely by surprise; his entire force was captured or killed, and though he himself managed to escape with a single ship, he was soon forced to run it aground and tried to reach Macedon by land. He was intercepted on his way by some soldiers of Lysimachos and executed (Diod. XVIII 72,3–4; Polyainos IV 6,8).

This brilliant stroke greatly enhanced Antigonos's reputation for military genius and freed him from further worry of Polyperchon interfering in Asia. He at once set out to deal with Eumenes. The fleet, decked with victory garlands and the prows of the destroyed enemy ships, was despatched to Phoenicia to eliminate the fleet being raised by Eumenes. The journey down the coast of Asia Minor served the additional purpose of advertising Antigonos's victory. Eumenes had already sent his fleet north under the command of Sosigenes, who had with him a large sum of money. The two fleets met near Rhosos in Kilikia, but no battle was fought: when the Phoenicians saw the ornaments of victory on Antigonos's fleet they changed sides at once, taking the money with them. Sosigenes managed to get away to sea and is heard of no more (Polyainos IV 6,9). Since the naval war was now at an end, Nikanor sailed away with Kassandros's ships to Peiraieus, entering the harbor in triumph (Diod. XVIII 75,1). In

12. Kleitos was seeking to gain the adherence of the cities of the Propontis, and the battle took place near Byzantion (Diod. XVIII 72,3–4); Byzantion aided Antigonos immediately after the battle (Diod. XVIII 72,6): apparently Kleitos had been pressuring or even besieging Byzantion. Diodoros reports Nikanor's losses as seventeen ships sunk and about forty captured, the rest escaping to Chalkedon (XVIII 72,4). Polyainos IV 6,8 has Nikanor lose seventy ships, and a bit later self-consistently speaks of sixty ships being left to Antigonos. Since the two accounts are otherwise so similar as to indicate that they must have drawn on the same source (see Engel loc.cit. n. 11), I suppose that Polyainos's figure is probably correct (*contra* Engel) and that Diodoros has simply omitted to list the ships that were disabled in the action, but not captured or sunk—about thirteen in number.

Greece Polyperchon's situation had gone from bad to worse during 317, with most of the cities adhering to Kassandros's cause, disgusted by Polyperchon's lack of energy. Shortly before Nikanor arrived, Kassandros had secured full control over Athens, placing his friend Demetrios of Phaleron in charge as *epimelētēs* (Diod. XVIII 74,1–3).

Meanwhile, Antigonos settled his affairs in Asia Minor and selected from his army 20,000 infantry and 4,000 cavalry with which to knock out Eumenes before he could do further damage. With this force he marched across Asia Minor to Kilikia, intending to fight it out with Eumenes in Syria. Eumenes somehow had advance knowledge of his movements, however, and hurried out of Phoenicia and across Syria into Mesopotamia, with the idea of gathering support in the upper satrapies for a showdown with Antigonos (Diod. XVIII 73,1–2).[13] He won the support of Amphimachos, the satrap of Mesopotamia (see Diod. XVIII 39,6 and XIX 27,4), and then moved down into northern Babylonia, where he went into winter quarters with his army at a place called Karōn Kōmai. While there he negotiated with Seleukos, satrap of Babylonia, and Peithon Krateua, satrap of Media, who was with Seleukos at Babylon, vainly seeking their aid against Antigonos (Diod. XIX 12,1–2).[14] Antigonos, finding Eumenes gone when he reached Syria, presumably took some time to secure control of Kilikia and northern Syria and then followed after Eumenes. He marched into Mesopotamia, and there went into winter quarters with his army (Diod. XIX 15,6, and cf. 13,5).

In Europe, Polyperchon had made the mistake in 317 of leaving King Philippos and his wife Eurydike unsupervised in Macedon. Eurydike, resentful of her subordination and of Polyperchon's repeated overtures to Olympias and scornful of Polyperchon's abilities after his repeated setbacks, decided to take control of affairs in her husband's name (Diod. XIX 11,1). Connected with this was perhaps

13. At XVIII 73,3–4 Diodoros gives a summary preview of events he later narrates more fully at XIX 12,1–13,7 and gives two valuable pieces of information omitted in the later, fuller account: XVIII 73,4 gives the figures for Eumenes' army when he won his way across the Tigris into Susiane and Persia as 15,000 foot and 3,300 horse; XVIII 73,3 relates that Eumenes suffered losses in a night attack by local inhabitants near the Tigris, and that he suffered further losses to Seleukos near the Euphrates. The rivers are here given in the wrong order: Seleukos inflicted losses on Eumenes near the Tigris (Diod. XIX 12,5–13,2); the night attack by locals must have occurred when Eumenes was preparing to cross the Euphrates, and is not elsewhere attested.

14. The reason professed by Seleukos and Peithon was adherence to the arrangements of Triparadeisos. Though they claimed to be at all times ready to be of service to the kings (Diod. XIX 12,1–13,1), they ignored Polyperchon's orders, claiming in despite of Eumenes and Polyperchon that *their* side (that of the victors of Triparadeisos) represented the true interests of the kings.

an expedition into Macedon by Kassandros, taking advantage of Polyperchon's absence.[15] At any rate, according to Justin (XIV 5), Eurydike wrote to Polyperchon depriving him of the regency and ordering him to hand over his army to Kassandros, and also wrote to Antigonos in Asia. Kassandros, strengthened by his new authority, made a campaign into the Peloponnesos, and in his absence Polyperchon and Olympias invaded Macedon with an army furnished by her cousin, King Aiakides of Epeiros. Eurydike went out to meet them in battle, but her Macedonians went over to Olympias at once, and both Philippos Arrhidaios and Eurydike were captured (Diod. XIX 11,2–3; Justin XIV 5,1–10). Olympias had the unlucky king and his misguided wife assassinated, Philippos Arrhidaios having occupied the throne for six years and four months (Diod. XIX 11,5), which places the assassination in about October of 317. Olympias then sought to establish control over Macedon by instituting a veritable reign of terror against Kassandros's sympathizers (Diod. XIX 11,8–9).

In Asia, Eumenes' failed negotiations with Seleukos and Peithon forced him to leave his winter quarters early, for he was in great need of supplies (Diod. XIX 12,3–4) and had Antigonos's hostile army behind him in Mesopotamia and the equally hostile Seleukos and Peithon to his south. In Susiane, Eumenes expected to replenish his supplies, to fill his empty coffers from the treasury at Susa and to summon the forces of the upper satrapies to aid his cause, which he represented as that of the kings. His attempts to cross the Tigris were at first thwarted by Seleukos, but he eventually won his crossing, as Seleukos simply became anxious to get Eumenes out of his satrapy (Diod. XIX 12,5–13,5). Once in Susiane, Eumenes marched his army in three columns to Susa, living off the land as they went, and sent letters to the upper satraps, ordering them in the kings' names to meet him with their forces at Susa (Diod. XIX 13,6–7).

Eumenes was very lucky at this time in that the forces of the upper satrapies were already combined together into a single army and ready to respond to his summons. For while the events outlined above had been going on in Europe and western Asia, there had been hostilities in inner Asia also. In the settlement of Triparadeisos in summer 320, Peithon Krateua, a most ambitious man, received the satrapy of Media, probably the strongest of the upper satrapies. He

15. An invasion of Macedon by Kassandros at this time is attested by Diod. XVIII 75,1 and XIX 35,7 and implied by Justin XIV 5,3–5; this presumably was the catalyst for Eurydike's actions.

may also have been named, then or shortly afterwards, as overseer of the upper satrapies (στρατηγὸς τῶν ἄνω σατραπειῶν); he is thus introduced by Diodoros at XIX 14,1 and it is not clear whether the title was granted or usurped.[16] At any rate, as the strongest leader in the upper satrapies, he tried to rearrange the commands in these satrapies to make them more amenable to his control, his first step being the murder of Philippos, satrap of Parthia, whom he replaced with his own brother, Eudamos. The other satraps in inner Asia were quick to perceive their danger and united all their forces under Peukestas, the satrap of Persia, defeated Peithon, and drove him out of Parthia (Diod. XIX 14,1–2).[17] Peithon returned to Media, and then went on to Babylon to try to persuade Seleukos to back him in an attempt to reassert his authority (Diod. XIX 14,3).

These events evidently occurred only a short time before Eumenes' arrival in Babylonia, for when he got there, Peithon was with Seleukos at Babylon (Diod. XIX 12,1–13,1), and when he advanced into Susiane at the beginning of 316, he found the forces of the upper satrapies still in the field as a united army led by Peukestas (Diod. XIX 14,4–8). Eumenes' army at this time consisted of 15,000 infantry and 3,300 cavalry (Diod. XVIII 73,4); the army of the satraps amounted to some 18,700 infantry, 120 elephants, and 4,600 cavalry (Diod. XIX 14,8); together these were a very considerable force, with which Eumenes could look forward with some confidence to doing battle with Antigonos. When the allied satraps first joined Eumenes in Susiane, there was a wrangle over the leadership of the combined force, Peukestas and Antigenes putting forward rival claims against Eumenes. However, Eumenes' authorization from the kings to dispose of the funds in the royal treasury at Susa greatly strengthened his hand, and he was able to maintain his authority (Diod. XIX 15,1–5).[18]

---

16. Bengtson, *Strategie,* 1:179–80, assumes (with little argument) that Peithon usurped the post, which is certainly possible; the view that Peithon was formally granted the position at Triparadeisos was put forward by Beloch, *GG,* 4.1:91–92; but see most recently the discussion of Schober, *Gesch. Babyloniens,* pp. 74–78, arguing cogently for Bengtson's view.

17. Diod. XIX 14,1 actually gives "Philotas" in error for Philippos, who was named satrap of Parthia at Triparadeisos (Diod. XVIII 39,6; Arrian *Met' Alex.* 1,35) and had been made satrap of Baktria at the earlier division in Babylon (Diod. XVIII 3,3). For an excellent recent account of the war in the upper satrapies, see now Schober, *Gesch. Babyloniens,* pp. 74–79.

18. The decision of the upper satraps to take Eumenes' side without doubt stemmed directly from the fact that Peithon and his ally Seleukos had chosen to oppose Eumenes and side with Antigonos; *contra* Schober, *Gesch. Babyloniens,* pp. 79–80, who implausibly reverses the order and suggests that Peithon and Seleukos sided with Antigonos because the upper satraps had *already* in 317 opted for Eumenes.

Antigonos, meanwhile, had left his winter quarters in Mesopotamia and was hurrying after Eumenes when he received word from Seleukos of Eumenes' crossing into Susiane and of the aid in the form of the army of the upper satrapies that awaited him there (Diod. XIX 13,5; 15,6). Accordingly, Antigonos slowed his march and began to enrol additional troops, since it was clear that he would now need considerably more than the 20,000 foot and 4,000 cavalry he had with him (Diod. XIX 15,6).[19] He made an alliance with Seleukos and Peithon, receiving further troops from them, presumably cavalry, as they are earlier reported to have had no infantry (Diod. XIX 13,3), and crossed the Tigris by pontoon bridge into Susiane (Diod. XIX 17,1–2). When Eumenes heard of Antigonos's approach, he ordered Xenophilos, the man in charge of the citadel and treasury at Susa, to refuse to have dealings with Antigonos, and himself marched away southeastward towards Persia. He crossed the river Pasitigris and encamped behind it, posting pickets along it to warn him of Antigonos's approach, and clearly intending to contest the crossing. He also prevailed upon Peukestas to send to Persia for light infantry reinforcements (Diod. XIX 17,3–7).

Antigonos marched to Susa, where he found the citadel held against him and the treasury closed to him. He appointed Seleukos satrap of Susiane for the time being, giving him a sufficient force to besiege Susa. Then he broke camp and marched against Eumenes, arriving at the river Kopratas, a tributary of the Pasitigris, towards the end of June or beginning of July 316 (Diod. XIX 18,1–2). The river, narrow but deep and swift, required boats to cross, of which Antigonos had only a few. These he used to send over an advance force, ordering the soldiers to construct a camp with moat and palisade as a base for the rest of the army. About 3,000 infantry and 400 cavalry crossed in this way, and in addition 6,000 foragers (= light infantry?) crossed the river in scattered groups. However, Eumenes arrived upon the scene with 4,000 foot and 1,300 horse, attacked Antigonos's unprepared force and routed it with ease. Many of Antigonos's troops who had crossed were killed, and some 4,000 are said to have been captured, while Antigonos could only look on helplessly from across the river (Diod. XIX 18,3–7; Plut. *Eum.*

19. Antigonos presumably sent for further detachments of his army from Asia Minor, for he set out in 317 without his elephants (seventy in number: Arrian *Met' Alex.* 1,43), whereas at the battles of Paraitakene and Gabiene in autumn 316 and winter 316/15 he had his elephants with him (Diod. XIX 27,1 and 40,1).

14,1–2).[20] Faced with this disaster, Antigonos decided to abandon the attempt to cross the river and turned back northward, marching up to the river Eulaios, where he rested his troops while considering what to do. He decided that his best move would be to march up into Media; there he could replenish his funds from the treasury at Ekbatana, strengthen his army with the addition of horses, cavalry, and pack animals, and threaten the upper satrapies (Diod. XIX 19,1–2).

A difficult decision faced Antigonos in selecting the route to Media. The safest route involved a 40-day march up the Tigris valley and along the Babylon-Ekbatana road, but as it was the middle of summer, the heat would be intense, and his soldiers had already suffered much from the heat in Susiane. The alternative was the short route through the Kossaian mountains, a 9-day march through cool hill country, but made difficult by the fierce tribesmen, who were in the habit of exacting tribute from those passing through their country, opposing by force any who refused to pay. Antigonos was determined to use this route, but was not disposed to pay for his passage. Though Diodoros (following Hieronymos?) attributes this unwillingness to pay to Antigonos's pride, it is likely that it had more to do with his lack of money: the six hundred talents he had seized at

20. Diod. XIX 18–44 lays great emphasis on the sufferings and heavy losses of Antigonos's troops in the campaigns of 316: for example, at 18,2, many men die from extreme heat; at 18,5–7, 4,000 men are captured by Eumenes and many others killed; at 19,1 many again succumb to heat; at 19,5–8, many are killed by the Kossaioi. At the battles of Paraitakene (31,5–32,1) and Gabiene (43,1), Antigonos's men sustain disproportionately heavy losses, and 37,5 stresses their sufferings when marching through a desert. This theme is echoed by Plut. *Eum.* 14,1; Polyainos IV 6,10; 11; 13; Justin XIV 3,5; and is accepted at face value by some modern scholars (e.g., Hornblower, *Hieronymus,* pp. 217–19). Analysis of actual troop strengths exposes considerable exaggeration, however: despite all the apparent disasters of Diod. XIX 18,2–19,8, Antigonos's army at Paraitakene had 28,000 heavy infantry, 10,600 cavalry, 65 elephants, and a mass of light infantry, so his losses cannot have been so high unless his original army was huge. Investigation of two specific units confirms one's skepticism: in 320 Antigonos received from Antipatros 70 elephants and 8,500 Macedonian infantry (Arrian 1,43); though the elephants are specifically said to have suffered heavily under attack from the Kossaioi, there were still 65 of them at Paraitakene; though the Macedonians went through the campaigns of 319 as well as all the suffering of Diod. XIX 18,2–19,8, Antigonos still had at Paraitakene "nearly 8,000 Macedonians, whom Antipatros had given him" (Diod. XIX 29,3). Clearly Antigonos's losses were more modest than Diodoros's narrative suggests. By contrast to the suffering of Antigonos's men, Diod. XIX has parallel passages on Eumenes' troops: at 21,2–23,2, they march through a land of healthful climate and abundant supplies, and are feasted at Persepolis; at Gabiene (43,1), the 3,000 Argyraspids most implausibly take on Antigonos's entire phalanx (22,000 men!) and rout it completely, killing 5,000 without losing a man themselves. Apparently Diodoros's source, presumably Eumenes's kinsman Hieronymos, exaggerated the losses and suffering of Antigonos's troops to glorify Eumenes by comparison.

Ephesos in 318 must have been much depleted, and though he *may* have been able to replenish his funds from the treasury at Kyinda in 317, he had been unable to draw any money from the treasury at Susa and must by mid 316 have been very low on funds. It cost huge sums to maintain in the field a large army of mostly mercenary character, and Antigonos could not afford to give money he needed to pay his troops to the Kossaioi (Diod. XIX 19,2–4).

He selected a large force of peltasts, archers, slingers, and other light-armed troops, which he placed under the command of Nearchos with orders to march in advance and secure the narrowest and most dangerous passes. Posting the rest of the light infantry along the route, Antigonos himself led the heavy infantry, and placed the rearguard—presumably made up of the cavalry and the baggage—under Peithon. Though facing severe opposition, Antigonos thus brought his army through into Media nine days after setting out (Diod. XIX 19,4–8). There he supplied the troops with everything they needed, and went out of his way to mingle with them in the friendliest way, to make them forget the struggles and losses of the past months. He drew five hundred talents for the soldiers' pay from the treasury at Ekbatana, and Peithon brought in reinforcements of 2,000 cavalry, 1,000 spare horses to replace those lost during spring and summer, and plenty of pack animals, which were distributed to the soldiers (Diod. XIX 20,1–4). Thus Antigonos prepared his army for further campaigning.

Antigonos's move to Media was shrewd, but risky. It opened a way for Eumenes to march back to Asia Minor, which would be a heavy blow against Antigonos and Kassandros; but by threatening the upper satrapies, it played on the fears of the satraps. If Eumenes and Antigenes had been able to persuade these satraps to march west with them, things would have looked grim for Antigonos, but as it happened the satraps refused to go, so that Eumenes was left with the choice of marching back with his own force or staying in the east. Since splitting up the army would have played straight into Antigonos's hand, Eumenes decided to stay in the east, and the whole army marched down into Persia to Persepolis, where they encamped and were grandly fêted by Peukestas (Diod. XIX 21,1–22,3; Plut. *Eum.* 14,3). There followed some dissension in the army, with Peukestas reviving his claim to the leadership, but Eumenes overcame this new challenge by a clever trick and seized the opportunity he had thus created to secure himself further by two shifts. He arraigned Sibyrtios, one of Peukestas's main supporters, for treason, forcing him to flee for his life; and he borrowed four hundred talents from the satraps. Thus he made the satraps fear to cross him, and he held their money hostage for their future loyalty (Diod. XIX 23,1–24,3).[21]

The summer of 316 was by now well advanced, and Antigonos moved southward from Media towards Persia in the hope of yet being able to decide the war before the end of the campaigning season. News of this move soon reached Eumenes, who likewise broke camp and advanced north to meet Antigonos. After some delay caused by an illness Eumenes incurred through overindulgence at a banquet (Diod. XIX 24,4–5), the two armies drew together in the region called Paraitakene, between Media and Persia. Antigonos hoped to force and win a decisive battle. He drew up his army in a strong defensive position, but Eumenes likewise drew up his army in a strong position. The two armies surveyed each other for a while, but being separated by a river and a ravine which neither side was disposed to cross to launch an attack, they encamped where they were, less than half a mile apart (Plut. *Eum.* 14,3–15,2; Diod. XIX 24,6–25,2). For four days they lived off the surrounding countryside; on the fifth, when supplies were running very short, Antigonos attempted to induce the enemy to come over to his side by making them lavish promises, but had no success (Diod. XIX 25,2–7).

That night, therefore, Antigonos decided to march away to the neighboring region of Gabiene, where the countryside was rich and unplundered. However, in the midst of the preparations to move, some of his men deserted to Eumenes and reported Antigonos's preparations to march away. Eumenes quickly divined Antigonos's intentions and decided to try to reach Gabiene first. He paid some mercenaries to desert to Antigonos and report plans for an attack to be made that night on his camp. While Antigonos kept his army under arms in expectation of this attack, Eumenes managed to steal away and get a substantial head start on the way to Gabiene. However, Antigonos soon learned from scouts how he had been tricked by Eumenes and gave pursuit. Realizing that he could not hope to catch up with Eumenes traveling with his entire army, he left the main body under the command of Peithon with orders to march on at moderate speed, and himself gave chase with the cavalry alone. In this way he caught up with Eumenes' rearguard at dawn, just as Eumenes was debouching from hilly country into a broad plain. Antigonos

21. Eumenes' trick is also described by Polyainos IV 8,3. The story of Eumenes borrowing money from the satraps is recounted rather earlier by Plut. *Eum.* 13,6 (before the battle at the Kopratas), but this is not to be preferred to Diodoros.

posted his cavalry in plain view on the crest of the hills, and Eumenes—seeing this and fearing that Antigonos's entire army was there and would attack him in rear if he moved on—stopped his march and drew up his army for battle (Diod. XIX 26,1–9).

Thus the rest of Antigonos's army had time to come up, and both sides now prepared to fight. Antigonos's army at this battle—the battle of Paraitakene—consisted of 28,000 heavy infantry, 10,600 cavalry, 65 elephants, and an unspecified number of light infantry. Eumenes commanded some 35,000 infantry (heavy and light), 6,300 cavalry, and 125 elephants.[22] Antigonos probably had an overall advantage in numbers, certainly in numbers of cavalry and of heavy phalanx infantry. Eumenes, however, besides having more elephants and a large number of excellent Persian light infantry, had what was probably the best unit of heavy infantry the world had yet seen: the Macedonian Silver Shields, 3,000 strong. Eumenes drew up his battle order first, and Antigonos, being able to view Eumenes' disposition at leisure from his hillside, drew up his own army accordingly (see fig. 3). Both stationed their best cavalry on their right wings under their own command, intending to decline battle with their left and strike with their right after the fashion of Alexander. Opposite the formidable Silver Shields, Antigonos placed his relatively expendable mercenaries, while his left wing under Peithon was made up of a mass of light cavalry, with orders not to come to close grips with Eumenes' heavy right-wing cavalry. Antigonos's son Demetrios, aged about twenty, was with his father on the right for his first major battle (Diod. XIX 29,4).

Diodoros mentions the awe-inspiring sight of Antigonos's army as it marched down from the hills to give battle (XIX 26,10), making it clear that his account derives from an eyewitness, obviously Hieronymos of Kardia. The battle was fought in three phases: Peithon ignored his orders to hang back, attacking Eumenes' heavy cavalry with his more numerous light cavalry, and was driven back to the foothills in rout; the two phalanxes came to grips and, after a hard struggle, the experience of the Silver Shields prevailed and Antigonos's phalanx was also driven back to the hills; but despite the reverses to his left and center, Antigonos kept his head and charged

22. This battle is fully and carefully described by Kromayer and Kahnes in *Antike Schlachtfelder,* ed. Kromayer and Veith, 4:393–424; cf. also Scullard, *The Elephant in the Greek and Roman World,* pp. 86–90; and for a more recent description, Devine, *AncW* 12, nos. 3/4 (1985):75–86. As often, there are discrepancies in Diodoros's numbers, but these are cleared up by Kromayer and Veith and Devine, except that Kromayer and Veith cast doubt on Diodoros's figure of 2,200 Tarentines (XIX 29,2), for reasons of probability that seem to me inadequate.

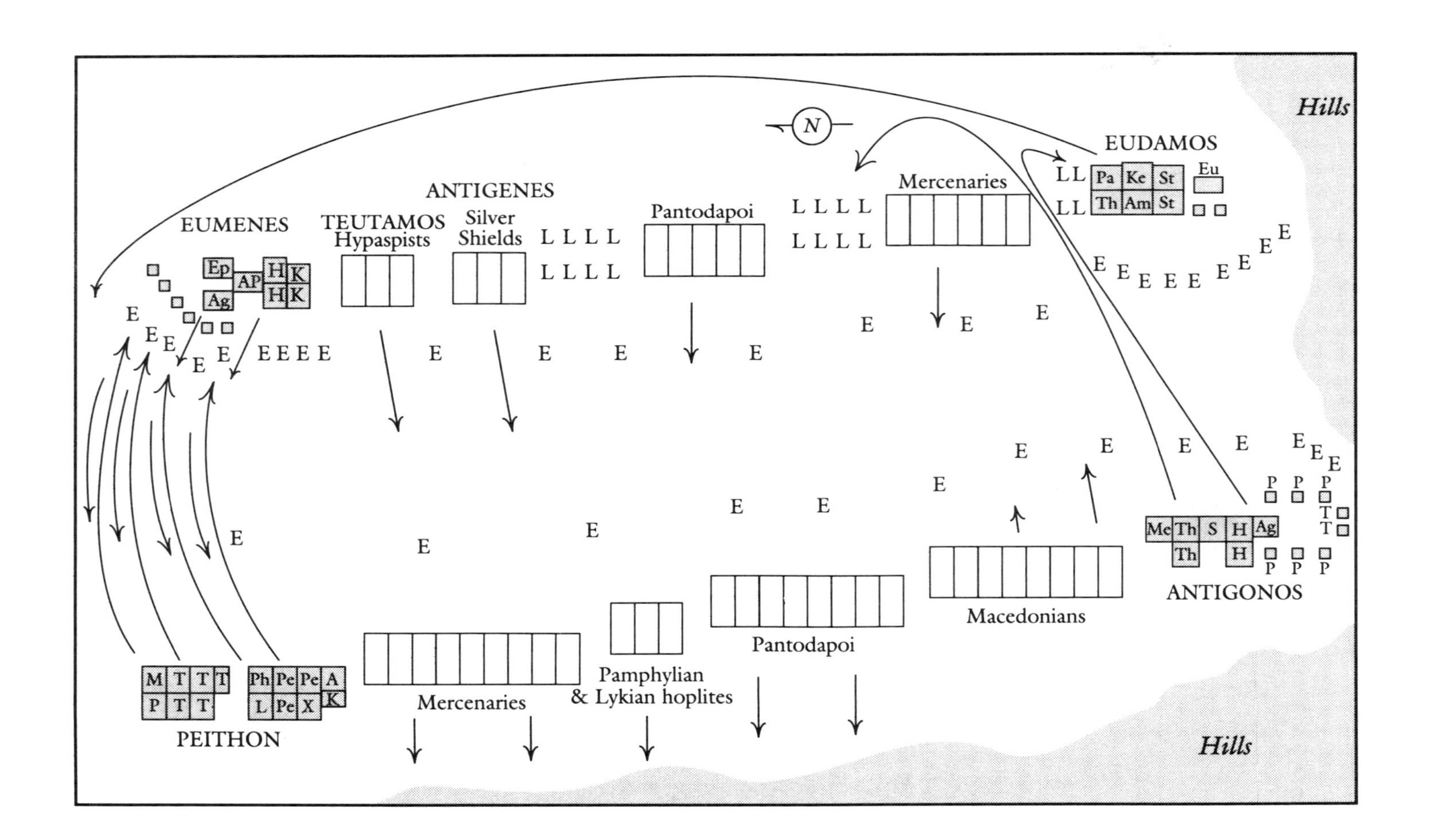
Hills
N
EUDAMOS
Eu
Mercenaries
ANTIGENES
EUMENES
TEUTAMOS
Hypaspists
Silver
Shields
Pantodapoi
ANTIGONOS
Macedonians
Pantodapoi
Pamphylian
& Lykian hoplites
Mercenaries
PEITHON
Hills

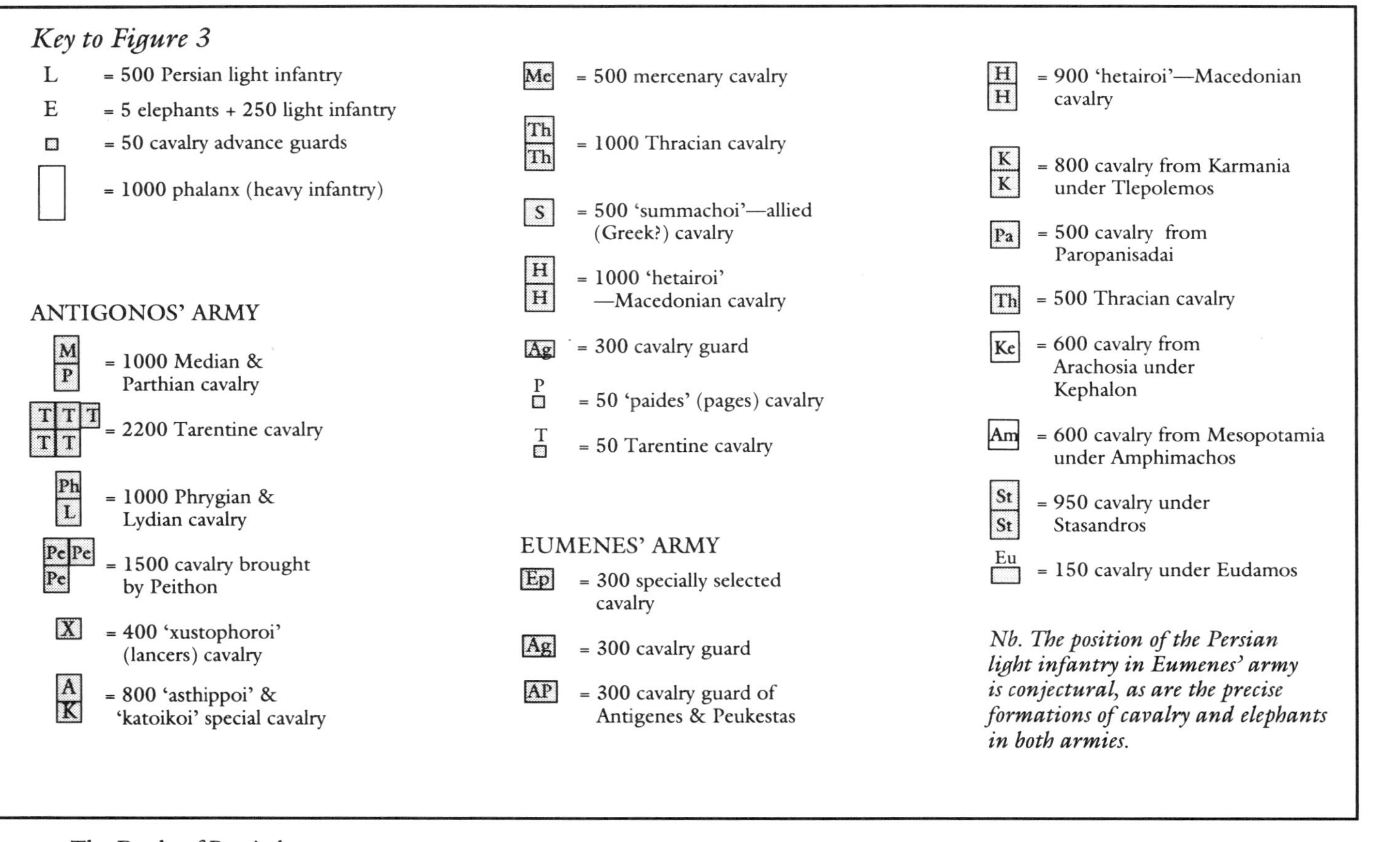

Figure 3. The Battle of Paraitakene

with his heavy cavalry into the gap that opened between Eumenes' left and center as his phalanx advanced, routing the light cavalry on Eumenes' left and forcing Eumenes' victorious phalanx to halt and about-face. Antigonos then sent orders to his phalanx and light cavalry to form a new line of battle along the foothills.

Though the sun had already set, the two armies thus reformed about 125 yards apart, a little less than four miles from the site of the original battle. By the time all was ready to renew battle, however, it was nearly midnight, and both sides were too exhausted, after a night of marching and a day of fighting, to fight again. Accordingly, Eumenes decided to march back to the original site of battle and occupy it, taking up the dead; but once they were moving back, his troops insisted on returning right to their baggage, some distance away, and camping there for the night. Antigonos, who had his troops better in hand, marched his army forward to occupy the battle site, and encamped there for the night, claiming the victory as being in possession of the field of battle and the enemy dead. However, his casualties were far more numerous than those of Eumenes (Diod. XIX 30,1–31,5).[23]

Antigonos wished to conceal this disparity in losses from Eumenes, and he also wished to fulfill his original purpose of marching away from Eumenes into unplundered country. He therefore began rapidly to dispose of his own dead at dawn the next day, and when a herald arrived from Eumenes to ask for his dead to be handed over, Antigonos detained him. That day he buried his dead, rested and fed his men, and then sent Eumenes' herald back to him with the announcement that he would hand over the dead next day. When darkness fell, however, he broke camp and marched his entire army away, making a forced march in order to put a long distance between himself and Eumenes (Diod. XIX 32,1–2; Polyainos IV 6,10). Antigonos took his army to southern Media, and since the year was nearing its end, he there went into winter quarters; Eumenes buried his own dead magnificently, and marched his army to Gabiene, where he established his winter quarters (Diod. XIX 32,3; 34,7–8). But Antigonos had still not given up hope of ending the war quickly, and when he learned that Eumenes had divided his army for wintering into many small detachments, which were scattered widely around Gabiene, he formed a plan to make a surprise attack and mop up

23. Despite my comments in n. 20 on exaggeration by the sources of the disparity between losses suffered by Antigonos and Eumenes in this campaign, the subsequent course of the campaign makes it clear that there was a considerable disparity at the battle of Paraitakene.

Eumenes' army before it could be gathered together (Diod. XIX 37,1; Polyainos IV 6,11).

The winter quarters of the two armies were separated from each other by a distance of twenty-five days' march by the road, which led through well-peopled countryside, but only by a distance of nine days' march as the crow flies (Diod. XIX 34,8). The march would be across waterless, treeless desert, but it was this route which Antigonos proposed to take. He ordered his troops to prepare food and water for ten days' march, giving it out publicly that he intended to invade Armenia. When all was ready, he led his army into the desert, setting out towards the end of December 316, at about the time of the winter solstice (Diod. XIX 37,3). Since the desert was an open plain surrounded by highlands, he gave orders that no fires were to be lit at night lest they should be observed from the bordering highlands and reported to Eumenes. During this march occurred the famous incident when some soldiers, not realizing he was present, stood outside Antigonos's tent cursing him, until he called out, "You'll be sorry if you don't go farther off to curse me!" rather than coming out to discipline them (Plut. *Apophth. Ant.* 10; *Mor.* 457e; Seneca *De ira* III 22,2), the sort of story that gets passed around the camp and wins a commander his soldiers' affection. However, some soldiers went beyond complaints, for the nights were so cold that on the fifth night they disobeyed his orders and lit fires. What Antigonos had feared then happened: the fires were observed, and the presence of a great camp in the desert was reported by the locals to Peukestas and Eumenes (Diod. XIX 37,2–6; Plut. *Eum.* 15,3–4; Polyainos IV 6,11 and 8,4).[24]

Eumenes and Peukestas were now in an awkward position, for while the most distant of their winter camps were six days' march away (Diod. XIX 39,1), the enemy were only some four days' march distant. Peukestas wished to retire to the further reaches of Gabiene and there gather the army, but Eumenes rose to the occasion with a bolder plan. He gathered together a body of troops and, marking out on the hills overlooking the desert an area the size of a large army

24. It is worth stressing again the complementary nature of Diodoros's and Polyainos's accounts: they are here, as elsewhere, virtually the same in outline, with some striking verbal similarities, but their different interests cause them to focus on different details. That the episode of the cursing soldiers occurred during this march is evident from Plutarch's information (*Apophth. Ant.* 10) that it was during a winter campaign in terrain lacking all supplies, which exactly fits this occasion. Antigonos was in general a commander who inspired confidence and affection in his men by cracking jokes with them and laughing in a booming voice (Plut. *Eum.* 15,2; *Dem.* 28,4).

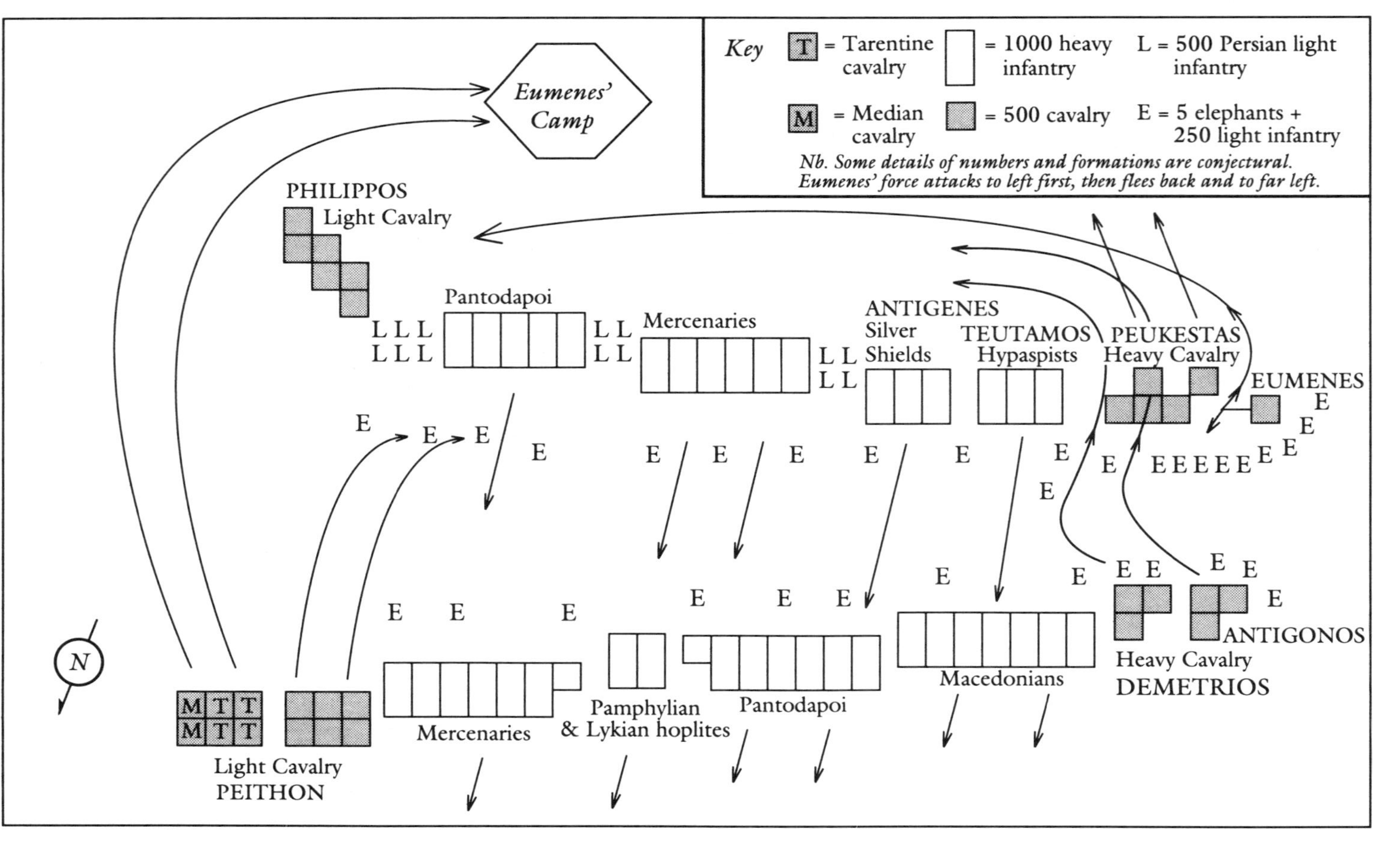

Figure 4. The Battle of Gabiene

camp, he had each soldier light and tend a campfire during the night so as to give the impression that a large army was encamped there. This was reported by local hillmen to Peithon and Antigonos, who supposed that Eumenes' entire army was at hand and were appalled. Antigonos at once gave up his plan and turned aside into inhabited country to rest and refresh his army (Diod. XIX 38,1–6; Plut. *Eum.* 15,4–7; Polyainos IV 8,4). Meanwhile Eumenes constructed a fortified camp and gathered his army for a decisive battle. This he managed to do, despite the enemy's proximity, except that his elephants were somewhat slow to come in, and were almost captured by surprise by a raiding column sent out by Antigonos (Diod. XIX 39,1–6). A few days later, the armies drew together and encamped opposite each other about five miles apart. They were on a broad plain, entirely uncultivated because of the loose, sandy, and salty soil (Diod. XIX 39,6 and 42,1; Polyainos IV 6,13). Here the two armies were marched out and drawn up for battle (see fig. 4).

Antigonos's strength at this battle was 22,000 heavy infantry, 9,000 cavalry, 65 elephants, and an unknown number of light infantry. He was decidedly superior to Eumenes in cavalry, and his strategy was to strike with his heavy cavalry, stationed on the right under Demetrios and himself, while his phalanx and light cavalry under Peithon on the left stood on the defensive. Eumenes observed Antigonos's dispositions before making his own. His army amounted to 36,700 infantry (both heavy and light), 6,000 cavalry, and 114 elephants; his plan was to refuse battle on the right, to check Antigonos's cavalry with his left, where he stationed himself with the best heavy cavalry, preventing a repeat of Antigonos's battle-saving exploit at Paraitakene, and to win with his incomparable heavy infantry (Diod. XIX 40,1–4; Plut. *Eum.* 16,3–4).

Before the battle began, Antigenes, the commander of the Silver Shields, sent a horseman over to where Antigonos's Macedonians were stationed to rebuke and threaten them in the name of the Silver Shields, who were of course the old guard battalion of Philip and Alexander.[25] This produced despondency among Antigonos's Macedonians, while a great cheer went up from Eumenes' ranks, and at

25. This passage shows that the *argyraspides* of the Diadoch era were the same as Alexander's *hypaspistai* and Philip's *pezetairoi*. The depiction of them as τοὺς μετὰ Φιλίππου καὶ Ἀλεξάνδρου τὰ ὅλα κατειργασμένους strongly implies this. Though this identity is generally accepted, it was recently challenged by Lock, *Historia* 26 (1977):373–78, but has since been firmly and rightly restated by Anson, *Historia* 30 (1981):117–20; for the identity of Alexander's *hypaspistai* and Philip's *pezetairoi*, see Griffith in Hammond and Griffith, *History of Macedonia*, 2:703–9. For a full account of the battle of Gabiene, see Devine, *AncW* 12, nos. 3/4 (1985):87–96.

this psychological moment Eumenes gave the signal for battle. The first to engage were the skirmishing screens of elephants and light infantry drawn up in front of the armies. At once a great cloud of dust was raised, obscuring much of the action. Antigonos observed this and immediately took advantage of it. He selected a body of Median and Tarentine light cavalry and ordered them to ride around the edge of the battle to Eumenes' camp, which was about one thousand yards behind Eumenes' line; there they were to seize Eumenes' baggage train and carry it back to Antigonos's camp. Because of the great clouds of dust, this maneuver went entirely unnoticed by Eumenes' army, and finding the enemy camp inadequately guarded, Antigonos's troops captured and carried off the entire baggage train, containing the wives, children, servants, and accumulated savings of Eumenes' army (Diod. XIX 42,1–3; Plut. *Eum.* 16,5–6; Polyainos IV 6,13).[26]

Meanwhile Antigonos led his right-wing cavalry in a charge against Eumenes' left wing. Evidently riding around the screen of elephants and light infantry, who were fighting fiercely against those of Eumenes, Antigonos charged towards Eumenes' cavalry in a great cloud of dust, unnerving the enemy to such a degree that Peukestas fled immediately with most of the cavalry. Eumenes, stationed on the extreme left with his own following, tried to retrieve the situation by charging upon Antigonos's flank; but though they fought fiercely, trying to force their way towards Antigonos himself, they were too much outnumbered and were driven back. As the battle of the elephants and skirmishers was then decided by the death of Eumenes' leading elephant, Eumenes broke off the action on this wing and rode with his attendants to his right wing, where he took command of the light cavalry, which had not yet come into action. While the cavalry battle was thus being won by Antigonos, however, Eumenes' heavy infantry had come to grips with Antigonos's phalanx and, spearheaded by the invincible Silver Shields, had won a clear victory.

26. The sources, including Justin XIV 3–4 and Nepos *Eum.* 10,2, are unanimous in attributing Eumenes' downfall to this stratagem of Antigonos. Its success illustrates a basic flaw in Eumenes' generalship: that he did not really understand the character of his men. He had lost his baggage train before, at Orkynia, with disastrous results to the morale of his men, and rejected an opportunity to inflict a similar blow on Antigonos's army right after that battle; here again he seems to have taken inadequate precautions to secure his army's baggage, showing that he underestimated its importance to his men. E. M. Anson has recently suggested in his "Eumenes of Cardia" that Eumenes' ultimate failure was not so much due to his being a Greek among Macedonians as to the simple fact that he failed to win any clear and decisive success over Antigonos; one might add to this that he did not understand the character and aspirations of his troops and so never managed to impose his authority on them in the way that men like Antigonos, Ptolemy, and Seleukos did.

Eumenes now attempted to get Peukestas and his cavalry, who had escaped quite unharmed, to join with him in renewing the cavalry battle and recapturing the baggage train, but they refused to comply, retreating even further instead. Antigonos had in any case formed his cavalry into a screen between Eumenes and the battlefield, and ordered Peithon to attack Eumenes' phalanx in flank and rear with his cavalry. This forced Eumenes' heavy infantry to break off their victorious pursuit, but being battle-hardened veterans, they formed a square and succeeded in withdrawing safely from the field of battle and rejoining Peukestas and Eumenes. In spite of the success of the infantry, it was clear that the main honors of the battle had gone to Antigonos, and hence recriminations began at once in Eumenes' camp. Peukestas was blamed for his retreat, the satraps wanted to retire as quickly as possible into the upper satrapies, while Eumenes tried to persuade everyone to stay and try the issue of battle once again. The decisive opinion, however, was that of the Macedonian Silver Shields: as soon as they heard that Antigonos had captured their wives, children, and money, they decided that they had had enough of the war and opened negotiations with Antigonos to retrieve their property (Diod. XIX 42,4–43,8; Plut. *Eum.* 16,4–17,1; Polyainos IV 6,13).

A deal was struck whereby Antigonos was to hand back the captured baggage train in return for the delivery to him of Eumenes and a promise of future allegiance. Peukestas, with his 10,000 Persian archers and slingers, came in on the deal, and most of the others in the camp followed suit. The Silver Shields arrested Eumenes before he was aware of the treachery afoot against him, and Antigonos sent a trusted officer named Nikanor to take charge of him. The war was thus at an end. Some of the satraps and generals, for example, Tlepolemos of Karmania, made their escape from the scene. A few, such as Antigenes, the former commander of the Silver Shields; Eudamos, the elephantarch; and Kephalon, were executed by Antigonos.[27] Most of the enemy men and officers were simply received into Antigonos's service—notably Hieronymos of Kardia; Mithri-

27. Diod. XIX 44,1 makes it clear that the men selected by Antigonos for execution were those persistently hostile to him. Antigenes' career in this respect is clear; his peculiarly cruel punishment (burnt alive in a pit) is puzzling unless it could be that he had caused the execution of Antigonos's friend Philotas (see app. 3, no. 95) and suffered this fate in revenge. Eudamos was one of the stauncher supporters of Eumenes (Plut. *Eum.* 16,2), and commanded the left wing of Eumenes' army at Paraitakene (see Diod. XIX 30,3 and 30,9). For Kephalon, the MSS of Diodoros in fact read "Kelbanon" (RX) or "Kebalon" (F); it was seen by Heckel, *BN* 15 (1980):43–45, that the MSS should be emended to Kephalona, the man whom Eumenes placed in command of Sibyrtios's contingent after the latter's flight (Diod. XIX 27,4).

dates, son of Ariobarzanes; Peukestas; and probably Philippos and Phoinix of Tenedos.[28] Eumenes was placed under heavy guard in the keeping of an officer named Onomarchos while Antigonos pondered his fate, to decide which he held a council of friends. Demetrios and Nearchos urged him to spare Eumenes' life, and Antigonos was himself reportedly disinclined to kill Eumenes, but felt unable to trust him after the Nora episode, and most of the *synedrion* were insistent that Eumenes must be killed. So it was decided, then, and Eumenes met his end, his body being handed over for burial to his friends (Diod. XIX 43,8–44,3; Plut. *Eum.* 17,1–19,1; Nepos *Eum.* 10,3–13,1).[29] Antigonos then took the combined army back to Media to winter quarters, it being about the middle of January 315.

While the war in Asia was unfolding in the manner described, the war in Europe was being won by Antigonos's ally Kassandros. As noted, at the end of 317 Olympias and Polyperchon had managed to capture and execute Philippos Arrhidaios and his wife Eurydike, and were now ruling Macedon in the name of the young Alexandros IV. Olympias, however, did her cause no good by conducting a reign of terror against Kassandros's friends, relatives, and sympathizers. Kassandros, with characteristic energy, abandoned his undertakings in the Peloponnesos and hurried to Macedon with a large army, using rafts to bypass Thermopylai, which a strong force of Aitolians was holding against him. He despatched forces to hold at bay Polyperchon, who was in Perrhaibia with an army, and Aiakides of Epeiros, who sought to come to Olympias's aid. Olympias herself went with her retinue to Pydna, where she was closely besieged by Kassandros over the winter of 316/15 and starved into surrender. Kassandros had her formally tried for treason and sentenced to death, the relatives of her own victims carrying out the sentence. Her most loyal supporter, Aristonous, was murdered by Kassandros; Polyperchon's army was corrupted by bribery and Polyperchon himself forced to flee; Aiakides was ejected from the throne of Epeiros by his own people, who

---

28. See on these men app. 3, nos. 51, 73, 90, 93, and 96 respectively.

29. The sources vary somewhat on precisely how Eumenes died: Diodoros simply says Antigonos had him put to death (ἀνεῖλε τὸν ἄνδρα); Plutarch more circumstantially has Antigonos order Eumenes to be deprived of food and then a few days later send a man to kill him; Justin XIV 4 does not even record Eumenes' death, though he later alludes to it at XV 1; Nepos has Eumenes killed without Antigonos's knowledge. It is clear that there was a tradition that sought to absolve Antigonos of responsibility for Eumenes' death, playing up their old friendship and laying the principal blame on Antigonos's *philoi,* who feared the influence Eumenes might wield at Antigonos's court if he were allowed to live. This probably originated with Hieronymos, justifying his serving under the killer of his friend, fellow-citizen, and perhaps kinsman Eumenes.

preferred to make an alliance with Kassandros. Thus Kassandros won full control of Macedon by the spring of 315 (Diod. XIX 31,1–36,6; 49,1–51,6; Justin XIV 5–6).

Antigonos had spread his winter quarters widely over Media, himself wintering near Ekbatana. During the winter reports were brought in that Peithon was courting the favor of the troops in the more distant parts of Media with a view to revolt, a worrying prospect as Peithon had great prestige and ability. However, Antigonos publicly discounted the rumors and gave out that he fully trusted Peithon and planned to make him general of the upper satrapies with a large military force—5,000 Macedonian infantry and 1,000 Thracians (cavalry?) according to Polyainos IV 6,14. Peithon was taken in and quickly traveled to Antigonos's camp with great expectations; but Antigonos had him arrested, tried him for treason before his *synedrion,* obtained a guilty verdict, and had him executed (Diod. XIX 46,1–4; Polyainos IV 6,14). Antigonos then gathered his army together ready to move off; he appointed the Mede Orontobates satrap of Media and made Hippostratos general of the upper satrapies, with a force of 3,500 mercenaries.[30] He took charge of the royal treasure at Ekbatana, 5,000 talents of uncoined silver, and then marched south to Persia (Diod. XIX 46,5–6).

The march to Persepolis took twenty days, and Antigonos there received a royal reception from the natives. He now held a grand *synedrion* of his friends to arrange a reorganization of the upper satrapies. Tlepolemos of Karmania and Stasanor of Baktria could not be dislodged without military action and were therefore permitted to retain their satrapies, though hostile; the same applied to Oxyartes of the Paropanisadai (the Hindu Kush), and the former Indian satrapies were apparently not even discussed, these having already cast off the Macedonian yoke.[31] The former satrap of Areia/Drangiane, Stasandros, must have been captured or killed, for to this satrapy Antigonos sent a replacement (see app. 3, nos. 38 and 39). The existing satrap of Arachosia, Sibyrtios, had only narrowly escaped death at Eumenes' hands, as narrated above, and was consequently now well disposed towards Antigonos, who summoned him to Persepolis and confirmed him in his satrapy. Since Sibyrtios was responsible for the frontier with the rebellious Indians in Arachosia, and since Antigonos wished to break up the Silver Shields, who wielded far too much

30. See app. 3, no. 54, and cf. Schober, *Gesch. Babyloniens,* pp. 84–90.

31. See on the matter of the Indian satrapies between 323 and 315 the excellent treatment of Schober, *Gesch. Babyloniens,* pp. 90–93.

influence as a unit for Antigonos's comfort, 1,000 of the unruliest Silver Shields were assigned to Sibyrtios for the frontier war, with instructions to regard them as expendable (Diod. XIX 48,3–4; Polyainos IV 6,15; Plut. *Eum.* 19,2).[32] Moreover Peukestas, who was extremely popular in his satrapy, the dangerously powerful Persia, was deposed and promised suitable alternative employment in the western portions of Antigonos's empire (see app. 3, no. 90). Though some of the leading Persians were very angry at this, Antigonos quelled the protest and appointed Asklepiodoros ruler of Persia, with sufficient troops to enforce his authority (Diod. XIX 48,5).

It was probably at Persepolis that Antigonos decided to send Nikanor to Media to take over as general of the upper satrapies; though the evidence is unclear, Hippostratos may have died soon after Antigonos's departure (see app. 3, nos. 54 and 79). At any rate, the east had now been satisfactorily ordered: the extreme east had been virtually given up, except for Areia/Drangiane, Arachosia, and the supervisory position of the general of the upper satrapies, with a substantial army at his back; Media and Persia, the most powerful eastern satrapies, were firmly held. Antigonos left Persepolis and marched north to Susa. On his way he was met by Xenophilos, the guardian of Susa, who had surrendered to Seleukos (presumably when news of Eumenes' defeat and death arrived), and who had been sent by Seleukos to Antigonos with instructions to obey the latter in all things. Antigonos received Xenophilos into the circle of his friends, but probably did not continue his command at Susa. The treasure at Susa, amounting to 15,000 talents, was taken over by Antigonos; with the 5,000 talents from Ekbatana and a further 5,000 talents in booty and gifts, Antigonos's treasury now contained the magnificent sum of 25,000 talents (Diod. XIX 48,5–8). He prepared a great caravan to carry this treasure and set out with it towards Babylonia, leaving a native named Aspeisas as satrap of Susiane (Diod. XIX 55,1).

The march to Babylon took twenty-two days, and Antigonos was there given a magnificent reception by Seleukos. However, relations between Antigonos and Seleukos soon became strained. It is probable that Antigonos was already inclined to be suspicious of

32. See ibid. on the probability that Sibyrtios had problems along his border with India. Plutarch seems to imply that all of the Silver Shields were given to Sibyrtios, but the more reliable Diodoros states that only the most troublesome (τοὺς ταραχωδεστάτους) were thus assigned, while Polyainos specifies that these were 1,000 in number, and that the other Silver Shields were assigned to garrison duty in various out-of-the-way forts.

Seleukos as the able, popular, and ambitious head of a rich satrapy containing Alexander's last capital, Babylon. An open rupture occurred, according to Appian (*Syr.* 53), when Seleukos one day punished a *hēgemōn* without consulting Antigonos; the latter thereupon angrily demanded that Seleukos account for the revenues of the satrapy. Seleukos denied any such obligation, and the dispute grew heated. Eventually, calling to mind the examples of Peithon, son of Krateuas (killed), and Peukestas (deposed), Seleukos concluded that he had better make himself scarce, and fled from Babylon through Mesopotamia and Syria to Egypt, where he found refuge with Ptolemy (Diod. XIX 55,2–5). Antigonos, at first pleased to see the back of Seleukos without having to put him to death, is said to have been influenced by the prophecies of some Chaldaian astrologers concerning Seleukos's subsequent fate to despatch men to pursue and kill him (Diod. XIX 55,6–7: probably merely an invention *ex eventu*).[33] Anyway, Antigonos gave Babylonia to Peithon, son of Agenor, formerly in charge of one of the Indian satrapies, who had joined him during this year (315). Most likely Mesopotamia was joined with Babylonia into one great satrapy under Peithon, for it is recorded by Appian (*Syr.* 53) that Antigonos deposed Blitor, satrap of Mesopotamia, for aiding Seleukos's escape, and no successor is ever mentioned.[34]

Antigonos then left Babylonia and marched with his army and treasure caravan through Mesopotamia and up to Kilikia, where he arrived at Mallos after the setting of Orion (November 315). He established his troops in winter quarters in Kilikia and added to his treasure the royal moneys at Kyinda—10,000 talents. In addition to the vast treasure he now possessed, he is reported to have had annual revenue from his empire of 11,000 talents; this enormous wealth put him in a marvelous position to maintain his great armies and undertake whatever projects he might wish, but it also brought him the

33. Hadley, *Historia* 18 (1969):142–52, argues that this prophecy, along with other prophecies and legends concerning Seleukos, was recounted by Hieronymos in an excursus just after his account of the battle of Ipsos, and is hence genuine. There are two fallacies in his argument: (i) that because Diodoros recounts this story it must come from Hieronymos and (ii) that whatever was recounted by Hieronymos must be true. There is no evidence that Hieronymos recounted this or any other prophecy or legend portending Seleukos's greatness, nor is it likely that he did so; and even if he did, the prophecy is so detailed (Seleukos will rule all of Asia and Antigonos will die in battle against him) as to come under strong suspicion of being *ex eventu*.

34. See Diod. XIX 55,4 for the appointment of Peithon, son of Agenor, as satrap of Babylonia, and for the conjecture that he was also the satrap of Mesopotamia, see app. 3, no. 88, and chap. 7 at n. 57. On Blitor, evidently an appointee of Antigonos's, see app. 3, no. 24.

envy of the other dynasts (Diod. XIX 56,4–5). Seleukos, arriving in Egypt, had been warmly received by Ptolemy and found in him a ready audience for his accusations against Antigonos. Together they also sent to Kassandros and Lysimachos, who were ruling Macedon and Thrace respectively, proposing a common alliance against Antigonos. The latter, foreseeing this development, had already sent envoys to Ptolemy, Kassandros, and Lysimachos from Babylon, urging them not to break off their friendly relations with him; but the arguments of Seleukos prevailed, and the four dynasts prepared an ultimatum to deliver to Antigonos, with the threat of war if he should refuse to comply (Diod. XIX 56,1–57,1; Appian *Syr.* 53).

Though his authority had seemed secure with his victory over Eumenes, the western dynasts were unwilling to see Antigonos rule all of Asia. Thus, as the Second Diadoch War ended, were sown the seeds of the Third Diadoch War, which began early in 314 and pitted Antigonos against Ptolemy, Seleukos, Kassandros, and Lysimachos. Ptolemy was at this time in control of Kyrene, Koile Syria, and Phoenicia, in addition to Egypt, and also enjoyed great influence in Cyprus. Lysimachos was still not in full control of Thrace, and was less formidable than his partners. Kassandros ruled Macedon and controlled King Alexandros IV, whom he kept under guard at Amphipolis with his mother, Roxane (Diod. XIX 52,4). He was perhaps the most formidable of the coalition. During the year 315 he had allied himself to the Argead royal house by marrying Philip's daughter Thessalonike; he had founded a city named Kassandreia after himself at the neck of the Pallene peninsula, near the site of ancient Potidaia; he had refounded the city of Thebes, thereby considerably augmenting his prestige in Greece; and he had forced Polyperchon and his son Alexandros entirely onto the defensive in Aitolia and the Peloponnesos respectively (Diod. XIX 52,1–54,4). It seems that the coalition may already have initiated hostilities against Antigonos in late 315, for an army of Kassandros is heard of operating in northern Kappadokia and besieging Amisos early in 314 (Diod. XIX 57,4), and there may also have been some action against Antigonos's navy in the waters off Cyprus.[35] However, the formal declaration of war depended upon the response Antigonos should make to the ultimatum the coalition planned to send him at the beginning of the year 314,

35. Doubts have been expressed as to whether Kassandros could really have had an army operating in Kappadokia in 315/14, and the name is sometimes altered to Asandros, but see now Seibert, *Ptolemaios I*, pp. 157–63, arguing convincingly in favor of the retention of Kassandros. On naval warfare around Cyprus in 315, see app. 3, no. 44.

though given the way they framed it, they could have entertained little doubt as to the outcome.

THE THIRD DIADOCH WAR (314–311 B.C.)

When Antigonos moved out of his winter quarters in Kilikia early in 314 and began to march south into upper Syria, he was met by envoys from the allied dynasts Ptolemy, Kassandros, and Lysimachos. He called a *synedrion* and introduced these envoys into it to state their masters' demands. These were that Kappadokia and Lykia should be ceded to Kassandros, Hellespontine Phrygia to Lysimachos, all of Syria to Ptolemy, and Babylonia to Seleukos, and that he should share with these dynasts the treasures he had accumulated.[36] If he failed to comply with these demands, the dynasts threatened him with war (Diod. XIX 57,1). The allies justified this extraordinary set of demands as their fair share in a war in which they too had taken part. Obviously Seleukos had every right to feel hard done by, and it was by no means unfair for the allied dynasts to claim a share of the treasures which all of the Macedonians had captured under Alexander's leadership. But this does not apply to the territorial demands of Lysimachos and Ptolemy, who had played no significant part in the Second Diadoch War and had undergone none of the dangers and hardships faced by Antigonos and his forces in winning that war; Kassandros, who had contributed significantly to the war effort, held Macedon and Greece as his reward, and for this he had the aid

36. I list the territorial demands as in the text of Diod. XIX 57,1; many modern scholars are not satisfied with this and wish to emend in some fashion. Droysen, *Geschichte des Hellenismus,* 2:6, suggests that here as elsewhere in Diodoros "Kasandros" (*sic*) has been mistakenly used for Asandros, satrap of Karia, and he is followed by Wesseling and Fischer in their editions of Diodoros. However, Diod. XIX 61,2 indicates that Asandros only joined the coalition against Antigonos at a later stage; and Seibert, *Ptolemaios I,* pp. 159–63, has rightly pointed out that in 301 Kassandros took territories in Asia Minor (albeit in the name of his brother Pleistarchos), so that there is nothing inherently impossible or improbable in him demanding such territories in 315/14. Other scholars doubt that Kassandros would have demanded such widely separated regions as Kappadokia and Lykia. Since the fact that Kassandros claimed Kappadokia seems to be established by the presence of his army under Asklepiodoros there in 314, scholars have emended Lykia either to Kilikia (Tarn, *CAH,* 6:484) or to Lydia (Aucello, *RFIC,* n.s., 35 [1957]:382–404, followed by Wehrli, *Antigone et Démétrios,* pp. 43–48). Either emendation is possible; neither seems inherently more probable than what the text gives (i.e., Lykia), so it seems best to retain the text as it stands (cf. the cautionary remarks of Engel, *Untersuchungen,* p. 56 n. 261, who points out that any emendation of the text can be no more than hypothetical).

furnished him by Antigonos in 318 to thank.[37] There was no justification for the demand that Antigonos cede Syria and half of Asia Minor to these dynasts: this was simply an attempt to cut him down to size.

Perhaps this ultimatum by the allied dynasts was intended as an initial bargaining position, to be modified in response to whatever Antigonos should offer as a counterproposal. If so, the dynasts misjudged their man: Antigonos clearly had no intention of making territorial concessions, and he was angered rather than cowed or impressed by the threat of war. He had sent messages to the dynasts in 315 urging them to remain his friends, and was met in return by demands which must have seemed outrageous to him (cf. Justin XV 1,2). His only answer was to advise the dynasts to be ready, then, for war (Diod. XIX 57,2; Appian *Syr.* 53); and indeed it is hard to believe that the allies did not foresee and even expect this response to their ultimatum. Thus began the Third Diadoch War. A strange feature of this war is the lack of energy and urgency with which it seems to have been conducted by the allied dynasts in the first year, 314, in spite of the fact that they had spent the latter half of 315 discussing the idea of common action against Antigonos, and even appear to have begun military operations. Kassandros had sent a force into Kappadokia to make good his claim to that region (Diod. XIX 57,4), and there is also the matter of Antigonos's fleet. As recounted above, Antigonos had a large fleet in 317, especially after capturing most of Kleitos's Macedonian fleet and Eumenes' Phoenician fleet; yet in 314 we find that Antigonos had only a handful of ships (Diod. XIX 58,1). Ptolemy, we learn from Diodoros, had carried off the fleets of the Phoenicians to Egypt (XIX 58,2), and Kassandros may have sent a fleet to help crush Antigonos's navy near Cyprus (see app. 3, no. 44 on Hagnon of Teos).

The results of these actions are recorded by Diodoros: at the beginning of 314, Antigonos had no fleet, Ptolemy held the Phoenician cities and fleet, and Kassandros's general Asklepiodoros was besieging Amisos in northern Kappadokia (Diod. XIX 58,1–2; 59,2; 57,4; and 60,2). In spite of the favorable position they had thus won for themselves and the time they had had to prepare, however, the allied dynasts do not seem to have been ready in 314 for full-scale

37. See Diod. XVIII 68,1 and Paus. I 6,7 on Kassandros's ingratitude in making war on Antigonos, his former benefactor.

hostilities with Antigonos (Diod. XIX 57,3).[38] Antigonos immediately seized the initiative. Recognizing in Ptolemy and Kassandros his most formidable opponents, he took a series of steps to put them on the defensive. Against Kassandros's forces in Kappadokia, Antigonos sent his nephew Polemaios with a large army—its exact size is not given, but we learn later (Diod. XIX 68,6) that it exceeded 8,300 foot and 600 horse; Polemaios's instructions were to evict Kassandros's army from Kappadokia and raise the siege of Amisos, and then to proceed to the Hellespont and there take up a position to prevent Kassandros crossing with more troops. At the same time Antigonos sent his friend Aristodemos of Miletos to the Peloponnesos with 1,000 talents and instructions to raise a large force of mercenaries and campaign against Kassandros's positions there, and also to seek an alliance with Polyperchon and his son Alexandros, who were still holding out against Kassandros with a considerable army in the Peloponnesos and could prove useful allies now that Kassandros had turned against Antigonos (Diod. XIX 57,4–5).

Against Ptolemy Antigonos prepared blows in Cyprus and Palestine, the two outposts on which Ptolemy relied to prevent attacks on Egypt. A diplomatic mission headed by a certain Agesilaos was despatched to Cyprus to try to persuade the city-kings there to support Antigonos, while Antigonos himself set out with his army to Phoenicia to deprive Ptolemy of that region and Koile Syria (Diod. XIX 57,4; Appian *Syr.* 53). Antigonos further realized that, his main advantage against the coalition being the distance separating Ptolemy from Kassandros and Lysimachos, the best way to confirm and extend the position of holding interior lines, with all of the strategic advantages entailed thereby, was to secure firm control of the sea, which was the avenue for communication and mutual support between Ptolemy and his allies in Europe. Accordingly, having encamped near Tyre, which was held by a Ptolemaic garrison, Antigonos summoned the governors of Syria and the kings of the Phoenician cities not garrisoned by Ptolemy to a meeting, at which he gave instructions for the building of a great fleet. The timber was readily available from the slopes of Lebanon and of the Taurus range

38. Diodoros's statement may mean that the dynasts were unprepared for the immediacy of Antigonos's rejection of their demands, supposing that there would be a lengthy period of negotiations before it came to war, and so were not ready to deal with the scale and speed of Antigonos's measures against them.

in Kilikia; shipyards were set up in the Phoenician cities of Tripolis, Sidon, and Byblos, and a fourth in Kilikia. In addition, Antigonos had previously sent ambassadors to Rhodes, who negotiated an agreement whereby the Rhodians were to build ships for Antigonos from timber he would send to Rhodes for the purpose (Diod. XIX 57,4; 58,1–5). It is clear too that Antigonos sent to his dependencies in the Hellespontine region to provide ships, for ships from there subsequently joined him at Tyre (Diod. XIX 62,7).

Having made these arrangements, Antigonos initiated a siege of Tyre, cutting off the city's land communications. A full siege could, however, only be achieved when a fleet was ready to blockade Tyre's sea communications, a fact quickly emphasized by Ptolemy, who sent out a fleet of 100 ships under Seleukos (Diod. XIX 58,5–6). Though it is not stated by Diodoros, one imagines that Seleukos must have provisioned Tyre, and perhaps brought in reinforcements; he then sailed contemptuously right past Antigonos's camp and on up the coast. This created a bad impression in Antigonos's camp, especially as it was clearly Seleukos's intention to ravage the coasts of Asia Minor, and there was as yet nothing to be done about him. However, Antigonos alleviated this bad impression by affirming that he would take the sea with a large fleet that very year, and meanwhile sent to his nephew Polemaios to move with his army to Ionia to prevent Seleukos from securing any of the cities there (Diod. XIX 58,6 and 60,3–4). At this point, too, Antigonos's envoy Agesilaos returned from Cyprus with news of not inconsiderable successes there. For though Nikokreon of Salamis and his allies Pasikrates of Soloi and Nikokles of Paphos continued to support Ptolemy, with whom they had already allied themselves in 320 (Arrian *Met' Alex.* 24,6), the rulers of Kition, Marion, Lapethos, Keryneia, and Amathous had been persuaded to cast in their lot with Antigonos (Diod. XIX 59,1, and cf. 62,6 for Amathous).

Upon receipt of this news, Antigonos left a senior officer named Andronikos of Olynthos to press the siege of Tyre with 3,000 soldiers, while he himself marched into southern Palestine with the rest of his army; there he ejected Ptolemy's last garrisons at Joppa and Gaza, thus securing control of all of Syria and Palestine, with the exception of Tyre (Diod. XIX 59,2). He then returned to Tyre to continue the siege. Ptolemy, meanwhile, seems to have heard of the situation on Cyprus, and despatched 3,000 men to help Nikokreon against the kings who had gone over to Antigonos (Diod. XIX 62,3). The Ptolemaic fleet under Seleukos had sailed up to Ionia; of its activities there or elsewhere the sources tell us nothing, except that towards autumn Seleukos was at Erythrai laying siege to the place, but was forced to leave hurriedly with nothing accomplished when Antigonos's general Polemaios arrived in Ionia (Diod. XIX 60,3–4). Polemaios, it will be recalled, had been sent out in early spring of 314 with a large army to recover control of Kappadokia. This he performed apparently with ease, whereupon he marched along the Black Sea coast through Paphlagonia to Bithynia, making on the way an alliance with the tyrant Dionysios of Herakleia Pontika, cemented by marrying the tyrant's daughter (Memnon in *FGrH,* no. 434 F 4,6). In Bithynia the dynast Zipoites was making war on the cities of Chalkedon and Astakos with a view to increasing his power; to this Polemaios put a stop, requiring Zipoites to ally himself with Antigonos and hand over hostages, and also enrolling the two Greek cities Chalkedon and Astakos as allies of Antigonos. He then received Antigonos's instructions to go to the aid of Ionia, where he arrived in time to thwart Seleukos at Erythrai (Diod. XIX 60,2–4). Since the year must by then have been well advanced, one presumes that Polemaios and his troops wintered in Ionia or Lydia.

While his nephew Polemaios had thus been confirming Antigonos's control over Asia Minor, his friend Aristodemos had not been inactive in the Peloponnesos. Having been sent there early in the year with 1,000 talents, he had negotiated an agreement with the Spartan government that enabled him to recruit 8,000 mercenaries.[39] He then opened negotiations with Polyperchon and Alexandros, eventually managing to persuade them that it was to their advantage to ally themselves with Antigonos. Polyperchon, still nominally the regent (*epimelētēs*) of the empire, reached an accord with Antigonos involving a redefinition of the powers of both men, and Polyperchon's son Alexandros traveled to Asia to meet Antigonos and confirm the deal, joining Antigonos in his camp at Tyre around midsummer 314 (Diod. XIX 60,1 and 61,1).

After conferring with Alexandros, Antigonos called a general meeting of his soldiers and everyone else present in the camp and delivered a harangue against Kassandros, accusing him of the murder of Olympias and imprisonment of the young king Alexandros IV and his mother Roxane, and of forcibly marrying Philip II's daughter

---

39. Possibly at the mercenary fair at Cape Tainaron; see Parke, *Greek Mercenary Soldiers,* p. 218, and Griffith, *Mercenaries,* p. 52, and cf. Griffith, pp. 259–60, on Tainaron as the mercenary fair par excellence in the late fourth century.

Thessalonike. He charged that Kassandros aimed to usurp the throne, adducing as proof the foundation of Kassandreia, and he also held the refoundation of Thebes against Kassandros. When the assembled throng expressed its approval of his speech, he introduced a motion calling on Kassandros to destroy the two cities just mentioned, hand over the king and Roxane, and in general yield obedience to Antigonos as the man who had succeeded to the regency of the empire; in addition it was specified that the Greeks were to be free, ungarrisoned, and autonomous. This motion the meeting duly approved, and Antigonos took steps to have it widely broadcast, sending messengers with copies to the cities, peoples, and dynasts. He hoped to confirm the Asian satraps in support of himself and to strike a double blow against Kassandros by espousing the cause of the young king and winning over the Greeks with the prospect of liberty. Alexandros was given 500 talents and returned to the Peloponnesos (Diod. XIX 61,1–5).

The proclamation of Tyre marked a major new stage in Antigonos's plans. Up to this point, one can distinguish three stages in his rise after Alexander's death: the first is his participation in the coalition challenging the settlement of Babylon; the second is his appointment as overseer of Asia under the overall authority of Antipatros; and the third is when he used the death of Antipatros to establish his authority in Asia as subject only to the kings—that is, in practice, as being valid until Alexandros IV should come of age and decide on a new disposition of the empire. We now seem to have reached a fourth stage, in that Antigonos claimed to be regent and for the first time laid claim to authority over the whole of the Macedonian Empire. However, the Tyre proclamation was principally a piece of propaganda, aimed especially at undermining Kassandros's position in Macedon and Greece, and in general put out as a response to the harsh ultimatum submitted to Antigonos at the beginning of 314 by the allied dynasts. It is not clear, consequently, how far Antigonos's claim to have succeeded to the regency represented a genuine political aim.

It is clear from Diodoros, however, that the basis on which Antigonos rested his claim to have succeeded to the regency was a rather disreputable deal with Polyperchon.[40] In theory, since Polyper-

40. Such a deal was suggested by Heuss, *Hermes* 73 (1938):149 n. 1, and accepted by Rosen, *AClass* 10 (1967):78–81; it has been disputed by Simpson, *Historia* 6 (1957):371–73, arguing from the Macedonian constitution, but this has now been discredited (see above chap. 2 n. 1). Furthermore there is no justification in the sources for Simpson's assumption that Polyperchon no longer regarded himself as the legal *epimelētēs* for the kingdom in 315. It is clear

chon had been directly named regent by Antipatros, he could in his turn nominate a successor to himself; but since Antigonos had never acknowledged the legitimacy of Antipatros's procedure in appointing Polyperchon regent, it was certainly cynical and inconsistent on his part to claim to succeed to the regency through Polyperchon. Nevertheless, Diodoros's account shows that that is what Antigonos did: he sent Aristodemos to Greece to negotiate with Polyperchon (XIX 57,5). Aristodemos did this and struck a bargain by which Polyperchon was to be *stratēgos* of the Peloponnesos (XIX 60,1: note the implied relinquishing of the regency and Antigonos's assumption of authority in Europe). Polyperchon's son Alexandros brought news of this deal to Antigonos (XIX 61,1), and only after conferring with Alexandros did Antigonos for the first time claim to have succeeded to the regency.[41]

Obviously Antigonos was not worried about the inconsistency of accepting the regency from Polyperchon: he had been Kassandros's ally against Polyperchon; now he wanted Polyperchon as an ally against Kassandros. What mattered for purposes of propaganda was to establish some claim, however implausible or inconsistent, to having received the regency from some source more "legitimate" than his own personal fiat; his assembled army and followers at Tyre were not likely to examine the origin of the claim with any rigor before enthusiastically approving, and the views of his enemies hardly mattered.

But could Antigonos seriously expect to make good so nebulous a claim to the regency? He may in fact have had no such expectation: he had not wanted war with the western dynasts, but had been presented with unacceptable demands by them; the claim to the regency was a weapon for the ensuing war, for it could be pressed or dropped according to how the war went and what concessions could be won from the enemy. The Tyre proclamation also carried a sting

---

from Diod. XVIII 48,4 that Antipatros in 319/18 simply appointed Polyperchon regent by his own authority; hence Polyperchon could in theory hand over his authority to an appointee of his own if he so wished.

41. Diod. XIX 61,3: *τῶι καθεσταμένωι στρατηγῶι καὶ τῆς βασιλείας παρειληφότι τὴν ἐπιμέλειαν*. In the first part of this phrase Antigonos refers to his appointment as *stratēgos* in Asia by Antipatros in 320, showing that he regarded this as being still valid in 314; in the second part Antigonos claims that he has succeeded (*παρειληφότι*) to the *epimeleia* of the *basileia*. The use of the verb *παραλαμβάνω*, whose primary meaning is "*receive from* another, esp. of persons succeeding to an office, etc." (Liddell and Scott s.v.), seems to show that Antigonos claimed to have legally succeeded to the regency, by which he can only mean that he was appointed by Polyperchon.

in its tail, however, for the Greeks were devoted to the principle of autonomy and by no means reconciled to Macedonian rule by their past defeats. The goodwill and military aid of the Greeks were not to be sneezed at; at the very least Antigonos could hope through their interventions to keep Kassandros so busy at home as to be unable to menace him in Asia.[42]

Having broadcast this proclamation far and wide, then, Antigonos turned his attention back to the siege of Tyre, which the maturation of his ship-building enterprises now enabled him to render fully effective. For a substantial number of ships had been built and equipped in Phoenicia, and the first batch of those built at Rhodes now also came in. With these Antigonos sailed out and established a full naval blockade of Tyre. The siege dragged on through the winter of 314/13 and into late spring or early summer 313, lasting a year and three months in all, but starvation eventually forced the besieged to capitulate, and Antigonos was then able to dismiss the Ptolemaic garrison and install one of his own (Diod. XIX 61,5). During all this time, it seems, Ptolemy made no effort to raise the siege; however, he was evidently impressed by Antigonos's proclamation concerning the freedom of the Greeks, for he issued a similar proclamation of his own, perhaps towards the end of 314. At about the same time, he also succeeded in making an ally of Asandros, the satrap of Karia, who had probably been put under pressure by Antigonos's nephew Polemaios (then in Ionia with a large force) to declare his allegiance to Antigonos (Diod. XIX 62,1–2 and cf. 62,5). It looks as if Asandros then sailed in the winter of 314/13 to Europe, doubtless to ally himself with Kassandros too and seek aid from him. At any rate, Asandros is attested as having been in Athens in January 313, where he was honored for some sort of military aid to the city—perhaps against pirates.[43] It seems likely that his visit was aimed at gaining the support of Demetrios of Phaleron and/or Dionysios, the commander of Kassandros's garrison in Mounychia, for his negotiations with Kassandros.

---

42. It is worth noting that Antigonos's proclamation at Tyre specifically singled out Kassandros for attack, doubtless in an attempt to isolate him and so fragment the enemy coalition. On the importance Antigonos attached to good relations with the Greeks, see chap. 6 below.

43. *IG* II^2 450, an Athenian inscription honoring Asandros for his goodwill towards Athens and permitting him to set up a statue of himself in Athens, dates from the 11th of Gamelion in the archonship of Nikodoros (= January 313). It refers to him as *παραγενόμενος εἰς τὴμ / πόλιν* (lines 18–19), which is to say, he was actually in Athens about this time. Lines 19–21 record that Asandros lent the Athenians his own ships and soldiers for some purpose,

The year 313 saw rather more determined efforts on the part of Ptolemy and Kassandros to get to grips with Antigonos than hitherto. Ptolemy sent out to Cyprus a grand force under the command of his brother Menelaos, consisting of 10,000 mercenaries, led by an Athenian officer named Myrmidon, and 100 ships, with a certain Polykleitos as admiral. On Cyprus this force linked up with Seleukos and his fleet, who had presumably wintered there, and a council of war was held. Polykleitos was sent with 50 ships to fight Antigonos's allies in the Peloponnesos, Myrmidon and his mercenaries were to aid Asandros in Karia, and Seleukos and Menelaos with the rest of the fleet (150 ships) remained in Cyprus, where they captured Keryneia and Lapethos, persuaded the rulers of Marion and Amathous to support Ptolemy, and placed Kition under siege (Diod. XIX 62,3–6). Meanwhile Kassandros marched from Macedon with an army early in 313 and entered the Peloponnesos. After campaigning there with mixed success, he proceeded to the Argolid, where he presided over the Nemean games (ca. July 313) and then returned to Macedon. His most significant success was persuading Alexandros to desert Antigonos. Alexandros was offered the post of *stratēgos* of the Peloponnesos with an army and, Aristodemos being absent in Aitolia (Diod. XIX 63,3–64,4; 66,1), readily acceded.

In the meantime Antigonos had brought the siege of Tyre to a successful close and, being joined there by a squadron of ships from the Hellespont (40 strong, under the admiral Themison of Samos) and another from the Hellespont and Rhodes (80 strong, under Antigonos's nephew Dioskourides), had gathered a great fleet of 240 ships (Diod. XIX 62,7–8). Of these Antigonos ordered 50 to sail to the Peloponnesos to aid the cause there;[44] the remaining 190 he placed under the command of Dioskourides, with orders to sail round the

which is now lost, as the inscription is broken at this point. Droysen, *Geschichte des Hellenismus,* 2:25 n. 1, suggests the Athenian naval expedition to Lemnos ordered by Kassandros (Diod. XIX 68,3). Since this expedition coincided with an expedition sent by Kassandros to aid Asandros, who was in severe military difficulties, against Antigonos's general Polemaios, it is unlikely that Asandros would at the same time have sent his own forces away to help Athens, nor does Diodoros know of it. The events of Diod. XIX 68,3 in fact occurred late in 313, and we can only guess at the purpose for which Asandros gave aid to Athens.

44. It has long been thought (e.g., by Beloch, *GG,* 4.1:122 n. 3, and Bengtson, *Strategie,* 1:149 n. 3) that the fifty ships of Diod. XIX 62,9 were identical to the fifty ships sent to the Peloponnesos under the command of Telesphoros by Antigonos after he had captured Karia (see Diod. XIX 74,1). This is impossible: the first fifty ships were sent directly after the fall of Tyre, from Phoenicia (Diod. XIX 62,7–9); Telesphoros was sent a year later, after Antigonos had moved to Karia (Diod. XIX 69,1–3 and 74,1).

Aegean and persuade the islands to ally themselves with him (Diod. XIX 62,9). This mission of Dioskourides was no doubt responsible for the adhesion to Antigonos's cause of the islands of Lemnos and Imbros, hitherto under Athenian control, and the creation of a League of the Cycladic Islands centered on Delos, which had also been under Athenian control until 314.[45] Apparently while Dioskourides was sailing about engaged on this task, the Ptolemaic admiral Polykleitos, after sailing with his 50 ships to the Peloponnesos and back, ambushed an Antigonid army and fleet proceeding along the Kilikian coast, capturing both with their commanders, and then sailed back to Egypt (Diod. XIX 64,4–8). Antigonos sent Ptolemy an envoy to ransom the general and some of the other prisoners (officers presumably) and propose a meeting at Ekregma—which lies between Pelousion and Gaza on the north coast of the Sinai—to discuss peace. At this meeting Ptolemy's demands proved to be more than Antigonos was prepared to agree to, however, so it proved fruitless (Diod. XIX 64,8).

Back in Greece, Antigonos's friend Aristodemos won a diplomatic success at the autumn (313) assembly of the Aitolian League, persuading the Aitolians to support Antigonos. He then crossed back to the Peloponnesos with his mercenaries and fought Alexandros at Kyllene, liberated the Achaian cities of Patrai and Aigion from Kassandros's garrisons, and returned to Aitolia. His troops at Aigion helped the city of Dymai to eject its garrison, despite a bloody intervention by Alexandros (Diod. XIX 66,1–6), who was shortly thereafter assassinated near Sikyon (Diod. XIX 67,1–2). When Kassandros heard of Aristodemos's success with the Aitolians, he came

45. Dioskourides' task was to guarantee the safety of the allies and win over the islands that had not yet entered the alliance (Diod. XIX 62,9), implying that some of the Aegean islands were already allies of Antigonos; these must surely have been the islands of the eastern Aegean, such as Rhodes (cf. Diod. XIX 58,5; 61,5; and 62,7), Samos (see Habicht, *AM* 72 [1957]:169–70 and 183–86 for two inscriptions recording friendly relations between Antigonos and Samos predating 306), and Chios (see, e.g., Dunst, *Klio* 37 [1959]:63–68). See further pp. 207–25 below on these islands and on Lemnos and Imbros. Athenian control over Delos is last attested in summer 314 (see Tréheux, "Dernières Années de Delos"), whereafter Delos evidently revolted from Athens. Some recent discussions date this revolt and Dioskourides' setting up of the island league in the second half of 314 (thus, e.g., Merker, *Historia* 19 [1970]:141–60); but see now Buraselis, *Das hellenistische Makedonien*, pp. 41–43, 60–67. Buraselis very plausibly suggests (pp. 41–42) that the liberation of Delos from Athens could have been arranged by the Hellespontine fleets of Themison and Dioskourides in 314 (cf. Diod. XIX 62,7), whereas the foundation of the island league would more likely have been owing to Dioskourides' mission in 313 (Diod. XIX 62,9).

south himself, persuaded the Akarnanians to ally with him, and campaigned successfully along the Adriatic coast. With his western border thus greatly strengthened, he returned to Macedon and decided, despite the fact that the year must by now have been far advanced, to send an army to the aid of his ally Asandros (Diod. XIX 67,3–7; 68,2). Evidently the 10,000 mercenaries of Myrmidon had failed against Polemaios, who seems to have reduced Asandros to sore straits. Besides sending an army to Karia, Kassandros also wrote to the *phrourarchos* Dionysios and Demetrios of Phaleron in Athens, ordering them to send a fleet of twenty ships to try to recapture Lemnos, possibly with the intention of distracting Antigonos's admiral Dioskourides from interfering with the sailing of the Karian expedition.[46] The squadron was duly sent out under the command of an officer named Aristoteles, who effected a junction with Seleukos. Together they ravaged the island, but when Seleukos for some reason sailed away to Kos, Dioskourides swooped down with Antigonos's fleet and captured most of Aristoteles' ships (Diod. XIX 68,3–4).

In the meantime, Kassandros's Karian expedition, under the command of Prepelaos, succeeded in reaching Karia, escorted by a fleet of thirty-six ships from Pydna in Macedon.[47] Having joined up there with Asandros, Prepelaos discussed with the satrap how to conduct the campaign. They decided to try a surprise attack on Polemaios's troops, and selected a force of 8,000 foot and 200 horse, which they sent out to this end under the general Eupolemos, apparently one of Prepelaos's lieutenants.[48] Eupolemos marched with his army to a place called Kaprima, evidently in northern Karia, and encamped there while preparing his surprise attack. However, some deserters from Eupolemos's force caused his presence and plans to become

46. Such, at least, seems to me to be the most plausible reason why Kassandros should have ordered the Athenians to undertake this expedition at this particular time, so late in the year.

47. For these Pydnaian ships, see Diod. XIX 69,2–3 and cf. Hauben, *AncSoc* 9 (1978):47–54, rejecting attempts to emend them away.

48. From Diod. XIX 68,5: "Asandros and Prepelaos commanded the force which Kassandros had sent to Asia," it might be supposed that Asandros was in Macedon late in 313 and sailed from there with Prepelaos, but this is without doubt a false impression created by Diodoros's abbreviation of his source, for Asandros could hardly have left Karia while it was under heavy attack by Polemaios. However, once Prepelaos and his expedition reached Karia, Asandros's territory, he would naturally have deferred to Asandros's authority. The Eupolemos mentioned here was clearly an officer of Kassandros (see Diod. XIX 68,7; and cf. Buraselis, *Das hellenistische Makedonien*, p. 10), but he is a controversial figure on whom see now Billows, "Anatolian Dynasts: The Case of the Macedonian Eupolemos in Karia."

known. Polemaios hastily gathered 8,300 foot soldiers and 600 cavalry from the nearest camps and marched against Eupolemos, reaching his fortified camp in the middle of the night. An immediate attack on the sleeping and unwary enemy enabled Polemaios to capture the entire force with ease, including Eupolemos (Diod. XIX 68,5–7)

Polemaios evidently sent an immediate report on all of this to Antigonos, who now decided to march into Asia Minor himself. To guard against a possible incursion into Syria by Ptolemy, Antigonos left his son Demetrios with a large army and four experienced advisers, who had all served under Alexander: Peithon, son of Agenor, who had been called specially from his Babylonian satrapy; Nearchos the Cretan; Philippos, probably a former officer of Eumenes, who had been with Antigonos since Gabiene; and Andronikos of Olynthos, who appears to have been the general of the garrison at Tyre (Diod. XIX 69,1; see app. 3, nos. 9, 77, 88, and 93 for details on the careers of these four advisers). Antigonos himself marched into Kilikia with the main army and, after being prevented initially from crossing the Taurus by the winter snows, found a pass that was still open and marched over to Phrygia, where he quartered his army near Kelainai for the winter. He also ordered his admiral Medeios of Larissa to sail up from Phoenicia with a fleet, presumably of new ships from the Phoenician shipyards.[49] Medeios happened to fall in on his way with the thirty-six Pydnaian ships of Kassandros and captured them all (Diod. XIX 69,2–3); this completed the disaster of Kassandros's Karian expedition.

These reverses, and the presence of Antigonos with a great army in Phrygia, apparently convinced Asandros that further resistance would be futile and caused him to negotiate with Antigonos. An agreement was reached whereby Asandros was to hand over all of his soldiers to Antigonos, leave the Greek cities on his coast free and autonomous, and continue to govern Karia as a subordinate and ally of Antigonos. Prepelaos was presumably permitted to return to Macedon with the remnants of his force, and also it seems with Eupolemos, who is shortly afterwards found serving Kassandros in Boiotia (Diod. XIX 77,6). Asandros handed over his brother Agathon as hostage for his good faith in this agreement, but a few days later he had second thoughts and, arranging for his brother to escape from Antigonos's custody, sent urgent messages to Ptolemy and

49. This must be supposed to be the case, as Dioskourides is attested as campaigning with the main fleet at Lemnos at about this time (Diod. XIX 68,3–4).

Seleukos begging for help (Diod. XIX 64,1–2). Antigonos was understandably enraged at this and quickly prepared a devastating blow that removed Asandros from the political scene. Calling out his troops from their winter quarters, probably about the end of January 312, Antigonos captured all of Karia in the space of a few weeks in a brilliant demonstration of the use of superior force and exterior lines (see map 4). His forces were divided into three or four columns: the first, under his former enemy Dokimos,[50] was dispatched down the Maiandros valley to liberate the great Greek city of Miletos, with the aid of the fleet under Medeios; the second column consisted of Polemaios's army, and was sent through central Karia from east to west, reaching the coast at Iasos; another force may have been sent under Peukestas to Theangela (see app. 3, no. 90); and Antigonos himself led the main column from Tralleis in northern Karia, which he besieged and captured, in a great north-south march through central Karia and down to the southern Karian coast at Kaunos, whither he summoned Medeios and the fleet to aid in capturing the city (Diod. XIX 64,3–6).[51]

Having secured control over Karia, Antigonos turned his thoughts to retaliation against Kassandros, despatching his nephew Telesphoros with a fleet of fifty ships and a sizeable body of troops to the Peloponnesos. There Telesphoros rapidly succeeded in expelling all enemy garrisons except those maintained by Alexandros's widow, Kratesipolis, in Sikyon and Korinth (Diod. XIX 64,1–2). In this same spring a revolt against Lysimachos was under way in the Greek cities of the northwestern Black Sea coast. The leading role was played by Kallatis, but Istria and Odessos also joined. The latter two were quickly recaptured by Lysimachos, who had marched north with a large army; while he was besieging Kallatis, however, Antigonos sent a fleet under Lykon and an army under Pausanias to the aid of this city, and also persuaded the Thracian dynast Seuthes to rebel against

50. On this man, see app. 3, no. 35.

51. The Milesian *stephanēphoroi* list records the liberation of Miletos by Antigonos in the year of the *stephanēphoros* Hippomachos, that is, March 313 to February (or early March) 312 (see Rehm, *Milet,* 1, no. 123, and cf. *Syll,* no. 322). Since it is clear that Antigonos's campaign in Karia took place in the winter of 313/12, the liberation of Miletos should be dated to early or middle February 312. Hence the whole Karian campaign evidently took place early in the year 312. Antigonos's strategy can be easily reconstructed from Diodoros's narrative, brief and lacking in detail as it is, for the facts pretty much speak for themselves: the liberation of Miletos by Dokimos and Medeios, the liberation of Iasos by Polemaios (for which cf. also Blümel, *I. Iasos,* 1, no. 2), Peukestas's presence at Theangela, and Antigonos's activity first at Tralleis and then Kaunos indicate a sophisticated plan along the lines I have indicated.

Lysimachos. News of this quickly reached Lysimachos, who left a body of troops to continue the siege of Kallatis, and himself marched south to intercept Pausanias. Obliged to do battle with Seuthes at a pass through the Haimos Mountains, he won a bloody victory, and subsequently cornered and captured Pausanias and his troops. He killed Pausanias and enrolled most of the soldiers in his own army, though he allowed Antigonos to ransom some of them (Diod. XIX 73,1–10). Antigonos's fleet under Lykon presumably reached Kallatis safely and aided the city; the siege there continued for several years (still on in 310: Diod. XX 25,1) and the outcome is not recorded, though doubtless Lysimachos eventually won.

Just after Antigonos had concluded his campaign in Karia, envoys arrived in his camp from Aitolia to confirm their alliance with him as negotiated by Aristodemos the previous autumn, and with them came envoys from Boiotia, also to conclude an alliance, perhaps being themselves allied with the Aitolians.[52] About this time Antigonos and Kassandros met at the Hellespont to discuss terms for peace, but were unable to come to any agreement (Diod. XIX 64,6; *OGIS,* no. 5, lines 5–9). In thus negotiating separately with one of his enemies for the second time (cf. the earlier meeting with Ptolemy at Ekregma), it is clear that Antigonos was pursuing his strategy of trying to split the enemy coalition, but had not yet caused any of them enough loss to succeed.

Kassandros now decided to launch a new assault against Antigonos's allies in Greece. He began by sailing against the city of Oreos on Euboia with 30 ships and besieging it. Aid for the city soon appeared in the form of Telesphoros from the Peloponnesos with 20 ships and 1,000 soldiers, and the admiral Medeios with 100 ships from Asia. These broke Kassandros's blockade, using fire against his ships and burning four of them, the rest narrowly escaping. Medeios, however, was summoned back to Asia,[53] while reinforcements came

52. The order of events in the early part of 312 as I have given it here differs considerably from that given by Diodoros in XIX 73–75; the reason for this change is that the Milesian *stephanēphoroi* list proves Antigonos's Karian campaign to have occurred at the very beginning of 312 (see n. 51 above), so that Diod. XIX 75 belongs chronologically before XIX 74, and indeed before much of the information in XIX 73. In recounting the events at Kallatis, which began in 313, but went on into 312 and beyond, Diodoros got ahead of himself chronologically, and the events recounted in XIX 74–75 thus appear out of sequence.

53. This is not directly stated in the sources but is clear from two facts: Kassandros, after receiving reinforcements from Athens, was able to defeat the forces besieging him, and the Athenians at this date cannot possibly have sent him a large enough fleet to be able to take on the combined fleets of Telesphoros and Medeios (120 ships); moreover, at Diod. XIX 77,2,

to Kassandros from Athens under Thymochares the Sphettian, enabling Kassandros to sail out and defeat Telesphoros's squadron, sinking one ship and capturing three (Diod. XIX 64,6–8, and cf. *IG* II[2] 682 [= *Syll.* no. 409], lines 14–18). But Medeios had been summoned to Asia only to receive reinforcements and act as escort to a major new force which Antigonos had prepared to settle matters finally in Greece. Its leader was Polemaios, Antigonos's nephew and right-hand man, who was made commander in chief of all Antigonos's forces and affairs in Greece and given an army of 5,000 foot and 500 horse and a fleet of 150 sail under Medeios. With this force Polemaios sailed into the Boiotian harbor of Bathys on the Euripos, where he was joined by 2,200 foot and 1,300 horse from the Boiotian League, which was allied with Antigonos (Diod. XIX 77,2–4).

Polemaios's arrival in Greece probably occurred about the middle of the summer 312. He summoned the Antigonid forces from Oreos and concentrated his army at Salganeus on the Euripos, which he fortified and from where he hoped to be able to capture Chalkis, Kassandros's only major stronghold in Euboia.[54] This shrewd move was sufficient to cause Kassandros to abandon the siege of Oreos and hurry to Chalkis, concentrating his forces there against Polemaios. Antigonos had a counter to this, however: he recalled Medeios and the fleet to Asia and marched with his army to the Hellespontine region as if to cross into Europe and invade Macedon. When Kassandros learned of this, he left his brother Pleistarchos in command of Chalkis and crossed to the mainland. There he secured Oropos and Thebes, left his general Eupolemos in charge, and then returned hurriedly to Macedon (Diod. XIX 77,4–6). Whether Antigonos really meant to cross to Europe that year seems doubtful; with full control of the sea, he certainly could have if he had wished to, but the season was by now rather late for such a major operation. At any rate, when Antigonos reached the Propontis, he negotiated with Byzantion for an alliance, but this city, at the urging of Lysimachos, preferred to remain neutral. An alliance with Byzantion would have

Medeios is back in Asia and is sent to Greece again, this time with 150 ships, under the overall command of Polemaios. This is an instance of Diodoros leaving out important information due to extreme abbreviation of his source.

54. Bakhuizen, *Salganeus*, pp. 104–30, argues that the impressive remains of fortifications visible at Salganeus must have been constructed by Polemaios (Diod. XIX 77,4), but this is disputed by Picard, *Chalcis*, p. 256, showing that these fortifications cannot be those built by Polemaios, since they were clearly intended for operations against Boiotia, whereas Polemaios's enemy was in Chalkis.

given Antigonos a secure base of operations in Europe; without it Antigonos gave up any idea of crossing that year, and turned his thoughts instead to establishing winter quarters for his army (Diod. XIX 77,6–7).

Kassandros's absence from Greece had the effect Antigonos had hoped for: Polemaios was able to capture Chalkis without difficulty. He removed Kassandros's garrison, but did not install one of his own in its place, thus emphasizing Antigonos's policy that the Greek cities should be autonomous and ungarrisoned. Eretria and Karystos joined Antigonos's alliance at this time. Polemaios crossed back to Boiotia and attacked Kassandros's garrison in Oropos, capturing it and handing the city back to the Boiotian League. Certain elements in Athens had for some time been sending secret messages to Antigonos asking him to liberate the city, and Polemaios now invaded Attica. This emboldened the anti-Kassandros faction to come out in the open. They forced Kassandros's *epimelētēs* to negotiate a truce with Polemaios and send ambassadors to Antigonos to discuss an alliance.[55] Polemaios, meanwhile, returned to Boiotia and attacked Kassandros's garrison in the Kadmea at Thebes, capturing it and so freeing Thebes of its garrison. He then proceeded into Phokis, drove out Kassandros's garrisons in that region, and moved thence into Opuntian Lokris, where he initiated a siege of Opous (Diod. XIX 78,2–5). The outcome is not recorded, but doubtless the city capitulated, and Polemaios must have gone into winter quarters in central Greece, having cleared out all Kassandros's garrisons south of Thermopylai except that at Mounychia in Attica.

While these events were transpiring in Asia Minor and Greece, the year 312 saw action on Antigonos's southern front too. As noted, he had left his son Demetrios in Syria with a large army and several senior advisers to counter any possible attack by Ptolemy and Seleukos (Diod. XIX 69,1).[56] Early in the summer Ptolemy had to deal with a revolt against his authority in Kyrene. When this had been settled, he traveled with a great force to Cyprus, where some of the

55. Nothing further is heard of this embassy: the negotiations evidently came to naught.

56. Any account of the campaigns surrounding the battle of Gaza must necessarily rely on Diod. XIX 79–93, by far the most detailed and reliable of our sources. Many other sources mention the battle of Gaza—Plut. *Dem.* 5,1–6,3; Appian *Syr.* 54; Paus. I 6,5; Josephus *Contra Apionem* I 184–85; Justin XV 1,6–9; Marm. Par. (*FGrH*, no. 239b), sec. 16—but none adds much reliable information to Diodoros's account, though they do perpetuate various errors: for example, Plutarch's statement (*Dem.* 5,2) that Antigonos *sent* Demetrios to Syria from Phrygia on receiving news of Ptolemy's raid on Cyprus and Syria, and Appian's statement (*Syr.* 54) that Seleukos set out for Babylon *immediately* after the battle of Gaza, both convincingly refuted by Diodoros's more detailed account.

kings were still, or again, intriguing with Antigonos. Ptolemy now killed or arrested the rulers of Kition, Lapethos, Keryneia, and Marion as being friendly towards Antigonos and/or hostile to himself, and established his friend Nikokreon of Salamis firmly as general over Cyprus (Diod. XIX 79,1–5). Next he raided Antigonos's territories, sacking Poseideion and Potamoi Karōn in Syria and Mallos in Kilikia, thereby giving his troops their fill of plunder and rapine, and then sailed back to Egypt (Diod. XIX 79,6–7; 80,3).

Demetrios was encamped with his army in southern Palestine to counter any major land invasion. When news arrived of Ptolemy's raid on northern Syria, Demetrios showed his inexperience by rushing headlong to the scene of this raid with the more mobile part of his army, arriving too late and having to return south again immediately with nothing achieved (Diod. XIX 80,1–2). Demetrios then concluded that Ptolemy would not invade any more that year and sent his men into winter quarters. And indeed it seems likely that Ptolemy would have rested content with his actions in Cyprus and Kilikia had it not been for the promptings of Seleukos to adopt a bolder policy.[57] At Seleukos's urging, however, Ptolemy decided to mount an invasion of Palestine despite the lateness of the season, and to this end began to bring together a large army (Diod. XIX 80,3).

About the end of the year 312 Ptolemy marched from Egypt via Pelousion along the northern edge of the Sinai Peninsula with an army of 18,000 infantry and 4,000 cavalry. The army comprised contingents of Macedonians and mercenaries—numbers not specified—and a *plēthos* (mass) of Egyptians, many of whom were employed only as porters, though others were soldiers (Diod. XIX 80,4). Receiving timely intelligence of Ptolemy's march, Demetrios recalled his troops from their winter quarters and concentrated them at Gaza. His army consisted of 11,000 heavy infantry, some 2,000–3,000 light infantry, 4,400 cavalry, and forty-three elephants, so the two armies appear to have been fairly evenly matched.[58] Demetrios's advisers, concerned at his inexperience compared to Ptolemy and

57. For the motivating role played by Seleukos in getting Ptolemy to adopt offensive plans, and his importance in helping to carry these plans out, see Seibert, *Ptolemaios I,* pp. 77–79, 144–45, 170; Mehl, *Seleukos Nikator,* 1:82–89. For the chronology adopted here, see Errington and Hauben, cited in n. 67 below.

58. Diodoros lists Demetrios's army twice (XIX 69,1 and 82,2–4), with major differences, doubtless because of dispositions made by Demetrios during the year 312. Detailed modern accounts of the battle may be found in *Antike Schlachtfelder,* ed. Kromayer and Veith, 4:435–46, and Seibert *Ptolemaios I,* pp. 164–75; also now Devine, *AClass* 27 (1984):31–40. Kromayer and Veith argue wrongly that the 18,000 men of Ptolemy were all heavy infantry; see Seibert's arguments at pp. 166–67.

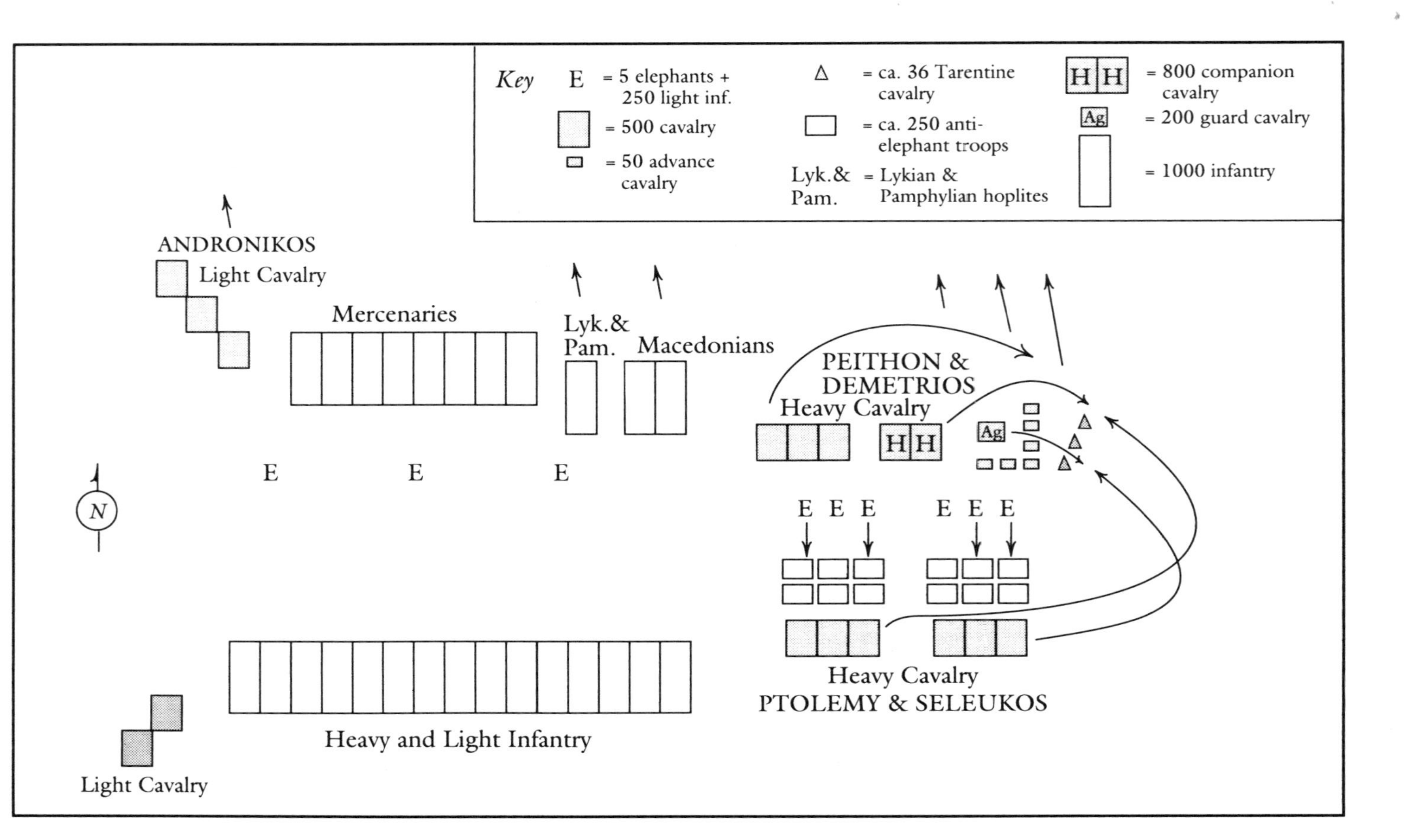

Figure 5. The Battle of Gaza

Seleukos, urged him to send for Antigonos and avoid battle, but Demetrios was determined to fight (Diod. XIX 81,1). In his co-commander Peithon and in Nearchos, at least, he had generals of comparable experience to that of Ptolemy and Seleukos, while his other important generals, Philippos and Andronikos, were also veterans of Alexander's campaigns (Diod. XIX 69,1; cf. app. 3, nos. 9, 77, 88, and 93).

The battle plan evolved by Demetrios and Peithon distinctly resembled that of Antigonos at Paraitakene and Gabiene. A weak right wing under Andronikos was to hang back and avoid closing with the enemy, while the infantry were to advance behind a skirmishing screen of elephants and light infantry, and the battle was to be decided by a strong left wing of 2,900 cavalry under Demetrios and Peithon, behind a strong screen of thirty elephants and 1,500 light infantry (see fig. 5). This, if unoriginal, was a sound battle plan, which had every chance of producing a successful outcome had it not been for the excessive confidence placed in the elephants—Ptolemy being without any of these beasts. As a screen from behind which to charge with one's cavalry, elephants had proved useful at Paraitakene and Gabiene, and Seleukos was to prove their effectiveness as an anti-cavalry screen at Ipsos in 301; but as an attacking force in themselves, elephants were effective in ancient warfare only against enemies who had not encountered them before and were overawed by their size and strength. Seleukos and Ptolemy had encountered elephants before.[59] They prepared a special troop of men equipped with iron spikes linked with chains to be spread out in the path of the elephants' charge, thus rendering them unable to proceed because of the tenderness of their feet. Their battle plan was based on Demetrios's battle array: against Demetrios's strong left wing, they opposed their right wing consisting of 3,000 heavy cavalry, which they commanded themselves, with the anti-elephant troop in front together with a large body of archers and javelin men, who had orders to concentrate their fire on the elephants and their mahouts. Their phalanx was stationed drawn back, with the remaining 1,000 cavalry withdrawn on the left (Diod. XIX 83,1–3).

The fighting essentially consisted of a fierce, but confused and indecisive, cavalry scrimmage between the heavy cavalry forces of

59. They had both come up against elephants in India with Alexander, especially Seleukos, who had commanded part of Alexander's infantry against the 200 elephants of Poros at the battle of the Hydaspes (see, e.g., Tarn, *HMND*, pp. 93–94). On the elephants in the battle of Gaza, see Scullard, *The Elephant in the Greek and Roman World*, pp. 95–97.

Demetrios's left and Ptolemy's right, and a charge by Demetrios's elephants that was intended to decide the battle. It did. The spikes arrayed by Ptolemy's anti-elephant corps stopped the beasts in their tracks, whereupon his archers and javelineers shot down the mahouts and captured the elephants themselves. This disaster shattered the morale of Demetrios's cavalry, which turned to panic-stricken flight (Diod. XIX 83,3–84,5). Demetrios attempted for a while to rally his cavalry, but when he found that their flight could not be checked, he too left the field of battle. As far as Gaza the flight remained reasonably ordered, but there wild confusion resulted as the troops tried to rescue their baggage, so that Ptolemy's pursuing forces were able to capture the city with ease. Demetrios himself continued straight on to Azotos, some 35 miles (270 stades) north of Gaza, which he reached about midnight. From there he sent a herald to treat concerning the burial of his dead, who numbered about 500, mostly cavalry (Diod. XIX 84,5–85,3).[60] Andronikos and the right-wing cavalry escaped, and Andronikos went to Tyre to hold it against Ptolemy (Diod. XIX 86,1–2). Since Diodoros names Peithon and a certain Boiotos, otherwise unknown, as the most distinguished of Demetrios's dead, Nearchos and Philippos must also have escaped. Of the phalanx, which never really came to grips with the enemy, some discarded their heavy equipment and escaped from the field of battle, but about 8,000 surrendered to Ptolemy. He magnanimously returned Demetrios's personal baggage and attendants to him (having presumably captured these in Gaza) and permitted him to recover and bury his dead; his own dead he gave a magnificent funeral; the 8,000 captives he sent to Egypt to be settled there as colonists (Diod. XIX 85,2–4).

Demetrios now retreated to Tripolis in northern Phoenicia, where he rallied the remnants of his army (with 500 dead and rather more than 8,000 captured, some 8,000–9,000 remain unaccounted for) and summoned reinforcements from the garrisons of upper Syria and from Kilikia; he also wrote to Antigonos reporting what had happened and urging him to send help. Meanwhile Ptolemy and Seleukos advanced through southern Palestine, capturing the cities one by one. Ake, Joppa, Samaria, and Sidon were all captured with ease, but at Tyre they met with determined resistance from Andronikos (Diod. XIX 84,4–86,1, and cf. 94,7). This was most important,

60. Plut. *Dem.* 5,2 gives Demetrios's dead as 5,000, a simple error (*pentakischiliōn* for *pentakosiōn*): see Seibert, *Ptolemaios I*, pp. 164–75.

for it gave Demetrios more time to organize the defense of upper Syria. Ptolemy's blandishments and offers of bribes had no effect on the loyal Andronikos, but eventually his soldiers mutinied and drove him out, the city and Andronikos thus falling into Ptolemy's hands (see further app. 3, no. 9). At this time, presumably about the end of January 311, Seleukos asked Ptolemy to give him a force with which to attempt to reach Babylonia and recover his satrapy (Diod. XIX 86,1–5). Ptolemy agreed, and sent Seleukos off with a force of either 800 foot and 200 horse (Diod. XIX 90,1), or 1,000 foot and 300 horse (Appian *Syr.* 54). This appears at first sight a hare-brained venture, but when one considers that Seleukos was marching in the dead of winter through regions denuded of their enemy garrisons, against a satrapy whose satrap (Peithon) was dead, the risk seems a good deal less.[61]

At any rate, Seleukos marched off with his tiny army, and Ptolemy gave his attention to further exploiting his victory. While he presumably occupied himself with organizing his conquests in southern Palestine, he sent his general Killes with a major portion of the army to drive Demetrios out of northern Phoenicia. Killes, however, fatally underestimated Demetrios, who had by now built up quite a respectable army again. When he heard from his scouts that Killes and his army were approaching and had encamped rather carelessly at a place called Myous, Demetrios made a forced night march with his army and reached the enemy camp around dawn. His attack took Killes and his men completely by surprise, so that he was able to capture the camp and general, and most of his army with hardly a blow being struck (Diod. XIX 93,1–2; Plut. *Dem.* 6,1–2). His prisoners came to some 7,000 men according to Plutarch, thus making up for most of his losses at Gaza, and after consulting with Antigonos, he reciprocated Ptolemy's magnanimity after Gaza by sending back to him Killes and his staff with splendid gifts (Plut. *Dem.* 6,2–3). Demetrios then prudently encamped with his army in a strong position surrounded by marshes, until Antigonos could join him. The latter came down to Syria with a great army early in 311, as soon as the Taurus passes were clear of snow (Diod. XIX 93,3–4).

When Ptolemy heard that Antigonos had joined Demetrios with his army, he called a *synedrion* of his friends to discuss their best course

61. An account of Seleukos's actions after leaving Tyre follows at the beginning of chap. 4 below.

of action, and the unanimous advice opposed risking a battle against a general of Antigonos's caliber with a greatly superior army. Accordingly Ptolemy evacuated Palestine, destroying the forts at Ake, Samaria, Joppa, and Gaza, and returned to Egypt determined to conduct his defense, if necessary, from behind the Pelousiac branch of the Nile (Diod. XIX 93,5–7). Antigonos was thus able to reoccupy Phoenicia and Koile Syria in peace, but did not at once venture to attack Ptolemy in Egypt, being no doubt daunted by the memory of how Perdikkas had fared in 320. Instead, he began operations against the Nabataian Arabs, whose capital was at Petra in what is now southwestern Jordan.[62] This was presumably intended to prepare for an invasion of Egypt, for to an army marching across the northern Sinai, the Nabataians could be either valuable allies and a source of supplies or exceedingly dangerous foes upon a wide-open flank; but it is possible that an interest in the trade route in incense from the Red Sea lands also played a part in Antigonos's decision to subjugate the Nabataians, who were the middlemen in this trade.[63]

Antigonos selected one of his friends named Athenaios (app. 3, no. 22) and sent him with 4,000 light infantry and 600 cavalry to make a raid on Petra to carry off hostages and booty, well knowing that only by holding their families and possessions hostage could he easily subdue the Nabataians, as they would otherwise simply melt away into the desert with their families and flocks and lead him a merry dance trying to deal with them (Diod. XIX 94,1–95,1). Athenaios's surprise attack was initially successful, but subsequent carelessness permitted the Nabataians to take him by surprise in turn and destroy his force, only about 50 horsemen escaping (Diod. XIX 95,2–5).

When the Nabataians wrote to Antigonos complaining of this attack, he agreed with their complaints and criticized Athenaios as having carried out an entirely unauthorized attack, hoping to lull them thus into a false sense of security. But after maintaining friendly relations with the Nabataians for a while, he fitted out another expedition, consisting of 4,000 light infantry and 4,000 cavalry, and sent Demetrios with it to chastise them. Demetrios, taking supplies

62. See F. Abel, *Rev. Biblique* 46 (1937):373–91, and A. Negev, *Palestine Exploration Quarterly* 8/9 (1976/77):125–33, for accounts of the Nabataians and Antigonos's expeditions against them and for the identification of Diodoros's *τινος Πέτρας* (XIX 95,1 et al.) with Petra in southwestern Jordan. Cf. also most recently Bowersock, *Roman Arabia*, pp. 12–16, and Browning, *Petra*, pp. 33–35.

63. For Antigonos's interest in the frankincense trade from Arabia, see Theophrastos *Hist. plant.* IX 4,8 and Pliny *NH* XII 56; and cf. Browning, *Petra*, pp. 33–35.

for many days, marched to Petra through the desert, but the Nabataians were on the alert, and when he reached Petra he found that they had dispersed with their forces and flocks, leaving only a sizeable garrison to guard their property in the virtually unassailable stronghold. After making an unsuccessful attack, Demetrios was therefore easily persuaded by the Nabataians to discuss terms and, being given hostages and gifts by them (including 700 camels according to Plutarch, *Dem.* 7,1), he made peace with them and marched away (Diod. XIX 96,1–98,1). On his way back to Antigonos, he marched by the Dead Sea and observed the gathering there of asphalt, a product much in demand in Egypt for its use in embalming. When Antigonos heard Demetrios's report, he accepted the treaty with the Nabataians somewhat grudgingly, but was interested to hear of the asphalt production at the Dead Sea. Since developments in Europe now demanded his attention, he left Hieronymos of Kardia in charge of Palestine, with orders to take over the asphalt sources at the Dead Sea and raise revenue therefrom, and turned to more important matters (Diod. XIX 100,1–2).[64]

In the winter of 312/11 Antigonos's nephew Telesphoros, who had been subordinated to Antigonos's other nephew Polemaios when the latter was made commander in chief of all Antigonos's forces in Greece, decided to rebel as a result, considering this subordination to be insulting. Though he did some initial damage to Antigonos's position (see app. 3, no. 111), Polemaios soon restored the situation and persuaded Telesphoros to give up his schemes (Diod. XIX 87,1–3). Telesphoros was apparently forgiven by Antigonos, for he went in the entourage of Demetrios to Athens in 307/6 (Diogenes Laertios V 79).

Polemaios was now in control of all Greece south of Thermopylai except Korinth and Sikyon (still held by Polyperchon), and Athens (where Kassandros's nominees were still in power), and was allied with the Aitolians in addition. Kassandros recognized that he was beaten for the time being and opened negotiations with Polemaios with a view to establishing a truce and bringing the war to an end. Antigonos's friend Aristodemos, who was still in Greece as a subordinate of Polemaios, was sent to Asia about mid 311 to confer with Antigonos on these talks, bringing with him Kassandros's friend Prepelaos, who was acting as plenipotentiary of both Kassandros and

---

64. For Hieronymos's position and activities, see app. 3, no. 51.

Lysimachos (*OGIS,* no. 5, lines 9–29).[65] Agreement was speedily reached on the basis of acceptance of the status quo and an express affirmation of the principle of autonomy for the Greeks, as enunciated by Antigonos's Tyre proclamation of 314. Kassandros and Lysimachos thus abandoned their ally Ptolemy, who was naturally very worried at the prospect of having to fight on against Antigonos alone when he heard of this peace agreement. He therefore quickly sent envoys to Antigonos seeking to be included in the peace. Antigonos readily agreed, and sent a diplomatic mission headed by Aristodemos, with Aischylos and Hegesias as his colleagues, to make peace with Ptolemy too (*OGIS,* no. 5, lines 30–53).

Such is Antigonos's own account of how this peace came about, preserved in his letter circulated to the Greek cities, of which the example sent to Skepsis survives. Diodoros preserves only a brief account of the terms of the peace as they were finally settled and agreed upon in the latter half of 311 (XIX 105,1). It was specified that until the coming of age of Alexandros IV, the empire was to be ruled by the four dynasts who were signatories to the peace, the division of powers being the following: Kassandros was, like his father Antipatros, to be *stratēgos* of Europe; Lysimachos was to rule over Thrace, and Ptolemy over Egypt and the adjacent cities of Libya and Arabia; and Antigonos was to hold sway over all of Asia. The Greek cities were to be autonomous. Excluded from direct participation in the peace were Polyperchon and Seleukos; they were implicitly placed under the authority of Kassandros and Antigonos respectively, who were evidently given a free hand to deal with them more or less as they saw fit.[66]

By this peace treaty Antigonos attained the zenith of his power.

---

65. *OGIS,* no. 5, a letter from Antigonos to the people of Skepsis, details the negotiations preceding the conclusion of peace in 311 and his efforts to have the principle of Greek autonomy enshrined in that peace. Though one must beware of Antigonos's desire to present himself and his actions in the best possible light in this letter (thus the strong insistence on his efforts on behalf of Greek freedom throughout), there is no reason to doubt that the facts presented here by Antigonos are essentially true. On the identification of Aristodemos and Ptolemaios, named as arranging this peace, as Antigonos's diplomat and nephew of those names, see app. 3, nos. 16 and 100.

66. Some modern scholars have held that Seleukos must have been included in the peace because Ptolemy and the other dynasts could not have just let him drop: thus, for example, Beloch, *GG,* 4.1:133–34; Costanzi, *AUT,* n.s., 1, no. 4 (1916):1–20; and others. Against this view, which seems to me utterly untenable, based as it is on purely subjective grounds of probability, see, for example, Neppi Modona, *Athenaeum* 11 (1933):3–9; R. H. Simpson, *JHS* 74 (1954):25–31; Cloché, *CRAI* (1957):134–39.

His strategy of creating trouble for each of the enemy dynasts in his own sphere of influence had ultimately proved too much for them and had broken their coalition. Of the demands placed before Antigonos at the beginning of 314, not one was achieved in the peace that concluded the Third Diadoch War: Antigonos was recognized as ruler of all Asia and retained possession of the treasures he had accumulated. The claim Antigonos had made to the regency of the empire was of course given up under the terms of the peace, which looks at first sight like a setback. This is more apparent than real, however. The claim was made as part of the proclamation of Tyre, which I have shown above to have been a propaganda counterblast to the harsh demands of the allied dynasts. Antigonos had not desired war with them, but had tried to persuade them to accept his position as ruler of Asia (Diod. XIX 56,4). This he had now achieved, and that it had been his real aim throughout the war is indicated by the peace negotiations he had undertaken in mid 313 with Ptolemy at Ekregma (Diod. XIX 64,8), and in early 312 with Kassandros near the Hellespont (Diod. XIX 75,6; *OGIS,* no. 5, lines 1–10). In both cases Antigonos seems to have initiated the talks, and in both cases they seem to have been broken off due to the demands made by the other party. Evidently Ptolemy and Kassandros were then not yet willing to break their coalition and retract the demands of 314; but Antigonos did ultimately force them to take these steps, and the claim to the regency was promptly dropped when this happened. This was then, it seems, essentially a concession Antigonos could make without giving up any of his real war aims.

In several respects, indeed, Antigonos had made substantial gains. He had conquered Karia and brought the dynasts of the northern Anatolian coast—Dionysios and Zipoites—into his alliance system, thus rounding off his control of Asia Minor. Kassandros and Lysimachos had not only been forced to give up their territorial and monetary demands: they had had to confirm the autonomy of the Greeks proclaimed by Antigonos at Tyre, while Antigonos's alliances with many of the Greek states (e.g., the League of the Islanders, the Aitolians, the Boiotians, and the Euboian cities) gave him a strong foothold in Greece, which was protected by his commander Polemaios with his army, though nominal supervision of Greece reverted to Kassandros as general of Europe. By inducing Kassandros and Lysimachos to make a separate peace, moreover, Antigonos had forced Ptolemy into a corner where he had little choice but to accept his loss of Syria and Palestine to Antigonos and to throw Seleukos to the wolves. This peace was, then, a triumph for the now 71-year-old Antigonos.[67]

Despite the fact that Antigonos's rule over Asia was now recognized by the western dynasts, however, certain problems remained. Antigonos's power, indeed the power of all the dynasts, was temporary, exercised during the minority of Alexandros IV, who was now growing up. It remained to be seen whether and how Antigonos could free his power from Argead suzerainty and pass it on to his sons. Moreover, there was one leader, Seleukos, who had not recognized Antigonos's authority over Asia; and though Seleukos seemed a negligible figure in 311, events were already occurring in inner Asia that proved he was not.

67. This interpretation rests on a chronology of Seleukos's activities in the east that is new: it results from the demonstration of Errington (*Hermes* 105 [1977]:478–504), Hauben (*AJPh* 94 [1973]:256–67), and others that the battle of Gaza occurred in the winter of 312/11. Seleukos therefore only returned to Babylon in spring 311, and his campaigns to recover Babylonia and defeat Antigonos's overseer of the upper satrapies occurred during summer and autumn of 311 and were unknown in the west when the Peace of the Dynasts was concluded.

4

Antigonos's Assumption of the Kingship

The Peace of the Dynasts in late summer of 311 basically parceled out the Macedonian Empire between the four dynasts who signed it: Antigonos, Kassandros, Ptolemy, and Lysimachos, with Antigonos getting the lion's share. In spite of its essential character as a *division* of the empire, however, it still maintained the idea of a unified empire ruled by the legitimate Argead king, Alexandros IV, thereby reminding the world of this youth's existence. He was now twelve years old, and had for the past five years been living in seclusion at Amphipolis under close guard by officers of Kassandros, ostensibly for his own protection. He constituted a major problem for all of the dynasts, who had spent twelve years of toil and danger establishing themselves in power over various parts of the empire, but were faced with the likelihood of being required to relinquish their power in a few years when Alexandros grew up and assumed his prerogatives as ruler. In particular, he was a problem for Kassandros in Macedon, where voices began to be raised asking when the young king was to be brought out of seclusion and trained to rule (Diod. XIX 105,2). Kassandros faced this problem with typical ruthless realism: he sent orders to his officer at Amphipolis to kill Alexandros and his mother and bury them secretly. With the king dead, he and the other dynasts were relieved of anxiety; each of them held his territory now as "spear-won land," and each began to cherish hopes of royal status for himself (Diod. XIX 105,2–4).

The dominant feature of the next five years (310–306), then, is a jockeying for position by the major dynasts with a view to the assumption of royal status, in which the surviving women of the Argead clan, Kleopatra and Thessalonike, assumed considerable importance. In the case of Antigonos, a prominent feature of these years was his handing over of the direct conduct of military affairs to his sons, Philippos and, above all, Demetrios, devoting himself instead to the consolidation of his realm by founding cities, settling troops, and organizing an efficient administrative system, all of which will be investigated in part 2 of this work. A result is that Antigonos, now well into his seventies, recedes into the background in our sources, which from 310 onwards focus more and more on Demetrios; but that Antigonos continued to keep the direction of affairs firmly under his control is shown by frequent reports in the sources of Demetrios's receipt of and obedience to instructions from his father.

THE LEAD-UP TO ROYAL STATUS (310–306 B.C.)

The question facing all of the dynasts was whether, when, and how to assume the kingship, and how widely to interpret the claim to power inherent in such status. In view of this uncertainty and concomitant competition, it is obvious that the peace of 311 would not long have survived the death of Alexandros IV; but in fact it was already a dead letter even before the king's death. For in the winter of 311/10 news arrived in the west of Seleukos's activities in inner Asia, activities which constituted a major blow to Antigonos's power and at once stirred his former enemies into renewed warfare against him. By all rational calculation, Seleukos's expedition should have been a forlorn hope, and it is not surprising therefore that the dynasts should have bowed to Antigonos's pressure to leave out Seleukos in making peace in the late summer of 311. Seleukos, however, was the sort of man who makes up by energy, daring, and sheer talent for what he lacks in resources, and his expedition was as a result successful beyond the stoutest expectations that could have been entertained when he set out.

He left the camp of Ptolemy with his small force shortly after Tyre had fallen into Ptolemy's hands due to the mutiny of Antigonos's garrison against their general, Andronikos.[1] Since the battle of Gaza occured in the winter of 312/11, presumably not earlier than the middle of December 312, and since the events described by

1. So Diod. XIX 88,1–5, whose account is detailed, self-consistent, and plausible, and certainly to be preferred to Appian's brief statement (*Syr.* 54) that Seleukos set out for Babylon immediately (*autika*) after the battle of Gaza. On the primacy to be accorded Diodoros among the extant sources, see further app. 1, pp. 341–46.

Diodoros as the aftermath of the battle (burial of the dead; despatch of prisoners to Egypt; operations against Phoenician cities, culminating in the siege of Tyre: XIX 85,1–86,2) clearly occupied a number of weeks, it is unlikely that Seleukos set out earlier than late January 311.[2] His route from Tyre to Babylon was necessarily not the direct one, for that would have taken him through the Syrian desert, where he could not have found water and supplies for his force; in fact he followed the course of the so-called "fertile crescent"—north from Tyre, most probably up the Orontes Valley (he had to avoid the coast, where Demetrios was gathering a new force at Tripolis), and then east to the Euphrates. He probably crossed this river near the site where he later founded a colony with the suggestive name Nikephorion ("bringer of victory"). From there he marched to Karrhai (Harran) in northern Mesopotamia (now in southern Turkey). At Karrhai there was a colony of Macedonian veterans, whom Seleukos recruited into his army by a mixture of force and persuasion (Diod. XIX 91,1). Then he turned south and eventually marched into Babylonia. His success in marching safely through northern Syria and Mesopotamia was clearly due in large part to the facts that it was the middle of winter, that the country had been denuded of its garrisons by Demetrios's summoning of them to Tripolis to form his new army (Diod. XIX 85,5), and that Peithon, the satrap of Babylonia and (probably) Mesopotamia, had died at Gaza.

Setting out in late January and marching by this long and circuitous route, with a pause at Karrhai, Seleukos cannot have reached Babylonia before late March. Nor did he make straight for Babylon: he rounded up support from the inhabitants of the countryside first, and was further strengthened when one of the Antigonid district commanders, a certain Polyarchos, came over to him with 1,000 soldiers (Diod. XIX 91,1–3). Seleukos finally entered Babylon some time after the beginning of April 311,[3] there to deal with the last

---

2. This dating is consistent with the known date of the beginning of the Seleukid era (i.e., 1st Nissan [= 3 April] 311 B.C., see, e.g., Sachs and Wiseman, *Iraq* 16 [1954]:202–12), and with the "Babylonian Chronicle" in Grayson, *Assyrian and Babylonian Chronicles,* no. 10, pp. 115–19, which indicates at rev. lines 4–8 that Seleukos was back in Babylon in the spring of 311.

3. This follows from the two facts that the Babylonians dated the beginning of the Seleukid era (which was connected with Seleukos's return to Babylon in 311) from the 1st of Nissan (see n. 2 above), and that it was the habit of the Babylonians to date such matters from the beginning of the year *in which* they occurred—thus, for example, the first year of Philippos III Arrhidaios was reckoned to be the year April 323 to March 322, even though Alexander did not in fact die and Phillippos Arrhidaios did not succeed to the throne until June 323 (see for this, e.g., Grayson, *Bab. Chron.,* pp. 25–26, and cf. Schober, *Gesch. Babyloniens,* pp. 46–73). Hence Seleukos must have returned to Babylon after the beginning of Nissan 311, most probably in middle or late April, or even early May.

Antigonid loyalists in the satrapy, who had taken refuge in the citadel of Babylon led by its commander, Diphilos. These men held out for a long time against Seleukos's siege, but were eventually overcome, Seleukos taking the citadel by storm some time in August (Diod. XIX 91,3–4; Bab. Chron., rev. lines 5–8). In the citadel Seleukos found many of his friends and retainers, who had been placed there under guard by Antigonos after Seleukos's flight in 315; having freed these, he began further strengthening his forces against the inevitable Antigonid counterattack (Diod. XIX 91,5).

The first Antigonid response to Seleukos's coup came not from the west, where Antigonos and Demetrios were occupied with reestablishing control over Palestine, campaigning against the Nabataians, and then negotiating the Peace of the Dynasts, but from the east. Antigonos's general of the upper satrapies, Nikanor, was stationed in Media with a substantial force, and as soon as he heard of Seleukos's activities, he gathered further troops from the Iranian satrapies. Then he set out against Seleukos in late summer 311 with an army of over 10,000 foot and 7,000 horse, drawn in large part from Media and Persia. Against this army Seleukos could muster only 3,000 foot and 400 horse, being obliged to leave behind a force under the command of his trusted friend Patrokles to guard Babylonia from possible western attacks (Diod. XIX 92,1–2; 100,5; Bab. Chron., rev. lines 9–10).[4] Nikanor should have been able to crush Seleukos with ease, but this did not happen. Seleukos reached and crossed the Tigris before Nikanor and, learning somehow Nikanor's whereabouts and line of march, he concealed his small army in ambush in marshes near the river. Nikanor reached the Tigris and found no troops to oppose him there, hearing reports instead that Seleukos and his men had fled from his approach.[5] Accordingly, he encamped at a way station, foolishly neglecting to keep a proper watch. Thus Seleukos's attack in the middle of the night took his men completely by surprise, causing panic and confusion, in which Nikanor's army quickly surrendered to Seleukos.[6] Nikanor himself escaped with a handful of loyal friends and fled through the desert back towards

4. For this man's career, see *RE* s.v. Patrokles no. 5 [Gisinger].

5. Diod. XIX 92,3 says "when Nikanor arrived at the Tigris river he did not find the enemy there, and he encamped at a royal way-station, believing that they had fled further" (sc., than they in fact had). Apparently Nikanor heard rumors that Seleukos and his troops had come to the Tigris and then fled from his approach; perhaps these rumors were spread at the instance of Seleukos himself.

6. For further details, see app. 3, nos. 38 and 79.

Media, while Seleukos, now at the head of a formidable force, had no difficulty in seizing all of Susiane (Diod. XIX 92,3–5).

Seleukos placed an officer named Euteles over Susiane (Diod. XIX 100,5–6), and moved to eastern Susiane, where in November he negotiated a pact of some sort with the Kossaioi in the mountains between Susiane and Media (Bab. Chron., rev. lines 11–12: the Guti = the Kossaioi). He clearly planned to invade Media in the spring. Meanwhile he wintered in eastern Susiane with his army, sending messengers to Ptolemy with an account of his successes (Diod. XIX 92,5). Nikanor likewise sent urgent messages to Antigonos from Media reporting the disasters incurred at Seleukos's hands and seeking aid (Diod. XIX 100,3). The news of Seleukos's victories came as a surprise in the west and prompted a shake-up of political alignments, ending the peace. Ptolemy had promised Seleukos further aid when he set off from Tyre early in 311; he had made peace with Antigonos only because he was afraid to fight on alone after Kassandros and Lysimachos had made peace, but now Seleukos emerged as a powerful ally, offering a real hope of cutting down Antigonos's power. Hence at the beginning of spring 310, scarcely six months or so after concluding peace with Antigonos, Ptolemy sent an expeditionary force to Kilikia Trachea, an attack on Antigonos that he justified publicly by the claim that Antigonos was infringing the Greek autonomy clause of the peace by garrisoning Greek cities (Diod. XX 19,3–4). He probably also sent troops to Seleukos across the Arabian desert: the event is reported in passing and without any indication of date by Arrian (*Indika* 43,4–5), but it fits the circumstances of this time.[7] At any rate, Ptolemy's aim with his expedition to Kilikia was obviously to weaken Antigonos further, and by distracting him to enable Seleukos to do more damage in inner Asia.

Meanwhile others in the west took advantage of the situation to attack Antigonos, including even his nephew Polemaios. In spite of the advancement Polemaios had received and the trust placed in him by Antigonos, he felt himself insufficiently honored and appreciated. The reason may have been the advancement of Antigonos's sons Demetrios and Philippos; these young men were now grown up and

7. Tarn, *CR* 40 (1926):13–15, and *CAH*, 6:502, suggests that Arrian was referring to an embassy sent to Seleukos by Ptolemy in 302 to persuade him to join a new coalition against Antigonos; but Schober, *Gesch. Babyloniens*, pp. 128–29, points out that Arrian seems to imply more than an ambassador or two crossing the desert (he refers to Cambyses' army crossing this desert and compares "those sent by Ptolemaios to Seleukos in Babylon") and plausibly argues that Arrian in fact refers to aid sent by Ptolemy to Seleukos in 310–309.

it was clear that Demetrios would in future be Antigonos's right-hand man, not Polemaios. He could not accept this and aimed to create an independent realm for himself in Greece based on Boiotia and Euboia.[8] To this end he made an alliance early in 310 with Kassandros, who thereby also broke the peace with Antigonos. Polemaios also arranged for the governor of the Hellespontine region in Asia Minor, a friend of his named Phoinix whom he had himself placed in power there in 314, to rebel against Antigonos, sending him soldiers and bidding him garrison the cities and forts and refuse all obedience to Antigonos (Diod. XX 19,2).

Antigonos reacted to these difficulties with decision. The most important matters were to regain full control in Asia Minor, to distract Kassandros from active intervention, and to try to aid Nikanor. Accordingly he sent his younger son Philippos with an army to fight Phoinix and recover Hellespontine Phrygia, and Demetrios with another army to drive Ptolemy's force out of Kilikia. Kassandros he seems to have dealt with indirectly, for the hitherto impotent Polyperchon now tried to regain his power in Macedon, apparently with Antigonos's support. Polyperchon obtained from Pergamon a youth named Herakles, reputedly an illegitimate son of Alexander the Great, whom he proposed to raise to the Macedonian throne, and he could hardly have got him from Asia Minor without the cooperation of Antigonos.[9] It seems very likely that the whole operation set up by Polyperchon was originally planned by Antigonos. Whoever Herakles really was, it must have been Antigonos who installed him at Pergamon and had him brought up there as a son of Alexander, presumably with a view to eventual use against Kassandros. Moreover Polyperchon had hitherto been reduced to a position of no importance and almost complete powerlessness in the Peloponnesos, but now suddenly managed to raise a great army, talk the Aitolians into joining him, and find the funds to finance a major campaign (Diod. XX 20,1–4). The Aitolians were allies of Antigonos, and it

8. For Polemaios's realm in Central Greece, see, for example, Picard, *Chalcis*, pp. 225–61, and Gullath, *Gesch. Boiotiens*, pp. 159–66. An epigraphical testimony to Polemaios's realm is *IG* II^2 469, on which see further app. 3, no. 125.

9. Since Herakles had been brought up in Pergamon and was fetched thence by Polyperchon, he must have been raised under the auspices of and handed over to Polyperchon by Antigonos, in whose realm Pergamon lay. That Antigonos was behind the Herakles episode was seen already by Tarn, *JHS* 41 (1921):18–28, and P. A. Brunt, *RFIC* 103 (1975):22–34, see esp. p. 32 n. 1. As to whether or not Herakles was really the son of Alexander, Brunt's arguments seem to show, as against Tarn, that he could have been, but I don't think it can be proved.

seems probable that it was he who persuaded them to back Polyperchon and provided Polyperchon with money as well as a pretender to the throne. At any rate, the whole operation was a very shrewd blow against Kassandros.

After making very careful preparations, both organizational and propagandistic, Polyperchon marched in 309 with an army of 20,000 infantry and 1,000 cavalry to invade Macedon via the region of Tymphaia, his own homeland.[10] Here Kassandros opposed him with an army, but his Macedonians were disaffected—no doubt because of the rumors of his having murdered Alexandros—and he greatly feared that they might go over to the party of Herakles: the traditional loyalty to the Argead house was evidently still strong (Diod. XX 20,4 and 28,1). Kassandros characteristically resorted to diplomacy, and with typical persuasiveness induced Polyperchon to murder Herakles by promising to restore to him all his properties and estates in Macedon, make him general of the Peloponnesos, and give him an army of 4,000 Macedonian infantry and 500 Thessalian cavalry. On this basis the two agreed, and, Herakles having been killed, Polyperchon marched south with his new army to take up his position in the Peloponnesos (Diod. XX 28,1–4). He never again played an important role, though he seems to have outlived both Antigonos and Kassandros (Plut. *Pyrrhos* 8,3).[11]

Returning to matters in Asia in 310, Demetrios defeated Ptolemy's army with ease and recovered control of Kilikia (Diod. XX 19,5). He was then given the job of leading a counterattack against Seleukos. At Damascus in Syria he gathered an army of 15,000 infantry (5,000 of them Macedonians) and 4,000 cavalry and marched towards Mesopotamia (Diod. XIX 100,4–5). Seleukos at this time had invaded Media to deal with the fresh opposition Nikanor was trying to organize there, and in a second battle defeated Nikanor again, personally killing him according to Appian (*Syr.* 55).[12] While

---

10. See for this Berve, vol. 2, no. 654.

11. The ease with which Kassandros induced Polyperchon to drop his scheme and murder Herakles is perhaps a further indication that the plan concerning Herakles did not originate with Polyperchon, and that he was hence not totally committed to it. Though Polyperchon briefly made common cause with Antigonos twice in the period 314–309, he was obviously never very committed to this course, doubtless seeing in Antigonos the chief cause of his fall from supreme power in 318/17.

12. Appian says that Seleukos killed Nikanor in battle with his own hand; since Nikanor escaped from the battle by the Tigris, this could only have occurred in a second battle fought between Seleukos and Nikanor in Media. This was recently doubted by Marasco, *Appiano*, pp. 51–55, but for no good reason in my view.

Seleukos was busy adding Media and Persia to his conquests, his officer in charge of Babylonia, Patrokles, had to deal with Demetrios's invasion. Since he did not have an adequate force to meet Demetrios in open battle, he decided to adopt a delaying strategy. Garrisoning the citadels of Babylon, he sent the civilians to Susiane, or into the trans-Euphrates regions, and prepared to obstruct Demetrios's operations making use of the waterworks of the satrapy as defenses (Diod. XIX 100,5–6). This campaign seems to have taken a considerable time, with Patrokles moving his troops about the satrapy to hinder Demetrios as much as possible, while sending urgent calls for help to Seleukos in Media; the Babylonian Chronicle (rev. lines 15–17) shows that Demetrios arrived in southern Mesopotamia in August 310 and campaigned there through the summer and autumn and into the winter. He entered the deserted city of Babylon and besieged the citadels, capturing and plundering one, but being unable to storm the other (Diod. XIX 100,6–7; Plut. *Dem.* 7,2; Bab. Chron., rev. lines 24–25). In February of 309 (Bab. Chron., rev. lines 25–29) he brought most of his troops out of Babylon and thoroughly plundered the surrounding region and the town of Cuthah (see also Plut. *Dem.* 7,3); he then made ready to return to Syria and Asia Minor, leaving his general Archelaos with 5,000 infantry and 1,000 cavalry (7,000 men according to Plutarch) in charge of Babylon with orders to continue the siege of the second citadel (Diod. XIX 100,7; Plut. *Dem.* 7,2–3; Bab. Chron., rev. lines 30–31). Demetrios himself with the rest of the army marched down to the sea and into Asia Minor, arriving in Karia in the summer of 309 just in time to stop Ptolemy capturing Halikarnassos, which he was then besieging (Plut. *Dem.* 7,3).[13] Meanwhile Seleukos, who had refused to be distracted from his operations in Media and Persia by Demetrios, reentered Babylonia and reconquered it after extensive campaigning against the force left behind by Demetrios, which seems to have caused widespread devastation (Bab. Chron., rev. lines 34–41).

In Europe, Kassandros's deal with Polyperchon had eliminated the threat to his position in Macedon, but presumably at the same time violated his pact with Polemaios, who can hardly have been

13. Plutarch's synchronism of the return of Demetrios from Babylonia with Ptolemy's Karian campaign in 309 is a valuable chronological pointer for Demetrios's whole Babylonian campaign, and together with the Bab. Chron. (cited in n. 2 above) anchors the chronology I have here adopted, which involves a considerable rearrangement in the order of events as narrated by Diodoros. The chronological change is based on the evidence of the Bab. Chron. taken together with various Greek sources, such as the Marmor Parium, Plutarch, and Diodoros, but the arguments are too long and complex to be given here: I plan to publish a separate paper on this.

happy with the position granted Polyperchon in Greece. Polemaios accordingly turned away from Kassandros, and sought an accommodation instead with Ptolemy (Diod. XX 27,3). Ptolemy had at this time embarked on very ambitious schemes, stimulated perhaps by the example of Seleukos. Early in 310 he had had first to deal with difficulties in Cyprus, where Antigonos, not content with simply defeating Ptolemy's attack on Kilikia, had persuaded Ptolemy's friend Nikokles to change allegiance. Ptolemy heard of this in time to prevent a serious situation from arising; he sent agents who, in cooperation with his brother Menelaos, who was still on Cyprus with an army, surrounded Nikokles in his palace and forced him to commit suicide (Diod. XX 21,1–3).[14] Having dealt with this situation, Ptolemy was not put off by the defeat inflicted on his forces in Kilikia, but prepared to set forth himself on a major expedition.

Ptolemy had accused Antigonos early in 310 of breaking the provision of the peace of 311 that called for the Greek cities to be autonomous, and in connection with this he is reported (Diod. XX 19,4) to have solicited the Greek cities in the influence spheres of Kassandros and Lysimachos to join him in an anti-Antigonos crusade. Evidently Ptolemy was putting forward very wide claims of leadership, such as were likely to bring him into conflict with other dynasts besides Antigonos. In the spring of 309 he sailed with a large force from Egypt and attacked Antigonos's positions in Lykia and Karia, capturing Phaselis, Xanthos, Kaunos, Iasos, and Myndos (Diod. XX 27,1–2; 37,1; Blümel, *I. Iasos,* 1, no. 2), but failing to capture Halikarnassos due to the timely arrival of Demetrios to succor the city (Plut. *Dem.* 7,3). These various sieges must obviously have taken some time and the summer must have been well advanced by the time Demetrios arrived to put a stop to Ptolemy's successes in Karia. Ptolemy now withdrew to Kos, where he established his forces for the time being and prepared to strike further blows against Antigonos by diplomatic means. He was in contact with Antigonos's nephew Polemaios and with Kleopatra, the sister of Alexander the Great, who was still residing in Sardis at this time under Antigonos's supervision.[15]

---

14. It used to be thought that there was a confusion in Diodoros between Nikokles of Paphos and Nikokreon of Salamis here (thus, e.g., Seibert, *Ptolemaios I,* p. 185), but see now against this view, Gesche, *Chiron* 4 (1974):103–25, and Bagnall, *Ptolemaic Administration,* pp. 39–40.

15. On the projects and activities of Ptolemy at this time (310–308), see Seibert, *Ptolemaios I,* pp. 184–89. Kleopatra settled at Sardis in 321 (Arrian *Met' Alex.* 1,26; 1,40; 25,2–8) and was still there in 309, watched over by Antigonos's *epimelētēs* in Sardis (Diod. XX 37,3–5).

Ptolemy and Polemaios arrived at some sort of agreement for common action, in pursuance of which Polemaios sailed from Chalkis with a substantial force to join Ptolemy at Kos. Most likely Ptolemy planned to undertake further operations along the coast of Asia Minor with the aid of Polemaios, who must have had a certain influence in the region left over from his campaigns there on Antigonos's behalf in 314–312.[16] Kleopatra, whose long residence at Sardis had given her ample opportunity to gain influence in the region, would also have been a help there. However, Polemaios was not a man to be used easily; he considered himself Ptolemy's equal and thereby quickly became suspect to Ptolemy, who arrested him, forced him to take poison, and took over his troops (Diod. XX 27,3). The murder of Polemaios naturally harmed Ptolemy's chances of making further progress on the Asia Minor coast, but there was still the Kleopatra card to be played.

The precise details of Ptolemy's negotiations with Kleopatra are lost, but they must have occurred during the latter part of 309 and winter 309/8 when Ptolemy was residing at Kos. Kleopatra was dissatisfied with her life under Antigonos's supervision at Sardis and was persuaded by Ptolemy to marry him, apparently with a view to assuming the royal power, possibly on a joint basis.[17] Ptolemy was thus playing for very high stakes at this time. Kleopatra actually set out to join Ptolemy, but failed to evade the vigilance of Antigonos's governor at Sardis, who prevented her from leaving and, after due consultation with Antigonos, had her assassinated by some of her women (Diod. XX 37,3–5). Balked of his prospects in Asia Minor, Ptolemy turned his attention to Greece, where Polemaios's death had left something of a power vacuum. In spring of 308 Ptolemy sailed across the Aegean and put in at Korinth. There he made an agreement with Kratesipolis, the widow of Polyperchon's son Alexandros, who was still in charge of Korinth and Sikyon; he took over these two cities, and issued a proclamation announcing the liberation of all the Greek cities and asking them to send representatives to Korinth to discuss Greek freedom. Evidently he intended to revive the so-called "League of Korinth" of Philip and Alexander, a further indication that he was

16. This is the convincing hypothesis of Seibert, *Ptolemaios I*, pp. 185–86. Add now also to Seibert's argument the treaty between the Karian city of Iasos and Ptolemy, which must date from 309, and which mentions Polemaios several times in the preamble, though the text at that point is unfortunately too broken to make out what was said of Polemaios there (Blümel, *I. Iasos*, 1, no. 2).

17. Seibert, *Ptolemaios I*, p. 187; id., *Dynastische Verbindungen*, pp. 19–20, 23–24.

aiming at royal status.[18] However, though many of the Peloponnesian cities promised him support, none actually materialized. In his anger Ptolemy established garrisons in Sikyon and Korinth and, making peace with Kassandros, gave up his plans and sailed back to Egypt (Diod. XX 37,1–2).

While these events were taking place, Antigonos seems to have been in Asia Minor watching the development of the situation. We have seen that he reacted to the setbacks of 310 by sending Philippos to the Hellespont and Demetrios to Kilikia and then Babylonia, probably also arranging for Polyperchon to challenge Kassandros with the pretender Herakles, and negotiating with Nikokles of Paphos to bring Cyprus over to his side. In 309 he apparently followed his younger son Philippos to the Hellespontine region, to aid in reorganizing that district after the rebellion of Phoinix, for he founded—evidently in the years 309–307—three cities and a military colony in Hellespontine Phrygia.[19] These foundations—Antigoneia Troas, Antigoneia-by-Daskylion, Antigoneia Bithyniake, and the fortress of Antigoneia-by-Kyzikos—must have been part of the settlement of the region in the aftermath of Phoinix's activities, as well as being outposts against possible trouble from Lysimachos, who was busy at this very time founding the city of Lysimacheia on the northern side of the Hellespont (Diod. XX 29,1). When Kleopatra's attempt to ally herself with Ptolemy was reported to him, he gave orders for her to be killed; but in order to escape the odium of the deed, he had the women who had carried it out punished and arranged a royal funeral

18. For the agreement with Kratesipolis, see Polyainos VIII 58: she handed over Korinth to Ptolemy against the wishes of her own garrison there. Ptolemy's attempt to refound the "League of Korinth" can be deduced from Diod. XX 37,1–2 and the Suda s.v. Demetrios Antigonou; cf. the analysis of Seibert, *Dynastische Verbindungen*, pp. 23–24, and *Ptolemaios I*, pp. 180–82, 187–88. The Suda reports that Ptolemy had at this time an alliance with Demetrios, with clauses guaranteeing the freedom of the Greeks and mutual support. This passage has been carefully analyzed by Seibert, *Ptolemaios I*, pp. 180–83, and shown to consist of three parts: the notice of the alliance; an account of Demetrios's freeing of Athens and Megara in 307; and an account of Ptolemy's activity in Greece in 308. Since the passage contains a number of errors and omissions and is chronologically unsound, Seibert is highly skeptical of this supposed treaty (which is absent from the more detailed treatment of Diodoros and was unknown to Plutarch as well). Seibert proposes, rightly I think, that the author of the Suda has carelessly tacked together a notice of the treaty between Demetrios and Ptolemy in 298/97 (Plut. *Dem.* 32; *Pyrrhos* 4) with quite unrelated information about their (in fact mutually hostile) activities in 308 and 307.

19. On these foundations and their dates, see chap. 8 below at n. 30. It may be that an embassy to Antigonos from the League of Ilion (*Syll.*, no. 330, lines 8–9), was also connected with Antigonos's settlement of the Hellespontine region ca. 309–308, as the absence of the title *basileus* for Antigonos indicates that the embassy was sent before 306.

for Kleopatra, apparently coming down to Sardis in person to see to these matters in the winter of 309/8 (so Diod. XX 37,6 seems to imply).

Since the situation in Asia Minor and Greece had made it necessary for Demetrios to leave Babylonia early in 309 without accomplishing a proper reconquest of the region, whereas Seleukos had succeeded in establishing control over Media, Persia, and Susiane, and had returned to Babylonia in 309 to set about driving Demetrios's general Archelaos out, apparently with success, it was clear that the eastern situation required Antigonos's attention. It looks as if Antigonos intervened in person, presumably some time in 308, for Polyainos (IV 9,1) preserves an account of a battle between Seleukos and Antigonos that can hardly belong to any other time.[20] This battle, doubtless fought in southern Mesopotamia or northern Babylonia, ended Antigonos's involvement with the upper satrapies and demonstrated the decline in his powers as a battle leader. When the two armies met, they fought a drawn battle and both retired to their camps for the night; but whereas Antigonos's army disarmed and went to sleep, Seleukos ordered his men to dine and rest in full armor and in their ranks. He then launched a surprise assault towards morning and won a simple victory, though apparently not an overwhelming one, since Antigonos clearly escaped unharmed and the battle is passed over by the rest of our historical sources.

After this battle, won by precisely the kind of surprise tactics that Seleukos had used against Nikanor in 311 and that Antigonos had himself used with conspicuous success earlier in his career, Antigonos apparently gave up any idea of reconquering the upper satrapies (for the time being at least), and it seems probable that he and Seleukos patched up some kind of peace agreement. For Seleukos hereafter turned his attention to securing control over Baktria, Karmania, and Areia/Drangiane in the east and campaigned against the Indian ruler Chandragupta (Sandrokottos in the Greco-Roman sources: Appian *Syr.* 55; Justin XV 4,12–21), while Antigonos concentrated his attention on events in the west.[21] The boundary between their respective

---

20. Polyainos gives no indication of date or location of this battle, but the period when Seleukos was reestablishing his control in Babylonia is the only possible time; cf. Schober, *Gesch. Babyloniens*, pp. 129–31. Schober locates this battle by reference to Appian *Syriaka* 57, where it is said that Seleukos founded Nikephorion to commemorate a victory he had won; but it seems to me that Nikephorion lies a good deal too far north to have been the site of Polyainos's battle.

21. See further Schober, *Gesch. Babyloniens*, pp. 133–39, and on Seleukos's subsequent campaigns in the east, ibid., pp. 143–93; and cf. Tarn, *CAH*, 6:494, for the peace between

spheres of authority after 308 cannot be determined, but must be presumed to have been somewhere in Mesopotamia: it seems most likely that Seleukos gained control of southern Mesopotamia, while Antigonos retained the areas of Mesopotamia adjacent to Syria and Anatolia.

By the end of 308, then, Antigonos could more or less regard three major areas of conflict as settled. The upper satrapies, always peripheral to his interest, had been ceded to Seleukos. The north coast of Asia Minor had been pacified, and Lysimachos was evidently still too busy in Thrace to present any immediate threat to Antigonos. Moreover, during the latter part of 309 and 308 Demetrios must certainly have recaptured the cities of Karia and Lykia that Ptolemy had conquered in the first half of 309, and the latter had withdrawn to Egypt.[22] What remained to be settled was the question of Greece, where the rebellion of Polemaios, Polyperchon's decision to side with Kassandros, and the activities of Ptolemy had between them virtually destroyed Antigonos's influence, though it seems that after Polemaios's death some of his troops reverted to loyalty to Antigonos (see, e.g., *IG* II^2 469). While Antigonos's loss of the upper satrapies did not greatly diminish his military power or do too much damage to his financial resources, the loss of a strong position in Greece could have a much more unsettling effect if it were to prevent him from obtaining the Greek manpower he needed as administrators of his realm, settlers in his colonies, and mercenaries for his army.

Accordingly in 307 Antigonos prepared to launch a great new expedition to Greece, with the ultimate aim of driving Kassandros's and Ptolemy's garrisons and allies out of Greece and once and for all making it his own sphere of influence. The key to Kassandros's position in Greece, which had maintained his power and influence in the Greek world throughout the previous decade, was Athens, which was ruled by Kassandros's friend and *epimelētēs* Demetrios of Phaleron and Kassandros's officer Dionysios, who occupied Mounychia with a strong Macedonian garrison (Diod. XX 45,1–2). Hence it was at Athens that Antigonos prepared to strike first, in the hope that liberating the greatest bastion of democracy and center of Greek culture would create enough of a sensation in Greece to smooth his

Antigonos and Seleukos, and pp. 502–3, for Seleukos's campaigns in the east between 308 and 303.

22. Note that in 306 Demetrios was able to use the coastal cities of Karia, Lykia, and Kilikia as a recruiting ground and base for his invasion of Cyprus: Diod. XX 46,6–47,1; see also XX 82,4, where Demetrios uses Loryma in Karia as his base for the war against Rhodes.

path in the other cities (Plut. *Dem.* 8,1–2 and *Mor.* 182e–f). The leader of the expedition was Demetrios, who was given 250 ships, a large army, and 5,000 talents for this campaign. With him, too, went many of Antigonos's top officers and advisers, chief among them the admiral Medeios of Larissa and the diplomatic troubleshooter Aristodemos of Miletos.[23]

It was decided that the best way to achieve a rapid result at Athens was to effect a surprise coup de main. Already in 312 there had been elements in Athens who were favorable to Antigonos (Diod. XIX 78,4), and it may be that there were still people in Athens who could be counted on in 307. At any rate, great care was taken that the object of the expedition being prepared should not become known: Demetrios did not tell the pilots of his ships where they were bound, but ordered them to follow the flagship and gave them sealed instructions to be opened only if they became separated from the fleet (Polyainos IV 7,2).[24] In this way the aim of attacking Kassandros's position at Athens was kept a secret, and it was a completely unsuspecting Attica that Demetrios approached in the late spring of 307. At Cape Sounion, Demetrios ordered the main body of his fleet to heave to, while he selected twenty of the best ships and sailed up the Attic coast with them on a route as if making for Salamis. The object was to give the impression that they were going to sail past Peiraieus, and this impression was indeed created, the Athenians assuming that the twenty ships were a squadron of Ptolemy's sailing up to Korinth, where there was a Ptolemaic garrison (Polyainos IV 7,6; Plut. *Dem.* 8,3–4). At the last moment, however, Demetrios changed course and swooped into Peiraieus where, in the confusion and panic of the Athenian authorities, he gained control of the harbor and brought in the rest of his fleet. Though Dionysios and the Athenian generals did their best at this stage to organize resistance, Demetrios's troops were

23. On Aristodemos and Medeios, see app. 3, nos. 16 and 68; and see also app. 3, nos. 1, 12, and 86 for some other prominent aides of Demetrios in his Greek campaigns.

24. In his Teubner ed. of Polyainos and "Über die Quellen und den Wert den Strategemensammlung Polyäns," p. 628, Melber tentatively attributes this stratagem of Demetrios to the year 301 after the battle of Ipsos, following Droysen, *Geschichte des Hellenismus,* 2:221; Schubert, *JClPh,* suppl. 9 (1877/78):725, refers it to Demetrios's expedition to Athens in 295 (cf. Plut. *Dem.* 33,1–2). However, the former hypothesis can be summarily dismissed, as Plut. *Dem.* 30,2–3 shows that there was nothing secret about Demetrios sailing to Europe in 301; and Schubert's hypothesis likewise finds no support in the text of Plut. *Dem.* 33,1–2, where secrecy and surprise are not mentioned as either aimed at or achieved by Demetrios. It seems to me that Schmidt, *Dem. Pol. in Graeciam,* p. 5, is correct in attributing Polyainos's strategem to 307, when we see clearly from Plut. *Dem.* 8,3–4 that Demetrios did aim at and achieve secrecy in crossing to Europe to take Athens by surprise.

able to force a landing, and the heralds of Demetrios cried the policy of Antigonos and Demetrios to liberate Athens and restore the ancestral constitution to such effect that most of the Athenians went over to Demetrios forthwith (Polyainos IV 7,6; Plut. *Dem.* 8,4–9,1; Diod. XX 45,2–3).[25]

Thus, about the beginning of June (the 26th day of the Attic month Thargelion: Plut. *Dem.* 8,3), Demetrios managed to secure control of all of Peiraieus, except the garrison fort of Mounychia, with scarcely a blow being struck. He immediately established siege works around Mounychia and entered into negotiations with the Athenians, who were keen to receive him. Demetrios of Phaleron recognized that his position was now untenable, and after diplomatic exchanges involving Aristodemos of Miletos, he was given a safe-conduct to Thebes and the old democracy was restored in Athens under the leadership of Stratokles of Diomea and Demochares of Leukonoe, the nephew of Demosthenes.[26] Demetrios then launched a full-scale assault on Mounychia. After two days of continuous assault by artillery and men fighting in relays, the fort was stormed and the garrison was forced to surrender.[27] Mounychia was razed to the ground to assure the Athenians that Antigonos and Demetrios were serious in their intent to free the city.

The enthusiasm evoked by these events in Athens was extraordinary. A decree moved by Stratokles was passed in the Athenian assembly granting Antigonos and Demetrios an impressive array of honors: gilded statues of them were to be set up in a chariot next to the statues of the tyrannicides Harmodios and Aristogeiton in the agora (a unique honor, for it was otherwise forbidden to place statues near those of the tyrannicides);[28] they were to receive honorary

25. There are certain discrepancies between these three sources; I follow Polyainos and Diodoros, who seem to me more reliable here than Plutarch, whose account is highly theatrical (see n. 27 below).

26. See, for example, Ferguson, *Hellenistic Athens*, pp. 95–117, and Shear, *Kallias of Sphettos*, pp. 47–48.

27. Plut. *Dem.* 9,2–10,1 has Demetrios capture Mounychia only *after* the liberation of Megara, whereas Diod. XX 45,5–46,3 reports that Demetrios *first* captured Mounychia, entered Athens in triumph, and only then moved on to Megara. I prefer Diodoros's more factual and logical seeming version to Plutarch's, which is theatrical and anecdotal, concentrating on Demetrios's near capture during a secret amorous encounter with Kratesipolis (*Dem.* 9,3–4) and on one of the king-philosopher encounters so beloved by the anecdotal sources (cf., e.g., Alexander's reputed meeting with Diogenes the Cynic: Plut. *Alex.* 14,1–3) between Demetrios and the Megarian philosopher Stilpon.

28. See, for example, *IG* II^2 450 (= *Syll.*, no. 320), lines 30–33 (honors for Asandros the Karian satrap, from 313); *IG* II^2 646, lines 37–40 (honors for Herodoros, from 294); and cf. Habicht, *Gottmenschentum*, pp. 46–47 and n. 15.

"crowns" of two hundred talents; two new tribes were created and named Antigonis and Demetrias in their honor; an altar was consecrated to them under the name of the "Saviours" and an annual sacrifice, procession, and games were instituted;[29] and their portraits were to be woven into the *peplos* annually dedicated to Athena at the festival of the Panathenaia (Diod. XX 46,2; cf. also Plut. *Dem.* 10,3–13,2, who, however, exaggerates the honors accorded at this time, adding some fictitious ones and others actually granted Demetrios only some years later).[30] A formal alliance was established between Athens and Antigonos, and Demetrios promised on Antigonos's behalf to give to Athens 150,000 *medimnoi* of grain and timber sufficient to build 100 warships (Diod. XX 46,1; Plut. *Dem.* 10,1).[31] An embassy was despatched to Antigonos to report the honors bestowed on him and the alliance established, and meanwhile Demetrios turned his attention to Megara, where Kassandros still had a garrison.

Megara was captured by Demetrios without any great difficulty, and there too he restored the ancestral constitution and left the city free, though there was a certain amount of plundering by his troops (Diod. XX 46,3; Plut. *Dem.* 9,2–6). He then returned to Athens, where instructions from Antigonos now arrived. In response to the embassy of the Athenians, Antigonos sent them the 150,000 *medimnoi* of corn and the ship timber already promised by Demetrios, and in addition gave to Athens 150 talents in silver and gold coin and restored to Athenian control the islands of Lemnos and Imbros (Diod.

29. For full discussion, see Habicht, *Gottmenschentum*, pp. 44–48. Epigraphical testimonia to the cult of the Sotēres are listed in ibid., p. 45 n. 12, and show that the cult continued until the 230s (see *Syll.*, no. 487, line 12, from 235/34). On the significance of the "deification" of Antigonos and Demetrios, see further pp. 234–36 below.

30. Plutarch reports, for example, that the Athenians decreed that the priest of the Sotēres was to be the eponymous officer of subsequent years, instead of the archon, which is decisively refuted by abundant epigraphical testimony; further that an altar was set up to "Demetrios Kataibates" at the point where Demetrios stepped down from his chariot in Athens, which Habicht, *Gottmenschentum*, pp. 48–49, shows belongs rather to 304; see, in general, ibid., pp. 44–55. A further honor accorded Antigonos and Demetrios in 307, though mentioned by neither Diodoros nor Plutarch, is the naming of two new sacred triremes *Antigonis* and *Demetrias* after the two dynasts: Suda s.v. Paraloi; Photios s.v. Paralos and Paraloi; schol. Demosth. XXI 171 (ed. Dindorff II 637); Bekker, *Anekdota Graeca*, 1:267,21; and cf. Habicht, *Gottmenschentum*, p. 45 n. 10.

31. While Diodoros speaks of timber for 100 *nausin*, Plutarch specifically says for *triēreis*. However, from Diod. XX 50,3 it seems that the ships in fact built were *tetrēreis* (30 of them fought with Demetrios at the battle of Salamis in Cyprus in 306); Plutarch is here using the word *triēreis* loosely to mean simply "warships" (for this usage, see Hauben, *Chiron* 6 [1976]:4 n. 32).

XX 46 4; *IG* II² 1492b [= *Syll.*, no. 334], lines 5–12, 27–31, 40–42).[32] To Demetrios he sent orders to prepare to sail down to Cyprus with his force to attack the position of Ptolemy there. Before leaving Greece however, Demetrios was to call a meeting of representatives from all the Greek states allied to Antigonos (presumably including Aitolia, Boiotia, Chalkis, Eretria, and Karystos at this time, in addition to Athens and Megara),[33] to discuss measures for their common safety against a counterattack by Kassandros (Diod. XX 46,5). Demetrios remained at Athens over the winter of 307/6 organizing this meeting, and sought without success to suborn Ptolemy's garrison commander over Korinth and Sikyon. He also married at this time an upper-class Athenian lady reputed to be a descendant of Miltiades; this was Eurydike, the widow of Ophellas, Ptolemy's former general over Kyrene—so the marriage might have more than one political use (Plut. *Dem.* 14,1–15,1).

At the beginning of spring 306 Demetrios sailed from Athens to begin operations against Ptolemy's forces on Cyprus. With him as allies went 30 Athenian quadriremes, presumably newly built over the winter from the timber sent by Antigonos; by way of reciprocation Demetrios seems to have left some of his troops in Athens to help against the expected counterattack by Kassandros.[34]

In accordance with his father's orders, Demetrios first sailed across the Aegean to Karia. There he summoned the Rhodians, who were or had been allies of Antigonos, but were now becoming very friendly with Ptolemy, to join in the war against Ptolemy, but they refused.[35] Coasting along, then, to Kilikia, where he enrolled additional ships and troops, Demetrios crossed over to Cyprus with an army of 15,000 infantry and 400 cavalry, and a fleet whose numbers are uncertain, but may have been rather more than 110 triremes and

---

32. See further Pritchett, *AJPh,* 58 (1937):329–33, arguing that the Athenian inscriptions *IG* II² 675 and 525 preserve official record of this embassy; cf. Habicht, *Gesch. Athens,* pp. 198–99.

33. The alliance with Athens is attested at Diod. XX 46,1; presumably Megara too made an alliance with Antigonos after being liberated, though this is not specifically attested. Antigonos's other alliances in Greece in 307 must be those formed in the years 314–312: Aitolia and Boiotia (Diod. XIX 75,6), Eretria and Karystos (Diod. XIX 78,3), Chalkis (Diod. XIX 78,2, and cf. *IG* II² 485 + 563 [see Ad. Wilhelm, *AM* 39 (1914):279] and *IG* II² 491), and no doubt other cities. Probably this meeting of allied cities was intended as the first step towards setting up a league of mainland Greek states, see further pp. 228–30 below.

34. See for this app. 3, nos. 48, 102, and 125.

35. On the relations between Rhodes and Antigonos and between Rhodes and Ptolemy at this time, see pp. 202–3 and 207–8 below.

quadriremes plus 53 heavier ships (fives, sixes and sevens—the latter being the largest warships available to him).[36]

It was Antigonos's intention to drive Ptolemy completely out of Cyprus and make the island his own. In the years 314–309 Cyprus had persistently been used by Ptolemy as a staging post for raids against Antigonos's long, exposed Mediterranean coastline in Syria and southern Asia Minor, and Antigonos now meant to put a stop to this. At the same time, Antigonos himself was in upper Syria near the mouth of the river Orontes, where he was founding a city named Antigoneia, which was to be the new capital of his empire and serve as a center from which to keep a watch over his lands in Mesopotamia and Palestine against possible encroachments by Seleukos or Ptolemy (Diod. XX 47,5).

Ptolemy's general over the island of Cyprus was his brother Menelaos, who had concentrated his forces against Demetrios's attack, amounting to 12,000 infantry, 800 cavalry, and 60 ships. Demetrios landed near Karpasia on the northeastern peninsula of the island and stormed this town and its neighbor Ourania. He then left his fleet with a strong guard and marched against Salamis. Menelaos came out to meet him, and a battle was fought some five miles from Salamis. Demetrios was victorious, driving Menelaos back into Salamis with the loss of 1,000 dead and nearly 3,000 captured, whom he sent to Antigonos in Syria (Diod. XX 47,1–4). In Salamis, Menelaos hastily prepared the city for a siege and sent a message to Ptolemy reporting his defeat and asking for rapid aid. Demetrios meanwhile marshalled his siege train, and brought his fleet around to blockade the city by sea. The siege of Salamis was the first of the series of great sieges that earned for Demetrios his nickname Poliorketes—the Besieger of Cities—and the first time we hear of him preparing one of his great siege towers, the *helēpolis*. This was a nine-story tower on wheels, constructed to overtop the city wall, towards which it was slowly wheeled, while heavy stone-throwing artillery on the lower levels of the siege tower battered the wall and light catapults and stone throwers on the upper levels drove the defenders off the wall.[37] In addition Demetrios had two huge battering rams made, with large protective penthouses (Diod. XX 47,7–48,3).

Demetrios launched his assault on Salamis and, after destroying a large section of the wall, nearly captured the place. However, Menelaos managed to burn much of the siege machinery in a surprise night

36. See n. 38 below for problems with the numbers given at Diod. XX 47,1.

37. For Demetrios's siege machinery, see Marsden, *Greek and Roman Artillery*, via indices s.v. Demetrius Poliorcetes.

sortie, and meanwhile Ptolemy arrived from Egypt with a great force and landed at Paphos. There he gathered further forces from the allied Cypriote cities, and then moved on to Kition, about twenty-five miles from Salamis (Diod. XX 48,4–49,1). His force now amounted to 140 warships, all quadriremes and quinqueremes, and over 200 transports carrying an army of more than 10,000 men in addition to all sorts of baggage. If he could effect a junction with Menelaos, his fleet would clearly be superior to that of Demetrios, and he sent messages to Menelaos to try to arrange this (Diod. XX 49,2–3; Polyainos IV 7,7; Plut. *Dem.* 16,1).

Demetrios received intelligence of Ptolemy's arrival and approach and quickly took steps to prevent Menelaos's squadron from joining Ptolemy's fleet. He embarked the best of his soldiers on his ships as marines, also setting up catapults and stone-throwers on the larger ships, and sailed out with his entire fleet to an anchorage outside the harbor entrance of Salamis, bottling up Menelaos inside (Diod. XX 49,4–5). Demetrios had acquired some ships from the Cypriote cities he had captured (Diod. XX 50,2), and his warships seem to have totaled 180.[38] Ptolemy, unaware of Demetrios's move, undertook a night dash from Kition to Salamis, hoping to sail into the city by surprise and unopposed; but when early in the morning he sailed around a headland and into view of Salamis, he found Demetrios's fleet drawn up waiting for him. Ptolemy's hope now was that in the course of the battle Menelaos would sail out with his 60 ships and attack Demetrios's fleet in rear. He ordered his transports to drop back and drew up his warships in line, massing most of his larger ships on the left, where he commanded in person (Diod. XX 50,5–6; Polyainos IV 7,7).

Demetrios had already drawn up his fleet for battle when Ptolemy appeared. Well aware of the danger presented by Menelaos's squadron, he nevertheless undertook a bold gamble: he detached only 10

38. At XX 47, 1 Diodoros says Demetrios had 110 "swift-sailing triremes" and 53 "heavier *stratiōtidai*" plus sufficient *poria* to act as troop transporters. Evidently there is an error; since the *poria* were to transport the troops, the "troop transporters" (*stratiōtidai*) must in fact have been heavier *warships*, a fact confirmed by the presence in Demetrios's fleet at Salamis of at least 20 *pentēreis*, 10 *hexēreis*, and 7 *heptēreis* (Diod. XX 50,1–3). Furthermore, the 110 triremes must in fact include quadriremes, of which Demetrios had at least 30 (Diod. XX 50,3). There were thus 163 warships in Demetrios's original fleet, to which he added ships captured on Cyprus (Diod. XX 50,2), and Diodoros's total here for the fleet of 108 plus 10 must be an error. Polyainos IV 7,7 and Plut. *Dem.* 16,1–2 give Demetrios either 180 or 190 warships; I think the former is closer to the truth. Ptolemy needed only to combine with Menelaos in order to achieve superiority over Demetrios (200 to 180), but blockading Menelaos's 60 ships with only 10 of his own gave Demetrios sufficient superiority over Ptolemy's fleet to win the day (see further Hauben, *Chiron* 6 [1976]:1–5).

quinqueremes to blockade the narrow exit from Salamis's harbor, hoping that the numerical superiority of 170 to 140 ships thus obtained over Ptolemy would enable him to win the battle before Menelaos could free the harbor mouth and sail out to Ptolemy's aid. He had drawn up part of his army on the shore, ordering the cavalry to ride up and down and rescue or capture shipwrecked swimmers.

Demetrios had his fleet arranged with his best ships—7 Phoenician sevens, 30 Athenian quadriremes, 10 sixes, and 10 quinqueremes—massed on the left flank, all commanded by the admiral Medeios, who himself was present aboard his flagship, one of the Phoenician sevens (Diod. XX 49,6–50,4; Plut. *Dem.* 16,1–2). Ptolemy had thus copied Demetrios's arrangement, and the battle was in effect a race to see which of the two dynasts could first defeat the enemy's right wing and turn to attack the enemy's center. The loser in this race would be forced to withdraw with his own strong left wing or face the risk of encirclement, and there was the added question of whether or not Menelaos would succeed in breaking out of Salamis in time to intervene.

As things turned out, it was Demetrios who won the race and pulled off his gamble. He himself is reported to have fought brilliantly on his flagship, and the Athenian contingent seems to have distinguished itself particularly, for Demetrios subsequently gave Athens 1,200 suits of armor from the spoils of victory (Plut. *Dem.* 17,1; Diod. XX 52,1–2). Demetrios crushed Ptolemy's right wing and also put to flight his center; though Ptolemy was victorious with his own left wing, when he turned towards the center of the battle, he found that he was too late, and could only join the rest of his fleet in flight. Meanwhile Menelaos's 60 ships engaged Demetrios's 10 quinqueremes at the harbor mouth and, after a fierce struggle, managed to force their way out, only to find that Ptolemy had already lost the battle; they accordingly had no option but to return to Salamis. The battle thus ended in a brilliant victory for Demetrios. He sent out transports to pick up survivors, and towed the captured and damaged ships to land. Of his own fleet, 20 ships were damaged, but all were rescued and repaired; of the enemy Demetrios captured 40 intact and disabled about 80, which he brought to land full of water. In addition, he captured over 100 of Ptolemy's transports, with 8,000 soldiers on board and much baggage, money, and military equipment (Diod. XX 51,1–52,6; Plut. *Dem.* 16,2–3).[39]

---

39. Diod. XX 49,4–52,5 recounts the battle at greatest length, and it is his account that I have essentially followed. Though Polyainos IV 7,7 is rather different, it seems to me that he

After this crushing defeat Ptolemy sailed back to Egypt with the remnant of his fleet. Menelaos was forced to surrender Salamis to Demetrios, so that the latter acquired a further 60 ships and 8,000 soldiers. He swiftly took over all of the forts and cities of Cyprus and enrolled the captured Ptolemaic soldiery, amounting to some 16,000 infantry and 600 cavalry, in his own army thus doubling its size (Diod. XX 53,1; Plut. *Dem.* 16,4).[40] Ptolemy's friends and relatives among the captives, including Menelaos and Ptolemy's illegitimate son Leontiskos, were sent back to Ptolemy with their personal baggage in a magnanimous gesture; and Demetrios sent his flagship to Syria with Aristodemos of Miletos to report the victory to Antigonos (Plut. *Dem.* 17,1–2; Diod. XX 53,1; Justin XV 2,7).

THE ASSUMPTION OF THE KINGSHIP AND ITS MEANING

The importance of Demetrios's victory at Salamis, a victory reminiscent of the great successes won by Antigonos himself in earlier years, went far beyond its immediate result in the conquest of Cyprus, for it was used by Antigonos as the occasion to assume the royal title. Since the Argead dynasty had come to an end with the murder of Alexandros IV in 310—or perhaps with that of Herakles in 309—the Macedonian Empire had been left not only kingless, but without the possibility of a legitimate successor being found. Only two options were open, therefore: either Macedon and the empire would switch to a non-monarchical form of government or a new dynasty/dynasties would claim the kingship. In fact, the position of the great Macedonian dynasts had been that of kings in all but name since at least 315, when Alexandros IV was placed in protective custody at Amphipolis by Kassandros. The regency thereafter effectively fell

and Diodoros are not really at odds, the discrepancies being due more to careless abbreviation on Polyainos's part than to real differences in their information. Plut. *Dem.* 16,1–3, though a scanty account of the battle, confirms the blockading force of only 10 ships, but exaggerates the scale of Ptolemy's losses; Diodoros's more modest statement at XX 52,6 that 40 ships were captured whole and 80 disabled, implying that Ptolemy escaped with about 20 ships, seems more reliable.

40. Plut. *Dem.* 16,4 writes of Menelaos handing over to Demetrios 12,000 infantry and 1,200 cavalry at his surrender, which agrees roughly with Diodoros's figure for the original size of Menelaos's force (12,000 infantry and ca. 800 cavalry: Diod. XX 47,3) but fails to take into account Menelaos's losses in his battle against Demetrios near Salamis (1,000 dead and 3,000 captured: Diod. XX 47,3), of which Plutarch appears to be ignorant. At *Dem.* 17,5 Plut. gives the total number of soldiers Demetrios captured as 16,800, which agrees well with Diodoros's figure of 16,600 at XX 53,1.

into abeyance, and the great dynasts made war upon each other overtly in their own interests. It was thus obvious that only the second option was a real possibility: it was just a matter of time before one or more of the dynasts took the step of assuming royal status. What remained to be seen was who would assume the royal title first, and how, and when; also how widely he would seek to interpret his claim to kingship, and what the reaction of the other dynasts would be.

Of the various dynasts who might aspire to kingship, Lysimachos was not in so strong a position in Thrace that he could afford the risk of being the first to proclaim himself king; likewise the position of Seleukos in inner Asia was hardly secure enough, even after he had apparently come to terms with Antigonos ca. 308, to encourage him to take this step, though he seems to have received royal honors from his Asian subjects (as had Antigonos already in 315 in Persia and Babylonia).[41] Kassandros was superficially in a strong position to take the lead, since he ruled Macedon and by his wife Thessalonike had sons who were grandsons of the great Philip, but in view of the odium attaching to him as the murderer of Olympias and Alexandros IV—the rightful king—he too could not take the political risk of being the first to call himself king. The left Ptolemy and Antigonos, the two who were clearly in the strongest position to assume the title of *basileus*. I have suggested above that Ptolemy's activities in 309 and 308—particularly the attempt to arrange a marriage with Kleopatra and the plan to form a Hellenic alliance—may have been intended to pave the way for an assumption of the royal title. As it was, these activities failed, and Ptolemy did not assume the royal title first.

Antigonos did so: he was the wealthiest and most powerful of the dynasts and the one who could point to the most distinguished military and administrative record, a not unimportant point, as the power of all of the dynasts rested in great part on the personal charisma they had won by their military and administrative successes and ability. According to Plutarch, in fact (*Dem.* 10,3), the Athenians had already addressed Antigonos as king in 307, showing that the idea was in the air. But Antigonos's victories had all been won before the death of Alexandros IV, and the proclamation of royal status for himself really called for a great and famous victory to make it con-

41. Plut. *Dem.* 18,3 attests Seleukos's royal honors before 306; that he was not actually accounted king at this time is clear from the continuation of reckoning by Alexandros IV's reign (see e.g., Sachs and Wiseman, *Iraq* 16 [1954]:202–11). Royal honors for Antigonos in 315 are attested by Diod. XIX 48,1 (Persia) and 55,2 (Babylonia).

vincing and memorable. Moreover, Antigonos was an old man who could not realistically expect to live much longer; thus the matter of royal status was to him without doubt as much as anything a question of the succession to his power, for which there existed at the time no legal or institutional mechanism. It was of the utmost significance to him, therefore, that his son Demetrios had won a sensational victory over a rival dynast and former companion of Alexander the Great, and had so proved himself to be worthy to receive the power built up by Antigonos.

As regards the actual coronation of Antigonos, Plutarch *Dem.* 17,2–18,1 records an elaborate charade played by the "arch-flatterer" Aristodemos, who is supposed to have landed from his ship alone and, refusing to give any indication of the news he bore, to have advanced slowly to the royal palace in Antigoneia, gathering as he went an anxious throng. Meeting the by now very worried Antigonos at the palace gate, he cried aloud, "Hail, King Antigonos!" and described the great victory won. Enthused by the report of this great victory, the assembled crowd thereupon took up Aristodemos's use of the royal title and acclaimed Antigonos as king, and Antigonos's friends came forward with a royal diadem, which they bound on his head.

Though Plutarch's account is highly rhetorical and has some unlikely aspects, it should not be summarily dismissed as complete fiction.[42] But Aristodemos was far from being a mere "arch-flatterer" as Plutarch makes him out to be: he was in fact one of Antigonos's most senior advisers and aides (see app. 3, no. 16 for a full review of his career). I believe there is a genuine historical basis to the charade recounted by Plutarch, the key to which is provided by the fact that when Aristodemos came out with his apparently wholly unexpected greeting and report of victory, the *philoi* of Antigonos had a diadem ready with which to crown him as king. In other words, we are here dealing with a prearranged coup de théâtre: Antigonos must already have had word of Demetrios's victory, for as we have seen Demetrios waited to secure full control of Cyprus before sending Aristodemos to Antigoneia. Aristodemos and the friends of Antigonos were thus taking part in an elaborate show staged to impress the multitude, awe

42. Müller, *Antigonos Monophthalmos*, pp. 80–81, demonstrates that Plutarch's account is built up in the form of a theater piece and concludes that it comes most probably from one of the so-called "tragic" historians, e.g., Douris of Samos. This seems plausible, but is no grounds for rejecting the story entirely, even if one must discount much of the "color"; see now the excellent treatment of Gruen, "Coronation of the Diadochoi," pp. 255–57 and nn. 12, 13.

it into vigorously acclaiming Antigonos's assumption of the royal title, and thus lend the authority of popular backing to his elevation to royal status. The moving spirit behind this was obviously Antigonos himself, just as it was he who promptly conferred royal status on Demetrios as well, sending him a diadem to wear and addressing him in an accompanying letter as "King Demetrios" (Plut. *Dem.* 18,1). The point was to show for propaganda purposes that Antigonos was not simply usurping royal status himself, but being elevated by the wishes and action of his assembled *philoi,* soldiers, and subjects, moved by their recognition of his obviously "royal" qualities. This kingship was thus not a merely personal assertion, but an expression of real authority over an important power bloc.

The nature of the kingship assumed by Antigonos in 306 needs to be examined: what were the intended and actual ramifications of this act? Here I shall only discuss the foreign policy aspects of Antigonos's and Demetrios's elevation to royal status, reserving the details of the royal powers and methods of rule for discussion in chapter seven below. Clearly, as I have already suggested, one important effect aimed at by Antigonos was to institutionalize his power in such a way as to provide for the succession of Demetrios to that power. The fact that Antigonos's first royal act was to name Demetrios co-king makes this clear, buttressed by the fact that Antigonos was a very old man whose physical fitness was in decline. Inevitably, however, Antigonos's act has been seen by modern scholars in the light of his supposed dream of reuniting the empire of Alexander; in other words, it is usually assumed that in taking the title of *basileus,* Antigonos merely took the last step in his long project of securing rule over Alexander's entire empire.[43] The fact is, however, that even if Demetrios's victory over Ptolemy gave hope that it might be possible to eliminate Ptolemy entirely and annex Egypt, there were still three other dynasts in charge of major portions of Alexander's empire who could not be reduced to submission merely by Antigonos proclaiming himself king.

Obviously it was impossible for Antigonos to know exactly what the reaction of the other dynasts to his assumption of royal status

---

43. Thus, for example, Tarn, *CAH,* 6:495–502; Will, *Histoire politique,* 1:74–75; Müller, *Antigonos Monophthalmos,* pp. 88–89. Hauben, *AncSoc* 5 (1974):105–17, draws support for this idea from an anecdote recording that Demetrios and his boon companions scorned and rejected the claims to kingship of the other Diadochoi, but Gruen, "Coronation of the Diadochoi," pp. 259–60, shows that this anecdote in fact belongs to the 290s and so tells us nothing about Antigonos's conception of his kingship.

would be, but the thought that they would simply do likewise must have crossed his mind. To suppose that he wished to be regarded as the successor of Alexander or even of the Achaemenids is hardly feasible: even at the height of his power in 315–311, Antigonos had made no serious attempt to control the far eastern portions of the empire of the Achaemenids and Alexander, and since then he had had to concede the loss of the Iranian lands and much of Mesopotamia to Seleukos. Nor does he seem to have been greatly disturbed by this: Antigonos was interested in the Mediterranean and Aegean lands—Syria, Palestine, Anatolia, and Greece—rather than inner Asia. In declaring himself king, he was in the first place affirming and institutionalizing his power and making it hereditary; but the kingship of Antigonos was personal, not territorial or national. Antigonos proclaimed himself and his son to be "kingly" persons, the proof of this lying in their deeds and abilities: hence the timing of the proclamation after Demetrios's smashing victory at Salamis. The proclamation should not, then, be regarded as a claim specifically to supreme power over all of Alexander's empire. Neither should it be regarded as limited to particular territories.[44] In practice, however, real limits to Antigonos's power had to be, and were, acknowledged. Not all of these limits were involuntary: as noted, for example, Antigonos was uninterested in the far east, and he pursued a policy of autonomy for the Greek city-states (see chapter 6 below).

The new status of Antigonos and Demetrios as kings was immediately accepted in their realm and sphere of influence; it remained to be seen what the reaction of the other dynasts would be, and what form Antigonos's future relations with them would take. As to the former, Ptolemy assumed the royal title in early 304, immediately followed by Seleukos, Lysimachos, and Kassandros.[45] This signaled the definite breakup of the empire into separate realms, a situation which had already existed de facto since 314. It did not, however, signify the dissolution of the empire into precise territorial kingdoms: each of the five dynasts claimed for himself and his descendants the title *basileus;* some of them were prepared to recognize others as kings

44. A new historical fragment (*P. Köln,* 6 [1987], no. 247) explicitly claims that in taking the kingship Antigonos aimed to rule all of Alexander's empire, but this proves only that this idea was already prevalent in Rhodian history writing of the late third/early second centuries B.C., of which this fragment is an example, not that this was really Antigonos's aim; see further app. 1, "Addendum."

45. For full discussions of the circumstances and timing, see Müller, *Antigonos Monophthalmos,* pp. 93–104; Gruen, "Coronation of the Diadochoi," pp. 253–71.

some of the time; none of them seems to have been ready to acknowledge definite and permanent boundaries to his area of rule.[46] It is only by understanding Diadoch, and especially Antigonid, kingship as intensely personal that one can, for example, explain the peculiar phenomenon of kings without kingdoms (Demetrios between 301 and 294, Antigonos Gonatas from 283 to 277), and also the chronic fluctuations of the Diadoch kingdoms between 306 and the mid third century: it was left to the second and third generations of Hellenistic kings to accept the territorial nature of their kingdoms.[47]

As to the matter of Antigonos's relations with the other dynasts, his rise to kingship initiated a new phase in his foreign policy, in which he in turn attempted entirely to eliminate Ptolemy and Kassandros, the two dynasts who had been most consistently and dangerously hostile to him in the period 315–306. This policy perhaps sprang from disillusionment with the peace of 311, which had lasted only a few months and mitigated the hostility of the rival dynasts towards him not one whit. Nevertheless, it demonstrates that Antigonos acknowledged no definite limits to his power as king, which he attempted to enforce over Ptolemy in 306 and over Kassandros in 302. In assuming the kingship, then, Antigonos clearly did assert his primacy over the rival dynasts, who had spent the past eight years trying to cut down his power; and by proclaiming Demetrios king at the same time he advertised to the world that his son's success proved that he had what no rival yet had—an heir worthy to rule the Macedonians in the future.

---

46. For example, Kassandros, Lysimachos, Ptolemy, and Seleukos recognized each other when they formed their coalition against Antigonos in 302 and subsequently divided up his empire; Seleukos and Demetrios recognized each other when Seleukos married Demetrios's daughter Stratonike ca. 297 and the two kings fêted each other royally (Plut. *Dem.* 31,1–32,2). In private, however, Demetrios scorned the pretensions of the other kings (Plut. *Dem.* 25,4–5). Seleukos and Ptolemy, though remaining friends, never recognized each other's claims to Koile Syria (Diod. XXI 1,5); Seleukos would not permit Demetrios to retain any territories on the Asian continent (Plut. *Dem.* 32,4–33,1); Seleukos and Lysimachos ultimately settled the matter of mutual recognition on the battlefield of Kurupedion in 282, when Lysimachos was slain and Seleukos seized his entire realm.

47. Note, for example, Polybios's practice of referring to Philippos V as king of Macedon (II 70,8), to Antiochos III as holding the kingdom of Syria (II 71,4–5), and to the "kings of Syria" (i.e, the Seleukids) at V 34,6; see further the Adulis inscription of Ptolemy III (*OGIS*, no. 54), in which the king enumerates the lands of his ancestral domain, and the negotiations about ancestral territorial rights in Koile Syria between Antiochos III and Ptolemy IV in 219/18 (Polybios V 67).

5

The Final Years

The assumption of the kingship in autumn of 306 opens the final phase of the life of Antigonos, who was about seventy-six years old at that time. The last years of Antigonos's life were spent in attempts to consolidate his power and position, partly by administrative work within the kingdom, on which the sources are unfortunately very reticent, and partly by aggressive actions aimed at eliminating some of his persistent external enemies. These actions, mostly led by Demetrios, form the dominant theme in our sources for the period 306–301, the last five years of Antigonos's life. These years were also marked by a physical decline in Antigonos himself. At some point, possibly in 305,[1] Antigonos suffered a serious, indeed near-fatal, illness. Though he recovered and passed the episode off saying, "It was not so bad; for the illness has reminded us not to be proud, as we are but mortal" (Plut. *Mor.* 182b = *Apophth. Ant.* 6), it clearly affected him seriously. Plutarch has left a telling description of the old king in his final years, his huge body now run to fat and suffering from the shortness of breath and lack of energy natural to a combination of old age and excessive corpulence (Plut. *Dem.* 19,1–2). Another hard blow would have been the untimely death of Antigonos's younger son, Philippos, in autumn 306, shortly after the assumption

1. That Antigonos's illness recorded by Plut. *Mor.* 182b occurred in 305 may be implied by Plutarch's information that it was after the Egyptian expedition in late autumn 306 that Antigonos ceased to play an active role in military affairs and became seriously overweight (*Dem.* 19, 1–2). No activity by Antigonos is recorded for 305 except the issuing of a proclamation about Rhodian traders (Polyainos IV 6,16).

of the kingship (Diod. XX 73,1). Antigonos gave Philippos a royal burial at Antigoneia, but did not allow his grief to interfere with carrying on his business.

ATTEMPTS TO ELIMINATE RIVALS (306–302 B.C.)

Ptolemy had been a thorn in Antigonos's side for a long time, and the crushing defeat inflicted by Demetrios offered real hope of being able to get rid of him once and for all if the battle of Salamis were only followed up quickly enough and in sufficient force. In his letter to Demetrios naming him as co-king, Antigonos summoned his son to meet him at Antigoneia with a considerable part of his fleet, and, still in 306, a great expeditionary force was gathered there to march against Egypt: 80,000 infantry, 8,000 cavalry, and eighty-three elephants, and a fleet of 150 warships and 100 transports carrying supplies (Diod. XX 73,1–2). With these forces Antigonos moved south through Palestine to Gaza, he himself commanding the army and Demetrios the fleet, which coasted along with the army. At Gaza he was joined by a great troop of camels brought to him by some allied Arabs; evidently his relations with the Arab tribes of the Dead Sea and Sinai regions had improved since 311. The camels were to carry 130,000 *medimnoi* of wheat and a large stock of fodder for the animals on the expedition. The military machines were conveyed in wagons, and in addition there were the 100 transports of the fleet. With all of this Antigonos expected to reach the Nile without too much hardship.

Eight days before the setting of the Pleiades (i.e., about October 23rd), Antigonos ordered his men to take up ten days' ration each and marched from Gaza towards Egypt, the fleet setting out about midnight of (presumably) the next day (Diod. XX 73,3–74,1). He was taking a risk in setting out so late in the year; Diodoros tells us that some of the pilots of the fleet were not very happy about it, and it seems that the admiral Medeios may have advised against it, to judge from a story in Plutarch of how Medeios is supposed to have dreamed that the expedition would fail (*Dem.* 19,1–2). However, great victories are not won without great risks being taken, and by waiting until the next spring Antigonos would have lost the chance to capitalize on Demetrios's victory at Salamis, giving Ptolemy a whole winter in which to prepare his defenses. Though Antigonos has been blamed by some modern historians for ignoring "expert" advice (e.g., by

Hornblower, *Hieronymus,* pp. 219–20), the fact is that despite running into a heavy storm and losing a few ships, Demetrios and his fleet managed to reach Kasios near the Egyptian border, ride out the storm, and effect a junction there with Antigonos and the army (Diod. XX 74,1–5). Antigonos erred not in ignoring the "experts" who counseled against the expedition, but in preparing for it on too grand a scale. His army of 88,000 men, not counting camp followers, was undoubtedly several times greater than the army Ptolemy could field against him, but, more important, would be exceedingly difficult to control and maintain unless it proved possible to break across the Pelousiac branch of the Nile and into Egypt very quickly. Antigonos would have been better advised to take an army only half the size; this would have been more manageable and easily maintained, yet probably still far larger than Ptolemy's army.[2]

At any rate, Antigonos safely reached the Nile with his army and fleet and camped about a quarter of a mile from the river. Ptolemy had already established a string of loyal garrisons along the Pelousiac branch of the Nile, and he sent out men in boats to offer large bribes to any soldier of Antigonos who would desert to him. After the rough march through the desert, many of Antigonos's mercenaries were inclined to take up Ptolemy's offer, but Antigonos drove off the boats with archers, slingers, and catapults, and tortured some of the would-be deserters *pour décourager les autres* (Diod. XX 74,5–75,3). Having thereby quelled the desertions for the moment, Antigonos set in train his plans for forcing a crossing into Egypt. With the knowledge of Perdikkas's failure in 320, Antigonos was not inclined to try to advance directly across the river against determined opposition. It was to obviate this that he had brought a fleet with him: Demetrios was to sail along the coast and effect a landing behind the Pelousiac mouth of the Nile, thereby turning Ptolemy's defensive position and enabling Antigonos to cross the river with relative ease. When the ships which had been scattered or turned back by the storm had arrived at Antigonos's camp, then, Demetrios set out with the whole fleet, sailing to a place called Pseudostomos. There he attempted a

2. The scale of Antigonos's preparations for this campaign and the cautious way in which he conducted it contrast strongly with the daring he displayed in his campaigns of 319–16, bearing out the judgment of him preserved by Polyainos (IV 6,5) that Antigonos was more daring the weaker his position, and more cautious as his position grew stronger (and he consequently had more to lose). Since Ptolemy had suffered losses amounting to over 20,000 soldiers in 306 (see chap. 4 n. 40) and most of his fleet, it is unlikely he could have put in the field an army of anywhere near 44,000 men at the end of the year unless he had recruited huge numbers of untrained Egyptians, who would scarcely have been a match for Antigonos's men.

landing, but was driven off by the local garrison's fire of all sorts of missile weapons.

After this initial failure, Demetrios made for another mouth of the Nile, called the Phatnitikon, sailing there by night, having ordered the pilots to follow the light on the masthead of his flagship. Unfortunately, many of the pilots failed to carry out this order, and the fleet was scattered. When Demetrios arrived at his objective at daybreak, he wasted a lot of time sending out swift ships to round up the ships that had got lost. Meanwhile Ptolemy arrived at Phatnitikon with substantial reinforcements and prevented Demetrios from landing there. As Demetrios was sailing back along the coast looking for another place to try a landing, a violent storm arose, in the course of which three quadriremes and a number of transports were lost, and Demetrios struggled back to Antigonos's camp with the rest of the fleet, having achieved nothing (Diod. XX 75,4–76,2).[3] The failure of the fleet to turn Ptolemy's defensive position on the Pelousiac branch of the Nile precipitated a very serious situation for Antigonos; he could not maintain his vast army much longer where they were, so that he must either attack immediately across the river, or retire to Palestine. In view of the height of the river, Ptolemy's well-prepared defenses, and the memory of Perdikkas's disaster, the former was not a very alluring option. Not surprisingly, then, when Antigonos called a meeting of the army council, it was decided to cut their losses and return to Palestine at once, which the army and fleet then did in safety (Diod. XX 76,3–6). This campaign thus turned out to be a major setback for Antigonos, though his losses were insignificant except in prestige. Nevertheless, the expedition had had every chance of success when it set out. Its ignominious failure must clearly be laid at the door of Demetrios and the pilots of his fleet, whose poor performance in seeking to make a landing beyond the Pelousiac Nile scotched Antigonos's strategy for the campaign and forced the retreat.[4]

3. Diod. XX 75,4 gives the impression that Antigonos himself led the fleet, as he simply writes "he sailed to the place called Pseudostomon," and the last person mentioned (at XX 75,3) is Antigonos. However, at XX 76,1 it is clearly stated that it was Demetrios who led the fleet, as was to be expected from XX 73,2 and 74,1. Hence the apparent implication at XX 75,4 that Antigonos did so must simply be an error in Diodoros's abbreviation of his source.

4. Seibert, *Ptolemaios I,* pp. 208–22, criticizes Antigonos's "fehlerhafte Strategie und Gesamtplanung des Feldzuges" (p. 222), which in his view caused Antigonos's failure: Antigonos planned to march across the Nile Delta to assault Alexandria, an impracticable strategy owing to the many streams, canals, and marshes of the delta area, which would enable Ptolemy to hold up Antigonos virtually indefinitely; Antigonos should have planned to march south to Memphis, which is how Antiochos IV and Mithridates of Pergamon later successfully invaded Egypt. More recently Hauben has pointed out (*OLP* 6/7 [1975/76]:267–71) that Diod. XX 76,3–4 indicates that Antigonos *did* plan to proceed down the Pelousiac branch of the Nile

Originally it was intended to return to Egypt the following year, after more thorough preparation and at a time of year when the Nile was lower and easier to cross (Diod. XX 76,5). However, before this plan ever matured, a side issue intervened and reached such major proportions that the whole question of Egypt was shelved and never returned to, namely the siege of Rhodes. The Rhodians had been allies of Antigonos during the Third Diadoch War, but had refused to join Demetrios's campaign on Cyprus in 306. They had, in fact, become very friendly towards Ptolemy, being the main middlemen in Egypt's important grain trade with Greece.[5] When Demetrios summoned them to the war against Ptolemy, the Rhodians seem to have

---

towards Memphis with both his army and his fleet, but that by holding the Nile with his river craft, which could outmaneuver triremes and quadriremes on the narrow river, Ptolemy prevented Antigonos from achieving this (he refers also to the very brief description of Paus. I 6,6, which seems to me to add nothing to Diodoros's account). I think neither is entirely correct: it was clearly Antigonos's primary strategic aim on reaching Egypt to eliminate Ptolemy's main army, which was concentrated on the west bank of the Pelousiac Nile, thus damaging what remained of Ptolemy's prestige and opening the way into Egypt. To achieve this, a frontal assault across the Nile, whether near Pelousion or near Memphis, was not likely to succeed. This is why it was vital for Demetrios to land troops in the delta region, to attack Ptolemy's defensive positions along the Pelousiac Nile in the rear and thus enable Antigonos's main force to launch an attack across the river with a good prospect of success. With Ptolemy's major defensive positions and forces thus shattered, his credibility would have been irreparably harmed and Antigonos would have proceeded (as Hauben rightly concludes from Diodoros) along the Pelousiac Nile to Memphis, his army marching along *both* banks and his fleet accompanying him.

5. For a quite good recent treatment of Rhodes in the Diadoch period, see Hauben, *Historia* 26 (1977):307–39, and on the Rhodians' position as middlemen in Egypt's trade with Greece, see esp. the works Hauben cites at p. 335 n. 122. However, Hauben's treatment of the Rhodians' foreign policy in this period as reported at Diod. XX 81,1–4 is inadequate, for he essentially accepts Diodoros at face value (see pp. 318–21). In fact, this chapter of Diodoros is mostly anachronistic or downright fictitious; its main points are as follows: (1) Rhodes was strong in sea power and exceptionally well governed, and a Rhodian alliance was sought by all the dynasts, but it farsightedly preferred to maintain a neutrality friendly to all; (2) Rhodes fought the pirates and purged the seas of them; (3) Alexander the Great deposited his testament at Rhodes and honored it above all cities; (4) in general, Rhodes maintained friendship with all rulers, but most of all with Ptolemy, because of the revenues from its Egyptian trade. Taking these points in order:

1. At the siege of Rhodes in 305/4, the Rhodians sent out squadrons of three (Diod. XX 84,5), three (Diod. XX 88,4), nine (Diod. XX 93,2), and "some" (evidently not many more than three: Diod. XX 97,5–6) warships, which hardly argues for great naval strength at this time. Diodoros is describing Rhodes of the third and early second centuries, when it was a strong sea power and adopted a neutral foreign policy (see, e.g., Polybios XXX 5,6–8), whereas during the years 314–311 Rhodes supported Antigonos against Ptolemy and Kassandros, even concluding an alliance with him (Diod. XIX 58,5; 61,5; 62,7; 64,5–7; 77,3).

2. Rhodes purging the seas of pirates belongs to the third century; Hauben's suggestion that the participation of pirates in Demetrios's campaign against Rhodes was because of a desire to retaliate for Rhodes's police actions against them does not

claimed to have some sort of treaty with or concerning Ptolemy that freed them from any obligation to aid Demetrios, though the matter is very obscure.[6] In any case, Antigonos was clearly very annoyed that Rhodes was edging into the Ptolemaic camp. When planning his Egyptian expedition in the second half of 306, he sent a squadron of ships to prevent any trade between Rhodes and Egypt, but the Rhodians managed to drive this squadron away and evidently continued their trade. Antigonos took this as a *casus belli,* and informed the Rhodians of the fact in no uncertain terms (Diod. XX 81,4–82,2).

Consequently Antigonos's first move at the beginning of 305 was against Rhodes. The Rhodians were alarmed at the prospect of war with Antigonos; they voted him signal honors and sent an embassy to apprise him of the fact and to beg him to permit them to remain friendly with Ptolemy. Antigonos, however, was not prepared to let them off so lightly, no doubt regarding the humbling of Rhodes as the first step in his continued campaign against Ptolemy. He despatched Demetrios with an expeditionary force well equipped with siege engines to bring Rhodes to heel, and the Rhodians were indeed frightened into sending ambassadors to Demetrios agreeing to join in Antigonos's war against Ptolemy (Diod. XX 82,2–3). However, Demetrios insisted upon receiving 100 hostages from the most prominent families, and on being allowed to enter Rhodes with his whole

---

carry conviction: the pirates aided Demetrios as his allies and in the hope of enrichment (Diod. XX 82,4–5); it is more likely that Rhodes's bitter operations against the pirates in the third century were a retaliation for their attack on Rhodes under Demetrios!

3. Not even Hauben lends any credence to the story of Alexander's testament, which (as Hauben says, p. 319) "has absolutely no basis in historical fact and corresponds to the Rhodian interpolations in the Alexander Romance."

4. Rhodes had in fact helped Antigonos against Ptolemy and Kassandros in 314–311, and even had an alliance with him; friendship with Ptolemy may have had its origin in 309/8, as Hauben suggests (p. 336); the trade with Egypt had no doubt already started up in the Diadoch era, but its heyday was in the third and early second centuries, and in the late fourth century much of Rhodes's trade was in fact with Asia Minor and Syria, as may be seen from Antigonos's proclamation recorded by Polyainos IV 6,16.

Hence Diod. XX 81,1–4 merely shows that his account of the siege of Rhodes was drawn from a late-third- or second-century source of strongly pro-Rhodian tendencies. It provides no reliable insights into the background of the conflict with Antigonos other than the observation that Rhodes inclined more and more towards Ptolemy for essentially economic reasons. The most recent discussion of Rhodes in the Diadoch period, that of Berthold, *Rhodes in the Hellenistic Age,* esp. at pp. 63–67, takes essentially the same position as Hauben.

6. See pp. 202–3 and 207–8 below for a fuller discussion of this.

fleet. At this the Rhodians jibbed, fearing that Demetrios was planning a coup d'état in Rhodes, and resolved to resist him at whatever cost. Demetrios concentrated his forces for the siege of Rhodes at Loryma on the Karian coast opposite the island: he had 200 warships of various sizes, over 170 transport ships carrying vast amounts of siege machinery, ammunition, and other supplies, and almost 40,000 soldiers, including cavalry and a considerable number of pirates who were serving as his allies. In addition, there are said to have been close to 1,000 private vessels owned by traders and privateers accompanying him in the hopes of making some profit out of the impending conflict (Diod. XX 82,3–5).

Landing beside the city of Rhodes, Demetrios thoroughly ravaged the island, built a great fortified camp for his army and an artificial harbor for his fleet, and set about constructing siege engines. After vainly pleading for peace several times, the Rhodians set their forces in order: resident aliens and other non-Rhodians who did not wish to fight were sent out of the city, and there remained some 7,000 fighting men to defend Rhodes. They sent urgent messages to Ptolemy, Kassandros, and Lysimachos requesting aid, and passed a number of measures intended to bolster the ardor of the fighting men (Diod. XX 83,1–85,5). Diodoros gives an extremely long and detailed account of this siege (XX 85,5–88,9 and 91,1–99,3); here only its main features will be briefly reviewed.[7]

The siege lasted over a year and can be divided into two phases: in the first Demetrios concentrated on sea-born attacks aimed at capturing the harbor of Rhodes; in the second he gave up naval warfare and attempted to storm Rhodes from the landward side. In both phases enormous effort and ingenuity was expended on the creation of unprecedented and highly impressive siege machinery and other equipment, which seized the imagination of ancient authors (see e.g., Plut. *Dem.* 20–21), and established the reputations of Demetrios ("the Besieger" as he was henceforth known) and his engineers.[8] In spite of this, the siege was ultimately unsuccessful, a result which the huge disparity of force in Demetrios's favor should have made impossible. One cannot escape the conclusion that, more even than the heroic resistance of the Rhodians and the aid they received from Ptolemy, Kassandros, and Lysimachos, a number of blunders by Demetrios were responsible.

7. For full modern treatments of the siege, see, for example, Wehrli, *Antigone et Démétrios,* pp. 207–14 and Seibert, *Ptolemaios I,* pp. 225–30.

8. See app. 3, nos. 37, 47, and 124 for Demetrios's engineers.

In the first phase of the siege, Demetrios launched an all-out attack on the Rhodian harbor with extraordinary floating siege machinery, capturing the harbor mole and distracting the Rhodians with simultaneous assaults on their land fortifications; but after eight days of struggle, he called off the attack to rest his men for a week. Thus he of course also gave a week's respite to the desperately hard-pressed and outnumbered defenders, who were then able to beat off Demetrios's renewed assault. Obviously this respite was a mistake. After Demetrios switched to land assaults, naval operations seem to have been conducted highly negligently. Tiny squadrons of Rhodian ships were able to sail out and do disproportionate damage to Demetrios's shipping, and reinforcements seem to have been able to sail into Rhodes at will. Though it is notorious that ancient oared galleys were inefficient at blockading, it is clear that Demetrios's 200 ships should have been able to limit access to Rhodes's harbor if properly used.[9] Finally, during the land assault phase, Demetrios managed to breach the Rhodian defenses enough to infiltrate troops into the heart of Rhodes at night with orders to cooperate from within with a dawn assault from without; but he sent in only 1,500 men, who proved too few and were annihilated by the Rhodians at the same time as the assault from without was beaten off.[10]

At this point, with the siege threatening to drag on well into 304, Antigonos decided that enough was enough and sent instructions to Demetrios to end the business on the best terms he could; and at about the same time Ptolemy sent to the Rhodians pledging his continued support for their cause, but advising them to agree to terms with Antigonos if possible. The Aitolian League sent an embassy to mediate the dispute in spring of 304, and the two sides took the opportunity to reach a settlement. It was agreed that Rhodes should remain free, ungarrisoned, and financially independent, and should not be obliged ever to fight against Ptolemy, but the Rhodians were otherwise to be allies of Antigonos, and were required to furnish 100 hostages. Thus the siege ended in a compromise, with both sides

9. For the Rhodian squadrons of between three and nine ships and the damage they inflicted, see Diod. XX 84,5; 88,4; 93,2–5; 97,5–6; Plut. *Dem.* 22,1. For reinforcements and supplies sailing unmolested into Rhodes, see Diod. XX 88,9; 96,1–3; 97,6; 98,1. Gomme, *Essays in Greek History and Literature*, pp. 190ff., points out that ancient galleys could not blockade effectively, but Demetrios had two hundred ships and could surely have had squadrons of them patrolling turn and turn about to and fro in front of the harbor entrance to prevent access and egress.

10. For some further details on the land assaults on Rhodes, see app. 3, nos. 6, 8, and 66.

giving ground, but it cannot be denied that in view of the immense resources committed to it under Demetrios's personal leadership, the failure to win a clear victory represented a sharp blow to Antigonid prestige. The Rhodians honored Lysimachos and Kassandros with statues for the aid they had sent; in gratitude for Ptolemy's greater help they voted him divine honors under the title Sotēr (Diod. XX 100,2–4), no doubt in imitation of the cult of Antigonos and Demetrios instituted in Athens in 307; and it was towards the end of the siege that Ptolemy and the other dynasts responded to Antigonos's assumption of the kingship by proclaiming themselves kings as well.[11]

Antigonos now (early summer 304) sent Demetrios to Greece, where his presence was badly needed to deal with efforts by Kassandros to reconquer Athens.[12] At the beginning of 304, it seems, Kassandros had managed to capture Salamis and invest Athens quite closely, and Athenian appeals to Antigonos and Demetrios for help were consequently fairly desperate (Plut. *Dem.* 23,1). Demetrios assembled 330 ships—the number doubtless includes both warships and transports—and a large army, and, after sailing through the Cyclades, landed at Aulis in Boiotia, in the rear of Kassandros's forces besieging Athens. The Boiotian League had at this time incorporated both Chalkis and Eretria on Euboia and was cooperating with Kassandros. Demetrios freed the Euboian cities and frightened the Boiotians into renewing their alliance with Antigonos; he also renewed the alliance with the Aitolians, Kassandros's perennial enemies, and in one swift campaign he raised the siege of Athens and cleared all of central Greece up to Thermopylai of Kassandros's forces, driving Kassandros home to Macedon in headlong flight and capturing the city of Heraklea, where 6,000 Macedonian soldiers came over to him. He then turned back south and took Kenchreai, the port of Korinth, captured the garrisons of Kassandros in the Attic forts of Phyle and Panakton, which he handed back to Athens, and entered Athens in triumph at the end of 304 (Diod. XX 100,5–6; Plut. *Dem.* 23,1–3; *IG* XII.9 192).[13]

---

11. For the dates and circumstances of the other dynasts' assumption of royal status, see the works cited in chap. 4 n. 45 above.

12. For a review of the modern literature on the war between Athens and Kassandros in 307–304, which is now generally recognized to be the so-called Four-Years' War (Plut. *Mor.* 851d), see Seibert, *Diadochen,* pp. 141–42, and Habicht, *Pausanias,* pp. 78–80.

13. Cf. on these events the excellent recent treatment of Gullath, *Gesch. Boiotiens,* pp. 179–83; a recently published inscription provides new evidence of Kassandros holding Athenian frontier forts at this time: Matthaiou, *Horos* 4 (1986):19–23.

This record of signal achievement Demetrios sullied by his activities over the winter of 304/3, when he dwelt hubristically and dissolutely in the Parthenon and involved himself in the factional politics of Athens. He interfered in a power struggle between the Athenian politicians Stratokles and Demochares, in which Stratokles won with Demetrios's support and Demochares was exiled (Plut. *Dem.* 24,3–5).[14] Though this interference was doubtless merely an expression of Demetrios's arrogance, it was unwise, since it cast into doubt the sincerity of Antigonos's policy of freeing the Greeks and made it seem that Demetrios would simply prove another Kassandros, merely backing a different faction in Athens. And perhaps this impression was in many ways right. At any rate, planning was also going ahead during this winter to invade and liberate the Peloponnesos, a necessary preliminary towards setting up a league of the free Greek city-states.

At the beginning of spring 303 Demetrios moved with his army into the Peloponnesos via Kenchreai, which he had captured in the previous year. From Kenchreai he decided to make his first attack not, as one would naturally expect, on Korinth, but on Sikyon, which was still held by a garrison of Ptolemy's (Diod. XX 102,2). To further his aim of surprise, Demetrios tarried at Kenchreai for several days, engaged on various sorts of pleasurable pursuits, while covertly preparing his attack. He apparently established a squadron of ships in the Gulf of Korinth, for when he was ready, he ordered some ships to sail by night to attack the harbor of Sikyon, while mercenaries under his officer Diodoros were in the same night to march around Sikyon and attack from the west along the Pellene road, and he himself led an attack from the east (Polyainos IV 7,3). Sikyon was thus captured with ease. The garrison withdrew to the acropolis, but surrendered shortly afterwards when Demetrios agreed to let them return to Egypt (Diod. XX 102,2; Polyainos IV 7,3). He persuaded the Sikyonians to move their main habitation from the harbor to their acropolis, where they would be more secure against future enemies, and received divine honors for liberating the city (Diod. XX 102,2–4; Plut. *Dem.* 25,2).[15]

---

14. Also Plut. *Mor.* 851d–e = Ps.-Plut. *X Orat.* This power struggle evidently lasted some time, possibly well into the year 303, with Demochares' exile occurring about the middle of that year; see L. C. Smith, *Historia* 11 (1962): 114–18, and cf. Ferguson, *Hellenistic Athens,* pp. 119–22, and Shear, *Kallias of Sphettos,* pp. 47–51.

15. Diodoros and Plutarch state that Sikyon was renamed Demetrias, which seems of rather doubtful historicity in view of an inscription of just this period (last years of the fourth century) recording a treaty between Athens and Sikyon and referring to Demetrios (line 2) and

Demetrios's next target was Korinth, which in 303 was held by a garrison of Kassandros under Prepelaos. There were elements in Korinth who were in sympathy with Demetrios and promised to betray the city to him. Emboldened by his success at Sikyon, Demetrios decided to employ the same tactics at Korinth and was again successful: he set out for Korinth at night, sending one column of troops round to attack from the direction of Lechaion (i.e., from the north) and himself marching up to the south gate, where his friends let him into the city, the other citizens and the garrison all being busy defending the Lechaion gate (Polyainos IV 7,8; Diod. XX 103,1).[16] The garrison troops took refuge on two hills—Sisypheion and Akrokorinthos—but when Demetrios rapidly took Sisypheion by storm, Prepelaos and his men on Akrokorinthos were intimidated into surrendering on terms and returning to Kassandros, leaving Demetrios in full control of Korinth and the Isthmos (Diod. XX 103,2–4).[17] These successes, gained with minimal losses in a few weeks of February/March 303, made a deep impression on the Greeks: the Athenians, for example, who had a contingent of soldiers serving with Demetrios, vowed annual sacrifices to Athena Nike, Good Fortune, and the Saviours (i.e., Antigonos and Demetrios) for the successes thus gained with few or no casualties among their citizens serving with Demetrios.[18]

The Korinthians, we are told, were garrisoned by Demetrios until the end of the war at their own request (perhaps really at the request of the pro-Antigonid faction), and Demetrios moved on to campaign in the Argolid, Achaia, and Arkadia. Inscriptions attest to his capture

---

the Sotēres (i.e., Antigonos and Demetrios; line 3), which consistently names Sikyon and the Sikyonians (e.g., lines 10, 12, 15), not Demetrias and the Demetrieis: E. Schweigert, *Hesperia* 8 (1939):35–41, no. 9 (and cf. Schmitt, *Staatsverträge*, pp. 61–63, no. 445). Recently, however, H. Taeuber has suggested that a city named Demetrias in an Arkadian inscription of early Hellenistic date may be Sikyon (*ZPE* 42 [1981]:179–92). Taeuber suggests that Sikyon was indeed renamed Demetrias in 303, but resumed its ancient name in 301 after the battle of Ipsos.

16. Polyainos literally refers to the "mountain gate," which must correspond to the gate mentioned by Pausanias II 5,4, speaking of a mountain road leading from the Teneatic gate to Tenea "in the interior" (sc., to the south): cf. Bon, Carpenter, and Parsons, *Corinth* 3.2, pp. 48, 65. Lechaion was Korinth's port to the north.

17. Diodoros speaks of Sisypheion and Akrokorinthos as separate hills, though Strabo VIII 379 seems to indicate that Sisypheion was actually part of Akrokorinthos: perhaps one should regard it as a spur or saddle below the peak of Akrokorinthos.

18. On this decree, see Woodhead in *Edson Studies*, ed. Dell, pp. 357–67, for the text and Robert, *REG* 62 (1949):109–13, for a good interpretation. The decree shows that Demetrios had already won significant successes by March of 303, for it belongs to Elaphebolion (March/April) of 303 (see Woodhead, loc. cit.). See further for a laudatory inscription set up by Athenian troops serving with Demetrios at this time Moretti, *ISE*, no. 7.

and liberation of Troizen and Epidauros, and towards the end of June he was in control of Argos, where he presided at the festival of the Heraia (Plut. *Dem.* 25,1–2).[19] While he was in Argos, Demetrios contracted his third marriage, to Deidameia the sister of Pyrrhos of Epeiros, a marriage which offered him two advantages: since Deidamia was a relative of Olympias and had been betrothed originally to Alexandros IV, Demetrios gained a link to ancient royalty by marrying her; and as she was the sister of the reigning king of Epeiros, Demetrios acquired a valuable ally against Kassandros, for Kassandros was an enemy of Pyrrhos (Plut. *Dem.* 25,2; *Pyrrhos* 3,1–4,2). Demetrios then went on to liberate the cities of Achaia and brought over to his side all of Arkadia except Mantinea, apparently meeting serious resistance only at Orchomenos. There the garrison installed by Polyperchon held out against him for a while, but he eventually took the place by storm. Since no aid was forthcoming from Kassandros or Polyperchon (who was apparently lying low in Messenia at this time),[20] this led the other forts and cities to go over to Demetrios without delay, including the important city of Elis (Diod. XX 103,4–7; *IG* IV².1 68 V, lines 136–37). With the northern and central Peloponnesos thus brought into the Antigonid camp by the end of the autumn of 303, plans could be laid for the creation of the great league of Greek cities that was to institutionalize Antigonid influence in Greece while enshrining Antigonos's policy of making the Greek cities autonomous.

The plans for the creation of this league seem to have occupied Demetrios through the winter of 303/2. They came to a head in the spring of 302, when a meeting of representatives from all of the Greek mainland cities now allied with Antigonos and Demetrios met during the Isthmian games at Korinth—the site of the meeting being no doubt chosen in conscious imitation of Philip II. Antigonos could thus strengthen his claim to be the true king of the Macedonians, heir to Philip's policies; and even the Greeks at this time looked back on the era of Philip and Alexander as a more pleasant period than the

19. For Epidauros, see *IG* IV².1 68 (text of League of Korinth treaty) and 58 (honors for Alkaios of Ainos, an officer of Demetrios as we know from *IG* II² 495); for Troizen, see Michel, *RIG*, no. 452 (and cf. Wilhelm, "Att. Urk.," pt. 1, pp. 37–44 for the date and significance of this inscription; also app. 3, no. 120). On Argos, see W. W. Ferguson, *Hesperia* 17 (1948):121 and nn. 23 and 24; the time of the Heraia at Argos was apparently the second half of June.

20. Thus, at least, Beloch, *GG*,4.2:444–45; Plut. *Pyrrhos* 8,3 seems to indicate that Polyperchon *may* have lived on into the third century, despite his advanced age as a near contemporary of Antigonos (cf. Diod. XVIII 48,4 and Plut. *Dem.* 3,3: Antigonos and Polyperchon are respectively the oldest and "almost the oldest" of Alexander's successors).

succeeding decades (see, e.g., Plut. *Phokion* 29,1–2).[21] At any rate, at this Isthmian conference the assembled delegates of the city-states of the northern and central Peloponnesos and of central Greece approved a constitution for the league, much of which is preserved in a large (but in places fragmentary) inscription from Epidauros (*IG* IV².1 68), and elected Antigonos and Demetrios leaders of the Greeks for the duration of the war (Plut. *Dem.* 25,3). The constitution of the "League of Korinth" was quite complex (see pp. 228–30 below for a full discussion), but its main purpose was clearly to set up a sort of "United States of Greece," with Antigonos and Demetrios and their heirs more or less in the position of permanent presidents: the individual cities were to be autonomous and ungarrisoned, but the conduct of foreign policy and maintenance of peace and security were essentially handed over to a representative *synedrion,* chaired by the Antigonid representatives in time of war and set to meet regularly at the Panhellenic games in peacetime.

While Demetrios had been busy in Greece in these years (304–303), Antigonos was in Asia, presumably occupied with the peaceful administration of his realm: he prepared, for example, a synoikism of the Ionian cities of Teos and Lebedos ca. 303 (see *Syll.* 344), and was also busy overseeing the building of his new capital of Antigoneia-on-the-Orontes, where he planned to celebrate a great festival in 302 (Diod. XX 108,1). In the winter of 303/2 Kassandros, alarmed at the loss of his entire position in Greece south of Thermopylai, which he evidently felt unable to reverse, and worried by Demetrios's preparations to campaign further against him in Thessaly and Macedon, opened negotiations with Antigonos with a view to establishing peace (Diod. XX 106,1–2). However, Antigonos, possibly disgusted by the extremely short duration of his previous peace treaty with Kassandros in 311, and convinced that Demetrios was now in a

21. The date of the founding of the League of Korinth (i.e., at the Isthmia of 302) was established by Robert, *Hellenica,* 2:15–33 at 26–28. Philip established his Hellenic alliance at a common council of the Greeks at Korinth (Diod. XVI 89,2; Justin IX 5,1–4); hence no doubt Ptolemy's attempt to call a *synedrion* of the Greeks at Korinth in 308 (chap. 4 n. 18 above), and likewise the location of Demetrios's *synedrion* of the Greeks. The Macedonians remained devoted to the memory of Philip and Alexander: cf. the difficulties of Kassandros in dealing with Alexander's alleged son Herakles in 309 (Diod. XX 28,1–2); the hatred of the Macedonians for Antipatros, the son of Kassandros, for killing his mother, Philip's daughter Thessalonike, and on account of Kassandros's crimes against Alexander's family (Plut *Dem.* 36,1–37,2); and the alleged speech of Demetrios to the Macedonians in 295, recalling to them his father's service with Philip and Alexander (Justin XVI 1,8–17). It therefore made sense for Antigonos to emphasize his own connection with Philip, and he may in fact have been involved with Philip's *synedrion* at Korinth in 338 (see pp. 29–30 above).

position to finish off Kassandros in one more campaign, would agree to no terms short of complete surrender by Kassandros. At this Kassandros called upon Lysimachos, his long-term ally and by now a personal friend, and the two kings met to discuss the situation (Diod. XX 106,2–3). Lysimachos was by no means blind to the threat to his own power that would inevitably arise should Antigonos and Demetrios succeed in annexing Thessaly and Macedon, and he had evidently at last managed to establish firm control over Thrace, being thus free to act against Antigonos.

These two kings, then, decided to take joint steps against Antigonos, the first being to attempt to revive the coalition of 314–311 by diplomatic representations to Ptolemy and Seleukos (Diod. XX 106,3–5). After his own brush with Antigonos in 306, Ptolemy needed little convincing to join with them. Seleukos had established his eastern boundaries after a difficult campaign against the Indian ruler Chandragupta Maurya, giving up his claims to the lands of the Indus valley and receiving in return 500 war elephants from Chandragupta,[22] and he too was easily persuaded to join in this new coalition against Antigonos, doubtless fearing that Antigonos was not yet entirely reconciled to his loss of the upper satrapies. Thus was prepared what may be called the Fourth Diadoch War, in which the four allied kings agreed to a concerted military offensive in an attempt to break Antigonos and Demetrios once and for all (Diod. XX 106,5; Plut. *Dem.* 28,1). The strategy of the alliance was for Kassandros to block Demetrios in Thessaly with part of his army, while the rest of his army under Prepelaos was to join Lysimachos in an invasion of Asia Minor and the forces of Seleukos and Ptolemy were to invade Antigonos's realm from the east and south.

Kassandros accordingly sent Prepelaos with his troops to join Lysimachos and himself moved to Thessaly with the rest of his army—29,000 infantry and 2,000 cavalry—to face Demetrios. Meanwhile Demetrios, besides attending the Isthmia to inaugurate the

22. The 500 elephants given to Seleukos by Chandragupta are reported by Strabo (XV 724 and XVI 752) and by Plutarch (*Alex.* 52), and seem to be confirmed by the testimony of Diod. (XX 113,4) that Seleukos brought 480 elephants with him to Kappadokia in 302, and of Plutarch (*Dem.* 28,3) that 400 elephants fought for Seleukos and Lysimachos at Ipsos. Tarn, *JHS* 60 (1940):84–89, casts doubt on this tradition, but the original numbers in the sources have been convincingly defended by Bar-Kochva, *Seleucid Army*, pp. 76–77, who explains the numbers 500, 480, and 400 by natural wastage on the march from India to Kappadokia and the coldness of the Kappadokian winter, and points out that Seleukos's use of his elephants at the battle of Ipsos as a cavalry screen shows that he must indeed have had an unusually large number of the beasts (cf. more recently Schober, *Gesch. Babyloniens*, pp. 183–86, rejecting Tarn's view and accepting the sources' numbers).

League of Korinth, had wasted time at Athens having himself initiated into the Eleusinian mysteries in a highly irregular fashion, calculated to outrage religious feeling and dispell the goodwill he had previously acquired in Athens (Plut. *Dem.* 26,1–3; Diod. XX 110,1). Having satisfied this religious whim, Demetrios gathered his army and fleet at Chalkis in Euboia to proceed against Kassandros. Demetrios's army now consisted of 48,000 heavy infantry (8,000 Macedonians, 15,000 mercenaries, and 25,000 Greek allies), 8,000 light infantry and 1,500 cavalry, making him far superior to Kassandros. Since the latter had by this time garrisoned the passes into Thessaly against his passage, Demetrios embarked his army on his ships and sailed from Euboia across to Thessaly, landing at the port of Larisa Kremaste in Phthiotis (Diod. XX 110,2–4; cf. *IG* XII.9 210). He had no difficulty in arresting Kassandros's garrison in Larisa, quickly captured some other small towns in Phthiotis, and then took up position with his army against Kassandros, who had garrisoned Pherai and Phthiotic Thebes to guard his rear and encamped in a strong position to thwart Demetrios.

The two armies remained thus encamped opposite each other for a considerable time without any significant action resulting, despite the fact that battle lines were frequently drawn up. Diodoros (XX 110,5) records that both were awaiting some decision of events in Asia Minor, and while this was natural enough for Kassandros, it indicates a culpable lack of energy on the part of Demetrios, who ought to have been able to use his massive superiority in infantry to gain some important success during the course of this summer. It is true that the advance of Prepelaos along the coast of western Asia Minor distracted Demetrios, requiring him to send aid there (Diod. XX 107,3 and 5; cf. *OGIS*, no. 9); but in Thessaly the sum of Demetrios's success was the liberation of Pherai and the capture of Kassandros's garrison there (Diod. XX 110,6). And while Demetrios was thus failing to capitalize on his military superiority vis-à-vis Kassandros in Thessaly, Kassandros's allies were enjoying all too much success in Asia Minor.

THE CAMPAIGN OF IPSOS (302–301 B.C.)

Lysimachos and Prepelaos crossed the Hellespont with their forces early in 302 and landed near Lampsakos and Parion, which quickly came over to them. From there they marched down to the Troad and took Sigeion by storm, installing a garrison in the place, and then divided their forces: Prepelaos marched down to the west coast through Aiolia and Ionia, while Lysimachos undertook a campaign in the interior of western Anatolia (Diod. XX 107,2). First, however, Lysimachos sat down to besiege Abydos, but he gave up the siege when help arrived for the city from Demetrios. Instead, Lysimachos marched into the interior of Hellespontine Phrygia and, winning most of it over without (apparently) much resistance, proceeded into greater Phrygia down the great north-south road to Synnada, which he besieged. Dokimos, presumably the man who had formerly been an adherent of Perdikkas and Alketas,[23] was in charge of Synnada and the surrounding region at this time. He had already shown in 317/16 that he had no scruples over treason (see Diod. XIX 16,1–4), and on this occasion he quickly betrayed the trust of Antigonos and went over to Lysimachos, handing over to him Synnada and the treasure Antigonos held there (Diod. XX 107,2–4; Paus. I 8,1).

While Lysimachos was thus advancing successfully into Phrygia, Prepelaos was enjoying similar success in Aiolia and Ionia, where he seized Adramyttion in passing and pressed down to Ephesos, which he captured without much of a struggle. There he found and released the one hundred Rhodian hostages taken by Demetrios in 304. He also destroyed all the ships in the harbor, altered the constitution of Ephesos, established his own supporters in power, and left a garrison to hold the city (Diod. XX 107,4; 111,3; *I. Ephesos,* 5, no. 1449 [= *Syll.*, no. 358]).[24] Prepelaos next took over Teos and Kolophon, but further progress on the coast of Ionia was impeded by the arrival of reinforcements by sea, which secured Klazomenai and Erythrai against him and caused him to turn inland (Diod. XX 107,5; *OGIS,* no. 9). He marched on Sardis and persuaded the general in charge of the region, one Phoinix, to desert Antigonos and let him into Sardis. However, Antigonos's commander of the citadel of Sardis and the royal treasure held there was loyal, and Prepelaos's success was thus only partial (Diod. XX 107,5).

Antigonos was at his new capital of Antigoneia-on-the-Orontes in spring of 302, organizing a great festival with athletic and dramatic competitions to inaugurate the new city. When word reached him of Lysimachos's invasion and the losses caused by the treachery of his generals, however, he cancelled the festival immediately, richly com-

23. See on this app. 3, no. 35 below.

24. For the correct interpretation of this inscription, showing that it records the stationing of a garrison in Ephesos, see Robert, *Hellenica,* 3:79–85.

pensating the disappointed performers, and prepared to march to Asia Minor with his army. It was at this time that the loss of his younger son Philippos and his nephew Polemaios must have been most regretted by Antigonos, who was obliged at the age of eighty and in poor physical condition to undertake in person a strenuous campaign against younger and more energetic opponents. Nevertheless, Antigonos began his campaign with some of his old energy and despatch. Marching with great rapidity, he moved first to Tarsos, where he gave his army three months' pay to ensure its loyalty and in addition equipped himself with 3,000 talents to defray the expense of the war, drawing for all this on the great treasury at Kyinda. Then he crossed the Taurus mountains, and proceeded through Lykaonia and Phrygia, restoring the local *stratēgoi* to loyalty to him as he went (Diod. XX 108,1–3).

As Antigonos approached through southern Phrygia, Lysimachos was apparently still in the region of Synnada, having probably been joined there by Prepelaos.[25] He held a council to decide what to do, and since his army was inferior to that of Antigonos, it was decided to avoid a battle until Seleukos arrived from inner Asia. In the meantime it was necessary to occupy Antigonos and maintain a position in Asia Minor to make a junction with Seleukos possible. Accordingly Lysimachos selected a strong position and made a fortified encampment with palisade and ditch, where he awaited Antigonos's arrival. Antigonos, finding that Lysimachos would not come out to battle, occupied the approaches to Lysimachos's camp in force so as to cut off his supplies. Lysimachos then broke out by night and made a forced march of about 50 miles (400 stades) to Dorylaion, where he established a new camp beside the river Thymbres (the modern Porsuk), there being ample supplies of food in Dorylaion. He fortified this new camp with a triple stockade and a deep ditch (Diod. XX 108,4–7).

Antigonos followed Lysimachos and set about besieging the latter's new camp, sending for siege engines with which to assault the fortifications and establishing his own line of field works around the camp to shut Lysimachos and his army in. By now he must have known the full scale of the task facing him, as he learned of the

25. This is nowhere specifically recorded, but seems inevitable, as otherwise there ought to be some report in the sources of how Prepelaos fared when Demetrios landed in Ionia at the end of 302 (Diod. XX 111,3); from Diodoros's silence concerning Prepelaos there, it seems evident that Prepelaos had already left Ionia and Lydia to join Lysimachos against Antigonos in Phrygia.

situation in Thessaly, of Prepelaos's presence in Asia, and of Seleukos marching through Mesopotamia and Armenia towards Kappadokia to enter the field against him. In addition, Ptolemy fulfilled his part in the strategy of the coalition by invading Palestine at the head of a strong force, but instead of marching rapidly north towards Asia Minor to play a part in events there, he spent his time taking over the cities of Palestine and establishing garrisons in them (Diod. XX 113,1).[26] Antigonos's position was thus becoming critical, but a decisive victory by Demetrios in Thessaly or by himself over Lysimachos could have restored the situation at once. He therefore pressed his siege of Lysimachos strongly, defeating repeated attempts by Lysimachos to prevent his enclosing the latter's camp with field fortifications. However, as his enclosure of Lysimachos's camp was nearing completion, Lysimachos took the opportunity of a particularly dark and stormy night to break out and slip away through the gap that yet remained, marching away northward along a ridge of high ground. Antigonos set out in pursuit at daybreak, marching parallel to Lysimachos's column through the plains, but great rainstorms turned them into a sea of mud, in which he lost many of his pack animals and even some of his soldiers. His endurance broke at this, and he decided to call a halt and go into winter quarters (Diod. XX 109,1–4).

Antigonos had already taken measures to delay or turn back Seleukos and Ptolemy: a swift raiding column had, it seems, crossed the Euphrates and descended on Babylonia, capturing Babylon behind Seleukos's back; and men had been sent to spread rumors in Palestine of a great battle fought in Asia Minor between Antigonos and the forces of Lysimachos and Seleukos, in which the latter two had been decisively defeated, freeing Antigonos to march against Ptolemy.[27] The cautious Ptolemy was deceived by these rumors and hurried back to Egypt, after first securing with garrisons the cities he had already captured in Palestine (Diod. XX 113,1–2); but Seleukos was in no wise deflected from his purpose and brought his army down into Kappadokia, where he went into winter quarters late in 302 with 20,000 infantry, about 12,000 cavalry, 100 scythed chariots,

26. Tarn, *CAH*, 6:504, attributes Ptolemy's brief campaign in Palestine to "spring 301," but it is in fact clear from Diod. XX 112–13 that it occurred at the end of 302; at 112 Diodoros reports the crossing of Pleistarchos from Odessos to Herakleia Pontika to join Lysimachos in winter quarters at the end of 302, and at the beginning of 113 he introduces his account of Ptolemy's campaign with the clear chronological indication "During these same days . . . ."

27. For the raiding column Antigonos sent to occupy Babylon behind Seleukos's back, see now Mehl, *Seleukos Nikator*, 1:196–98.

and 480 elephants (Diod. XX 113,4).[28] When Antigonos found that he was unable to prevent Lysimachos's escape northward and that Seleukos had not been deflected from his march into Anatolia, he realized that the issue of the war must be decided by a major battle in western Anatolia and sent instructions recalling Demetrios from his sterile encounter with Kassandros, ordering him to bring his army to Asia Minor as soon as possible (Diod. XX 109,5). Demetrios patched up a truce with Kassandros, in which it was specified that all Greek cities were to be free and that the further terms of peace were to be effective only if ratified by Antigonos (Diod. XX 111,1–2; Marmor Parium [*FGrH,* no. 239b], sec. 26).

In point of fact the truce between Demetrios and Kassandros was simply a device allowing for immediate disengagement of their forces, as neither of them really intended to abide by it. Demetrios sailed off with his army to Asia Minor, and once he was gone Kassandros recovered control of Thessaly. He then sent a large part of his army (12,000 foot and 500 horse) under his brother Pleistarchos to join Lysimachos and Prepelaos in Asia Minor (Diod. XX 111,2; 112,1). Demetrios sailed across the Aegean to Ephesos, which surrendered to him almost at once; he dismissed on terms the garrison of Prepelaos, and installed a garrison of his own on the acropolis. During the late autumn of this year (302), Demetrios carried out one of his characteristic whirlwind campaigns, recovering all of the areas of western Anatolia lost to Prepelaos and Lysimachos. The various cities were brought back to allegiance to Antigonos in a campaign northward up the west coast of Asia Minor, culminating in a sharp battle near Lampsakos between Demetrios and a force left there by Lysimachos, which Demetrios won, capturing Parion and Lampsakos and part of Lysimachos's baggage train, which had been left there (Diod. XX 111,3; Polyainos IV 12,1). Demetrios then proceeded to the Bosporos, where he built a fortified camp in the territory of Chalkedon and established a garrison of 3,000 soldiers and 30 warships to guard the crossing from Europe to Asia, and the passage through the Bosporos. He then went into winter quarters with the rest of his army in the cities of the Hellespontine region (Diod. XX 111,3).

After escaping from Antigonos at Dorylaion, Lysimachos and his army had retreated north towards Herakleia Pontika and set up

28. Diodoros actually says "more than 100" scythed chariots; Plut. *Dem.* 28,3 gives Seleukos and Lysimachos 120 chariots at Ipsos in 301. For the number of elephants, see n. 22 above.

winter quarters in the plain of Salonia, presumably the region between Herakleia on the coast and the modern city of Bolu. By marrying the widow of Herakleia's former tyrant, Dionysios, Lysimachos got control of Herakleia, which served him as a base and source of supplies (Diod. XX 109,6–7). Pleistarchos and his reinforcements for Lysimachos marched across Macedon and Thrace to the coast of the sea of Marmara, but found on arriving that the cities on the Asian coast had already been occupied by Demetrios, so that they could not safely cross there. Instead, Pleistarchos marched up the Black Sea coast to Odessos and prepared to cross from there straight to Herakleia. Since he could not find enough ships to ferry his entire force at once, he divided it into three parts to cross separately. The first contingent crossed safely to Herakleia, but the second was captured by Demetrios's 30 ships from the Bosporos. Pleistarchos gathered new ships from somewhere and set out to cross with the last contingent, but ran into a great storm that wrecked most of the ships. Pleistarchos was washed ashore still alive, but only 33 of the 500 men on his ship survived, and one can scarcely suppose that more than 1,000 or so of this last contingent got across. Thus only some 5,000 of the 12,500 men sent by Kassandros would have reached Lysimachos (Diod. XX 112,1–4).

These reinforcements would not even have been enough to replace other losses incurred by Lysimachos during the winter 302/1 as a result of Demetrios's capture of part of his baggage at Lampsakos. For this baggage happened to belong to mercenaries from the Danubian tribe of the Autariatai serving with Lysimachos, men who were more attached to their baggage than to their general, the more so as Lysimachos had evidently got into arrears with their pay. Accordingly 2,000 of the Autariatai deserted to Antigonos, and with them went 800 Lykians and Pamphylians.[29] These were all well received by Antigonos, who paid them what Lysimachos owed them and gave them gifts besides. Fearing the other 5,000 Autariatai would also desert, Lysimachos led them out into open country on a pretext and had them massacred (Diod. XX 113,3; Polyainos IV 12,7).[30]

29. It seems strange that Lysimachos should have been able to recruit such a large body of Lykians and Pamphylians from the territory of his perennial enemy Antigonos; perhaps these men were survivors from the army of Antigonos's general Pausanias, captured by Lysimachos in 312 and enrolled in his own army (Diod. XIX 73,10), which would help to explain why they deserted to Antigonos at this time.

30. Polyainos records Demetrios's capture of the baggage of the Autariatai at Lampsakos and Lysimachos's consequent massacre of some 5,000 of them lest they desert to Antigonos; Diodoros records the actual desertion of some 2,000 Autariatai to Antigonos. Since both events

The year 301 opened, then, with four armies in the field in northwestern Asia Minor: those of Demetrios and Antigonos wintering near the Hellespont and around Dorylaion respectively; and those of Lysimachos and Seleukos, which had wintered near Herakleia and in western Kappadokia respectively. Since Diodoros, our major source for the Diadoch period, ends his twentieth book with the winter of 302, and his subsequent books are preserved only in minor fragments and excerpts, the details of the campaign that led up to the battle of Ipsos are irretrievably lost, and only a rather vague picture of the battle itself can be gathered from the only two sources that offer any details: Plutarch *Dem.* 28–29 and Diodoros XXI 1,1–4b.[31] At the beginning of spring, Lysimachos and Seleukos must have left their winter quarters and marched towards each other, since they badly needed to effect a junction before Antigonos and Demetrios could overwhelm them separately. One may reasonably conjecture that Lysimachos, marching southeastward from the vicinity of modern Bolu, would have met Seleukos marching down the Royal Road somewhere near Ankyra. Meanwhile Demetrios must have joined Antigonos near Dorylaion. Such a course of events explains why the battle was fought near Synnada at Ipsos (probably the modern village of Sipsin, just north of the Dolay Çay river near modern Afyonkarahissar, and some forty miles north of ancient Synnada);[32] for from Ankyra Lysimachos and Seleukos would have thrust down the Royal

occurred in the winter of 302/1, it is obvious that there must be some connection between the facts reported by Polyainos and Diodoros; my reconstruction here seems most plausible. For dissension in Antigonos's camp at this same time, see app. 3, nos. 72 and 73.

31. For a full list of sources mentioning the battle of Ipsos, see Bar-Kochva, *Seleucid Army*, p. 107 n. 7. The only full-scale modern reconstructions of the battle are ibid., pp. 106–10, and Mehl, *Seleukos Nikator*, 1:200–207. I find Bar-Kochva's exculpation of Demetrios's pursuit of the defeated cavalry in front of him unconvincing: he suggests that Demetrios may have been intending to capture the enemy's baggage, like Antigonos at Gabiene, but there is no indication of this in the sources, and it is not the sort of task one would give one's main body of heavy cavalry, leaving the infantry meanwhile in the lurch. Bar-Kochva also suggests that the enemy cavalry under Antiochos had not been sufficiently disrupted for Demetrios to give up the pursuit, but a good cavalry general should never lose touch with the rest of his army, which it is his duty to support, whether he has managed thoroughly to disrupt the cavalry directly opposing him or not. Bar-Kochva suggests, too, that the army of Seleukos and Lysimachos was fired with the thought of plundering Antigonos's royal treasure at Synnada, but fails to notice that this had in fact already been captured by Lysimachos in the previous year (Diod. XX 107,4). Some useful comments on the battle of Ipsos can be found in Tarn, *HMND*, pp. 35–36, 68–69, 96.

32. See for this Honigmann, *Byzantion* 10 (1935):647–51, and cf. Robert, *Hellenica*, 7:217–18 n. 7, defending Honigmann against baseless criticism by Ramsay. Cf. also Bar-Kochva, *Seleucid Army*, p. 107; Wehrli, *Antigone et Démétrios*, p. 70; Mehl, *Seleukos Nikator*, 1:203.

Road towards Synnada, thus threatening Sardis and Kelainai, the most important centers of Antigonid power in Asia Minor.

Evidently Antigonos and Demetrios must have hurried south to intercept Seleukos and Lysimachos and cover the threatened regions of Lydia and Phrygia, and so the two great armies came together in the plain around Sipsin on the north bank of the Dolay Çay, near where the north-south road between Dorylaion and Synnada met the Royal Road (see map 6). Here, on the broad flat plain of the Dolay Çay,[33] the last act of Antigonos's life unfolded. The combined army of Antigonos and Demetrios amounted to 70,000 infantry, 10,000 cavalry, and 75 elephants. The army led by Seleukos and Lysimachos was inferior in infantry at 64,000 men (though the troops of Lysimachos and Kassandros, which made up 44,000 of this number, were of excellent quality), but superior in cavalry, and they were able to field at least 400 elephants (Plut. *Dem.* 28,3).[34] However, a great part of Seleukos's cavalry (by far the majority of the cavalry in the allied camp) were light horse archers and javelineers—presumably Iranians—who could not be used for a mass charge (Diod. XX 113,4). It is probable, therefore, that Antigonos and Demetrios had a preponderance of heavy cavalry, and it was on this that they counted in the battle.

Plutarch records (*Dem.* 28,2–29,2) that Antigonos approached the coming conflict in a subdued mood. It was his habit in approaching great battles to display exaggerated cheerfulness and confidence, making boastful speeches and jokes to impress the troops; on this occasion, too, he is said to have remarked that he would scatter the enemies gathered against him like a flock of birds, with a single stone and a single shout. However, on the whole he was thoughtful rather than exuberant, and he spent much time closeted in private discussions with Demetrios, even holding an assembly of his army to hear him affirm Demetrios's position as his successor. On the day of the battle itself, Antigonos is said to have tripped and fallen on his face while leaving his tent—a bad omen—and to have prayed on rising for

---

33. For a brief description of this plain, see G. Radet, *REA* 38(1936):263; he had visited the region in 1893.

34. The precise number of cavalry fielded by Seleukos and Lysimachos is in doubt. Plut. *Dem.* 28,3 speaks of 500 more cavalry than Antigonos, that is, 10,500, but Bar-Kochva, *Seleucid Army*, p. 107 n. 11, points to the fact that Seleukos brought 12,000 cavalry with him from the east in 302 (Diod. XX 113,4) and argues that since Lysimachos must also have contributed some cavalry, the total of the allies' cavalry should have been nearer 15,000 than 10,500. Accordingly he suggests that there is an error in Plutarch's text, supporting this by the similar error between 500 and 5,000 in Plutarch's text at *Dem.* 5,2.

either victory or death before defeat. Some of this gloom is no doubt *ex eventu* elaboration of the facts, but it is reasonable to suppose that Antigonos, approaching such a crucial and dangerous battle at the age of eighty-one and in poor physical condition, should have taken into account the possibility of not surviving the conflict and hence discussed the state of the realm and its future needs with Demetrios and confirmed the latter's position as his successor. And it seems that Antigonos really was determined not to survive a defeat.

The battle of Ipsos was a turning point in history. A decisive victory for Antigonos and Demetrios would have enabled Antigonos to recover control over such of the upper satrapies as he wished, and Kassandros—a great part of whose army fought at Ipsos—would not have had sufficient strength to withstand a new assault on Macedon. Only Ptolemy would have been left of Antigonos's enemies, and he could have been dealt with at leisure. On the other hand, defeat would throw into the melting pot all of Antigonos's achievements of the past twenty years, and it is not surprising that Antigonos should have decided to conquer or die, for at his age he could hardly make a new start or relish the prospect of life as a fugitive or captive. The exact plans and dispositions of the two armies for the battle are not recorded in our extant sources. We know from Plutarch (*Dem.* 29,3) that most of Antigonos's heavy cavalry was massed on one wing under the personal command of Demetrios, who was indeed the battle leader of Antigonos's army. Opposite Demetrios was drawn up a large part of Seleukos's cavalry under his son Antiochos. Antigonos evidently took up his station with his phalanx, which was intended to play a defensive role in the battle, as was the weak cavalry wing, which must have been marshalled in a withdrawn position. The plan was for Demetrios to charge with the heavy cavalry, drive away the cavalry of Antiochos, and then take the enemy phalanx in flank and rear.[35]

Antigonos's 75 elephants must be presumed to have been drawn up as a screen in front of his phalanx and defensive wing, interspersed with light infantry (as was usual). Opposite them would have been the enemy phalanx with a similar screen of elephants—perhaps numbering 100 or so—under the command of Lysimachos, for it is recorded that one phase of the battle consisted of a fierce and even

35. At least, one may reasonably assume that this was the battle plan from Demetrios's actions: he charged and routed the cavalry opposite him, drove them off the field, and then turned back towards the main battle and the infantry (Plut. *Dem.* 29,3). Unfortunately, Demetrios had pursued the enemy cavalry too far and left the rest of the battle too long, enabling Seleukos to block his return to the battle with a screen of elephants, which the horses would not approach.

struggle between Antigonos's elephants and elephants under Lysimachos (Diod. XXI 1,2). The total number of elephants fielded by Seleukos and Lysimachos in the battle is said to have been 400 (see n.22 above), the majority of them—perhaps some 300 in number—stationed in a body under the command of Seleukos himself. When Demetrios charged with his cavalry, the cavalry of Antiochos was driven back in real or pretended flight[36] and drew Demetrios away from the battlefield in pursuit. Seleukos then drew up his elephants in a screen, preventing Demetrios's cavalry from returning to the field of battle to attack Lysimachos's phalanx in rear (Plut. *Dem.* 29,3, and cf. *Pyrrhos* 4,3). Having thus neutralized Demetrios and the heavy cavalry, Seleukos took his light horse archers and javelineers, who had presumably until then been arrayed on the withdrawn flank, and led them in a maneuver outflanking and encircling Antigonos's phalanx, which they harassed from a distance.

Thus faced with the double threat of the enemy phalanx under Lysimachos in front and Seleukos's light cavalry in flank and rear, Antigonos's phalanx quickly caved in, a large part of it surrendering to the enemy and the rest turning to flight (Plut. *Dem.* 29,3–4). At this point the battle could perhaps still have been turned into a draw, like the battle of Paraitakene in 316, if Demetrios could have yet attacked Lysimachos's phalanx in rear, and it is said that Antigonos hoped for this to the last. At any rate, when his phalanx was broken, the old king refused to leave the field of battle, and when warned by one of his attendants that a mass of the enemy was bearing down to attack him, he coolly replied, "Who else but me should they attack?" Since Demetrios failed to return to the battle despite his father's faith in him, Antigonos was eventually abandoned by his guards and attendants and went down in a cloud of javelins, only one faithful friend, Thorax of Larissa, remaining by his body (Plut. *Dem.* 29,4–5). So, refusing to survive defeat, Antigonos died, having outlived all of his contemporaries with the possible exception of Polyperchon. Demetrios, to whose classic error of pursuing too far the defeat must be attributed, fled from the battle with 4,000 of the cavalry, gathering in addition 5,000 infantry in the course of his flight. He went to Ephesos and took ship on his fleet to start a new career as sea king (Plut. *Dem.* 30,1–2). The body of Antigonos was given a royal burial by his enemies (Diod. XXI 1,4b), probably thanks to Seleukos, the most

36. Tarn, *HMND*, pp. 68–69, suggests that the flight of Seleukos's cavalry under Antiochos was a deliberate ploy decided on in advance by Seleukos in order to lure Demetrios away from the battle and enable his return to be blocked.

magnanimous as well as the most able of Antigonos's opponents; and the Asian empire of Antigonos was divided up between the conquerors.

EPITAPH

The ultimately unsuccessful aggressiveness of Antigonos's last years has colored the judgments of him by both ancient and modern commentators alike. Diodoros (XXI 1,1) and Plutarch (*Dem.* 28,2), for example, pronounced final judgments on Antigonos as a man flawed and ultimately brought to ruin by excessive and overweening ambition. These verdicts were clearly influenced by the events of the last years of Antigonos's life, but have the effect of pronouncements on his entire career, and unjustly so: one need only imagine how different the closing judgments on Antigonos would have been had he died in (say) 303, or had he won the battle of Ipsos, to see that this is so. Nevertheless, these judgments have been taken over by many modern scholars. Historians like Jouguet, Wehrli, and Hornblower—to pick a few examples more or less at random—express negative judgments on Antigonos's abilities or invidious comparisons with Alexander, which seem to me wholly to miss the mark.[37]

Unlike Alexander, who was the universally recognized king of a united people, Antigonos had to build up his own power piecemeal and faced the determined opposition of able and well-trained leaders with forces of the same type and background as his own, so that comparisons between the success of Alexander and the ultimate failure of Antigonos are beside the point. It is a fact that for over twenty years Antigonos was the most successful general and statesman in an age of unusually many able political and military leaders. Of course he occasionally miscalculated and made errors; and to say that his ambition led to his ultimate failure is as obviously and insignificantly true as to say that his ambition led to his earlier successes: without great ambition one does not seek great power, and if one does not seek great power, one does not create the opportunity for either the great successes or the great failures that mark the careers of ambitious men.

That Antigonos should have avoided the risk of a decisive battle like that fought at Ipsos by being conciliatory towards the other

37. Jouguet, *Macedonian Imperialism,* p. 136; Hornblower, *Hieronymus of Cardia,* pp. 211–23; Wehrli, *Antigone et Démétrios,* p. 135.

dynasts is the judgment of hindsight—a judgment which would be exactly the opposite had he won the battle, as he might have done; and that Antigonos could in the long run have avoided a showdown with his rival dynasts is far from certain. One might call to mind Machiavelli's principle that to make concessions in order to avoid war is usually merely to postpone the war to one's own disadvantage (*Il principe* III). Even if Antigonos had successfully avoided war during his own lifetime, it is possible (not to say likely) that his son Demetrios would ultimately have faced such a battle as that fought at Ipsos in 301, quite likely with the same disastrous consequences. For if the sources show one thing, it is that the failures of Antigonos's later career were for the most part due to the excessive trust he placed in the abilities of Demetrios, brilliant though Demetrios was capable of being on occasion. The serious reverse at Gaza, the failure of the Egyptian expedition, the debacle of the siege of Rhodes, and the final disaster at Ipsos itself were all due in great part to errors on the part of Demetrios, who simply lacked the consistent political, strategic, and tactical sureness of touch which marked out Antigonos as the greatest of the Diadochoi, and which were required if Demetrios were to play the role intended for him by Antigonos satisfactorily.

Part II

Antigonos as Ruler of a Hellenistic Empire

6

Antigonos's Relations with the Greeks

As ruler of Asia a factor of prime importance to Antigonos was a supply of Greco-Macedonian manpower to fill his armies, administration, and colonies. The major source of such manpower was the Greek city-states of Asia Minor and Greece proper, but the latter were under the hegemony of the ruler of Macedon, Antigonos's rival Kassandros. Good relations with the Greeks therefore served a twofold purpose for Antigonos: to encourage Greeks to take service with him; and to make difficulties for Kassandros, turning his overlordship of Greece as far as possible from a source of strength into one of weakness. In seeking a way to bring the Greeks into his own sphere of influence, while at the same time retaining their goodwill, Antigonos hit upon the idea of promoting local autonomy for the Greek city-states, the very well-spring of their political and cultural life, and setting himself up as their protector and benefactor. In doing this, Antigonos defined the ground rules for political interaction between Hellenistic monarchs and the Greek *poleis* throughout the Hellenistic era.[1] But the idea of basing his policy on the autonomy principle did

---

1. See, for example, Gruen, *Hellenistic World and the Coming of Rome,* 1:132–57. Orth, *Königliche Machtanspruch,* has shown that under the early Seleukids the relations between the monarchs and the Greek cities, though still using the idea of autonomy and royal benefactions as a framework, became redolent with cynicism and hypocrisy on both sides, and this trend certainly pertained to the other dynasties besides the Seleukids and became more notable as time passed. But under Antigonos, who first pressed the idea of Greek autonomy as a general principle, cynicism and hypocrisy, even if present to some extent, are much less marked. Indeed, Orth himself repeatedly contrasts the more liberal and friendly relations between Greek cities and Antigonos with those of the same cities and the Seleukids (see, e.g., pp. 48–50, 80–81, 94–95).

not spring newborn into Antigonos's mind: this principle had developed as an ideal in Greece during the fourth century and needed only to be adapted by Antigonos to fit his needs.

COMMON PEACES AND AUTONOMY IN THE FOURTH CENTURY B.C.

The fourth century B.C. was a difficult era for the Greek city-states. The Peloponnesian War had a disastrous effect upon Athenian power and confidence, upon Spartan manpower, upon the cohesion of the Spartan alliance, and upon the internal political stability of states all around the Greek world. Moreover, it was a war that settled little, in spite of its seemingly decisive outcome. Within eight years of its end, the Greek world was at war once more: in Asia Minor the Spartans attempted to reverse their cession of the Asiatic Greeks to the Persians, while in mainland Greece they faced a coalition of old enemies (Athens and Argos) and recalcitrant allies (Korinth and Boiotia). Out of this renewed warfare emerged two significant developments, which were to play a major role in Greek history for the next few centuries. One was the principle that all Greek states should unite in peace and respect one another's freedom and autonomy. This was established by the so-called Peace of Antalkidas that ended the warfare in 387. The second is illustrated by the other name given to this peace—the King's Peace. It was brought about by the intervention of the Persian king, who sent down a rescript setting out the terms and threatening war to any Greek states that rejected the peace.[2] Thus was established the principle that a foreign superpower might set itself up as the guarantor of peace and autonomy in the Greek world, the *rector* of the Greeks.

The Peace of Antalkidas itself did not last long, but the ideas embodied in it remained. In only half a century, no fewer than six of these "common peaces" were made[3]—perhaps even more if one includes some dubious cases. Two facts stand out clearly in all this. In

2. Xenophon *Hellenika* V 1,25–32; esp. 1,31: "King Artaxerxes asserts . . . that the other Hellenic cities both great and small should be autonomous . . . and whoever do not observe this peace, against them I shall make war"; and cf. also Diod. XIV 110,3 giving the same terms and threat, and Isokrates VIII 16.

3. In 387, 375, 371 (Sparta), 371 (Athens), 362, and 338; for sources and full discussion, see Ryder, *Koine Eirene*. Possible, but dubious, other examples are a reputed common peace in 366/65 (see, e.g., Xen. *Hell.* VII 1,33–40), and the Peace of Philokrates in 346 (thus [Demosthenes] VII 20–32).

the first place, attractive as the idea of a common peace guaranteeing the autonomy of all the *poleis* was to the Greeks in principle, they were incapable of putting the principle into practice on more than a very transitory basis. Secondly, it is evident that Persia could not sustain the role of *rector* of Greece: the center of Persian power was too far from mainland Greece, and Persia was in any case a state in decay, plagued by secessions and maintained largely by the efforts of Greek mercenaries. Though Persia's influence is recorded in connection with several of the common peaces after 387, its aim seems largely to have been to effect peace in Greece in order to liberate Greek manpower to supply its own wants as mercenaries.[4]

Nevertheless, conditions in Greece after 362 (the battle of Mantinea) favored intervention by a strong, centralized power. After close to a century of internecine warfare (ca. 460–360), the two strongest states in Greece—Sparta and Athens—had been cut down to size, while Thebes had proved unable to fill their shoes. In the Peloponnesos Sparta was ringed by the hostile states of Messene, Megalopolis, and Argos, which prevented it from regaining its old power. The revival of Athenian sea power was impaired by the bitter struggle of the Social War (357–355), which seriously weakened the so-called Second Athenian League. Thebes, by wantonly provoking the Phokians, brought upon itself the Third Sacred War (ca. 356–346), which neither side was able to win: it simply dragged on, causing great losses and suffering to both sides, fatally injuring Thebes's leadership in Central Greece, and providing the arena for Philip of Macedon to intervene in Greek affairs. As is well known, Philip intervened several times in the war and eventually brought it to a close, in the process establishing himself as *archōn* of Thessaly and gaining representation in the Amphiktyonic League.[5]

To those Greeks who could see it, the writing was now on the wall. By uniting Thessaly to a strong and stable Macedon, Philip had created far the strongest military power in Greece and put himself in a position to intervene decisively in Greek affairs. Some welcomed the prospect of Macedonian hegemony: Isokrates published a pam-

---

4. A good survey of Persian history in this period can be found in Frye's recent book *A History of Ancient Iran*. For Persia's interest in promoting peace in order to secure Greek mercenaries, see Diod. XV 38,1–2 (375 B.C.); XV 50,4 (371 B.C., Sparta); and cf. the peace proposals of Ariobarzanes' agent Philiskos in 368 (Xen. *Hell.* VII 1,27; Diod. XV 70,2), and Pelopidas's mission to Persia in 367 (Xen. *Hell.* VII 1,33–40).

5. On all of the above, see, e.g., R. Sealey, *A History of the Greek City States ca. 700–338 B.C.* (Berkeley, 1976), pp. 438–95; J. Cargill, *The Second Athenian League: Empire or Free Alliance* (Berkeley, 1981); J. Buckler, *The Theban Hegemony, 371–362 B.C.*. (Cambridge, Mass., 1980).

phlet calling on Philip to compose the quarrels of the Greeks and unite them under his leadership for a crusade against Persia in Asia Minor.[6] Others, such as Demosthenes, pursued a policy of balking Philip in every enterprise. In the event, of course, Philip succeeded in defeating Athens and Thebes, cowing Sparta, and uniting all of Greece except the sullen Spartans under his leadership. The system he used for uniting Greece was precisely that of the common peace.[7]

The common peace of Philip was clearly a descendant of the Peace of Antalkidas: it was in fact a new King's Peace. Like the Peace of Antalkidas it was concluded under pressure of the threat of superior force, though unlike Artaxerxes II, Philip does not seem to have made the threat explicit in the peace terms. Instead, there were included in the terms provisions for common enforcement of the peace against any aggressor. There were a *hēgemōn,* or leader; a *synedrion* (council) of representatives from the Greek states, officers who were to see to the maintenance of the peace in conjunction with the *hēgemōn* (*οἱ ἐπὶ τῆι κοινῆι φυλακῆι*: [Demosth.] XVII 15); and provisions for the raising of forces from all the participants in the peace to join in chastising the breaker of the peace.[8] All of this can be seen as a development of what we saw in the Peace of Antalkidas ("whoever do not observe this peace, against them I [Artaxerxes] will make war with those who wish to do so"; see n. 1 above), and of ideas expressed in the common peace agreed on at Athens in 371 ("if anyone takes the field against any one of the cities which have sworn this oath, I will come to her aid with all my strength": Xen. *Hell.* VI 5,2). It differed from the earlier common peaces, however, in having an institutionalized system for enforcing the peace. In this respect, the common peace of Philip showed a number of similarities to the Second Athenian League, a symmachy (alliance)with a *hēgemōn* (Athens), a *synedrion,* provisions for joint military action, and the stated purpose of

6. Isokrates *Philippos;* cf. also his two letters to Philip (= oration V and letters 2 and 3 in the 1910 Blass ed. [Teubner]).

7. That the treaty of 338/37 was a treaty of "common peace" and not a symmachy has been conclusively established to my mind by Heuss, *Hermes* 73 (1938):171–86, and Ryder, *Koine Eirene,* 150–62, based especially upon [Demosthenes] XVII and upon the inscription recording the Athenian oath to Philip; see Tod, *GHI,* 2, no. 177 (= *Syll.,* no. 260). All the evidence points to a common peace: see esp. [Demosth.] XVII 2 and 4; Plut. *Phok.* 16,4; Diod. XVII 9,5; and cf. Justin XI 3,2.

8. Here I follow Ryder, *Koine Eirene,* 154–57, against Heuss, op.cit. n. 7, p. 180, in believing that the treaty of 338/37 did provide for a permanent *hēgēmon,* and that Philip (and after him Alexander) was so appointed: see Tod, *GHI,* 2, no. 177, lines 11–12; Diod. XVII 4,1–2; and cf. Justin XI 3,2.

defending the freedom and autonomy of its members in accordance with the Peace of Antalkidas.[9]

It is understandable, then, that the common peace of 338 has often been regarded as a hegemonic symmachy similar to the Peloponnesian League and the two Athenian Leagues. However, Philip was clever enough to avoid the form of such a league,[10] which had become hated by the Greek states after their experiences with Athens and Sparta, while obtaining much of its substance under the acceptable format of the common peace, one of the major stipulations of which was the guarantee of the freedom and autonomy of all Greek states who were signatories. In this respect the Hellenic Peace Treaty of 338 (as I shall henceforth call it) was particularly explicit, requiring that the territorial integrity and existing constitutions of all states be respected, and that the exiles of the various states not receive help from the signatories of the peace.[11] By this Hellenic Peace Treaty, then, Philip and his successor, Alexander, were made overseers of the peace and stability of Greece and the Greek states, but were given neither rights of interference in the internal affairs of the cities nor power to influence their foreign policies, except if they should contravene the terms of the peace. The war with Persia was decided upon by a vote of the *synedrion* on the grounds that Persia was disrupting the peace of Greece,[12] and Philip (and later Alexander) was appointed general with full power to conduct the war. This empowered them to require military contingents from the Greek states and to punish states which entered into relations with Persia as traitors, but gave them no other rights or powers over the internal or external affairs of the cities.

---

9. For the Second Athenian League, see *IG* II^2 43 (= Tod, *GHI,* 2, no. 123), lines 9–15: "so that the Lakedaimonians may permit the Greeks, being free and autonomous, to have peace . . . and so that the common peace to which the Greeks and the king swore according to the treaties may be enforced and remain forever"; see also Diod. XV 28,3–4 on the *synedrion* and the hegemony of Athens.

10. The hegemonic league was characterized by the words *ὁ δεῖνα καὶ οἱ σύμμαχοι* (see, e.g., *IG* II^2 43, line 49; Thucydides II 7,1), and by some stipulation that bound the allies' foreign policy, for example, *τοὺς αὐτοὺς φίλους καὶ ἐχθροὺς νομίζειν* or *στρατεύειν ὅπηι ἂν Λακεδαιμόνιοι ἡγῶνται.*

11. Tod, *GHI,* 2, no. 177, lines 4–18; [Demosth.] XVII 4; 10; 16; and further Schmitt, *Staatsverträge,* 3, no. 403.

12. See Arrian *Anab.* II 4–9, Alexander's letter to Dareios after Issos justifying his invasion of the Persian Empire: "Since I was appointed hegemon of the Greeks . . . and your emissaries attempted to harm my friends and to disrupt the peace, which I had established among the Greeks, I have campaigned against you, you having initiated the enmity."

The Hellenic Peace Treaty was a very subtle device, which gave the Macedonian king (in view of his personal power and prestige) a great deal of room to achieve his aims in Greece, while keeping the outward signs and manifestations of Macedonian control at the barest minimum, though there were apparently garrisons at Thebes (Arrian *Anab.* I 7,1; Diod. XVII 8,7) and Ambrakia (Diod. XVII 3,3). As Alexander's career of conquest progressed, however, the relationship between Macedon and Greece changed. After the dismissal of the Greek contingents by Alexander at Ekbatana in 330, no more is heard of the Hellenic Treaty. Antipatros had already infringed its terms, altering constitutions and establishing garrisons, in the process of settling the Spartan war.[13] And there is no reason to suppose that Alexander was in disagreement with this policy. We never hear of directives from him to Antipatros to change his policy, though he was in close touch with him most of the time.[14] On the contrary, when Alexander returned from India in 324 he himself treated the Hellenic Treaty as a dead letter, evidently regarding the Greeks quite simply as his subjects. For his decree of that year ordering the recall of all the exiles by all Greek states contravened the treaty and showed that the freedom and autonomy of the Greek cities were at an end as far as Alexander was concerned.[15]

Since the terms *freedom* and *autonomy* are central to the theme of this chapter, it is important to determine what exactly they signified to the Greeks. The major concept is that of *eleutheria,* normally translated as "freedom." This is in origin an all-embracing term that can best be defined by pointing to its opposite, *douleia,* or "slavery." It was in the nature of the Greek *polis* to wish to be *eleutherē* in the widest sense of the term, which is to say free from any and all

---

13. Alexander dismissed the Greek allies at Ekbatana in 330 (Arrian *Anab.* III 19,5–6); tyrannies in Peloponnesos in 331 are attested by [Demosth.] XVII 7 and 10 and Paus. VII 27,7; already before Agis of Sparta had definitely "revolted" there was a Macedonian force in Peloponnesos under one Korrhagos (Aischines III 165; Deinarchos I 34; Curtius VI 1,20). Antipatros did, however, refer the question of how to punish Sparta to the Hellenic *synedrion,* which in turn referred the matter to Alexander (Diod. XVII 73,5–6).

14. He was, for example, kept up to date on the Peloponnesian situation: he sent a fleet to Greece to help Antipatros from Tyre in early 331 (Arrian III 6,2); in December 331 he sent Antipatros money to finance his operations (Arrian III 16,10); and he received word of Antipatros's victory (Curtius VII 4,32).

15. Note that Alexander's exiles decree does not even allude to the existence of the Hellenic Treaty and the *synedrion:* it addresses the exiles themselves, promising them forcible aid from Antipatros if their cities hesitate to take them back (Diod. XVIII 8,4). We have two inscriptions describing the actual return of some of these exiles, from Mytilene (*IG* XII.2 6) and Tegea (*Syll.,* no. 307); see further Diod. XVII 109,1; Curtius X 9,4; Hypereides *Against Demosth.* 18; Athenaios XIII 538b; and cf. Justin XIII 5,2.

restrictions upon its internal and external workings and activities. This happy state of existence was, of course, fairly rare, and over the centuries a number of ways in which *eleutheria* might be to some extent limited, without thereby being entirely abolished, came to be recognized. One of these led to the regular coupling of the term *autonomia,* which literally means "having one's own laws [or constitution]," with *eleutheria.* This coupling is the outcome of sixth- and fifth-century events, when it was found that the hegemonic states like Athens and Sparta might impose on other states a particular kind of constitution and then leave them "free" in the well-founded expectation that under the imposed constitution the state's leaders would see to it that the state followed the hegemonic power's lead in foreign policy. Hence the importance of *autonomia* in the fourth century (cf., e.g., nn. 1 and 9 above): it came to be more or less accepted by the majority of city-states that their freedom in the sphere of foreign policy was bound to be limited, but they objected strongly to interference in their internal affairs.

Ultimately, the term *autonomia* came to be virtually synonymous with *eleutheria,*[16] but it is worth noting the difference: their virtual synonymity in the Hellenistic era was a shrinkage of the concept of freedom rather than an expansion of the concept of autonomy. By the Peace of Antalkidas the Greek states had enshrined the notion that all *poleis* on the Greek mainland should be autonomous as one of the fundamental principles of international usage, but had ipso facto acknowledged limitations upon their foreign policies. By the Hellenic Treaty of 338 the foreign policies of the Greek city-states were all but abolished (in effect, that is, not by the explicit terms of the treaty). *Eleutheria* thus meant in essence simply the state of not being actually and legally subject to a foreign power (e.g., Macedon), even if bound to it by various obligations. Hence its similarity to autonomy. It should be noted, however, that there are two other terms that came to be frequently associated with freedom and autonomy: *aphorologētos* (exempt from taxation) and *aphrourētos* (free from garrisoning). A city might be officially free and autonomous, and yet subject to taxation and garrisoning.[17] This again illustrates the shrinking of the term *eleutheria.* The great powers of the Hellenistic era were in a

16. See on this, for example, Jones, *Greek City,* pp. 96–102. On the development of the term *autonomia* in the fifth century, see now Ostwald, *Autonomia.*

17. In 303, for example, Korinth requested Demetrios to garrison the city for the duration of the war against Kassandros (Diod. XX 103,3); in the first part of the third century we find that Erythrai, an autonomous city, had paid taxes to the Seleukids (Welles, *RC,* no. 15).

position to impose a definition of *eleutheria* to suit their own convenience, which might exclude from it a number of the old freedoms; hence we find increasingly specific terminology, which, for example, led Erythrai in the mid third century to state that it had been *autonomos* and *aphorologētos* under Alexander and Antigonos, and Flamininus in 196 B.C. to specify that the Greek cities were to be free, untaxed, ungarrisoned, and autonomous.[18]

Much as the term *eleutheria* might shrink in extension, though, it could not be divorced from autonomy, which came to be viewed as the most basic and essential ingredient of freedom: hence the virtual synonymity of *eleutheria* and *autonomia* in the Hellenistic period. Whatever unpleasant limitations a Greek city might find itself reluctantly (or sometimes even willingly) enduring, no Greek city would ever readily countenance interference with its own laws and customs and constitution by a foreign power: that, at least, was clearly opposed to freedom. This is demonstrated by the extreme unpopularity of Antipatros and Kassandros in Greece as a result of their policy of establishing pro-Macedonian oligarchies or tyrannies in the Greek cities.[19] Similarly, Antigonos Gonatas was later very unpopular as a result of his policy of establishing tyrannies in the cities (Plut. *Arat.* 23–24). This illustrates another development: though people of all political persuasions might use the cry of "reestablishing the ancestral constitution" to seek legitimacy for their particular version of *autonomia,* it came more and more to be generally accepted that a democratic constitution was the only sort truly commensurate with autonomy.[20]

---

18. For Erythrai, see Welles, *RC,* no. 15, lines 21–23 (= *OGIS,* no. 223); on Flamininus's declaration, see Polybios XVIII 46,5: *ἐλευθέρους, ἀφρουρήτους, ἀφορολογήτους, νόμοις χρωμένους τοῖς πατρίοις* (and cf. Plut. *Flam.* 10,4, using the same words). In general on the concept of *eleutheria* in the Greek cities in the Hellenistic period, see now Mastrocinque, *AIV* 135 (1976/77):1–23.

19. This is best exemplified by the case of Athens, which rushed joyfully to overthrow Antipatros's post–Lamian War regime in 318, after Polyperchon's edict (Diod. XVIII 64,1–6), and later welcomed Demetrios with open arms in 307 (Plut. *Dem.* 8–9).

20. This is attested already in inscriptions from the end of the fourth century, for example, *IG* XII.9 192 (= *Syll.,* no. 323) from Eretria, recording that the *demos* has been liberated and democracy restored; and cf. *IG* XI.4 556, from Delos, mentioning freedom and democracy together at lines 12–13. For a slightly later period, see *OGIS,* no. 229, lines 10–11, where Smyrna in the mid third century praises Seleukos II for preserving its "autonomy and democracy"; and *OGIS,* no. 222, lines 14–16, where the Ionian League invites Antiochos I to protect the freedom and democracy of the Ionian cities. Of course, the term democracy was used very loosely in the Hellenistic period, and it would be wrong to imagine that all Hellenistic cities that claimed to be "democratic" had a constitution anything like that of Athens in the fifth

In the Hellenistic period, then, one may broadly state that to establish in or over a city a governor, a tyrant, or an oligarchy, was to deprive it of freedom. To allow it to run its own internal affairs, with assembly, council, and magistrates, and usually a more or less democratic constitution, amounted to granting it freedom. The imposition of a garrison or some form of financial contribution (even direct taxation) did not amount to depriving a city of freedom, though it clearly infringed its freedom. Not even the most philhellene and freedom-loving kings permitted the Greek cities to have a fully independent foreign policy. These are important facts to bear in mind when discussing Antigonos Monophthalmos's attitude to the Greeks, for he combined a claim and reputation for favoring the freedom of the Greeks with a great deal of interference in the affairs of various Greek cities. It is all too easy either, by looking at the claims he made about freeing the Greeks and his reputation among the Greeks, to exaggerate his commitment to Greek freedom or, by looking at his interference with Greek cities in his sphere of influence, to shrug off his pronouncements about Greek freedom as hypocrisy.[21]

ANTIGONOS'S CAREER IN RELATION TO THE GREEKS

The first known contact between Antigonos and a Greek *polis* is his activity in connection with Priene in 334, known from a Prienian decree honoring him. It is conjectured that he was despatched by Alexander to receive the submission of Priene, in the same way as Alkimachos was sent to take over the northern Ionian and Aiolian communities.[22] Of Antigonos's years as satrap of Phrygia nothing relevant is known until 318, when he deplored the attack of the satrap Arrhidaios on the city of Kyzikos on the grounds that it was an allied Greek city, guilty of no offense (Diod. XVIII 52,3). These two

century, but it is noteworthy that it seemed important at least to claim to be a democracy: see further Musti, *SCO* 15 (1966):138–45, showing that in the Seleukid Empire the terms *autonomia* and *demokratia* became virtually synonymous.

21. For example, among the three major modern treatments of Antigonos's policy towards the Greeks (Heuss, *Hermes* 73 [1938]:133–94; Simpson, *Historia* 8 [1959]:385–409; Wehrli, *Antigone et Démétrios*, pp. 103–29), Wehrli accuses Heuss with some justice of exaggerating Antigonos's commitment to Greek freedom, while himself undoubtedly falling into the opposite error.

22. Hiller von Gaertringen, *I. Priene*, no. 2, cf. Briant, *Antigone le Borgne*, pp. 37–40; for Alkimachos's mission, see Arrian *Anab.* I 18,1.

incidents, though in themselves by no means of major significance, are the first hints of Antigonos's later attitude towards the Greek cities. In 318 he drove Arrhidaios and Kleitos from their satrapies of Hellespontine Phrygia and Lydia, and in taking these areas over brought a large number of Greek cities into his sphere of influence. We hear that he expelled the garrisons with which Kleitos had secured the major cities (and by implication those of Arrhidaios also), and in particular we hear that he took over Ephesos with the aid of partisans within the city (Diod. XVIII 52,5–8); but we hear nothing of his own dispensations with regard to these satrapies and cities. In 317, of course, he marched east after Eumenes, and had no further dealings with Greek cities for several years.

Meanwhile a significant event had occurred in Greece, with the issuing by Polyperchon late in 319 of his edict concerning the Greek cities. This edict was a promise to the Greek cities to reverse the enactments of Antipatros after the Lamian War, abolish the oligarchies, and restore to the cities the constitutions they had enjoyed under Philip and Alexander. The precise significance of this edict—whether it amounted to an attempt to renew the Hellenic Treaty of Philip and Alexander or was merely an attempt to enlist the support of the "democratic" factions in Greece against Kassandros—is disputed. The latter view is argued forcefully by Heuss, who points out that the edict as preserved by Diodoros contains none of the important catchwords of the Hellenic Treaty—*eleutheria, autonomia, koinē eirēnē*—and in fact more or less explicitly confirms Alexander's exiles decree, which had contravened the Hellenic Treaty.[23] Against Heuss, Klaus Rosen claims that Polyperchon did attempt to renew the Hellenic Treaty,[24] but his arguments are not convincing. He claims that for the sake of brevity Diodoros, or his source, Hieronymos, has left out the section of the edict that referred to a common peace and the freedom and autonomy of the Greek cities. To bolster this argument he points to the fact that the Athenians interpreted the decree as offering them autonomy; and indeed it did, since it envisaged reestablishing the pre–Lamian War situation.[25] However, the edict quite explicitly proposes to honor all the edicts (*diagrammata*) of

23. See Heuss, *Hermes* 73 (1938):143–46. Polyperchon's edict is given by Diod. at XVIII 56,1–8.

24. Rosen, *AClass* 10 (1967):64–68.

25. The purpose and content of Polyperchon's edict are clearly stated by Diodoros: "It was decided to free the cities throughout Greece, and to overthrow the oligarchies established by Antipatros" (XVIII 55,2); "We [i.e., Philippos Arrhidaios] are preparing peace for you [the Greeks], and the constitutions which you had under Philip and Alexander, and shall act in

Alexander, evidently including the exiles decree, and therefore it does (as Heuss argues) seek to restore the situation of Greece as in Alexander's last years, when the Hellenic Treaty was already a dead letter. One should note in particular the orders given by King Philippos Arrhidaios to the Greeks in this edict to take back those exiled under Antipatros and to obey Polyperchon, and the threat of punishment for noncompliance at the end.[26] Clearly this decree did not amount to a reestablishment of the principle of Greek autonomy.

Limited as the significance of Polyperchon's edict may be for Greek freedom, however, it is nevertheless a liberal move compared to the policy pursued by Kassandros. Wehrli has rightly pointed out that the fact that Antigonos was a supporter of Kassandros at this time was a notable blot on his reputation among the Greeks.[27] This support of Kassandros makes it clear that Antigonos, in the years 318–315 at least, pursued a purely pragmatic policy, which took account of Greek freedom only when it might bring him political advantage.

When Antigonos returned from the interior of Asia to the Mediterranean coastlands in 314 and found himself confronted by the four western dynasts, he made his famous Tyre proclamation espousing the cause of Greek freedom and autonomy. Specifically, he stated that all Greeks should be free, autonomous, and ungarrisoned, and he sent out messengers to report on this decree in the hope that the news would cause the Greeks to regard him as their friend and make trouble for Kassandros.[28] The primary motive behind the Tyre proclamation was clearly to incite mainland Greeks to rebel against Kassandros. Thus far one may conclude that it was purely a politico-military maneuver, devoid of any broader policy or idealistic content. But one must remember here that after Kassandros, the person most affected

future according to the edicts previously written concerning you" (XVIII 56,3). Under Philip and Alexander the Greek cities were ungarrisoned, autonomous, and ruled by democracies, and the fact that the Athenians interpreted Polyperchon's edict as granting them freedom from garrison and a democratic constitution (so Diod. XVIII 64,3 et al.) is not a problem, and does not require the insertion of further clauses into the edict, as Beloch (*GG*, 4.1:100 n. 1) and Rosen have supposed.

26. Diod. XVIII 56,4: "We restore those driven out or exiled from the cities by our generals after the time when Alexander crossed to Asia"; XVIII 56,8: "We have charged Polyperchon to deal with these and other matters; you, therefore, as we have written to you before, obey him: for those who do not do what we have written, we shall not overlook." These orders and threats are an infringement of Greek autonomy that is hardly consonant with a revival of the Hellenic Treaty. See further the arbitrary orders sent to Argos and other Peloponnesian cities by Polyperchon (Diod. XVIII 57,1; 69,3–4).

27. Wehrli, *Antigone et Démétrios*, pp. 108–9.

28. See Diod. XIX 61,3–4 and cf. Wehrli, *Antigone et Démétrios*, pp. 110–11.

by the decree was Antigonos himself, since his own sphere of influence in Asia Minor contained the greatest number of Greek cities outside of the Greek mainland. In enunciating a policy of Greek autonomy and freedom from garrisons, Antigonos was as likely to cause trouble for himself as for Kassandros unless he genuinely applied the policy in Asia Minor.

Another significant fact is the tenacity with which Antigonos subsequently stuck to the policy of Greek freedom. Between 314 and 311 Antigonos and his generals secured firm control of Asia Minor, the Aegean islands, and mainland Greece south of Thermopylai—with the exception of Athens, Korinth, Sikyon, and perhaps a few other towns in the Peloponnesos. Nevertheless, by the peace of 311 the freedom and autonomy of the Greeks were once more insisted upon, without doubt at Antigonos's prompting.[29] In this instance Antigonos was limiting his own freedom of action with regard to the Greeks more than anyone else's. It can be claimed that as long as Kassandros held Macedon, Antigonos needed the goodwill of the Greeks as a tool against him, and there is some truth to this. But Antigonos could equally well have garrisoned the Greek cities and maintained a strong force under Polemaios, his nephew, to hold Greece against Kassandros, relying on might rather than goodwill to maintain his power in Greece.

The rebellion of Polemaios collapsed Antigonos's entire position in mainland Greece and gave Ptolemy an opportunity to intervene. Already in 314 Ptolemy had followed Antigonos's proclamation of Greek freedom with a similar declaration (Diod. XIX 62,1–2), but he had as far as we know done nothing about it: since there were almost no Greek cities in Ptolemy's own territories (only Naukratis, Alexandria, Kyrene, and some Cyprian cities), the proclamation was a cheap piece of propaganda. In 310 he accused Antigonos of violating Greek freedom by garrisoning some cities and sent an expedition to Kilikia, which apparently seized some cities there, but was then driven off by Demetrios.[30] In the next year Ptolemy himself sailed north and took

29. A brief summary of the treaty is given by Diod. XIX 105,1; it is clear from the Skepsis inscriptions (*OGIS*, nos. 5 and 6) that the clause concerning Greek freedom was included at Antigonos's behest. Cf. also the consistent propagandizing of Antigonos and his generals in Greece in these years (see, e.g., Diod. XIX 64,2; 66,3; 74,1; 77,2; 78,2; 78,5; 87,5; and Moretti, *ISE*, no. 71).

30. Diod. XX 19,3–5. The term used by Diodoros for the activity of Ptolemy's general Leonidas—*πόλεις . . . ἐχειρώσατο*—does not point to a particularly "liberating" undertaking.

Phaselis, Xanthos, Kaunos, and Kos.[31] Thereupon he entered into negotiations with Antigonos's nephew Polemaios, whom he lured to Kos and murdered. Sailing then to the Isthmos, he took over Korinth, Megara, and Sikyon, and called upon the cities of Peloponnesos to join him in a freedom crusade. Finding that the Peloponnesians did not respond to his call, he garrisoned the three cities he had taken, made peace with Kassandros, and sailed back to Egypt.[32] This was the extent of Ptolemy's efforts on behalf of Greek freedom, and it is not very impressive. One might note also that Polyperchon, that other champion of Greek autonomy, was little more than a small-time dynast during the years 313–302, preserving some shreds of power by maintaining mercenary garrisons in various Peloponnesian towns, with or without the aid of Kassandros.

In contrast to this, Antigonos, despite the setbacks of 310–308, still clung determinedly to his policy of Greek autonomy, and in 307 he sent his son Demetrios with a great armada to free Athens from Kassandros's control. In 306 he ordered his son, who had by then freed Athens and Megara and established democracies in those cities, to summon delegates from all the Greek states to discuss their common security,[33] while Demetrios himself was to sail to Cyprus to fight Ptolemy. It was in the context of the war against Ptolemy that

31. Diod. XX 27,1–3. Ptolemy also evidently captured Myndos (Diod. XX 37,1) and Iasos (Blümel, *I. Iasos,* vol. 1, no. 2). The Iasos inscription records an agreement between Iasos and Ptolemy made before the latter became king, by which he bound himself to maintain Iasos as ἐλεύθερον καὶ αὐτόνομον καὶ ἀφρούρητον καὶ ἀφορολόγητον (lines 50–51, 54–55). Mention at the beginning of the inscription of Polemaios and troops left in the region by him makes it clear that the decree must belong to 309, and shows that at this date and in this region Ptolemy was living up to his claims concerning Greek freedom. It seems that Ptolemy also at this time attempted to take Halikarnassos, but was prevented by the timely arrival of Demetrios (Plut. *Dem.* 7,3; and cf. Seibert, *Ptolemaios I,* p. 186 and n. 33).

32. So Diod. XX 27,3 and 37,1–2; and cf. Seibert, *Ptolemaios I,* pp. 184–89. Some historians (e.g., Will, *Histoire politique,* 1:61–63) have concluded on the basis of a passage in the Suda (s.v. Demetrios lemma 431) that a treaty was made between Demetrios and Ptolemy to free Greece in 309/8, and have inferred further that it was as a result of this treaty that Ptolemy assassinated Polemaios. Seibert, however, has shown conclusively (op. cit. pp. 180–83) that the Suda passage is a nest of errors and confusions and is not to be believed. Attempts to connect the Suda passage with Diod. XX 37 and 45 (so, e.g., Rosen, *AClass* 10 [1967]:85–6) do not convince, for the words used and order of events are entirely different, whereas we see that in a passage where the Suda was really following Diod. (Suda s.v. Demetrios lemma 429 [p. 41, lines 2–10, in Adler ed.] = Diod. XIX 81,3–4) there is an almost word-for-word correspondence.

33. Diod. XX 46,5: "He wrote to his son Demetrios ordering him to bring together representatives of the allied cities to consult in common concerning the needs of Hellas." This is seen by many, and I think rightly, as the first step towards creating a Hellenic League. As to who the "allied cities" could have been, see chap. 4 n. 33 above.

the siege of Rhodes, the other event commonly used to show the opportunism and insincerity of Antigonos's policy of Greek freedom, occurred.

Antigonos and Rhodes had made an alliance in 312, and in 306 Demetrios summoned the Rhodians to take part in the war against Ptolemy.[34] The Rhodians refused to obey the summons, and this was viewed by Antigonos and Demetrios as a *casus belli*. As we have no idea of the terms of the alliance between Antigonos and Rhodes, it is impossible to tell whether or not Antigonos was legally justified: the Rhodians appear to have claimed that they had no obligation to Antigonos, whether because they had no treaty with him, because the treaty did not oblige them to fight Ptolemy, or because they had a conflicting alliance with Ptolemy.[35] Under pressure the Rhodians were prepared to submit to Antigonos's demands: it was only Demetrios's demand to be received into Rhodes with his fleet that actually precipitated war.[36] Moreover, the Greek states—including Athens and Aitolia—that mediated between Demetrios and Rhodes do not seem to have ceased to regard Antigonos as the patron of Greek liberty as a result of this siege.[37] One might conclude from this that perhaps the Rhodians were indeed in the process of breaking a treaty of alliance with Antigonos and switching sides to Ptolemy, so that Antigonos's punitive action was regarded internationally as at least legally justified, if unwelcome.

The upshot was that the Rhodians eventually renewed their alliance with Antigonos, but won the concession of a clause explicitly

---

34. Diod. XIX 77,3: ἐποιήσατο δὲ καὶ πρὸς Ῥοδίους συμμαχίαν. Diod. XX 46,6: καὶ κομισθεὶς ἐπὶ Καρίας παρεκάλει τοὺς Ῥοδίους πρὸς τὸν κατὰ Πτολεμαίου πόλεμον.

35. The precise situation can no longer be ascertained with certainty from the sources. The alliance with Antigonos is certain, but its terms and duration are unknown: it may have been aimed only at freeing the Greeks. However, since Demetrios had come into conflict with Ptolemy's garrisons at Korinth and Sikyon, and since there were Greek cities on Cyprus, Antigonos may have represented his war with Ptolemy as waged to free the Greeks (see Plut. *Dem.* 9 and 15, and esp. 8: Antigonos and Demetrios were fired with an ambition to free all of Greece, which had been enslaved by Kassandros and *Ptolemy*). Moser, *Politik Ptolemaios' I,* pp. 65–66, argues that the Rhodians had a treaty with Ptolemy from 315 on, but his arguments have now been thoroughly discredited by Seibert, *Ptolemaios I,* pp. 225–30, whose treatment of this problem is excellent.

36. Diod. XX 82,3: under Antigonos's threats, the Rhodians at first agreed to his demands that they join in the war against Ptolemy, but when Demetrios unwisely insisted in addition on receiving 100 hostages and permission to bring his whole fleet into the harbor of Rhodes, the Rhodians determined to fight, fearing that Demetrios intended to carry out a coup.

37. The first city to attempt to mediate was Knidos (Diod. XX 95,4); Athens is mentioned as a mediator by Diod. XX 98,2–3 (along with other Greek cities) and Plut. *Dem.* 22; Aitolia by Diod. XX 99,3. The Athenians, of course, immediately begged Demetrios to intervene again in Greece as a "liberator" (Plut. *Dem.* 23).

exempting them from any hostilities against Ptolemy (Diod. XX 99,3). Demetrios sailed back to Greece and spent the years 303 and 302 liberating all Greece from Kassandros and setting up the Hellenic League. This organization, a substantial portion of whose charter has been preserved in an inscription from Epidauros,[38] was a symmachy whose purpose was to ensure the freedom, peace, and security of the Greek states under the benevolent hegemony of Antigonos and Demetrios. Though the surviving portions of the Epidauros inscription do not happen to preserve the words *eleutheria* or *autonomia,* there is a clause prescribing common action to be taken against the imposition of garrisons (lines 13–15), and common peace is mentioned several times.

This brief survey has shown, then, that from 314 until the end of his life in 301, Antigonos consistently maintained as one of the major elements of his foreign policy an express commitment to autonomy and freedom from garrisons for the Greek cities. In contrast, Polyperchon never committed himself to the principle of autonomy as a general policy, but only in a restricted way at a certain phase in his career. Ptolemy committed himself to autonomy and the removal of garrisons twice (in 314 and in 311–309), but the first time did nothing about it, and the second time overtly went back on the policy by garrisoning Korinth and Sikyon. As far as we can tell, Kassandros and Lysimachos were opposed to the idea of Greek autonomy,[39] though both were induced by Antigonos to pay lip service to the policy in the peace treaty of 311. Seleukos had no independent contact with the Greeks in this period, though later he seems to have espoused the cause of Greek autonomy along with many other elements of An-

38. *IG* IV^2.1, no. 68; cf. also Schmitt, *Staatsverträge,* 3, no. 446, for a revised edition with bibliography and commentary, and Austin, *Hellenistic World,* no. 43, pp. 76–78, for an English translation of the most important fragment.

39. I don't think anyone would claim that Kassandros ever supported Greek autonomy; for Lysimachos the situation is more complex. He may have claimed to be liberating Greek cities in Asia Minor that came over to him in 302 (see Diod. XX 107,2 on Lampsakos and Parion) though he garrisoned Sigeion (Diod. loc. cit), and his general Prepelaos installed a garrison at Ephesos (see *Syll.*, no. 353 and Robert, *Hellenica,* 3:79–85). He maintained excellent relations with Athens (see *IG* II^2 657, 662, and 663), but subjugated the Greek cities of the western Black Sea area (see, e.g., Diod. XIX 73,1–10 on the efforts of Kallatis, Istria, and Odessos to free themselves from Lysimachos's garrisons), and later had an evil reputation in Ionia (see on this Will, *Histoire politique,* 1:84–85). All in all he cannot be claimed as a champion of Greek autonomy: this is also conceded by S. M. Burstein, *AncW* 3 (1980):73–79, who otherwise paints a more favorable picture of Lysimachos's relations with the Greek cities than I assume was the case; and the hatred many of the cities felt for Lysimachos's oppression is well brought out by Orth, *Königliche Machtanspruch,* pp. 26–28, 81, 104–6, 126–29, 132–34.

tigonos's policies.[40] What are we to make, then, of Wehrli's statement that "tous les diadoques, sans exception, font de l'autonomie des cités un thème de propagande qu'ils brandissent face à leurs adversaires,"[41] with which he dismisses Antigonos's claim to a special relationship with the Greeks? In fact, Wehrli is well aware that this statement is invalid with regard to Kassandros; but leaving aside the exaggeration, Wehrli does have a case that needs to be answered.

Wehrli, as I have mentioned above, concentrates most on the negative aspects of Antigonos's involvement with the Greeks: his opportunism, the political advantages he derived from proclaiming Greek freedom, the many instances in which his treatment of the Greek cities fell short of according them complete liberty. It is by insisting on a very literal sense of *eleutheria* that Wehrli shows up the stark limitations of Antigonos's policy. This was, perhaps, salutary after the rather too encomiastic treatment of Heuss and others.[42] But Wehrli himself fails to do justice to the tenacity with which Antigonos stuck to the general policy of Greek autonomy, despite limitations and occasional violations, throughout this period. We need not suppose that Antigonos was actuated by any sentimental considerations of philhellenism in order to rebut charges of insincerity or hypocrisy. For Antigonos's policy was an act of statesmanship; to quote R. H. Simpson: "He had determined to bring the Greek cities to his side, and he saw that the surest way to do this was to appeal to the strongest instinct of the Greeks, the will for autonomy and independence, which was at the same time the most vital element of their political life."[43] Other courses were open to him, particularly in 311, and again in 302, and the fact that he strove to maintain as far as possible the policy he had enunciated in 314 should be laid to his credit as an act of wise and considerate statesmanship.

It did not, of course, always prove possible for Antigonos to maintain his policy in its strictest sense, but it should be remembered that throughout the period we are dealing with, except for a few brief months in 311/10, he was constantly at war with some or all of the

40. Seleukos's only contact with the Greek cities in the period under discussion came during his few years as a Ptolemaic admiral, 314–312 (Diod. XIX 58,5; 60,4; 62,4–6; 68,3–4). In this period, then, one cannot find any evidence for Seleukos as a patron of Greek liberty, except insofar as Ptolemy was such in 314–312.

41. Wehrli, *Antigone et Démétrios*, p. 126.

42. For example, Ulrich von Wilamowitz-Moellendorff, *Hellenistische Dichtung in der Zeit des Kallimachos* (Berlin, 1924), 1:6; P. Roussel, *Histoire grecque* (Paris, 1945), 4:388.

43. Simpson, *Historia* 8 (1959):406.

other Macedonian dynasts. In the face of the repeated expeditions sent by Ptolemy to the coast of Asia Minor, the occasional garrisoning of cities along that coast can hardly be held to negate their autonomy, and the situation in mainland Greece was similar with regard to Kassandros. What matters is that Antigonos far eclipsed the other dynasts in the scrupulousness of his behavior towards the Greeks, and this can be seen in his posthumous reputation among them. In the judgment of Plutarch (*Dem.* 8): "None of the kings who succeeded Alexander ever waged a nobler or juster war than this," which Antigonos and Demetrios fought "to restore freedom to all of Greece, which had been enslaved by the rule of Kassandros and Ptolemy."[44]

ANTIGONOS'S RELATIONS WITH INDIVIDUAL *POLEIS*

It is only through a detailed examination of what is known of Antigonos's dealings with Greek cities that we can measure the extent to which he really lived up to his propaganda claims and reach a definite verdict on his relations with the Greeks. The evidence of his contacts with Greek cities will be dealt with under three headings: the Asiatic cities (including the islands off the coast of Asia and the Black Sea region); the islanders; and the mainland Greeks.

The Asiatic Cities

The first recorded contact between Antigonos and a Greek city occurred when he was apparently delegated by Alexander to see to the submission/liberation of Priene in 334 (see n. 22 above). Since Antigonos was satrap of Phrygia in the years 333–321, he is unlikely to have had extensive dealings with Greek cities during that period, though as caretaker (apparently) of the satrapy of Lykia/Pamphylia from 329/28 on, and full satrap of the region after 323, he would have had a number of city-states under his authority.[45] Most of these, such as Xanthos, Telmessos, Patara, Myra, Perge, and Side, cannot really be termed Greek (though many of these later did establish claims to

44. Impressive words, even allowing for the possibility that they may originate with the pro-Antigonid historian Hieronymos. See also esp. Welles, *RC*, no. 15, a letter of Antiochos I or II to Erythrai in the 260s, in response to an Erythraian embassy which had reminded him (lines 21–23) that under Antigonos's rule they had been autonomous and exempt from taxation; and cf. Orth, *Königliche Machtanspruch*, pp. 81, 94.

45. See chap. 1, n. 86 above for Antigonos's position with regard to Lykia/Pamphylia.

Greek ancestry), but even at this date Phaselis and Aspendos were already considered Greek cities.[46] At any rate, for my purposes it hardly seems worthwhile to insist on a distinction between genuinely Hellenic cities and the various Karian, Lykian, and Kilikian city-states. Antigonos's authority in this region was interrupted by his expulsion at the hands of Perdikkas in 321, and after his return he was busy elsewhere until 314. After that date, his authority over southern Asia Minor was more or less an established fact, though Ptolemy from time to time seized a few cities along the coast. Due to the rarity of Hellenistic inscriptions from this area, little can be said about Antigonos's relations with the coastal city-states.

Our only real evidence of Antigonos's dealings with the cities of Anatolia's south coast comes precisely from the literary evidence on Ptolemy's various expeditions to the area. It may be significant that when in 310 Ptolemy accused Antigonos of breaking the peace of 311 by maintaining garrisons in some of the cities, his (Ptolemy's) first action was to send an expedition under his general Leonidas to Kilikia Trachea. Here Leonidas "liberated" (Diod. XX 19,3–5 says simply "subdued"—*ἐχειρώσατο*) the cities; one should probably think here of such places as Soloi, Elaioussa, and Kelenderis. However, Demetrios immediately recovered these cities. Ptolemy followed this up by himself sailing north and, avoiding Demetrios's forces in Kilikia, capturing Phaselis, Xanthos, Kaunos, Myndos, Iasos, and Kos.[47] Perhaps, then, Antigonos maintained garrisons in these south coast cities: garrisons are definitely recorded by Diodoros for the non-Greek cities of Kaunos and Xanthos, though it seems that there was no Antigonid garrison at Kos.[48] We also hear of Antigonid troops

46. Aspendos was supposed to be an Argive colony (Strabo XIV 3,9); Phaselis was a Dorian colony (Herodotos II 178), supposedly founded by Rhodian Lindos (Steph. Byz. s.v. Gela; Athenaios VII 297f). For the claims of other Lykian and Kilikian cities to Greek ancestry, see, for example, the cases of Side (Arrian *Anab.* I 26,4: the Sidetans were colonists from Kyme, who miraculously began to speak a barbarian language as soon as they landed) and Soloi (Strabo XIV 5,8: colonized by Achaians and Rhodians). For new evidence of claims to Greek status by Aspendos and Kilikian Soloi in the late fourth century, based on the notion of Argive colonization, see the new Argive decree from Nemea published by Stroud, *Hesperia* 53 (1984):193–216.

47. See n. 31 above; and on Ptolemy's broader plans at this time, see chap. 4 nn. 15 and 16 above.

48. Ptolemy seems to have sailed into Kos more or less unopposed (Diod. XX 27,2–3); Sherwin-White, *Ancient Cos*, pp. 82–85, suggests that Kos remained essentially in Ptolemy's "sphere" from 313 down to Demetrios's victory in 306: there is no evidence as yet published to decide this, other than Ptolemy's stay there in 309/8, which the Koans were not in a position to prevent. Purely from geography, it seems to me much more likely that Kos would already have been friendly with Antigonos in this period.

stationed in the interior in Karia, and at Pogla in the Kabalia district of the border between Pisidia and Lykia.[49] It may be that the uncertainty of the peace with Ptolemy, and the proximity of Cyprus (at this date under Ptolemaic control), led Antigonos to treat the south coast city-states in the same fashion as the native interior, where the stationing of troops was an accepted fact.

At any rate the evidence becomes fuller when we move on to the cities of the Aegean coast, starting with Rhodes. Antigonos originally had a very friendly relationship with the Rhodians. When Ptolemy, Kassandros, Lysimachos, and Seleukos combined against him in 314 and he decided that he would need a fleet to combat this coalition, he sent diplomats to Rhodes who established friendship and an agreement whereby Antigonos might employ the Rhodian dockyards to build ships.[50] Subsequently the Rhodians concluded an alliance with Antigonos in 312, perhaps with the stated purpose of liberating the Greeks (see Diod. XIX 77,3). At some date prior to 305 the Rhodians voted Antigonos a variety of honors, of which the only one specifically mentioned in our sources is the erection of statues of Antigonos and his son Demetrios.[51] The siege of Rhodes by Demetrios in 305/4 is usually regarded as a major infringement by Antigonos of his policy of granting autonomy to the Greeks. However, in the absence of precise knowledge of the terms and duration of Antigonos's symmachy with Rhodes, judgment on this point should be suspended. For it was, of course, recognized by the ancient Greeks that when a partner to an alliance failed to live up to his obligations, the other partner had the right to attempt to force him to do so. If this was the case with Antigonos and Rhodes, then Antigonos could not properly be considered to be infringing Rhodian autonomy(for they had entered into the alliance of their own free will), unless and until he

49. Troops of Antigonos in Karia: *AM* 72 (1957):188–90, Samian decree honoring Hipparchos Heniochou Kyrenaios who (line 7) [τεταγμένος] ἐγ Καρίαι displayed goodwill towards Samians who were στρατευομένων παρ' αὐτῶι (line 9); Antigonid troops in the Kabalia: Segrè, *TC*, no. 8, records Kalymnians stationed under an officer of Antigonos at Mogla, which is doubtless the same place as Pogla in the Kabalia of Ptolemy *Geog.* V 5 (a lapicidal error M for Π according to Hiller von Gaertringen, *Gnomon* 15 [1939]:630).

50. Diod. XIX 57,4; 58,5: the Rhodians agreed to build ships for Antigonos from timber imported by him for the purpose. The fact that these ships were to be used against Ptolemy is noteworthy: ships actually built are recorded by Diod. at XIX 62,7 (eighty ships from the Hellespont and Rhodes) and 64,5 (an unspecified number of ships from Rhodes with Karian crews). A fairly good modern treatment of Rhodes and its relations with Antigonos in this period is Hauben, *Historia* 26 (1977):307–39, esp. 316–39.

51. Diod. XX 93,6–7: the Rhodians decided not to abrogate the honors of Antigonos despite the current hostilities (304 B.C.).

were to establish a governor and garrision on the island after the siege. In any case, the siege failed and was concluded by a treaty which left Rhodes free, autonomous, and ungarrisoned, but still an ally of Antigonos.[52]

Opposite Rhodes lies the coast of Karia, which came into Antigonos's hands in 312, conquered by him from the Macedonian satrap Asandros. Antigonos himself captured Kaunos in that year, and though Ptolemy occupied the place in 309, one assumes that it was soon retaken by Antigonid forces. It was from the coast of Karia, presumably in this region, that Demetrios in 306 summoned the Rhodians to join him in the war against Ptolemy (Diod. XX 46,6). Knidos, on the long promontory of Asia Minor between Rhodes and Kos, is attested as being autonomous under Antigonos by its role as attempted mediator in the war between Demetrios and Rhodes, for the Rhodians would hardly have listened for a moment to "mediators" subject to Antigonos.[53] Halikarnassos is also attested as under Antigonos's protection: Ptolemy attempted to seize the place, presumably in 309, but was prevented by the timely arrival of Demetrios. Plutarch's description of this leaves open the possibility of an Antigonid garrison being stationed there, but an interesting diplomatic exchange between Halikarnassos and its mother city, Troizen, makes this unlikely. The city of Troizen (in the Peloponnesos) honored one Zenodotos, the son of Baukideus, from Halikarnassos for helping to free Troizen and expel a garrison stationed there. The context is clearly Demetrios's campaign in the Peloponnesos in 303, and Zenodotos must have been an officer in Demetrios's army. The Troizenians sent an embassy to Halikarnassos to announce the honors they were paying to Zenodotos, and the Halikarnassians passed a decree in response. This exchange surely proves that Halikarnassos was free and ungarrisoned, as the Troizenians would hardly otherwise have been so tactless as to send an announcement of their own good fortune in this respect.[54]

---

52. Diod. XX 99,3; Demetrios did receive 100 hostages for the future good behavior of Rhodes; they were sent to Ephesos, where Prepelaos found them in 302 and sent them home (Diod. XX 107,4).

53. Diod. XX 95,4–5. The Knidians are represented as acting entirely independently in this matter, though they were doubtless allied to Antigonos like the later mediators Athens and Aitolia (and like Rhodes, for that matter). It is possible, of course, that Antigonos, who seems to have been anxious to end the siege (cf. Diod. XX 99,1), could have suggested to the Knidians that they act as mediators. Their trade may have been adversely affected by the hostilities so near by.

54. On Ptolemy's attempt to seize Halikarnassos, see Plut. *Dem.* 7; on Zenodotos, see app. 3, no. 120.

Between the two promontories of Knidos and Halikarnassos lies the island of Kos. In 314/13 Seleukos seems to have used Kos as his naval base, and in 309/8 Ptolemy did the same. It seems likely that in between these dates the island was in Antigonos's sphere, though there is at present no sure evidence of this. At any rate, by 303 Kos was an autonomous and democratic city in Antigonos's sphere of influence, as we learn from the famous inscription preserving Antigonos's regulations on the synoikism of Teos and Lebedos, in which we find that the two cities have agreed to use the constitution of Kos until a new constitution can be drawn up for them, and Antigonos reports that he has accordingly written to Kos for a copy of its constitution. Another inscription, found on Kos, records honors awarded to Koans who had arbitrated, apparently at the request of Antigonos, in a dispute between Klazomenai and a neighboring town, perhaps Kolophon. There was, further, a temple and cult of an Antigonos on Kos, who may have been Monophthalmos. There exist, it seems, other inscriptions shedding further light on Antigonos's relations with Kos, which have not yet been published, though found more than sixty years ago.[55]

The island of Kalymna appears to have had an alliance with Antigonos, as we see from a decree of the island honoring an officer of Antigonos named Moschion, who had troops from Kalymna stationed under him at Pogla in the Kabalia district.[56] The use of troops from allied Greek cities by Antigonos is several times recorded.

The city of Iasos on the Karian coast was captured for Antigonos by his nephew Polemaios in 313. It appears from a long inscription found there in the sixties by the Italian excavators that Polemaios left a body of troops at Iasos (cf. n. 31 above). The inscription records three-way negotiations between the Iasians, the troops left by Polemaios, and Ptolemy, presumably in 309. The city is to become an ally

55. *Syll.*, no. 344 (= Welles, *RC*, nos. 3 and 4), lines 58–66, for Kos in the Teos inscription; Kos's arbitration at Klazomenai: G. Pugliese Carratelli, *PP* 33 (1978):153–56(= *SEG*, 28, no. 697); Segrè, *RPAA* 17 (1941):30–34, reports an inscription from Kos referring to a temple (*hieron*) of an Antigonos that required to be maintained or restored in the time of Antigonos Doson, so that the temple was perhaps built in the time of Monophthalmos or Gonatas to honor one of those monarchs; Segrè also mentions (op. cit., pp. 30–31) that there are unpublished documents from Kos demonstrating its relations with Antigonos before 306; on Antigonos and Kos in general, cf. Sherwin-White, *Ancient Cos*, pp. 82–90, showing that Kos was free and a democracy at this time.

56. See Segrè, *TC*, no. 8, and cf. n. 49 above. The officer mentioned in the inscription, Moschion, son of Moirichos, may be the same man as the diplomat sent by Antigonos to Rhodes in 314 (see app. 3, no. 75).

of Ptolemy, and the troops are either to leave peacefully or, if they wish, settle at Iasos. There is strong insistence on the fact that Iasos, as Ptolemy's ally, is to be free, autonomous, ungarrisoned, and exempt from taxation. Whether this is to be understood as the Iasians demanding from Ptolemy the same status as they had enjoyed under Antigonos, or whether we should understand that under Antigonos the Iasians had not felt quite free and autonomous, is unclear. Antigonos is not mentioned in the extant text, and it is not certain under what circumstances the troops mentioned were stationed at Iasos.[57]

A particularly interesting testimony concerning Antigonos's policy in Ionia comes from Miletos. Diodoros records (XIX 75,3–4) that Antigonos's generals Medeios and Dokimos liberated Miletos from Asandros's garrison, and restored the city's autonomy. The list of eponymous *stephanēphoroi* found in the Delphinion gives the Milesian version, under the stephanephorate of Hippomachos son of Theron (313/12): "Under this man the city was made free and autonomous by Antigonos, and the democracy was restored."[58] Interesting, too, is the case of Priene, which is illuminated by a number of Athenian decrees concerning diplomatic exchanges between Athens and Priene immediately after the liberation of Athens by Demetrios.[59] Although the inscriptions are all very fragmentary, it is clear at least that the Prienians congratulated the Athenians on recovering their freedom and ancestral constitution, and they may have made a gift of some sort. Athenian financial records of this period (archonship of Anaxikrates: 307/6) mention the receipt of "crowns" from Miletos, Ephesos, Tenedos, Myrina, and Peparethos, while embassies similar to that from Priene are recorded from Kolophon, Tenos, Paros, Myrlea,

57. Polemaios "liberates" Iasos: Diod. XIX 75,5; for Ptolemy at Iasos see Blümel, *I. Iasos*, 1, nos. 2 and 3; on the Antigonid troops at Iasos, see further pp. 300–301 below.

58. Rehm, *Milet*, 1, no. 123 (cf. *Syll.*, no. 322, giving the parts relevant to Antigonos). A letter of Ptolemy II to Miletos (Welles, *RC*, no. 14) mentions that Ptolemy I had at some date relieved the Milesians of harsh taxes imposed by "some of the kings" (τινες τῶμ βασιλέων) (lines 5–8). It has been suggested (e.g., by Welles, p. 75) that "some of the kings" refers to Antigonos; the problem is that so far as we know Ptolemy I was at no time in control of Miletos. Welles suggests that the occasion referred to could be 314/13, when Ptolemy was allied with Asandros, who controlled Miletos. He fails to notice that in that case it could not have been Antigonos who imposed the taxes. It seems more likely that the kings referred to are Demetrios (after 301, when he needed cash) and Lysimachos (see Rehm, *Milet*, 1, no. 138, for the harsh exactions of Lysimachos, which Miletos had to borrow to pay); see further on this Orth, *Königliche Machtanspruch*, pp. 24–30. For Miletos under Antigonos, see also *IG* II^2 1129, a Milesian decree from soon after the expulsion of Asandros, mentioning the restoration of the *patrios politeia*.

59. See *IG* II^2 564, 565, 566, 567; *Suppl. inscr. Att.*, 2.5: 39–46; *SEG*, 3, no. 86; and cf. Wilhelm, "Att. Urk.," pt. 5, pp. 166–75.

and a city whose name is no longer preserved. In the case of the latter, a gift of some talents of silver is mentioned, and Kolophon also seems to have offered help.[60] It looks as if a lot of the Greek cities in Antigonos's sphere rushed to congratulate Athens and offer aid, and it is natural to assume that these cities already had what they were congratulating Athens for recovering, i.e., freedom and autonomy. It might be conjectured that Antigonos, who himself sent money, corn, and wood for ships to the relief of Athens in 307/6, encouraged the Greek cities also to help Athens.

Another aspect of Antigonos's relations with the Greek cities is illustrated by Prienian inscriptions, namely his role as an arbitrator in disputes between cities. Priene and Samos had a dispute over a piece of land on Cape Mykale going back to the seventh century. A very long inscription of the early second century recording a Rhodian arbitration includes a complete history of the dispute and the various wars and arbitrations it had caused. Antigonos appears as one of these arbitrators (along with the likes of Alexander, Lysimachos, Antiochos et al.). His arbitration seems to have been a particularly significant one, for it is again mentioned (together with the Rhodian arbitration) in a decree of the Roman Senate from the second half of the second century B.C., settling another outbreak of the feud. It seems that the appearance of any new power in the area was used variously by Samos and Priene to revive the dispute in the hope of overturning a previous unfavorable arbitration. Of course, such arbitrations were an invidious task, and Antigonos seems on other occasions to have preferred to nominate some Greek city agreeable to both parties to arbitrate disputes about which he received appeals.[61]

International arbitrations were no new thing in the Greek world at this time, but Antigonos seems to have been an innovator in a related field. An inscription from the Aiolic city of Kyme records that judges from Magnesia came to the city to settle a large backlog of

60. For the gift of "crowns" by various cities in 307/6, see *IG* II² 1485 and 1486; for the embassies, see *IG* II² 456 and 470 (Kolophon, probably offering help: 470, lines 14–15 . . . *καὶ ἀφεστ[άλκασι ..11..]ιαν ἑκατὸν*), 466 (Tenos), 557 (an unknown city, which sent [line 3] several talents of silver), 573 (Paros), and 703 (Myrlea; cf. B. Meritt, *Hesperia* 5 [1936]:201–5 for the date of this decree, 305/4—archonship of Euxenippos).

61. Rhodian arbitration: Hiller von Gaertringen, *I. Priene,* no. 37, mentioning Antigonos at lines 141–49 (and cf. ibid., *Nachträge* ad loc. for the identification of this Antigonos as Monophthalmos, rather than Doson as H. von G. at first opined); *I. Priene,* no. 40 gives the Roman arbitration (reprinted in Sherk, *Roman Documents* 10a) referring to Antigonos at lines 8–9. Antigonos had Mytilene arbitrate disputes between Teos and Lebedos (*Syll.,* no. 344, lines 27–30), and let Kos arbitrate between Klazomenai and a neighbor (*SEG,* 28, no. 697).

court cases in accordance with a *diagramma* from Antigonos. This became a common phenomenon during the Hellenistic period: it seems that the cumbersome jury systems of the cities were unable to handle the volume of business, and the Greeks did not trust their own fellow citizens to be impartial—hence the recourse to citizens of another *polis*. The Kyme case is the earliest known, dating from before the assumption of the royal title by Antigonos. It appears that the Kymeans, unable to handle their lawsuits, appealed to Antigonos to intervene, and Antigonos adapted the international arbitration system by requesting Magnesia (-on-Mt. Sipylos?) to send some respected citizens to dispense rapid justice in the suits. The idea caught on, and was widely used in the third century.[62] In this way Antigonos both solved the problem and avoided meddling personally in the internal affairs of Kyme: he had, in any case, enough pressing business without having to judge local lawsuits.

A large number of inscriptions exist illustrating Antigonos's excellent relations with Samos, including more than a dozen decrees honoring officers and diplomats of Antigonos for various benefactions. It is an attestation to the widespread influence, perhaps even to the genuine popularity, of Antigonos and his rule that we possess more decrees of Greek cities honoring subordinates of his—including substantial "dossiers" from Athens, Ephesos, Eretria, and Megara, as well as Samos—than of any other single Hellenistic monarch. The Samians apparently had an alliance with Antigonos: a decree honoring the Antigonid officer Hipparchos of Kyrene lauds him for his goodwill towards Samian soldiers stationed with him in Karia. There was a festival of Antigoneia kai Demetrieia at Samos, and the Samians apparently had a tribe named after Antigonos's son Demetrios.[63] Ephesos too seems to have maintained good relations with Antigonos, as we learn from a number of extant decrees, in particular a recently published decree showing that the Ephesians won from Antigonos some form of *ateleia*.[64]

62. *OGIS*, no. 7 (= Engelmann, *I. Kyme*, no. 1) is the decree of Kyme honoring the Magnesian judges; cf. on the institution of bringing in foreign judges, and the role played by the Diadochoi in this, Robert, "Les Juges étrangers dans la cité grecque."

63. On Samos and Antigonos, see Schede, *AM* 44 (1919):4–19, and Habicht, *AM* 72 (1957):152–208, 260–65. The festival of Antigoneia kai Demetrieia is attested in Schede, no. 7 (= *SEG*, 1, no. 362), while we learn of a *phylē* named after Demetrios from Schede no. 5K (= *SEG*, 1, no. 355). Cf. further Shipley, *History of Samos*, pp. 170–74.

64. For Ephesos's relations with Antigonos and Demetrios, see *Syll.*, no. 352 (the Ephesians congratulate Demetrios and Antigonos, perhaps on the victory of Salamis) and *OGIS*, no. 9 (honors for a friend and officer of Demetrios who has helped Ephesos in 302), and cf. Keil, *JÖAI* 16, no. 1 (1913):231–44, nos. Ig, IIIb, and IIIe; Engelmann, Knibbe, and

Of Erythrai I have already remarked above (see n. 44) that it was autonomous and *aphorologētos* under Antigonos. From Kolophon, too, we have an inscription recording that Antigonos gave the city its freedom. The inscription dates from before 306 (Antigonos is not yet king), and it appears that Antigonos may have been instrumental in helping Kolophon to expand and rebuild its city walls.[65] Strabo records that in the case of Smyrna, it was Antigonos who reestablished the city, synoikizing the villages into which it had been broken up after the Lydian sack in 627, though the project was apparently only completed by Lysimachos after Antigonos's death.[66] The best known of Antigonos's synoikisms is that of Teos and Lebedos, many of the details of which are preserved in a long inscription containing the better part of two letters from Antigonos to the people of Teos and Lebedos.[67] In addition to the light these letters shed on the synoikism itself, they are also valuable sources of information on how Antigonos dealt with Greek cities.

Teos and Lebedos, situated close together on the southern shore of the neck of the Erythrai peninsula, were ancient Ionic foundations. The attempt to synoikize them is one of the charges often laid against Antigonos as an infringement of the autonomy principle. It is possible that this is a legitimate charge, but there is no evidence for it. Antigonos's letters are responses giving his advice on problems raised by the people of Teos and Lebedos, and give the impression (no doubt deliberately) that the synoikism was wanted by the two cities and that Antigonos was merely helping them achieve their aim. He is scrupulous to phrase each of his decisions as advice (ὠιόμεθα δεῖν: "we thought it right that . . .") and presents himself as the impartial

Merkelbach, *I. Ephesos,* 5, nos. 1450, 1451, and 6, no. 2003. See Knibbe and Iplikçioglu, *JÖAI* 53 (1982):130–31, no. 6, for a decree granting Aristodemos of Miletos citizenship for helping the Ephesians obtain *ateleia* from the king, presumably freedom from a tax on importing goods from the royal lands, or the like.

65. See Meritt, *AJPh* 56 (1935):361 for the inscription, and Robert, *RPh,* 3d ser., 10 (1936):158–61, for date and commentary; and cf. Wehrli, *Antigone et Démétrios,* pp. 90–92, suggesting that Antigonos may have helped Kolophon expand at this time, reabsorbing its port town of Notion.

66. Strabo XIV 1,37, and cf. Wehrli, *Antigone et Démétrios,* p. 92, suggesting that the appearance of the name in an Athenian inscription of 387/86 (*IG* II² 28, line 19 = *Syll.*, no. 136) refutes Strabo, which of course it does not: the name Smyrna and the people, the Smyrnaians, continued to exist, though the town had been broken up into several villages (just as Mantinea existed as a name and people after being broken up into several villages by Agesilaos and Agesipolis; see Xen. *Hell.* V 2,1–7).

67. See most conveniently Welles, *RC,* nos. 3 and 4 (= *Syll.*, no. 344) and cf. Wehrli, *Antigone et Démétrios,* pp. 87–89: Welles and Wehrli take a very different view from that which I argue here.

mediator between the two interest groups of Lebedians and Teans, with the interests of both at heart. In this role he does, at one point, express himself more strongly, when he proposes to review the new code of laws that is to be drawn up and threatens punishment for anyone who has proposed an "inopportune" law (lines 54–55).

The date of the synoikism is clearly ca. 303, for Antigonos was king already, but never had time to complete it (Teos was occupied by Prepelaos on behalf of Lysimachos in 302: Diod. XX 107,4–5). We know that in 304/3 there was an earthquake in Ionia,[68] and it seems natural to connect the synoikism with this event, for there is mention (lines 5–14) of the necessity of demolishing some buildings at Teos, perhaps even amounting to the greater part of the city. It seems likely that Lebedos was largely destroyed, and that Teos had suffered considerable damage, but that it was not yet clear what proportion of the houses were beyond repair. The fact that after the abandonment of this synoikism the Lebedians did not simply return to their old town, but were transferred by Lysimachos to Ephesos, seems to me to increase the likelihood of this assumption. It seems then that the synoikism was not simply an arbitrary act by Antigonos, but a response to an emergency. It is, of course, possible that when Lebedos and Teos appealed to Antigonos for help after the earthquake, they did not anticipate what form it would take. They would doubtless not have dared to refuse when he replied advising them to synoikize and offering his assistance in the matter, even if his advice was unwelcome.

The above reconstruction is conjectural, but it is at least based on the actual tone and contents of the surviving documents and on other known facts. Moreover, once synoikized the new, larger city would itself be an autonomous, sovereign *polis*. Antigonos gives every appearance of striving to keep his direct involvement in the cities' affairs to a minimum. They are to draw up their own new law code (though he assumes the right of veto, no doubt to assure fair play as between the two peoples). In the meantime they can use the law code of a city agreeable to themselves, Kos. Disputes between them are to be arbitrated by another Greek city mutually agreed upon, in this case Mytilene. Though he is personally against the import of corn by Greek cities, he nevertheless concedes to their wishes in this matter, with a gentle reminder that they can obtain supplies of corn from his own royal lands in nearby Lydia (lines 80–94). No one will suppose

68. See Marm. Par. in *FGrH*, no. 239b, sec. 24; and cf. Ad. Wilhelm, *AM* 22 (1897): 212–13.

that Antigonos was acting from entirely disinterested motives in all of this; but what is noticeable is the trouble he takes to spare the feelings of the Greek cities concerned, and as far as possible to serve the best interests of the cities (while ultimately, of course, serving those of himself and his realm as well).

Antigonos's other great synoikism was that which created Antigoneia (later Alexandria) Troas. We know very little of the details of this one, being dependent on several notices in Strabo.[69] Antigoneia was formed from a number of tiny towns on the central Troad coast, opposite Tenedos, and included a few small towns further inland in the Skamander valley. Most of these towns—Larissa, Kolonai, Hamaxitos, Neandria, Kebrene—were utterly insignificant, and may have been glad to be combined into a city of size and importance. This is not the case, however, with Skepsis, which Strabo in two passages states to have been included in the synoikism. The Skepsians seem to have joined unwillingly, and were subsequently enabled to return home by Lysimachos. Not only does Antigonos seem to have been morally in the wrong here: the most puzzling aspect of this move is the geography of it. For Skepsis is a very long way inland, separated from the site of Antigoneia by two ranges of hills and more than twice as far away as Kebrene, which was otherwise the most distant outpost of the synoikism. It is as hard to imagine why Antigonos would have made the geographical decision to include Skepsis (rather than much nearer towns like, say, Assos or Gargara) as it is to see why he damaged his reputation on Greek autonomy in this regard.[70]

However that may be, the new city was a success. Under the name Alexandria Troas, it became far the most important city of the region, while Skepsis remained a free city in its own right after escaping from the synoikism. Antigonos's earlier relations with Skepsis had been excellent: it is from Skepsis that our best contemporary evidence of his widespread propaganda for Greek autonomy comes.[71] The famous Skepsis inscription contains a letter from An-

69. Strabo XIII 593; 597; 604; 607. Cf. also on Antigoneia/Alexandria Robert, *Etudes de numismatique grecque*, pp. 5–100, esp. pp. 5–40.

70. One thing that may have been in Antigonos's mind when founding Antigoneia Troas—as in founding Antigoneia Bithynika (Nikaia), Antigoneia Kyzikena, and Antigoneia by Daskyleion—was the growing strength of Lysimachos in Thrace, and his new city of Lysimacheia on the Chersonnesos. The establishment of these three towns and one fort (A. Kyzikena is called a *phrourion* by Steph. Byz. s.v.) in a chain along the Hellespontine region suggests that military considerations played a role in their location.

71. See *OGIS*, nos. 5 and 6, and cf. Austin, *Hellenistic World*, nos. 31 and 32, for English translations; a commentary on *OGIS*, no. 5 (Antigonos's letter) can be found in Welles, *RC*, no. 1.

tigonos to the Skepsians outlining the course of the peace negotiations of 312/11 as they related to the interests of the Greek cities, and a decree passed by the Skepsians in response. From the letter, which was clearly a pamphlet circulated around all the Greek cities in his sphere, we learn that Antigonos laid great stress on the commitment to Greek autonomy embodied in the peace treaty as a major success on his part. We also learn that Antigonos regarded the Greek cities as his allies, and as such received from them troops and/or financial contributions for the war effort (lines 42–45), and requested them to swear to the peace terms concerning Greek freedom and autonomy (lines 53–56).[72] The Skepsian response to Antigonos's letter shows that they were already before this time celebrating a festival with sacrifices and games in honor of Antigonos; now (in 311) they decided to expand this into a full-blown cult with *temenos,* altar, and cult statue in recognition of his services to the cause of Greek freedom and autonomy (so *OGIS,* no. 6, lines 10–26).

Another case in which Antigonos is seen carefully respecting the autonomy of a Greek city is provided by a set of inscriptions from Eresos on Lesbos concerning the Eresian law on tyranny which provided for the perpetual banishment of the descendants of tyrants. The sons of Agonippos, a tyrant of the 330s, appealed to Antigonos ca. 306/5 for reinstatement at Eresos; Antigonos wrote a letter on their behalf, but when the Eresians stood firmly by their law, he accepted their stance. It is his letter confirming their right to perpetuate the exile of Agonippos's sons that is partially preserved.[73]

Of the cities on the Propontis, Antigonos had been friendly with Kyzikos as early as 318, when he saved it from Arrhidaios, and with Chalkedon since 317, when it was his base in the naval war against Kleitos.[74] At the same period, he was already friendly with Byzantion, a friendship which continued throughout his reign, though the city preferred to remain neutral in his conflict with Lysimachos.[75] His

72. This is built up by Heuss (*Hermes* 73 (1938):153–59) into a *koinē eirēnē,* but in the absence of a *synedrion* of the Greeks to debate and conclude peace, Heuss's case is not really convincing—though Antigonos no doubt had the "common peace" idea in mind when he asked the Greek cities to swear an oath that "all the Greeks would help to protect each other's freedom and autonomy" (*OGIS,* no. 5, lines 54–56).

73. *OGIS,* no. 8 (= Welles, *RC,* no. 2); for a commentary, esp. on Agonippos and the other tyrants of Eresos, see Heisserer, *Alexander the Great and the Greeks,* pp. 27–77.

74. Kyzikos: Diod. XVIII 52,1–3; Chalkedon: Diod. XVIII 72,4.

75. Antigonos was aided by the Byzantines against Kleitos (Diod. XVIII 72,5–6), and though they refused to ally with him against Lysimachos in 312 (Diod. XIX 77,7), he appears to have remained on good terms with them, as we learn from some inscriptions found at

concern for the cities in the Black Sea region is shown by the campaign of his nephew Polemaios in this area in 314, when he saved Amisos from siege by the Macedonian Asklepiodoros, apparently made an alliance with Dionysios of Herakleia, and protected Chalkedon and Astakos from Zipoites of Bithynia and made alliance with them.[76] Antigonos also aided the cities on the north coast of the Black Sea in their attempt to free themselves from Lysimachos in 313–311, sending aid to Kallatis in particular in the form of two expeditions, one by land and one by sea (Diod. XIX 73,1–10).

Finally, mention should be made of the leagues of cities in relation to Antigonos. We know, from epigraphic sources only, of a revived version of the old Ionic League, and of a League of Ilion that may or may not be the same as a League of Aiolians also attested. The dates when these leagues were revived are obscure, but they are firmly attested in the time of Antigonos.

The earliest certainly datable mention of the revived Ionian League is in the letter of Antigonos concerning the synoikism of Teos and Lebedos, the very first lines of which record his stipulation that the two cities shall in future send joint representatives to the Panionion (the meeting place of the Ionian League in the territory of Priene).[77] The league was hence functioning by 303/2 at the latest, though two very fragmentary inscriptions concerning it are probably to be dated a little earlier. One is a decision of the council of the Ionian League to allow the Lebedians to set up a stele in the Panionion, which is to be dated to the fourth century, not only on linguistic grounds (Ionic dialect instead of *koinē*), but also on the grounds that in the third century the Lebedians were first moved from Teos to Ephesos, and when enabled to return home by Ptolemy called their city Ptolemais.[78] The other is a tiny fragment from Erythrai with the very beginning of a decree of the Ionians and Aiolians, again to be dated in the fourth century on the grounds of use of the Ionic dialect.[79]

Olympia (*Syll.*, nos. 349, 350, 351) recording a Byzantine decree honoring and congratulating kings Antigonos and Demetrios (i.e., dating from 306–301), and the dedications on statue bases set up for the two monarchs by the Byzantines (and cf. Paus. VI 15,7, mistakenly identifying the Antigonos thus honored as Gonatas).

76. For the activities of Polemaios, see app. 3, no. 100.

77. *Syll.*, no. 344, lines 1–2 (= Welles, *RC*, no. 3).

78. For Lysimachos moving the Lebedians to Ephesos (which was renamed Arsinoeia), see Paus. I 9,7; for Lebedos renamed Ptolemais ca. 266 see, for example, Kern, *I. Magnesia M.*, nos. 53 and 79. The Lebedians seem to have resumed their old name for a time in the 260s: *OGIS*, no. 222, line 46.

79. Engelmann and Merkelbach, *I. Erythrai und Klazomenai*, no. 16.

As far as this goes, then, it would be possible to attribute the refounding of the Ionian League to the time of Antigonos, perhaps to Antigonos himself.[80] However, there are later inscriptions, and testimony from Strabo, recording the existence of a league festival (first attested ca. 268–262) in honor of Alexander, which has led most scholars to conclude that Alexander must have refounded the league. Habicht has argued this most forcefully, pointing out that the festival was probably celebrated on Alexander's birthday and that festivals founded posthumously to honor individuals were never celebrated on that individual's birthday. This argument is not, however, quite decisive. Habicht claims that cults of Alexander were almost certainly established in many Ionian towns in the immediate aftermath of Alexander's liberation of the area, and if the Ionian League only subsequently (i.e., after Alexander's death) established its Alexandreia, it would most likely have followed its various member cities in setting the date for the festival—that is, Alexander's birthday.[81] The lack of any mention of the league during Alexander's lifetime, and even during the greater part of Antigonos's reign, is a disturbing factor. If the league was in fact refounded by Antigonos, the original festival would doubtless have been called the Antigoneia, but this would have been discontinued by Lysimachos. One might conjecture that, just as Lysimachos caused Antigoneia Troas to be renamed Alexandria, he may have caused the Ionian League to rename its festival the Alexandreia. Certainty can only be obtained if new evidence appears, but it is at least clear that Antigonos happily countenanced the league's existence.[82]

The evidence for the League of Ilion and/or Aiolian League is even more confused. Again, no clear date of inception is known, and the honor of having founded the league is variously assigned to Alexander or Antigonos. No evidence connecting Alexander with the League of Ilion exists, other than his general goodwill towards Ilion

80. So, for example, Tarn, *Alexander,* 1:32; 2:231ff.

81. Habicht, *Gottmenschentum,* pp. 17–25; against Habicht, Badian ("Deification of Alexander the Great," in *Edson Studies,* ed. Dell, pp. 59–63) has questioned the truth of the proposition that cults of the dead were never instituted on the person's birthday, and has argued forcefully that *if* any cults were founded in Asia Minor in Alexander's lifetime (and the evidence is far from conclusive), that most likely occurred during the last years of Alexander's reign. On the refounding of the Ionian League, see further T. Lenschau, *RE* s.v. Iones, cols. 1890–92, also arguing for Alexander as the person responsible.

82. It is also, of course, entirely possible that Antigonos himself requested the league to honor Alexander in its festival, as an act of piety; he also, for example, throughout his reign struck the coin-types of Alexander.

and care for its interests.[83] A number of decrees honoring one Malousios of Gargara (a small town on the south coast of the Troad) attest to the existence of the league in the time of Antigonos and its relations with Antigonos.[84] Malousios had aided in providing for the expenses of an embassy sent to Antigonos before 306 (no royal title for Antigonos in line 9) and again when another embassy was sent to Antigonos as king (lines 23–26). This latter embassy had a mission concerning the freedom and autonomy of the cities, again an indication of Antigonos's interest in the subject, and should perhaps be connected with the hostilities in the area in early 302, when Lysimachos held part of the Troad for a while.[85] The league calls itself τῶν πόλεων τῶν κοινωνουσῶν τοῦ ἱεροῦ (sc., of Athena at Ilion). It had a *synedrion,* which evidently met at the sacred precinct of Athena, and celebrated games dedicated to Athena. Besides Ilion, only Gargara and Lampsakos are known for certain to have been members.[86]

There is also some evidence for a League of Aiolians. The fragment from Erythrai of a decree of the Aiolians and Ionians (see n. 79 above) attests to its existence. There are also coins, small bronze pieces and a few silver coins with the legend AIOLE that date from the late fourth and early third centuries and have been tentatively attributed to Lesbos or to some otherwise unknown small town named "Aioleion" or the like.[87] Given the inscriptional evidence, however, it now seems likely that an alternative hypothesis proposed, namely, that the coins were struck by a revived Aiolian League, is correct. The question is, was this the same as the League of Ilion, or was it quite separate? Robert has pointed out that the cities of the Troad were mostly of Aiolic origin, and that in the Hellenistic period one meets with the designations "Aiolian from Assos" and "Aiolian from Alexandria," just as one finds "Aiolian from Kyme" or "Aiolian from Myrina," in inscriptions. Moreover, the two precisely known find

83. See, for example, Arrian *Anab.* I 11,7–12,1; Plut. *Alex.* 15; Diod. XVII 17,3; Justin XI 5,12; Strabo XIII 1,26; and cf. Diod. XVIII 4,5 on the "last plans" of Alexander.

84. *Syll.*, no. 330 gives these decrees, six in number.

85. Diod. XX 107,1–3; the embassy may have interceded for Lampsakos and Parion, which had gone over to Lysimachos voluntarily, but were recaptured by Demetrios in the same year (Diod. XX 111,3).

86. *Syll.*, no. 330, lines 21 (Gargara) and 59 (Lampsakos); cf. *CIG,* 2, nos. 3601–4 for other inscriptions of the League of Ilion.

87. See on this subject Robert, *Etudes de numismatique grecque,* pp. 92–100, positing the theory that the coins derive from a city called "Aioleion." A new and rather wild theory on this coinage, involving no fewer than three separate leagues in the Troad under Antigonos, has been put forward by Lazzarini, *RIM* 85 (1983):3–15, but this seems to make the situation overly complex.

spots of the Aiolian coinage (all of which comes from Asia Minor) are Kebrene and Assos in the Troad. It seems likely that the Aiolians of the inscription and the coins were none other than the cities that shared in the sanctuary of Athena at Ilion—that is, that the "Aiolian League" and the "League of Ilion" are one and the same institution.[88]

One may conclude, then, that many of the Greek cities of Asia Minor were organized in the time of Antigonos (and perhaps by Antigonos) into two leagues centered on the cult sites at Ilion and the Panionion. It was, of course, with the cities of Asia Minor that Antigonos was most closely associated, and for the longest time, as Asia Minor was throughout his career the very heartland of his power. It is therefore significant that Antigonos's relations with these cities turn out to have been on the whole (with one or two relatively minor exceptions) consistent with his stated policy of respecting Greek autonomy.

The Islanders

The earliest known contact of Antigonos with the Greeks of the islands came in 313, when he sent out a fleet under his nephew Dioskourides to protect the islands and coastal cities from Ptolemy's fleet under Seleukos and to invite them to join his symmachy. In the second half of 314, the island of Delos was emancipated from Athenian control, as we know from the cessation of the official Athenian dedications at the temple each year. Also, at some date before 306 a League of the Islanders was set up centered on Delos (the κοινὸν τῶν Νησιωτῶν), which instituted a cult of Antigonos. These three facts have been brought together to show that under Antigonos's auspices the islands were "liberated" in 313 and united in a common federation, the League of the Islanders, which was allied with Antigonos and had a festival of Antigoneia as part of a founder's cult in Antigonos's honor.[89] This reconstruction is now generally accepted to be correct.

88. Robert, *Etudes de numismatique grecque*, pp. 95–96, for find spots of the coins, and for Aiolians in the Troad in general, pp. 96–97; it should be noted that in the review of *I. Erythrai und Klazomenai* in "Bull. ép.," 1973 (= *REG* 86 [1973]:140), Robert sticks to his guns on the theory of the otherwise unknown town of Aioleion. The types of the coins are Athena/Thunderbolt (silver) and female deity (Hera?)/Thunderbolt (bronze): could these refer to the Athena of Ilion?

89. The expedition of Dioskourides: Diod. XIX 62,9; on the date of Delos's liberation from Athens, see, for example, Th. Homolle, *BCH* 15 (1891):149–55, and cf. chap. 3 n. 45 above; the foundation of the League of the Islanders and the Antigoneia on Delos are known from the inscriptions *IG* XI.4 1036 and *IG* XI.2 154a, the latter dating to 296 and mentioning

The form or institutional structure of the island league in Antigonos's time is very imperfectly known. Though the league had quite a long subsequent history, it is best known from inscriptions describing it as it was under the Ptolemies, from ca. 287 until some not precisely specifiable date about the middle of the third century.[90] It is clear that the league had a religious aspect, centering on the cult of Apollo at Delos, and on a cult of Antigonos and (after 306) Demetrios; likewise, there was later a cult of the Ptolemies, with a festival of Ptolemaieia. We find that both under Antigonos and his son and under the Ptolemies, the league had a *synedrion;* it is further almost certain that under Antigonos and Demetrios, as under the Ptolemies, the head of the league was a *nēsiarchos* appointed by the king.[91] In view of these similarities, it seems reasonable to suppose that the Ptolemies, when they took over the league, left it much as it had been instituted by Antigonos, and that evidence from the Ptolemaic period can be used (with due caution) for the Antigonid period.

The League of the Islanders was not just a religious organization or a league of allied states, but a full-fledged federal state. This is indicated by three points: first the existence of the *nēsiarchos* as chief officer of the league (a sort of president of the islands); second, the fact that the *synedrion* had the power to require *syntaxeis* (financial contri-

---

the Antigoneia at line 42; some important modern works on the League of the Islanders are: König, *Bund der Nesioten;* Guggenmos, *Geschichte des Nesiotenbundes*; Tarn, *Antigonos Gonatas,* app. 5; W. Schwahn, *RE* s.v. Sympoliteia, sec. 5.19; Merker, *Historia* 19 (1970):141–60. All agree that Antigonos I founded the league ca. 314. See now further the discussion of Buraselis, *Das hellenistische Makedonien,* pp. 41–43, 60–67, pointing to the year 313 for the league's foundation.

90. The date when Ptolemaic control of the islands collapsed depends on the dates assigned to the sea battles of Kos and Andros, about which there appear to be almost as many theories as historians. A good account of the league's institutions, with all of the evidence, can be found in W. Schwahn, *RE* s.v. Sympoliteia, sec. 5.19; and on the league in its Ptolemaic phase, see Bagnall, *Ptolemaic Administration,* pp. 136–58.

91. For the Antigoneia and Demetrieia, celebrated in alternate years from (most probably) 306 on, see *IG* XI.4 1036; for the Ptolemaieia see, for example, P. Roussel, *BCH* 31 (1907):344, no. 3, lines 23–25. *Synedrion* under Antigonos: *IG* XI.4 1036, lines 7, 36, 45; under Ptolemies: *IG* XI.4 1037, 1038, etc. *Nēsiarchos* under the Ptolemies: *IG* XI.4 1125, 1126, and cf. Merker, *Historia* 19 (1970):150–53; the case for a *nēsiarchos* under Antigonos and Demetrios is more complex: it rests on a jest recorded by Phylarchos *apud* Athenaios VI 261b and Plut. *Dem.* 25, which suggests that Demetrios did have a *nēsiarchos* (the various other kings of the time are described by Demetrios's courtiers by official titles such as *nauarchos* (Ptolemy), *elephantarchos* (Seleukos), *gazophylax* (Lysimachos), and *nēsiarchos* (Agathokles), the point being that Antigonos and Demetrios are the only real kings). Merker, op. cit., pp. 152–53, suggests that the Apollodoros, son of Apollonios of Kyzikos, who seems to have been *nēsiarchos* in the early 280s and/or late 290s probably held office under Demetrios.

butions) from the member states and to inflict punishment for noncompliance; third, and most decisive, the fact that the *synedrion* was empowered to confer on benefactors the citizenship of all the member states at once, which appears to imply further that citizens of the member states enjoyed isopolity in each other's communities.[92] In all probability the *nēsiarchos* presided over the *synedrion*, and the *synedrion* was the sovereign body of the league, there being no league assembly (travel problems would have made such an assembly impracticable, even if it was ever considered). Decisions of the league *synedrion* were to be inscribed at Delos and in all the member states.

The league was also militarily active. Infantry forces from the league seem to have campaigned in the Peloponnesos, perhaps with Telesphoros or Polemaios in 312/11, from which one can infer that the term *symmachia* in Diodoros (XIX 62,9) is to be understood literally, and that the island league had a treaty of alliance with Antigonos. On other occasions, the league no doubt provided naval forces, and the league forces were evidently commanded by the *nēsiarchos*.[93] In terms of membership, the league was clearly based on the Cyclades. Attested as members, besides Delos, are Mykonos, Kythnos, and Keos, and probably also Ios, in the time of Antigonos; under the Ptolemies we also find Andros, Naxos, Amorgos, and Paros attested as members.[94] In all probability all of the Cycladic islands were in the league, but it seems unlikely that, in the time of Antigonos at least, other Aegean islands were also members. There is no reason to associate any of the large islands off the coast of Asia Minor with the league: Samos and Chios, in particular, would have been members rather of the Ionian League.[95] Moreover, Lemnos and

92. *Syntaxeis* levied by the *synedrion: IG* XI.4 1036, under Antigonos. For the granting of citizenship there is no evidence from the Antigonid period; for the Ptolemaic period see, for example, *IG* XI.4 1039 and 1046, and cf. 1040 and 1042 for the award of other honors valid on all the islands; there is no reason to suppose things were different in this respect under Antigonos and Demetrios.

93. For island troops in the Peloponnesos, see the inscription found at Nemea and published by Geagan, *Hesperia* 37, no. 4 (1968):381–84. For naval forces apparently supplied by the league (at a later period) and for the *nēsiarchos* as commander of such forces, see *OGIS,* no. 773 and Dittenberger's commentary in n. 4.

94. For Mykonos, Kythnos, and Keos in the Antigonid period, see Geagan, loc. cit. n. 93; for Ios, see *IG* XII, suppl. 168; on the Ptolemaic period, see *IG* XII.7 506 (Delos, Kythnos, Naxos, Amorgos, Andros), *IG* XII.5,2 1069 (Keos), Michel, *RIG,* no. 534 (Paros).

95. See Herodotos I 142; and on the Hellenistic *koinon,* see, for example, *Syll.,* no. 368 (esp. at n. 1) for a decree of 289/88 mentioning the "13 cities" of the league (i.e., including Chios and Samos), and Engelmann and Merkelbach, *I. Erythrai und Klazomenai,* no. 75, for Chios actually cited as a member of the league.

Imbros, the other islands of whose relations with Antigonos we have evidence, were clearly not members of the league. Lemnos revolted from Athens (then under the rule of Kassandros's nominee, Demetrios of Phaleron) in 314/13, contemporaneously with Delos, preferring the promises of Antigonos to the realities of Kassandros's rule. Imbros no doubt went over to Antigonos at the same time. Antigonos's admiral Dioskourides protected Lemnos against an Athenian attempt to reconquer it with the aid of Ptolemy's fleet under Seleukos. Thereafter the two islands remained under Antigonos, apparently with protective garrisons, until the liberation of Athens in 307, when Antigonos handed them back to Athenian control.[96]

We have two inscriptions recording the nature of Antigonos's patronage of the Cycladic islands, from Delos and from Ios. The former (*IG* XI.4 566) is clearly to be attributed to Antigonos Monophthalmos because of the mention, besides "King Antigonos" in line 6, of "the kings" in line 7, and of "King Demetrios" in lines 15–16. Mention of an Antigonos and a Demetrios as co-kings in this way can only refer to Monophthalmos and Poliorketes in the years 306–301.[97] This inscription is extremely fragmentary, but the main drift is clear enough: ambassadors are to be sent to Antigonos to report honors accorded him and hand over "crowns" and the award of *xenia;* they are to emphasize the goodwill of the people towards him; there are further mentions of gold crowns and bronze statues. In lines 10–12 we find some of the reasons for all this: Antigonos is to be invited to maintain the situation, presumably established by him, whereby Delos has a democratic constitution and the people live "harmoniously" (ὁμ[ο]ν[οο]ῦντες) "in a free city," having indeed their "ancestral" laws (lines 16–17).

The inscription from Ios (*IG* XII, suppl. 168) was attributed to the late fourth century by the original editors, Klaffenbach and Hiller von Gaertringen, on the basis of the letterforms. Hence the King Antigonos whom it concerns was identified as Monophthalmos,

96. For Lemnos joining Antigonos and so forth, see Diod. XIX 68,3–4; Antigonos removes his garrison from Imbros in 307 and hands it back to Athens: Diod. XX 46,4; Athens receives tribute from Lemnos and Imbros in 305/4: *IG* II^2 1492b, lines 124–38; cf. also *IG* II^2 550 for mention of Antigonos and Lemnos. Since Antigonos handed the islands over to Athenian control, they cannot have been in the island league.

97. Only Antigonos Monophthalmos and his son Demetrios are known to have been joint rulers; attempts to argue that Antigonos Gonatas and Demetrios II ruled jointly (see, e.g., Will, *Histoire politique,* 1:344, 347 for bibliography) do not carry conviction.

correctly in my view, though this has been disputed.[98] What chiefly convinces me that the attribution to Monophthalmos is correct is a comparison of this inscription with that from Delos, for they are very similar. We read at line 3, "He gave to the people of Ios their ancestral laws" and at line 12 "so that we may guard the city in harmony" (ὁμονοο̣[ῦ]ντες) "and without strife" (ἀ̣σ̣τα̣σί[αστοι]). Now the first of these statements is merely conventional phraseology, but the second—and especially the use of the term ὁμονοοῦντες—is not, and its appearance in these two decrees from Cycladic islands in the early Hellenistic period strongly suggests that both refer to the same man and occasion: Antigonos Monophthalmos, ca. 306. Antigonos is to be awarded a gold crown of 2,000 drachmai, he is given the title of Sotēr (which the Athenians had, of course, already bestowed on him in 307), and good-news sacrifices are ordained (lines 5–6), presumably referring to news of Salamis and the assumption of the royal title by Antigonos. Doubtless there was originally a companion decree honoring Demetrios.

If the above interpretation is correct, we have three decrees from the islands dating to ca. 306—one by the *synedrion* of the league, one by the Delians, and one by the people of Ios. Two of the three make reference to Antigonos's earlier benefits to the islands, all three laud and congratulate him on the occasion of his accession to royal status and his son's great victory, the latter two making explicit reference to the freedom, autonomy, and harmony thus secured for the islands. There is one further piece of evidence about the Cyclades in this period. When Ptolemy cruised through the Cyclades in 308 on his way to Korinth, he "liberated Andros and drove out the garrison" (Diod. XX 37,1). If this garrison was placed there by Antigonos,

98. For example, by Habicht, *Gottmenschentum*, pp. 65–73, though he declares himself less convinced that attribution to Monophthalmos is impossible in the *Nachträge* to the 2d ed. at pp. 256–57. The problem is that Antigonos is only introduced in line 2 of the inscription, in a way that normally implies that benefactions by ancestors of the honorand have been lauded first, which is not appropriate for Antigonos Monophthalmos but is for Gonatas or Doson. Habicht considers and rejects the possibilities of reference to Monophthalmos's son Demetrios in line 1 (the solution of Klaffenbach and Hiller von Gaertringen), or of mention of Antigonos as private person in line 1 and as king in line 2. There is, however, another solution: based on Diod. XIX 62,9, one could restore the first two lines:

> [———ἐπειδὴ πρότερον Διοσκουρίδης ὁ στρατηγὸς τοῦ Ἀντιγόνου πολλῶν καὶ/ μεγάλων ἀγαθῶ]ν ἄιτιος γεγένηται τῆι π[ό]λει, νῦν τε Ἀντίγονος ὁ βα[σιλεὺς . . .

There is room for this (the editors plausibly restore line 4 with 119 letters), and the decree would thus refer to Antigonos's earlier benefactions via his nephew and general Dioskourides, before turning to praise of his current benefactions.

which is nowhere stated but is clearly possible, it would certainly represent a mark against him. However, the garrison was more probably established by Antigonos's rebellious nephew Polemaios, who had himself passed through the Cyclades with considerable forces in 309 on his way to meet Ptolemy at Kos.[99] Whatever may be the truth of this matter, it is clear that on the whole Antigonos's relations with the islanders were cordial.

The Mainland Greeks

Antigonos's earliest known contacts with the Greeks of the mainland are those that must have resulted from his position as general of the Greek allies in Alexander's army in 334. Subsequently there is a long gap when, as satrap of Phrygia, his contacts with the Greeks must have been minimal and in any case we hear virtually nothing about him. It is interesting to note, though, that when he fled from Perdikkas to Antipatros in 321, he embarked on Attic ships and hence presumably reached Antipatros via Athens. Again, when he sailed back to Asia early in the following spring, he had a number of Athenian ships with him, no doubt the same ships that had brought him to Europe the year before.[100] As a friend of Antipatros and his son Kassandros, Antigonos was not, in the years 320–315, an outstanding friend of the mainland Greeks or proponent of autonomy for them. With the Tyre declaration of 314, however, this changed.

In the wake of the declaration at Tyre that all Greeks were to be free, ungarrisoned, and autonomous, Antigonos despatched three successive expeditions to Greece to try to bring this about. The first, under his close friend Aristodemos, succeeded in freeing much of the Peloponnesos by means of an alliance with Polyperchon and Alexandros, and in persuading the Aitolians to become Antigonos's allies. The work in the Peloponnesos was undone, however, when Kassandros persuaded Alexandros to change sides again.[101] In 312, therefore, Antigonos sent out another expedition under his nephew Telesphoros, who did much to restore the situation in the Peloponnesos. Antigonos felt that yet more was needed and in mid 312 despatched a third, and by far the largest, expedition under another nephew, Polemaios. When this man succeeded in driving Kassandros's garri-

99. See on this Diod. XX 27,3; and cf. Seibert, *Ptolemaios I,* p. 188 n. 41, for the suggestion that the garrison on Andros was Polemaios's.

100. Antigonos sailed from Asia on Attic ships: Diod. XVIII 23,4; he returned to Asia with Athenian ships: Arrian *Met' Alex.* 25,1; and cf. Hauben, *ZPE* 19 (1974):62–64.

101. For the expedition of Aristodemos, see app. 3, no. 16.

son out of Chalkis, he "left the Chalkidians without a garrison, so that it would be clear that Antigonos truly intended to free the Greeks" (Diod. XIX 78,2). Polemaios's successes liberated all of Greece up to Thermopylai, with the exception of Athens and a few Peloponnesian towns, and brought Kassandros to the negotiating table.[102] In the subsequent peace, the freedom of the Greeks was, of course, strongly reiterated.

During the course of the hostilities, Boiotia had made an alliance with Antigonos, and we also hear of Eretria and Karystos entering the symmachy of Antigonos; even the Athenians sent envoys to Antigonos about an alliance. It is clear that at this date Antigonos was already operating in Greece through a network of alliances. Interesting to note is, incidentally, the expulsion by Polemaios of Kassandros's garrison from Thebes in 312, leaving the city free. The Tyre declaration had ordered Kassandros to destory this city again as an enemy of Macedon, which fact has been used by Wehrli to demonstrate the insincerity of Antigonos's declaration of Greek freedom. Antigonos's actions show, however, that it was his orders to Kassandros regarding the Thebans and Olynthians that were empty propaganda, rather than the declaration of Greek freedom. Not only was Thebes left intact and free in 312, but a few years later (ca. 304) we actually find Demetrios contributing funds towards the rebuilding of the city.[103]

The treason of Polemaios in 310 undid most of Antigonos's work in Greece, but in 307 he determined to try again, this time through his son Demetrios. What was actually in his mind at this juncture cannot be known, but the sentiments later attributed to him by Greek tradition are worth noting; for we find among Antigonos's apophthegms in Plutarch the statement that by making the Greeks free, "his repute, kindled in Greece as on a lofty height, would spread like beacon-fires throughout the inhabited world."[104] At any rate, Demetrios sailed into Athens with a huge armada and amidst great public rejoicing expelled Demetrios of Phaleron, drove out the garrison from Mounychia, and reestablished the Athenian democracy. He also liberated Megara at this time. The enthusiasm aroused by these events

---

102. For Telesphoros, see app. 3, no. 111; for Polemaios, app. 3, no. 100.

103. Polemaios and Thebes: Diod. XIX 78,5 (ἠλευθέρωσε τὰς Θήβας); for Demetrios giving money to Thebes, see Holleaux, *Etudes*, 1:1–40, dealing with an inscription from Thebes recording gifts towards the rebuilding (*IG* VII 2419 = *Syll.*, no. 337), with Demetrios's gift at lines 30–34.

104. Plut. *Mor.* 182f, and cf. Plut. *Dem.* 8 for a variant.

was extraordinary. Honors were showered upon Antigonos and Demetrios (see pp. 149–50 above).[105]

The upshot was that Antigonos was hugely popular in Athens at this time, and these actions would not have gone unnoticed in the rest of Greece either. Athens now made an alliance with Antigonos, as no doubt did Megara, though that happens not to be attested. As a result of the alliance with Athens, we find thirty Athenian ships fighting in Antigonos's navy at the battle of Salamis in 306 (Diod. XX 50,3), a draft of Athenian settlers helping to populate Antigoneia-on-the-Orontes (see pp. 303–4 below), and a body of Athenian soldiers fighting under Antigonos and Demetrios at the battle of Ipsos (*IG* II^2 657, lines 16–26). We have from Athens at least a score of inscriptions honoring friends and officers of Antigonos and Demetrios between 307–301 (not counting various dubious cases); there are also a large number of honorary inscriptions from Megara (no less than eighteen) honoring various individuals: only four of them refer explicitly to Demetrios, but they are all so alike that the chances are most of them honor officers in Demetrios's army, especially as seven of the nineteen men mentioned are Asiatics, an unexpectedly high proportion.[106] After the Cyprian/Rhodian interlude, Demetrios returned to Greece in 304, liberating Euboia, central Greece, and the Peloponnesos in the course of the next two years. Again honorary inscriptions attest to Antigonid popularity at Eretria, Epidauros, and Troizen. On a less positive note, Demetrios's personal arrogance began to cause discontent in some circles at Athens.[107]

---

105. For the honors bestowed on Antigonos and Demetrios by Athens, see Diod. XX 46,1–2 and Plut. *Dem.* 10–13 (with some exaggeration); for the state galley *Antigonis,* see Bekker, *Anekdota Graeca* 1:267,21, and schol. Demosth. XXI 171 (ed. Dindorff II 637); for gifts of Antigonos to Athens, see Diod. XX 46,4, and cf. *IG* II^2 1492b at lines 97–103 (140 talents), 120–22 (timber), 133–34 (Lemnos and Imbros under Athenian control).

106. For Athenian decrees honoring Antigonid officers, see *IG* II^2 459, 469,471, 486, 492, 495, 496 (+ 507), 498, 538, 555, 558, 559 (+ 568), 560, 562, 646, 773; *SEG,* 14, no. 60; *Hesperia* 7 (1938), p. 297, no. 22, p. 301, no. 25; Herzog, *RFIC,* n.s., 20 (1942):12–13, no. 6a; Koumanoudes, *Horos* 4 (1986):11–18; Matthaiou, *Horos* 4 (1986):19–23 (= a total of twenty-two; there are probably more). For the Megarian decrees, see *IG* VII 1–14, 3473; *ABSA* 19 (1912–13):82–85, nos. I–III; there are men from Eresos, Erythrai (two men), Halikarnassos (three men), and Iasos; *IG* VII 1, 4, 5, and 6 are certainly officers of Demetrios; on the date and significance of these decrees, see now Urban, *Wachstum und Krise des Achaiischen Bundes,* pp. 66–70.

107. For decrees honoring Antigonid officers at Eretria, see *IG* XII.9 198, 199, 210, and 212 (and cf. nos 197, 200, 201); at Epidauros, see *IG* IV^2.1 58 (and cf. nos. 49, 51, and 53); for Troizen, see app. 3, no. 120 below. On the discontent aroused at Athens by Demetrios's behavior in 304–2, see now Shear, *Kallias of Sphettos,* pp. 49–51. Possibly connected with this is the fact that Antigonos and Demetrios seem to have had some Athenians under arrest in Asia in 301 (*IG* II^2 657, lines 26–29), no doubt suspected sympathizers with Kassandros and Lysimachos, as they were sought out and freed by Lysimachos's agents after Ipsos.

However, the most significant act for Antigonos's Greek policy was the foundation of a Hellenic League at Korinth in spring 302. The event is attested by Plutarch and by a number of inscriptions.[108] By far the most important is the Epidaurian inscription, which is a copy of the league's charter and gives us a great deal of detailed information on its institutions. The league was a full symmachy, which is not surprising: I have noted again and again Antigonos's liking for cementing his relations with Greek states by an alliance. Speaking now only of mainland Greece, between 314 and 306 he concluded alliances with Aitolia, Boiotia, Eretria, Karystos, and Athens. These are the alliances explicitly attested: there is no reason to doubt that alliances also existed with the likes of Sparta, Elis, Chalkis, and Megara, to name just a few.[109] In late 307, when recalling his son Demetrios to Asia to face Ptolemy, Antigonos instructed him to summon a meeting of representatives from all of the Greek allies to consult about their common safety. This should doubtless be seen as the first step towards bringing together the various alliances in Greece into one big alliance system.[110] The process was completed by Demetrios some four years later.

The charter of the league is preserved for us, then, in five substantial fragments of what must originally have been a very long document indeed. Fragments 1 through 4 all preserve details of the league's purpose and organization; fragment 5 has part of the oath sworn by members. Fragment 1 specifies (lines 7–10) that the Greeks are to be in a relation of friendship and alliance to Antigonos and Demetrios and their descendants "so as to have the same friends and enemies"; and (lines 13–15) that anyone who makes war on one of the allies, imposes a garrison, or harms the *βασιλεία* of Antigonos and Demetrios is to be an enemy of all of the allies. Fragment 2 is very imperfect (only the left edge remains: a dozen or so letters per line), but it apparently mentioned duties of the league members, and particularly (lines 34–37) the duty of abiding by the agreement, with punishment for noncompliance and rewards for informers.

108. Plut. *Dem.* 25; *IG* IV².1 68; *Hesperia* 9 (1940):348–51; Daux, *Delphes,* p. 351, no. 2; and see also Robert, *Hellenica,* 2:15–33, discussing the epigraphic testimony and establishing the date of the league's foundation (spring 302).

109. See, e.g., Diod. XIX 60,1 (Sparta); 87,1–3 (Elis); 77,4–78,2 (Chalkis, and cf. *IG* II² 469, 491, and 563 + 485); XX 46,3 (Megara, and cf. Plut. *Dem.* 9).

110. Diod. XX 46,5, and cf. Simpson, *Historia* 8 (1959):396.

Fragment 3, the best preserved and most interesting section, deals with the league institutions, particularly the *synedrion*. It is specified that all agents of the league are to enjoy safety in going about its business, and violators of this rule are to be seized by the local authorities and handed over to the *synedrion* for punishment (lines 60–66). The *synedrion* is to convene at the sacred games in peacetime, in wartime whenever and wherever convenient, as decided by the council and the general who represents the kings (lines 66–73). The decisions of the *synedrion* are to be binding (*kyria*), and the quorum is set at one-half; councillors are not to be impeached at home on account of the proceedings at the *synedrion* (lines 73–76). There are to be five *proedroi* (presidents or chairmen), chosen from among the councillors, but not more than one from any city; they are to prepare the agenda together with the secretaries and see to the orderly conduct of affairs; and anyone who has business he thinks should be discussed at the *synedrion* must present it in writing to the *proedroi* (lines 76–87). It is specified that during a joint war, the representatives of the kings are to preside (line 91). Cities which fail to send their representatives to the council are to be fined; likewise, fines are specified for failure to send troops assessed for the common war effort, at different rates according to the different kinds of soldiers—cavalry, heavy infantry, and so on (lines 92–99). It is decreed, finally, in fragment 5 (lines 133–39) that all participants are to set up copies of the treaty and oath at their most important cult site, for example, the Eleians at Olympia.

This brief review of the most important points of the Epidauros inscription reveals a highly organized institution that was clearly intended to last, and that one could almost call a "United States of Greece," with the Antigonid monarch as hereditary president and commander in chief and a house of representatives to formulate policy. Particularly significant is the provision for regular meetings of the *synedrion* even in peacetime, at which business affecting the kings and the Greeks was to be discussed and states or individuals that were getting out of line were to be dealt with. Antigonos evidently intended to establish harmony and cooperation once and for all in Greece under the leadership of his dynasty, and he sought to make the Greeks his partners in this endeavor. His position in peacetime would be that of a state represented in the *synedrion,* like the other Greek states, though with important security functions. Hence, he does not appear to have intended to rule the Greeks as a master, but rather to lead them as a friend.[111] Surely there can be little doubt that the system outlined in the Epidauros inscription would have been a great boon to Greece if it had ever actually been firmly established.

The Hellenic League of Antigonos is obviously a descendant of the Hellenic Treaty of Philip II and of the "Second Athenian League," but so far as we can tell it was more broadly conceived than either of these. The great advance made by Antigonos was in providing for a system of peacetime governance under which problems between states could be discussed and the league as a whole made a real part of the life of Greece. The organizations of Athens and Philip, though they already had much of the institutional content of Antigonos's league, were essentially directed towards fighting common enemies, of which an oath of the members to maintain peace among themselves was merely a necessary corollary. Antigonos seems to have planned to combine the hegemonic league system with the common peace system into a single institution that would combine his own interest (leadership of the Greeks) with the best interests of the Greeks (harmonious self-rule).

It may be thought that I have presented too rosy a picture of Antigonos's policy and intentions with respect to the Hellenic League, but in truth I have merely interpreted the evidence of the document recording its institutions. This paints the picture itself, although naturally one does not know to what extent Antigonos would have lived up to what seem to have been his intentions in 303/2. Since the Hellenic League basically died with Antigonos on the field of Ipsos in 301, we shall never know how well or how badly this league would have fared. Given the arrogant and unstable character of Demetrios, one suspects that it was doomed from the start.

In any event, Antigonos's relations with the mainland Greeks were always colored by the presence of Kassandros in Macedon, which made Antigonos's policy of "freedom for the Greeks" profitable and ensured his popularity among them. Final evaluation of Antigonos's dealings with the Greeks, then, should be based mostly on his relations with the Asiatic Greeks, whose overlord he was for more than a decade.

---

111. For a full discussion of the Hellenic League of the Epidauros inscription, see Larsen, *CPh*, 20 and 21 (1925 and 1926):313–29 and 52–71 resp. (and cf. also Larsen, *Representative Government in Greek and Roman History*, chap. 3). Larsen's conclusions differ somewhat from mine (e.g., he is convinced that Antigonos's League was just a revival of a league founded by Philip II; he denies that Antigonos and Demetrios would normally have sent some *synedroi* to represent them in the council, like the other members, but see line 91 of the inscription). On the whole, however, his treatment is thorough and illuminating.

GREEK REACTIONS TO ANTIGONOS

At the start of this chapter I remarked that the fourth century was a difficult era for the Greek cities: this is especially true of the last two decades of the century. The dismemberment of Alexander's empire created a situation in which the Greeks were torn between their own desire for independence, the determination of Kassandros to control them as a source of strength to be kept to himself and denied to his rivals, and the determination of those rivals—Antigonos and Ptolemy—to disrupt Kassandros's control. The kingdoms that Antigonos and Ptolemy were building required large numbers of Greeks to help control and run them. Hence the importance to Antigonos (and Ptolemy) of the Greek cities, both of Asia Minor and of Europe.

Antigonos was clearly determined to bring the largest possible number of Greek cities under his aegis, and in the face of stiff competition from Ptolemy and Kassandros he could not afford to leave such cities entirely independent: he could not, that is, countenance their defection to his rivals. Two paths were open to him. He could follow the example of Kassandros and try to control the Greek cities by garrisons and strong-arm tactics, or he could seek to gain the goodwill of the Greeks. Both policies had drawbacks: the former in the commitment of large numbers of troops to garrison duty and the certainty of unpopularity; the latter in the uncertainty of the practical worth of Greek goodwill. To his credit, Antigonos chose the latter path, which required from him something of a tightrope act in striving to combine the maximum of autonomy for the cities with the necessary minimum of control by himself.

It seems that since he had to limit the freedom of the cities somehow, Antigonos chose the symmachy as his tool to this end. The examples of Rhodes, Samos, Kalymna, the Skepsis decree, Astakos and Chalkedon, and the League of the Islanders (not to mention the various mainland Greek alliances) indicate that he most probably built up a network of alliances that bound all the Greek states within his sphere of influence to him. The advantages are obvious: in making such an alliance, Antigonos recognized the Greek city as a sovereign state, but he could limit the foreign policies of these city-states by the terms of the alliances, binding them to his cause and giving himself justification for attacking any that defected from him. Thus, too, he could obtain aid in money and manpower without having to resort to extortion.

This policy was pleasing to the Greeks because it recognized their autonomy and strictly defined and limited their obligations to Antigonos. It also suited Antigonos no doubt because it limited the amount of time and effort he would have to put into the governance of the Greeks. For that dealing with the Greek cities could be a very time-consuming business can be seen at a glance by looking at the complex provisions in Antigonos's two letters on the synoikism of Teos and Lebedos.

It is doubtless in this context that one should place Antigonos's liking for leagues of Greek cities. The more cities could be gathered together into such organizations, the better, for it enormously simplified his diplomacy. Instead of having thirteen embassies from Ionia to listen to, he might have to hear only one, from the Ionian League; and if he himself had something to communicate to the Ionians, he could send an ambassador to a meeting at the Panionion. Significantly, the later leagues that we hear of—the island and Hellenic leagues—seem to be far more highly developed than those of Asia Minor. Whether or not Antigonos had anything to do with the revitalization of the Ionian and Ilian leagues, he evidently found the league as an institution much to his taste and worth developing.

In general, Antigonos's administrative involvement with the Greek cities was very slight. Their foreign and defense policies were in his hands, and for purposes connected with warfare he might require contributions of money, men, or ships from them, or occasionally even interfere with them in other ways. But on the whole it seems that he involved himself with the affairs of the Greek cities only when appealed to, and even then usually preferred (as in the cases of Kyme and Klazomenai) to request another Greek city to do the work, restricting himself to the sending of a *diagramma* giving guidelines for the law tribunal, international arbitration, or whatever. Moreover, it is evident that Antigonos for the most part used Greeks in his dealings with the Greek states. Men like Aristodemos of Miletos, Medeios of Larissa, Nikomedes of Kos, and Adeimantos of Lampsakos, all very well known figures in Antigonos's diplomatic activities with respect to the Greeks, are only the most important representatives of a host of Greek collaborators who appear in the Greek inscriptions as aides of Antigonos and Demetrios in their relations with the Greek cities. Though Antigonos had many Macedonians and a number of Asians in his service, it seems that he preferred when practicable to send a Greek to Greeks. The most notable exceptions, Dioskourides, Telesphoros, and Polemaios, were all three members of his family (nephews), and are thus to be viewed as particularly personal representatives—and no doubt he felt better able to trust them with major independent commands (wrongly as it turned out).

This scrupulous thoughtfulness probably explains Antigonos's generally excellent reputation among the Greeks. That the mentions of Antigonos in the contemporary epigraphic sources should have been highly complimentary was only to be expected: a Greek state would not normally refer to a ruler in an inscribed document except to compliment him for some benefaction or other.[112] Noteworthy, however, is the fact that even posthumously Antigonos continued to be highly regarded for his relations with the Greek cities: recall in this context the third-century inscription from Erythrai pointing out that Antigonos had given the city its freedom, and the verdict of Plutarch on Antigonos's efforts on behalf of Greek freedom. The policy which Antigonos enunciated in his Tyre proclamation and pursued steadfastly throughout the remainder of his career became the standard policy of virtually all great powers towards the Greek cities, down to and including Rome in the second century B.C.. The enthusiasm aroused by Antigonos's espousal of the cause of Greek freedom and the successes he gained thereby were such as could not be ignored by later powers.[113]

The contemporary records attest abundantly to that enthusiasm and success. The responses of the Greek cities to Antigonos's activities may be roughly divided into three categories, based on the type of honors accorded by the Greek cities: there were the standard honors awarded to Antigonos's various officers and aides—*proxenia,* citizenship, crowns, statues, preferential access to council and people, and so on; there were the more or less standard honors awarded to Antigonos himself and members of his family, such as *xenia,* crowns, good-news or thanks offerings, statues, preferential access to council and people; and there were the divine honors accorded Antigonos and members of his family—cults with altars, sacrifices, festivals, divine epithets, cult statues, and the like.

There are extant a host of inscriptions from Greek cities all around the Aegean honoring Antigonos's various friends and subordinates: many of these have been referred to already (see especially nn. 63, 64, 106, and 107 above), and the evidence is presented in full in my

---

112. But see for an important contrast the uncomplimentary mention of Kassandros in several Athenian public documents (e.g., *IG* II^2 469 and 467); and cf. for a private document the curse tablet directed against Kassandros and his officers in Jordan, *AM* 95 (1980):225–36.

113. For the continued effect of Antigonos's policy of freedom of the Greeks in the Hellenistic period to Rome's conquest, see the works cited in n. 1 above.

prosopographical appendix (app. 3 below).[114] There are, as far as I can tell, more of such decrees honoring friends of Antigonos than of any other single Hellenistic monarch, an attestation not only of the influence and authority of Antigonos, but also of the genuine enthusiasm and popularity he evoked as the first monarch to make Greek autonomy a firm plank in his general policy. The Greeks could not fail to perceive the self-interest and cynicism behind the claims and counterclaims of subsequent monarchs and themselves became cynical in awarding even the highest honors in order to encourage a friendly interest in them by powerful persons. However, self-interest and cynicism, even if present (as they probably were to some degree), were not so evident in the case of Antigonos, the first and most tenacious proponent of this policy, so that the genuine popularity evoked by Antigonos's policy need not be doubted. And the mainland Greeks, at least, had a tradition going back to 387 of looking to Asian rulers as potential liberators from oppressors nearer at hand.

The various honors bestowed on Antigonos and his immediate family are a further attestation of the success of Antigonos's propaganda. Instances of what I have called the "standard honors" (as opposed to divine or quasi-divine honors) are numerous, and the evidence has mostly been alluded to already: the states concerned are Priene, Ephesos, Delos, Ios, Rhodes, and Byzantion. The most significant of these honors were those involving actual outlays of money: crowns and statues; and of these the statues were the more important, since they formed a lasting reminder of the benefactions conferred by Antigonos and so must have spread his repute and perpetuated his fame. One should not underestimate the significance of the fact that visitors to the greatest Panhellenic shrines—Olympia, Delphi, and Delos—and the greatest Greek cities of the Hellenistic age—Athens and Rhodes—would there have seen statues of Antigonos and his son Demetrios.[115]

Most important of the honors accorded Antigonos by the Greek cities, however, were those of a divine nature: cults of Antigonos of one sort or another are definitely attested at Skepsis, Samos, Athens, and Delos, and less certain evidence may refer to cults at Kos, Rhodes, and Ios.[116] Most likely there were cults in numerous other

114. See also for an excellent discussion of the nature and purpose of these decrees Herman, *Talanta* 12/13 (1980/81):103–49.

115. See for these statues *Syll.*, nos. 349–51 and Paus. VI 15,7 (Olympia); Paus. X 10,2 (Delphi); *IG* XI.4 566 and 1036 (Delos); Diod. XX 46,2 (Athens); and Diod. XX 93,6 (Rhodes).

116. Cult at Skepsis: *OGIS*, no. 6; at Athens: there are many *testimonia* proving the establishment of the cult and showing that it continued to the 230s at least (see Habicht,

cities of which no evidence survives, especially in cities in Asia Minor. There were Greek precedents for the rendering of divine honors to a mortal, but until Alexander the Great, at least, they were isolated cases; and if the recent tendency to doubt the existence of widespread cults of Alexander during his lifetime is correct,[117] then Antigonos would have been the first man to receive divine honors widely in the Greek world while still alive. Again these cults attest to the enormous impact the career and policies of Antigonos had on his contemporaries, such that in seeking to praise him adequately, they felt the need to break down the traditional barriers between the human and the divine, something that had been done before on a widespread basis, if ever, only in the case of the superhuman-seeming Alexander.

The location, nature, and meaning of the various cults of Antigonos and his family around the Greek world have been exhaustively reviewed and analyzed by Habicht in *Gottmenschentum und griechische Städte* (see especially pp. 42–79). Besides cults of Antigonos and Demetrios, we have evidence also for cults of Phila, the wife of Demetrios, and Stratonike, either the wife of Antigonos or the daughter of Demetrios.[118] What needs to be pointed out is that, though divine honors and a cult subsequently became a regular and institutionalized feature of Hellenistic monarchies,[119] passing thence to the Roman emperors, and though this was clearly a development of the cults of Alexander and Antigonos and their contemporaries, it was in no wise part of Antigonos's policy to seek divine honors as far as we can tell. In every known case of a cult for Antigonos, the initiative in instituting it seems to have come entirely from the Greek city concerned, being a way of expressing gratitude for some benefaction conferred and hope of future benefits.

The raising of Antigonos to "divine" status, with at Athens at least—and perhaps at Ios—the cult epithet Sotēr, is a reflection of his

Gottmenschentum, pp. 44–48, for details); at Samos: *SEG*, 1, no. 362 mentioning a festival of Antigoneia kai Demetrieia; at Delos: *IG* XI.4 1036. For the possibility of a cult of Antigonos at Kos, see above n. 55; for the conjecture of a cult on Rhodes, see Habicht, op. cit., pp. 73–74; and for a possible cult of Antigonos on Ios, see the use of the epithet "Sotēr," typically a cult title, for Antigonos by the people of Ios in *IG* XII, suppl. 168.

117. See, for example, Badian in *Edson Studies*, ed. Dell, pp. 27–71.

118. Cult of Phila at Athens: Athenaios VI 225c and VI 254a (a fragment of the contemporary comic poet Alexis); for Stratonike, see the Delian inscription *IG* XI.4 415 from ca. 300 mentioning a cult statue (*agalma*) of Stratonike, generally assumed to be Demetrios's daughter, though I fail to see why, in view of the date, it cannot just as well pertain to Demetrios's mother.

119. See for this, for example, Bikerman, *Institutions des Séleucides*, pp. 236–58.

prestige and authority, not of any policy of seeking to elevate himself above mortal status. It demonstrates again the enthusiasm that his espousal of the principle that the Greek cities should be free and ungarrisoned aroused. Particularly interesting in this respect is the fact that at Athens even private citizens were moved to offer homage of their own to Antigonos and Demetrios as quasi-divine patrons of Greek liberty.[120] One must bear in mind, therefore, that while the various honors accorded Antigonos by the Greek cities became standard in the Hellenistic period, they were not so already in Antigonos's own lifetime, being then first evoked by his career and policies. Habicht (*Gottmenschentum,* pp. 240–41) rightly points to the contrast with Kassandros, who was not liked or honored by the Greeks.

Here, indeed, we touch on the central issue in passing judgment on Antigonos's relations with the Greeks. He was not motivated by a disinterested love of the Greeks, or of freedom as such; he did limit the freedom of the Greeks; his pronouncements of Greek autonomy were self-interested. But having decided, as a self-interested act of statesmanship, on a policy of gaining the goodwill of the Greeks, he applied it with all the rigor and tenacity that circumstances permitted, and so deserves to be called the most philhellene of the kings of his time, for he could have acted otherwise. From the Greek point of view, it would no doubt have been better if there had been no Philip and Alexander, and no Diadochoi, to disturb their independence; but given the reality, an Antigonos was clearly preferable to a Kassandros or Lysimachos, or even a Ptolemy. One wonders, finally, whether the policy Antigonos chose was a wise one from the point of view of his own interests. I think that on the whole it was. It is always better to rule through goodwill than through force when possible, and Antigonos had the power and wealth not to need to keep a tight rein on the Greek cities. More significantly, as a Macedonian king of Asian "barbarians," he needed to be able to attract Greeks to his service, and a good reputation among the Greeks would have been very useful to him in this respect. It is noteworthy that Ptolemy was his chief rival for Greek goodwill, and that subsequently the Seleukids, Ptolemies, and Attalids all sought to maintain good repute among the Greeks.

---

120. *IG* III^2 3424 (and cf. Wilhelm, *AE,* 1937, pp. 203–7, for an improved text) is a dedicatory inscription of an altar to the Sotēres, Antigonos and Demetrios, by at least eleven private citizens; Moretti, *ISE,* no. 7, records cult honors paid to Demetrios "the Great" by Athenian volunteers who had fought with him in the Peloponnesos in 303/2.

7

Antigonos's Administration of His Asian Realm

The realm under Antigonos's direct or indirect rule in Asia fluctuated considerably during the years 320–301, starting as just his old satrapy of Phrygia/Lykaonia/Pisidia/Lykia/Pamphylia; encompassing at its greatest extent virtually all of Asia Minor west of the rivers Iris and Euphrates, Syria and Palestine, and the upper satrapies as far as Areia/Drangiane and Arachosia; and in its last and most stable phase (310–301) comprising essentially Anatolia and Syria/Palestine. It is the aim of this and the following chapter to give as far as is possible an account of how Antigonos ruled this realm, what sort of institutions and policies, whether inherited from predecessors or newly invented, he established, and to what extent he is therefore to be considered the precursor of the Seleukids, who eventually took over his realm. The evidence on which this attempt is based is scanty and inadequate: the literary sources were by and large not interested in social, institutional, and economic history, so that one must rely on brief scattered references in them and on the slightly more forthcoming epigraphic source material in trying to reconstruct this aspect of Antigonos's career. The result is that any such reconstruction must necessarily be incomplete and to a certain extent hypothetical, but there is enough source material to justify the attempt, particularly as it seems likely to shed some very interesting light on the origins of Seleukid institutions and policies.

THE GEOGRAPHY OF ANTIGONOS'S ASIAN REALM

The heart of Antigonos's empire, ruled by him virtually uninterruptedly from 317 to 302, was western Asia Minor and Syria/Palestine (though Palestine was conquered by Antigonos only in 314). Apart from the coast lands, which were subject to occasional raids by Ptolemaic fleets (though these had no lasting effect), these regions enjoyed an era of relative peace under Antigonos's rule. Upon Antigonos's return from inner Asia in 315, it is true, a campaign by his nephew Polemaios was needed to assert his authority in Kappadokia and to establish it in Paphlagonia and Bithynia. Moreover, Karia was conquered only in 313–312; the rebellion of Polemaios and Phoinix in 310 briefly interrupted Antigonos's control of the Hellespontine region and necessitated fighting there; and the battle of Gaza in the winter of 312/11 caused a brief interruption of Antigonid control over Palestine. But these interruptions of the peace of the region were brief and local; overall, the region enjoyed fifteen years of peace under Antigonos as far as we can tell from the sources.[1] For though he was constantly at war, the fighting occurred almost entirely outside his realm.

This period of peace formed a profound contrast to that ushered in by the invasion of Asia Minor by Lysimachos in 302, which led to extensive and recurrent campaigning in and around the region that disturbed its peace again and again in the next century or so. It seems that during the decades after Antigonos's death, his rule was looked back on as a pleasant period and his demise was regretted: see, for example, the anecdote of the Phrygian peasant who, when found digging a large hole and asked what he was doing, responded sadly that he was looking for Antigonos (recorded by Plutarch *Phok.* 29,1–2).

It must be emphasized that statements in some modern works to the effect that parts of Asia Minor such as Pisidia or Kappadokia and Paphlagonia were never really under Macedonian control seem to be entirely erroneous as far as the period of Antigonos's rule is con-

1. This needs to be emphasized as a number of modern scholars (e.g., Wehrli, *Antigone et Démétrios*, p. 102) speak of the lands ruled by Antigonos as ravaged by continuous warfare during his reign, failing thereby to distinguish the continual military activity of Antigonos against his rivals—which took place almost entirely on the edges or outside of his realm—from the generally peaceful condition of the lands over which Antigonos ruled.

cerned.[2] Antigonos asserted his authority in Pisidia in 319 in the course of the campaign against Alketas, and won control of Kappadokia and Paphlagonia by his own campaigning early in 319 and by the subsequent efforts of his generals Menandros and Polemaios. There is no evidence of any difficulties or trouble in either of these regions during the rest of Antigonos's rule. Statements of the sort made, for example, by Jouguet (*Macedonian Imperialism,* p. 348) that "even in Asia Minor, certain regions, such as Pisidia, were not reduced" (sc., by Antigonos) rest on no evidential basis whatever and in fact ignore the evidence (Diod. XVIII 44,1–47,4) that shows Antigonos campaigning successfully in Pisidia in 319 and imposing his will on Termessos.[3]

It is difficult to say how far east Antigonos's authority extended at any time during his rule. As to Asia Minor, there is no evidence that Antigonos's rule extended beyond Kappadokia into Armenia, nor is it particularly likely. Since his territories certainly extended at least as far east as Amisos in northern Asia Minor (Diod. XIX 57,4; 60,2), and probably as far as the Euphrates in the south (though this is, admittedly, a conjecture), it seems best to posit an eastern boundary corresponding roughly to a line between the headwaters of the Eu-

---

2. See, for example, Jones, *Cities,* p. 149, suggesting that after Eumenes left Kappadokia "the country relapsed into anarchy. This state of affairs proved the opportunity of a Persian noble, Mithridates"; here the entire rule of Antigonos over Kappadokia between 318 and 302 is passed over as if it never happened, though it is well attested by Diod. (XVIII 59,1–2; XIX 60,2). Likewise Griffith, *Mercenaries,* pp. 182–83, states flatly that Kappadokia and Pontos (Paphlagonia) were never securely held by Antigonos. Appian *Mithrid.* 9 ascribes the founding of the Pontic kingdom by Mithridates Ktistes to "the embarrassment of the Macedonian power," by which he undoubtedly refers to the confusion in Asia Minor engendered by the Ipsos campaign.

3. Tarn, *CAH,* 6:489, claims Bithynia and western Pisidia were independent of Antigonos, as does Jouguet, *Macedonian Imperialism,* p. 348. Diod. XVIII 44,1–47,4 shows that Antigonos conquered western Pisidia in 319, basing his power there at Kretopolis and receiving the submission of the authorities of Termessos, and though at XVIII 47,2 Diod. states that Termessos's young men engaged in brigandage against Antigonos's lands in revenge for the death of Alketas, this does not show that Pisidia was independent, nor is any serious trouble in the region ever reported afterwards. Again, at Diod. XIX 60,3 it is reported that Antigonos's general Polemaios entered Bithynia with a large army and prevented Zipoites from capturing Astakos and Chalkedon, overawing him into making an alliance with Antigonos and extracting hostages, information which hardly agrees with Jouguet's statement (loc. cit.) that "They [i.e., Astakos and Chalkedon] were saved by a strategem of Antigonos, but Bithynia remained independent." Worthy of note is the fact that Zipoites remained quiescent as far as we know for the rest of Antigonos's reign, but immediately after Ipsos, he became very active, asserting his independence against Lysimachos, assuming the royal title, and expanding his realm (see C. Habicht, *RE* s.v. Zipoites).

phrates and the lower course of the river Iris for Antigonos's realm in Asia Minor, though he no doubt had a certain influence in Armenia (see map 5). East of Syria the satrapies of Mesopotamia, Babylonia, Media, Susiane, and Persia were all conquered by Antigonos during his eastern *anabasis* in 317–315. In addition, he was able in 315 to place a subordinate of his own in charge of Areia/Drangiane and also received the submission of Sibyrtios, the satrap of Arachosia. It is hard to believe, however, that his control of these latter two satrapies was ever much more than nominal, and the same may be said of the authority he appears to have claimed over Baktria and Karmania in 315, recognizing the incumbent satraps there (Diod. XIX 48,1) and perhaps receiving nominal messages of submission from them.

It is certain that Antigonos genuinely ruled over the five aforementioned important areas, which he had personally visited with his army in 317–315 and over which he had placed his own satraps. However, his rule here turned out to be of short duration, as Seleukos recaptured Babylonia in 311 and thence conquered Susiane, Media, and Persia, as well as regions further east. What is not clear is the fate of Mesopotamia after 311: one can only conjecture that Antigonos retained control of the parts of it adjacent to Syria and Asia Minor, while Seleukos took over those portions of it situated nearer Babylonia and Media. Effectively, then, Antigonos's realm was much the same as the territories in Asia later held by the Roman Empire: Asia Minor as far as the border of Armenia and Syria/Palestine up to the Euphrates, with some territory in Mesopotamia.[4] The available evidence suggests that Antigonos was at heart not greatly interested in the regions east of the Euphrates: his conquests there in the first place were only the result of his duel with Eumenes, and he refrained from establishing control over Baktria and Karmania when he certainly had the power to do so in 315. His efforts to recover the upper satrapies from Seleukos in 310–308 seem to have been distinctly half-hearted, and were probably due more to a (justified) fear of Seleukos's new power than to a powerful interest in the upper satrapies. The removal of the great royal treasures of Ekbatana and Susa to safekeeping in the western treasuries such as Kyinda in 315 (Diod. XIX 48,7–8; 55,1) should probably be understood as indicating that Antigonos had no

4. See maps 3 and 5 for Antigonos's empire ca. 315 and ca. 303. In Syria/Palestine Antigonos's rule went as far south as Gaza (Diod. XIX 59,2; 80,5; XX 73,3); he failed in his attempt to extend it further southeastward at the expense of the Nabataians (Diod. XIX 94,1–98,1), though he seems to have gained some influence among them (Diod. XIX 97,3–98,1; Plut. *Dem.* 7,1; Theophr. *Hist. plant.* IX 4,8).

intention of ever returning to the east and was not too confident of being able to keep control of the farther east.

Even so, the territories ruled by Antigonos were extensive, wealthy, and productive of all kinds of resources. In the great river valleys of western Asia Minor, the valley of the Orontes in Syria, the valley of the middle Euphrates, and the valley of the Sea of Galilee and the Jordan in Palestine, Antigonos held vast and fertile arable lands. The Troad and the plateau of Phrygia and Kappadokia provided pasture in abundance for cattle and horses. The forests of the Black Sea coast and of Kilikia and the Lebanon provided an unfailing supply of timber of all sorts, and a variety of important minerals were mined or quarried in Anatolia and Syria in ancient times.[5] In addition to these economic resources, moreover, these regions provided manpower. The evidence of our sources shows that Antigonos made extensive use of the military peoples of Asia Minor in his armies, and his navies were certainly largely manned by Phoenicians, Kilikians, and Ionian Greeks—we even hear of Karian crews in one flotilla (for details on all this, see app. 2 below). The power of Antigonos was certainly founded upon Greco-Macedonian armies and Persian treasure, both indirectly inherited from Alexander, but it was maintained by the resources of the territories Antigonos ruled, which made him the strongest of the dynasts who succeeded Alexander.

For most of his career the capital of Antigonos's huge realm was the city of Kelainai in Phrygia, which had been his seat as satrap of Phrygia and Lykaonia during the reign of Alexander. This fact was long ago recognized by Ulrich Koehler in an important article on Antigonos's realm,[6] and can be documented from the literary sources, which show Antigonos again and again using Kelainai as his winter quarters and the starting point for various expeditions (e.g., Diod. XVIII 52,1: 318 B.C.; XIX 69,2: 313/12 B.C.; XIX 93,4 and Plut. *Dem.* 6,3: 312/11 B.C.). Kelainai was particularly suitable as a capital for the Anatolian part of the realm, since it was at the crossroads of the great east-west road running from Ephesos via the Kilikian gates to Tarsos and on into Syria and the north-south road that led from the Bosporos via Dorylaion and Synnada (where it crossed the Persian Royal Road) to Kelainai and on over the Klimax pass in Pisidia to the Pamphylian coast.

5. See, for example, Heichelheim, "Roman Syria," and Broughton, "Roman Asia Minor," on these and the other resources of these regions.

6. Koehler, *SDAW*, 1898, pp. 824–43.

In 306 Antigonos founded a new capital city, Antigoneia, on the river Orontes in Syria, close to the later site of the Seleukid capital Antioch. The city was a large one, having a perimeter of seventy stades (about seven and a half miles), Diodoros reports, and its location was (to quote Diodoros) "naturally well suited to watching over Babylon and the upper satrapies, as well as lower Syria and the satrapies near Egypt" (Diod. XX 47,5). It was clearly founded with strategic considerations in mind, controlling the lower Orontes Valley and thereby upper Syria and the routes into Anatolia, the upper Orontes Valley and hence Koile Syria and the main north-south route from Syria to Palestine, and the main routes from Syria into Mesopotamia and so to the upper satrapies. It should not be supposed, however, that Antigoneia *replaced* Kelainai as capital of the Antigonid empire—the very concept of a capital being in any case anachronistic if understood too institutionally. Most likely Kelainai remained the most important base and center of Antigonos's power in Asia Minor, while Antigoneia was his administrative center for Syria and Palestine, so that one should think rather of two "capitals" (like Antioch-on-the-Orontes and Seleukeia-on-the-Tigris in the Seleukid empire afterwards).[7] Though Antigonos seems to have spent the years 306–302 at Antigoneia, he no doubt spent the last winter of his life, when he was back in Phrygia preparing for the campaign of Ipsos, at his old capital of Kelainai.

ANTIGONOS'S KINGSHIP AND INSTRUMENTS OF RULE

Like the transformation of the Diadochoi themselves from satraps to kings, the development of administrative institutions and policies in the Diadoch kingdoms was obviously a gradual, evolutionary process. However, in the case of Antigonos's realm at least, this evolution can no longer be traced in the surviving sources. We get no more than occasional glimpses of policies and institutions. The only way any worthwhile analysis and synthesis can be carried out is to treat the fifteen or so years of Antigonos's rule as monolithic, interpreting evidence for any part of his reign as being more or less valid for the whole (though it is possible to trace something of an evolution from the Argeads and Achaemenids through Antigonos to the Seleukids). One concomitant of the need to treat the period from

7. See, for example, Jouguet, *Macedonian Imperialism,* pp. 367–72.

roughly 317 to 302 as a monolithic whole is that Antigonos is mostly viewed in this chapter as a ruler *tout court,* without regard to his rise from satrap to *stratēgos* of Asia and eventually to king in 306.

Of course, the theoretical basis of Antigonos's power varied greatly within the period from the conference of Triparadeisos to the proclamation of Tyre, the Peace of the Dynasts, and ultimately his assumption of royal status at Antigoneia. There was not, however, a great deal of difference in the actual nature of Antigonos's power and rule: whether officially the plenipotentiary under some title or other of an absentee and infant king or holding power *suo iure* as king, Antigonos (and, as far as we can tell, the other Diadochoi) acted as ruler and owner of his territories with full authority to administer them as he saw fit.[8] For the purposes of this chapter, therefore, I take the evolution of the Diadochoi into kings as a given fact, employing the benefits of hindsight in a fashion that may lead to occasional anachronisms, but that is justified (I think) by the fragmentary nature of the sources and by the supremely independent and self-confident rule of Antigonos and the other Diadochoi even in the period when their power was officially temporary and subordinate to that of the Argead king.

The power of the Argead kings of Macedon was not institutionally limited, and as commander in chief, administrator, chief judge, and head of religion, the king of Macedon virtually personified the state. The same seems in essence to have been the case with the Achaemenid kings of the Persian Empire;[9] but in practice both the Argead and the Achaemenid rulers had their power limited somewhat by the existence in Macedon and Persia of a hereditary nobility with large estates, roots and influence among the populace, and a traditional hereditary claim to a certain status (the *hetaireia* in Macedon) or certain offices (in the Persian Empire).[10] The power of the Hellenistic kings—at least those in Asia and Egypt—was not

---

8. Indicative of this, for example, is the fact that several of the dynasts founded cities bearing their own names (normally a royal prerogative) long before they assumed the royal title: Kassandros built Kassandreia in 315 (Diod. XVIII 52,2–3; 61,2); Lysimachos built Lysimacheia in 309 (Diod. XX 29,1); Antigonos founded Antigoneia-on-the-Orontes before assuming the royal title in 306 (Diod. XX 47,5).

9. See, for example, Frye, *History of Ancient Iran,* pp. 106–20, esp. pp. 106–9.

10. In ibid., p. 116, Frye goes so far as to say that "this nobility held the real power in the empire"; satrapal posts clearly had a strong tendency to become hereditary in the Persian empire (cf. Frye, p. 115); in addition the families of the six helpers of Dareios I in gaining the throne seem to have formed a special hereditary elite in the empire, owning extensive lands and holding special positions at court (Frye, p. 102).

limited in this fashion, since the Greco-Macedonian conquest had greatly diminished the traditional influence and claims of the native aristocracies, while the Greeks and Macedonians had no hereditary claims to anything outside their homelands. If the Argead kingship had survived, it is possible that the Macedonian nobility might have been able to transfer its traditional privileges and influence to the Asian empire, as the Persian nobility seems to have done in the Persian Empire, though some modern scholars have noted an increasingly autocratic disposition to Alexander the Great's rule as his conquests in Asia proceeded,[11] which created friction between Alexander and some of the Macedonians. But the Macedonian nobility fragmented in the power struggles consequent upon Alexander's death and the dissolution of the Argead monarchy, and the influence of individual Macedonians, Greeks, or Asians became dependent on their personal relationship with those who managed to seize leading positions in the empire as it broke up.

As a consequence the Hellenistic kings, though their kingship was clearly based on Argead and Achaemenid kingship, enjoyed a more absolute power than had been the case even in those earlier, already fairly absolutist, monarchies;[12] and this was a direct outcome of the events of the Diadoch period. As is now generally recognized, the royal power of the Diadochoi was at least de facto based on personal charisma and what the Germans call *Siegerrecht,* the right of the military victor. This finds expression in the ancient sources in the term "spear-won land" (δορίκτητος χώρα), which appears several times in Diodoros as the basis for the territorial power of the Diadochoi (see Diod. XVIII 39,5: Ptolemy in 320; XVIII 43,1: Ptolemy in 319; XIX 85,3: Antigonos in 312/11; XIX 105,5: all of the Diadochoi in 311; XX 76,7: Ptolemy in 305). The principle of the right of the victor to hold his spear-won land had been expressed by Alexander when he cast a spear into Asia from his ship while crossing the Hellespont in 334 (Diod. XVII 17,2), and it was doubtless in imitation of Alexander that the Diadochoi adopted the principle.[13] Hence Antigonos and the other dynasts actually regarded themselves as the owners of their realms by right of military conquest, in addition to

---

11. See in particular Badian, *TAPhA* 91 (1960):324–38; *JHS* 81 (1961):16–43; and *AUMLA* 17 (1962):80–91.

12. Thus also, for example, Habicht, *VSWG* 45 (1958) 1–16, esp. at pp. 7, 13–14.

13. On the notion of "spear-won land," see Schmitthenner, *Saeculum* 19 (1968):31–46; Instinski, *Alexander der Grosse am Hellespont;* Müller, *Antigonos Monophthalmos,* pp. 116–21; Mehl *AncSoc* 11/12 (1980/81):173–212.

holding the traditional royal prerogatives of supreme military command, absolute control of administration and foreign policy, and supreme judicial authority; and this set the pattern for Hellenistic kingship in general.[14]

Despite the lack of institutional or traditional checks on their power, however, there were, of course, limitations to the power of the Diadochoi even after they had become kings. As compared with the later Hellenistic Seleukid, Antigonid, or Lagid monarchs, for example, Antigonos and the Diadochoi were relatively more dependent on the support of their friends, and especially of the leading Macedonians among them, because they were first seeking to establish for themselves royal status and hence superiority over the other Macedonian nobles, whereas the later Hellenistic kings enjoyed established and undisputed legitimacy as kings. This relative dependence and a consciousness of the ultimately usurpatory nature of their power, which carried with it the possibility of others seeking to follow their example or step into their shoes, was no doubt largely responsible for the occasionally rather harsh and suspicious attitude of the Diadochoi towards friends and allies.[15] Antigonos was not free of this kind of attitude, which is perhaps behind the implied charge of Plutarch (*Sertorius* 1,4) that Antigonos was not as faithful towards his friends as he should have been; but it is clear nevertheless that Antigonos took seriously the duties as well as the privileges of power and patronage. Two anecdotes recorded by Plutarch (*Apophth. Ant.* 8 and 9 at *Moralia* 182c) show that Antigonos rejected as fit only for barbarians the notion that a king could do as he pleased without regard to what is honorable (*τὰ καλὰ*) and what is just (*τὰ δίκαια*), and that he brought this principle into practice even where his immediate relatives were concerned, insisting on trying a lawsuit involving his half-brother Marsyas in public so that there could be no suspicion of favoritism or injustice.[16]

14. See Habicht, *VSWG* 45 (1958):1–16; Müller, *Antigonos Monophthalmos*, pp. 105–21.

15. For examples of this, see Introduction above, esp. at nn. 26 and 27.

16. The group of anecdotes and *obiter dicta* preserved by Plutarch at *Mor.* 182a–183a as the *Apophthegmata Antigonou* are unfortunately not all concerned with Antigonos Monophthalmos, a number of them (e.g., 7, 15, 17) having to do more probably with Antigonos Gonatas. In general, however, it is clear that most of them do concern Monophthalmos, and indeed Plutarch even has a separate heading at *Mor.* 183c–d with five *apophthegmata* of Antigonos Gonatas. Of the two anecdotes I cite here apropos of Antigonos's views on justice, no. 9 certainly concerns Monophthalmos, since it refers to his half-brother Marsyas (for whom see app. 3, no. 67); and no. 8 should likewise be attributed to Monophthalmos, since it is closely connected both by its place in Plutarch's list and its subject matter with no. 9.

It is obvious that, however absolute the authority of Hellenistic kingship as an institution, no king could in fact rule the vast territories won and handed down to their successors by the Diadochoi without a great deal of help from a host of variously qualified aides and advisers. The Argead kings had had the *synedrion* (council) of their *hetairoi* to help them run their affairs, and it is amply documented that in the Hellenistic kingdoms the institution of the *synedrion* continued in place, with the difference that its members were called *philoi* (friends) instead of *hetairoi* (companions).[17] We are fortunate in having four passages in Diodoros that show this council of state in action in Antigonos's reign, neatly exemplifying the ruler's reliance on his *synedrion* and its wide sphere of competence, encompassing essentially every aspect of the ruler's activities.

The first of the four Diodoros passages is XVIII 50,5, recording that Antigonos consulted with his *synedrion* on the state of the empire and the policy he planned to pursue after the death of Antipatros in autumn 319. Diod. XIX 46,4 informs us that Antigonos summoned his *synedrion* to try Peithon Krateua when the latter was suspected of treachery early in 315 and easily obtained a guilty verdict; and Diod. XIX 48,1 reports that later in the same year Antigonos's *synedrion* held a session at Persepolis to help him decide the administrative arrangements and appointments to be made in the upper satrapies. The fourth passage—Diod. XIX 57,1—tells us that when ambassadors from the four allied western dynasts came to Antigonos in early 314 with their ultimatum and threat of war, he called his *synedrion* into session to receive them. From these it may be concluded, then, that the *synedrion* might be consulted on the general policy to be followed, on important judicial decisions, on administrative matters, and on foreign policy; and it must be emphasized that in none of these four instances is there any suggestion or hint that the summoning of a *synedrion* was in any way unusual or exceptional. The opposite is rather the case: when we read at XIX 46,4 that Antigonos accused Peithon before τοῖς μετέχουσι τοῦ συνεδρίου and at XIX 57,1 that ambassadors were εἰσαχθέντες εἰς τὸ συνέδριον, the impression is given that the *synedrion* was an established institution at the court of Antigonos, and this is without doubt in accordance with the facts.

Though the four passages adduced above are the only ones in which the *synedrion* of Antigonos is explicitly attested by name, there are other passages in Diodoros and also in Plutarch that are most

17. Habicht, *VSWG* 45 (1958):2–5; Herman, *Talanta* 12/13 (1980/81): 115–17.

probably to be interpreted as referring to activities of the *synedrion*. This can be virtually proved in one instance for both Diodoros and Plutarch, who speak of Antigonos deliberating what to do with Eumenes after the battle of Gabiene (Diod. XIX 44,2: ἐβουλεύετο; Plut. *Eum.* 18,3: βουλευόμενος), while on this same subject the Latin writer Cornelius Nepos speaks of Antigonos deciding Eumenes' fate at a *consilium* with his *amicis* (Nepos *Eum.* 12,1–3), and it is clear that this must be a translation of *synedrion* and *philoi* in Nepos's Greek source. Evidently, then, we should understand Diodoros and Plutarch to mean that Antigonos consulted his *synedrion* when they say that he "took counsel" concerning the fate of Eumenes. Likewise we can reasonably assume meetings of the *synedrion* to be referred to when Plutarch speaks of "those present" (τοὺς παρόντας) at Antigonos's parley with Eumenes at Nora in 319 (Plut. *Eum.* 8,3); when we read that Antigonos viewed the disposition of Eumenes' army in Paraitakene surrounded by his *philoi* (Plut. *Eum.* 15,2); when in 307, apropos of the decision to send a great expedition to Attica, one of the *philoi* advised Antigonos to garrison Athens (Plut. *Dem.* 8,2); and when Antigonos consulted the leaders of his army as to the best course of action after Demetrios's fleet had failed to turn Ptolemy's defensive position in Egypt in 306 (Diod. XX 76,5).[18]

In each of the above instances, when we try to imagine the circumstances—who were "those present" at the parley with Eumenes and why were they there; when and in what circumstances did one of the *philoi* advise Antigonos what to do with Athens; and so forth—it is clear enough that the obvious context was a session of the *synedrion* to hear what was being planned and offer advice. Other similar instances could be adduced, but these should suffice to make the point, and they indicate that in addition to the areas of general policy, judicial matters, administrative affairs, and foreign policy, the *synedrion* was regularly consulted on military matters also, and we may be sure that the advice of the *synedrion* would likewise be sought in regard to financial and any other concerns of Antigonos. It is clear from a number of the passages mentioned above (especially from Diod. XVIII 50,5 and XIX 48,1), as well as from later Hellenistic practice, that the persons who made up the *synedrion* were called the king's *philoi*, or friends. The change in terminology from *hetairoi* to

18. At Diod. XX 76,5 the text seems to be corrupt, as it reads: "bringing [or calling] together the camp [*to stratopedon*] and the leaders"; Madvig suggests reading *to stratēgikon* (i.e., the generals), whereas Fischer proposes adding *kata* before *to stratopedon* and striking *kai* after it, so that the text would record that the leaders were brought together *in* the camp. Whatever emendation one accepts, it seems a military *synedrion* is referred to by Diodoros here.

philoi seems to originate with the Diadochoi, therefore, and is likely due to their originally non-royal status, when their entourages consisted not of royal *hetaireiai* but of groups of personal friends.[19]

This can be documented by reference to Diod. XVIII 22,4, which describes how Antigonos, then merely the satrap of Phrygia and Lykia/Pamphylia, fled from the wrath of Perdikkas in late 321 taking with him his personal friends (μετὰ τῶν ἰδίων φίλων), and that it required several ships to transport these people to Europe. Evidently these *philoi* who fled with Antigonos in 321 must have formed the nucleus of the body of *philoi* who formed his *synedrion* as ruler and eventually king of Asia. These early *philoi,* who were apparently not few in number, had presumably formed his personal staff as satrap at Kelainai and continued to be part of it after his rapid rise to greater power. An example appears to be the Macedonian Theotimides, son of Theophilos (see app. 3, no. 115). From the staff of the satrap, then, must have grown the staff of the dynast and king, and the activities of the *philoi* were not, of course, limited to accompanying Antigonos about his travels and campaigns and forming the membership of his *synedrion*. No fewer than 128 persons serving under Antigonos or his generals can be identified in the surviving sources (see app. 3 below), but unfortunately only 19 of them are specifically called *philoi* or referred to in such a way that they can be identified as *philoi* with near certainty.[20] Most of these 19 were clearly officers in Antigonos's armies, but a number of them are recorded to have fulfilled diplomatic tasks (Aristodemos) or administrative duties (Hieronymos; Peithon, son of Agenor), to have been financial officials (Xenophilos) or at least to have given financial advice (Aristodemos), or to have been simply close advisers (Boiotos) or courtiers/attendants (Mithridates; Thorax).

In short, this small sample of 19 makes it clear that the *philoi* fulfilled a wide variety of tasks and duties on Antigonos's behalf: the

19. Of course it might be argued that the use of the term *philoi* for the Diadoch period by Diodoros et al. is anachronistic, derived from later Hellenistic usage. But note the contemporary evidence of inscriptions from Athens and Eretria honoring Eupolis, Sotimos, and Kleochares as *philoi* of the kings (i.e., Antigonos and Demetrios): *IG* II^2 486; *Horos* 4 (1986):11–18; *IG* XII.9 199; and cf. app. 3, nos. 40, 110, and 58.

20. The nineteen men concerned are Alexandros, Andronikos, Archelaos, Aristodemos, Athenaios, Boiotos, Diphilos, Eupolis, Hieronymos, Kleochares, Medeios, Mithridates, Nearchos, Peithon, Philippos, Philotas, Sotimos, Thorax, and Xenophilos, for all of whom see app. 3 below. Not all of these men are directly called *philoi* in the sources, but the designation is at least clearly implied for all of them. For example, at Diod. XIX 91,3 Diphilos is named as the leader of those men in Babylon who in 311 preserved their *philia* towards Antigonos, which clearly implies that Diphilos was a *philos*. Similar arguments lead to the same conclusion for Andronikos, Hieronymos, and Nearchos; the rest are all directly called *philoi* in the sources.

preponderance of military men is without doubt due rather to the predominantly military interests of the literary sources than to a genuine preponderance of the scale indicated (11 of the 19 are mentioned only in a military context). Moreover, the title *philos* can be ascribed with confidence to a great many of those 109 men for whom it is not specifically attested (one thinks here especially of such men as Agesilaos, Aischylos, Demarchos, Dokimos, Euagoras, Hippostratos, Idomeneus, Leonidas, Nikanor, Nikomedes, Menandros, Peukestas, and Theotimides: see app. 3 *sub nom.*), and it is in fact likely that the great majority of the 128 men were *philoi* of Antigonos.[21] The *philoi* provided a pool of available manpower for any important task Antigonos needed to have done: commanding armies or troops, administering provinces or districts, guarding fortresses or treasuries, undertaking embassies, leading fleets or flotillas, conducting inquiries or trials, looking after financial affairs, or simply being ready to accompany and support, advise and amuse the king. Indeed, as Habicht remarks of the *philoi* of the Hellenistic kings,[22] in many cases we find the same man successively undertaking a whole range of different tasks and duties: the best case in point under Antigonos is Aristodemos of Miletos: military commander, diplomat, financial adviser, friend, and general troubleshooter.

Under the later Hellenistic kings the *philoi* became considerably stratified into classes of varying degrees of influence and proximity to the king.[23] Such stratification is not observable yet under Antigonos, but there is some indication of the existence of a sort of inner circle, which may have been the first step towards this later stratification. Naturally not all of those who were called *philoi* were actually personal friends of Antigonos; in most cases the relationship between ruler and *philos* was simply one of mutual advantage, as was clearly the case with Antigonos's acceptance of Xenophilos among his *philoi*, as recorded by Diodoros XIX 48,6, for example. That Antigonos did

21. This can be shown from the cases of some of those who are clearly attested as *philoi* of Antigonos: for example, Aristodemos of Miletos, who crops up frequently as an important helper and adviser of Antigonos in Diodoros, Plut. *Dem.*, and epigraphical sources, is never called a *philos* except at Plut. *Dem.* 9,1 and in a rather silly anecdote at Plut. *Mor.* 182d (= *Apophth. Ant.* 11); the case is similar for Medeios of Larissa, another important aide of Antigonos, attested as a *philos* only at Plut. *Dem.* 29,1, where he is said to have had a prophetic dream about the Egyptian expedition in 306. If it were not for these few inconsequential snippets, Aristodemos and Medeios would be among those not actually attested as *philoi*, though they clearly were such; we may be sure that most, if not all, of the men in app. 3 were in fact *philoi* of Antigonos.

22. Habicht, *VSWG* 45 (1958):2–4.

23. Ibid., pp. 15–16; Bikerman, *Institutions des Séleucides*, pp. 40–50.

have an inner circle of genuine friends who were informed and consulted about even the most delicate matters is suggested by the case of a certain Boiotos, reported by Diodoros XIX 85,2. This man, who is otherwise entirely unknown, is said to have been one of Antigonos's most distinguished friends, having lived with him for many years and shared in all his state secrets.[24] Since nothing suggests that he was ever used as a general or diplomat or given any other post of authority, it seems likely that he was simply what Diodoros says, a close and trusted personal friend and adviser of Antigonos. And obscure as he is, Boiotos is not likely to have been the only friend Antigonos trusted even with matters kept secret from the *synedrion* as a whole. Other men who appear to have enjoyed his complete trust are Aristodemos of Miletos, Andronikos of Olynthos (see especially Diod. XIX 86,1–2 for the loyalty of this man), Medeios of Larissa, and Nearchos the Cretan, to name just a few. It seems likely that Antigonos at all times had with him a number of highly trusted advisers with whom he could discuss matters and plans too delicate to be publicly discussed in the *synedrion*.

The basic picture, then, is of an absolute ruler who had in his employ a body of men called his *philoi* who formed the membership of his council of state (*synedrion*) and the pool of manpower on which he drew for his officers and officials. The standing and influence of an individual *philos* clearly depended on his relationship—close or distant, trusted or merely utilized—with Antigonos, and there was probably an inner circle of more important *philoi* (cf. Diod. XIX 48,6: τοῖς μεγίστοις τῶν φίλων). Although the *philoi* had no standing beyond that given by their relationship with the king, their importance and influence in the realm should not be underestimated. The ruler was absolutely dependent on his *philoi* for getting the work of government done, and though he could easily replace individual *philoi*, he needed the class as a whole. The vital significance of the *philoi* as a class is illustrated by the details of Antigonos's elevation to royal status: according to Plutarch's credible story, it was his *philos* Aristodemos who hailed Antigonos as king, and the other *philoi* who then brought forward a diadem and "crowned" him (Plut. *Dem.* 17,5–18,1).

24. On Boiotos, see app. 3, no. 25. For distinctions of grade or status among Antigonos's *philoi*, see further the case of Xenophilos, who is said to have been received into the circle of Antigonos's greatest friends in 315 (Diod. XIX 48,6).

CENTRAL ADMINISTRATIVE INSTITUTIONS AND PRACTICES

The running of Antigonos's realm, which was a vast agglomeration of territories very different in nature from the relatively monolithic modern nation state, must have been an exceedingly complex business, and it must be emphasized again here that our sources are inadequate. In the Achaemenid court and empire a certain hierarchy is discernible, and a fairly detailed hierarchy can be traced in the Seleukid court and empire,[25] but the sources for Antigonos's relatively brief reign are not so forthcoming. Furthermore, the distinction between domestic and foreign policy in Antigonos's realm was far from clear-cut and indeed largely nonexistent: for the realm included on its western seaboard a large number of officially autonomous Greek cities; there were also various dynasts ruling large or small territories whose degree of subjection to Antigonos is highly problematic now and was probably not clear even in Antigonos's own time (for example, Zipoites of Bithynia, Dionysios of Herakleia Pontika, Mithridates of Kios); and even some of Antigonos's satraps were halfway independent (for example, Sibyrtios of Arachosia, Peithon of Babylonia). In addition Antigonos's *philoi* did not normally make a career in the military, or in diplomacy, or in finance, but often practiced any or all of these nowadays distinct fields of endeavor indiscriminately.

The result is that it is not possible to establish exact categories of activity and to set out hierarchies of office within those categories. Certain kinds of specialization of expertise can be discerned, however, and to discuss Antigonos's administration coherently some framework is needed to order the evidence. A number of broad categories are used, therefore, with the proviso that they cannot be strictly defined and that there is often considerable overlap between them. They are: the *Administrative and Diplomatic Category*, the *Financial Category*, the *Judicial Category*, the *Military Category*, and the *Naval Category*.

The *Administrative and Diplomatic Category* comprises the officials, institutions and practices by which Antigonos organized and expedited the receipt of embassies and other visitors at court, the drafting of decrees, regulations, and correspondence, and the conveyance of

25. For the Achaemenid court, see, for example, Frye, *History of Ancient Iran*, pp. 106–10; for the Seleukid court, Bikerman, *Institutions des Séleucides*, pp. 31–50.

these to the appropriate destinations. There was a constant stream of visitors to Antigonos's court both from within his realm and from without. Obviously there must have been arrangements for the reception of such visitors, some categorization of them according to the nature and importance of their visits, and a procedure for setting up an interview with Antigonos himself or for having them dealt with by a subordinate if their business did not warrant Antigonos's personal attention. Testimony to the stream of visitors to court and to their reception comes from a considerable number of inscriptions from various Greek cities. Many of these inscriptions honor friends of Antigonos dwelling at his court for helping citizens of the city concerned who had come to the court for some reason;[26] more important are some inscriptions recording the despatch of embassies to Antigonos and, in particular, a relatively small, but highly significant, subset of these that honors men at Antigonos's court for helping these embassies.[27]

Clearly both the private visitors and the public ambassadors flowing to and from Antigonos's court were regularly helped there by someone among Antigonos's *philoi*. It might be thought that this was a purely private affair between the *philos* in question and the particular visitor, but it seems more likely that at least some of the *philoi* who made themselves useful to persons visiting Antigonos were in fact officials appointed to the duty of interviewing persons arriving at court and arranging for their business to be dealt with in some way. Particularly suggestive is the case of Nikomedes of Kos, who was honored by at least thirteen different Greek cities, in several cases explicitly for aiding embassies to Antigonos (see app. 3, no. 82).

26. See, for example, R. Herzog, *RFIC*, n.s., 20 (1942):12–13, recording that many Greek cities praised Nikomedes of Kos for helping private citizens and public embassies who had arrived at Antigonos's court, and giving a (heavily restored) text of one of these honorary decrees, that from Athens.

27. Epigraphically attested embassies to Antigonos are: two from Samos (Habicht *AM* 72 (1957):169–71, 187–88, nos. 3 and 21); two from the League of Ilion (*Syll.*, no. 330); two from Teos and Lebedos concerning the proposed synoikism ca. 303 (*Syll.*, no. 344); one from Priene over the boundary dispute with Samos (*I. Priene*, no. 37, lines 114–15); one from Byzantion (*Syll.*, no. 349); one from Delos (*IG* XI.4 566); one from Eresos (*OGIS*, no. 8); and one or two from Ephesos (*JÖAI* 53 [1981–82]:130–32; *JÖAI* 16 [1913]:223, no. 1g). Of these the two from Samos and the two Ephesian inscriptions (for the connection of the latter with Antigonos, see Hauben, *Callicrates*, pp. 16–21) all mention aid given to the ambassadors by friends of Antigonos: Nikomedes of Kos, Drakon of Kos, Aristodemos of Miletos, and Kallikrates respectively. Other embassies are recorded by the literary sources: for example, embassies from Athens in 312 (Diod. XIX 77,4) and 307 (Diod. XX 46,4 and cf. Pritchett, *AJPh* 58 (1937):329–33), and from Aitolia and Boiotia in 312 (Diod. XIX 75,6).

Obviously it is most unlikely that Nikomedes' efforts on behalf of so many cities were due purely to his own goodwill and contacts with those cities; rather he was charged by Antigonos with receiving visitors and embassies, interviewing them, finding them accommodation, and arranging for them to be dealt with by Antigonos himself or some other high official, or seeing to the despatch of their business in some other way. Another man who may have had the same sort of job was Drakon of Kos, recorded to have helped a Samian embassy to Antigonos (*SEG,* 1, no. 354). That such embassies may at times have been dealt with by someone other than Antigonos seems to be suggested by an Ephesian inscription honoring Aristodemos of Miletos for helping an Ephesian embassy win a tax concession from Antigonos: Aristodemos was surely too senior a man to have the task of a receptionist; more likely the Ephesian embassy was referred to him in lieu of an interview with Antigonos himself, and had its case essentially decided by Aristodemos subject to Antigonos's ultimate approval.[28]

It seems, then, that Antigonos had at his court a number of officials specially designated to look after visitors to the court, Nikomedes of Kos being apparently one of the more important of them. In addition, since Antigonos would not have had time personally to see every person or embassy with a request to make or business to take care of, a number of senior advisers like Aristodemos took on the task of dealing with the less important matters. No doubt there would have been regular meetings of the *synedrion* at which men like Aristodemos would report briefly on the affairs they had dealt with and obtain Antigonos's formal approval of their decisions. The more important matters were obviously dealt with by Antigonos personally, as was the case, for example, with the ambassadors from Ptolemy, Kassandros, and Lysimachos in 314, or with the ambassadors from Teos and Lebedos concerning the proposed synoikism of their two cities ca. 303 (see *Syll.,* no. 344, passim, especially lines 72ff.). It should be pointed out also that whereas our evidence comes exclusively from the Greek world, there must in addition have been regular

28. See Knibbe and Iplikçioglu, *JÖAI* 53 (1982):130–32; the decree praises Aristodemos for helping the Ephesian embassy win some sort of *ateleia* from the king. He must have advised Antigonos to make this award either before or when the embassy was received by the king, or he must have made the award himself, with Antigonos merely approving it. In view of Aristodemos's very high standing and importance and the relatively trivial nature of the Ephesians' business, the latter seems most likely.

messengers coming to Antigonos from the various native dynasts and communities and his own satraps and other administrators scattered around Asia,[29] who were presumably taken care of in much the same way.

Besides having persons coming to his court, Antigonos was constantly sending out various kinds of ambassadors, messengers, and dispatch riders himself, and it is clear that he maintained at his disposal a large staff of people capable of performing these tasks and furthermore took care of the communications network in his realm. Ambassadors to important dynasts and cities would need to be of fairly high rank and ability, and were doubtless selected simply from the available members of the *synedrion*. We hear of a number of such ambassadors in Diodoros and in the Skepsis inscription, but there is no sign of any particular specialization except in the case of Aristodemos of Miletos, who is repeatedly recorded as being involved in diplomatic negotiations at the highest level and of the most delicate sort, acting as ambassador to Polyperchon, Ptolemy, and Demetrios of Phaleron among others (see app. 3, no. 16). Apart from these top-level people, however, it is known that Antigonos had in his service a body of ordinary messengers: Diodoros (XIX 57,5) informs us that by the beginning of 314 Antigonos had organized throughout his empire a system of fire-signals and dispatch-carriers (*bibliaphoroi*), and later in the year 314 he sent out men to all the Greek cities and the generals and satraps in Asia with reports on the proclamation of Tyre (Diod. XIX 61,3–4). Clearly there were two corps of messengers: one spread out around the empire to form relays carrying dispatches to and from the various parts of the realm, and one concentrated at Antigonos's court to carry special messages or general directives that he from time to time sent out.[30] Another occasion when a general missive to various parts of the realm was sent out seems to have been the Peace of the Dynasts, for Antigonos's letter to Skepsis that is preserved is a copy of a circular obviously sent out to all the Greek cities to report on the clause guaranteeing Greek autonomy embodied in the peace.[31]

---

29. See, for example, the case of the messenger who came to Antigonos from Nikanor in winter 311/10: Diod. XIX 100,3.

30. Note, e.g., the messengers regularly sent with instructions to Demetrios (Diod. XX 46,5; 73,1; 99,1; 109,5; 111,1); also the *bibliaphoros* who came to Antigonos from Nikanor (above n. 29).

31. On this see, for example, Welles, *RC*, no. 1, p. 8; and note that in the Skepsians' reply

We have seen, then, that Antigonos had organized fairly sophisticated arrangements to take care of the in- and out-flow of business and the people conducting it to and from his court; it remains to see how all of this business was actually processed. This, too, must have required a considerable special staff, including people with particular expertise to advise on the various complex administrative, legal, and financial matters that needed to be dealt with. Again our best source for specific problems Antigonos had to deal with is a number of Greek inscriptions. For example, Antigonos sent an edict (*diagramma*) regulating the settling of a backlog of court cases at Kyme by Magnesian arbitrators (*OGIS,* no. 7); he sent another edict regulating the arbitration of a boundary dispute between Klazomenai and Kolophon by Kos (*SEG,* 28, no. 697); he personally arbitrated a long-standing dispute between Samos and Priene (*I. Priene,* no. 37 and no. 40, line 9); he established guidelines for a host of problems connected with the synoikism of Teos and Lebedos (*Syll.*, no. 344); he had a copy of the peace treaty of 311, of an oath to be sworn confirming it, and an account of the treaty's purpose and coming about drawn up and sent to the Greek cities (*OGIS,* no. 5); he had an inquiry made into either the boundaries, the tax obligations, or the existing titles (or all three) of some estates in Lydia, which he then awarded to a certain Mnesimachos (Buckler and Robinson, *Sardis VII,* no. 1). Other business is recorded or can be inferred: the sending of financial and material relief to Athens in 307 (Diod. XX 46,4; *IG* II^2 1492b); the recruitment and transportation of colonists for his new cities, and the organization of said cities.

All of this cannot have been seen to by Antigonos on his own. The legal problems of Greek cities, for example, would have been largely beyond his ken, and to draw up regulatory edicts or even constitutions for new cities he must have had the services of Greek legal experts who were familiar with the problems involved. Antigonos cannot have had time to write up edicts, reports on negotiations, and the like himself: he must have had a staff of secretaries to help him with the voluminous correspondence involved in running a large empire. Likewise, to keep track of the business of the empire, there must have been records kept and an archivist or archivists in charge of them. Polyainos IV 6,2 says that Antigonos kept records of

to Antigonos's letter (*OGIS*, no. 6), the Akios who is praised as Antigonos's messenger was clearly one of these *bibliaphoroi*.

all his diplomatic correspondence and was in the habit of having the appropriate records brought to him for his perusal before interviewing embassies, thus impressing them with his grasp of past relations between himself and their cities or rulers.[32] In short, Antigonos clearly had at his court a well-organized chancery, to borrow the term Welles uses in *Royal Correspondence in the Hellenistic Period*. The actual processing of the business of the realm must have been done by the various experts of the royal chancery, under Antigonos's ultimate direction and supervision. In outline, then, the system of conducting business at Antigonos's court ran as follows: persons arriving with news, requests, or whatever would be received by special staff, who would, according to the nature of their business, organize an appropriate interview with Antigonos or a senior adviser; the interview would take place, with the interviewer being assisted by specialist advisers (Antigonos might call a meeting of the *synedrion* for something really important); the decisions taken would be drafted into decrees or edicts or letters by the secretaries in the chancery and copies deposited in the record office; and the decrees, letters, or whatever would be sent to their destination either in the hands of those come to seek them or by means of the royal messenger service.

Turning to the second, *Financial Category*, some consideration must be given to the regulation of income and expenditure in the running of the empire and in connection with Antigonos's various projects—military, colonizing, or other. In the course of his conquest of Asia, Antigonos had amassed a vast treasure from the various treasuries of Alexander and the Achaemenids. The treasury at Ekbatana in Media yielded 5,000 talents of silver (Diod. XIX 46,6), that at Susa 15,000 talents' weight of gold and silver (Diod. XIX 48,7), and the treasury at Kyinda in Kilikia yielded a further 10,000 talents (Diod. XIX 56,5). In addition, Antigonos brought with him from the east 5,000 talents in booty and gifts of various sorts, mostly no doubt from satraps who had sided with Eumenes and now sought to placate him (see Diod. XIX 48,7–8). In all, then, Antigonos had a grand treasure of 35,000 talents, which formed the solid foundation of his

32. Unfortunately it is not absolutely clear whether the Antigonos of this Polyainos strategem is Monophthalmos or his grandson Gonatas to whom Polyainos IV 6,1 and 3 clearly refer. Polyainos was capable of mixing a Monophthalmos anecdote in with several of Gonatas: see, for example, the case of Polyainos IV 6,19 (Monophthalmos), which is surrounded by IV 6,17 and 18 and IV 6,20 (all Gonatas); at any rate, it is highly likely that both Antigonoi would have had archives.

power, for this immense wealth enabled him to recruit armies, build navies, and found cities almost at will.

Much of this treasure was held by Antigonos at a number of great royal treasuries, probably the most important of which was Kyinda in Kilikia.[33] It was from Kyinda that Antigonos drew a fighting fund of some 3,000 talents for the campaign in 302/1 that culminated in the battle of Ipsos (Diod. XX 108,2–3); when Demetrios raided it a few years after Ipsos, he was still able to carry off 1,200 talents (Plut. *Dem.* 32,1). There was another royal treasury at Synnada in Phrygia (Diod. XX 107,3–4), and it seems likely that Pergamon and Sardis, which were important treasuries of Lysimachos's after Ipsos (see Strabo XIII 623 and Paus. I 8,1 for Pergamon; Polyainos IV 9,4 for Sardis), were already royal treasuries of Antigonos's before that time (cf. Diod. XX 107,5 for the citadel of Sardis as an important royal stronghold under Antigonos). These treasuries were guarded by special royal officers named *gazophylakes,*[34] and were presumably used as the regional centers for the collection of tribute and the disbursement of pay to garrison troops, administrative officials, and the like. There may well have been other such treasuries we hear nothing of.

More important at present is the fact that Antigonos seems to have kept with him at all times a mobile royal treasury, from which he met the large regular expenses of his court and standing army and the special expenses of great projects like campaigns and city foundations. Early in 314, for example, he gave Aristodemos of Miletos 1,000 talents to raise a mercenary army in Greece, and later in that year he gave 500 talents as a fighting fund to Polyperchon's son Alexandros (Diod. XIX 57,5; 61,5); in 307 he sent at least 140 talents of gold and silver to Athens for the war with Kassandros (*IG* II^2 1492b), and in 302 he paid out 200 talents to the various athletes and artists he had assembled for a great festival at Antigoneia (Diod. XX 108,1). Obviously he must have had guards and financial officers in charge of this treasury, though no positive evidence of their existence happens to have survived.

Though Antigonos's treasure was a great one, even 35,000 talents is not an inexhaustible supply of money when one maintains armies on the scale he did, to say nothing of other expenditures. Diodoros

33. On the importance of the treasury at Kyinda, see, for example, Simpson *Historia* 6 (1957):503–4.

34. For this title, see Plut. *Dem.* 25,4–5 and the comments of Hauben *AncSoc* 5 (1974):105–17.

informs us at XIX 56,5 that Antigonos's annual revenue amounted to 11,000 talents. This probably includes the revenues from the upper satrapies, which Antigonos lost after 311, but even after that his annual revenues in tribute, presents, and other contributions must have been considerable. The "tribute" here represents the money derived annually from the "tribute-paying" (*phorologētos*) territories of Asia, which was presumably first gathered into local treasuries and then forwarded, in whole or in part according to need, to Antigonos's court. The Greek cities were exempt from tribute (see chapter 6 above), but they nevertheless contributed to Antigonos's finances in a number of ways. In the first place there were the so-called "crowns" of gold or silver that Greek cities frequently voted Antigonos as marks of esteem and goodwill: examples are the 100 gold staters voted him by Skepsis in 311 (*OGIS,* no. 6, lines 27–28); the 200 talents reputedly voted by Athens in 307 (Diod. XX 46,2—the figure seems excessive); gold crowns of value no longer preserved voted by Delos ca. 306–302 (*IG* XI.4 566); and the gold crown of 2,000 drachmas voted by Ios ca. 306–302 (*IG* XII, suppl. 168). Other examples are known; the voting of such "crowns" was a regular procedure when news of any great success won by Antigonos or Demetrios came in (for example the Skepsis crown and one awarded to Antigonos by Ephesos ca. 306–302: *I. Ephesos,* 5, no. 1448).

In addition to these voluntary presents, Antigonos got other contributions from the Greek cities in wartime, for the cities were required to help pay the costs of Antigonos's wars. This is recorded by Antigonos himself in his letter to the Skepsians (*OGIS,* no. 5, lines 43–45), where he expresses regret that these contributions may have proved burdensome to the Greek cities. The size of the contributions cannot even be guessed at in the absence of any figures in our sources,[35] but the total is likely to have represented a considerable,

35. Wehrli, *Antigone et Démétrios,* pp. 100–101, speaks of the heavy contributions exacted from the Greek cities by Demetrios after 301, and describes Demetrios as the "continuator of the policy of Antigonos"; in fact, however, since the revenues of Asia were lost to Demetrios after the battle of Ipsos, he was forced to exact what money he could from the Greek cities around the Aegean to maintain his fleet, the sole remaining source of his continuing power. Hence his position after 301 was utterly different from that of Antigonos before 301, and his fiscal policy thus has no bearing on that pursued by Antigonos. In particular Wehrli cites the claim made by Diog. Laert. II 140 that Demetrios exacted a tribute of 200 talents per year from Eretria on Euboia as evidence for Antigonos's heavy financial demands on the Greek cities. In the first place, however, all the evidence indicates that Antigonos exacted no regular tribute from the Greek cities (see chap. 6 above passim); and in the second place Diogenes' figure of 200 talents is wildly exaggerated as an annual tribute paid by Eretria. It is hard to believe that

though irregular, income. One other source of money that should be mentioned is war booty. Antigonos brought back 5,000 talents in booty and gifts from his eastern *anabasis* in 315; certain of his other campaigns were also highly profitable, in particular the defeat of Ptolemy and conquest of Cyprus by Demetrios in 306 (see Diod. XX 49,1–52,6; Plut. *Dem.* 16,2–3).

Thus Antigonos's financial resources in treasure, regular revenues, and irregular or occasional income were huge. His expenditures were also huge: I have listed some of his extraordinary outlays above, and in addition must be computed the cost of maintaining a large court, military forces that may have totaled in excess of 120,000 men, and a large navy (see app. 2 below for details). Even so, his expenditures are unlikely to have outrun his income, and he could evidently afford to reject the advice of Aristodemos that he curtail his extravagant expenditures (*Apophth. Ant.* 11 at Plut. *Mor.* 182c). Intriguing is Antigonos's arrangement of the money supply in the realm: even after he had become king, he did not strike coins with his own name or likeness, continuing instead the minting of Alexander coinage. The reason for this can only be guessed at: the international popularity of the Alexander coinage and the fact that much of the treasure he had captured was probably in Alexander coins may have been factors.

On the *Judicial Category* in Antigonos's central administrative institutions and policies, there is not a great deal to be said. As king, Antigonos was the chief judge and source of law in the empire, and we have seen from the two anecdotes in Plutarch (*Mor.* 182c) alluded to above that he took seriously the prevailing notions of justice both as lawmaker and as judge. We possess no legal code for Antigonos's realm, of course, nor is it likely that any such thing ever existed. Each of the peoples, tribes, and cities of the realm would have had their own local laws and customs, and in addition there would have been the overall *administrative* law of the empire, flexible no doubt and most probably largely borrowed from Persian precedents. Antigonos's role as lawmaker is likely to have been more interpretative than innovative: one thinks of cases such as the appeals to Antigonos by Kyme, and by Klazomenai and Kolophon to settle backlogs of court cases or local boundary disputes. Antigonos limited his role in

---

Eretria, which was in the Hellenistic period neither a very large nor an important city, could have furnished 200 talents as a one-time payment without the gravest difficulty; that the city paid such a sum annually is incredible.

such cases to laying down the rules by which others were bidden to arbitrate.[36] Similarly, in the proposed synoikism of Teos and Lebedos, Antigonos limited himself to receiving and approving the constitution to be drawn up by a panel of Teans and Lebedians (*Syll.*, no. 344, lines 44–55).

While Antigonos avoided the invidious position of laying down the law to Greek cities or of judging right and wrong between them, preferring in most cases to lay down the rules and let others make the play, he would have been less sensitive about sending out edicts and fiats to his subject territories. Even here, however, judicial interference is likely to have been kept to a minimum for obvious practical reasons: for most purposes local laws or traditions and local tribunals or judges would have sufficed. On important issues Antigonos may have promulgated new rules or laws, and important law suits (i.e., those involving powerful interests) may have found their way to Antigonos's court. For the latter, the evidence of the cases of Eumenes and Peithon suggests that Antigonos employed his *synedrion* as a sort of supreme court, thereby conforming to the practice of Alexander and previous Macedonian kings, who preferred to test the reaction of their main supporters before condemning persons of power and influence (cf. chapter 1, n. 17, above). Thus Antigonos may either have prosecuted a case before the *synedrion* himself, seeking the approval of his *philoi* before inflicting punishment, or simply have presided as judge over a meeting of the *synedrion* at which a legal dispute was thrashed out, evading by this openness possible charges of favoritism or jobbery. One field where Antigonos may have engaged in more extensive lawmaking was in establishing constitutions for his newly founded cities or for Hellenized Asian cities; even here though, it is possible that he preferred to find other solutions (see further p. 309 below).

Turning now to the *Military Category*, it is obvious that it was the military element of his rule and realm that took up most of Antigonos's time and resources, for he was above all a military leader and

36. So in the case of Kyme (*OGIS*, no. 7) he nominated judges from Magnesia to try the backlog of cases; in the case of Klazomenai and Kolophon (G. Pugliese Carratelli, *PP* 33 [1978]:151–57) the city of Kos was named as arbitrator; in the event of possible disputes between the peoples of Teos and Lebedos in the course of their synoikism, Antigonos named Mytilene as arbitrator (*Syll.*, no. 344, lines 27–30). We do know of one case in which Antigonos acted as arbitrator himself, namely that of the eternal dispute between Samos and Priene over territory on Cape Mykale, which every sovereign over the region was called upon to decide anew it seems (*I. Priene*, no. 37, esp. lines 140–48 for Antigonos's arbitration).

owed his power and throne to his success in that capacity. Throughout his rule Antigonos maintained vast military forces, which can be divided into two basic categories: garrison troops scattered throughout his empire, and a standing army or armies concentrated under his own direct command and under the command of leading generals such as his nephew Polemaios and his son Demetrios. On the former, the garrison troops, we are very poorly informed, and these in any case belong to the subject matter of the section below dealing with provincial institutions. We are much better informed about the standing army, due to the simple fact that it was of course involved in the campaigns and battles which are the main theme of the literary sources. Besides expeditionary forces sent out at various times for various purposes, and under the command of various generals, it is clear that throughout the period of his rule from 320 on, Antigonos kept near his own person and under his own command a large army, the mainstay of his power.[37] This probably consistently numbered about 40,000 infantry and 5,000 cavalry; its nucleus was a strong contingent of Macedonians, making up perhaps as much as a quarter of the total, while the remainder consisted of a large body of Greek mercenaries and forces drawn from the peoples of his empire (on all this, see app. 2).

It is greatly to be regretted that nothing is known of the command structure, recruitment, and training of this army. All that can really be said is that Antigonos was the commander in chief; that the force was drawn from a variety of sources, of which at least the subject territories may have been subject to forced levies; that the army was essentially professional, and hence mercenary, in character in spite of whatever recourse there may have been to levying troops; and that it was certainly a highly trained and highly competent force to judge by its successes under the command of Antigonos and his generals.[38] The army was one of the major burdens on the treasury. The soldiers received pay (*misthos*); rations, or a money equivalent for their purchase (*sitēresion*); and often arms, uniforms, boots, and other equip-

37. This can be amply documented from Diodoros's history; I refrain from citing passages for the years 320–315, when Antigonos was engaged in his long war with Eumenes and hence continually with his army; thereafter one might note, for example, Diod. XIX 59,1–2 (314 B.C.), XIX 69,2 (late 313), XIX 77,5 (312 B.C.), XIX 93,4 (311), XX 47,4–5 (306 *init.*), XX 73,1–2 (end of 306), XX 108,1–2 (302).

38. For the professional and indeed largely mercenary character of Diadoch armies, see Tarn, *HMND,* pp. 23–24; Griffith, *Mercenaries,* pp. 38–56.

ment.[39] The cost of all of this cannot be determined, but must have been very great, as we can tell from the one aspect of it for which some computation can be made: the *misthos*. In the late fourth century the standard pay for a Greek mercenary was four obols per day (see, e.g., Parke, *Greek Mercenary Soldiers*, p. 233), and the Macedonian and Asian troops can hardly have been paid less. When one takes into account the higher pay of soldiers on double or triple pay (awarded for good service and doubtless carrying with it duties like those of a corporal or sergeant today), the much higher pay of the various ranks of officers, and the occasional gifts and bounties that must have been distributed to keep the soldiers content in times when there was no booty to supplement the pay, it would not be excessive to reckon the average expenditure at a drachma (six obols) per man per day. The *misthos* for 40,000 infantry would thus amount to at least 2,435 talents a year, and in addition to this there would be the pay of the cavalry and of such other forces as were under arms on expeditions or in garrisons.

Within the great standing army that Antigonos kept permanently mobilized, some special units call for separate discussion. Among the cavalry at the battle of Paraitakene (Diod. XIX 29,4–5), we hear of 300 making up Antigonos's *agēma* (guard), 300 *paides*, and 1,000 Companion cavalry (*hetairoi*). These units are of considerable interest as shedding light on continuity and change from the Macedonian army of Alexander to the Hellenistic armies. In Alexander's army the Macedonian heavy cavalry were called the *hetairoi*, or Companion cavalary (see, e.g., Arrian *Anab.* I 14,1; II 8,9; III 11,8), and it is obvious that the unit of the same name in Antigonos's army would likewise have been made up of Macedonian heavy cavalry. This unit can in fact be traced back to the latter half of 320, when Antipatros gave Antigonos troops to fight Eumenes including 8,500 Macedonian infantry and a body of Companion cavalry (Arrian *Met' Alex.* 1,43: the number of the cavalry is lost owing to a corruption in the text; see

39. For the *sitos* or *sitēresion*, paid either in cash or in kind, see, for example, Griffith, *Mercenaries*, pp. 264–316; and on this and other equipment, see also W. K. Pritchett, *The Greek State at War*, 1:3–25. As to the *sitos*, it seems likely that Antigonos paid this to his troops in kind out of the agricultural surpluses of his royal domains; but the expense of equipment must have been great, and he would probably also have had to give his troops donatives and bonuses in lieu of booty during periods when there were no campaigns. Antigonos thoroughly understood the vital importance of the financial side of warfare: in 302 for the Ipsos campaign he gave his troops three months' pay in advance and carried with him a fund of 3,000 talents for future needs (Diod. XX 108,2–3); when some troops of Lysimachos deserted to him later in the same year, he paid them the arrears owed to them by Lysimachos (Diod. XX 113,3).

further app. 2 below); subsequently Demetrios had 800 Companion cavalry at the battle of Gaza (Diod. XIX 82,3). Evidently Antigonos continued to use the terminology of Alexander's army, though by 311 or 301 there cannot have been many men left in his Macedonian cavalry who had been in Alexander's Companion cavalry; and even later under the Seleukids the cavalry drawn from Greco-Macedonian settlers in Asia continued to be called *hetairoi*.[40]

One point of difference between the cavalry of Alexander and that of Antigonos is that under the former the *agēma,* or guard, was part of the *hetairoi,* being simply the royal squadron (ἴλη βασιλικὴ) of the Companion cavalry, whereas under Antigonos it seems that the *agēma* (300 strong like Alexander's royal squadron) had been separated out as an independent unit. This, too, is paralleled by later Seleukid usage.[41] The *agēma* was Antigonos's personal bodyguard in battle (see Diod. XIX 29,5) and presumably outside of battle too: for example, the unit of cavalry Antigonos had with him at Triparadeisos, with which he overawed the mutinying infantry of the royal army and rescued Antipatros (Polyainos IV 6,4), was most probably his *agēma,* and the same can be said of the bodyguards (*doryphoroi*) with whom he protected Eumenes during the parley at Nora in 319 (see Plut. *Eum.* 10,4). This unit was obviously made up of Antigonos's most trusted friends and retainers (one thinks of Thorax of Larissa, who stayed by Antigonos's side to the bitter end at the battle of Ipsos: Plut. *Dem.* 29,4–5), its original nucleus being no doubt those "*philoi*" who had fled with Antigonos from Asia in 321 (Diod. XVIII 23,4). Besides his own *agēma,* Antigonos also employed guards for his closest relatives: at the battle of Gaza, Demetrios fought surrounded by a guard of 200 selected cavalry, including all his *philoi* (Diod. XIX 82,1); Demetrios's wife Phila had a bodyguard (*phylakē*) captained by a Lykian officer named Demarchos (*Syll.* 333, an inscription from Samos honoring him); and it can be deduced from Diod. XIX 16,3–4 that Antigonos's wife Stratonike also had a bodyguard.[42]

40. See for this Bar-Kochva, *Seleucid Army,* pp. 67–73.

41. Ibid. for the *agēma* of the Seleukids; on Alexander's *ilē basilikē,* see Berve, 1:104–12, esp. p. 109.

42. Diod. XIX 16,1–5 concerns the attempt at escape by ex-Perdikkans imprisoned by Antigonos in a stronghold in southern Phrygia in 317–16. We hear that Stratonike was near the place when they were besieged by the garrisons of Antigonos's nearby *phrouria,* and that one of the besieged, Dokimos, sent a message to her, evidently with an offer to betray the place. This man and a companion then secretly left the stronghold and joined Stratonike, who handed them over *eis phylakēn,* the *phylakē* here being presumably her bodyguard.

The third cavalry unit which calls for special attention is that of the 300 *paides,* organized into six squadrons of (probably) 50 each.[43] These *paides* clearly functioned in battle as an additional bodyguard for Antigonos, being drawn up in front and on the flank of his *agēma* (Diod. XIX 29,5), and we know from the sources on Philip and Alexander of a unit functioning as a bodyguard and called *paides:* Philip had instituted the practice of having the teenaged sons of the nobility serve as his "Pages" (to use the term normally given as the English equivalent of these *paides*), guarding and waiting on him and thus learning to be loyal and courageous *hetairoi,* and the practice was continued by Alexander (see Aelian *VH* 14, 48; Arrian *Anab.* IV 12,7–13,4). Obviously the 300 *paides* with Antigonos were not "slaves" but "Pages", the sons of his distinguished friends and followers serving him in the same way that similar *paides* had served Philip and Alexander.[44] Though they are mentioned in the extant sources only on the single occasion of the battle of Paraitakene, there is every reason to suppose that they were a regular unit in Antigonos's army and court, another of his many borrowings from the institutions of Philip and Alexander.

Of course, the cavalry of Antigonos was not by any means made up exclusively of Macedonians: we also hear of contingents of Thracians, Medes and Parthians, Lydians and Phrygians, and (naturally) Greeks. Likewise the infantry was made up of various nationalities: the heavy (phalanx) infantry was based on a core of Macedonians, fleshed out with large contingents of Greek mercenaries, Asiatics armed in the Macedonian fashion, and Lykian and Pamphylian hoplites; there were also large numbers of light infantry of mostly Asian origins (Persian archers, slingers, and javelineers; peltasts in part drawn doubtless from Pisidian mountaineers and the like), but including bodies of Cretan archers and no doubt Greek and Thracian mercenary peltasts (see app. 2 below). Whether Antigonos's Macedonian phalanx troops were called *pezetairoi* like those of Alexander is

43. In vol. 9 of the Loeb ed. of Diodoros, p. 309, R. M. Geer translates ἐκ τῶν ἰδίων παίδων εἶλαι τρεῖς (XIX 29,5) as "there were three troops from his own slaves," whereas it is clear that in this context the *paides* are youths, not slaves. I give the number of these "Pages" as three hundred here; Diodoros actually speaks of six *ilai* in two groups of three, and it is commonly assumed that each of these *ilai* numbered some fifty men (thus, e.g., Geer loc.cit.; Launey, *Recherches,* p. 96 n. 1).

44. For the *paides* under Philip and Alexander, see further Berve, 1:37–39; for *basilikoi paides* under the Seleukids, see Bikerman, *Institutions des Séleucides,* pp. 37–38; clearly the *paides* of Antigonos were of the same sort.

not recorded, but there is one interesting passage in Polyainos (IV 6,8) that mentions Antigonos having in his army *hypaspistai:* he placed the bravest of them on the defeated ships of Nikanor to make sure these ships would fight properly in the dawn attack by which he overwhelmed Kleitos's victorious fleet in 317. If the word *hypaspistai* is derived from the primary source for Polyainos's strategem, as is likely of such an unusual term, it would seem that Antigonos had organized in his army a crack guard regiment named after Alexander's famous *hypaspistai,* who in the Diadoch period were known as *argyraspides* (Silver Shields).[45]

In general, then, Antigonos's army was very much modeled on that of Philip and Alexander, as was indeed to be expected. The officer corps, especially in the upper echelons, seems to have been mostly of Macedonian extraction, although Greek and Asian officers are known (see app. 3 below for this). The precise titles and promotion ladder for officers cannot be confidently restored, though it was no doubt much like that in the armies of Alexander and the Seleukids.[46] At any rate, the top officers, in charge of independent army units whether as satrapial garrisons or as expeditionary forces, were called *stratēgoi* (for this title, see Bengtson, *Strategie,* 1:180–209). Other military titles we hear of are *hēgemones* (Diod. XX 76,5; Plut. *Mor.* 182a = *Apophth. Ant.* 2), *chiliarchoi* (see the inscription in Buckler and Robinson, *Sardis VII,* no. 1, and cf. at Diod. XIX 91,3 the officer Polyarchos), and for commanders of forts and strongholds *epimelētai* (Diod. XX 37,5) and *phrourarchoi* (Diod. XIX 16,1). The high state of training of Antigonos's army is well illustrated by his campaigns, in which he often successfully undertook extraordinary route marches, special night operations, and operations in difficult terrain. Some indication of the discipline by which he maintained this state of training and preparedness is given by Plutarch's anecdote at *Apophth. Ant.* 2 (= *Mor.* 182a) describing how Antigonos once saw some soldiers occupying their leisure by playing ball but still wearing their armor. When he sought out their officers to commend them for instilling such zeal in their men, he found them busy drinking, and accordingly demoted them instead and promoted the zealous soldiers in their places.

---

45. See chap. 3 n. 25 above for the *argyraspides* in the Diadoch period; this unit was broken up by Antigonos in 315, part of them being sent to Arachosia and the rest to garrisons in Media (Diod. XIX 48,3–4; Polyainos IV 6,15). The Seleukid army subsequently had units named both *hypaspistai* and *argyraspides:* Bar-Kochva, *Seleucid Army,* pp. 58–66.

46. Berve, 1:201–8; Bar-Kochva, *Seleucid Army,* pp. 85–93.

Of Antigonos's commissariat not much more can be said than that it seems to have been effective, since his men seem always to have been well supplied. The *aposkeuē,* or baggage train, formed an important part of ancient armies in general, and Antigonos was (unlike Eumenes) strongly aware of its particular importance to an army of essentially mercenary character. He won several major successes by capturing the enemy's baggage and thereby undermining the morale of the enemy troops, and was generally careful to guard his own baggage well. In 316 we hear of him courting the favor of his troops after some unusual hardships by providing them with pack animals for their baggage (Diod. XIX 20, 1–4). We also hear several times of the care Antigonos took to see to it that he had money on hand to pay his men (Diod. XVIII 52,7; XIX 20,1–4; XX 108,2–3), in which connection I have noted above the mobile treasury he seems to have kept with him at all times. Though the details of his supply, pay, and baggage system escape us, then, there is good reason to suppose that he understood their significance and saw to it that they were properly organized.

Concerning the final, *Naval Category,* it should be pointed out that Antigonos fully understood the importance of sea power to a realm based on the Aegean and eastern Mediterranean coast lands, and hence maintained a strong standing navy based on Phoenicia, Kilikia, Ionia, and the Nesiotic League, and also on the Hellespontine cities. He initially won control of the sea by his victory over Kleitos in 317 and subsequent capture of the Phoenician fleet organized by Eumenes (Polyainos IV 6,8 and 9), but in 314 he was forced to start again from scratch after Ptolemy took over the fleets of the Phoenician cities during his absence in the east. Diodoros describes how Antigonos set up shipyards in Phoenicia at Tripolis, Byblos, and Sidon, in Kilikia and on Rhodes, and how with the aid of the Phoenician rulers and the governors of Syria he organized gangs of men and beasts totaling 8,000 men and 1,000 pairs of draught animals to cut timber on Mt. Lebanon and Mt. Taurus and transport it to the shipyards, where sawyers and shipwrights turned out warships (Diod. XIX 58,2–6). The fleets thus built must undoubtedly have been mostly manned by Phoenicians and Kilikians, though the ships built at Rhodes would presumably have been manned by crews drawn from the Ionian cities, and we hear of one contingent of the Rhodian-built ships having Karian crews (Diod. XIX 64,5). In addition to the products of these shipyards, Antigonos also drew a number of ships from the Hellespont (Diod. XIX 62,7), and by 313 he had a fleet of 240 ships.

From this time on Antigonos was able to use the sea much as he wished, and his hegemony at sea was confirmed by victory over the navy of Kassandros in 313 (Diod. XIX 69,3, where the Pydnaian ships must belong to Kassandros), and by the crushing victory of Demetrios over Ptolemy's main battle fleet and the subsequent capture of Cyprus in 306 (Diod. XX 49,1–53,1). Antigonos was not content to build only triremes and quadriremes: bigger and more powerful ships were built for his navy, and at the battle of Salamis we find in his fleet ships as big as sixes (*hexēreis*) and sevens (*heptēreis*), as well as quinqueremes and lighter ships.[47] Antigonos several times sent out battle fleets of close to 200 ships, and in addition he often had smaller squadrons out on detached service (see further app. 2 below for his fleets); and he also had troop transporters and other support ships, most impressively attested at the start of the famous siege of Rhodes (Diod. XX 82,4).

Despite the undoubted presence of Phoenician, Kilikian, and Karian crews on his ships, no person of such nationality is securely attested as an officer in Antigonos's navy (but see app. 3, nos. 113 and 132, below for two possibilities). The known naval officers of Antigonos were mostly Greeks, examples being Themison of Samos and Hegesippos of Halikarnassos (see app. 3, nos. 46 and 112). Though he placed his (Macedonian) nephews Dioskourides, Telesphoros, and Polemaios in command of great fleets (usually combined with armies) at various times, and later his son Demetrios also, it looks as if the specifically naval side of things was almost entirely in the hands of Greek officers.[48] During the amphibious campaigns around Cyprus in 306, Demetrios was commander in chief, but the admiral (*nauarchos*) was apparently Medeios of Larissa, under whom there was the chief pilot (*archikubernētēs*), Pleistias of Kos. Medeios, in particular, crops up repeatedly during the years 313–304 as *nauarchos* (for his career see app. 3, no. 68), so as to suggest to Hauben (n. 48 above, with plausible arguments) that he was Antigonos's regularly instituted admiral in chief, with the chief pilot Pleistias as second-in-command. If this is correct, it argues a considerable institutionalized hierarchy in Antigonos's navy, which would be most interesting, though no more is known about it. At any rate, it is clear again that Antigonos gave his usual thorough care and attention to the creation and organization of

---

47. On the development of the great ships of the Hellenistic era, see especially Tarn, *HMND,* pp. 122–52; warships larger than quinqueremes are first mentioned in our sources in the fleet built for Antigonos in Phoenicia in 314: Diod. XIX 62,8.

48. For this and what follows, cf. Hauben, *Vlootbevelhebberschap*.

his navy, the most potent force in the eastern Mediterranean between 313 and 301.

PROVINCIAL ADMINISTRATIVE INSTITUTIONS

In an empire the size of Antigonos's much of the business of administration is not under the direct control of the ruler, but takes place on a regional or provincial basis, being in the hands of local governors and their subordinates. At its height Antigonos's empire was virtually coextensive with the old Persian Empire, and it was at all times made up of parts of the Persian Empire and the subsequent empire of Alexander. It is to be expected, therefore, that Antigonos's organization of provincial administration was in many ways inspired by the institutions and practices of the Persian Empire: Alexander's administration seems to have been essentially a continuation of that of the Persians (see pp. 46–47 above), and Antigonos himself had served for thirteen years as the satrap of the old Persian satrapy of greater Phrygia under Alexander. In a recent study of Persian provincial administration,[49] Michael Weiskopf concludes that the most prominent characteristic of Achaemenid administration, in Anatolia at least, was its lack of any fixed and rigid structure. The general framework of the administration was the division of the empire into satrapies, each with a satrap at its head, but within the satrapy no fixed structure or hierarchy is discernible, and the boundaries of the satrapies were themselves often fluid. We do hear of a variety of subordinate officials within a satrapy, most notably the royal secretary and the military commander, and there were local landholders and dynasts, some of them indigenous and some from important Persian families. The exact power, influence, and sphere of competence of any individual, however, seems always to have been as much dependent on his relations with king and court as on his official title and position.

Given this fluid and flexible nature of the Achaemenid administration, it is not surprising that Antigonos's provincial administration, insofar as it can be reconstructed from the sources, appears to have been characterized by a similar flexibility, the more so as Antigonos's rule was essentially based on a military conquest and he never had an extended period of peace and leisure to organize a consistent and

49. Weiskopf, "Achaemenid Systems for Governing Anatolia."

logical system of administration. In many ways Antigonos's administrative setup in the empire shows signs of being derived from a military occupation and administration, differing between one region and another according to circumstance and displaying its military origin by its ranks. Despite the fact that they bore military titles like *stratēgos* and *chiliarchos,* the powers and competences of Antigonos's governors were by no means limited to the military sphere. No clear divisions between administrative, military, judicial, and financial responsibilities are discernible in the provincial administration: individual governors and officials often seem to have been charged simultaneously with authority over several or all of these areas of responsibility. In particular the governors of provinces or regions, whether called satraps or *stratēgoi*, were responsible for every aspect of the governing of their provinces, including all of the above spheres and, of course, the maintenance of internal security and of the effectiveness of the parts of the empirewide communications network that passed through their provinces.

The titles, competences, and hierarchy of provincial governors and officials as organized by Antigonos naturally fall into two groups: (1) *upper level* administrators, meaning those directly appointed by Antigonos himself to important posts, normally posts that were autonomous or semiautonomous under Antigonos's supreme power; and (2) *lower level* officials appointed by, or directly responsible to, a superior other than Antigonos himself, normally the satrap or *stratēgos* of the province.

I term the *upper level* administrators holders of posts that were "autonomous or semiautonomous under Antigonos's supreme power" because, though these men were mostly in full charge of their provinces or whatever with only Antigonos over them, there were in Antigonos's empire a number of supra-provincial officers who exercised part of Antigonos's authority over the provincial governors in some areas. The best known is the so-called "*stratēgos* of the upper satrapies," who between 315 and 311 was stationed in Media with a large army to enforce Antigonos's authority east of the Tigris.[50] The first mention of a "generalship of the upper satrapies" in our sources is at Diod. XIX 14,1, where Peithon, son of Krateuas, is recorded as assuming this position in 317, but he was opposed by the combined forces of the upper satraps (Diod. XIX 14,1–3). Subsequently, early

50. See on this Bengtson, *Strategie,* 1:176–86; and more recently Schober, *Gesch. Babyloniens,* pp. 84–85, 98–90, 97–98.

in 315, Antigonos put about a report that he intended formally to appoint Peithon *stratēgos* of the upper satrapies, with an army of 5,000 Macedonian infantry and 1,000 Thracians (cavalry?),[51] as we learn from Diodoros and Polyainos (discussed in detail, pp. 105–6 above).

In origin, then, the generalship of the upper satrapies was not Antigonos's idea. His offer of this post was only a bait to trap Peithon, an exceptionally ambitious man reported to be plotting against Antigonos. However, Antigonos actually did appoint a *stratēgos* of the upper satrapies (though not Peithon, who was executed): after the wars of 317 and 316 Antigonos knew very well the strength and potential for trouble of the satrapies of inner Asia, and he needed to make some arrangement to contain it in view of his own imminent departure for the Mediterranean region.[52] The setting up of a trusted overseer with a force large enough to intervene quickly and decisively in case of trouble or defections among the upper satraps was the obvious answer. There is no evidence or reason to suggest that this *stratēgos* held any authority to intervene in the internal administration of the upper satrapies, though he did have the power to call out the satraps and their local forces to join him in the event of trouble or war,[53] and there must have been an arrangement for him to draw money for his needs and to pay his staff and troops from the revenues of the upper satrapies (for the royal treasures had been removed by Antigonos). The *stratēgos* originally appointed by Antigonos in 315 was one Hippostratos, who was given a force of 3,500 mercenary infantry and some cavalry, perhaps the 1,000 Thracians; but he was soon replaced, perhaps in the same year, by the Macedonian Nikanor, who held the post until killed by Seleukos in 310.[54]

51. One would naturally expect a general of a considerable force to receive cavalry as well as infantry; it is interesting to note that the only Thracians mentioned in Antigonos's army in 316 are 1,000 Thracian cavalry at the battle of Paraitakene (Diod. XIX 29,4), and it seems likely to me therefore that the 1,000 Thracians he said he planned to leave with Peithon in 315 were that cavalry unit.

52. Antigonos, of course, never again ventured east of the Tigris himself and doubtless planned not to from 315 on; however, in Stasanor, Tlepolemos, and Oxyartes, he was leaving behind some powerful satraps not very well disposed to himself (Diod. XIX 48,1–2), and he needed to make preparations in case they should cause trouble.

53. Thus, for example, the Median satrap Orontobates fought together with the *stratēgos* Hippostratos against the rebellious partisans of Peithon in 315 (Diod. XIX 47,1–3); and when Nikanor marched as *stratēgos* of the upper satrapies to fight Seleukos in 311, he had in his army the provincial troops of Media and Persia (Diod. XIX 92,1–4).

54. Diod. XIX 46,5–6 says, as the text stands, only that Hippostratos received 3,500 mercenary infantry, but there is clearly a lacuna in the text, for these infantry are introduced as *pezous men* and there is no corresponding *de* clause: this missing clause must have mentioned some cavalry, as was noted by Fischer in the Teubner ed. of Diodoros, and one thinks at once

Whereas the *stratēgos* of the upper satrapies seems to have been entirely a military official, this was not necessarily the case with the other supra-provincial offices known under Antigonos, though most of them do seem to have had their origin in military requirements. Like the generalship of the upper satrapies, these other great commands were essentially intended to enable military power on a wide scale to be exercised by one official in the absence of Antigonos himself. For example, in 314 when Antigonos was busy campaigning in Syria and Palestine, he sent his nephew Polemaios into Asia Minor with a large force on a mission which ultimately encompassed Kappadokia, Paphlagonia, the Hellespontine region, Ionia, and Karia. Clearly Polemaios was in effect Antigonos's *locum tenens* in Asia Minor in 314–313; likewise, when Antigonos crossed into Asia Minor in late 313, he left his son Demetrios in charge of all of Syria and Palestine. While the primary purpose of the commands of Polemaios and Demetrios was military, we find that Polemaios was able to appoint a governor of the Hellespontine region (Diod. XX 19,2), which indicates that he had administrative powers also; and there is no reason to suppose that Demetrios's power in Syria was limited to the military sphere. On the other hand, the commands of these two were temporary, emergency measures designed to enable actual or potential crises to be dealt with in the absence of the ruler himself, while the generalship of the upper satrapies was a permanent institution.[55]

These commands, then, illustrate the essential flexibility of Antigonos's administration, which was always tailored to particular needs rather than schematized according to some system. A further example of this is the marked difference between provincial governorships in the eastern part of Antigonos's empire—that is, east of the Euphrates—and in the western part: for in the east we find men with the Persian title of satrap ruling the old Persian satrapies, while in the west the governors seem to have been called *strategoi* or by some other Greek title, and it is not immediately clear whether they ruled satrapies or areas larger or smaller than the Persian satrapies. We are fully informed about Antigonos's provincial arrangements in the upper

---

of the 1,000 Thracians discussed in n. 51 above. On the position of Hippostratos and his replacement by Nikanor, I follow Schober against Bengtson (both cited at n. 50 above); see also app. 3, nos. 54 and 79.

55. Indeed, this institution of a generalship of the upper satrapies seems to have been copied by the Seleukids during much of their reign at least: see, for example, the remarks of Schober, *Gesch. Babyloniens*, p. 90, and Bengtson, *Strategie*, 1:186, and cf. the position of the Seleukid *stratēgos* Molon in inner Asia at the time of Antiochos III (Polybios V 40,7–54,7).

satrapies by Diodoros, who gives the information at the conclusion of his account of Antigonos's war with Eumenes (Diod. XIX 46,5; 48,1–5; 55,1). The far eastern satraps Stasanor of Baktria, Oxyartes of the Paropanisadai, and Tlepolemos of Karmania were confirmed because they were beyond Antigonos's reach or interest; Sibyrtios of Arachosia was confirmed in his satrapy as being friendly to Antigonos, and was given reinforcements in addition. Antigonos's new appointments were Euagoras in Areia/Drangiane, Orontobates in Media, Asklepiodoros in Persia, and Aspeisas in Susiane. It is remarkable that two of the four appointees—the Mede Orontobates and Aspeisas of Susa—were natives of their satrapies: evidently Antigonos sought to conciliate the eastern peoples, and the general impression of his organization is that it was intended to settle the upper satrapies in such a way that they would not again demand his personal attention.[56]

A special case seems to have been Antigonos's treatment of Babylonia and Mesopotamia, which were perhaps combined into one large satrapy under Peithon, son of Agenor. When Antigonos first entered Mesopotamia he apparently established a certain Blitor there as satrap (see app. 3, no. 24), while he of course recognized his ally Seleukos as satrap of Babylonia. In 315, however, he fell out with Seleukos, causing him to flee for his life to Ptolemy, and he then deposed Blitor for having helped Seleukos escape. Whereas we are told that Peithon replaced Seleukos, no new satrap of Mesopotamia is ever mentioned; but when Peithon was summoned to Syria in 313/12 to help Demetrios hold Palestine against a possible attack by Ptolemy and Seleukos, he must have come through Mesopotamia, and it is indeed from the satrap of neighboring Mesopotamia that one would expect help for Syria to be summoned. I suspect, therefore, that Babylonia and Mesopotamia were combined into one super-satrapy by Antigonos, holding as they did an important position in the middle between the upper satrapies (in which Antigonos was not greatly interested) and Antigonos's heartlands of Syria and Anatolia.[57]

In contrast to the fairly full information we have for the appointees to governorships in the east, relatively little is directly known

56. For Antigonos's lack of interest in the far east, cf. the remarks of Goukowsky, *Essai*, p. 119.

57. This seems the more likely in that Babylonia and Mesopotamia had been combined into one great satrapy before under the Achaemenids: see Frye, *History of Ancient Iran*, pp. 113–14.

about Antigonos's governors in Syria and Anatolia. We are not told who if anyone Antigonos set in the place of the deposed Eumenes, Alketas, Kleitos, and Arrhidaios when he conquered the various satrapies of Anatolia in 319–317; nor are we subsequently told of a successor to Asandros in Karia or of specific governors of Syria. The evidence relevant to governorships in these regions is, in short, not plentiful and does not offer a picture of a consistent system.[58] Most scholars concentrate on a passage of Diodoros (XX 107,3–5) that mentions Dokimos and Phoinix as governors in Phrygia and Lydia with the title of *stratēgos,* but they come to very different conclusions based on this evidence. Koehler, for example, argues that Antigonos broke up the satrapies of Asia Minor and Syria into smaller regions under *stratēgoi;* Tarn, on the contrary, suggests that Antigonos combined the Persian satrapies into a handful of huge "generalships." Bengtson holds against Koehler that the old satrapies were not broken up, but simply had *stratēgoi* placed over them instead of satraps, though he is inclined to accept in part Tarn's thesis of the joining together of several satrapies under one *stratēgos;* and Wehrli follows the first part of Bengtson's thesis, making the *stratēgoi* rulers of satrapies, without apparently noticing that Bengtson in part accepts Tarn's theory.[59] It must be said at once against Tarn, Bengtson, and Wehrli that Koehler's view accords well with the evidence of Diodoros about Dokimos and Phoinix, which in no wise implies that Dokimos's authority extended beyond Synnada and a few surrounding places (Diod. XX 107,4) or that that of Phoinix covered anything

58. The evidence: in 314 Polemaios was *stratēgos* of the Hellespontine region (στρατηγὸς τῶν περὶ Ἑλλήσποντον: Memnon in *FGrH,* no. 434 F 4,6); in 310 Polemaios's friend Phoinix was called *epistatēs* of the same region (Diod. XX 19,2 calling the region a satrapy); in 311 Antigonos made Hieronymos *epimelētēs* in charge of the Dead Sea bitumen production (Diod. XIX 100,1–2), but Josephus implies that Hieronymos was actually governor of [Koile?] Syria (τὴν Συρίαν ἐπετρόπευεν: *Contra Apionem* I 213–4); in 302 Lysimachos captured Synnada as a result of Antigonos's *stratēgos* Dokimos going over to him (Diod. XX 107,3–4; Paus. I 8,1), and Prepelaos had the city (but not the acropolis) of Sardis betrayed to him by Antigonos's *stratēgos* Phoinix (Diod. XX 107,5); in 314 the *hyparchoi* of Syria were summoned by Antigonos for instructions on the ship-building program he then instituted (Diod. XIX 58,1–2).

59. Koehler, *SDAW,* 1898, pp. 824–43; Tarn, *CAH,* 6:489; Bengtson, *Strategie,* 1:197–209; Wehrli, *Antigone et Démétrios,* pp. 95–97. The problem of Antigonos's provincial governorships in Asia Minor has been unnecessarily complicated by those (e.g., Wehrli) who adduce the agreement reached by Antigonos with Asandros in late 313 whereby Asandros was to be permitted to remain satrap of Karia after submitting to Antigonos and handing over all his troops (Diod. XIX 75,1). As Bengtson shows (*Strategie,* 1:205–6), this is an exceptional case, which has no bearing on Antigonos's general administrative arrangements; in any case, because of Asandros's treachery the agreement was never properly put into effect.

other than the city of Sardis and perhaps its surrounding territory (Diod. XX 107,5).

The matter is not quite so simple, however, that Koehler's thesis can be forthwith accepted and the arguments of Bengtson et al. dismissed. A problem for Bengtson's theory is that Diodoros conspicuously fails to call Dokimos *stratēgos* of Phrygia or Phoinix *stratēgos* of Lydia, though he elsewhere does specify when people are in charge of such regions. The point made by Bengtson that through all of Lysimachos's conquest of Hellespontine Phrygia and greater Phrygia we only hear of Dokimos as *stratēgos*, and that likewise we only hear of Phoinix in Lydia, is probably to be explained by Diodoros's extremely compressed narrative here—so compressed that he fails even to mention Lysimachos's move from the Hellespontine region into greater Phrygia (at least as the text of Diod. XX 107,3 stands). On the other hand when we read at Diod. XX 108,1 that Antigonos heard of the desertion (ἀπόστασιν) of his *stratēgoi* and at Diod. XX 108,3 that, having now crossed the Taurus with his army, Antigonos restored to their former alliance the deserters (ἀφεστηκότας) in Lykaonia and upper Phrygia, the implication seems to be that the ἀφεστηκότας were *stratēgoi* and that there were hence *stratēgoi*—several of them—in Lykaonia and upper Phrygia besides Dokimos.[60] This seems to negate the arguments of Tarn and Bengtson.

There remains a problem in the fact that regions continue to be called satrapies by Diodoros even when they do not appear to have had satraps over them, as at XX 19,2 where the Hellespontine region is called a satrapy in 310. This could lead to the conclusion that Antigonos retained the Persian satrapies in Asia Minor as in the east, but before we reach this conclusion with Bengtson and Wehrli, it is surely necessary to decide what is meant by the term *satrapy* and how technically precise a meaning it has. There are passages in Diodoros where he seems to use the word *satrapy* either with the general meaning of a region under one governor or else anachronistically: at XX 98,1 for example Diodoros speaks of the "satrapy of Idumea," whereas at XX 95,2 he refers to "the eparchy of Idumea." In all probability neither of these terms should be taken literally—the Seleukids may conceivably have had a satrapy or eparchy of Idumea, but

60. Particularly interesting to note is that *stratēgoi* who are called *aphestēkotas* are placed by Diodoros as being in Lykaonia and upper Phrygia, whereas in his account of Lysimachos's campaign Diodoros brings him no further south or east than Synnada (Diod. XX 107,1–4), a long way from Lykaonia: clearly Diodoros is here once again guilty of excessive abbreviation.

not Antigonos[61]—and in any case the use of both to refer to the same district indicates that Diodoros did not take care to be technically accurate in using these terms. The same may be said when at XIX 44,4 Diodoros refers to the eparchy of Rhagai in Media, where *eparchy* probably just means district and should not be taken to indicate that Media had been broken up into eparchies with eparchs over them.

Since, then, Diodoros at times uses the term *satrapy* loosely, it would be dangerous to conclude from the reference to the Hellespontine satrapy at XX 19,2 that the Persian satrapies continued to exist in Asia Minor. For one thing the term *satrapy* might be applied, as in the case of Idumea, to a region other than (and considerably smaller than!) a Persian satrapy; and besides the word might be used simply as a geographical term.[62] In the case of the Hellespontine satrapy, it is interesting to note that whereas under Alexander the satrapy included Paphlagonia (Arrian *Anab.* II 4,1–2), at the conference of Babylon this region was taken from it and added to Kappadokia under Eumenes (Diod. XVIII 3,1), and there is no reason to suppose that this reduction of Hellespontine Phrygia was ever subsequently undone. Furthermore, when the sources refer specifically to the administrative region of Antigonos they speak of the Hellespont only—not of Hellespontine Phrygia (Diod. XX 19,2: *τῆς ἐφ' Ἑλλησπόντωι σατραπείας*; Memnon [= *FGrH*, no. 434] F 4,6: *στρατηγὸς . . . τῶν περὶ τὸν Ἑλλήσποντον*). The earlier satrapy of Leonnatos and Arrhidaios is always called "Hellespontine Phrygia" (see Diod. XVIII 3,1; 12,1; 39,6; 51,1), and this name is likewise commonly used to refer to the geographical region of northwestern Asia Minor (for example, at Diod. XVIII 5,4; XIX 57,1; XX 107,3). It could be argued, then, that the "satrapy" of which Polemaios was *stratēgos* and Phoinix later *epistatēs* was not Hellespontine Phrygia but only the region actually along the Hellespont and Sea of Marmara, a much smaller district.[63]

61. Antigonos in fact met with nothing but defeats in this region: see Diod. XIX 94,1–100,2.

62. Under the Achaemenid system, all of Palestine, Koile Syria, Syria proper, and (at times it seems) Mesopotamia formed one satrapy (see Frye, *History of Ancient Iran*, pp. 113–14). Note further that Diodoros apparently refers to "the satrapies [*sic*] near Egypt" at XX 47,5 (though the MSS are not unanimous in giving this reading; see the *app. crit.* of Fischer in the Teubner ed.), which is another instance of either an imprecise or an anachronistic use of the term *satrapy*.

63. Cf. Diod. XIX 57,4 which seems to suggest that Polemaios's command along the Hellespont was in origin purely military in nature and concerned with the prevention of troop crossings under either Lysimachos or Kassandros.

There is in fact no clear evidence to suggest that the Persian satrapies in Asia Minor and Syria/Palestine continued to be primary administrative units under Antigonos after 314 at the latest. The fact that we do not hear of a single satrap in these areas, in sharp contrast to the east under Antigonos, is a strong *e silentio* argument against the continuation of the Persian satrapies. The titles *hyparchos, stratēgos, epistatēs,* and *epimelētēs,* applied by the sources to what are clearly administrative officials,[64] suggest rather that Antigonos appointed no satraps in the western part of his empire, but instead placed officials with a variety of titles in charge of portions of satrapies such as Synnada and the surrounding region (Dokimos), the region around Sardis (Phoinix), and Koile Syria (Hieronymos). Koehler appears, therefore, to be essentially right, though he is overschematic in assuming that all such governors were called *stratēgoi*: we hear of *stratēgoi* in Phrygia, Lydia, and Lykaonia, but the region along the Hellespont had an *epistatēs,* Syria seems to have had several *hyparchoi,* and Koile Syria at least one *epimelētēs*. True, one cannot by any means insist upon the technical accuracy of these terms in Diodoros or assume that they were necessarily the titles actually used by Antigonos for these officials. The term *stratēgos,* however, is likely to be accurate, for it seems that under Lysimachos Asia Minor continued to be governed by such *stratēgoi,* and subsequently under the Seleukids *stratēgos* was the title of the governor of a "satrapy," and it seems reasonable to assume that these usages derived from Antigonos's administrative *stratēgoi*.[65]

No precise information is forthcoming about the sphere of competence of these *stratēgoi* and other governors, but there is no reason to suppose that they did not exercise full civil and military authority, with everything entailed thereby, within their districts. The *stratēgos* Dokimos was clearly in charge of financial affairs and of colonization within his district (see n. 64 above), as well as being the military commander. The same would have been true of the other governors. An exception to this full control seems to have been formed by a

64. The *stratēgos* Dokimos for example, was evidently in charge of the royal treasury at Synnada (Diod. XX 107,4), and had the authority to found a garrison colony near Synnada at Dokimeion (see, e.g., Tscherikower, *Städtegründungen,* p. 35), which indicates that he had full administrative as well as military authority in his region. For the use by Diodoros of the term *hyparchos,* to refer to a satrap-type administrator, see, for example, the case of Asklepiodoros, placed in charge of Persia by Antigonos in 315 (Diod. XIX 48,5).

65. For *stratēgoi* under Lysimachos, see Bengtson, *Strategie,* 1:209–23; for governors in Asia Minor with the title *stratēgos* under the Seleukids, see, for example, the case of Meleagros, the governor of Hellespontine Phrygia under Antiochos I (*OGIS,* no. 220).

number of great royal strongholds held by virtually autonomous commanders: we hear of an *epimelētēs* directly responsible to Antigonos being in charge of Sardis in 309/8 (Diod. XX 37,5), and in 302 one Philippos was in charge of the acropolis of Sardis and apparently independent of the regional *stratēgos*, Phoinix (Diod. XX 107,5). The Diphilos who commanded the citadel of Babylon for Antigonos in 311 was most likely in a similar position of independence (Diod. XIX 91,3), and the same was probably true at Susa (cf. the position of Xenophilos there in 316: Diod. XIX 17,3; 18,1; 48,6). Likewise, the reliable senior officer Andronikos of Olynthos was apparently Antigonos's immediate subordinate in charge of Tyre,[66] and there is every reason to suppose that the *gazophylax* of the royal treasury at Kyinda and whoever was in charge of Kelainai in Antigonos's absence would have been directly subordinate to Antigonos.

The picture that emerges, then, is of relatively small administrative regions under military governors with full civil authority and a string of major forts at strategic points like Sardis, Kelainai, Tyre, Babylon, and Susa held by special royal commanders with large garrisons.[67] The reason for such an organization is easily guessed. Since Antigonos himself spent the years 314–301 in Asia Minor and Syria, he was able to supervise the governing of these areas fairly closely and could afford to break them up into smaller regions than had been customary under the Persians and Alexander. He thus reduced the power of the individual governors, and so, while giving them full civil and military competence within their districts, obviated the possibility that any of them might rebel and seek to emulate his own rise and that of the other great Diadochoi from satrap to independent dynast. The resistance of Asandros of Karia and the rebellion (inspired by Polemaios) of Phoinix on the Hellespont showed what was to be feared along these lines. The strategic strong points under specially trusted royal governors would have been intended as an extra guard against possible rebellions and invasions: it is noteworthy that Andronikos held up Ptolemy at Tyre in early 311, that Diphilos organized the resistance to Seleukos at Babylon in 311,

66. This is to be deduced from Diod. XIX 59,2: Andronikos is left in charge of the siege of Tyre for a time by Antigonos in 314; and Diod. XIX 86,1–2: Andronikos is *phrourarchos* of Tyre in early 311. No doubt Andronikos was selected to be one of Demetrios's four advisers in Syria in 313/12 (Diod. XIX 69,1 and 82,4) because of his key position as *phrourarchos* of Tyre with a large military force.

67. Such garrisons are, at any rate, specifically attested by Diodorus at Babylon (XIX 92,3–4), Tyre (XIX 86,1–2), and Sardis (XX 107,5).

and that it was Philippos's stubborn loyalty that saved the key position of the Sardis acropolis for Antigonos in 302.

One final point that needs to be made concerning the upper level of administration in Antigonos's realm is that a number of (usually native) dynasts were permitted to retain their power in various regions of the realm. The precise degree of subjection of these allied dynasts to Antigonos is not known, and it was doubtless in any case variable: the examples known to us are Mithridates of Kios, Zipoites of Bithynia, Dionysios of Herakleia, and the kings of several Phoenician cities, notably Sidon, Byblos, and Tripolis. Of these the Phoenician kings were clearly subject, able to be summoned and ordered to set up shipyards and build a navy for Antigonos (Diod. XIX 58,1–4); likewise Mithridates of Kios is definitely described as a subject (ὑπήκοος) of Antigonos, and the latter was able to have him executed when he suspected him of treason (Diod. XX 111,4). Zipoites and Dionysios are only described as allies of Antigonos, however (see Diod. XIX 60,3 and Memnon F 4,6 respectively), but it is noteworthy that Zipoites furnished Antigonos with hostages and Dionysios made Antigonos the guardian of his sons (Memnon F 4,9). Doubtless, therefore, these dynasts too were essentially subject to Antigonos's authority, though for political reasons they were permitted to remain nominally independent allies. In general, Antigonos's reason for leaving such dynasts in power would have been the political one of not wishing to stir up trouble unnecessarily or do violence to the national sentiments of such peoples as the Bithynians, the Phoenicians, and the Herakleots, who could be very difficult to deal with if roused. Again, this is an indicator of the flexibility of Antigonos's administration.

Under the regional *stratēgoi* and other governors, there must have been a host of lesser officials forming the *lower level* of provincial administration: men subordinate to and usually doubtless appointed by the regional governors. The kind of officials that might be expected to serve under regional *stratēgoi* or (in the east) satraps can be learned from a famous passage in Plutarch's *Eumenes* (3,7) which tells us that upon receiving Kappadokia from Perdikkas, Eumenes "entrusted the cities to his own friends, established garrison commanders, and left such judges and financial officials as he wished," the Greek terms for these four kinds of officials being *philoi, phrourarchoi, dikastai,* and *dioikētai.*

This passage of Plutarch has been analyzed by P. Briant, who shows in the first place the exemplary nature of this proceeding of

Eumenes, and in the second place the remarkable continuity it shows between the Persian administration and that of the Diadochoi and Seleukids.[68] Obviously, Antigonos must have been in part responsible for any such continuity, and it is hence natural to look for these various kinds of officials under Antigonos and his governors.

I have rendered *dioikētēs* as "financial official" above, but it is in fact not absolutely clear what the exact significance of the term was: Briant (*Rois, tributs et paysans*, p. 24) understands it in the sense I have given, with the further elucidation, based on Seleukid parallels, that some of these officials must have been in charge of tribute collection and others of managing the royal lands; the *Greek-English Lexicon* of Liddell and Scott renders it as "governor, administrator . . . esp. financial controller." Particularly interesting for Antigonid practice are two pieces of evidence: in the famous Mnesimachos inscription (Buckler and Robinson, *Sardis VII*, no. 1) the tribute due from the estates of Mnesimachos is specified as owing to chiliarchies under named chiliarchs (Pytheos and Sagarios are the two whose names survive);[69] and at Diodoros XIX 91,3 we read that when Seleukos invaded Babylonia in 311 to wrest it from Antigonos, he was joined by an officer named Polyarchos who was in charge of a *dioikēsis* and had under him a little more than 1,000 soldiers. Thus we have tribute officials in Lydia with the title *chiliarchos* (captain of a detachment of 1,000 men), and in Babylonia a captain of 1,000 men who was apparently a *dioikētēs* (financial controller). The obvious conclusion seems to be that under Antigonos's rule the regions of the empire were divided up into financial (tribute) districts called chiliarchies because at the head of each stood a chiliarch whose sphere of competence (*dioikēsis*) included oversight of the tribute collection and com-

68. Briant, *Rois, tributs et paysans*, pp. 15–30.

69. For the date of the Mnesimachos inscription—in the time of Antigonos Monophthalmos—see Debord, *Aspects*, app. 5 at pp. 244–51. He points out that though the inscription is of the late third century, the document is of the sort that would be reinscribed if damaged, and demonstrates that this must indeed have happened because of the administrative officers called chiliarchs (not found under the Seleukids), the assessment of *phoros* in gold (the Seleukids used silver), and the many non-Greek names in the document (uncommon in Lydia by the late third century); all point to a late fourth century date, as does the mention of Antigonos as the awarder of the estate in the document. Atkinson, *Historia* 21 (1972):62–64, attempts to date the document later than ca. 240 on the grounds of the appearance in it of the personal name Kaikos, which she takes to be a reference to Attalos I's victory over the Gauls near the river Kaikos ca. 240: however, see the Delian inscriptions *IG* XI.2 154a, lines 24, 44 (296 B.C.), and *IG* XI.2 142, line 43 (end of the fourth century), for much earlier occurrences of Kaikos as a personal name, which demolishes Atkinson's argument.

mand of the troops (nominally 1,000 in number, though there was doubtless much variation) stationed or settled in the district.

For *dikastai* in Antigonos's empire the evidence is not so direct. However, besides the inherent probability that there would have been district judges in the realm, for justice must have been administered somehow, there is one piece of evidence that may refer to such a *dikastēs*. This is again a mention in the Mnesimachos inscription cited above, in the first two lines of which we read "Chaireas having enquired . . . and later Antigonos awarded the estate to me."[70] The text here is unfortunately fragmentary, so that it is not certain what the background and point of Chaireas's enquiry (the Greek is ἐπερωτήσαντος Χαιρέου) was, but it seems at least plausible to suppose that what was enquired about was the existing title(s) of the lands to be granted to Mnesimachos, so that he should not be awarded lands already held by someone else and so that the boundaries of the lands might be ascertained to be settled.[71] In fact we read further in the inscription of a division being made (διαιρέσεως γενομένης: line 13) by which two men named Pytheos and Adrastos held separate sections of land within the estate granted to Mnesimachos. Possibly the enquiry of Chaireas was connected with determining the rights of these two men within the overall estate granted to Mnesimachos, and it was clearly based on the results of Chaireas's activities that Antigonos "awarded" or "adjudged" (ἐπέκρινε) the estate to Mnesimachos.[72] If this is correct, as seems likely, Chaireas would probably have been acting in some sort of judicial capacity, and hence may have been a *dikastēs*, though on this occasion—since the enquiry concerned royal land—the final decision rested with the king.

In the case of *phrourarchoi* we are on firmer ground, for a passage of Diodoros specifically records the existence of such officers under Antigonos. At XIX 16,1–3 Diodoros informs us that between 319 and 316 the captured Perdikkan leaders Attalos, Polemon, Dokimos, and five others were kept imprisoned by Antigonos in a fortress

70. A full translation is given in Austin, *Hellenistic World*, no. 181 at p. 295.

71. Cf. the grant of land to a certain Aristodikides by Antiochos I (Welles, *RC*, nos. 10–13), which specifies that the titles of the lands granted to Aristodikides are to be investigated to determine whether the estates have already been given to someone else (in which case Aristodikides will receive different land); and see also the case of the estate granted to Laodike by Antiochos II (Welles, *RC*, nos. 18–20), in which it is specified that the precise boundaries of the estate are to be determined by an on-the-spot investigation by the local hyparch and the deed of sale and record of boundaries are to be filed at the record office in Sardis.

72. For the use of the verb *epikrinein* to indicate the granting of an estate by royal fiat, see the examples cited by Buckler and Robinson, *Sardis VII*, p. 6, and id., *AJA* 16 (1912):70.

(presumably in the border region between Phrygia and Pisidia) under the *phrourarchos* Xenopeithes, and that when these men managed to free themselves and kill Xenopeithes, troops quickly arrived from nearby *phrouria* (forts) to besiege them. Evidently southern Phrygia and Pisidia, at least, were dotted with such forts, each with a garrison and a *phrourarchos* under Antigonos; indeed, as Briant points out (*Rois, tributs et paysans,* pp. 20–21), such *phrouria* are attested throughout Asia Minor from Persian times down to the time of Mithridates VI of Pontos (first century B.C.), and so there is no reason to suppose that under Antigonos the *phrouria* with their *phrourarchoi* were limited to the region implied in Diodoros's account of Attalos and his companions. These *phrouria,* such as that in which Attalos and the others were imprisoned and that of Nora in Kappadokia where Eumenes was besieged by Antigonos, were typically small forts on easily defensible rock bastions, well supplied with water and kept stocked with food and fuel (i.e., corn and wood) in case of emergencies. They formed thus a chain of local defense points, reinforcing the security of the realm. Of course these *phrourarchoi* must be distinguished from the men in charge of great royal strongholds like Sardis, Kelainai, and Tyre, who are also occasionally called *phrourarchoi* (see, e.g., Diod. XIX 86,1–2, where Andronikos is called the *phrourarchos* of Tyre), and also from the commanders of garrisons sometimes placed in other important cities,[73] both of these types being royal rather than local appointees.

The fourth type of local officials mentioned in the Plutarch passage, the *philoi,* were of course the personal staff of the governor, and every governor would have had such a staff. Antigonos himself, when satrap of Phrygia, had his staff of *philoi* (see Diod. XVIII 23,4), and in the case of Antigonos's *stratēgos* Dokimos, for example, we learn that in 302 he had on his staff the Philetairos who later became dynast of Pergamon and founded the Attalid empire (Pausanias I 8,1, where Philetairos is not explicitly called a *philos* of Dokimos, though it seems to be implied that he was a member of Dokimos's personal staff and hence his *philos*). From the text of Plutarch it would seem that one typical task of these *philoi* was to govern the towns and cities of the region on behalf of the satrap or *stratēgos,* though they doubtless had other tasks also, and in fact it seems likely that most of the *dioikētai, dikastai,* and *phrourarchoi* of the region would have been counted among the *philoi* of the regional governor.

73. On these latter officers, see, for example, Bengtson, *Strategie,* 1:190–97.

Meager as the evidence is, then, it is sufficient to establish the *probability* that the brief account of the setting up of a regional administration given by Plutarch *Eum.* 3,7 is valid for the regions/satrapies of Antigonos's realm. At the head of each region stood a satrap or *stratēgos,* each with his own personal staff of *philoi.* Apart from the men serving as aides and assistants on the governor's staff, there were in each region a number of important officials, chief of whom were doubtless the *chiliarchoi,* who combined military and financial responsibilities and were thus like *stratēgoi* on a smaller scale. Besides these *chiliarchoi* there were judicial officials and governors of the towns and cities, both types of officials probably directly subordinate to the *stratēgos* or satrap, and *phrourarchoi* in charge of small garrisons in natural strongholds, probably subordinate to the local *chiliarchoi.*[74] It is not possible to give a full picture of the working of this administrative setup, for the sources do not permit it. We do, however, have some further information concerning its most important aspect, the gathering of tribute: it is fairly obvious that the main point of providing good government in the regions of the empire, seeking to ensure security, administering justice, and so forth, was to ensure the regular flow of tribute into Antigonos's treasuries, so that the army, court, and bureaucracy could be maintained and the empire remain a going concern.

From the Mnesimachos inscription (for which see n. 69 above) it appears that in Antigonos's empire the duty of collecting the tribute (*phoros*) fell to the chiliarchs, since the chiliarchies there appear as tribute districts (see Buckler and Robinson, *Sardis VII,* no. 1, lines 5–10). Two kinds of rural unit are there described as being responsible for paying the tribute: villages (*kōmai*) and lots (*klēroi*). Concerning the former of these, it is interesting to note that small villages might be assigned to a larger village for the purpose of tribute paying (*Sardis VII,* no. 1,4–5); under the term *klēroi* we should probably understand allotments of land to soldier-settlers to be meant.[75] The authorities of the village community and the owner of the *klēros,* then, were re-

74. The garrisons of the *phrouria* mentioned at Diod. XIX 16,1–5 were clearly very small: there were 400 soldiers in the *phrourion* in which Attalos and his associates were being held captive, and some 900 men subsequently gathered from the surrounding *phrouria* to besiege the place. These garrisons were surely too small to have been autonomous, but on the other hand if in each district there were troops under the chiliarch in addition to the garrisons of the *phrouria,* then the number of garrison troops in Asia Minor alone would have been huge. It is clear that in fact the garrisons of the *phrouria* must have been the troops of the chiliarchs.

75. See in this sense, for example, Buckler and Robinson, *AJA* 16 (1912):54–55.

sponsible for paying in the tribute to the local chiliarch, the assessment being in gold staters and obols. Apparently, therefore, the villages and allotment holders were required to sell sufficient produce to provide their tribute in cash, thereby easing considerably the task of the chiliarch, who had merely to collect, audit, and store, use, or forward to higher authorities the cash tribute. Obviously the chiliarchs must have had local treasuries in which to collect and store the tribute money: no doubt some of the *phrouria* served this purpose. Obviously also, part of the tribute collected must have been earmarked for the chiliarch's use, to pay his expenses and the wages of his staff and troops, and so on. The rest must have been forwarded to the regional government and thence to the king.

The fact that Mnesimachos's estates could be valued by the annual tribute owing on them implies the existence of local record offices where the tribute owed by each village and allotment was recorded, and that these records included specifications of the boundaries and (in the case of allotments) titles of the lands in the region: in other words, there must have been land registers.[76] It would be on the basis of such land registers that the chiliarch could audit the tribute annually, that an official like Chaireas could inquire concerning land ownership, and that the worth of the land as collateral could be determined by those making loans against it, like the temple wardens of Artemis at Sardis in the Mnesimachos inscription. Such land registers would doubtless already have been set up by the Persians when they determined the tribute to be paid by the regions of their empire; Antigonos's administration would in all likelihood simply have taken them over, and their continued existence is attested in the Seleukid period (see n. 76).

I have already pointed out, citing Briant's well-known article (see n. 68 above), that the offices attested under Eumenes and Antigonos seem also to be attested under the Seleukids. An exception is the office of *chiliarch,* a title which does not appear among the extant documentation of the Seleukid empire. However, it does emerge from various sources that Seleukid governors had under them regional officers named *hyparchs,* their districts being named hyparchies,[77] and it seems likely to me that these are simply Antigonos's chiliarchies under a

76. For the existence of land registers in the Seleukid period, see Westermann, *CPh* 16 (1921):12–19; cf. Tarn, *Alexander,* 2:22 n. 5.

77. An example is the hyparch ——krates, who was a subordinate of the *stratēgos* Metrophanes and charged with surveying the estate sold to Laodike by Antiochos II (Welles, *RC,* no. 20).

new name. The literary sources for the period of Alexander and Antigonos seem to use hyparch as an occasional synonym for satrap (see, e.g., Diod. XIX 48,5 where the new satrap of Persia appointed by Antigonos in 315 is termed a hyparch), or simply to mean governor of a region (as at Diod. XIX 58,1–2 where Antigonos summons the hyparchs of Syria). Under the Seleukids the hyparch was definitely a subordinate of a regional satrap or *stratēgos,* and it is hence natural to suppose that this term was then first applied to the district officers who had been called chiliarchs under Antigonos.

To any ruler at the close of the fourth century, and above all to Antigonos, given his experience, there were two models of imperial administration to draw on in setting up a system of rule: that of Philip in Macedon, and that of the Achaemenids in Asia. The salient points of Philip's system of rule are its reliance on his reformed army as the basis and main support of his power, expansion of the ruling class and binding of it to his interests by the granting of revocable estates on royal and conquered land, and the use of colonization and population transfers to establish his rule firmly over conquered territories. All three of these elements were prominent in the rule of Antigonos: we have seen that his administration was very much based on a military pattern, and in the next chapter I shall show that he was a great colonizer, and had begun to establish a ruling class of *philoi* on estates in Asia held at his pleasure.

Based on a recent review of the Achaemenid empire in R. N. Frye's *History of Ancient Iran* (pp. 106–20), one may characterize the Achaemenid administration as follows. Around the king at court there seems to have been a council, or at least a circle, of friends and advisers, if the Greek sources that speak of such institutions are to be trusted. At any rate, there was a considerable bureaucracy at the court—a chancery—though it is not possible to establish a hierarchy. The documents mention treasurers, tax and tribute collectors, overseers of rations, and other such functionaries, but it is often difficult to separate the functions of these officials from each other. There was a well-organized empirewide communications network of roads and messengers to expedite royal administration. Provincial organization, though everywhere based on the satrapial model, seems to have been very varied. By and large the satrapies seem to have been divided into subunits, either under local dynasts or under subgovernors, whose main function was to collect taxes, which were many and varied and payable mostly in kind. Land was measured, registered, and taxed extensively, and estates of conquered land were sometimes given by the king in "fief" as payment for military service.

Again, most of this is very much like what we have seen in Antigonos's empire, and there can be little doubt that this is because of his continuation of Achaemenid institutions and practices. Antigonos's work was hence mostly of selection and reorganization. He firmly established Macedonian-style military institutions in Asia and a Greco-Macedonian ruling elite. He broke up the Persian satrapies in the west, at least, into smaller governorships under military governors. The communications system was refurbished, and the tribute system set on a new footing by the introduction of cash payment, though this was no doubt still based on the Achaemenid land registers and tax assessments, since the Mnesimachos inscription speaks of payment in gold (rather than silver) coinage, and measures land as requiring so-and-so many *artabas* of seed (a Persian measure: see Buckler and Robinson, *Sardis VII,* no. 1, lines 15–16). The system of chiliarchies, if not a new invention of Antigonos's, was at least doubtless a rationalization of the Persian subdivision of satrapies.[78] In other words, Antigonos took over the Achaemenid administrative system and adapted it to the requirements of his rule, introducing many Greco-Macedonian elements and practices and thus setting the administration of his realm on a new and more efficient footing.

The ultimate importance of all this is of course that most of Antigonos's realm became the heartland of the Seleukid empire, and that the Seleukids seem to have continued and built on Antigonos's work of organization. What has emerged from this study is that by 302 Antigonos had set up a complete Hellenistic state in western Asia, with practically all of the typical practices and institutions already present, albeit often in a relatively undeveloped form. The monarchy, with a co-regency to establish the succession; the *synedrion* and the *philoi;* the chancery and the communications system; the *stratēgiai* and the smaller administrative districts (chiliarchies/hyparchies); and as we shall see in the next chapter, the estate holders and *katoikoi,* as well as the new and old Hellenic *poleis,* autonomous but in alliance with the king: all these were as characteristic of the Seleukid empire as they were of Antigonos's realm, and they establish Antigonos's role as proto-founder (as it were) of the Seleukid empire, and especially as the middleman transmitting the practices and institutions of Philip and the Achaemenids to the early Seleukids.

---

78. Though Xenophon mentions Persian chiliarchs at *Oikonomikos* 4,7 and *Kyropaidia* VIII 6,1, it is clear that these were purely officers of garrisons, if they ever really existed.

8

Economic, Settlement, and Cultural Policies

ECONOMIC POLICY

If there is one aspect of Antigonos's rule that might be thought beyond hope of elucidation, it is his economic policy, for the ancient sources as a rule have almost nothing to say directly about economic matters, and it might even be doubted in principle whether Antigonos had anything that could be called an economic policy. However, there are in fact in our extant sources certain pieces of information indicating that Antigonos did have something of an economic policy, which enable us to discern at least some of its outlines. Of course, part of the evidence concerns Antigonos's financial arrangements and institutions, and some of this has already been discussed under the heading of his central institutions, but it is clear that Antigonos had an economic policy that went beyond the mere mechanical oversight of tribute and tax collection, though the latter played an important part in it. The discussion of this economic policy may be divided into two areas—external and internal—concerned respectively with matters of import and export (i.e., the promotion or impeding of trade between his empire and other lands) and with the rural and urban economies of the lands within Antigonos's empire.

Concerning Antigonos's *external* economic policy, there is not a great deal to be said, but that little is of great interest, for it seems that Antigonos anticipated the later Hellenistic states of the Seleukids and, above all, the Ptolemies in seeking to establish state monopolies and to make his empire self-sufficient as far as possible. This was argued convincingly in an important article by Préaux,[1] based on a section of Antigonos's correspondence concerning the synoikism of Teos and Lebedos preserved in a famous inscription (see *Syll.*, no. 344; Welles, *Royal Correspondence in the Hellenistic Period* [henceforth cited as *RC*], nos. 3 and 4). In an interesting passage in the first of Antigonos's two preserved letters concerning this synoikism (Welles, *RC,* no. 3, lines 72–101), Antigonos grudgingly permits the people of the two towns to set up a fund for the import of corn to assure themselves of an adequate food supply. Antigonos states (at lines 80–90) that his general policy has been not to permit cities to import corn, preferring that they should obtain their supplies from the tributary territory of his own empire. His justification is that he does not wish the cities to become indebted as a result of excessive imports, and other inscriptions showing the financial difficulties some cities got into as a result of this practice lend color to this (see on this, for example, the commentary of Welles, *RC,* p. 29). However, it is obvious that it was also his desire that regions within his realm should as much as possible rely on each other for the necessities of life, rather than obtaining them from outside.

In fact it is clear from Antigonos's statement of policy that he sought to establish a grain monopoly within his sphere of influence, with the realm supplied exclusively from his own tributary lands. Two important reasons for this are that it was necessary for the peasants of the tributary lands to find a ready market for their produce so that their village authorities could pay the cash tribute in gold to the chiliarchs, and that Antigonos obtained large amounts of produce from his royal estate lands for which he also required a ready market.[2] Financial reasons aside, there were political considerations, in that the major grain exporter of the eastern Mediterranean area was Egypt, governed by Antigonos's rival Ptolemy, whose economy Antigonos would not wish to see boosted by the import of Egyptian grain into

1. Préaux, *CE* 29 (1954):312–27.

2. That the tribute was paid in cash is shown by the Mnesimachos inscription (Buckler and Robinson, *Sardis VII*, no. 1), where the villages of Tobalmoura, Tandos, and Kombdilipia are described as owing fifty gold staters annually (lines 4–6), and other villages and *klēroi* are also mentioned as owing tribute in gold staters and obols. The estate of Mnesimachos produced also a further surplus, which provided Mnesimachos's personal revenues (see lines 11–13); undoubtedly Antigonos held extensive royal lands which, unlike Mnesimachos's estate, had not yet been handed over to one of his *philoi,* from which Antigonos derived an agricultural surplus.

his own empire. Such a political desire for economic self-sufficiency receives some slight support from a notice in Theophrastos (*Hist. plant.* IV 8,4; cf. Pliny *NH* XIII 73) concerning the papyrus plant: he reports that besides in Egypt it also grew around a lake in Syria and that Antigonos thence derived a supply to make cables for his ships. The reference appears to be in the first instance to Antigonos's naval building program of 314/13 (Diod. XIX 58,1–6), thus primarily reflecting Antigonos's military rather than economic preoccupations. However, papyrus cables were not only used for naval vessels, and neither was papyrus exclusively used for cables; the development of an independent source of papyrus seems to be an indication of Antigonos's desire to make his realm self-sufficient, just as the Attalids later promoted the development of parchment so that they would not be dependent on papyrus from Egypt.[3]

There are other indications that Antigonos was aware of the economic and hence political importance of trade and sought to encourage, control, and exploit it. Another passage in Theophrastos (*Hist. plant.* IX 4,8) reports that Antigonos was interested in the trade in frankincense from the Red Sea area, and persuaded the Arab traders who brought the incense to the Mediterranean to bring him logs of the frankincense tree (cf. also Pliny *NH* XII 56). It may be that his attempt to conquer the Nabataians of Petra, the middlemen in this trade, was in part inspired by an interest in securing control of the frankincense trade (see Diod. XX 94,1–98,1), and that when this failed he persuaded the traders to bring him frankincense plants in the hope of cultivating them within his realm. The notion that Antigonos might have gone to war partly from economic motives should not be dismissed: that such motives had some weight with him is attested by his attempt to take over bitumen production on the Dead Sea (Diod. XX 98,1–100,2), hoping to find in it a profitable source of revenue (and perhaps to put pressure on Egypt, the main market for the bitumen).

Further evidence of economic policy comes from the Teos inscription (Welles, *RC,* no. 3) at lines 94–101, where Antigonos lays down rules for the export of foodstuffs from the territory of the proposed synoikism (see also Welles's commentary, *RC,* p. 30). Antigonos introduced a new provision that farmers wishing to export

---

3. On the Attalid promotion of parchment production, see, for example, Hansen, *Attalids of Pergamon*, pp. 214–15; on sources of papyrus outside Egypt, see N. Lewis, *Papyrus in Classical Antiquity* (Oxford, 1974), taking—it must be said—a rather skeptical view.

need not bring their produce to the city agora first in order to pay the duties; instead they could just declare to the *agoranomos* their intention to export a stated quantity of produce, pay the relevant duties, and then export it direct. This was clearly designed to facilitate exports, which shows Antigonos's interest in promoting a surplus of exports over imports in his empire. Again certain aspects of the hostilities between Antigonos and Rhodes in 306–304 were probably connected with trade. Rostovtzeff has noted (*SEHHW,* 3:1354 n. 42) that Antigonos's rivalry with Ptolemy of Egypt as a grain exporter (Asia Minor, Syria, and Cyprus producing surpluses of grain for export) may have been in part responsible for their rivalry to secure paramount influence with Rhodes, which was playing an increasingly important role in the grain trade. This idea is supported by the fact that when in 306 Antigonos decided on hostilities with Egypt, he sent a naval flotilla to disrupt trade between Egypt and Rhodes (Diod. XX 82,1–2); and that during the later siege of Rhodes in 305–304, Antigonos attempted to bring over to his side all Rhodian seamen and traders operating in Syria, Phoenicia, Kilikia, and Pamphylia by promising them the freedom of the ports in his realm if they would abstain from aiding Rhodes (Polyainos IV 6,16).

While it is not possible, then, to describe Antigonos's foreign trade policy in detail, there is sufficient evidence to indicate that he was interested in this matter, took at least occasional initiatives connected with it, had in general a policy of promoting a healthy surplus of exports over imports in the foreign trade of his empire, and sought to promote self-sufficiency within the empire and to set up a government monopoly in the grain trade.

Turning to his *internal* economic policy, this was probably primarily fiscal in nature—that is, concerned with securing as high an income as possible and regulating his expenditures. That this is how economic policy was regarded in Antigonos's time is directly attested by Ps.-Aristotle *Oikonomikos* II, which is of early Hellenistic date (it mentions in all its examples of economic activity no person or event later than ca. 320).[4] It has long been recognized that the description (at sec. 1, 1–4) of the royal and satrapial economies refers essentially to late Persian times and the period of Alexander and Antigonos (see, e.g., Rostovtzeff, *SEHHW,* 1:441). The author speaks of the royal

---

4. For Ps.-Aristotle *Oikonomikos,* see the Budé edition of A. Wartelle (Paris, 1968), which gives a translation and brief commentary. A fuller commentary was given by van Groningen, *Aristote: Le Deuxième Livre de l'Economique.*

economy being concerned with coinage (i.e., the money supply), with imports and exports (glossed as taxes on these, sent to the king by the satraps),[5] and with expenses: in other words we are here dealing with income (from taxation), the production of coinage, and outlays—all strictly fiscal matters. Likewise the section on the satrapial economy deals exclusively with the governor's finances, deriving from agricultural tribute, from mining, from harbor, land, sales, and cattle taxes, and from poll taxes and taxes on manufacture.

The interest of all this is that it provides us with certain insights into the internal economic organization of Asia in the late fourth century. It appears that the tribute (*phoros* or *ekphorion*) was at least notionally set at one-tenth of agricultural produce, though since we read in the Mnesimachos inscription of a fixed cash tribute, this "tithe" was probably established as a tenth of the average yearly yield, so that the tribute would not vary with good or bad years. Furthermore, it would seem that most economic activity was taxed, as were land and agricultural animals, the latter again at one-tenth. The statement that all products of the earth such as gold, silver, copper, and so on, formed part of the state revenues indicates that in Asia at this time all minerals were considered state property and the mining of them was a royal monopoly. It is not my purpose here to analyze this information in depth and see exactly how far we may be justified in applying it to Antigonos's rule, for this would demand too much space.[6] It suffices to indicate that in general the late-fourth-century date of Ps.-Aristotle's work invites its application to Antigonos, and that nothing obviously rules such an application out. The kinds of taxes and revenues described therefore form an eloquent commentary on certain anecdotes concerning Antigonos's financial administration, for he is said (Plut. *Mor.* 182a = *Apophth. Ant.* 1) to have been more exigent in his demands for money than Alexander, and to have justified this by remarking that whereas Alexander had reaped Asia, he was reduced to gleaning it.

---

5. Thus, at any rate, Wartelle in the Budé ed. (cited in n. 4 above), who in his translation at pp. 9–10 and n. 1 on p. 10 interprets the term *tagēi* in the text as "contribution," which it is clear from the context is sent to the king by the satraps out of import and export taxes (and cf., in the same sense, the Loeb ed. [G. C. Armstrong] at pp. 346–47).

6. Rostovtzeff draws conclusions for the economy of the Seleukid empire from his analysis of the text (*SEHHW,* 1:440–72), and it can therefore hardly be considered an illegitimate proceeding to use its information for Antigonos's empire too; indeed, Rostovtzeff suggests that the author of the pamphlet may have "had in mind and tried implicitly to characterize . . . the kingdom of Antigonus the One-eyed" (p. 441).

This anecdote suggests that in practice there was considerable leeway in the interpretation and application of the various taxes and tributes imposed on the peoples of the empire,[7] and that Antigonos was relatively strict and rigorous in his application of taxes. On the other hand, another anecdote (Plut. *Phok.* 39,1) records that under the even harsher regime of Lysimachos, the peasants of Asia Minor regretted Antigonos's demise, so that in general one might perhaps characterize Antigonos's taxation policy as strict but fair. That the peasantry of Asia Minor were by and large quite well off under Antigonos's rule is further suggested by a passage in Plutarch's *Eumenes* (8,4–5) which tells us that in the early winter of 320/19 Eumenes plundered greater Phrygia to pay his troops,[8] that region having been for the previous thirteen years under Antigonos's governance as satrap. The countryside is described as being full of people and flocks, indicating that it had prospered under Antigonos's governance. There is no reason to suppose that Asia Minor and Syria were less well treated by Antigonos as king than Phrygia had been by Antigonos as satrap. In short, it may reasonably be claimed that so far as he could, Antigonos promoted agricultural productivity and rural prosperity. The already-cited regulation in the edict concerning the Teos/Lebedos synoikism, making it easier for farmers to export produce by freeing them from the obligation of first bringing their produce to the agora of the local city or port of exit, will also have aimed at this.

This is about as much as can reasonably be said about Antigonos's economic policy. To be sure, the establishment of Greco-Macedonian friends and supporters as proprietors of large estates of royal land (for instance, the frequently adduced Mnesimachos: Buckler and Robinson, *Sardis VII,* no. 1), the settling of soldier-colonists on plots of royal land, and the establishment of new or larger Greek cities (colonies and synoikisms), may have had as consequences increased agricultural efficiency and productivity and increased economic activity; and this may well have been to some extent a planned and

7. This notion is supported by many of the anecdotes in section 2 of Ps.-Aristotle *Oikonomikos* II, which are in quite a few instances concerned with the shifts of various satraps such as Mausolos and (under Alexander) Kleomenes of Egypt to interpret their taxation rights widely.

8. See also on this episode the new palimpsest fragment of Arrian's *Met' Alex.* published by Noret in *AC* 52 (1983):235–42. An excellent analysis and discussion of the episode is Briant, *Rois, tributs et paysans,* pp. 56–73.

intended effect. However, the main reason for this activity was probably not economic but political and military.

What does need to be discussed in connection with Antigonos's economic policy is the coinage produced in his realm. Antigonos's attitude to coinage and the money supply is hard to determine, because he struck no coins in his own name; instead throughout his reign the mints of Asia continued to produce Alexander coinage, whether due to deliberate policy of Antigonos or on their own initiative. Consequently any attempt at an in-depth investigation of Antigonos's coining would involve a study of the posthumous Alexander coinage, which is beyond the scope of this work. The failure of Antigonos to put his name on the coinage in his realm is the more surprising in that his satrap of Susiane felt at liberty to put *his* name (Aspeisas) on the Alexander coins minted at Susa (see app. 3, no. 21). The facts that Tyre after 307 became an important mint site for Alexander coinage and that Demetrios subsequently produced his own coinage with his own name, suggest that the continuation of the popular Alexander coinage under Antigonos was a deliberate policy, whether from economic or propagandist motives one cannot say. At any rate a number of important mints within Antigonos's realm kept the empire supplied with coinage of Alexander's type throughout this period: mints at Susa, Babylon, Sidon, and Ake may be mentioned, for example.[9] In the absence of any evidence as to why Antigonos elected, unlike his rivals and his own son, to continue to mint Alexander coinage exclusively, any further discussion of Antigonos's coining policy would be the merest speculation, which is better avoided.

SETTLEMENT POLICY: URBANIZATION AND COLONIZATION

As foreign conquerors the Macedonian rulers of Asia—Alexander no less than Antigonos and the Seleukids—found it necessary to promote the establishment in Asia of large numbers of Greco-Macedonian settlers to act as a kind of permanent garrison of the conquered lands and to provide a continuous supply of manpower for the army

9. On Antigonos's mints and coining policy, see the brief comments of Tarn in *CAH*, 6:487–88. Some recent bibliography on the thorny problems of the posthumous Alexander coinage is given by Seibert, *Diadochen*, p. 55; for the reopening of Tyre as an Antigonid mint producing Alexander coins in 307/6, see Merker, *AncSoc* 5 (1974):119–26.

and the bureaucracy of the new empire. Although Alexander seems to have sought to coopt the Iranian ruling class as partners in the running of the empire,[10] and although we shall see in the section on Antigonos's cultural policy below that Antigonos to a certain extent followed this policy, it is obvious that the Macedonian rulers of Asia had in the first place to rely on Greco-Macedonian helpers and soldiers, the only people whose most vital interests as inhabitants of Asia required them to support the Macedonian rulers. Handsome tribute is regularly paid to Alexander's pioneering work as a founder of Greco-Macedonian colonies in Asia (already briefly discussed in chapter 1 above), and every work discussing the Greco-Macedonian colonization of Asia recognizes the major contributions of Seleukos and his son Antiochos in this respect (see now, e.g., Cohen, *Seleucid Colonies*, pp. 1–14). Between these, however, the colonizing activity of Antigonos is too often passed over with only a brief acknowledgement that he, too, made a contribution.[11]

Several modern scholars have, in fact, recognized that Antigonos's settlement of Greeks and Macedonians in Asia must have been of fundamental importance. In *Die hellenistischen Städtegründungen,* for example, Tscherikower remarks (at pp. 154–55): "Dass Antigonos der bedeutendste unter den unmittelbaren Nachfolgern Alexanders gewesen ist [i.e., as a founder of cities], wird man trotz der mangelhaften Überlieferung zugeben müssen" and "Dass Antigonos als grosser Städtegründer von seinem Nachfolger gepriesen worden wäre wenn er einen Nachfolger gehabt hätte, steht ausser Zweifel." More recently Goukowsky has pointed out that a simple calculation of the potential provenance of Greco-Macedonian colonists in Asia shows that Antigonos must have anticipated much of Seleukos's work.[12] For Seleukos was never in a position to draw recruits for his colonies from Macedon, and neither could he draw upon Greek manpower with anything like the ease Antigonos could.

10. Though there is no agreement on what exactly Alexander was aiming at with regard to the Persians and other Asian peoples and their role in his empire, it is generally agreed that at the very least he planned to use the Persians to help run his empire, this being widely attested in the sources; see, for example, the review and discussion of modern scholarship in Seibert, *Alexander der Grosse,* 186–92.

11. In *Seleucid Colonies,* for example, Cohen makes only scant reference to the work of colonizing done by Antigonos, on which much of the Seleukid colonizing was based; and Wehrli, *Antigone et Démétrios,* pp. 79–93, gives only a very incomplete review of Antigonos's colonizing activities.

12. Goukowsky, "Un Aspect de l'administration d'Alexandre," p. 15 n. 27.

By and large Seleukos must have worked mostly with Greeks and Macedonians already in Asia, which is to say the soldiers and settlers of Antigonos. Indeed, in the case of Antioch and Apamea-on-the-Orontes we are explicitly told by sources that Seleukos founded the cities with settlers who were already present.[13]

Since most of Antigonos's colonizing activity is not recorded in the sources, any full treatment of it must be largely speculative. However, sufficient evidence does survive to show that he was a large-scale colonizer by any reckoning. Moreover, since the cities he is directly recorded as having founded, such as Antigoneia Troas, Antigoneia in Bithynia, and Antigoneia-on-the-Orontes, are reported to have been refounded under new names after his death (as Alexandria Troas, Nikaia, and Antioch respectively), there is every reason to suppose that original foundations of Antigonos's may have been behind many colonies of the Seleukids, and that many of the Macedonian settlements in Asia whose founders are not known may go back to him. Antigonos's settlement policy will be reviewed under five basic headings: care for Greek cities already existing in Asia; Hellenizing of native Asian cities; foundation of entirely new Greek cities; establishment of military colonies which lacked city status; and settling of individual colonists, whether as large estate holders or as soldier-settlers.

As ruler of Asia Minor and Syria/Palestine, Antigonos was fortunate in already having within his realm a considerable Greek element in the form of the old Greek cities established along the coasts of these territories; from Amisos on the Black Sea all the way round the Anatolian coast down to Poseideion in Syria, there were a host of Greek cities of varying sizes and antiquity. A large number of men from these cities are attested in Antigonos's service (see app. 3 for details), and they formed a natural source of supply for officials and officers, mercenary soldiers, and drafts of settlers. It was Antigonos's policy to foster and strengthen this existing Greek element as much as possible. It is clear from the evidence on his relations with the Greek cities that he treated them well and respected their autonomy as far as was consonant with his own security needs as ruler of Asia. What calls for special attention here is his synoikizing activity, which led to the foundation of Antigoneia Troas, the reestablishment of the city of

13. For Antioch-on-the-Orontes, see, for example, Strabo XVI 719 and Diod. XX 47,5–6 (mistakenly calling it Seleukeia). As to Apamea, Strabo records at XVI 752 that the place was called Pella by the first Macedonian settlers, who were hence already settled on the site when Seleukos founded this city of Apamea there.

Smyrna, and the reintegration of Kolophon and its port town of Notion, and which envisioned the synoikism of Teos and Lebedos.

Antigonos's synoikizing was intended to strengthen the Greek cities involved by making them more viable economic and political units. In this he was spectacularly successful in the cases of Antigoneia Troas and Smyrna, which were in Hellenistic and Roman times two of the most flourishing cities of western Asia Minor. Only Strabo reports Antigonos's synoikizing of these cities, stating that he founded Antigoneia Troas (later Alexandria Troas after Lysimachos changed its name) from a number of mostly utterly insignificant Aiolic communities in the Troad: Hamaxitos, Kebrene, Chrysa, Larissa, Kolonai, Neandria, Sigia (on the old site of which Antigoneia was actually founded), and Skepsis—a more important city, which was later given back its independent status by Lysimachos (Strabo XIII 593, 597, and 604).[14] Smyrna had been sacked and razed by the Lydians in the seventh century and had broken up into a number of small villages, and it was on Antigonos's initiative that these were abandoned and the people came back together into a single city, though the process of synoikizing was apparently completed only after Antigonos's death by Lysimachos (Strabo XIV 646). The extension of the city of Kolophon is epigraphically attested, and though Antigonos is explicitly mentioned only as having guaranteed the city's autonomy, it is commonly hypothesized (and surely rightly) that Antigonos was in fact behind the extension of the city.[15] The projected synoikism of Teos and Lebedos, finally, is attested by the famous inscription, which contains portions of two letters by Antigonos setting out arrangements and regulations for the synoikism (see *Syll.*, no. 344; Welles, *RC,* nos. 3 and 4).

Besides fostering and strengthening the Greek cities of the coast, it is highly probable that Antigonos strengthened the native cities in the interior and in particular sought to introduce a Greco-Macedonian population element and turn them into Hellenic *poleis*. Three examples of this may be adduced, unfortunately none of them absolutely secure. In the first place there is the case of Karrhai (= the ancient Mesopotamian city of Harran), where Seleukos, in the winter of

14. On Antigoneia/Alexandria Troas, see Tscherikower, *Städtegründungen,* p. 16, and Robert, *Etudes de numismatique grecque,* pp. 1–55.

15. The inscription in question was first published by B. D. Meritt, *AJPh* 56 (1935):385–97, and was more fully and correctly discussed and analyzed by Robert, *RPh,* 3d ser., 10 (1936):158–64. For the theory that Antigonos was behind the synoikism of Kolophon and Notion, see, for example, Wehrli, *Antigone et Démétrios,* pp. 89–91.

312/11, came upon a colony of Macedonians, some of whom he compelled to join his small army for the attack on Babylonia (Diod. XIX 91,1); the Macedonian colony at Karrhai is also attested by Dio Cassius (XXXVII 5,5), speaking of the time of Pompey. When we wonder who could have established a colony of Macedonians at Karrhai before 312, and consider that the colonists were still of an age for active campaigning in 312/11, the obvious answer is that Antigonos most probably founded the colony around 315/14. It is also probable that Antigonos considerably Hellenized the ancient Phrygian city of Kelainai, which was his satrapial seat and his residence as ruler from 333 to 306. There is no direct evidence of this other than Antigonos's well-attested sojourns at Kelainai, but since Antiochos I founded the Greek city of Apamea Kibotos close by the site of Kelainai, using the population of Kelainai as settlers (Strabo XII 577–78), it may be regarded as almost certain that the population of Kelainai already contained a large Greco-Macedonian element and that this was due to Antigonos (see in this sense, e.g., Tscherikower, *Städtegründungen*, pp. 155–56). The third example is Synnada, which is known to have had a Macedonian colony probably dating from the late fourth century (Tscherikower, *Städtegründungen*, p. 35). This city, near the modern Afyonkarahisar, is first mentioned in the sources as a center of Antigonos's power and seat of his *stratēgos* Dokimos in 302 (Diod. XX 107,3–4). Besides Macedonians, Ionian and Dorian settlers are attested by the city's coinage (see Ruge, *RE*, s.v. Synnada). The colony was most probably founded by Antigonos, perhaps on the site of an earlier Phrygian community.[16]

Several new cities are attested as having been founded by Antigonos, and more can be plausibly conjectured. The sources directly attest to three cities named Antigoneia after himself: near Bithynia (later renamed Nikaia by Lysimachos), at the site of Daskyleion in Hellespontine Phrygia, and on the river Orontes in upper Syria (near the later site of Antioch). The first of these, Antigoneia/Nikaia, was

16. That Synnada was an old Phrygian city Hellenized in the Diadoch period is suggested by the ancient, mythological foundation legend it subsequently adopted (for which see, for example, Jones, *Greek City*, pp. 45, 49–50). The site was an important one, on the Royal Road at its junction with the north-south road from the Bosporos to Pamphylia via Dorylaion, Kelainai, and the Klimax pass over the Taurus; and it is hence hard to believe that it had been entirely overlooked as a site for settlement until the time of Antigonos. Nevertheless, the mention of it as the seat of Antigonos's *stratēgos* Dokimos and site of a royal treasury of Antigonos is the earliest clearly datable attestation of its existence. For the notion that it was colonized by Antigonos, see, for example, Tscherikower, *Städtegründungen*, pp. 35, 156.

founded on the eastern shore of Lake Ascania at the site of modern Iznik, in a position where it could watch over Bithynia and the cities of the Propontis, as well as the north-south routes from Europe into Asia Minor via the Bosporos (Strabo XII 565; Steph. Byz. s.v. Nikaia). Antigoneia by Daskyleion is mentioned only by Stephanos of Byzantion (s.v. Antigoneia); Daskyleion was the seat of the Persian satraps of Hellespontine Phrygia and hence an important place, though it does not seem to have been a city (see the description of it in Xenophon *Hellenika* IV 1,15–16). Recent exploratory excavations have established its site as being on the southeastern shore of Lake Manyas and have shown the presence of Persian and early Hellenistic remains.[17] However, the place does not seem ever to have grown into an important city, though having a strategic location for overseeing Hellespontine Phrygia.

The most important of the three was undoubtedly Antigoneia-on-the-Orontes, which was Antigonos's residence from 306 to 302. It is the only one of Antigonos's foundations for which we have relatively full and accurate information on the date of foundation, the number and provenance of the colonists, and the size of the city; this is due to the face that Diodoros reports its foundation in 306 (Diod. XX 47,5) and that later writers interested in the great and famous city of Antioch were necessarily interested in Antigoneia, because Antioch was basically a re-foundation of Antigoneia at an adjacent site and using the population of Antigoneia.[18] The site of this Antigoneia seems to have been inland somewhat from Antioch, near the point where the tributary from the lake north-east of Antioch (the modern Lake Amik) joins the Orontes; ancient ruins have been found there and the identification of these with Antigoneia, already made in Kiepert's atlas of the ancient world (*Atlas antiquus* V map 1), is accepted by Downey in his monographs on Antioch.[19] Despite the destruction of Antigoneia by Seleukos in 301, the place is mentioned as still existing in 53 B.C. by Dio Cassius XL 39,1–2; presumably it continued to be inhabited by a remnant of its former population and became a *kome* of Antioch, as Tscherikower conjectures (*Städtegründungen*, p. 61).

17. See, for example, the *Princeton Encyclopedia of Classical Sites*, ed. R. Stillwell (Princeton, 1976), p. 259, citing the relevant bibliography.

18. For sources, see, for example, Downey, *Ancient Antioch*, pp. 29–39, and Jones, *Cities*, pp. 237–38, 242–43.

19. For example, at *Ancient Antioch*, p. 29 n. 7, citing the report of the eighteenth-century traveler Pococke, who saw ancient ruins at this site.

Besides these three clearly attested new cities, several other cities may be conjectured to have been founded by Antigonos. On the Gulf of Issos the modern city of Iskenderun occupies the site of an early Hellenistic foundation usually called Alexandria-by-Issos, though the city was actually many miles south of the town of Issos. In spite of a late tradition that the city was founded by Alexander himself—obviously simply deduced from the name Alexandria—it is clear that it was in fact founded by one of the successors, the obvious candidates being Antigonos and Seleukos (see in this sense, e.g., Tscherikower *Städtegründungen,* pp. 58–59). Of the two, the former is the more likely candidate. Strabo tells us that the successors of Alexander considered it an act of piety to name a city after Alexander and that Lysimachos renamed Antigoneia Troas after Alexander (Strabo XIII 593). Ptolemy similarly put his energy into building up the famous Alexandria in Egypt. Appian tells us that Seleukos named some cities in honor of Alexander, and mentions Alexandropolis in India and Alexandreschata in Scythia (Appian *Syr.* 57). If, as seems implied by Strabo, Antigonos also followed this practice, Alexandria-by-Issos is an obvious place to have been founded by him, for as a port it was clearly intended to serve as the end-point of the great trade route from inner Asia through upper Mesopotamia, and, just as it now is the port of Antakya, to serve as the port of upper Syria.[20] Seleukos built Seleukia-in-Pieria to fulfill this function, so we should most probably link the building of Alexandria with the foundation of Antigoneia-on-the-Orontes, with which it would have been connected by the excellent route still used.

A large number of military colonies (*katoikiai*) that probably did not, in origin at least, possess the status of *poleis* are known to have been founded in Asia Minor, Syria/Palestine, and Media, and it is commonly supposed that Antigonos was responsible for some.[21] Again, a few can be singled out as being particularly plausible, while for the rest it can only be said that one should not automatically assume a Seleukid founder for any of these *katoikiai*. Stephanos mentions a *phrourion* called Antigoneia in the Kyzikene some fifty stades west of Kyzikos on the coast (Steph. Byz. s.v. Antigoneia).

20. On Alexandria-by-Issos as a port serving the route into inner Asia via the lower Orontes valley and upper Mesopotamia, see, for example, Benzinger, *RE* s.v. Alexandria, no. 15. Wehrli, *Antigone et Démétrios,* p. 79, points to the likelihood that this town was intended to be the port of Antigoneia, just as Seleukia in fact became the port of Antioch.

21. See, for example, the remarks of Tscherikower, *Städtegründungen,* pp. 154–59, and Griffith, *Mercenaries,* pp. 149–53.

Approximately at the right distance from Kyzikos on the coast of the Kyzikene (i.e., the large peninsula jutting out into the Sea of Marmara by Kyzikos) lay the ancient town or village of Artake, at the site of modern Erdek (on this place, see Hirschfeld, *RE,* s.v. Artake no. 1). Possibly the fort called Antigoneia was the base of a garrison/colony settled near Artake by Antigonos to secure the Kyzikene against possible attacks by Lysimachos. In Phrygia a little to the north of Synnada there was a small town called Dokimeion, obviously founded by Antigonos's *stratēgos* Dokimos. The place is called a *kōmē* (village) of Synnada by Strabo (XII 577) and Stephanos (Steph. Byz. s.v. Synnada), though its coinage seems to indicate that it later became a *polis*.[22] Its coins proclaim Macedonian origin, and it is probable that the place was originally a settlement of veterans who had served under Dokimos as garrison troops in Phrygia.

Concerning the great city of Apameia-on-the-Orontes, the military headquarters of the Seleukid empire, Strabo informs us (XVI 752) that the "first Macedonians" who settled there called the place Pella before it was named Apameia by Seleukos after his wife. Again the obvious inference is that Antigonos (who may well have been a native of Pella—see pp. 17–18 above) founded a colony of Macedonian *katoikoi* on this site with the name Pella, which Seleukos later refounded as a city and named Apameia (thus, e.g., Tscherikower, *Städtegründungen,* pp. 158–59). The same may have been the case with Seleukia-in-Pieria: Strabo informs us (XVI 2,8) that Seleukia was originally called Hydatos Potamoi; Diodoros knows of a town in upper Syria in 312 named Potamoi Karōn (XIX 79,6), near Poseideion at the mouth of the Orontes. These towns, named Potamoi from their location at the Orontes Delta, are presumably in fact one and the same place—to judge by the name Diodoros gives, perhaps a settlement of Karian veterans. Such a settlement, existing already in 312, can only have been founded by Antigonos; like Pella it was evidently resettled, expanded, and renamed by Seleukos.

The region of Rhagai in Media was settled by Greco-Macedonian colonists in the early Hellenistic period, and Tscherikower conjectured (*Stadtegründungen,* p. 159) that this might have been in part the work of Antigonos, citing in support of this hypothesis Diod. XIX 44,4, where the prominent mention of Rhagai as a site where Antigonos quartered soldiers in 316/15 may be the remnant of a longer notice in Hieronymos describing the settlement of soldiers there as

22. Tscherikower, *Städtegründungen,* p. 35.

garrison/colonists. In favor of this hypothesis, I would also adduce Polyainos IV 6,15 where we learn that of the 3,000 Macedonian *argyraspides,* a third were sent to Sibyrtios in Arachosia in 315, and the remaining 2,000 were stationed in various "secure and out-of-the-way sites" (χωρία . . . ἐχυρὰ καὶ δύσβατα) as garrisons. The description "secure and out-of-the-way" fits the region of Rhagai, in the northeastern corner of Media, very well, and it may be that the settling of these 2,000 Macedonian troublemakers as soldier-colonists in the Rhagai area is cryptically referred to by both Diodoros and Polyainos.

Other significant areas of Greco-Macedonian settlement were the so-called Dekapolis in Palestine, the region of Kilikia in southern Asia Minor, and Lydia in western Asia Minor, where a host of small towns boasted in Roman times of Macedonian origins: for example, Nakrasa, Thyateira, Mostene, and Hyrkanis (see Tscherikower, *Städtegründungen,* pp. 21–24). Again, it is possible that Antigonos had a hand in founding some of these settlements, though this cannot be proved.[23] There are, however, indications of Antigonos settling individual colonists on estates or farm plots in Lydia, in the already often cited Mnesimachos inscription. This records the granting by Antigonos of a large estate in the Sardian plain to Mnesimachos and of *klēroi* (lots) within it, mentioning two individuals named Pytheos and Adrastos as holders of part of the estate (perhaps the two *klēroi,* in which case these men would probably be soldier-settlers).[24] We can be sure that the facts we learn from the Mnesimachos inscription do not form an isolated case: note for example that Diodoros XIX 25,2 reports that in seeking to bring over to himself the army of Eumenes in 316, Antigonos promised to give them large gifts of land. Clearly, what Antigonos promised to deserters from Eumenes he must also have granted his own officers and soldiers. We may be sure that he gave many estates such as that of Mnesimachos to prominent supporters, and settled many soldiers as *klērouchoi* (allotment holders) on royal and other lands in Asia. An indication of this seems to be

23. On the Dekapolis in Palestine, and on Kilikia, see Tscherikower, *Städtegründungen,* pp. 157–59; from the simple calculation of numbers of Macedonian soldiers available to Antigonos and Seleukos respectively, it is likely that Antigonos played a major role in colonizing Asia Minor (see for this, e.g., Griffith, *Mercenaries,* pp. 149–53), though it must be borne in mind that Lysimachos too may have been active colonizing in this region between 301 and 282.

24. Thus quite plausibly, for example, Atkinson, *Historia* 21 (1972):70–71, though in other respects (such as dating, and the nature of Mnesimachos's contract with the temple wardens of Artemis) I disagree with her (see chap. 7 n. 69 above).

provided by an inscription from Iasos in Karia recording that soldiers established in nearby forts by Antigonos's general Polemaios held parcels of land in the region and were hence intended to remain settled there.[25]

Though I have broken down Antigonos's settlement activity into the above five types, this is simply a convenient way of arranging the evidence for analysis. There is no reason to suppose that Antigonos himself distinguished the categories I have identified above, and in fact there was clearly some overlap between the various types of settlement activity. For example, since Antigoneia Troas was an entirely new city, it had in some ways more in common with such new foundations as Antigoneia-on-the-Orontes than with synoikisms like those at Smyrna and Kolophon. Again it is not clear whether Synnada was a new foundation or an old Phrygian town now Hellenized, and similarly it is not certain to what extent there was already existing indigenous settlement at the sites of Antigoneia/Nikaia (previously called Ankore according to Steph. Byz. s.v. Nikaia) and Antigoneia/Daskyleion. Furthermore the distinction between individual settlers and soldiers settled together in *katoikiai* is not a clear one. Though the Mnesimachos inscription, if rightly interpreted, indicates that some soldiers were settled on individual lots or estates, it seems likely that it was more common for soldiers to be settled in groups according more or less to their military units, and as such they would also have received *klēroi* to farm. The colony at Karrhai appears to have been of this sort, and an inscription from Thyateira shows that in Seleukid times, at least, soldiers were sometimes settled as a unit, complete with officers.[26] The findings of this review of settlement activity by Antigonos are shown here in figure 6.

The fact that eighteen foundations or areas of colonization can be attributed to Antigonos with at least a fair degree of probability notwithstanding the extremely defective evidence shows that he certainly deserves to be considered the forerunner of the Seleukids in this respect. As mentioned above, the major reason for supposing even where evidence is lacking that Antigonos is nevertheless likely to have laid the foundation for the subsequent work of Seleukos is that Antigonos had greater access to Macedonian and Greek manpower

25. For this inscription, see Blümel, *I. Iasos,* 1, no. 2. From line 24 it emerges that some of the soldiers were *katoikountas* in Iasian territory, which may indicate that they had been settled there as garrison-colonists.

26. See *OGIS,* no. 211, a dedication to a King Seleukos by the officers and soldiers of the Macedonians at Thyateira.

1. ?Alexandria-by-Issos
2. Antigoneia-by-Daskyleion
3. Antigoneia Kyzikena
4. Antigoneia Bithyniake (Nikaia)
5. Antigoneia-on-the-Orontes (Antioch)
6. Antigoneia Troas (Alexandria)
7. Dokimeion
8. Iasos
9. ? Karrhai
10. ? Kelainai (Apameia Kibotos)
11. ? Kolophon
12. Lydia—settlers in plain of Sardis: Mnesimachos et al.
13. ? Pella (Apameia-on-the-Orontes)
14. ? Potamoi Karon/Hydatos (Seleukia-in-Pieria)
15. ? Rhagai in Media
16. Smyrna
17. ? Synnada
18. Teos/Lebedos

(Question mark indicates that colonizing by Antigonos is not certain; additional names in parentheses show later name changes by action of Lysimachos or the Seleukids.)

Figure 6. Cities or Regions Colonized by Antigonos

than was ever the case for Seleukos and his successors. In 320 Antigonos received 8,500 Macedonian infantrymen from Antipatros, and despite losses in battle between 319 and 315, the number of Macedonian troops in Antigonos's service would have risen considerably due to his incorporation of the armies of defeated rivals: the army of Eumenes in 319, that of Alketas and Attalos in the same year, the troops of Arrhidaios and Kleitos in 318/17, and the second army of Eumenes at the beginning of 315. All of these armies had Macedonian elements in them, sometimes substantial ones (see app. 2 below for details). Consequently Antigonos may conservatively be estimated to have had somewhere around 20,000 Macedonians (infantry and cavalry) in 315 to draw on for settlers.

Since Kassandros secured control of Macedon in 315, and at the end of that year became an enemy of Antigonos, no further drafts of Macedonian soldiers could be expected, and to maintain his Macedonian infantry and cavalry (and officer corps) Antigonos could henceforth only resort to the expedient of settling his own troops in Asia and drafting their sons into his army. As most of Antigonos's Macedonians were already veterans in 315, it must be assumed that he began to settle them in colonies long before his end in 301, and this is shown to be so by the evidence concerning Karrhai, Rhagai, Pella/Apameia, Potamoi/Seleukia, and so on. Seleukos cannot have had more than a handful of Macedonians in his service before 301, and though he would then have inherited part of Antigonos's army (which probably included 6,000 new Macedonians brought from Europe by Demetrios in 302: see Plut. *Dem.* 23,1), after the division with Lysimachos he would scarcely have received a sufficient number of Macedonians to carry out the extensive colonization attributed to him. Much of it must simply have been a completion/reorganization of colonization begun by Antigonos.

Of course, one should not suppose that those places attested as Macedonian foundations, or *katoikiai,* were peopled exclusively with Macedonians. There were never enough Macedonians in Asia to people the large number of cities and colonies attested to have had Macedonian settlers. In 316 a substantial element in Antigonos's army was formed by people of various (Asian?) origins (*pantodapoi*) armed in Macedonian fashion: it seems very likely that these men were settled together with Macedonians in the *katoikiai,* both by Antigonos and by the Seleukids. Their descendants would doubtless simply be considered "Macedonians." In addition a large number of the settlers in Asia were certainly Greeks. Undoubtedly many Greek mercenary soldiers received *klēroi* and were settled in *katoikiai* along with the Macedonians, the more so as the difference between Macedonians and Greeks rapidly became of little importance in Asia, particularly in late Hellenistic times. However, in the time of Antigonos the difference between Greek and Macedonian was still fresh, and probably most of the Greeks who settled in Asia preferred to do so as members of the new Greek *poleis* founded by Antigonos and the Seleukids.

The major source of settlers for the new *poleis,* however, was drafts of colonists from old Greek cities—those in Asia Minor certainly, and, under Antigonos at least, also the cities of mainland Greece. Again, since Antigonos had great influence in Greece from

314 on and essentially controlled the Greek cities of Asia Minor from 317 on, whereas Seleukos conquered Asia Minor only just before his death and had no particular influence in mainland Greece at any time, it may justly be assumed that many of Seleukos's new *poleis* built on foundations already laid by Antigonos. A case in point is the great Antioch-on-the-Orontes, which was peopled with the settlers of the nearby Antigoneia: 5,300 men, we are told, of Athenian and Macedonian origin.[27] Whereas Antigonos was in a position in 306 to obtain a large draft of colonists from Athens, such was never the case for Seleukos, who obtained his manpower simply from Antigonos's existing foundation. The mix of a large number of Greeks with some Macedonians appears to have been typical for Antigonos's foundations: Dio Chrysostom of Nikaia (formerly Antigoneia) tells us that the original settlers of this city were "Macedonians and the first of the Greeks" (Dio Chrys. *Orat.* XXXIX 1). His meaning is that the Greeks settled there were not drifting riffraff but proper colonists drawn from reputable Greek cities.

There were two relatively distinct strands to Antigonos's settlement policy. One was colonization, which refers to the policy of settling soldiers with *klēroi* in return for military service. This policy aimed to secure the military viability of the realm by arranging for a continuous supply of recruits for the army: in the first place, trustworthy Greeks and Macedonians, but also doubtless soldiers of other races.[28] The other strand was urbanization: the synoikism of small Greek *poleis,* the Hellenization and expansion of native cities, and the foundation of new *poleis.* This policy of building up an infrastructure of urban centers within the realm must partly have served a cultural purpose (Hellenization), partly a political function (as self-governing entities, the cities would not require constant administrative supervision, but would administer and watch over large areas of Asian territory), and partly an economic function (the cities could be expected to exploit their lands efficiently and to become centers of trade and manufacture). In some cases a further, distinct policy is discernible, as for example with the four Antigoneias (Troas, Kyzikena, Daskyleion, Nikaia) founded in the Hellespontine

27. Malalas, p. 201 (Bonn ed.), and cf. Jones, *Cities,* p. 238 and n. 16.

28. Examples of the latter may have been the Pytheos and Adrastos who are named in the Mnesimachos inscription as (apparently) soldier-settlers: they seem to have been Lydians (see Buckler and Robinson, *AJA* 16 [1912]:29, 38).

region between 310 and 307.[29] These foundations must have been intended to help settle the region after the rebellion of Phoinix in 310, and perhaps also to serve as outposts against the power of Lysimachos, who in 309 built Lysimacheia on the European side of the Hellespont (Diod. XX 29,1).

A final point that may be made concerns the success of Antigonos's foundations and synoikisms. Though some of these (such as Antigoneia-by-Daskyleion and Teos/Lebedos) never really got off the ground, many of the others had a lasting impact. Under their new names Alexandria Troas, Nikaia, and Antioch, three of Antigonos's foundations became cities of major importance in the Hellenistic world and later in the Roman Empire. Synnada grew to be the metropolis of northen Phrygia and one of the most flourishing cities in Asia Minor (see Ruge, *RE,* s.v.); and, as Apameia Kibotos and Apameia-on-the-Orontes respectively, the towns of Kelainai and Pella were also important urban centers. It is clear that Antigonos and his advisers made excellent choices in selecting locations for colonization and city foundation. There was nothing mean about Antigonos's settlement policy: for example, Antigoneia-on-the-Orontes is said to have been founded with a circuit of seventy stades (ca. seven and a half miles: Diod. XX 47,5); and with 5,300 adult male Greek and Macedonian settlers, its Greco-Macedonian population must have been about 20,000 including women and children—no doubt considerably larger still counting slaves and Asians. All in all then, Antigonos's settlement activity clearly played a considerable part in creating the Hellenistic world.

CULTURAL POLICY

Under the heading of cultural policy, two aspects of Antigonos's rule need to be discussed. In the first place, there is the question of what his attitude was to the native Asian peoples of his empire, and, connected with this, the matter of whether he consciously pursued a

29. The *terminus post quem* is 311, at which date Skepsis was still an independent community (*OGIS,* nos. 5 and 6), though subsequently brought into the synoikism of Antigoneia Troas (Strabo XIII 597); the *terminus ante quem* is the fact that in 306 Antigonos was in Syria founding Antigoneia-on-the-Orontes (Diod. XX 47,5), whereafter we know he was in Egypt and then again in Syria until 302. Hence only the years 310–307 remain for these cities to have been founded by Antigonos.

policy of Hellenization. Secondly, one should consider whether Antigonos—like the Ptolemies and Attalids, for example—encouraged or patronized letters and arts, or whether he was indifferent to cultural matters of this kind. The evidence on both of these questions is fragmentary and it is certainly the case that we can only seek to infer Antigonos's policy from the little that is known of his acts in regard to these matters; but enough is known for at least an outline of Antigonos's policy to be reconstructed.

Much has been made by the more encomiastic modern biographers of Alexander the Great—such as W. W. Tarn—of his plans to associate at least the Iranian upper class in the ruling of his empire, and it is usually supposed that when Alexander died the notion of allowing anyone other than Greeks and Macedonians a share in the running of the empire died with him.[30] In his article on the ruling class in the Hellenistic monarchies, Christian Habicht fleshes out this supposition somewhat by pointing out that a review of several hundred persons known to have held important positions in the Seleukid empire shows only some 2.5 percent to be of non–Greco-Macedonian race, and that even these few representatives of the Asian peoples made their mark almost exclusively in the third and subsequent generations after Alexander.[31] Antigonos's policy in this respect was more like Alexander's than that of the early Hellenistic monarchs: of the 128 friends and subordinates of Antigonos whom I have been able to identify, the ethnic origin of 82 is known or can be plausibly inferred; 9 of them were Asians—11 percent.[32] Though the sample is rather small, it is nevertheless striking that the percentage is more than four times that found by Habicht for the Seleukid empire, especially considering that our literary and epigraphical sources are almost exclusively Greek and

30. Thus, for example, Jones, *Greek City*, p. 6; Goukowsky, *Essai*, p. 119; Tarn, *CAH*, 6:433–37.

31. Habicht, *VSWG* 45 (1958):5.

32. The nine Asian natives are: Aspeisas of Susa, Demarchos son of Taron (Lykian), Mithridates of Kios and Mithridates Ktistes (Persians), Orontobates the Mede, Philetairos (Paphlagonian), Pytheos and Sagarios (Lydian), and Zipoites of Bithynia. Forty-six of the friends and subordinates of Antigonos I have been able to identify are of unknown ethnicity. Though all of them have Greek names, this does not necessarily mean that they were all Greeks or Macedonians, for by the late fourth century many Asians already had Greek names: for instance, Demarchos and Philetairos listed above, and one may also adduce the famous Phoenician Philokles, king of Sidon (for whom see, e.g., J. Seibert, *Historia* 19 [1970]:337–51). Among the above-mentioned forty-six subordinates of Antigonos, it might be conjectured, for example, that the Theodotos who commanded a flotilla manned by Karians in 313 (Diod. XIX 64,5–7) could himself have been a Karian; and the soldier-settler Adrastos may have been a Lydian.

tend to mention only those subordinates of Antigonos involved with Greek affairs.

In other words, it looks as if Antigonos adopted a fairly liberal and conciliatory policy towards the so-called "subject races" of the empire, that is, the various indigenous Asian peoples. This is a significant fact, if true, since Antigonos has sometimes been accused of being harsh and insensitive towards the Asian peoples, to the detriment of his ability to establish firm rule over them.[33] This evaluation of Antigonos's attitude towards the subject peoples is in essence based on a handful of passages in the sources: Diod. XIX 48,5, where Antigonos replaces the popular Peukestas as satrap of Persia and violently quells dissent over this move; Diod. XIX 92,4, where it is said that many of the Persian soldiers in the army of Antigonos's general Nikanor went over to Seleukos because they were offended by Antigonos's conduct; and the events around Babylonia (recorded by the Bab. Chron., rev. lines 1–43; Diod. XIX 90,1–91,2; Plut. *Dem.* 7,3) from which it transpires that the Babylonians preferred to be ruled by Seleukos rather than by Antigonos, and that Antigonos's forces ravaged Babylonia during the war with Seleukos and caused widespread destruction.

While all of this evidence does show that Peukestas and Seleukos were more popular among the Persians and Babylonians than Antigonos, it says very little as to his overall policy with regard to these peoples. The point is surely that as satraps of specific regions, men like Peukestas and Seleukos could devote themselves to the interests of the local inhabitants in a way Antigonos, who ruled these regions only from a great distance and by proxy, could not. Hence he was very likely to be relatively unpopular, an unpopularity probably caused more by his local satraps and generals than by any action or policy of his own devising.[34] The fact that Antigonos in 315 appointed natives—Orontobates the Mede and Aspeisas of Susa—to rule the important satrapies of Media and Susiane suggests that he wished to conciliate the Asian peoples as much as possible; these two

33. For this, see for example, Jouguet, *Macedonian Imperialism,* p. 136, and Schober, *Gesch. Babyloniens,* pp. 96–102.

34. One problem would have been that Antigonos was not very interested in the east except as a source of tribute. He would thus not have been led to cultivate the sort of personal popularity sought by men like Seleukos and Peukestas in their satrapies (for Antigonos's indifference to the east, see, e.g., Goukowsky, *Essai,* p. 119). In Asia Minor, on the contrary, his reputation was excellent.

men were in fact the only non-Greeks (or Macedonians) we hear of as appointed to such high offices by any of the Diadochoi after 320.

The appointment of these two Asians as satraps was not the only conciliatory gesture made by Antigonos during his reign. Unlike Lysimachos, for example, he left the Bithynian dynast Zipoites in undisturbed control of his native realm, being content with making an alliance and receiving hostages (for Lysimachos's attempts to conquer and oust the Bithynian dynast, see, e.g., Habicht, *RE,* s.v. Zipoites). Antigonos also permitted the Persian Mithridates to remain in control of his small territory around Kios, and even took Mithridates' homonymous nephew into his court circle (see app. 3, no. 73). The traditional city kings of Phoenicia were also permitted to remain in power by Antigonos (Diod. XIX 58,1–4), except at Tyre, which had a Ptolemaic garrison and which he consequently had to capture by force. It is clear, in short, that Antigonos tried to avoid upsetting the nationalistic sentiments of the Asian peoples, in many cases allowing them to be ruled by men of their own race so that they should not feel themselves to be under foreign oppression.

This point can be taken further, for the two local governors (chiliarchs) whose names survive in the Mnesimachos inscription from Sardis seem to have been natives of the region they governed, Lydia.[35] This is an important fact, since it is with the chiliarchs, the commanders of the local garrisons and collectors of the taxes, that the country inhabitants would have had most to do, and it hence shows sensitiveness to their susceptibilities to have natives in such posts. At least as far as his selection of administrative personnel went, Antigonos thus pursued a policy of conciliating and encouraging the Asian peoples; and when we find a Persian like the younger Mithridates prominent at Antigonos's court, and a Lykian named Demarchos, son of Taron, captaining the bodyguard of Antigonos's daughter-in-law, Phila (see *Syll.*, no. 333), it is reasonable to conclude that Antigonos had no strict policy of enforcing Greco-Macedonian predominance or of excluding Asians from the upper echelons of his service.

35. See app. 3, nos. 104 and 105, Pytheos and Sagarios, the latter bearing a typically Lydian matronymic "son of Koreis" (see Buckler and Robinson, *AJA* 16 [1912]:35). Atkinson, *Historia* 21 (1972):48 n. 4, claims that the word *Koreidos* must be a tribal affiliation, but her sole argument for this is the arbitrary assumption that both Pytheos and Sagarios must have been Macedonians, and in general her treatment of this inscription seems to me wrong in this as in other respects (see chap. 7 n. 69 above for discussion of this).

Nevertheless, there can be no question that in various ways, but above all by his policy of colonization and urbanization, Antigonos contributed considerably to the Hellenization of Asia. The handing over of huge tracts of Asian land as farms and estates to Greek and Macedonian soldiers and officers, and the foundation of a number of full-scale Hellenic *poleis,* with constitutions probably borrowed from one of the old Greek cities,[36] could not help but lead to a certain Hellenization of the areas affected. The question remains, however, to what extent Antigonos consciously aimed at Hellenization. In fact, the settlement policy of Antigonos is largely attributable to the requirements of security and administration rather than to a policy of Hellenization. New Greek cities and Asian cities colonized with Greco-Macedonians would both be bulwarks of the rule of the Macedonian monarchs, as the guarantors of their possession of Asian lands, and would take care of the administration of the territories in Asia allotted to them, thus lightening the administrative burden of the king. Men granted estates, or *klēroi,* by Antigonos would likewise relieve him of the administration of such areas of royal land, and would be loyally bound to the king by these grants, since such estates were revocable, the king retaining a right of "eminent domain."[37]

Ultimately the question of the extent to which Antigonos had a policy of Hellenization depends upon how one defines the term: if one means by it the introduction of a substantial Greco-Macedonian element permanently settled in Asia, then Antigonos was clearly a Hellenizer; but if one takes the term to mean a policy of seeking to acculturize the Asians into Hellenic ways, it may be doubted whether

---

36. That Antigonos may well have done this is indicated, for instance, by the Teos inscription (Welles, *RC,* no. 3) at lines 55–64, which stipulated that until such time as a new law code for the synoikism of Teos/Lebedos should have been drawn up, they were to use the constitution of Kos. Though this use of a constitution from another city was to be only temporary, in the case of new foundations it may well have been done on a permanent basis, as being easier and less potentially troublesome than drawing up a new code. In the case of Antigoneia/Antioch, for example, which was founded with a large number of Athenian settlers, Jones notes (*Cities,* p. 238) that the *boulē* numbered 600, the same as at Athens after 307, which suggests that the constitution of Antigoneia/Antioch may have been at least in part borrowed from that of Athens.

37. The Mnesimachos inscription (Buckler and Robinson, *Sardis VII,* no. 1) indicates at col. 2, lines 12–15, that the estate granted to Mnesimachos might be taken back by the king, which shows that Antigonos retained a right of proprietorship and that such estates were hence revocable. In general it is clear that estates and *klēroi* were awarded not only in return for past service but also with an expectation of future service, and that the soldiers settled on *klēroi* and their sons were liable for military service in return for their farming lots.

he had any such policy. The Hellenization of Asia in this sense seems, to the extent that it occurred at all, to have been merely an unpremeditated by-product of the fact that the ruling class in Asia under Antigonos and the Seleukids was Greco-Macedonian, which caused a number of ambitious Asians to adopt Greek names and try to break into the circles of privilege by assimilating Hellenic culture. Since as far as we can tell from our evidence Antigonos mostly used Macedonians and Greeks as high officers and officials, he may well have been responsible for a certain amount of Hellenization of this sort; but insofar as he was apparently readier to admit non-Greco-Macedonians to his service and the circle of his *philoi* than were the early Seleukids, he would have contributed relatively less than they to this form of Hellenization.

In effect, though Antigonos saw that his power must be based on a substantial stratum of Greeks and Macedonians in Asia who would be self-interestedly loyal to Macedonian rule, he does not seem to have entirely abandoned Alexander's hope of also being able to employ Asians in the running of his realm, and hence was not a thorough or conscious Hellenizer. Antigonos's extensive use of Asian manpower in his armies, in addition to his Asian officers and officials, is indicative of this. Lykians, Pamphylians, Lydians, Phrygians, Parthians, and Medes are all explicitly attested as serving in considerable numbers in Antigonos's armies, as are Karians and Kilikians in his navies (see app. 2 below). And these were not just marginal light infantry, there to make up numbers: the Medes and Parthians were among Antigonos's most important cavalry units in the war against Eumenes, and the Lydians and Phrygians were also cavalry; the Lykians and Pamphylians were heavy infantry, making up part of Antigonos's phalanx along with Macedonians and Greek mercenaries. In addition a substantial portion of Antigonos's heavy infantry phalanx was made up of men of mixed—but certainly mostly Asian—races, armed in the Macedonian fashion: the so-called *pantodapoi*.[38]

By incorporating Asians into his phalanx in this way, to make up nearly half of its total numbers, Antigonos made it clear, I think, that

---

38. For the use by Antigonos of Median, Parthian, Lydian, and Phrygian cavalry, and of Lykians, Pamphylians, and *pantodapoi* in his phalanx, see, for example, Diod. XIX 29,1–3. N.B., the phalanx is here (battle of Paraitakene in 316) made up of 9,000 Greek mercenaries, 3,000 Lykians and Pamphylians, 8,000 *pantodapoi,* and 8,000 Macedonians, so that considerably more than a third of the phalanx was made up of Asian troops. That the *pantodapoi* were at least predominantly of oriental race is shown by the fact that the Macedonian and Greek mercenary troops are listed separately; hence the *pantodapoi* can only have been Asians.

he meant to use and rely on the Asian peoples of his empire as well as the Greco-Macedonians, even if as a Macedonian himself he must needs rely on the latter in the first instance. In this, of course, he was following the example of the Achaemenids as well as of Alexander, for they too had used subject peoples in their armies and had allowed non-Persians to hold high offices in the empire: examples are the Karian Hekatomnid family, who were satraps of Karia in the fourth century, and the Kappadokian Datames, satrap of Kappadokia early in the same century. But of course the Persians remained the dominant people in the Achaemenid empire, just as the Greco-Macedonians were in the empire of Antigonos and the Seleukids.

Moving on to the question of whether Antigonos was a patron of arts and letters and encouraged Hellenic culture in that respect, one may answer unequivocally that he was and did. There is evidence in support of this statement, and though in sum it hardly suffices to place him on a level with Ptolemy or the Attalids, it shows nevertheless that Antigonos had a keen interest in Greek culture and fostered it at his court. One may start by recalling that Antigonos was himself a man who had evidently enjoyed a good education and showed a fair degree of wit and discrimination. Such anecdotes as we have concerning Antigonos's court do not show him, like his son Demetrios, indulging in excessive drinking or consorting with *hetairai,* but rather listening to or conversing with men of letters.

Two examples are reported by Plutarch in *Apophthegmata Antigonou* numbers 13 and 14 (at *Mor.* 182d–e), the first of which records an occasion when a young pupil of Anaximenes delivered an oration before Antigonos. When the latter sought further information, the young man was silent, and he was thereupon chided by Antigonos with a line from Euripides for declaiming by rote rather than from knowledge of the subject. The second anecdote likewise concerns Antigonos listening to an orator, whose pompous rhetoric he deflated. Another instance, also recorded by Plutarch (*Mor.* 11b–c), is the pressing dinner invitation Antigonos sent to the sophist Theokritos of Chios, who was evidently living at Antigonos's court at the time. The picture that emerges is of a man who encouraged men of learning and letters to visit his court, and who liked to listen to them declaim and to converse with them over dinner. He also seems to have had an interest in music, to judge from an anecdote preserved by Aelian (*VH* IX 36) about how Antigonos was listening to a harper and kept correcting him, to the latter's irritation—though since the same story is told of Philip, including exactly the same retort by the harper (see Plut. *Mor.* 179b), one cannot place much reliance on the genuineness of this anecdote.

At any rate, Antigonos's interest in and encouragement of men of letters is well attested and can be further illustrated from the number of historians who emerged from his court circle. Besides the famous Hieronymos of Kardia, a *philos* and aide of his in the period 315–301, who may well already have been working on his great contemporary history during those years, one might mention Marsyas of Pella, Antigonos's half-brother, and his friends Nearchos the Kretan and Medeios of Larissa. Marsyas wrote a history of Macedon from early times down to 330, Nearchos wrote a memoir on Alexander the Great and his own service under Alexander from the Indian campaign (327) to Alexander's death in 323, and Medeios wrote a book from which Strabo cites legends connecting the Armenians with Thessaly through a supposedly Thessalian eponymous ancestor, as well as other quasi-geographical legends, which seem to indicate that Medeios's book may have been a history of Alexander.[39] We have no way of knowing when Medeios wrote his book, but it is very likely that Nearchos and Marsyas wrote near the end of the fourth century, when they were at Antigonos's court.

It seems, then, that there was quite a circle of literary men at the court of Antigonos, and while there is no direct evidence that Antigonos actually encouraged these men in their writing, it has been suggested that Nearchos made propaganda in his book for the legitimacy of Alexander's supposed son Herakles in order to further Antigonos's political schemes for this youth (thus Pearson, *Lost Histories,* pp. 116–18), which would suggest that Antigonos may well have had some influence on the writing of Nearchos at least. Besides his evident keenness on literary conversation and his apparent interest in history writing, one may further point out that Antigonos patronized the greatest painters of his day, Apelles and Protogenes, both of whom painted portraits of him (Pliny *NH* XXXV 90; 96; and 106), a portrait of Antigonos by Apelles having especial fame and being subsequently displayed in the Asklepieion at Kos (Strabo XIV 657). Again, in 302 Antigonos planned to celebrate the founding of Antigoneia-on-the-Orontes with games and a festival, for which he

39. On Marsyas of Pella, see Heckel, *Hermes* 108 (1980):444–62; on Nearchos the Kretan, see Pearson, *Lost Histories,* pp. 111–49; and for Medeios of Larissa's book, see Jacoby, *FGrH,* no. 129. Nearchos is generally thought to have written his book between ca. 315 and 300 B.C., when he was certainly with Antigonos (see app. 3, no. 77); Marsyas clearly began to write after 330 and probably was with Antigonos from that date on.

had gathered athletes, musicians, and actors from all over Greece; and though military preoccupations forced him to abandon the festival, he distributed some 200 talents to the athletes and artists by way of compensation.

On the basis of the present evidence, one can hardly attribute to Antigonos a consistent or coherent cultural policy like Ptolemy's in founding the Mouseion at Alexandria, but it is reasonable to conclude that Antigonos had at least a strong interest in cultural matters, and that his court was not without attraction and rewards for men of literary, musical, or artistic accomplishment. Whereas Ptolemy after 301 enjoyed a long period of peaceful rule in which he could give his mind to peaceful pursuits, Antigonos enjoyed no such respite from constant preoccupation with wars and pressing political concerns, so that cultural interests can never have occupied more than a small portion of his time. While this prevented him from developing a full cultural policy, it makes the cultural interests that are attested for him all the more worthy of remark.

Conclusion

The picture of Antigonos as a state builder presented here in the last few chapters has taken us a long way from the traditional picture of the hubristic Antigonos yearning after Alexander's empire and ultimately failing. In a way the battle of Ipsos was for Antigonos as much as anything a propaganda failure: its negative outcome has turned historical enquiry away from investigation of his work in Asia and caused his achievements there to be largely underestimated and overlooked. If the battle had been won, Antigonos would be justly famous as the founder of an Antigonid empire in Asia. Though this did not happen, the fact remains that Antigonos was a brilliant and innovative general and a statesman whose career and policies profoundly affected the course of history in his own time and later, and whose work of colonizing and establishing an administrative system did not simply disappear, but became the basis on which the Seleukid dynasty founded its empire.

There can be little doubt that Antigonos was a great general, probably one of the best of the ancient world. His brilliant victories at Orkynia and Kretopolis in 319 and against Kleitos on the Hellespont in 317, and his coolness and resourcefulness in the long duel with Eumenes, highlighted by the great battles of Paraitakene and Gabiene, prove that he was a superb battle leader: determined, decisive, inventive, and controlled. He knew how to turn a setback into a victory and how to make a victory decisive; and he understood the capacities and temper of his men, a quality Eumenes, otherwise more or less Antigonos's equal as a general, seems to have lacked, to his undoing. Like the most famous generals of antiquity—Alexander and Caesar—Antigonos knew the importance of daring and surprise in warfare, and that these can best be achieved by speed; consequently he—again like Caesar and Alexander—demanded great exertions of his men, but like them he softened this by undergoing the same exertions himself (no mean feat for a man in his sixties) and by showing great solicitude for his men's well-being.[1] Diodoros's account of the war between Antigonos and Eumenes is a virtually unique document of ancient warfare in giving us a detailed depiction of a war between two truly first-rate generals leading similarly first-rate armies: perhaps only the accounts of the civil war between Caesar and Pompey are comparable in this respect. Antigonos's duel with Eumenes thus gives us uniquely valuable insights into the techniques and methods of early Hellenistic warfare.

In his famous book *Hellenistic Military and Naval Developments,* W. W. Tarn characterizes the spirit of warfare in the Diadoch period as one of professionalism and intense thoroughness (see pp. 43–44). Antigonos may be classed as the supreme professional in an age of professionals, and this is best illustrated by his attention to the technical and technological aspects of warfare. If one considers the surprise march across southern Asia Minor by which Antigonos was able to annihilate Alketas's army in 319 with barely a blow being struck, one thing stands out clearly as a prerequisite to this success, namely military intelligence: Antigonos had to know where Alketas and his army were encamped and how best to get there unnoticed. In premodern warfare there were basically three methods of intelligence gathering: reconnaissance by troops sent out to scout in advance; the interrogation of prisoners and deserters from the enemy; and the interrogation of natives and travelers in the regions in which one was campaigning. Antigonos used all three to good effect in his campaigns, with the result that he habitually knew a great deal about his enemies' strength, whereabouts, and plans.[2]

---

1. Illustrative of this are several passages in Diodoros and anecdotes in other sources. Diod. XIX 15,6: Antigonos refreshes his forces before leading them against Eumenes; Diod. XIX 18,1–2: Antigonos does everything in his power to minimize his men's suffering from summer heat; Diod. XIX 19,2: Antigonos delays for several days at Badake in Susiane to let his men recover from a march; Diod. XIX 20,1–4: Antigonos restores his army's health, wealth, and morale after a difficult march through Kossaian mountains; Plut. *Mor.* 457e and Seneca *De ira* 22,2: Antigonos's concern for his soldiers when he has led them into difficult terrain; Plut. *Pelopidas* 1,1–2: Antigonos provides the best medical care for one of his soldiers.

2. There are numerous examples: Diod. XIX 25,1 tells of Antigonos sending out scouts; at Plut. *Eum.* 15,1 Antigonos gets information from prisoners, and at Diod. XIX 26,4 from (sham) deserters; at Diod. XIX 38,4–5 and 39,2 Antigonos obtains important intelligence from

Indicative of Antigonos's attention to the technological side of war is his employment of field fortifications, apparently introduced into Greek warfare in the early fourth century by the Athenian *condottieri* Chabrias and Iphikrates,[3] and attested several times as used by Antigonos: it seems that it was his practice to fortify his camps with a trench and palisade when on campaign (Polyainos IV 6,19; Diod. XIX 18,4), and he also used similar field fortifications to besiege Nora in 319 (Diod. XVIII 41,6). Then there is the use of the most advanced forms of siege technology, attested in the Antigonid army under Demetrios on Cyprus and Rhodes in 306 to 304. Again, in the sphere of naval warfare, it is in Antigonos's navy that we first hear of the use of the extra-large ships that were a typical feature of Hellenistic naval warfare: it was in Antigonos's shipyards in Phoenicia in 314 that the first ships larger than quinqueremes seem to have been built (Diod. XIX 62,8), and *hexēreis* and *heptēreis* formed an important part of the Antigonid fleet at Cyprian Salamis in 306 (Diod. XX 50,3). In addition, the use of artillery—catapults and stonethrowers—in naval warfare was apparently pioneered in Antigonos's navy at the battle of Salamis (Diod. XX 49,4), a point overlooked by Tarn, who claims (*HMND*, pp. 120 and 152) that the Romans were the first to do this.

Turning to the field of strategy, again Antigonos has left clear evidence of being a master. An example of his expertise is his move from the river Kopratas to Media in 316, forcing his enemy to leave a position of strength and move into the more open Iranian plateau, where the battles of Paraitakene and Gabiene were fought. I have described in chapter 3 above how in early 312 Antigonos used superior force and exterior lines to annihilate Asandros in Karia in only a few weeks: a minor strategical masterpiece. The Third Diadoch War in general shows Antigonos's grasp of grand strategy: in a classic exposition of the use of interior lines and sea power, he created so much trouble for each of the dynasts allied against him that he broke

local shepherds and farmers in Gabiene concerning Eumenes' movements. Another instance of Antigonos knowing what his enemy was doing is the fact that in the winter of 316/15 he discovered that Eumenes' army was widely dispersed in its winter quarters and hence susceptible to surprise attack and defeat in detail (Diod. XIX 37,1–2; Plut. *Eum.* 15,3; Polyainos IV 6,11); how he acquired this information we are not told, but it is clear that Antigonos's intelligence system functioned superbly.

3. For the development of field fortifications by Chabrias, see M. Cary, *CAH,* 6:68, ascribing the use of them by the Athenians and Boiotians in 378/77 to Chabrias, on the basis presumably of Strabo XVII 803 combined with Diod. XV 32,2–5 and Xenophon *Hellenika* V 4,38–54. That Iphikrates used a trench and palisade to guard his field camps is attested as a peculiarity by *Apophth. Iphik.* 2 at Plut. *Mor.* 187a.

their alliance and forced them to make peace without achieving any of the aims for which they had gone to war. As a final point, one may note that Tarn (*HMND,* pp. 34–35) places Antigonos and Eumenes at the beginning of the development that gradually took the general out of the actual melee to a withdrawn position from which he could control the entire battle, basing this on the control and awareness of their entire armies and the course of the battles displayed by the two generals at Paraitakene and Gabiene.[4] From all of the above, it will be clear that Antigonos fully deserves the almost universal judgment of him as the ablest general among Alexander's successors,[5] indeed one of the great generals of any period.

Moving to an evaluation of Antigonos as a politician and statesman, it must be said that far from being the great hope for the maintenance of Alexander's empire intact, Antigonos was one of the prime movers in its breakup. The main cause of the outbreak of civil war in the Macedonian empire was an excess of ambition and an insufficient commitment to harmony and unity on the part of all the major leaders. The ambitions and lack of harmony among the major generals proved so important because there was simply no person or institution of universally accepted legitimacy and authority around whom or which the military forces of the empire could unite, given the incompetence (literally) of the kings, the mentally retarded Philippos III and the infant Alexandros IV. In this situation the soldiery inevitably ended up by simply backing whatever general commanded

4. This is particularly noteworthy for the battle of Gabiene, at which Antigonos put Peithon Krateua and Demetrios in charge of his two wings and stationed himself with the right wing under Demetrios: in giving up command of this wing, he evidently wished to train his son as a battle leader, but also enabled himself to take a more detached view of the battle as a whole, being able to observe the enormous dust clouds raised and make use of this to send a special force to capture Eumenes' baggage train. Tarn seems to be right in what he says about Antigonos and Eumenes, but it is possible that the real credit for initiating this important development, as so many others in warfare, may belong to Philip, who seems to have directed the battle of Chaironea in much the way Antigonos ran Gabiene.

5. Thus, for example, Diod. XVIII 23,3: Antigonos was the most effective of the generals (after Alexander's death); XVIII 73,1: Antigonos won a reputation for strategic brilliance by his victory over Kleitos on the Bosporos in 317; Plut. *Sertorius* 1,4: four very great generals were one-eyed—Philip, Antigonos, Hannibal, and Sertorius; Plut. *Mor.* 337a: Antigonos, Seleukos, and Perdikkas were able to give the appearance of life to Alexander's power, but after them it crumbled; Cary, *History of the Greek World,* p. 22: "As a leader of troops in the field he [Antigonos] excelled all his Macedonian colleagues and had no match except Eumenes"; Tarn, *CAH,* 6:463: "the first general of the time; he could get almost as much out of his men as Alexander"; even Jane Hornblower is forced to admit (*Hieronymus,* p. 223) that "his [Antigonos's] later career exemplified the new spirit of warfare in the Hellenistic age . . . a spirit of getting things done."

and paid them, so long as he could show some claim to derive his authority from and be exercising it in the interests of the Argead monarchy, and so long as he appeared to be or to be likely to prove a successful leader. It should be emphasized that none of the major leaders of the period can escape a share of blame for the conflicts that divided the empire, including of course Antigonos, who played a major role in precipitating the First Diadoch War and was a protagonist of all the subsequent conflicts.

What need to be examined are Antigonos's guiding aims and policies during the conflicts of the Diadoch period. The main ancient sources portray Antigonos as a man of overweening pride and arrogance, driven by a ruthless ambition to rule the whole empire of Alexander, and this picture of him has been accepted in the main by modern scholarship, which generally regards the leitmotif of the Diadoch period as being a struggle between centripetal leaders (Perdikkas and then Antigonos) seeking to maintain Alexander's empire intact and rule all of it, and centrifugal figures (Ptolemy, Kassandros, Lysimachos, Seleukos) who sought to divide up the empire and rule over some part of it. However, I believe that the interpretation of Antigonos's aims offered by the sources needs to be more carefully evaluated and considerably revised.

In books XVIII–XX of Diodoros's history, there are some eighteen passages that refer to Antigonos's excessive ambition, seven of them referring explicitly to a quest for supreme power, and there are in addition two similar passages in Plutarch's *Eumenes* and one in his *Demetrios*.[6] It must be noted, however, that all but six of these twenty-one passages come from the accounts of Antigonos's duel with Eumenes of Kardia, where they form a marked contrast to the much vaunted tact, diplomacy, and dedication to the interests of the kings with which Eumenes is credited by the sources.[7] A suspicion of bias naturally arises. Of the six passages attributing excessive ambition to Antigonos that are not given in connection with the war against Eumenes, three merely report the propaganda put out by the coalitions of Antigonos's enemies in 315 and 302 (Diod. XIX 55,4–

6. These are the relevant passages in Diod., those mentioning the quest for supreme power marked with an asterisk: XVIII 39,7; XVIII 41,5; XVIII 42,2; XVIII 47,5; *XVIII 50,1–2; *XVIII 50,5; XVIII 52,6–8; *XVIII 54,4; XVIII 57,3; XVIII 58,4; XVIII 62,3–4; XVIII 73,1; XIX 12,1; *XIX 55,4–56,2; XIX 61,4; *XX 37,4; *XX 106,2–4; *XXI 1,1. The passages from Plutarch are *Eum.* 3,3 and 12,1–2; *Dem.* 28,2.

7. See, for example, Plut. *Eum.* 11,1–2; 13,2–3; Diod. XVIII 53,6–7; 58,2–4; 60,1–3; 61,1–3; XIX 15,3–5; 44,2.

56,2; 61,4; XX 106,2–4), obviously not unbiased evidence of Antigonos's aims; one is the accusation that all the Diadochoi, Antigonos included, sought to marry Kleopatra in order to gain supreme power (Diod. XX 37,4), which is probably false;[8] and the other two are the closing judgments of Diodoros (XXI 1,1) and Plutarch (*Dem.* 28,2) that it was Antigonos's ambition which brought about his downfall in 301, judgments which really only reflect on the last years of Antigonos's life. The picture of Antigonos as arrogant and power-mad given by the sources, then, belongs essentially to the story of his struggle against Eumenes, being a literary device whereby Antigonos's rival was made to seem a hero. The originator of this contrast may well have been Hieronymos of Kardia, who, though a loyal officer of the Antigonids during the second half of his life, was a close friend and probably nephew of Eumenes of Kardia. It has been plausibly argued by Jane Hornblower that Hieronymos's historical work originated with an adulatory account of Eumenes' career, which eventually formed the basis of the early parts of his Diadoch history, and that though loyal to Antigonos after Eumenes' death, Hieronymos disapproved of his methods.[9]

The picture of Eumenes as a man of heroic loyalty destroyed by the disloyalty of others has been somewhat revised in recent works on his career,[10] and the same needs to be done for the negative picture of Antigonos. Indeed, in a number of recent works, a start has been made in nuancing our sources' characterization of Antigonos, attempting to show how his aims, policies, and ambitions grew with and adapted themselves to the changing circumstances with which he

---

8. Diodoros's statement that *all* the Diadochoi sought to marry Kleopatra in order to grasp supreme power comes in his summation of her life and importance when reporting her death. In fact, Kassandros married Philip's other daughter, Thessalonike, and had no need for Kleopatra; and since Kleopatra lived under Antigonos's control at Sardis from 320 to 309 (Arrian *Met' Alex.* 1,40; Diod. XX 37,5), if Antigonos had wanted to marry her, he would presumably have done so, by force if necessary. The same goes for Seibert's theory (*Dynastische Verbindungen*, pp. 22–23) that Antigonos actually wanted to marry her to Demetrios. The statement of Diodoros is doubtless simply an exaggeration based on the fact that three great leaders really *did* try to marry Kleopatra: Leonnatos (Plut. *Eum.* 3,5), Perdikkas (Arrian *Met' Alex.* 1,21 and 26; Diod. XVIII 23,1–4), and Ptolemy (Diod. XX 37,3).

9. Hornblower, *Hieronymus*, pp. 196–211; and on Hieronymos's history, cf. app. 1, pp. 329–33 below. It is noteworthy that almost every passage in Diodoros that speaks of Antigonos's excessive ambition, other than the five I have discounted in the text here, does so in a context where Eumenes is mentioned (the exceptions are XVIII 52,6–8 and 54,4), and in several there is an explicit or clearly implicit contrast with Eumenes' moderation and/or loyalty to the kings (Diod. XVIII 42,2; 57,3–4; 58,4; 62,3; 73,1–2; XIX 12,1).

10. Important in this respect are Westlake, "Eumenes of Cardia"; Anson, "Eumenes of Cardia," esp. pp. 176–202; and Hornblower, *Hieronymus*, pp. 196–211.

was confronted over the years 323–306,[11] but this needs to be taken further. A close examination of Antigonos's career shows no sign of him being fired and guided by a determined ambition to reunite and rule over the whole of Alexander's empire. His policy was much more opportunistic than that: he sought, like the other dynasts, to rule as much of the empire as he could bring under his sway and to deal with his peers and rivals in whatever way seemed necessary to his interests, whether by friendship and diplomacy or by war and confiscation.

Laying aside, then, the prejudices evoked by the (probably Hieronyman) characterization of Antigonos's role and aims as Eumenes' opponent, it is clear that like most successful political and military leaders in history, Antigonos was more concerned with overcoming immediate problems and making the most of what opportunities arose than with pursuing any grand design of universal conquest. Of all the Diadochoi, it was Seleukos who modeled himself most closely on Alexander in his aims and propaganda;[12] if one looks for a model for Antigonos, Philip is the far more likely candidate. A case can be made suggesting that Antigonos's conception of empire was modeled on that of Philip. The story of the peace terms proposed to Alexander by Dareios after the battle of Issos, ceding all of Asia west of the Euphrates to Alexander, and of Parmenion's advice to Alexander to accept, is well known (e.g., Arrian *Anab.* II 25,1–2). It is often thought that Parmenion, Philip's oldest and most trusted general, hereby showed what the aims of Philip's expedition against the Persians were to have been if he had lived to carry it out.[13] Antigonos was fundamentally not very interested in holding territory in inner Asia, being interested rather in western Asia, near the Mediterranean and Aegean seas, and in Greece and Macedon. It may well be, then, that in so far as Antigonos had general policy aims beyond seizing the

---

11. The first to begin reevaluation of Antigonos's career was Cloché, "Remarques sur les étapes de l'ambition d' Antigone Ier"; his views have led to a slight modification in the characterization of Antigonos in such works as Wehrli, *Antigone et Démétrios,* and Engel, *Untersuchungen,* but these have not gone far enough, still regarding Antigonos as obsessed with holding all of Alexander's empire.

12. See, for instance, the propaganda concerning himself and Alexander spread by Seleukos (Diod. XIX 90,3–4; Appian *Syr.* 56). Seleukos's eastern *anabasis* and war with Chandragupta were also reminiscent of Alexander (Appian *Syr.* 55; Justin XV 4,12–21); and in attacking and defeating Lysimachos at Kurupedion, he actually reunited all of Alexander's empire except Egypt and Palestine.

13. An interesting example of this line of thought is Toynbee, "If Ochus and Philip Had Lived On"; see also the remarks of Ellis, *Philip II and Macedonian Imperialism,* pp. 227–34.

opportunities that arose, these were to establish an empire in Asia Minor, Syria/Palestine, and Greek lands, based on the political ideas of Philip, Antigonos's contemporary and his leader for over twenty years.

But whatever his aims, it is clear that until the end of his life Antigonos was an extremely successful politician and statesman; and this success was clearly based on pragmatism, a great ability to perceive the potentialities and limitations in situations that arose and act accordingly. Here again Antigonos was following the model of Philip rather than of the romantic Alexander. The latter's exploits in Baktria and India might be the stuff of legend, but they did not make strategic sense in terms of creating and running a durable empire: those regions were simply too far away from Greece and Macedon to be easily held as part of a Greco-Macedonian empire, and they offered no advantages worth the cost of conquering and holding them. Antigonos's approach was realistic: he removed the great Persian treasures of the east to western Asia, and for the rest simply sought to prevent any power strong enough to become a threat to him from arising in the far east. His loss of the battle of Ipsos and the subsequent establishment of Seleukos as ruler of Asia meant a return to something more closely approximating Alexander's policy.

This was not a boon for Greco-Macedonian power in Asia: the Seleukids' involvements in the far east distracted their attention from Asia Minor, which was allowed gradually to pass into the hands of a number of relatively minor dynasts. Meanwhile the east simply ate up Seleukid energies and resources that might have been better spent elsewhere; ultimately the east proved impossible for the Seleukids to hold and was lost to the Greek world, but meanwhile the Seleukids had been decisively weakened by many years of being overextended and were unable to resist the new power of Rome advancing from the west. It was left to the Romans to reunify Asia Minor and join it to Syria and Palestine to form the eastern part of their empire.

Though the Seleukids did not follow Antigonos's lead in their geographical conception of empire, they do seem to have done so in their administrative practices. As an administrator, Antigonos was also clearly pragmatic rather than idealistic or original. His methods and practices were a mixture of adaptations from Philip and the Achaemenids, as seemed best suited to the regions and problems they were intended to deal with. In the fifteen or so years Antigonos ruled his western Asian empire, he established a fully functional administrative system based on extensive colonization of Asia with Greek and Macedonian manpower, on the division of the old Persian satrapies into smaller and more manageable units, often called *stratēgeiai*, and on the creation of subdivisions of these called chiliarchies (changed to hyparchies under the Seleukids), which actually undertook the most important task, tribute collection. There can be no doubt that the early Seleukids, especially Seleukos himself, largely rounded off work already well advanced by Antigonos when establishing their administrative system in western Asia—notably Syria and southern Asia Minor. All future study of administrative practices and procedures in the Seleukid empire should henceforth begin with Antigonos, if not further back with Philip and the Achaemenids.

Undoubtedly Antigonos's major lasting achievement was his administrative work in Asia Minor and Syria, where he forms a bridge between Philip and the Achaemenids on the one hand, and the early Seleukids on the other. The "Hellenization" of Asia Minor and Syria was perhaps the most important achievement of the early Hellenistic period, and Antigonos clearly deserves much of the credit for this. Wherever we have evidence for colonizing activity by Antigonos, we also have evidence for further activity by Lysimachos and/or the early Seleukids: Alexandria Troas, Nikaia, Antioch, Apameia Kibotos, Apameia-on-the-Orontes, and Seleukia-in-Pieria are just the most famous places where colonization by Antigonos seems to have preceded the more widely known work of his successors. Some of the most famous cities of the Hellenistic world thus owed their beginnings to Antigonos, whose importance in this respect is surpassed perhaps only by Seleukos Nikator, the great continuator of his colonization program.

If this were the only contribution Antigonos had made, it would be enough to merit the attention of modern historians, but this is in fact far from being the case. As the first of the Diadochoi to assume the status of *basileus*, Antigonos had a decisive impact on the nature of Hellenistic kingship and royalist ideology, absolutist and emphasizing the *aristeia* and *andreia* of the monarch, which gave him a personal charisma justifying his elevation to superhuman status. With the possible exception of Alexander, Antigonos was the first living monarch to be given divine honors and a cult epithet by his Greek subjects and allies, which became standard features of Hellenistic kingship. All of this had an important impact on philosophical ideas, treatises on kingship becoming one of the standard types of philosophical writing in the Hellenistic period and beyond, virtually to the present day.[14] The revelation that a man could become a king by his own merits had a profound effect on political and ethical ideas; a small echo of the sensation caused by this act of Antigonos and the other Diadochoi can be found as late as the Byzantine compendium known as the Suda, which preserves (given the examples used evidently from an early Hellenistic source) the following definition of kingship s.v. *basileia:* "It is neither descent [*phusis*] nor legitimacy [*to dikaion*] that gives monarchies to men, but the ability to command an army and handle affairs competently. Such was the case with Philip and with the Successors of Alexander."

Another important effect of Antigonos's assumption of royal status was the status of his posterity as kings: though he was not personally responsible for establishing his dynasty as kings of Macedon, and his own empire in Asia was lost to his heirs, it is obvious that without Antigonos Monophthalmos's extraordinary career and elevation of himself and his son to kingship, his grandson Antigonos Gonatas would never have been in a position to make himself king of Macedon and settle the dynasty firmly on that throne. And the influence of Monophthalmos on his descendants should not be underestimated. Antigonos Gonatas's interest in sea power and control of the Aegean is reminiscent of the policy of Monophthalmos; in 224/23 Antigonos Doson founded a Hellenic League in many ways similar to that founded under Monophthalmos's auspices in 302; and it is only recently, with the Swedish excavations under Crampa at Labraunda in Karia, that the continued Antigonid interest down to the time of Doson and Philippos V in dominion over parts of Asia Minor has come to be fully realized.[15]

---

14. A short and easily accessible review by Walbank of the Hellenistic ideas on kingship and the literature that arose about it can be found in the new edition (1984) of the *CAH,* 7.1:75–84. This literature was influential in Roman imperial times, when philosophy of course had to come to terms with the absolute rule of the Roman emperors; the "mirror of princes" was a standard literary genre throughout the Middle Ages—an example is Thomas Aquinas's *De regimine principum*—and into the Renaissance, when Machiavelli wrote *Il principe* drawing, among other things, on examples from the ancient world. Philosophical interest in kingship naturally remained high during the age of royal absolutism, and continued with the Enlightenment idea of the "enlightened despot." It received a further boost from Bonapartism, extensively modeled on Alexander and Caesar, and is still with us in this century, I think, in the guise of the Führer and Duce worship of the extreme right and the "personality cults" encouraged by leaders of the extreme left.

15. The results of the Labraunda excavations are published in *Svenska Istitutet i Athen: Skrifter,* vol. 4, esp. pt. 3 (inscriptions); for convenient historical summaries, see Walbank, *CAH,* 7.1:459–61, and Will, *Histoire politique,* 1:366–71.

The upshot of this study is, then, a total reevaluation of the career and significance of Antigonos Monophthalmos: instead of the failed emulator of Alexander, we have the founder of a dynasty, the successful general and statesman under whose auspices new advances in military and naval techniques and technology were made, the inventor of the political compromise under which the Greek city-states were integrated into the Hellenistic state system down to the time of the Roman conquest, the founder of cities and colonies, the dynast who helped to create and shape Hellenistic kingship, and the state-builder whose empire (under Seleukid control) was one of the great powers of the Hellenistic world, and could perhaps have been greater than it was if his geographical conception had been adhered to by the Seleukids. All of this can be simply summed up, I think, by saying that Antigonos is to be understood in terms of Philip's career rather than that of Alexander, and that it was Antigonos's achievement to pass on to the Hellenistic world some of the tradition of thorough and realistic statesmanship that marked Philip's brilliant career and achievements. It is in this light that Antigonos should take his place as one of the seminal figures in creating the Hellenistic world of the third and second centuries B.C.

Appendix 1

The Literary Sources

A major problem every ancient historian must face is that of defining his or her attitude towards the literary sources. This is more of a problem for some periods than for others, according to the nature (primary, secondary, fragmentary, or whatever) of the sources preserved, and their reliability. For the historian of the Diadochoi, a clear statement of attitude towards the sources is of paramount importance, because none of the primary sources have survived, and rival theories about the influence of the lost primary sources on the surviving literary source material, and consequently of the trustworthiness of the various secondary or even tertiary historical sources that are all that survive, have proliferated to an alarming extent. Anyone writing about the Diadochoi must therefore explain his or her attitude towards the many contradictory tenets of *Quellenforschung* put forward by modern scholars, so as to make plain and justify the relative importance he or she attributes to the various surviving sources.

It will not be possible here, for reasons of space, to give anything like a full analysis of modern *Quellenforschung:* due to the number and complexity of the theories proposed in the past hundred years or so, to do so would require an entirely separate study. The interested reader can find a fairly full review of the scholarship on the sources for this period in Seibert's *Zeitalter der Diadochen,* pp. 1–53. In general one may legitimately say that many of the theories put forward as *Quellenforschung* are more notable for ingenuity than for credibility. It does not speak well for the methods employed by scholars engaged in source criticism that in all too many cases the conclusions arrived at by able, and even eminent, scholars investigating the same problem by the same methods are irreconcilably opposed: a case in point is the study of the sources used by Diodoros for books XVIII–XX of his history, which has led scholars to divergent and all too often fanciful conclusions (cf. the remarks of Seibert, pp. 32–35).

One factor contributing significantly to the situation outlined above is, I think, an understandable desire on the part of modern researchers to arrive at definite conclusions when studying problems, although often the available evidence is simply inadequate to establish such conclusions. An indispensible quality for successful source criticism is the ability to recognize when a problem is insoluble in the present state of the evidence and a willingness to say so. To be of any use, *Quellenforschung* must be conducted according to rigorous rules of logic: too many researchers show a lamentable reluctance to wield Occam's Razor, which would certainly have eliminated some of the more involved theories of scholars seeking to establish the links between surviving secondary and lost primary sources.

This is particularly true of the tendency prevalent among certain scholars to posit intermediary writers between primary sources and surviving secondary historians, which intermediaries are then supposed to have done the actual work of collating and condensing the primary sources.[1] For example, when Diodoros tells us in the introduction to his history that he had read the works of a large number of earlier historians, and condensed them into one manageable work of universal history (Diod. I 3,1–4,5), some scholars insist that in fact Diodoros did nothing of the kind, but merely produced a shorter version of such a universal history written earlier by Agatharchides of Knidos (thus, e.g., Beloch, *GG*, 4.2:5) or by an anonymous Alexandrian (as is hypothesized by Vezin, *Eumenes von Kardia,* pp. 6–7). This kind of thing seems to rest on no basis other than the long discredited *Einquellenprinzip* of Heinrich Nissen,[2] and on a curious unwillingness to believe that any of our surviving secondary historians can actually have done any work. Too little is known of the lost histories of Agatharchides and other Hellenistic writers (e.g., Timagenes of Alexandria) who have been brought forward as putative intermediaries between the surviving sources and the primary historians; there is a vitiating circularity of reasoning in concluding that Diodoros based

1. For an extreme example, involving the invention of an entirely unknown historian as intermediary, see the study of C. Bottin on Diodoros's sources in *RBPh* 7 (1928):1307–27.

2. Expounded in H. Nissen, *Kritische Untersuchungen über die Quellen der vierten und fünften Dekade des Livius* (Berlin, 1863).

himself on such intermediaries because of the way he wrote, for example, and then deducing the methods and sources of the intermediaries from the methods and sources apparent in Diodoros.

In short, then, my attitude to *Quellenforschung* tends to be conservative and skeptical: conservative in that I prefer a simple and straightforward solution to a problem rather than a complex one; skeptical in that I doubt modern theories that are not based on fairly clear and unequivocal indications in the sources. So when Diodoros states the beginning, end point, and subject matter of a famous work of history in his book, I take this as an indication that Diodoros may actually have read that work of history, rather than constructing a hypothesis on how Diodoros must have obtained this information from an intermediary. Unless and until substantially larger remains of the various putative third- and second-century intermediate authors such as Agatharchides are found, it is simply impossible to determine whether and how and to what extent they were used by our surviving sources. And speculation along these lines is in any case irrelevant to my purposes here. In order to decide whether and to what extent the surviving sources on Diadoch history are believable, what is important is to try to see whether their narratives are intrinsically plausible and self-consistent, whether we can see any indications of what the ultimate primary sources for their information were or could have been, and whether we can in any way determine the reliability of those primary sources. I give here, therefore, first a brief survey of the lost primary sources, indicating what is known of them; and then a review of the major extant sources, above all of Diodoros of Sicily.

THE LOST PRIMARY SOURCES

Hieronymos of Kardia

The one fact that may be said to have been established beyond reasonable doubt by modern *Quellenforschung* on the Diadoch period is that Hieronymos of Kardia is the most important of the primary historians of the period, and that his work is the ultimate source for most of the factual material preserved in the surviving accounts.[3] Despite the very meager number and length of the fragments of his history that are preserved, certain aspects of the surviving source

3. See for this most recently and fully, Hornblower, *Hieronymus*. The extant fragments and *testimonia* of Hieronymos's history are given by Jacoby, *FGrH*, no. 154; and cf. Hornblower, *Hieronymus*, with a text of the fragments and commentary at pp. 238–62.

material, combined with what is known of Hieronymos's life and career, make this virtually certain. For the chief characteristic of our sources for the Diadoch period is their heavy emphasis on the careers and activities of Eumenes of Kardia, Antigonos Monophthalmos, and Demetrios Poliorketes; and Hieronymos of Kardia is known to have served successively as officer and administrator under these three men (see app. 3, no. 51 for a brief account of Hieronymos's career). He thus had every opportunity to learn the facts of the careers of these three men, but far less opportunity to learn about the other dynasts, Ptolemy, Seleukos, Lysimachos, and Kassandros; and furthermore his sympathy for the causes for which he himself had served would naturally have led him to give them a full-length treatment in his history.

There are other arguments that support the identification of Hieronymos as the ultimate source for most of our knowledge of the Diadoch period, but for reasons of space these cannot be gone into here.[4] The precise scale and organization of Hieronymos's history are not known. We have no citations of any book numbers, but that the work was a very long one is attested by Dionysios of Halikarnassos, who includes Hieronymos's history in a list of books so long and turgid that no one would read them to the end (*De comp. verb.* 4,30 = T 12). The history covered at least the fifty-year period between the deaths of Alexander (323) and Pyrrhos (272); a citation from it for the age of Mithridates Ktistes at his death in 266 ([Loukianos] *Makrōbioi* 13 = F 7) raises the possibility that Hieronymos continued his history down to that date, but this fact could equally well have been recorded as an aside when reporting some other information concerning Mithridates; no firm conclusion can be thus drawn from it, other than that Hieronymos was still alive and writing or revising his history in 266.

It has often been assumed, mostly from the fact that Hieronymos records the deaths of Pyrrhos and Mithridates, that he must have written his history late in life, when he was perhaps living in retirement in Macedon under Antigonos Gonatas after the latter had finally secured control over Macedon by the defeat and death of Pyrrhos: such at least is implied by the theory that he wrote his history after the publication of Douris of Samos's *Makedonika* and as a counterblast to

4. See Hornblower, *Hieronymus*, pp. 18–75, and the works cited by her there, esp. Brown, *AHR* 53 (1947):684–96. A full bibliography is also given by Seibert, *Diadochen*, pp. 2–9.

that work.[5] There is, however, no proof that this was so, and in fact Hornblower has pointed out very persuasively that the detailed treatment of the military and political affairs of the years 323–301 given by Hieronymos indicates that he must at least have been taking notes with the ultimate intention of writing a history during those years (Hornblower, *Hieronymus*, pp. 174–75). A suggestion put forward by a number of modern scholars that Hieronymos may have written his book in two parts—a history of the Diadochoi (published after Ipsos), and a history of the Epigonoi (published after 272)—seems to me very plausible.[6] Admittedly there is no sure evidence for this hypothesis, which is based on ancient citations of Hieronymos's book as variously a *History of the Diadochoi* and a *History of the Epigonoi;* but this suggests that like the book of his younger contemporary Nymphis of Herakleia, Hieronymos's work was entitled in full *A History of the Diadochoi and Epigonoi,* and that a division at the decisive battle of Ipsos gave rise to the distinction between Diadochoi and Epigonoi.[7]

However that may be, it is virtually sure that Hieronymos's book is at the root of most of what we know of the Diadoch period, and that the *Sachlichkeit* and general excellence of Diodoros's account in particular (our main source) are hence due to Hieronymos's possession of those qualities. But the fact that Hieronymos's book seems on the whole to have given a good, thorough, factual account of events

---

5. For this theory, see, for example, J. G. Droysen, *Hermes* 11 (1876):458–65; F. Jacoby, *RE* s.v. Hieronymos no. 10; also Hornblower, *Hieronymus*, pp. 234–35. There is no real evidence for this view, as Hornblower admits; it is suggested mostly by the fact that Douris's history seems to have ended with the year 281, whereas Hieronymos's went down at least to 272, but this is an unreliable indicator. There is evidence that seems to point the other way: Diod. XIX 44,4–5 refers to Antigonos quartering troops at Rhagai in Media in 316/15, presumably based on the eyewitness evidence of Hieronymos, who was then with Antigonos (Diod. XIX 44,3); Douris refers to the same matter in almost the same terms as Diodoros (F 54 in Jacoby), but Douris was not a witness to this event and must have got his information from elsewhere; presumably Hieronymos is the source of both Douris and Diodoros, from which it would follow that the first part of his history, at least, was published before Douris wrote.

6. See Müller, *Antigonos Monophthalmos*, pp. 7–12, citing earlier scholars who have argued for this (e.g., Susemihl, Schubert, Fontana).

7. The earliest testimony for the title of Hieronymos's book is Diod. XVIII 42,1: *τῶν Διαδόχων Ἱστορίαι*. In the first century A.D., Josephus *Contra Apionem* I 213 writes of Hieronymos's book as *Περὶ τῶν Διαδόχων*. Both authors refer explicitly to the part of Hieronymos's history covering the time of Antigonos (i.e., before 301). Dionysios of Halikarnassos cites Hieronymos for his account of Roman history, which must have been part of his treatment of Pyrrhos's western expedition, 280–275, calling the work *Περὶ τῶν Ἐπιγόνων* (*Ant. Rom.* I 5,4). This evidence, from relatively early sources in the cases of Diodoros and Dionysios (both first century B.C.), does seem to support the notion of a two-part book, with 301 as the divide; the title cited by the Byzantine Suda—*τὰ ἐπ' Ἀλεξάνδρωι πραχθέντα*—simply describes the contents. See further Hornblower, *Hieronymus*, pp. 76–79.

should not lead us to an exaggerated respect for Hieronymos and his work; nor should the fact that Hieronymos was evidently behind most of our information on the Diadoch period lead to dogmatic attributions to him of specific details. Each individual fact that does not have a provenance specified in its source must be treated initially as of unknown provenance and can only be attributed to Hieronymos if logical argument leads at least with some plausibility to that conclusion; and the fact that a piece of information can be plausibly attributed to Hieronymos must not automatically be assumed to guarantee its veracity and objectivity. Most individual pieces of information preserved in our surviving sources for the Diadoch period could just as plausibly come from a writer such as Douris or Diyllos as from Hieronymos; the case for Hieronymos as the originator of most of the information is a cumulative one, based on the tendencies observable in most of the information when taken together, and this cumulative argument clearly cannot be applied to an individual piece of information.

One of the most common errors made in *Quellenforschung* is to suppose that because the *cumulative* picture of a late writer seems to suggest a particular early source, one can therefore rightly attribute *specific* information in the late writer to that early source. But the fact that a writer's work gives *overall* an impression of having used a particular source clearly cannot logically prove that any *particular* piece of information is from that source, especially when the writer in question shows any indication of awareness of or use of other sources. If one argues from particular information that the writer in general used a specific source, and then argues back from the use of that source to attribute other particular information given by the writer to that source, one is clearly guilty of circular reasoning: one can argue from the particular to the general conclusion, but not from the general conclusion back to the particular again.

It is often said that in Hieronymos's book we have lost a work that would have ranked with the writings of Thucydides and Polybios if it had survived. This is high praise, and seems to be not undeserved to judge from Diodoros's books XVIII–XX, which were clearly for the most part derived from a superb historian. However, making this sort of judgment does not absolve one henceforth from taking a critical attitude towards what Hieronymos wrote. Polybios, for example, was an excellent historian, one of the best in the ancient world, but that does not mean that his book is ipso facto free from bias and errors of fact: indeed his bias against the Aitolians is well known to every reader of his book, and factual errors can also fairly easily be discovered.[8] Likewise the fact that Hieronymos seems to have been an excellent historian should not blind us to the possibility that his work may have contained errors and biases. For example, it has been argued very cogently by Hornblower (*Hieronymus,* pp. 196–211) that Hieronymos was distinctly biased towards Eumenes in his account of the years 323–316, writing in effect an apologia for Eumenes. It is particularly regrettable, therefore, that there has arisen among modern scholars something of a tendency to regard Hieronymos as unquestionably authoritative, and hence to refer information that one considers or wishes to be considered truthful to Hieronymos as source, while relegating facts one considers or wishes to be considered dubious to a different source, usually Douris, who is generally regarded as unreliable.

Douris of Samos

One of the most widely read histories of the Diadoch period was the *Makedonika* of Douris of Samos, a man who seems to have lived in the last decades of the fourth century and the first half of the third; his history of Macedon began with the year 370 (Diod. XV 60,6) and went down at least to the battle of Kurupedion in 281 (see F 55 = Pliny *NH* VIII 143, recording the death of Lysimachos), covering these years in at least twenty-three books (see F 15 = Athenaios XII 66, p. 546c–d, citing Douris's account of Demetrios's death in 283 from Douris's twenty-third book).[9] Some thirty-six fragments of the *Makedonika* survive (*FGrH* Fs 1–15 and 35–56), most of them concerned with what we would call anecdotal matter: tales of drunkenness and vice, flattery, the unusual and the marvellous, and anything reflecting discredit on historical personages certainly seem to have attracted Douris's interest. These fragments do not necessarily, however, give us a complete picture of Douris's history: sixteen of the fragments are from Athenaios's *Deipnosophistai,* which is just a huge collection of anecdotes from any and every source, and another seven are from various of the *Lives* of Plutarch, another writer mostly interested in anecdotal material.

In other words, there is a strong possibility that the mostly

8. An example is Polybios's placing of Saguntum north of the river Ebro at III 15,5 (implicitly) and III 30,3 (explicitly), though he is known to have visited Spain himself and elsewhere correctly places Saguntum south of the Ebro (III 14,9).

9. For Douris's fragments and *testimonia,* see Jacoby, *FGrH,* no. 76; see further Ed. Schwartz, *RE* s.v. Duris, no. 3, and Kebric, *In the Shadow of Macedon.*

anecdotal nature of the fragments of Douris is in part due to the interests of those who have preserved the fragments, and that Douris's history as a whole may not have been quite so anecdotal and unreliable as the fragments make it appear; and after all, thirty-six short fragments are a rather slender basis on which to form a judgment of a work twenty-three or more books long. Nevertheless, since the surviving fragments are all we have to go on, any attempt to evaluate Douris's history must be based on them, and it has to be said that they do not give the impression that Douris was a serious and reliable historian. It is not really possible in the present state of the evidence to say more about Douris as a historian than that he liked to retail stories reflecting badly on famous men and was interested in the marvellous and the sensational. Clearly so long a history as his *Makedonika* must have contained a great deal of straightforward factual matter, but we are not in a position to determine how he divided up his work, what his judgments on the trends of events were, or whether he was especially biased for or against particular leaders or peoples.[10]

Though Douris's history was widely read in antiquity (it is referred to or quoted from by, e.g., Didymos, Cicero, Strabo, and Pliny in addition to the already mentioned Diodoros, Plutarch, and Athenaios, as well as others), it is nevertheless not possible to determine with any degree of probability what influence he had on the surviving sources. Plutarch was evidently familiar with his work and may have used it quite extensively in his *Life of Demetrios,* though this is no more than conjecture.[11] The fact that Diodoros cites the beginning point of Douris's work (at XV 60,6) suggests that he may have read it, and some modern scholars have seen proof of this in the fact

10. Some scholars describe Douris as an anti-Macedonian historian (e.g., Kebric, *In the Shadow of Macedon,* pp. 9, 19–28), but there is no sound evidence for this: his critical portrayal of various Macedonian and pro-Macedonian leaders is more plausibly to be classed as moralistic than as anti-Macedonian, for he praises the pro-Macedonian Phokion (Plut. *Phok.* 4,2 and 17,6). In general it would be truer to say that he liked to elaborate on the disreputable qualities of great leaders, whether Macedonian or Greek, than that any pervasive anti-Macedonian bias or sentiment is discernible. The fact that he called his history *Makedonika* hardly suggests an anti-Macedonian bias; other than this, the evidence is simply insufficient for reasoned judgment.

11. Though Plutarch cites Douris in a number of his biographies (e.g., at *Alkib.* 32; *Demosth.* 19 and 23; *Alex.* 15 and 46; *Phokion* 4 and 17; *Eum.* 1), he does not happen to do so in his *Demet.;* but the portrayal of Demetrios by Plutarch is so similar to that in Douris's fragments 13 and 14 as to suggest that Plutarch may nevertheless have used Douris here as elsewhere: see further Kebric, *In the Shadow of Macedon,* pp. 55–60.

that F 54 of Douris corresponds closely with Diod. XIX 44,4–5 (a discussion of Rhagai in Media).[12] However, the discussion of Rhagai in Diodoros could just as easily come from Hieronymos (as, indeed, could that of Douris if Hieronymos was the earlier writer), and one such correspondence is not conclusive proof of anything. It is perhaps likely that Diodoros had read at least some of Douris's work, but no clear trace can be found of its utilization in Diodoros books XVIII–XX. Beyond this our present knowledge does not really permit us to go.

One aspect of the modern scholarship on Douris that does need to be discussed here is the attempt by Robert Kebric in his monograph *In the Shadow of Macedon: Duris of Samos* to draw conclusions about Douris's historical aims and methods from the few scanty facts known about his life, for Kebric deduces quite a close relationship between the family of Douris and Antigonos and Demetrios.[13] It is known (see T 2 = Athenaios VIII 18, p. 337d) that Douris was at some time tyrant of Samos, and a corrupt passage of Pausanias (VI 13,5 = T4) suggests that Douris's father, Kaios, may have been tyrant before him.[14] Kebric assumes that this tyranny occurred when Samos was in the sphere of influence of Antigonos and Demetrios, and goes so far as to refer to Antigonos as the "supporter" of the tyranny (p. 5), the "benefactor" of Douris's father (p. 8), and even to conjecture that Douris's father may have died fighting for Antigonos at Ipsos. All of this is conjecture, utterly unsupported by any clear evidence;[15] the dates of the tyranny of Douris and his father are unknown, and could as easily fall in the early third century as in the late fourth. In fact, since we have an abundance of inscriptions from Samos of the late

12. See, for example, A. Haake, *De Duride Samio Diodori auctore* (diss. Bonn, 1874); Beloch, *GG*, 4.1:497–80, esp. n. 2.

13. See Kebric, *In the Shadow of Macedon*, pp. 4–9.

14. Ibid., and Barron *CR*, n.s., 12 (1962):189–92.

15. Kebric's argument (*In the Shadow of Macedon*, pp. 5–6) is based essentially on the known presence of Douris and his brother Lynkeus in Athens at some time to study under Theophrastos, and Lynkeus's attendance in Athens at some festivities organized by Demetrios and Antigonos. However, the Antigonos in question is certainly Gonatas, for Monophthalmos cannot have been in Athens later than 321/20; and the festivities in question therefore certainly belong to the 290s. We know that Theophrastos lived until 286/85 (see, e.g., *OCD*[2] s.v. Theophrastos); clearly Douris and Lynkeus were hence in Athens *after* the death of Monophthalmos, in the 290s. Their presence in Athens, and Lynkeus's participation at a couple of parties, prove nothing about family links with the Antigonids: Lynkeus, for example, also attended a famous banquet thrown by Ptolemy (see n. 17 below); there is no reason to suppose that the guests at these functions were political adherents.

fourth century, in none of which there is even the slightest hint of a tyranny on the island,[16] whereas there are far fewer inscriptions from the first three or four decades of the third century, it would be easier to fit the tyranny into the third century, perhaps when Samos was in the power of Lysimachos or Ptolemy II.[17]

At any rate, there is no good reason to link Douris with Antigonos Monophthalmos: the evidence suggests rather that Douris was a contemporary of Antigonos's grandson Gonatas, and there is no trace of a pro-Antigonid bias in his fragments. Since much of Douris's history dealt with events from before his own lifetime, he must have drawn on earlier sources for his knowledge of these; moreover, as he was a very young man during the early Diadoch period and nothing suggests that he ever traveled in Asia or took part in the great events of the time, one wonders also what his sources of information for the Diadoch period can have been. From the fact that his history went down to 281 at least, it seems reasonable to conclude that he wrote after that year, that is, in the period ca. 280–260. In that case he may have been able to draw on earlier historians of the Diadoch period, for example, Hieronymos and Diyllos, for much of his factual material. In addition, however, he may well have conducted original research: for example, a number of Samians are known to have played roles in the conflicts of the Diadoch period,[18] and it is only reasonable to suppose that Douris could have questioned such men and their relatives to gain further information for his history; and he would in any case have had the normal knowledge of events of his own lifetime that a well-educated man does have.

Diyllos of Athens

The Athenian historian Diyllos wrote a general history of the period 357–297 in twenty-six books, as we know from the citations of his work by Diodoros (XVI 14,5; XXI 5). Unfortunately, all that

16. The early Hellenistic Samian inscriptions have been published by Schede, *AM* 44 (1919):4–24, and Habicht, *AM* 72 (1957):152–274.

17. Kebric argues (*In the Shadow of Macedon*, p. 9) that there could not have been a tyranny at Samos under Ptolemy II, but in fact no evidence exists to prove this: it would be as easy to fit in the tyranny under Ptolemy as under Antigonos or Demetrios. There is no evidence for Kebric's assertion that "Duris must have seen his tyranny fall with Lysimachus." For good relations between Lynkeus (Douris's brother) and Ptolemy, see his account of attending a banquet given by Ptolemy at some undetermined date (perhaps the 290s?): Athenaios III 100e, 101e–f, and IV 128a–b.

18. Examples are Themison of Samos, a naval officer of Antigonos (see app. 3, no. 112), and Kallikrates, son of Boiskos, admiral of Ptolemy I and II, on whom see Hauben, *Callikrates of Samos*.

is left of the work are six *testimonia* and four fragments, so it is not possible to form any clear idea of its nature and quality (though this has not, of course, prevented various scholars from making the attempt).[19] Nor can it ever be conclusively stated what influence, if any, Diyllos had on the surviving sources, though the fact that Diodoros cites him three times (in addition to the two already mentioned, there is a notice of the end of part 1 of Diyllos's work at Diod. XVI 76,6) permits one to suppose that he may well have been at least read by Diodoros. Furthermore, two of the *testimonia* and one of the fragments are from Plutarch (T 4 = *Mor.* 345e–f; T 5 and F 3 = *Mor.* 862b), so that it would appear that he was either used by Plutarch directly, or by an intermediate source utilized by Plutarch. Since his history ended in 297, it seems likely that he wrote it quite early in the third century, and it may therefore have been already extant and available as a source for such (probably younger) contemporary authors as Douris and Nymphis. The nature of one of the fragments raises the possibility (though no more) that Diyllos could have been well disposed towards Kassandros, and hence presumably opposed to the Antigonids, but beyond that conjecture it is not possible to go with any plausibility.[20]

Demochares of Athens

Demochares, from the Athenian deme Leukonoe, was the nephew of the great orator Demosthenes and a notable orator and politician in his own right, active in the late fourth and early third centuries. As a politician he seems to have followed the example of his famous uncle by adopting an anti-Macedonian stance: he was opposed to Kassandros and his governor at Athens, Demetrios of Phaleron, and was a prominent leader of the restored democracy after Demetrios Poliorketes had liberated Athens. However, it seems that

19. For the fragments and *testimonia,* see Jacoby, *FGrH,* no. 73; and for an evaluation see Ed. Schwartz, *RE* s.v. Diyllos, no. 2; full bibliography in Seibert, *Diadochen,* pp. 19–21. The most extreme attempt to find traces of Diyllos in the surviving sources is that of Schwahn, *Philologus* 86 (1931):145–68, making Diyllos the main source for Diodoros's history of Macedon and Greece in the Diadoch period. The evidence is simply insufficient to establish Schwahn's analysis; cf. Seibert, *Diadochen,* p. 21.

20. Diyllos F 1 describes Kassandros's burial of Philippos Arrhidaios and Eurydike, and holding of funeral games for them, actions that redound to his credit. Although nothing firm can be deduced from an isolated fragment, when it is combined with the fact that Diyllos ended his history with the deaths of Kassandros and his eldest son Philippos, it at least seems to warrant the conjecture that Diyllos may have had a particular (and friendly?) interest in Kassandros.

he soon became involved in a power struggle with Stratokles of Diomea, another anti-Macedonian leader, who was able to win with the support of Demetrios Poliorketes and drove Demochares into exile in 303.[21] Hence Demochares became, not unnaturally, an opponent of the Antigonids; he seems to have been mostly in exile during the early years of the third century, as Athens passed from Demetrios's control to that of the tyrant Lachares and back again to Demetrios's control in 295.

Either while he was in exile or after his return Demochares wrote a history of his own time in twenty-one books or more, covering at least the years between 322 (death of Demosthenes) and 289 (death of Agathokles).[22] Only four *testimonia* and eight fragments (of which several are doubtful) remain, so that again no firm impression of this work can be obtained. It seems likely that it concentrated rather on Athens and events there, and was certainly very scathing about the acts of Demochares' various political enemies in Athens, and of Demetrios (see Fs 1 and 2). Cicero (*Brutus* 286) regarded the history as being very rhetorical, and it is quite likely that Demochares did not even make a pretense of historical objectivity, but basically produced an immensely long pamphlet making propaganda for his own political notions and vilifying his enemies, missing no opportunity to introduce sensational and entertaining anecdotes. Nevertheless, it doubtless preserved much valuable information—just to have an account of events from the kind of anti-Macedonian viewpoint Demochares represented would be invaluable for us now—and it is likely that quite a bit of Plutarch's *Life of Demetrios* is ultimately derived from Demochares, especially those parts recording Demetrios's scandalous doings during his various stays in Athens.[23] Other

21. On Demochares, see, for example, H. Swoboda, *RE* s.v. Demochares, no. 6; on the dates of his exile, L. C. Smith, *Historia* 11 (1962):114–18; for his power struggle with Stratokles, see Shear, *Kallias of Sphettos,* pp. 47–51.

22. The *testimonia* and fragments can be found in Jacoby, *FGrH,* no. 75; the twenty-first book of the history is cited by Athenaios VI 253b–d (= F 2) referring to an event of the year 291; the latest event mentioned in the extant remains is the death of Agathokles in 289 (see F 5), which could have been discussed in the same or in a succeeding book. The exact beginning and ending dates of the work are unknown.

23. The two most significant fragments of Demochares we possess, Fs 1 and 2 drawn from Athenaios VI 252f–253d, both describe the scandalous flattery of Demetrios and his associates by the Athenians in the late 290s, and Plutarch's account of Demetrios's dealings with Athens also has much to say on the topic of flattery (*Dem.* 10–13 and 23–26). In addition Plutarch several times mentions Demochares specifically, quoting a witticism by Demochares at *Dem.* 24,5 and referring to his exile, and at *Dem.* 27,2 reporting another witticism about Demetrios by an unknown Demochares of Soloi, who is surely in fact our Demochares—"Solios" being a textual corruption of some sort.

than that, it is not possible to indicate what exact influence he could have had on our surviving sources, though (as with Douris and Diyllos) the possibility that some information could ultimately derive from him must be borne in mind.

Nymphis of Herakleia Pontika

On the basis of a history he wrote of his native city, Herakleia, of which we have substantial knowledge by way of Memnon's adaptation of it,[24] Nymphis appears to have been a fairly good historian. He wrote a general history of Alexander, the Diadochoi, and the Epigonoi, as we know from two bare references to it in the extant literature,[25] but it is clearly impossible to say anything substantive about it on such a slender basis. Its starting date was presumably 336 (beginning of Alexander's reign) and it probably covered the period down to 247/46 (death of Ptolemy II Philadelphos) in twenty-four books. Whether it had any influence, direct or indirect, on the extant sources it is impossible to say; it is unlikely to have had much influence, as it is never cited, though this argument from silence is far from decisive. Since it appears to have been written later than 246, it is likely that the author used the earlier historians dicussed above as sources; but Nymphis was an adult during the later Diadoch period at least (he was exiled from Herakleia for many years, apparently as an enemy of Lysimachos, after whose death in 281 he returned to his native city),[26] and so may well have had original contributions to make to Diadoch history as well as to the history of the Epigonoi.

Philochoros of Athens

A special place among the primary sources on the Diadoch period is taken by Philochoros, who wrote a history of Athens rather than a general history. Philochoros lived between ca. 340 and 260, and his

24. Memnon's work, preserved in an epitome by Photios, is published in Jacoby, *FGrH*, no. 434; it gave a history of Herakleia Pontika from 364 (the year Klearchos became tyrant of the city) to the time of Caesar. For the part of this history covering the period down to 281, at least, and possibly to 247, it is likely that Memnon relied heavily on Nymphis's history: see, for example, Jacoby, *FGrH*, vol. 3b, pp. 259–69.

25. See Jacoby, *FGrH*, no. 432 T 1 (the Suda) and F 17 (Aelian *NA* 17,3 concerning Troglodytes in Africa). Apart from the title of the work given by the Suda and the one not very informative fragment preserved by Aelian, this book has left no discernible impact on the extant sources. For bibliography on Nymphis, see Seibert, *Diadochen*, p. 22.

26. Nymphis's exile and his return to Herakleia soon after Lysimachos's death are attested by Memnon (*FGrH*, no. 434 F 7,3). As Jacoby notes (*FGrH*, vol. 3b, p. 259), Nymphis can hardly have been born later than ca. 310 if he was one of the most prominent Herakleian exiles in 281.

Atthis covered the period from mythological times down to his own day in seventeen books—though it was not finished when he died, executed by Antigonos Gonatas at the time of the Chremonidean War as a suspected Ptolemaic sympathizer.[27] The surviving fragments indicate that Philochoros had already reached the early Diadoch period in book 7, showing that the years 323–ca. 265 were treated in considerable detail, taking up eleven of the seventeen books; and since Antigonos Monophthalmos came into contact with Athens a number of times during his career, he must have figured in Philochoros's work. Events we hear of that may have been recorded by Philochoros are, for example: Antigonos's flight to Europe on Attic ships in 321 (Diod. XVIII 23,4); his return to Asia with ten Athenian ships in 320 (Arrian *Met' Alex.* 25,1); Antigonos's aid to Kassandros in 318–317, which enabled the latter to secure control of Athens (Diod. XVIII 54,3–4; 68,1–69,2); the defection from Athenian control to the alliance of Antigonos by the islands of Lemnos and Imbros in 313, and also the setting up of the Nesiotic League based on Delos (Diod. XIX 68,3–4; Tarn, *Ant. Gon.*, pp. 432–39); the campaigns of Antigonos's general Polemaios in central Greece in 312, and especially his invasion of Attica and the subsequent negotiations between Athens and Antigonos (Diod. XIX 78,3–4); and, of course, the expedition sent by Antigonos under Demetrios to liberate Athens in 307, and the subsequent events in the careers of Antigonos and Demetrios down to 301 (Diod. XX 44–46; 100–110; Plut. *Dem.* 8–26). Indeed, four of the fragments of Philochoros belonging to the years 307–301 refer to Antigonos or to Demetrios explicitly (Fs 66, 70, 165, 166).

The fact that these and other events may have been, and in some cases certainly were, treated by Philochoros in his *Atthis* does not, however, prove that the information preserved in the extant sources is actually based, whether directly or indirectly, on Philochoros: the same facts must also have been related in the other primary sources already discussed. Nevertheless, Philochoros was a famous historian, the last and greatest of the Atthidographers, and it would be an obvious step for later writers such as Plutarch or Arrian to have consulted Philochoros when their narratives impinged upon the affairs of Athens. Once again, then, the possibility that some of the extant information derives from Philochoros must be borne in mind.

27. On the *Atthis* of Philochoros, see Jacoby, *FGrH*, no. 329 (fragments and *testimonia*) and *FGrH*, vol. 3b, suppl. (commentary); Jacoby, *Atthis*, passim; and R. Laqueur, *RE* s.v. Philochoros.

DIODOROS AND THE OTHER EXTANT SOURCES

By far the most complete and useful extant source on the years between the death of Alexander the Great and the battle of Ipsos (323–301) is that given in books XVIII–XX of Diodoros of Sicily's *Library of History*. Diodoros wrote this, a universal history covering the period from mythological times to ca. 58 B.C. in forty books, between the fifties and the thirties B.C., which means that his is also our earliest extant account of the Diadoch period, written at the very end of what we call the Hellenistic era. The history is a compilation purporting to give in one work of manageable proportions an account of world history based on the works of the classic historians of earlier times; it neither has nor claims any originality beyond that of selection and emphasis: the selection of sources and of information given by the sources, and the emphasis placed upon certain events and historical figures. In particular Diodoros was a moralist of a rather naive type, who interlards his entire book with generally extremely commonplace moralizations; indeed, he states in the preface that he was attracted to the task because of the lessons he thought might be learned from history (I 3,1–8).

Since Diodoros gives our only surviving full-scale account not only of the Diadoch period but also of the reign of Philip II of Macedon, and is in addition one of the important subsidiary sources for the years 480–360 and for the reign of Alexander the Great, he has come in for a good deal of attention from practitioners of *Quellenforschung* in the past century. In that time he has been the subject of some extremely severe adverse criticism, and though in more recent times there has been a bit of a reaction in his favour, opinion on Diodoros is still rather dominated by the annihilating comments of some of the great German scholars: he is said by Niebuhr to have been spiritless, simple, and ignorant, one of the worst historians; and Mommsen speaks of the "unbelievable simplicity and even more unbelievable lack of conscience of this most wretched of all writers." Eduard Schwartz dismisses Diodoros's book as a particularly poor example of compilation that has survived by a combination of chance and the poor taste of the Christian reading public of the late Roman Empire who, unlike the well-educated pagans, were sufficiently *"anspruchslos"* to use Diodoros.[28] The excessive severity of these judg-

28. The judgments of Niebuhr, Mommsen, and Schwartz on Diodoros are quoted by

ments will be immediately apparent to any reader who compares the work of Diodoros with that of Justin (on whom see pp. 348–51 below); when judged against a genuinely wretched and incompetent writer like this, the solid merits of Diodoros stand out clearly. In fact, the chief criticism that can be made of Diodoros is simply that his powers of judgment and of sheer hard work were not up to the great task he had set himself.

Diodoros's account of the Diadoch period is actually excellent and well-balanced, though not without occasional errors and omissions. It is very probable that in the main it derives from Hieronymos of Kardia: this is proved beyond reasonable doubt by the general trend of the account, especially its concentration on Eumenes and the Antigonids, Hieronymos's employers. The problem is to determine whether Diodoros XVIII–XX is based exclusively on Hieronymos (as the followers of the *Einquellenprinzip* hold), or whether there is evidence of an admixture of one or more additional sources; further whether Diodoros used Hieronymos and his additional source(s) (if any) direct, or whether (as is held by a subsidiary branch of the *Einquellenprinzip* theorists) he merely used some middle or late Hellenistic source which had already done for him the work of condensing Hieronymos and adding information from other sources. It must suffice here to say that I do not believe in the *Einquellenprinzip;* that there are passages in Diod. XVIII–XX that are clearly not derived from Hieronymos because they are adulatory of Ptolemy (e.g., XVIII 28,2–6; 33,2–36,7; XIX 86,1–5; XX 100,3–4) or anachronistic (e.g., the account of Rhodian policy at Diod. XX 81,2–4); that Diodoros's citation of Douris's and Diyllos's histories is prima facie evidence for his having read those works; and that some passages in Diod. XVIII–XX can be at least as plausibly derived from Douris or Diyllos as from Hieronymos (e.g., Diod. XIX 52,5 = Diyllos F 1; prominent mention of Samos at XVIII 8,7 and 18,9 could be due to the local patriotism of Douris).[29]

Seibert, *Diadochen* pp. 27–28. See ibid., pp. 27–36, for a full review of modern scholarship on Diodoros.

29. The agreement between Diod. XIX 52,5 and Diyllos F 1 concerning the burial of Philippos Arrhidaios and Eurydike is striking: both mention Aigai as the place of burial, both mention the burial of Kynane (Eurydike's mother) at the same time, and both mention the holding of funeral games. Though one fragment is a slender basis on which to suggest that Diodoros used Diyllos, this seems quite plausible when we remember that Diodoros took the trouble to cite the beginning and end of Diyllos's history, and even the point at which the first *syntaxis* (volume) ended. The matter of the Samians' return from exile, mentioned at Diod. XVIII 8,7 and 18,9, was not of major historical significance and might easily have been left out

In short, I see no reason to disbelieve Diodoros's statement in his preface that he had read very widely among the more famous historians of the ancient world and that his book was a synthesis of that reading, rather than a series of excerpts from a few major sources, as claimed, for example, by Ed. Schwartz (*RE* s.v. Diodoros, col. 669). It has been claimed that Diodoros's preface is just a series of conventional *topoi* that are not to be taken seriously;[30] proof of this is seen in his claim to have traveled widely in Asia and Europe to see some of the important scenes of his history (I 4,1), which is regarded as simply taken from Polybios's praise of autopsy and travel. It is said that the only places Diodoros can be shown to have visited in person are Rome and Egypt, and that his erroneous placing of Nineveh on the Euphrates rather than the Tigris at II 3,2 proves he was probably never in Asia.[31]

Against this sort of criticism it can be pointed out that under ancient conditions visits to Egypt and Rome already represented unusually widespread travel for a man from the tiny city of Agyrion in Sicily, and the fact that Diodoros introduces no personal anecdotes is far from proving that he never visited Greece and Asia Minor (though no doubt he never went as far as Mesopotamia).[32] Again, the fact that Diodoros's claims in his preface are similar to those made by other historians in *their* prefaces, does not prove that they are untrue: if one were to analyze the prefaces of modern scholars, one might come up with a list of conventional *topoi* that could by the same logic be taken to prove that most of them are lying. Diodoros's claims concerning the amount of research and travel he did and the length of

---

by a historian like Hieronymos, but is certain to have been reported by Douris, whom it directly affected. Again, this is a far from conclusive argument—but Diodoros cited the beginning (and presumably, in the lost book XXI or XXII, the end) of Douris's history, and so certainly at least knew of its existence!

30. See, for example, Hornblower, *Hieronymus,* pp. 24–26, and the works cited by her there; but for a recent more favorable assessment, Sacks, *Hermes* 110 (1982):434–43.

31. Pointed out by, among others, C. H. Oldfather at vol. 1, p. xiii of his Loeb ed. of Diodoros, and Hornblower, *Hieronymus,* p. 25 n. 26.

32. It is well to recall that when Diodoros was researching and writing (ca. 65–30 B.C.) the Parthians held Mesopotamia and the lands further east, and the whole area of eastern Asia Minor, Syria, and Mesopotamia was repeatedly in turmoil with the campaigns of Pompey, Crassus, Caesar, and Antony. As to the erroneous siting of Nineveh, I fail to see how this proves that Diodoros never visited Asia, when he is here deriving his information from the fourth-century historian Ktesias (cited at II 2,2 as the authority for the description of oriental peoples and cities that follows); Ktesias is known for certain to have spent many years in Asia (he was court physician to the Persian king Artaxerxes Mnemon: see F. Jacoby, *RE* s.v. Ktesias, no. 1, col. 2033). If a man like Ktesias could be wrong about the site of Nineveh, Diodoros's following him in that error certainly cannot prove that he never visited Asia.

time he spent on his work may perhaps be a bit exaggerated, but there is no reason to dismiss them entirely.[33]

In all probability, then, Diodoros's account of Diadoch history in XVIII–XX of his *Bibliotheke* represents a synthesis of his reading of several historians who covered that period. Two of the historians whom Diodoros is likely to have read are Douris and Diyllos, and in all probability their histories had some influence on what Diodoros wrote, though we can only conjecture what that influence may have been. Some of Diodoros's information on the Lamian War and the career of Kassandros, for example, could come from Diyllos; and perhaps those parts of Diodoros XVIII–XX that deal in such adulatory terms with the career of Ptolemy could derive from the history of Douris of Samos, who wrote at a time when his native island was under Ptolemaic control and may even have been installed or at least recognized as tyrant of Samos by Ptolemy II.[34] In addition to these writers, Diodoros probably read at least one considerably later historian, for his account of the siege of Rhodes in 305/4 is introduced by a palpably anachronistic survey of Rhodian power and foreign policy, and the whole account is very plausibly thought to be derived in the main from the early-second-century historian Zenon of Rhodes.[35]

However, as already stated several times, Diodoros's major source in this part of his history was clearly Hieronymos of Kardia, whose concentration on the careers of Eumenes, Antigonos, and Demetrios is reflected in Diodoros's work. Though it has been doubted that Diodoros actually used Hieronymos directly, as opposed to getting his information via an intermediary, there is no good reason for this. Diodoros was well aware of the existence and nature of Hieronymos's history; he mentions Hieronymos four times (at XVIII 42,1 and 50,4; XIX 44,3 and 100,3), and each time refers to him as a historian, calling him in the first passage "the man who wrote the *History of the Diadochoi,*" and in the other passages simply "the man

33. Hornblower, *Hieronymus,* p. 25, argues at length that mentioning how long one had worked on a book was a *topos,* and she is clearly right; but this says nothing about the truth or falsity of the claim: modern historians often still adhere to this *topos* in their own introductions, quite truthfully (one supposes). In fact, Diodoros visited Egypt for his research during the 180th Olympiad (60–57 B.C.: Diod. I 44,1) and was still working on the book when Augustus planted a colony at Tauromenion (Diod. XVI 7,1), an event which occurred after 36 B.C. (see for the date, e.g., Schwartz, *RE* s.v. Diodoros, no. 38, col. 663): this covers a period of over twenty years and makes his claim to have spent some thirty years on the entire work quite plausible.

34. See my discussion on Douris at pp. 333–36 above.

35. For this see, for example, Hornblower, *Hieronymus,* pp. 56–59.

who wrote the history." Numerous specific passages of Diodoros can be assigned to the authority of Hieronymos beyond any reasonable doubt: the account at XVIII 50,4 of the proposals of alliance Antigonos sent to Eumenes through Hieronymos, for example; also the account of Hieronymos's failed attempt to take over the bitumen sources at the Dead Sea on Antigonos's behalf, and the surrounding account of the Nabataian Arabs in general, at XIX 98,1–100,2; and further the account of the duel of Eumenes and Antigonos in inner Asia between the end of 317 and the beginning of 315, in which Hieronymos certainly participated (XIX 12,1–34,8; 36,1–44,5; see esp. XIX 44,3 for Hieronymos's presence in Eumenes' entourage during these events). Moreover, Hieronymos's book was certainly still extant in Diodoros's day, for Diodoros's much younger contemporary Dionysios of Halikarnassos had access to a copy of it (see *De comp. verb.* 4,30, and cf. *Ant. Rom.* I 54). The only argument ever put forward for denying that Diodoros actually read Hieronymos depends on the assumption that Diodoros only ever uses a single source at a time; since there are elements in books XVIII–XX that cannot have come from Hieronymos, it would then follow that Diodoros must have used a later writer who epitomized Hieronymos and added extraneous matter.[36] But as soon as one dispenses with this arbitrary *Einquellenprinzip,* it becomes a logical absurdity to maintain that Diodoros did not actually read Hieronymos's book.

In fact, Diodoros deserves much credit for choosing as his main source for the history of the Diadoch period the evidently sober, factual, and reliable history of Hieronymos, rather than (say) the apparently much more sensational, but unreliable, *Makedonika* of Douris. Not that Diodoros's motives in electing to follow Hieronymos were those for which we now praise his choice: rather than the sobriety and reliability of Hieronymos's history, what is likely to have influenced Diodoros is the fascination of the careers of Eumenes, Antigonos, and Demetrios—Hieronymos's chief characters—whose rapid and extreme changes in fortune provided ample material for the sort of moralizing philosophical reflections that were among Diodoros's major interests in the writing of history (see, e.g., XVIII 53,1–4; XIX 48,3–4; 81,3–4; XXI 1,1; and cf. Diodoros's opening remarks at I 2,1–2). But whatever the reasons for Diodoros's choice of his sources, hc has produced what is in the main a very informative

36. Thus, for example, Vezin, *Eumenes von Kardia,* pp. 6–7, and Bottin, *RBPh* 7 (1928):1307–27.

and reliable account of the period 323–301. The reliability of Diodoros's account can be demonstrated in the case of numerous details from surviving contemporary epigraphic and numismatic evidence: many of the correspondences between such primary source material and books XVIII–XX of Diodoros are cited by Hornblower (*Hieronymus*, pp. 111–20), the most important being perhaps the Skepsis inscription (see *OGIS*, no. 5, and cf. Diod. XIX 75,6 and 105,1).

In general it may be said that without Diodoros XVIII–XX, no full history of the years 323–301 could be reconstructed, a fact whose truth is amply demonstrated by the wretchedness of the state of our knowledge of the years after 301, where only miserable fragments of Diodoros remain. All of the other sources, even the most important of them, are merely supplements to the seminal account of Diodoros: one might say that Diodoros gives us the body of our knowledge, while the other sources merely provide us with clothing in which to deck it out. Diodoros is so much more detailed and complete than the other sources that all investigation of the period must begin with him. The other sources should be used as supplements where they add credible details; where they disagree with Diodoros, the presumption must be that he is most probably correct, which is to say that he should be believed unless good reason can be shown for believing the variant source—Diodoros should be presumed innocent until shown guilty.

To this general predominance of Diodoros, however, there is one exception, in that the *Met' Alexandron* of Arrian should be given at least equal authority for the few years it covers. Arrian of Nikomedia is best known for his surviving work on Alexander the Great, generally considered the best of our sources for Alexander's career. He also, however, wrote a history (now lost) of events after Alexander's death, covering the years 323–320 in ten books. When one considers that the thirteen years of Alexander's reign fill only seven books in Arrian's treatment, it is clear that his account of the four years after Alexander's death went into extraordinary detail. Though we now possess only a brief (but excellent) epitome of this work by Photios and three substantial fragments of the work itself,[37] these represent a valuable supplement to Diodoros for the few years they cover.

37. For Arrian's *Ta Met' Alexandron* I use the text of A. Roos in the second edition, with corrections and additions by G. Wirth (Teubner, 1967), 2:253–86, 323–24. This gives the Photios epitome (from his *Myriobiblion*) as F 1 and the important Vatican palimpsest as Fs 24 and 25; in addition *PSI*, no. 1284, another fragment of Arrian, is given as a supplement at pp. 323–24, and one should see also the further restorations to this papyrus fragment by Wirth, *Klio* 46 (1965):283–88. In addition another palimpsest fragment, discovered in Gothenburg, was recently published by Noret, *AC* 52 (1983):235–42. For further bibliography, see also Seibert, *Diadochen*, pp. 46–49.

Arrian describes his historical method at the beginning of his history of Alexander, the *Anabasis,* indicating that he read a number of sources and combined what seemed to him the most trustworthy elements of the most trustworthy sources to form his own narrative.[38] There is no reason to suppose that his method in the *Met' Alexandron* was any different: the very length of the work proves that it must have combined information from a number of primary sources, for none of the primary sources can have treated the years 323–320 at anything like the same length.[39] This indicates that there was still a very substantial amount of source material available when Arrian wrote (second century A.D.), and Arrian is likely to have added rhetorical padding (speeches and the like) of his own. Scanty as the remains of his work are, they not only agree virtually entirely with Diodoros's account (thus confirming again Diodoros's accuracy), but also add considerable detail omitted by Diodoros, for example, concerning events in the second half of 320, where Diodoros passes over almost half a year in silence.

Besides Arrian, two other ancient writers can be used to supplement Diodoros: Plutarch and Polyainos. Plutarch's *Life of Eumenes* and sections 1–29 of his *Life of Demetrios* are useful sources, but their value should not be overrated. It is well known that Plutarch disclaimed any intention of writing strict history in his biographies,[40] and the anecdotal nature of his *Lives* backs up his disclaimer: he often used highly questionable source material, he ordered his narrative without strict regard for the chronological sequence of events if it suited him, and he often ignored events we consider important. Anyone who has worked on third-century history, where some of Plutarch's biographies are the fullest remaining sources, will appreciate that Plutarch is no match for Diodoros in the detail and accuracy of his historical accounts. Polyainos's *Stratagemata,* written in the mid second century A.D., is of value only on military affairs, to which it is restricted, but for these it provides much useful detail not found in Diodoros. The stratagems recorded by Polyainos agree by and large so well with Diodoros's narrative, and give such emphasis to Antigonos Monophthalmos, Eumenes of Kardia, and Demetrios Poliorketes, that it seems fairly clear that they derive (whether directly

38. Arrian *Anab.* I *init.;* see further Stadter, *Arrian of Nicomedia.*

39. See the remarks of Hornblower, *Hieronymus,* p. 99, and Stadter, *Arrian of Nicomedia,* pp. 144–52.

40. Thus Plut. *Alex.* 1,1–3; see further for a review of the modern scholarship on Plutarch's *Eumenes* and *Demetrios* the discussion in Seibert, *Diadochen,* pp. 42–44.

or indirectly) from Hieronymos of Kardia.[41] No in-depth study of the aims, methods, and sources of Polyainos has been undertaken since 1885, a sad lack in modern historiographical scholarship, but as far as can be determined, his knowledge of Macedonian and early Hellenistic military history seems to have been fairly accurate.[42]

Besides the major sources, we have a number of subsidiary literary sources, which add occasional helpful details to our knowledge. These are given in the list of sources included at the end of this work, and there is no need to discuss them here. Mention must, however, be made of Justin, who provides the only surviving connected narrative of the Diadoch period other than that of Diodoros. His epitome of Pompeius Trogus's *Historiae Philippicae,* produced at some time probably during the second or third centuries A.D., has been used by some scholars as one of the principal sources of the early Diadoch period (which is treated in books XIII–XV), a proceeding which seems wrong to me.[43] In my opinion Justin is a writer who should be accorded no independent authority, at least for any period on which an alternative source is available. The reason for this is the large number of errors, some of them minor, but many of them of major significance, that Justin can be shown to have perpetrated. Justin was a writer whose ineptness went so far that he was not even able to copy information given correctly by Trogus, and he certainly had no pretensions to being able to judge what was true or false in Trogus, whose reliability as a historian we can no longer judge. To establish the truth of these assertions, I shall indicate some of the major and minor blunders Justin can be shown from other sources to have perpetrated.

In his discussion of the dissensions at Babylon after the death of Alexander, Justin associates one Attalos with Meleagros as a leader of the pro-Arrhidaios infantry faction (XIII 3,2), and attributes to Attalos the attempt to assassinate Perdikkas (XIII 3,7–8), whereas our other sources make it clear that Meleagros instigated this assassination

---

41. This conclusion was drawn already by Melber, *JClPh,* suppl. 14 (1885):419–688, esp. 618–60. See also F. Lammerts, *RE* s.v. Polyainos, no. 8; Hornblower, *Hieronymus,* pp. 74–75; Seibert, *Diadochen,* p. 49.

42. The only thorough study of Polyainos is that by Melber cited in n. 41 above; Polyainos was himself of Macedonian origin, and thus had a special pride and interest in the military achievements of the Macedonian leaders of the late Classical and early Hellenistic eras: see the *prooemium* to his bk. IV.

43. For a review of the modern scholarship on Justin, see Seibert, *Diadochen,* pp. 51–53. A modern scholar who has committed what seem to me a number of historical blunders by placing too much reliance on Justin is P. Briant, for which see notes 45 and 47 below.

attempt, and show that Attalos was in fact a friend of Perdikkas and the husband of the latter's sister Atalante.[44] When recounting the Lamian War in Greece, Justin wrongly makes the fighting between Antipatros and the Greeks under Leosthenes occur at Herakleia (XIII 5,8) although the *Prologi* of Trogus's *Historiae* show that Trogus correctly centered the war at Lamia (Trogus *Prol.* 13). At XIII 6,1–3 Justin discusses the war fought by Perdikkas against the Kappadokian dynast Ariarathes, but comparison with Diod. XVIII 16,1–3 and 22,1–8 shows that Justin has committed the gross error of conflating with it Perdikkas's later campaign against Isauria in Pisidia, showing a total unawareness of the historical facts.[45] At XIII 8,5–8 Justin twice refers to Polyperchon as the man whom Eumenes met in battle, defeated, and killed in early 320, instead of Krateros, who is correctly so identified in Trogus *Prol.* 13; and Justin's utter carelessness with names is evident again and again in other sections of his epitome.[46]

In the opening section of book XIV, Justin discusses the activities of Eumenes in Asia Minor after the Macedonians in Egypt had condemned him to death, and reports that he first ravaged Aetolia (*sic*, though most editors emend to *Aeolia*), exacting contributions of money, and then moved to Sardis to do battle there with the enemy (XIV 1,6–7). Comparison with Arrian *Met' Alex.* 1,40–41 and Plut. *Eum.* 8,4–6 shows that Eumenes went to Sardis first, was persuaded by Kleopatra not to stay there, and then went to *Phrygia,* which he plundered to pay his troops. Justin's mention of Aetolia is doubtless

44. For Attalos, see Diod. XVIII 37,2–4 and Arrian *Met' Alex.* 24,1. On the role of Meleagros at Babylon, see Arrian *Met' Alex.* 1,2–3; Diod. XVIII 2,3 and 4,7–8; Curtius X 6,20–9,21 esp. at 8,1–7 (plot to murder Perdikkas). N.B. also that Justin's list of the satraps appointed at Babylon contains numerous errors, such as the assertion at XIII 4,15 that Nearchos was made satrap of Pamphylia and Lykia, and the naming at XIII 4,23 of Amyntas (rather than Philippos) as satrap of Baktria.

45. At XIII 6,1 Justin states: "Meanwhile, Perdikkas in war against Ariarathes, king of Kappadokia, brought him to battle but gained as victor no prize except wounds and dangers; for the enemy, retreating from the battlefield into the city, killed their wives and children and each burned his home with all possessions." The section from ". . . but gained as victor" on to the end of the description concerns Perdikkas's war against the Isaurians in Pisidia (see Diod. XVIII 22,1–8) and *not* Ariarathes. Yet in spite of the fact that Justin here has entirely overlooked Perdikkas's move with the royal army and the kings from Kappadokia into Pisidia (explicitly attested also by Plut. *Eum.* 3,7–4,1), Briant, *Antigone le Borgne,* pp. 192–98, accepts as authoritative the statement of Justin XIII 6,10 that Perdikkas subsequently held a council of war in Kappadokia, where he had left the kings—a piece of manifest nonsense.

46. That these errors were really made by Justin and not by an incompetent copyist seems to be proved by the fact that Orosius, using Justin as his source for his *Historiae adversum Paganos,* already found these errors in his copy of Justin and repeated them (Oros. III 23,6–23). For other important confusions of names, see n. 49 below.

due to a confusion with Polyperchon's contemporaneous war with the Aitolians, attested by Diod. XVIII 38,1–5. At XIV 2,4 Justin suggests that Eumenes, defeated by Antigonos and shut up in Nora, sought aid from Antipatros against Antigonos, and that such aid was actually sent; but Plut. *Eum.* 5,4–5 shows that Eumenes and Antipatros were bitter enemies, and Diod. XVIII 41,7–42,1 indicates that it was on the initiative of Antigonos that the position of Eumenes was referred to Antipatros. There was no question of aid coming to Eumenes from Antipatros (though aid was later sent by Arrhidaios, the satrap of Hellespontine Phrygia: Diod. XVIII 52,4).[47] Justin's account at XIV 2,6–3,21 of the war between Antigonos and Eumenes in 317–315, and of Eumenes' relations with the Argyraspids, is utterly inadequate, showing a preference for flabby rhetoric over historical fact, and a complete ignorance of the number, location, and outcomes of the battles fought between Antigonos and Eumenes in this period, to say nothing of any other operations by Antigonos; and again Trogus *Prol.* 14 shows greater knowledge than is displayed by Justin's epitome of Trogus.[48] Again at XV 2,3–4 Justin gets hopelessly confused between Alexander the Great's legitimate wife Roxane and her son Alexandros IV and the pretender Herakles and his mother Barsine, though again Trogus *Prol.* 15 indicates that Trogus gave the facts more correctly.[49]

Other errors by Justin could be adduced, but it should be clear by now that Justin was a thorough bungler who does not deserve to be

47. This obviously erroneous passage of Justin was taken seriously by Briant in *Rois, tributs et paysans,* pp. 84–86. Briant recognizes Justin's inability to keep names straight and his habit in epitomizing Trogus of totally confusing the train of events (p. 84 bottom), but still believes that Antipatros really was asked for aid against Antigonos by Eumenes, rather than following Diodoros in having the case of Eumenes referred to Antipatros by Antigonos.

48. Trogus *Prol.* 14 knows of Antigonos's expulsion of Eumenes from Kappadokia; his expulsion of Arrhidaios from Hellespontine Phrygia and of Kleitos from Lydia; the defeat of these two by Antigonos in the naval campaign near the Hellespont; and the war of Eumenes with the Argyraspids against Antigonos, culminating in Eumenes' final defeat and death. For all of this Justin substitutes a long account of Eumenes' relations with the Argyraspids having little in common with the sober and reliable account of Diodoros XIX, and not even showing awareness of the fact that two battles (Paraitakene and Gabiene) were fought between Eumenes and Antigonos in this war.

49. Trogus *Prol.* 15 reports that Kassandros killed one of Alexander's sons in Macedon, and that Polyperchon killed the other. Justin XV 2,1–5 has Kassandros kill Herakles and his mother Barsine to prevent him, being now fourteen years old, from assuming power as king, and adds that he likewise killed Alexander's other son and his mother Roxane. For a correct account, see Diod. XIX 105,2–3 (Kassandros ordered that Alexandros and his mother Roxane be killed) and XX 20,1–4 and 28,1–3 (Polyperchon first supported, then killed, Herakles, son of Barsine).

called a historian, and certainly cannot be used as a source of equal authority to Diodoros, Polyainos, or Plutarch, let alone be used to correct any of the latter. When Justin agrees with the principal sources, the agreement is rarely worth mentioning as it seldom adds to the authority of the information concerned; where he disagrees with the principal sources, the disagreement is to be decided in favor of the other sources and Justin's variant is rarely even worth mentioning. The only real use of Justin is that he does occasionally give a detail which, though not recorded by the major sources, is nevertheless in a context that the major sources show to be factual, and is in itself plausible and complementary to what the major sources relate. Such details may be accepted as probably true; examples are the mention at XIII 6,16 of Kleitos's command of a fleet for Perdikkas, and the activities of Eurydike recorded at XIV 5,1–5.

Consequently, the reader will find my narrative to be based in the main on Diodoros, Arrian, Plutarch, and Polyainos, with occasional additions from other sources. Of course this statement only applies to the literary sources: a number of inscriptions provide significant primary evidence of the first importance; of these, as of the minor literary sources, a full list is given in the list of sources.

ADDENDUM

K. Maresch has recently published a new historical fragment dealing with the assumption of kingship by Antigonos and Ptolemy (*P. Köln.*, 6 [1987]:96–109). The papyrus was written in the late second or first century B.C. and the presentation of the material betrays a strongly pro-Rhodian point of view. Accordingly Maresch conjectures, very plausibly in my view, that the author may be Zenon of Rhodes (for whom see *FGrH*, no. 523). The chief points of interest are that the papyrus presents Antigonos's aim as being to rule the whole *oikoumenē* just as Alexander had done (col. 1, lines 18–27), and that it places Ptolemy's assumption of the kingship as an immediate reaction to that of Antigonos (col. 2, lines 6–19). Maresch seems to view this as definite confirmation of these notions, already familiar to us from the other literary sources.

Needless to say the papyrus does not prove that Antigonos aimed at universal rule in the manner of Alexander, but merely that a pro-Rhodian source writing probably in the early second century presented this as his aim. The same goes for the date of Ptolemy's assumption of the kingship. The papyrus shows an anti-Antigonid bias in that it seems to have followed mention of Antigonos's "coronation" by a negative review of his earlier career, emphasizing his killing of rivals (Alketas and Eumenes are mentioned: F a, which is almost certainly the bottom part of col. 1; see p. 108), and states that the Rhodians and others deemed Ptolemy worthy of the kingship but feared Antigonos's assumption of it would prove oppressive (col. 2, lines 28–38). This papyrus may hence reveal the ultimate source of the view that Antigonos was oppressive and hubristic and aimed at universal rule: the pro-Rhodian historiography of the third and second centuries B.C.

Appendix 2

Antigonos's Military and Naval Forces

MILITARY FORCES

Numbers

A handful of passages in Diodoros's account of Diadoch history and Plutarch's *Life of Demetrios* give us an idea of the approximate size of Antigonos's military forces: Diod. XVIII 50,3 (319/18 B.C.); Diod. XX 73,2 (306 B.C.); Plut. *Dem.* 28,3 (301 B.C.).

Diod. XVIII 50,3 states that in the winter of 319/18, after the death of Antipatros, Antigonos reviewed his entire political and military position, and that he then had forces totaling 60,000 infantry, 10,000 cavalry, and thirty elephants. It seems clear that this is intended to be an expression of Antigonos's *total* military establishment from two facts: that Antigonos's *field* army in the campaigns of 319 amounted only to 40,000 infantry and 7,000 calvary (Diod. XVIII 45,1) and while he subsequently incorporated *some* of Alketas's army, this only amounted to 16,000 infantry and 900 cavalry, not all of whom joined Antigonos; and that Diodoros explicitly says at XVIII 50,3 that Antigonos planned if necessary to recruit further forces in addition to those enumerated, implying that those enumerated were *all* of Antigonos's forces at the time. One correction can be made to Diodoros's figures: Arrian *Met' Alex.* 1,43 says that Antigonos received seventy elephants from Antipatros, and this number seems to be confirmed by the fact that he had sixty-five a few years later in 316 (Diod. XIX 27,1).

Diod. XX 73,2 states that late in 306 Antigonos led an all-out attack on Egypt with an army of 80,000 infantry, 8,000 cavalry, and eighty-three elephants. This clearly represents an extreme military effort on Antigonos's part, being by a considerable margin the largest single force he ever mobilized, and being clearly a concentration of the great majority of the troops he then had under arms. Yet, as Griffith points out (*Mercenaries*, p. 51) "mercenary garrisons, if not an army of defense, must have been left in his [Antigonos's] northern territories" so that Griffith's estimate of at least 100,000 as the total troop strength of Antigonos's military forces at this time seems a conservative figure: perhaps 100,000 *infantry* plus at least 10,000 cavalry would be near the mark.

Plut. *Dem.* 28,3 informs us that at the battle of Ipsos in 301 Antigonos and Demetrios fielded more than 70,000 infantry, 10,000 cavalry, and seventy-five elephants. Again this battle clearly represented a supreme effort on the part of Antigonos, since he was then engaged in a life-or-death struggle, but he must nevertheless have had troops elsewhere: there was a very real danger from Ptolemy in the south (Diod. XX 113,1–2), and it seems that a flying column was sent to occupy Babylon in Seleukos's rear (see, e.g., Tarn *HMND*, p. 38). Accounting, therefore, for these troops and for garrisons in Syria/Palestine and elsewhere, a total of some 90,000–100,000 infantry and 12,000 cavalry seems likely for Antigonos's military establishment at this time.

It seems therefore that Antigonos's total military establishment rose from some 70,000 men in 319, when he controlled only part of Asia Minor, to somewhere in the region of 110,000 men in the period 306–301, when Asia Minor and Syria/Palestine were under his rule. Of these a very considerable number must at all times have been on garrison duty, and it seems unlikely that Antigonos normally had many more than 40,000 men in the central field army under his direct control: that is roughly the size of the army with which he fought Eumenes in 316 (Diod. XIX 27,1: 28,000 infantry, 8,500 cavalry, and an unspecified number of light infantry); and since the army with which Demetrios joined Antigonos from Europe in 302 numbered some 25,000 (Diod. XX 110,4: I do not count the 25,000 Greek allies or 8,000 pirates and the like there enumerated), it would seem that Antigonos marched into Asia Minor in 302 with about 45,000 men.

Provenance

Macedonians: The Macedonian core of Antigonos's army was formed by the 8,500 Macedonian infantry plus an uncertain number of (Macedonian) Companion cavalry handed over to Antigonos by Antipatros in 320 (Arrian *Met' Alex.* 1,43, and cf. chap. 2 n. 40 above). In the course of the years 319–317 Antigonos successively took over the military forces of Eumenes, Alketas, Arrhidaios, and Kleitos, each of which had some Macedonians as a nucleus. Numbers are extremely hard even to guess at, but the fact of a core of Macedonians in these armies is well attested: for Eumenes' army in 320/19, see Plut. *Eum.* 7,1 and 8,6–7; for the army of Alketas and Attalos, see Diod. XVIII 37,3–4, Arrian *Met' Alex.* 1,39, and Plut. *Eum.* 5,2; for Arrhidaios's force, see Diod. XVIII 51,1, speaking of 1,000 Macedonians under his command; and for Kleitos's force the significant fact is that he was sent to fight Antigonos by Polyperchon, who was then in charge of Macedon proper. Given the number of 1,000 for Arrhidaios's Macedonians, it would not be unreasonable to guess that by incorporating most of the armies listed above, Antigonos gained 5,000–8,000 new Macedonian troops. When Antigonos went east in 317/16, he seems to have left these Macedonians behind, since at the battles of Paraitakene and Gabiene we hear only of the Macedonians (now about 8,000) whom he had from Antipatros. By winning out over Eumenes, Antigonos gained a further 6,000 Macedonian infantrymen: 3,000 Argyraspids and 3,000 Hypaspists (Diod. XIX 28,1); 1,000 of these he gave to Sibyrtios for service in the east (Polyainos IV 6,15), but the rest he incorporated into his own forces either as garrison settlers or as regular troops. This brings Antigonos's Macedonians up to some 18,000 or so (fewer than 8,000 from Antipatros plus 5,000 or more in Asia Minor plus 5,000 from Eumenes). In addition there was the cavalry. At Paraitakene, Antigonos seems to have had somewhere between 1,800 and 2,400 Macedonian cavalry. At XIX 29,1–7 Diodoros mentions 1,000 *hetairoi* (certainly Macedonian), 800 *asthippoi* and *katoikoi* (also Macedonians: see Hammond, *CQ*, n.s., 28 [1978]:128–35, though *contra* Milns, *CQ* 31 [1981]:347–54), 300 *agēma,* and 300 *paides,* who would most likely have been *at least* in part Macedonians. After 316, therefore, Antigonos clearly had at least some 20,000 Macedonians in his Asian realm. A later addition to these were the 6,000 Macedonians who deserted from Kassandros to Demetrios in 304 (Plut. *Dem.* 23,1) and must have been brought by Demetrios to Asia in 302. Evidently, then, the total pool of manpower for Macedonian colonization in Asia in the early Diadoch period was in the region of 26,000–30,000 men.

Greeks: ·Greek troops appear in Antigonos's armies under two basic headings, *xenoi* (mercenaries) and *symmachoi* (allies). Taking the latter first, we hear of 500 cavalry *symmachoi* fighting for Antigonos at Paraitakene in 316 (Diod. XIX 29,4), and that they were Greeks appears by a process of elimination, since the cavalry of other nationalities at this battle are all specified as being Lydian, Median, or whatever. That Antigonos regularly used contingents of allied troops from the Greek cities appears from his letter to Skepsis in 311 (*OGIS*, no. 5, lines 41–43), and a number of such contingents happen to be epigraphically attested: *Samian* troops stationed in Karia (*SEG*, 1, no. 358), *Kalymnian* troops serving at Pogla in the Kabalia district (Segrè, *TC*, no. 8), *Athenian* soldiers considerably more than 300 in number serving in the Ipsos campaign (*IG* II^2 657, lines 16–26, though these could have been mercenaries), *Cycladic* forces apparently campaigning with Antigonid generals in the Peloponnesos ca. 312/11 (Geagan, *Hesperia* 37 [1968]:381–84). In addition one might notice the 25,000 allied troops from the Hellenic League who fought with Demetrios in Thessaly in 302 (Diod. XX 110,4). As to the *xenoi*, Antigonos at all times used huge numbers of mercenaries, and has been termed by Griffith (*Mercenaries*, p. 44) "the greatest employer of all" (sc., of mercenaries). That these *xenoi* were at the very least for the greater part Greeks has been taken as axiomatic and need not be doubted (see, e.g., Griffith, *Mercenaries*, p. 42: "the *xenoi*, the Greek mercenaries"). The non-Greek troops are invariably identified by their ethnics in our (Greek!) sources, and at one point Diodoros even specifically distinguishes some non-Greek mercenaries as *pantodapoi misthophoroi* rather than *xenoi* (Diod. XIX 29,4). It would take too long to list here all the various mercenary detachments mentioned as serving under Antigonos, but it is noteworthy that Antigonos's phalanx at Paraitakene contained a body of 9,000 Greek mercenaries and that at this same battle he had 2,200 Greek mercenary cavalry of the type called "Tarentines" (Diod. XIX 29,2–3), and that besides heavy infantry (hoplites and peltasts) and cavalry, Antigonos also used Greek mercenary light infantry: Cretan archers, attested, for example, during the siege of Rhodes (Diod. XX 85,3).

Asians and other barbarians: Besides Macedonian and Greek troops, Antigonos also made extensive use of barbarian troops, especially Asian levies. Our best source for this fact is Diodoros's thorough list of Antigonos's troop contingents at the battle of Paraitakene (Diod. XIX 29,1–7), though Asian troops are mentioned elsewhere too. At the battle of Paraitakene, Antigonos had in his phalanx 3,000 *Lykian* and *Pamphylian* heavy infantry, and such troops are mentioned again: 500 were left with Demetrios in Syria in 313 (Diod. XIX 69,1) and 1,000 later fought with Demetrios at the battle of Gaza (Diod.

XIX 82,4). There were 1,000 *Lydian* and *Phrygian* cavalry with Antigonos at Paraitakene, and also some 2,000 *Median* cavalry and about 500 *Parthian* horse archers. *Persian* light infantry were extensively used: Antigonos presumably took over the 500 archers and slingers who were with Arrhidaios in 320 (Diod. XVIII 51,1); he later left 400 of such troops with Demetrios in Syria, and 500 Persian slingers subsequently fought with Demetrios at Gaza (Diod. XIX 69,1; 82,3). In addition a large number of Persians fought in the army of Antigonos's general Nikanor in 311 (Diod. XIX 92,3–4). After his defeat at Gaza, Demetrios is said to have recruited new soldiers in *Kilikia,* and further recruiting there preceded his campaign in Cyprus in 306, at which time it seems likely that *Karian* troops were likewise recruited (Diod. XX 46,6; 47,1). Of non-Asian barbarians, we hear of 1,000 *Thracian* cavalry with Antigonos at Paraitakene, perhaps the same as the 1,000 Thracians supposed to be left with Peithon Krateua in 315 (Polyainos IV 6,14); also Antigonos received reinforcement of 2,000 Balkan *Autariatai,* who deserted to him from Lysimachos in 302 (Diod. XX 113,3). Most significant of all these, however, were evidently the *pantodapoi,* heavy infantry of mixed race armed in the Macedonian fashion, who are shown by the account of Paraitakene to have made up a substantial part of Antigonos's phalanx infantry. These were clearly mostly, if not exclusively, men of various Asian races (see Griffith, *Mercenaries,* pp. 42, 48–49), and formed one of the most important elements in Antigonos's field army in terms of role and numbers; we also hear of *pantodapoi* cavalry: 500 at Paraitakene and 1,500 at Gaza (Diod. XIX 82,3), where they are distinguished from the Macedonian cavalry (800 *hetairoi*) and from Greek mercenary cavalry (100 "Tarentines").

NAVAL FORCES

Numbers

Although Antigonos's naval forces were significant in the years 319–317, they were subsequently eclipsed during his absence in the east, and on his return to the Mediterranean lands in 314 he had to start building up a navy almost from scratch. By mid 313, after the end of the siege of Tyre, we are informed by Diod. XIX 62,7–8 that Antigonos had accumulated a navy of 240 ships of war (*naus makras*). This force was divided into two fleets of 50 and 190 ships respectively, the latter under the command of Dioskourides (Diod. XIX 62,9). At the end of 313, when Dioskourides was operating with his fleet at Lemnos (Diod. XIX 68,4), Antigonos summoned another fleet from Phoenicia to Karia, evidently therefore of new ships, commanded by Medeios of Larissa, and these captured all or most of 36 Pydnaian ships on their way to Karia (Diod. XIX 69,3). Since Medeios's fleet early in 312 turns out to be 100 strong (Diod. XIX 75,7), it seems likely that he set out from Phoenicia at the end of 313 with about 70 ships and reached 100 by incorporating the former Pydnaian ships into his fleet. In addition we hear early in 312 of Telesphoros being sent to the Peloponnesos by Antigonos with 50 ships (Diod. XIX 74,1), but it is not clear that these are separate from the numbers already enumerated: they could be the 50 ships mentioned above at Tyre, now summoned to serve as Telesphoros's fleet; they could be a detachment from Dioskourides' fleet; or they could be 50 different ships raised from the coastal cities of Asia Minor. Thus in 312 Antigonos evidently had between 340 and 390 warships on active service (50 + 190 + 100 [+ 50?]). This was an unusually large number, needed for the war against Ptolemy and Kassandros simultaneously. Subsequently we hear of Antigonos sending out fleets of 250 ships (Plut. *Dem.* 8,3) in 307; 180 or 190 ships at Salamis in Cyprus in 306 (Plut. *Dem.* 16,1–2; Polyainos IV 7,7 and see above chap. 4 n. 38); 150 warships and 100 transports for the invasion of Egypt in late 306 (Diod. XX 73,2); 200 warships and 170 transports to the siege of Rhodes in 305 (Diod. XX 82,4); and 330 ships, doubtless including both warships and transports, to Greece in 304 (Plut. *Dem.* 23,1). Hence it would seem that Antigonos was able regularly to maintain roughly 200 warships and upwards of 100 transport vessels during the period 307–302, and could significantly increase the number of warships if an unusual effort were necessary.

Provenance

Phoenicia: When Antigonos began to rebuild his navy in 314, the main effort of building took place in Phoenicia, at the cities of Sidon, Byblos, and Tripolis (Diod. XIX 58,1–4). By mid 313 there were 120 ships at Tyre, described by Diodoros as "the first to be finished of the ships that had been built in Phoenicia . . . including those captured at Tyre." It is clear that from this time on, Phoenicia was one of the bastions of Antigonos's naval strength: at the battle of Salamis in 306, we are told, the best ships in the Antigonid fleet were seven Phoenician *hexēreis,* on one of which Demetrios himself fought in this battle (Diod. XX 50,3 and 52,1). Though it is nowhere specifically stated, one can hardly doubt that the Phoenician ships in Antigonos's navy were mostly manned by Phoenician sailors.

Kilikia: During Antigonos's naval building program in 314, a shipyard was also established in Kilikia (Diod. XIX 58,4), and no doubt the ships built there were manned by Kilikians. When Demetrios started on his expedition to conquer Cyprus, we hear of him first putting in at Kilikia to gather additional men and ships, so that we cannot reasonably doubt that Kilikian ships fought at the battle of Salamis in 306 (Diod. XX 47,1).

Rhodes: The fifth shipyard established by Antigonos in 314 was on the island of Rhodes, whose people agreed to build ships for Antigonos from specially imported wood (Diod. XIX 58,5). At Diod. XIX 61,5 we hear of Antigonos summoning the ships built at Rhodes to Tyre; at XIX 62,7 we hear of Dioskourides joining Antigonos at Tyre with 80 ships from the Hellespont and Rhodes (i.e., 40 from each?); and at XIX 64,5 we hear that a flotilla of an unspecified number of ships built at Rhodes, but crewed by Karians, was captured by an admiral of Ptolemy's in 313. Whether these three pieces of information add up to two or three Rhodian flotillas is disputed (see Hauben, *Historia* 26 [1977]:322–27; two flotillas seems likely to be correct, cf. also Berthold, *Rhodes,* p. 61 n. 5). Whether any Rhodians actually served on these ships is not clear; at any rate in 312 the Rhodians made an alliance with Antigonos and furnished a squadron of 10 ships to his fleet sailing to liberate Greece (Diod. XIX 77,3).

Hellespont: Two squadrons of ships from the Hellespont are mentioned as joining Antigonos's navy in 313: one of 40 ships under the admiral Themison of Samos, and one of 80 ships of which some (perhaps half?) were actually from Rhodes (Diod. XIX 62,7). Doubtless "Hellespont" is here used loosely, and these ships may be assumed to have been gathered from the Greek cities allied to Antigonos along the Propontis and southern Black Sea coast, having congregated at the Hellespont and sailed thence to Tyre.

Karia: As noted above, Karian sailors are recorded crewing a squadron of ships built for Antigonos at Rhodes in 313 (Diod. XIX 64,5).

Athens: At the battle of Salamis in 306, 30 Athenian quadriremes fought in Demetrios's fleet against Ptolemy (Diod. XX 50,3). This is doubtless to be connected with the information that Demetrios made an alliance with Athens in 307 (Diod. XX 46,1) and engaged to have his father Antigonos provide them with wood to build 100 warships, which Antigonos indeed did (Diod. XX 46,4, and cf. *IG* II^2 1492b, lines 118–24, mentioning the presence of the wood at Athens). Evidently some ships were built already over the winter of 307/6 and sailed with Demetrios to Cyprus.

Eretria: An inscription (*IG* XII.9 210) preserves record of Eretrians serving under Demetrios on ships, no doubt in 302 (cf. Diod. XX 110,2).

Ionia and the Islands: Although no ships or sailors from these regions are recorded in Antigonos's navy, many officers are (see app. 3 below), and it seems likely that these regions would have contributed more than officers to his navy.

Appendix 3

A Prosopography of Antigonos's Friends and Subordinates

A considerable number of friends, officers, and diplomats of Antigonos are mentioned in our literary sources, and many more are known to us through the astonishing profusion of honorific inscriptions concerned with such men set up by the Greek cities and in part still surviving. This material is here gathered for the first time into a single survey, giving the full evidence to back up many assertions made in the text of this work, especially in part 2. The men who can be identified with certainty or a high degree of probability as subordinates of Antigonos are presented in alphabetical order with a list of relevant sources for each person, a biography based on the sources, and some further literature on that person if any is available. At the end there is a separate group of *Incerti et Anonymi,* the former men who may possibly have served under Antigonos, the latter a number of epigraphical attestations of subordinates of Antigonos whose names are no longer preserved.

In a prosopographical survey of this sort, a number of rather arbitrary decisions have to be made based on one's best judgment of the available material: who is to be relegated to the *Incerti,* for example, and when references in the sources to someone with a common name (e.g., Philippos) are to be identified as one person or several. My tendency is optimistic in both instances: I have probably kept persons in the main survey whom others would consider uncertain; and I have doubtless identified as concerned with one man references that others would keep separate as belonging to distinct individuals. On the other hand, it may be that some readers will find me too conservative in this respect, as I do separate some persons who have been identified and relegate to the *Incerti* some men who have confidently been claimed as Antigonid officers.

In general, I include only men who can be shown to have served under Antigonos or one of his generals between 323 and 301; included, therefore, are subordinates of Demetrios before Ipsos, and excluded any men who are only known to have served under Demetrios after Ipsos. Rival dynasts like Peithon Krateua and Seleukos, who both served with Antigonos for a time, are excluded since they were not really subordinates; other dynasts who ruled territories within Antigonos's general realm as his allies, e.g., Zipoites of Bithynia and Dionysios of Herakleia, have been included. The scope of this survey is thus much narrower than, say, Berve's work *Das Alexanderreich auf prosopografischer Grundlage* (cited simply as "Berve"), in the second part of which he seeks to review every person who can in any way be brought into contact with Alexander and his career, including Alexander's enemies. My aim has been more modest, and I hope that in bringing together the material here appended I have achieved a complete survey as far as the evidence currently goes.

The sources listed at the beginning of each biographical sketch should be exhaustive, at least in the present state of the evidence. I have not sought to achieve completeness, however, in the works listed under the heading "Further Reading" for each individual. New studies appear at too rapid a rate for that to be practical; I have therefore given only what seemed to me the most accessible and useful modern studies appropriate to each person here reviewed. The abbreviations of titles used here should be readily intelligible in combination with the bibliography at the end of this work. References to *RE* s.v. (often followed by a number) are to the article in the Pauly-Wissowa *Realencyclopädie* under the name of the person concerned; references to Berve followed by a number are to the entries in vol. 2 of his *Alexanderreich*. Two general articles which have not been cited in this appendix, but which are valuable discussions of the relationship between ruler and friend or subordinate in Hellenistic times, are Habicht, "Die herrschende Gesellschaft in den hellenistischen Monarchien," *VSWG* 45 (1958):1–16; and Herman, "The 'Friends' of the Early Hellenistic Rulers: Servants or Officials?" *Talanta* 11/12 (1980/81):103–49.

1. ADEIMANTOS, son of Androsthenes, of Lampsakos

Sources. Demochares *apud* Athenaios VI 253a (= *FGrH,* no. 75 F1); Dionysios Tryphonos *apud* Athenaios VI 255c; Diogenes Laertios

V 57; Strabo XIII 589; *IG* XII.9 198; Daux, *Delphes,* p. 351, no. 2; Moretti, *ISE,* no. 9.

Career. Adeimantos is reported by Strabo (XIII 589) to have been one of the four most famous men ever produced by Lampsakos (the other three being the logographos Charax; the rhetorician and historian Anaximenes; and Metrodoros, the friend of Epikouros). He was apparently a close friend of the philosopher Theophrastos, for Diogenes Laertios (V 57) informs us that he received one of the three copies of Theophrastos's testament.

More significantly for us, Adeimantos was one of the most important diplomats in Demetrios's service during his campaign to liberate Greece from Kassandros in 304–302. Decrees honoring him survive from both Eretria (*IG* XII.9 198) and Athens (Moretti, *ISE,* no. 9). The former granted him citizenship and a statue for his services to Eretria and to the cause of freedom of the Greeks; the latter is more specific about Adeimantos's activities. This inscription shows that Adeimantos was involved in the establishment of the League of Korinth by Demetrios, and was nominated by Demetrios to be one of the *proedroi* (presidents) of the *synedrion* (representative council) that governed the league. For his activities in connection with this league, the Athenians decided to award him public praise and a gold crown. As the inscription breaks off at that point, it is not known what other honors (if any) were granted Adeimantos.

However, Demochares, the son of Laches and nephew of Demosthenes, who was an opponent of Demetrios and hence of Adeimantos, reported that Adeimantos (whom he calls a flatterer of Demetrios) received heroic honors at Athens (see Athenaios VI 253a). It is not clear from Demochares' hostile account whether these heroic honors were awarded publicly by the city, but it is nonetheless a great honor for Adeimantos even if he was heroized only by some private individuals. We owe the preservation of this information to Athenaios, who also preserves another anecdote about Adeimantos, demonstrating his admiration for Demetrios's wife Phila (VI 255c): Adeimantos and some of his Athenian friends set up a temple and a cult statue of "Aphrodite Phila" in the deme of Thria. The existence of this cult of Phila as Aphrodite in Athens is confirmed by a fragment of the comic poet Alexis, also in Athenaios (VI 254a), where one of the characters drinks a toast to King Antigonos, his son Demetrios, and Aphrodite Phila.

We also have, finally, a letter from Adeimantos to Demetrios preserved in an inscription from Delphi (Daux, *Delphes,* p. 351, no. 2). The letter was written by Adeimantos in his capacity as president of the *synedrion* of the League of Korinth and reports to Demetrios that the Delphic Amphiktyons have passed a decree concerning him, which he forwards together with letters from the king's friends, and that the *synedrion* has also passed a decree. Unfortunately the subject matter of these decrees is lost, as the inscription breaks off after four lines.

Further reading. Robert, *Hellenica* 2 (1946):15–33; G. Daux, *AE,* 1953/54 (= *Mélanges Oikonomos*), pp. 245–54; Habicht, *Gottmenschentum,* pp. 55–58; Wehrli, *Antigone et Démétrios,* pp. 123–25; Badian and Martin, *ZPE* 61 (1985):167–72.

2. ADRASTOS

Sources. Buckler and Robinson, *Sardis VII,* no. 1.

Career. Adrastos is recorded in this inscription (the famous Mnesimachos inscription, for the date of which see P. Debord, below) as holding a farmstead in the plain of Sardis under Antigonos, which indicates that he was probably a soldier-settler of Antigonos. Nothing is recorded of his rank or activities.

Further reading. Debord, "L'Esclavage sacré," pp. 258–60; id., *Aspects,* app. 5, pp. 244–51.

3. AGESILAOS

Sources. Diodoros XIX 57,4; 59,1; and cf. XIX 62,6.

Career. Agesilaos was a diplomat in the service of Antigonos who was sent out on an important mission to Cyprus in 315 to try to win over some of the Cypriot dynasts to support Antigonos, rather than Ptolemy. He seems to have succeeded in winning over Pumathion of Kition, Praxippos of Lapethos, Stasioikos II of Marion, the king of Keryneia, and Androkles of Amathous. Given the importance of the mission and the successes obtained, Agesilaos would have been a fairly senior man who had been with Antigonos for some time and enjoyed a high degree of trust.

Further reading. Olshausen, *Prosopographie,* no. 62; Beloch, *GG,* 4.2:331ff.; Seibert, *Ptolemaios I,* pp. 143–44.

4. AISCHYLOS of Rhodes (?)

Sources. OGIS, no. 5, lines 5, 48 (= Welles, *RC,* no. 1); Arrian *Anab.* III 5,3; Curtius IV 8,4; Diodoros XVIII 52,7; *IG* II^2 569, lines 6, 9.

Career. The famous letter of Antigonos to the Skepsians (*OGIS,* no. 5) mentions Aischylos as a diplomat involved in the negotiations leading to the peace of 311. He was sent by Antigonos with Demarchos to Kassandros to arrange a conference at the Hellespont. After the successful conclusion of these negotiations, Aischylos was sent on to Ptolemy to include him in the peace and receive pledges from him on behalf of Antigonos. He was clearly a man of standing in Antigonos's service.

Interestingly, there is another mention of an Aischylos in connection with Antigonos. In 319 Aischylos of Rhodes was convoying 600 talents of silver to the kings in Macedon. When he put in at Ephesos, Antigonos intercepted the convoy and seized the money to pay his troops, as Diodoros informs us (XVIII 52,7). It seems likely that this Aischylos of Rhodes is the same man as Antigonos's diplomat; after all, once Antigonos had seized the 600 talents, Aischylos would have been better off joining Antigonos's service than sailing on to Macedon empty-handed. Aischylos of Rhodes was a former officer of Alexander's: he was one of the two officers left by Alexander in charge of the garrison troops in Egypt (Arrian *Anab.* III 5,3; Curtius IV 8,4). His experience in Egypt was no doubt a factor in Antigonos's choice of him for the mission to Ptolemy in 311.

A third mention of an Aischylos in connection with Antigonos, ignored so far by modern commentators, is in an Athenian inscription concerning the island of Lemnos (*IG* II^2 569). Lemnos was controlled by Antigonos in the years 313–307, when Athens was under Kassandros; but when Demetrios liberated Athens in 307, Antigonos returned to Athens the islands Lemnos and Imbros as a mark of friendship (Diod. XX 46,4 and cf. *IG* II^2 1492b, lines 124–38, mentioning tribute paid to Athens by the two islands in 306/5 B.C.). Though *IG* II^2 569 is very fragmentary, it seems that the inscription records this handing back of Lemnos to Athens in 307 by Antigonos (there is mention of freedom and of the restoration of the ancestral constitution). Aischylos is mentioned in lines 6 and 9, and could be either the departing Antigonid commander or the arriving Athenian officer. If one prefers the former interpretation (as I am inclined to do), it would seem that this is another mention of Aischylos of Rhodes, who would have been placed over Lemnos (and maybe Imbros too) by Antigonos between ca. 310 and 307.

Further reading: Olshausen, *Prosopographie,* no. 63; J. Kaerst, *RE* s.v., no. 12; P. Schoch, *RE* suppl. 4 (1924) s.v. nos. 12b and 12a; Berve, no. 35; Hauben, *Vlootbevelhebberschap,* pp. 7–9.

5. AKIOS

Sources. OGIS, no. 5, line 70 (= Welles, *RC,* no. 1); *OGIS,* no. 6, lines 1, 36 (cf. C. Michel, *REG* 32 [1919]:388–92).

Career. Akios is mentioned in Antigonos's letter to the Skepsians as the emissary bringing the letter from Antigonos to Skepsis. In the Skepsian decree responding to Antigonos's letter he is also mentioned, with praise for his goodwill towards the Skepsians. His position in Antigonos's service cannot have been very high-ranking, for the job of bringing a letter and a copy of a treaty to the relatively small and unimportant town of Skepsis (and, no doubt, to the other towns of the Troad) was not particularly significant.

Further reading. Olshausen, *Prosopographie,* no. 64; P. Schoch, *RE* suppl. 4 s.v., no. 12.

6. ALEXANDROS from Macedon

Sources. Diod. XX 94,5; *FGrH,* no. 533 F2 (= P. Berol. 11632), lines 35, 45.

Career. Alexandros was a friend and high-ranking officer of Demetrios's at the siege of Rhodes. Demetrios had attempted to persuade the mercenary captain Athenagoras of Miletos, who had been sent by Ptolemy to aid the Rhodians, to betray the city to him. Alexandros was sent into Rhodes through a secret tunnel to conclude the negotiations, but Athenagoras instead handed him over to the Rhodians, who decided to kill him. The Berlin papyrus informs us, however, that Demetrios arranged to ransom him (lines 47–48).

Further reading. Olshausen, *Prosopographie,* no. 73; J. Kaerst, *RE* s.v., no. 21; Launey, *Recherches,* pp.303, 1171.

7. ALKAIOS, son of Heraios, from Ainos

Sources. *IG* II² 495 (= Moretti, *ISE,* no. 6); *IG* IV².1 58.

Career. Alkaios served as an officer in Demetrios's forces in Greece in 304–302, as we know from an Athenian decree describing him as *διατρίβων παρὰ τῶι βασιλ[ε]ι Δημητρίωι.* Besides being honored by the Athenians, he was also praised as a public benefactor by the Epidaurians, presumably in connection with services rendered during Demetrios's Peloponnesian campaign in 303.

Further reading. P. Schoch, *RE* suppl. 4 s.v., no. 8a; Osborne, *Naturalisation in Athens,* no. D 60.

8. ALKIMOS from Epeiros

Sources: Diodoros XX 98,1–9; Plutarch *Demetrios* 21,4; *IG* II² 773.

Career. We learn from Diodoros and Plutarch that Alkimos was one of Demetrios's most valued officers at the siege of Rhodes, outstanding for his strength and courage. When the engineer Zoilos of Cyprus made two special suits of steel armor, Demetrios wore one himself and gave the other to Alkimos (Plut. *Dem.* 21,4–6). When a breach in the Rhodian wall had been created, Demetrios selected Alkimos and Mantias to lead a night attack with 1,500 picked men, to seize the agora at dawn and create a diversion that would enable a general assault on the walls outside to succeed. Unfortunately, the enterprise failed and both Alkimos and Mantias were killed trying to lead the picked force back out of Rhodes after some desperate fighting (Diod. XX 98,1–9).

An inscription from Athens (*IG* II^2 773; cf. Habicht below) suggests that Alkimos was with Demetrios in Greece in 307/6. The inscription, which is from the archonship of Koroibos (306/5), was in honor of an [A]lkim[os] who is no doubt this man. It may be that Alkimos made himself useful to the Athenians serving with Demetrios in Cyprus in 306. Unfortunately, only the prescript of the inscription is preserved, so that we know nothing of the nature of Alkimos's services to, or the honors bestowed on him by, Athens.

Further reading. J. Kirchner, *RE* s.v., no. 11; Habicht, *AJAH* 2, no. 1 (1977):37–39; Launey, *Recherches,* pp. 408, 1204.

9. ANDRONIKOS, son of Agerros (?), from Olynthos

Sources. Arrian *Anab.* III 23,9; 24,5; Curtius VII 3,3; Diodoros XIX 59,2; 69,1; 82,4; 86,1–2.

Career. Andronikos of Olynthos is reported to have accompanied Alexander throughout his expedition, and was hence one of Antigonos's more senior and valued officers. In 314 Antigonos left Andronikos in charge of the siege of Tyre (Diod. XIX 59,2), while he himself secured the southern coast of Palestine. In 312 Andronikos was one of the four senior officers left as advisers to Demetrios in Syria (Diod. XIX 69,1). Despite the cautious advice of his co-commanders, Demetrios fought and lost the battle of Gaza. Andronikos survived the battle, in which he commanded the right wing (Diod. XIX 82,4), and took command of the garrison at Tyre, attempting to hold the city for Antigonos and rudely rebuffing Ptolemy's attempts to subvert his loyalty. When the garrison mutinied and handed him over to Ptolemy, he was nevertheless well treated and became a friend of Ptolemy's (Diod. XIX 86,1–2). It is not clear whether he returned to Antigonos's service or remained thenceforth with Ptolemy.

Concerning his service with Alexander, it seems likely that the Andronikos, son of Agerros, who in 330 negotiated the surrender of the Greek ex-mercenaries of Dareios in Hyrkania and was then appointed their commander when they entered Alexander's service

(Arrian *Anab.* III 23,9; 24,5), was the same man as Andronikos of Olynthos. Berve (below) denies such an identification on the grounds that Agerros is a Macedonian name; but, if this is indeed so, there would be nothing very surprising about finding a Macedonian name in use at Olynthos, particularly in what was evidently a pro-Macedonian family. His use as a negotiator with, and then commander of, Greek mercenaries suggests that Andronikos, son of Agerros, could well have been a Greek himself, and hence none other than Andronikos of Olynthos. In 328 Andronikos took part in the operations against Satibarzanes in Areia (Curt. VII 3,3), after which nothing further is heard of him until he appears in Antigonos's army at Tyre.

Further reading. U. Wilcken, *RE* s.v., no. 11; J. Kaerst, *RE* s.v., no. 10; Launey, *Recherches,* pp. 301–4, 1170; Berve, nos. 78, 79.

10. ANTIGONOS, son of Demetrios, Macedonian

Sources. See J. Kaerst, *RE* s.v., no. 4.

Career. Antigonos, nicknamed Gonatas, was the grandson of Antigonos Monophthalmos, the son of Demetrios and Phila. Since he died in 240/39 reputedly aged eighty he must have been born in 319, which shows that his parents must have married in mid 320. Obviously, then, he grew up under the rule of and at the court of his grandfather, Monophthalmos. For an anecdote indicating his attachment to his grandfather, see Plutarch *Pyrrhos* 34,4, reporting that when he was shown the head of his dead enemy Pyrrhos, he did not rejoice but was saddened, seeing in this a reminder of the fate of his grandfather and father, who both experienced a similar reversal of fortune to that of Pyrrhos. Antigonos Gonatas was in fact imbued with the strong family loyalty that was such an attractive feature of the early Antigonids, being devoted to both of his parents and on the best of terms with his half-brother, Krateros (see Plut. *Dem.* 51,1–2 and 53,1–3 for Gonatas's devotion to Demetrios; Plut. *Mor.* 250f–253a and 486a for relations with Krateros).

Though the earliest activity recorded for Antigonos Gonatas is ca. 293, when he was left in charge of Boiotia by his father (Plut. *Dem.* 39,3–40,2), it is obvious that as grandson of Antigonos Monophthalmos and hence ultimately heir apparent to the Antigonid realm, he must have received a thorough training in military and administrative matters during the last years of Monophthalmos's life, when Gonatas was in his later teens. Presumably he would have held military posts, either in Asia or under Demetrios in Greece in the years 304–301, and he is likely to have fought with his father at the battle of Ipsos, just like the then 18-year-old Pyrrhos, Demetrios's brother-in-law (no.

102 below). Tarn suggests (*Ant. Gon.*, pp. 19–21) that at this time Antigonos would have been sent away by Demetrios to Kassandros together with his mother Phila, because of Demetrios's marriage with Deidameia; but there is no evidence for either Phila or Antigonos having been sent away by Demetrios, and the absurdity of assuming this of Antigonos at least is so patent that one scarcely need argue against it. In fact, Demetrios was married to his wives concomitantly and held them all in honor, but Phila in most honor as the first wife and mother of his eldest son (Plut. *Dem.* 14,2), so that Tarn's hypothesis is otiose. For Antigonos's further career, see the works listed below.

Further reading. J. Kaerst, *RE* s.v., no. 4; Tarn, *Antigonos Gonatas;* Fellmann, *Antigonos Gonatas . . . und die griechischen Staaten;* Edson, *CPh* 29 (1934):254–55; M. Chambers, *AJPh* 75 (1954):385–94; R. W. Mathisen, *AncW* 1 (1978):71–4; Buraselis, *Das hellenistische Makedonien.*

11. ANTISTHENES

Sources. Diodoros XX 50,1 and 52,5; cf. Plutarch *Demetrios* 16,1.

Career. Antisthenes was an officer in Demetrios's fleet in Cyprus in 306. During the great sea battle off Cyprian Salamis, Demetrios left Antisthenes with a detachment of ten ships to block the harbor of Salamis and prevent Menelaos from sailing out with his sixty ships to help his brother Ptolemy by attacking Demetrios in the rear. Though Antisthenes was eventually beaten by Menelaos and forced to flee to Demetrios's camp, he held out long enough to prevent Menelaos's sixty ships from taking part in the battle, in which Demetrios destroyed Ptolemy's fleet.

Further reading. J. Kirchner, *RE* s.v., no. 2; Hauben, *Vlootbevelhebberschap,* pp. 13, 114.

12. APOLLONIDES, son of Charops, from Kyzikos (?)

Sources. Plutarch *Demetrios* 50; *IG* II^2 492; *Syll.* no. 352, lines 11ff.; cf. also *SEG,* 16, no. 58.

Career. Apollonides evidently served under Demetrios with some distinction in the years 307–301 and became a good friend of the king. The Athenian decree honoring him (*IG* II^2 492), as restored by Adolf Wilhelm (see below), gives a survey of his dealings with Athens over a number of years down to ca. 302. He appears to have helped Athenian fugitives from the great naval battle in the Hellespont in 322, when the Athenians were decisively defeated by Kleitos during the Lamian War. The town of Kyzikos is mentioned in connection with this, and was hence perhaps his home town. The decree shows further that Apollonides was with Demetrios in Athens in 307/6, when Athens was liberated from Kassandros and the democracy restored. For services in connection with this, Apollonides was rewarded with Athenian citizenship in the deme Peiraieus. Habicht has suggested (see below) that the decree awarding citizenship is the fragment *SEG,* 16, no. 58 of 304/3, restoring in line 17 the name [Apollon]ides, but this is uncertain (see Koumanoudes below).

After retailing this earlier history, the Athenian decree records the decision to award further honors to Apollonides (a gold crown to be given at the Panathenaic festival) because of his aid to the cause of Greek freedom while serving under the kings (i.e., Antigonos and Demetrios). The reference seems to be to the campaign of Demetrios in 303/2 culminating in the founding of the Hellenic League, with which Apollonides was perhaps associated.

Apollonides is further attested as active under Antigonos and Demetrios by a decree from Ephesos (*Syll.*, no. 352) recording that he came there bearing good news and communicating the goodwill of the kings. The decree is usually dated to 302, but is perhaps rather from 306, the good news being of the battle of Cyprian Salamis and the assumption of kingship by Antigonos and Demetrios. The two kings are praised in the decree and awarded gold crowns, and good-news sacrifices are decreed on their behalf. At any rate, Apollonides was awarded Ephesian citizenship. Later, after the battle of Ipsos (and perhaps as a result of capture in that battle), Apollonides entered the service of Seleukos. Plutarch attests to this (*Dem.* 50), reporting that in 286 during Demetrios's desperate last campaign in Asia, it was Apollonides who—as an old friend of Demetrios's—was sent by Seleukos to persuade Demetrios to surrender.

Further reading. Olshausen, *Prosopographie,* nos. 65 and 74; Wilhelm, "Att. Urk." pt. 5, pp. 175ff.; Habicht, *Gottmenschentum,* p. 57 n. 9; J. Kirchner, *RE* s.v., no. 11; Wehrli, *Antigone et Démétrios,* p. 125 n. 147; Koumanoudes *Horos* 4 (1986):14–17.

13. APOLLONIOS, son of Dionysios, from Antigoneia

Sources. IG XII.9 210; and cf. Diodoros XX 110,2.

Career. Apollonios was one of three brothers serving under Demetrios in Greece in 304–302, who were honored by the people of Eretria for having been helpful to Eretrians serving under Demetrios with ships. Presumably the decree is from 302, and the campaign referred to is that of that year, when Demetrios sailed from Euboia to Thessaly, thus turning Kassandros's position at Thermopylai.

Further reading. Ad. Wilhelm, *AE,* 1892, pp. 119–25.

14. ARCHELAOS, from Macedon (?)

Sources. Diodoros XIX 100,7; cf. XVIII 37,4.

Career. A man of this name was left in charge of Tyre by Perdikkas in 321, and helped Perdikkas's brother-in-law Attalos to make good his escape when the latter was condemned to death after Perdikkas's demise. When Demetrios raided Babylonia in 310, he left behind an officer named Archelaos with 6,000 men to continue the siege of the citadel of Babylon. The two are probably one and the same man: a considerable number of Perdikkas's officers subsequently joined Antigonos (e.g., Medeios of Larissa, Dokimos). Archelaos's name and the important military commands entrusted to him suggest to me that he was probably Macedonian. His subsequent fate is unknown; for a possible earlier career under Alexander, see Berve, nos. 157 and 158.

Further reading. J. Kirchner, *RE* s.v., nos. 19 and 20.

15. ARCHESTRATOS, son of Nikon, from Macedon

Sources. OGIS, no. 9 (= *I. Ephesos,* 5, no. 1452); *IG* XI.2 161b, line 76; cf. also Diodoros XX 107,5.

Career. Archestratos is honored in an Ephesian inscription as an *oikeios* (close friend) of Demetrios, stationed as *stratēgos* at Klazomenai whence he protected Ephesian grain ships. Evidently Archestratos was in command of a body of ships based at Klazomenai. The date of the decree is probably 302, when Kassandros's general Prepelaos temporarily seized Ephesos, but lost it again and was prevented from seizing Klazomenai and Erythrai when Demetrios sent reinforcements by sea (Diod. XX 107,5). Most likely Archestratos was with Demetrios in Greece in 304–302, and was sent with a squadron to Ionia when reports arrived of the successes being won there by Prepelaos and Lysimachos (Diod. XX 107,5). Possibly the same man is the Archestratos mentioned in an inventory of dedications from Delos (*IG* XI.2 161b, line 76), for this list mentions a number of prominent figures of the Diadoch period known to us from other sources, including at least one who can be plausibly identified as an Antigonid officer (see Peukestas no. 90 below). Probably these men made the dedications while at Delos with Demetrios (who is also mentioned, at line 85) on one of his campaigns in the Aegean.

Further reading. Hauben, *Vlootbevelhebberschap,* pp. 14–18; J. Kaerst, *RE* s.v., no. 11; Launey, *Recherches,* pp. 304, 644, 1174; Bengtson, *Strategie,* 1:190–93, 196.

16. ARISTODEMOS, son of Parthenios, of Miletos

Sources. Diodoros XVIII 47,4; XIX 57,5; 60,1; 62,5; 63,3–64,4; 66,1–6; and cf. XX 53,1–2: Plutarch *Demetrios* 9 and 17; Plutarch *Mor.* 182d; *OGIS*, no. 5, lines 11, 48; *IG* II[2] 459; Rehm, *Milet,* 1, no. 123, line 11; Knibbe and Iplikçioglu, *JÖAI* 53 (1982):130–32.

Career. Aristodemos of Miletos was among Antigonos's oldest and most trusted friends and helpers, used by him frequently on important diplomatic missions and occasionally entrusted with military responsibilities as well. First mentioned in 319, he was then already well trusted by Antigonos, and it is possible that he had served with Antigonos when the latter was satrap of Phrygia (333–22). He may well have been one of those close friends who accompanied Antigonos on his flight from Asia to Antipatros in Macedon in 321. In 319 we hear from Diodoros (XVIII 47,4) that Antigonos received the news of Antipatros's death from Aristodemos at Kretopolis in Pisidia. Perhaps Aristodemos had been in Macedon and witnessed the death of Antipatros and succession of Polyperchon as regent of the empire. We know that earlier, having defeated Eumenes and shut him up in Nora, Antigonos had referred the matter of a settlement with him to Antipatros (id. 41,7), and Eumenes himself then sent envoys to Antipatros led by Hieronymos of Kardia (id. 42,1). Hieronymos returned from Macedon at the very time that Aristodemos brought Antigonos news of events there (id. 50,4), and it seems logical to assume that Aristodemos had been sent by Antigonos to Macedon with Hieronymos to secure free passage for the latter (as a companion of Eumenes he was an outlaw) and represent Antigonos in the negotiations concerning Eumenes' fate.

During the next few years, when Antigonos fought Eumenes for control of Asia, Aristodemos is not mentioned in our sources. In 314, however, when Ptolemy, Seleukos, Kassandros, and Lysimachos had formed a coalition against Antigonos, the latter sent Aristodemos with 1,000 talents to the Peloponnesos, instructing him to try to establish friendly relations with Polyperchon and his son Alexandros, and to raise mercenaries to fight against Kassandros in Greece. In this Aristodemos was outstandingly successful (Diod. XIX 57,5; 60,1; 62,5; 63,3–64,4). Landing in Lakonia, he enrolled 8,000 mercenaries, probably at the great mercenary fair on Cape Tainaron. He established friendship with Polyperchon and Alexandros, granting the former the title of general of the Peloponnesos on behalf of Antigonos and persuading the latter to sail to Tyre for an interview with Antigonos. Hearing of Aristodemos's successes, Kassandros himself came to the Pelponnesos to restore the situation there. Kassandros made a tour of the cities and strengthened his position considerably, but as soon as he had left again, Alexandros and Aristodemos went around subverting his arrangements once more. At this Kassandros had recourse to diplomacy, and by some important concessions he persuaded Alexandros to switch to his side.

At the time of this setback, Aristodemos was apparently in Aitolia, where he persuaded the Aitolian League to make an alliance with Antigonos (Diod. XIX 66,1–6). Having done so, he crossed back to the Peloponnesos with his mercenaries and saved the city of Kyllene, which was being besieged by Alexandros. He went on to liberate Patrai and Aigion in Achaia, though at the latter town his troops got out of hand and pillaged the place. He then crossed back to Aitolia, leaving a strong force at Aigion, which subsequently helped the people of neighboring Dyme to free themselves from Alexandros's garrison.

In 312 Antigonos sent two further expeditions to the Peloponnesos under his nephews Telesphoros and Polemaios, the latter of whom was made Antigonos's general in charge of Greek affairs and thus Aristodemos's superior. He brought all of Greece south of Thermopylai except Athens and a few Peloponnesian towns into Antigonos's control. Kassandros thereupon opened negotiations with Polemaios, as a result of which Aristodemos was sent with Kassandros's general Prepelaos to Antigonos to report upon the negotiations (*OGIS,* no. 5, line 11), and peace was made between Antigonos and Kassandros and Lysimachos, more or less on the basis of the status quo. When Ptolemy of Egypt applied to Antigonos to be included in the peace, Aristodemos was sent with Aischylos and Hegesias to Egypt to receive Ptolemy's pledges (*OGIS,* no. 5, line 48). Thus Aristodemos had much to do with bringing about the peace of 311.

In 307 Aristodemos accompanied Demetrios on his great expedition to Greece to liberate Athens (Plut. *Dem.* 9). He was sent, after Demetrios's seizure of Peiraieus, into Athens to negotiate with Demetrios of Phaleron, Kassandros's official in charge of Athens. As a result, Demetrios of Phaleron withdrew under safe conduct to Thebes, and Demetrios was able to announce the restoration of the Athenian democracy after ten years of rule by Kassandros's oligarchic agents. For his involvement in this, Aristodemos was honored by the Athenian people (*IG* II^2 459), though since only the prescript of their decree survives, we cannot tell precisely what honors they awarded him. No doubt Athenian citizenship would have been among them.

When Antigonos instructed Demetrios to sail down to Cyprus to face Ptolemy's forces there, Aristodemos sailed with him (306). He was present at the great naval battle near Cyprian Salamis, where Demetrios annihilated Ptolemy's fleet and captured all of Cyprus as a result. Aristodemos was chosen, no doubt as Antigonos's oldest friend present, to bring the good news of the battle to Antigonos (Plut. *Dem.* 17). In connection with this news, Plutarch describes a dramatic scene. Antigonos was at his new city of Antigoneia-on-the-Orontes in Syria, where Aristodemos came to meet him. A great crowd had gathered anxiously awaiting the news from Cyprus, and as Aristodemos came up to Antigonos by the gate of the palace, he cried out: "Hail, King Antigonos! We have defeated Ptolemy in a sea battle and captured Cyprus, and we have 12,800 soldiers as prisoners of war." At this, the crowd gave a great cheer and a diadem was brought to crown Antigonos as king. In this way Aristodemos was instrumental in the elevation of Antigonos (and his son Demetrios) to kingship. After what we have seen of Aristodemos's career, we shall hardly concur with Plutarch's description of Aristodemos in connection with this as a mere flatterer of Antigonos.

The crowning of Antigonos can be regarded as the high point of Aristodemos's long and distinguished diplomatic and military career, and his selection to play this role surely justifies describing him as the most important diplomat in Antigonos's service. Indeed, throughout his career he seems to have been selected by Antigonos and Demetrios for the most important and delicate diplomatic tasks, requiring tact, persuasiveness, loyalty, and in general ability of a high order. After his great moment at Antigoneia, we find Aristodemos back home in Miletos, where in 306/5 he filled the office of *stephanēphoros* (Rehm, *Milet,* 1, no. 123, line 11), the highest dignity Miletos had to offer. That he continued thereafter in Antigonos's service is shown by a recently published inscription from Ephesos (*JÖAI* 53 [1982]:130–32) honoring him with Ephesian citizenship for helping an Ephesian embassy to the king concerning freedom from taxation. The description of Antigonos as "the king" shows that the decree is later than 306. An anecdote preserved by Plutarch (*Mor.* 182d) shows Aristodemos as a top adviser at Antigonos's court, offering him financial advice (which, however, Antigonos rejected as too parsimonious). After this Aristodemos disappears from historical record.

Further reading. J. Kirchner, *RE* s.v., no. 16; P. Schoch, *RE* suppl. 4 s.v., no. 16; Habicht *AJAH* 2, no. 1 (1977):39 n. 3; Olshausen, *Prosopographie,* nos. 66 and 75; Gullath, *Gesch. Boiotiens,* pp. 161–63, and esp. n. 2 on p. 162.

17. ARISTON, Macedonian

Sources. Diodoros XIX 59,3; Arrian *Anab.* III 11,8.

Career. Diodoros informs us that during Antigonos's siege of Tyre in 314 an officer named Ariston handed over to Antigonos's daughter-in-law Phila the ashes and bones of Krateros, her former husband, for burial, having been entrusted with these by Eumenes in 321. It seems, then, that Ariston had been an officer of Eumenes, that he was a friend (perhaps even a distant relative) of Krateros, and that after Eumenes's defeat in 316 he entered Antigonos's service (for he was in Antigonos's camp at Tyre). Such a man would probably have seen service under Alexander too, and it has been suggested by Berve that the Ariston who led a squadron of the Companion cavalry at the battle of Gaugamela is the same man who took care of Krateros's remains for seven years.

Further reading. Berve, no. 137; J. Kirchner, *RE* s.v., no. 28.

18. ARRHIDAIOS, son of Alexandros, from Macedon

Sources. *IG* XII.9 212; *I. Ephesos,* 5, no. 1451.

Career. An inscription from Eretria (*IG* XII.9 212) records citizenship and other honors accorded to a former officer of King Alexander's named Arrhidaios, son of Alexandros, from Macedon. As an officer of the kings (i.e., Antigonos and Demetrios: based on personal inspection of the stone, I read *basileis* at the end of line 6), he had fought to free the Greek cities from their garrisons. The inscription probably dates from 303/2, when Demetrios had established his Hellenic League. Perhaps the same man is the Arrhidaios honored with citizenship by Ephesos, apparently about 316 (*I. Ephesos,* 5, no. 1451). Only one officer of Alexander's named Arrhidaios is known, namely, the man who at the conference in Babylon in 323 was charged with supervision of Alexander's funeral cortege (Diod. XVIII 3,5). It is possible that the man honored at Eretria was the same man, in which case Arrhidaios must have joined Antigonos's service after defeat and capture in the naval battle near Byzantion in 317, in which Arrhidaios fought against Antigonos.

Further reading. J. Kaerst, *RE* s.v., no. 5.

19. ASKLEPIADES of Byzantion

Sources. *IG* II^2 555.

Career. All that is known of Asklepiades comes from the second part of an Athenian decree granting honors to him. Since the first half is not preserved, we do not know what he had done to earn these honors, but whatever it was, it was connected with the activities of Demetrios to liberate the Greeks. The mention of *tous basileis* in line 4 makes it clear that Asklepiades was an officer of Antigonos and Demetrios. The extravagant nature of the honors awarded him (a crown of 1,000 drachmas' value, a bronze statue of 3,000 drachmas, and three ambassadors to report on this in Byzantion, as well as lesser honors) indicates that he must have been a very important man. The inscription dates from between 306 and 303: the *terminus post quem* is given by the use of *basileis* referring to Antigonos and Demetrios; the *terminus ante quem* is given by the crown of 1,000 drachmas, as in 303 a law was passed limiting the value of honorary crowns, and all subsequent decrees refer to a crown κατὰ τὸν νόμον. The mention of τοὺς ἄλλους Ἕλληνας in line 5, presumably referring to Demetrios's campaigns in central Greece and the Peloponnesos, makes it probable that Asklepiades accompanied Demetrios on his second expedition to Greece, and that the decree is thus from 304/3 B.C.

Further reading. None.

20. ASKLEPIODOROS (son of Philon?)

Sources. Diodoros XIX 48,5; Arrian *Anab*. III 16,4, and cf. Diodoros XIX 92,4.

Career. Asklepiodoros was the man selected by Antigonos in 315 to replace Peukestas as satrap of Persis (Diod. XIX 48,5). One would expect him to have had previous experience of the East and of administration. Hence it is tempting to identify him with the Asklepiodoros, son of Philon, who was placed in charge of financial administration in Babylonia by Alexander in 330 (Arrian *Anab*. III 16,4), though this cannot be proved. Two other Asklepiodoroi are known under Alexander, both military men (Berve, nos. 167 and 168). Asklepiodoros was evidently dead by 311, as Diodoros (XIX 92,4) in that year mentions a certain Euagoras as satrap of Persis. It is also possible, of course, that Asklepiodoros may simply have been replaced by Antigonos without our sources mentioning it.

Further reading. Berve, no. 169; J. Kaerst, *RE* s.v., nos. 6 and 9.

21. ASPEISAS, Persian or Elamite

Sources. Diodoros XIX 55,1; Robinson, *NC*, 5th ser., 1 (1921):37f.

Career. Aspeisas was appointed satrap of Susiane by Antigonos during his reordering of the eastern satrapies in 315 (Diod. XIX 55,1). Diodoros's report on this is confirmed by the finding of Asiatic posthumous Alexander coins bearing on the reverse the legend ASPEI-

SOU, which indicates that the coins were struck at Susa when Aspeisas was satrap. Diodoros calls the man a native of Susiane, which may indicate that he was an Elamite, or perhaps rather a Persian. Either way, he is one of the few non-Greek officers of Antigonos recorded in our sources.

Further reading. Hornblower, *Hieronymus of Cardia,* p. 116.

22. ATHENAIOS

Sources. Diodoros XIX 94,1–96,2.

Career. Athenaios was an officer in Antigonos's army in 312, when he was sent with 4,600 men under his command on an expedition to subdue the Nabataians of Petra, now in modern Jordan. He was initially very successful, capturing Petra in a surprise attack and seizing a large amount of booty. During his return march, however, he was careless after his success, and gave the Nabataians a chance to surprise him in a night attack. Athenaios's force was annihilated except for a small number of horsemen, who escaped to Antigonos. It is not clear whether Athenaios escaped with these men or died in the night attack. The former seems more probable in view of the complaints against Athenaios lodged by the Nabataians with Antigonos, who dissociated himself from Athenaios's actions. At any rate, no further employment of Athenaios is recorded.

Further reading. J. Kirchner, *RE* s.v., no. 1.

23. [BIAN]OR (?)

Sources. *SEG,* 16, no. 58 (= *Hesperia* 7 [1938]:297, no. 22); cf. A. Woodward, *ABSA* 51 (1956):5–6.

Career. An Athenian inscription in a very fragmentary state records honors for at least one envoy or officer of Demetrios's in the year of the archon Pherekles (304/3). The decree was moved by the noted pro-Antigonid politician Stratokles, on the same day as similar decrees for nos. 40 and 110 below. Line 1 preserves remains of a name in the genitive case (——oros), suggesting to Woodward the name Bianor (Theanor and Euenor are other possibilities). Several names of other honorands used to be restored at lines 15–16 (e.g., [A]n[t]ime[de]s, [Apollon]ides), but see now Koumanoudes (below) against this.

Further reading. Koumanoudes *Horos* 4 (1986):14–17.

24. BLITOR

Sources. Appian *Syr.* 53.

Career. Appian mentions that Antigonos removed Blitor from office as satrap of Mesopotamia in 315 for having allowed Seleukos to escape through his territory to Egypt. Since the satrap of Mesopotamia appointed at Triparadeisos was Amphimachos, who in 317 had joined Eumenes in his war against Antigonos (Diod. XVIII 39,6; XIX 27,4), one must suppose that Blitor was a subordinate of Antigonos himself, appointed satrap in 317 when Antigonos was wintering in Mesopotamia on his way to fight Eumenes (Diod. XIX 15,6).

Further reading. J. Kaerst, *RE* s.v. Blitor; Schober, *Gesch. Babyloniens*, pp. 88 and 95 n. 1.

25. BOIOTOS, Macedonian (?)

Sources. Diodoros XIX 85,2.

Career. Boiotos was one of those who died at the battle of Gaza in late 312, on which occasion Diodoros (i.e., Hieronymos?) says of him that he had for a long time lived with Antigonos and shared in all his state secrets (*μετεσχηκὼς παντὸς ἀπορρήτου*). Although this is the only mention of Boiotos in our sources, it suffices to permit the conjecture that he was probably a personal friend of Antigonos's long before 323, for he is presented here as one of Antigonos's most trusted confidants. On the same grounds Kirchner (see below) conjectures that he was probably Macedonian.

Further reading. J. Kirchner, *RE* s.v., no. 8.

26. BOURICHOS, Greek (?)

Sources. Diodoros XX 52,4; Demochares *apud* Athenaios VI 253a (= *FGrH*, no. 75 F 1).

Career. Bourichos was an officer under Demetrios at the battle of Salamis in Cyprus, and was charged, together with Neon (no. 78 below), with the task of picking up survivors after the battle (Diod. XX 52,4). Since Demochares names him together with the well-known Adeimantos of Lampsakos and Oxythemis of Larissa as a "flatterer" of Demetrios who received heroic honors at Athens, he must have been an important man, and probably a Greek like his two colleagues.

Further reading. U. Wilcken, *RE* s.v. Burichos; Habicht, *Gottmenschentum*, pp. 55–58; Hauben, *Vlootbevelhebberschap*, pp. 114–15.

27. CHAIREAS

Sources. Buckler and Robinson, *Sardis VII*, no. 1, line 1.

Career. The famous Mnesimachos inscription from Sardis mentions Chaireas as having conducted an inquiry into either the tenure or extent of an estate then awarded to Mnesimachos by Antigonos on the basis (presumably) of that inquiry. Hence it appears that Chaireas was a judicial or administrative official in Lydia under Antigonos. Nothing further is known of him.

Further reading. Debord, *Aspects,* app. 5, pp. 244–51.

28. DEMARCHOS, son of Taron, from Lykia

Sources. OGIS, no. 5, line 5; *Syll.,* no. 333.

Career. Demarchos is mentioned (according to a plausible restoration) in the Skepsis inscription (*OGIS,* no. 5, line 5) as a diplomat involved in the negotiations between Antigonos and Kassandros in 311. This is probably the same man as the Lykian Demarchos, son of Taron, who was captain of Phila's bodyguard ca. 305/4 according to a Samian inscription (*Syll.,* no. 333). The Samians praised him for having helped them during their exile (before 322), and for his continuing goodwill they granted him citizenship. A certain Demarchos is known to have been satrap of Hellespontine Phrygia between ca. 327 and 321 (Arrian *Met' Alex.* 1,6), but it is impossible to say whether this is the same man.

Further reading. J. Kirchner, *RE* s.v., no. 3; Olshausen, *Prosopographie,* no. 67; P. Schoch, *RE* suppl. 4 s.v., no. 6; Welles, *RC,* p. 9; and cf. Berve, no. 255; H. Willrich, *RE* s.v., no. 5.

29. DEMETRIOS, son of Antigonos, Macedonian

Sources. Diodoros XVIII 23,4; XIX 29,4; 40,1; 59,3; XIX 69,1–100,7 and XX passim; Plutarch *Demetrios* passim esp. 2,1–29,5; Plut. *Eum.* 18,3; Plut. *Pyr.* 4,2–3; for further sources, see J. Kaerst, *RE* s.v., no. 33.

Career. Nothing like a complete account of the career of Demetrios can be given here, for such would be unsuited to the scale of this prosopography. Suffice it to say that he is attested first in 321, when he fled with his father from Asia Minor to Greece (Diod. XVIII 23,4); that he accompanied his father throughout the eastern *anabasis* of 317–315, fighting beside Antigonos in the crucial battles of Paraitakene (Diod. XIX 29,4) and Gabiene, where he commanded the right wing cavalry (Diod. XIX 40,1), and pleading with his father to spare the life of Eumenes after the latter battle (Plut. *Eum.* 18,3); and that from 312 on he was his father's right-hand man and chief battle commander, culminating in his command of Antigonos's cavalry at the battle of Ipsos in 301, where his reckless pursuit of the defeated enemy cavalry seems to have been chiefly responsible for losing the battle. His relations with his father were never other than exemplary, as a number of anecdotes preserved by Plutarch attest (e.g., *Dem.* 3,1–2; 14,3; 19,3–6). For full-length treatments of Demetrios's career, see (besides chaps. 3–5 above) the works cited below.

Further reading. J. Kaerst, *RE* s.v., no. 33; Dimitrakos, *Demetrios Poliorketes und Athen;* Elkeles, *Demetrios der Städtebelagerer;* Manni, *Demetrio Poliorcete;* Wehrli, *Antigone et Démétrios;* Bengtson, *Herrschergestalten des Hellenismus,* pp. 64–90.

30. DIODOROS

Sources. Polyainos IV 7,3 and 4.

Career. Diodoros was an officer in command of mercenaries under Demetrios at Sikyon in 303, and hence presumably was with Demetrios throughout his second Greek campaign, 304–302. In 301 Demetrios made Diodoros *phrourarchos* at Ephesos after the battle of Ipsos, but when he heard reports that Diodoros was planning to betray the city to Lysimachos, he rushed back and deposed him.

Further reading. P. Schoch, *RE* suppl. 4 s.v., no. 19a; J. Kirchner, *RE* s.v., no. 20.

31. DIONYSIOS, Macedonian from Amphipolis (?)

Sources. *IG* II^2 560; Habicht *AM* 72 (1957), no. 4.

Career. An inscription from Athens of the period 306–301 contains a decree proposed by the prominent pro-Antigonid politician Stratokles to honor Dionysios and another man whose name is not preserved, who are officers of the kings (i.e., Antigonos and Demetrios). Since we know, then, of an officer of Antigonos named Dionysios, it is tempting to identify as the same man a Macedonian named Dionysios who was honored by the Samians (*AM* 72 [1957], no. 4) ca. 319–307. It is natural to assume that a Macedonian honored at Samos in this period is likely to have been an officer in one of the Hellenistic kingdoms, most probably that of Antigonos, in whose sphere of influence Samos was at this time. However, as the name Dionysios was very common, it is possible that we are dealing here with two separate officers of Antigonos's.

Further reading. P. Schoch, *RE* suppl. 4 s.v., no. 69a.

32. DIONYSIOS, son of Klearchos, of Herakleia Pontika

Sources. Diodoros XVI 88,5; XX 77,1; Nymphis *apud* Athenaios XII 549a–d (= *FGrH,* no. 432 F 10); Memnon in *FGrH,* no. 434 Fs 2,1; 3,1; 3,3; 4,1–9; Strabo XII 544; Poole, *BMC Pontos* 141–42 (coins of Dionysios).

Career. Dionysios of Herakleia was the son of the tyrant Klearchos of Herakleia and brother of the latter's successor, Timotheos, under whose rule in the 340s Dionysios was first allowed a share in the government of Herakleia (Memnon Fs 2,1; 3,1; 3,3). When Timotheos died in 337/36, Dionysios succeeded him as tyrant and ruled for thirty-two years, until 306/5 (Diod. XVI 88,5; XX 77,1). The destruction of Persian power in Asia Minor by Alexander gave Dionysios opportunities to expand his own power, which he exploited carefully and successfully; personal enemies at Alexander's court (exiles from Herakleia) were unable to harm him due to the advocacy on his behalf of Alexander's sister Kleopatra (Memnon F 4,1). After Alexander's death he married Amestris, the ex-wife of Krateros, and was an opponent of Perdikkas (Strabo XII 544; Memnon F 4,3–4); his power and wealth grew to such an extent that he was able to purchase the extraordinary personal belongings of the ex-tyrant Dionysios of Syracuse (Memnon F 4,5).

In 314, when Antigonos was strengthening his grip on Asia Minor, Dionysios came to an agreement with Antigonos's nephew Polemaios (no. 100 below), presumably recognizing Antigonos's sovereignty, and sealed the compact by marrying his daughter to Polemaios (Memnon F 4,6). At some time he served under Antigonos in Cyprus either (as Kaerst hypothesizes) in 306 against Ptolemy, or more probably against the Perdikkan forces on Cyprus in 320 (Memnon F 4,6; cf. Arrian *Met' Alex.* 24,6; 1,30). As a one-time officer of Antigonos's, a loyal ally, and a relative by marriage, it is not surprising that Dionysios prospered under Antigonos's rule of Asia. He received from his subjects the sobriquet of "the Good" (Chrēstos), and died in his fifty-sixth year, leaving two young sons (Klearchos and Oxathres), of whom Antigonos was named guardian (Memnon F 4, 8–9).

Further reading. J. Kaerst, *RE* s.v., no. 66; Burstein, *Outpost of Hellenism,* pp. 75–81.

33. DIOSKOURIDES, son of Polemaios (?), Macedonian

Sources. Diodoros XIX 62,7–9; 68,4.

Career. Dioskourides was a nephew of Antigonos's (Diod. XIX 62,9), so perhaps a brother of Antigonos's other nephew, Polemaios, son of Polemaios. He served under his uncle as an admiral in the years 314–313. When Antigonos was collecting a fleet, Dioskourides was apparently put in charge of ordering ships from the Hellespont and of the ship-building program on Rhodes, for we hear that in spring 313 he joined Antigonos at Tyre with 80 ships from the Hellespont and Rhodes (Diod. XIX 62,9). He was then sent out with 190 ships to tour the Aegean and bring the islands over to Antigonos's side. Since it appears that it was at this very time that the so-called League of the Islanders was founded under Antigonos's auspices, it is often supposed that Dioskourides' mission was what led to the foundation of this league (see esp. Buraselis, below). At the end of 313 we find Dioskourides still active with his fleet in the Aegean, when he protected the island of Lemnos, which had gone over to Antigonos, against an Athenian attack prompted by Kassandros (Diod. XIX 68,4). Subsequently we hear nothing more of Dioskourides. Perhaps he died young or was involved in the rebellion of his brother or cousin Polemaios against Antigonos.

Further reading. J. Kirchner, *RE* s.v. Dioscurides, no. 1; Guggenmos, *Geschichte des Nesiotenbundes,* pp. 27–29; Buraselis, *Das hellenistische Makedonien,* pp. 34, 41–44, 64–67; Hauben, *Vlootbevelhebberschap,* pp. 27–30.

34. DIPHILOS

Sources. Diodoros XIX 91,3–5.

Career. Diphilos was the officer placed in charge of the citadel of Babylon under Antigonos (315–311). When Seleukos returned to Babylonia in 311, Diphilos remained loyal to Antigonos and, in the absence of the satrap of Babylonia, Peithon (killed at the battle of Gaza), he led the resistance to Seleukos. Since some of the district officers went over to Seleukos, those loyal to Antigonos took refuge with Diphilos in the citadel of Babylon, but Seleukos was able to capture the place after a short siege. Diphilos's subsequent fate is not recorded.

Further reading. J. Kirchner, *RE* s.v., no. 8; Schober, *Gesch. Babyloniens,* pp. 95–97.

35. DOKIMOS, Macedonian

Sources. Arrian *Met' Alex.* 24,3–5; Plutarch *Eum.* 8; Diodoros XVIII 44,1–45,3; XIX 16, 1–5; 75,3–4; XX 107,3–4; Pausanias I 8,1; L. Robert, *RPh,* 3d ser., 8 (1934):267–68 (inscriptions and coins of Dokimeion); and cf. Polyainos IV 6,7.

Career. Although he is never mentioned in any history of Alexander, it is clear from the prominence of Dokimos immediately after Alexander's death that he must have been an important officer in Alexander's army. After the death of Alexander, he was a partisan of the regent Perdikkas, who quickly promoted him to the rank of satrap: in 321 Perdikkas sent him to replace the unreliable Archon as satrap of Babylonia, which Dokimos was able to do after a struggle

(Arrian *Met' Alex.* 24,3–5). After the death of Perdikkas, Dokimos was one of the prominent Perdikkans condemned to death by the Macedonians, and he fled from his satrapy to the other condemned Perdikkan leaders in Asia Minor, where in 320 he disputed Eumenes' right to lead the Perdikkan forces (Plut. *Eum.* 8).

The result of this dispute was a split in the Perdikkan camp, and Dokimos was one of the faction headed by Alketas and Attalos who removed to Pisidia. There they were attacked in a brilliant campaign by Antigonos in 319 and utterly routed. Dokimos, along with the other leaders Attalos, Polemon, and Philotas, was captured by Antigonos and imprisoned in a fortress near the Phrygian border (Diod. XVIII 44,1–45,3; Polyainos IV 6,7). In 316, while Antigonos was away in the east fighting Eumenes, Dokimos and his companions succeeded in surprising their guard and seizing control of the fortress which was their prison. This led immediately to a heated dispute between Dokimos, who wished to break out into the countryside and make good their escape, and Attalos, who wished to remain in the fortress and await help from Eumenes. When Dokimos lost the argument and the confederates found themselves besieged in the fort by Antigonid troops under Antigonos's wife, Stratonike, Dokimos decided to save himself by betraying his friends. Having established contact with Stratonike, he left the fort by a secret route with one friend and betrayed the secret route to the enemy. Attalos and the rest, after holding out in the fort for nearly a year, were captured and apparently killed (Diod. XIX 16,1–5).

Dokimos, meanwhile, seems to have entered the service of Antigonos, for we find a man with that name in 312 as general in charge of the expedition to liberate Miletos from the Macedonian dynast Asandros (Diod. XIX 75,3–4). He subsequently rose to be general in charge of the district around Synnada in central Phrygia, where he was permitted or even encouraged by Antigonos to found a town named Dokimeion after himself (Robert, *RPh,* 3d ser., 8 [1934]:267–68). When Antigonos was attacked by the coalition of 302 and Lysimachos invaded Asia Minor, however, Dokimos once again proved faithless, going over to Lysimachos and betraying to him Synnada and several royal treasuries (Diod. XX 107,3–4; Paus. I 8,1). His subsequent fate is unknown.

Further reading. J. Kaerst, *RE* s.v., nos. 4, 5; Berve, no. 285; Schober, *Gesch. Babyloniens,* pp. 38–41; Simpson, *Historia* 6 (1957):504–5; Hornblower, *Hieronymus,* pp. 125–26; Launey, *Recherches,* 1:342.

36. DRAKON, son of Straton, of Kos

Sources. Schede, *AM* 44 (1919), no. 5 H; Habicht, *AM* 72 (1957), no. 21.

Career. Drakon was an official at the court of Antigonos, as we learn from a decree honoring him from Samos (first published by Schede, improved by Habicht). The decree dates from the years 306–301 (Antigonos has the royal title) and mentions that Drakon gave aid to Samian ambassadors to Antigonos, from which it may be inferred that Drakon's duties at Antigonos's court were (whether in whole or in part) diplomatic. Nothing else is known of him.

Further reading. P. Schoch, *RE* suppl. 4 s.v., no. 12a; *SEG*, 1, no. 354.

37. EPIMACHOS of Athens

Sources. Vitruvius X 164; Athenaios *Peri mēch*. 27,2; cf. Plutarch *Demetrios* 21,1 and Diodoros XX 91.

Career. Epimachos was an architect and engineer in Antigonid employ who served with Demetrios at the siege of Rhodes and built the famous *helēpolis,* the great metal-clad siege tower on wheels which Demetrios employed against Rhodes, like the one he had used earlier at Cyprian Salamis (Diod. XX 48). Since the *helēpolis* built to capture Salamis was constructed in 306, only a year before the siege of Rhodes, it is likely that Epimachos was at least partly responsible for that siege tower also. Whether he continued in Demetrios's service later and was responsible for further works of military architecture and engineering is unknown; his name is preserved for us only through the fame of the Rhodian *helēpolis*.

Further reading. E. Fabricius, *RE* s.v., no. 3; Marsden, *Greek and Roman Artillery,* 1:107–8; 2:84–85; Wehrli, *Antigone et Démétrios,* pp. 208–11.

38. EUAGORAS

Sources. Diodoros XIX 48,2; 92,1–4.

Career. When Antigonos rearranged the upper satrapies in 315, he appointed a certain Euitos satrap of Areia/Drangiane, but when this man died immediately afterwards, he replaced him with Euagoras (Diod. XIX 48,2). From this appointment it is clear that Euagoras was a high-ranking and well-trusted officer under Antigonos, though this is the first time he appears in the sources. Diodoros characterizes him as "a man admired both for courage and shrewdness." Four years later, in 311, one "Euagros" is named as fighting in the army of

Nikanor, Antigonos's overseer of the upper satrapies (Diod. XIX 92,1–4). This man, who died in battle against Seleukos, is described as satrap of the Persians, and is thought to be none other than Euagoras. Hornblower (see below) points out that the descriptive phrase attached to the first mention of Euagoras by Diodoros is a device typically used by that writer to pick out a person who is going to appear more than once in his work. Presumably the satrap of Persia (Asklepiodoros, no. 20 above) died or was deposed some time after 315, and Euagoras was appointed to take his place, either instead of or in addition to the satrapy of Areia. Athenaios (*Deipnosophistai VI* 244f) mentions a certain hunchbacked parasite of Demetrios's also named Euagoras, who must be a different person, in view of the fact that the eastern satrap died in 311 before Demetrios was really prominent.

Further reading. H. Willrich, *RE* s.v. Euagoras, no. 10, and Euagros, no. 3; Hornblower, *Hieronymus,* p. 279 and n. 20.

39. EUITOS

Sources. Diodoros XIX 48,2.

Career. Euitos was appointed satrap of Areia/Drangiane by Antigonos in 315. Evidently he was a person of considerable trust and consequence in Antigonos's entourage, though nothing else is known of him. He died immediately after taking up his post, and was replaced by Euagoras.

Further reading. H. Willrich, *RE* s.v.

40. EUPOLIS

Sources. *IG* II^2 486.

Career. An Athenian decree of mid 303 (Skirophorion [= roughly June] of the archon-year of Pherekles [304/3]), proposed by the pro-Antigonid politician Stratokles, states that the king (i.e., Demetrios) had written warmly recommending Eupolis as a friend who had greatly benefited the kings (i.e., Antigonos and Demetrios) and the Athenian people. The inscription breaks off here, but it is evident that the decree went on to bestow honors on Eupolis, who was clearly a subordinate of Demetrios helping in the campaigns of 304–302 in some military or diplomatic capacity. The superscript of the decree preserves the fact that Eupolis was granted Athenian citizenship, as were the recipients of two other decrees proposed by Stratokles on the same day (see no. 23, [Bian]or, and no. 110, Sotimos).

Further reading. P. Schoch, *RE* suppl. 4 s.v., no. 2a; Ad. Wilhelm

AM 39 (1914):279–80; Osborne, *Naturalisation in Athens,* no. D 45; Koumanoudes, *Horos* 4 (1986):13–14.

41. EURYA[LOS or NAX]

Sources. Habicht, *AM* 72 (1957):186, no. 20.

Career. A Samian decree of the years 306–301 honored this man for some kind of benefaction performed (it seems, see line 4) in connection with a king or kings who must be Antigonos and/or Demetrios. Unfortunately, not enough remains of the inscription to say anything more than that this man was apparently an official in Antigonid employ.

Further reading. None.

42. EUTROPION

Sources. Plutarch *Mor.* 11, and cf. 633c.

Career. Eutropion is described in an anecdote of Plutarch's as a man who had at one time been an officer in Antigonos's army, but subsequently became his chief cook (*archimageiros*). He was sent to invite the sophist Theokritos of Chios to dinner; when Theokritos rejected the invitation with a witticism insulting Eutropion for being an *archimageiros* and Antigonos for having only one eye (calling him "Cyclops"), Eutropion reported the matter to Antigonos, who had Theokritos executed. It has been pointed out to me by Raphael Sealey that in all likelihood Plutarch has missed the point of Theokritos's witticism and so misinterpreted Eutropion's status. The term *mageiros* meant as much "butcher" as "cook" (see Liddell and Scott s.v.), and was sometimes used figuratively to refer to killers in the same way as the English word "butcher" is (see, for example, Eunapios *Lives of the Philosophers* 480: φονικήν τινα καὶ μαγειρώδην ψυχήν). Hence Eutropion was doubtless never other than a military officer—perhaps the captain of Antigonos's bodyguard?—whom Theokritos accused of being Antigonos's chief "butcher."

Further reading. H. Willrich, *RE* s.v.

43. GLAUKIPPOS, son of Dionysios, from Antigoneia

Sources. *IG* XII.9 210; and cf. Diodoros XX 110,2.

Career. Glaukippos was one of three brothers serving under Demetrios in Greece in 304–302 who were honored by the Eretrians for having been helpful to citizens of Eretria serving under Demetrios with ships. See further Apollonios, no. 13 above.

Further reading. Ad. Wilhelm, *AE,* 1892, pp. 119–25.

44. HAGNON, son of Kaballas, of Teos

Sources. Plutarch *Alex.* 22; 40; 55; id. *Mor.* 65d; Athenaios XII 539c; Aelian *VH* IX 3; Arrian *Indika* XVIII 8; Poole, *BMC Ionia,* 312, nos. 24, 25 (coins); *IG* II[2] 682 (= *Syll.*, no. 409, line 8); Keil, *JÖAI* 16, no. 1 (1913):231–44, no. II p.

Career. A number of anecdotes preserved by Plutarch, Athenaios, and Aelian record Hagnon of Teos as being a luxury-loving flatterer of Alexander the Great, gossip that simply means that he was an influential courtier whose wealth and power excited envy: Athenaios XII 539c (after Phylarchos and Agatharchides) records that he was one of Alexander's *hetairoi.* It has further been suggested (by Keil, above) that the Andron, son of Kabeleus, of Teos mentioned by Arrian (*Indika* XVIII 8) as one of the trierarchs in the fleet with which Alexander sailed down the Indus, was in fact Hagnon, son of Kaballas.

Keil published an Ephesian inscription honoring Hagnon for helping Ephesian ambassadors to Krateros, evidently in 320 when Krateros and Antipatros were in Asia Minor fighting against Eumenes and Perdikkas. From this inscription we learn (for the first time) Hagnon's patronymic, and the likeness between Ἄνδρων Καβήλεω and Ἅγνων Καβάλλα is indeed such as to lend plausibility to Keil's conjecture, given that one would not expect a small town like Teos to produce several men of importance at Alexander's court with very similar names (the patronymics are simply different spellings of the same name, cf. Robert below). Hagnon, then, was a courtier and naval officer under Alexander and after Alexander's death attached himself to Krateros.

Antigonos was also an ally of Krateros in 320, and it appears that Krateros's death led Hagnon to enter the service of Antigonos. An Athenian inscription (*IG* II[2] 682) records that Thymochares of Sphettos, as admiral of an Athenian naval contingent fighting off Cyprus, captured an enemy squadron commanded by Hagnon of Teos. Dittenberger suggests (*Syll.* no. 409 nn. 3, 4, and 5) that this refers to the hostilities around Cyprus in the archonship of Praxiboulos (315/14) between Antigonos and his enemies, described by Diodoros (XIX 59,1; 62,3–6). The inscription also mentions Praxiboulos's archonship (line 9) and Hauben supposes (see below) that the events around Cyprus described in lines 4–9 belong to that archonship. Hauben is probably correct, but the connection with Diod. XIX 59,1 and 62,3–6 must be abandoned, for Diodoros knows nothing of any Antigonid fleet active at Cyprus at that time (314 B.C.), but rather states specifically that Antigonos then had no naval forces (XIX 58,1). Antigonos did have a large navy at the end of 317, however, which must have been eliminated some time before 314. Perhaps, then, this inscription refers to fighting in late 315 that resulted in the destruction of Antigonos's naval forces led by Hagnon.

Berve (below) claims that the name Hagnon is too common to permit the assumption that the various references to a Hagnon in 330–314 all pertain to the same person. However, it is hard to believe that Teos produced two men named Hagnon who both served as high officers in the Macedonian courts and forces of this time. Hence, too, one may safely assume that the Tean magistrate Hagnon who minted coins in this period (Poole, *BMC Ionia,* 312, nos. 24, 25) is the same man. His fate subsequent to his capture by Thymochares is unknown.

Further reading. J. Sundwall, *RE* s.v., no. 3; Berve, no. 17; Keil, *JÖAI* 16, no. 1 (1913):242 and nn. 30, 31; Hauben, *ZPE* 13 (1974):62–64; id., *Vlootbevelhebberschap,* pp. 40–41; J. and L. Robert, "Bull. ép.," 1982, no. 30; Habicht, *AM* 72 (1957):162 n. 26.

45. HEGESIAS

Sources. OGIS, no. 5, line 48 (= Welles, *RC,* no. 1).

Career. Hegesias was one of the men sent by Antigonos in 311 to Egypt to receive Ptolemy's pledges to the peace of that year. He is named third after Aristodemos and Aischylos, and was hence presumably the most junior member of the embassy. Nothing else is known of him.

Further reading. P. Schoch, *RE* suppl. 4 s.v., no. 10a; Olshausen, *Prosopographie,* no. 68.

46. HEGESIPPOS of Halikarnassos

Sources. Diodoros XX 50,4.

Career. Diodoros informs us that at the battle of Cyprian Salamis against the fleet of Ptolemy in 306, Demetrios placed his right wing under the command of Hegesippos of Halikarnassos and Pleistias of Kos (who was also the chief pilot of his whole fleet). Hence, Hegesippos was a high-ranking naval officer in the Antigonid service, though nothing else is now known about him.

Further reading. J. Sundwall, *RE* s.v., no. 2; Hauben, *Vlootbevelhebberschap,* pp. 42, 119.

47. HEGETOR of Byzantion

Sources. Vitruvius X 15,2–6; Athenaios *Peri mēch.* 21,2; Anon. of Byzantion 230,1 (ed. R. Schneider, *Gött. Abh.* 11, no. 1 [1908/9]).

Career. Hegetor was one of the military engineers in Antigonid employ. He is specifically mentioned as having constructed special mantlets (or "tortoises") of amazing size at the siege of Rhodes. Though Hegetor, like the other two Antigonid military engineers Epimachos and Zoilos, is mentioned only in the context of the famous siege of Rhodes, his employ by Antigonos and Demetrios was doubtless not limited to that. It seems he wrote a book on military engineering (cf. Wehrli, below).

Further reading. J. H. Kroll, *RE* suppl. 6 s.v., no. 2; Marsden, *Greek and Roman Artillery,* 2:88; Wehrli, *Antigone et Démétrios,* pp. 204, 206, 208.

48. HERAKLEI[DES or TOS] of Erythrai

Sources. *IG* II[2] 1492b, lines 106, 116.

Career. An Athenian inscription bearing the records of the treasurers of Athena for the year 306/5 (archon Koroibos) mentions the disbursal of funds of two officers, Polykleitos the Athenian and Heraklei(des?) to Erythrai, who were evidently not officials of the Athenian state (see Polykleitos, no. 102 below). The money came from a gift of 140 talents donated by Antigonos (lines 97–103), and was evidently intended and used for military purposes (the money was disbursed to P., H., and "the generals"), so Polykleitos and Heraklei(des?) were probably officers in Antigonid employ left behind with a body of troops by Demetrios to help defend Athens against Kassandros.

Further reading. None.

49. HERODOROS, son of Ph——, from ——kos

Sources. *IG* II[2] 646.

Career. Herodoros was honored by the Athenians in 294 for helping to expedite their negotiations with Demetrios. In lines 9–10 the inscription records that Herodoros had already shown himself well-disposed to Athens in earlier times, when he was serving with (διατρίβων παρὰ) Antigonos the king. From this one can conclude that Herodoros was an official in Antigonos's employ in 306–301, and remained loyal to Demetrios after Ipsos. Of his ethnic only the letters ——κηνος are preserved, from which one may conjecture that he was from the Hellespontine region (Kyzikos, Lampsakos, or Astakos). His service with Antigonos and Demetrios appears to have been largely diplomatic in nature: in 295/94 he was involved in the peace negotiations between Athens and Demetrios, and no doubt his earlier goodwill was demonstrated during one of the diplomatic interchanges between Athens and Antigonos and Demetrios in 307–302.

Further reading. P. Schoch, *RE* suppl. 4 s.v., no. 3a; Habicht, *Untersuchungen,* pp. 4–7; *SEG,* 29, no. 95; Osborne, *Naturalisation in Athens,* no. D 68.

50. HIERON

Sources. Blümel, *I. Iasos,* 1, no. 2; cf. Diodoros XIX 75,5.

Career. Hieron was one of three officers named in the above inscription (see also nos. 65 and 108 below), which records a treaty between these officers, the people of Iasos, and Ptolemy. It dates without doubt from 309/8, when Ptolemy campaigned along the coast of Lykia and Karia (Diod. XX 27,1–3). They and their troops were apparently stationed in the area of Iasos by Polemaios, Antigonos's nephew and general (see line 10) who had captured Iasos on behalf of Antigonos in 312 (Diod. XIX 75,5). Hence it follows that Hieron and his two colleagues were in the service of Antigonos at least between about 312 and 309.

Further reading. Pugliese Carratelli, *ASAA,* n.s., 29/30 (1967/68):437–45, no. 1; J. and L. Robert, "Bull. ép.;" 1971, no. 620; Garlan, *ZPE* 18 (1975):193–98; Bagnall, *Ptolemaic Administration,* pp. 89–91.

51. HIERONYMOS of Kardia

Sources. Diodoros XVIII 42,1; 50,4; XIX 44,3; 100,1–3; Plutarch *Eum.* 12 and *Demetrios* 39,3–7; [Loukianos] *Makrobioi* 11; 13; 22; Josephus *Contra Apionem* I 213–14; Pausanias I 9,8; Appian *Mithridatika* 8; Suda s.v. Hieronymos Kardianos; and cf. Buschor, *Misc. Acad. Berol.* 2 (1950): 25–30.

Career. Hieronymos of Kardia, the great historian of the Diadochoi, is one of the most interesting men of his day. After having served successively under Eumenes of Kardia, Antigonos Monophthalmos, Demetrios, and Antigonos Gonatas, he reputedly lived to be 104, hale and hearty to the end ([Louk.] *Makrob.* 22, following the second-century B.C. historian Agatharchides). The precise termini of his life are not known: he is first mentioned serving under Eumenes in 319 (Diod. XVIII 42,1) and certainly lived to record in his history the death of Mithridates Ktistes of Pontos in 266 ([Louk.] *Makrob.* 13). He is described as the friend and fellow-citizen of Eumenes (Diod. XVIII 50,4), but was in fact almost certainly Eumenes' nephew. Eumenes was himself the son of a Hieronymos of Kardia (Arrian *Ind.* 18,7), and the common Greek custom which decreed that grandfather and grandson should have the same name suggests strongly that the father of Eumenes and the famous Hieronymos of Kardia stood in that relationship towards one another. Hieronymos should then be somewhat younger than Eumenes, who was born ca. 360 (he was 45 at the time of his death in winter 316/15: Nepos *Eum.* 13); one may reasonably place Hieronymos's birth ca. 350, and his death about the middle of the third century B.C..

Hieronymos was, then, a near contemporary of Alexander the Great (born 356), and it is likely that he would have accompanied his uncle Eumenes already for all or part of the latter's service under Alexander in Asia (cf. e.g., Hieronymos's contention that Alexander never passed through Kappadokia: Appian *Mith.* 8), and was present in Babylon when Alexander died. In 319 Eumenes, besieged at Nora by Antigonos, sent Hieronymos as his ambassador to treat with Antipatros in Macedon (Diod. XVIII 42,1). Hieronymos returned from Macedon bearing news of Antipatros's death and an offer of partnership from Antigonos (Diod. XVIII 50,4; Plut. *Eum.* 12), which Eumenes did not accept. During all of his subsequent vicissitudes, Eumenes was accompanied by Hieronymos, until the final battle with Antigonos at Gabiene in 316 that ended Eumenes' career and life. Hieronymos was wounded and captured in this battle; but Antigonos received him with kindness, won his trust, and persuaded him to enter his service (Diod. XIX 44,3). Thenceforth Hieronymos remained a loyal officer of the Antigonid monarchs.

We next hear of him in 311, when he was entrusted by Antigonos with the task of overseeing the collection of bitumen from the Dead Sea, which Antigonos hoped to make a valuable source of revenue (Diod. XIX 100,1–3), but which turned into a fiasco due to the violent oppositon of the local Arabs. Diodoros describes Hieronymos simply as the *epimelētēs* of this operation, but other evidence suggests that he may have had a wider competence. Josephus (*Contra Apionem* I 213–14) complains that Hieronymos made no mention whatsoever of the Jews in his history, despite the fact that he practically lived among them, having been placed in charge of Syria by Antigonos (τὴν Συρίαν ἐπετρόπευεν). Perhaps we should regard Hieronymos as being at this time governor of Koile Syria (modern Palestine) in which position the oversight of operations round the Dead Sea would naturally have fallen to him. How long he may have held this post is not known; in 301 he appears to have been with Antigonos at the battle of Ipsos in Phrygia, for the author of the *Makrobioi,* in citing Hieronymos for Antigonos's age at death, describes him as fighting with Antigonos ([Louk.] *Makrob.* 11: ὁ συστρατευόμενος αὐτῶι). He may have been honored by the Samians ca. 312–307, as a Samian inscription of this period (Buschor above, and cf. Habicht, *AM* 72

[1957]:259) honors a Kardian officer of Demetrios whose name no longer survives, but Hieronymos would exactly fill the gap.

After Ipsos he evidently fled along with Demetrios to Greece, for in 293 he was made governor of Thebes by Demetrios (Plut. *Dem.* 39, 3–7). He did not accompany Demetrios on his last desperate campaign in Asia in 286, remaining rather with Antigonos Gonatas, under whom he presumably passed the remainder of his long and eventful life. It is commonly supposed that he wrote his history in his old age under the patronage of Antigonos Gonatas, a supposition which finds support, at least as far as the later parts of it are concerned, from two passages in Pausanias, in which Hieronymos is accused of being unfairly favorable towards Gonatas (I 9,8) and yet excused for this because a man living under a king must necessarily write to please him (I 13,9). Nevertheless, the evident detail and accuracy of his work suggests that he must have taken notes of events not long after they happened, unless he was gifted with a truly phenomenal memory for detail.

Further reading. F. Jacoby, *RE* s.v., no. 10; id. *FGrH,* no. 154; Berve, no. 383; Brown, *AHR* 53 (1947):684–96; Reuss, *Hieronymos von Kardia;* Rosen, *AClass* 10 (1967):41–94; Hornblower, *Hieronymus;* Olshausen, *Prosopographie,* nos. 1, 69.

52. HIPPARCHOS, son of Heniochos, of Kyrene

Sources. Habicht, *AM* 72 (1957):188–90, no. 22.

Career. An inscription from Samos records a decree of the Samians honoring Hipparchos for kindness he has shown to Samian soldiers under his command in Karia, as well as for goodwill shown towards the Samians both before and after their exile (from which they returned in 322). Lines 5–6 refer to him as an officer of King Antigonos, which indicates that the decree belongs to the years 306–301 (the royal title). In lines 6–7 Hipparchos's current position is restored by Habicht as νῦṿ [τε τετα|γμένο]ς ἐγ Καρίαι, though in the *app. crit.* he gives an alternative restoration, proposed by Hiller von Gaertringen: ν[ῦν δὲ στρα|τηγῶν] ἐγ Καρίαι. Whichever is correct, it is clear that Hipparchos was a fairly high-ranking officer of Antigonos stationed in Karia, with (among others, no doubt) an allied contingent from Samos under his command.

Further reading. SEG, 1, no. 358.

53. HIPPODAMAS, son of Dionysios, from Antigoneia

Sources. IG XII.9 210; and cf. Diodoros XX 110,2.

Career. Hippodamas was one of three brothers serving under

Demetrios in Greece in 304–302 who were honored by the Eretrians for having been helpful to citizens of Eretria serving under Demetrios with ships. See further Apollonios, no. 13 above.

Further reading. Ad. Wilhelm, *AE*, 1892, pp. 119–25.

54. HIPPOSTRATOS (son of Oxythemis, from Larissa?)

Sources. Diodoros XIX 46,5–47,2; and cf. *Syll.*, no. 343, lines 6–7, 17–18.

Career. In early 315 Antigonos, having defeated Eumenes, was alarmed by reports that the powerful Peithon, son of Krateuas, satrap of Media, was contemplating revolt. He sent to Peithon offering to make him general in charge of all the upper satrapies, which offer brought Peithon to Antigonos's camp, where he was arrested, tried, and executed (Diod. XIX 46,1–4). In his place, Antigonos made the Mede Orontobates satrap of Media, and a certain Hippostratos was appointed general, with a force of 3,500 men. It is thought that the term *stratēgos* referring to Hippostratos (Diod. XIX 46,5) picks up the term στρατηγὸς τῶν ἄνω σατραπειῶν, the position offered to Peithon, and that Hippostratos held that post. The size of the force entrusted to him, and the fact that subsequently Antigonos did have a "general of the upper satrapies" in 311, namely Nikanor (Diod. XIX 100,3), support the notion that Hippostratos indeed held that post. The precise date of his replacement by Nikanor is not known, but it seems likely that it was quite shortly after his appointment, still in 315. For Orontobates and Hippostratos were attacked by a band of Peithon's supporters under Meleagros and Menoitas and fared rather badly against them (Diod. XIX 47,1–3). Perhaps this provided the occasion for Antigonos to appoint Nikanor: possibly Hippostratos (who is never heard of again) died in the first attack by Meleagros and his friends (cf. Schober, below).

The well-known officer and diplomat of Antigonos and Demetrios, Oxythemis of Larissa (no. 86 below), was the son of a Hippostratos and clearly the nephew of Antigonos's friend and admiral Medeios, son of Oxythemis, of Larissa (no. 68 below). It has been plausibly conjectured by Dittenberger (*Syll.*, no. 343 n. 1) that the general Hippostratos is the brother of Medeios and father of Oxythemis, serving Antigonos like the rest of his family. For a family tree, see Berve, no. 521 (Medeios).

Further reading. W. Otto, *RE* s.v., no. 5; Bengtson, *Strategie*, 1:181–83; Schober, *Gesch. Babyloniens*, pp. 85, 89–90.

55. HORISMOS, son of Damasistratos, of Elaia

Sources. Schede, *AM* 44 (1919):7–8, no. 5 I (= *SEG,* 1, no. 356).

Career. Horismos was honored by the Samians for the goodwill he showed towards them when they were in exile (before 322 B.C.), and more specifically after their return, when he was an officer of King Demetrios. The use of the royal title dates the inscription after 306; the reference to the exile of the Samians indicates that it belongs still in the fourth century; hence Horismos was in Antigonid employ ca. 306–301.

Further reading. P. Schoch, *RE* suppl. 4 s.v.

56. IDOMENEUS, Greek?

Sources. Diodoros XIX 57,4, and cf. 58,4–5; 61,5; 62,7; 64,5–7.

Career. Idomeneus was sent by Antigonos as ambassador to Rhodes in 314 (with Moschion, no. 75 below) to request the Rhodians to build warships for Antigonos. He was successful, the Rhodians agreeing to build ships from timber imported into Rhodes by Antigonos, and a considerable number were actually built (Diod. XIX 58,4–5; 61,5; 62,7; 64,5–7). Idomeneus' mission was an important one; his standing in Antigonos's service was clearly high, and as ambassador to the free republic of Rhodes, he was most probably a Greek.

Further reading. J. Sundwall, *RE* s.v., no. 3; Olshausen, *Prosopographie,* no. 70.

57. IOLAOS, son of K——, Macedonian

Sources. *IG* II² 561, and cf. Diodoros XX 46,4.

Career. A fragmentary Athenian inscription honors two men who are described as former bodyguards (*sōmatophylakes*) of King Alexander, presently serving under Antigonos, in which capacity they have in some way benefited Athens. Iolaos is one of the two men (the other is Philippos, no. 93 below), evidently a Macedonian both from his name and his former position under Alexander. The term *sōmatophylax* was used under Alexander the Great to designate a small group of very high-ranking officers who formed a sort of personal staff of the king. We are fairly well informed of the men who held this office by Arrian, and Iolaos and Philippos are not mentioned among them. For this reason Habicht, Burstein, and Heckel (below) have conjectured that these two men were *sōmatophylakes* of the boy-king Alexandros IV.

With this conclusion I cannot agree. The child Alexandros IV had no need of a personal staff of this sort, and the existence of such *sōmatophylakes* is never recorded for him. The term *sōmatophylax* was also used to describe the actual bodyguards of Alexander the Great, the first, or royal, *taxis* (1,000 strong) of the Hypaspists (see, e.g., Arrian *Anab.* III 17,2; IV 3,2 and 30,3; and cf. Berve, 1:123–25). It is doubtless in this sense that we should take the term in this inscription, and should infer that Philippos and Iolaos were officers of the Hypaspists under Alexander the Great. Iolaos, mentioned second, is likely to have been the more junior of the two. Of his patronymic, which was nine letters long, only the first is preserved (*K*). It would seem that about 307/6 (the inscription does not appear to use the royal title for Antigonos), Iolaos was serving in Antigonos's personal entourage, and perhaps made himself useful to the Athenian embassy which visited Antigonos about that time (Diod. XX 46,4). Nothing further seems to be known of him under either Alexander or Antigonos.

Further reading. P. Schoch, *RE* suppl. 4 s.v., no. 5a; Habicht, in *Akten VI Kongr. Epig.*, p. 373 n. 35; Burstein, *ZPE* 24 (1977):223–25; Heckel, *ZPE* 40 (1980):249–50; id., *ZPE* 44 (1981):75–77.

58. KLEOCHARES, son of Pytheas, Macedonian from Amphipolis

Sources. *IG* XII.9 199; also *IG* II[2] 559 + *IG* XII suppl., p. 178.

Career. Kleochares was honored with proxeny by the Eretrians. The context is made clear by lines 3–5, where he is described as a friend of "the kings" who has displayed goodwill towards the generals of the Greeks, and to the Eretrians in particular. Mention of "the kings" (i.e., Antigonos and Demetrios) and "the generals of the Greeks" (i.e., of the Hellenic League) effectively dates the inscription to 303–302, after Demetrios had established the Hellenic League. Kleochares was clearly an officer in the army with which Demetrios liberated Greece from Kassandros in 304–302, and it is as such that he showed goodwill to the Eretrians. He may also have been honored by Athens at about the same time (*IG* II[2] 559 + *IG* XII suppl., p. 178).

Further reading. P. Schoch, *RE* s.v., no. 3; I. Tsuntas, *AE,* 1887, p. 80, no. 2.

59. KLEON, son of Kleon, of Erythrai

Sources. *IG* VII 5.

Career. Kleon was an officer of Demetrios honored by the Megarians with proxeny. Since the King Demetrios concerned is to be identified as Demetrios Poliorketes (see Urban below), the activity of Kleon as an Antigonid officer should be placed in 304–302, during Demetrios's campaign to liberate Greece. See further no. 140 below on the nature and date of this decree and related inscriptions.

Further reading. Urban, *Wachstum und Krise des Achaiischen Bundes,* pp. 66–70.

60. KRATEROS, son of Krateros, Macedonian

Sources. Plutarch *Mor.* 250f–253a; 486a; Phlegon *Miracula* 32; Polyainos II 29,1; Frontinus *Strategemata* III 6,7; Th. Homolle, *BCH* 21 (1897):598ff. (and cf. Pliny *NH* XXXIV 64; Athenaios XV 696e); see also Diodoros XVIII 18,7; XIX 59,3; Plutarch *Demetrios* 14.

Career. The famous Krateros, son of Alexandros, who was one of Alexander the Great's top generals and died in battle against Eumenes of Kardia in 320 (cf. Berve, no. 446; F. Geyer, *RE* suppl. 4 s.v., no. 1a), was married in the winter of 322/21 to Phila, the daughter of Antipatros (Diod. XVIII 18,7). After Krateros's death and the conference of Triparadeisos in 320, Phila was married off by Antipatros to Demetrios, the son of Antigonos Monophthalmos (Diod. XIX 59,3; Plut. *Dem.* 14), who had by her his son Antigonos Gonatas (b. 319). Krateros, son of Krateros, was a half-brother of Antigonos Gonatas (Plut. *Mor.* 486a; Phlegon *Mir.* 32) and was hence the son of Krateros and Phila born about 320, perhaps shortly before the death of his father. He was evidently raised by his mother and step-father (Demetrios) at the Antigonid court, and remained throughout his life a loyal friend and supporter of his half-brother, Antigonos Gonatas (Plut. *Mor.* 250f–253a; 486a; Poly. II 29,1; Front. *Strat.* III 6,7; and cf. Tarn, below).

As a youth at the Antigonid court in the last quarter of the fourth century, Krateros must have received his military and administrative education in the Antigonid service in the years 305–301, when he would have been about 15–19 years old. No information is preserved on his service, but he would have been used as an officer by Antigonos and Demetrios (as was Demetrios's 18-year-old brother-in-law Pyrrhos at the battle of Ipsos: Plut. *Pyrrhos* 4). Krateros was from a great aristocratic family of the Macedonian canton Orestis (Arrian *Ind.* 18,5), and his father was one of the greatest men of his day; he himself was later Gonatas's right-hand man in Greece, and hence we can be sure that his training would not have been skimped. That he was instructed fully on the career of his own father can be seen from his dedication at Delphi of a monument depicting his father and Alexander hunting a lion, which his father had vowed to dedicate but did not live to do. Krateros presumably dedicated this piece at the end of the fourth or early in the third century (see Homolle, *BCH* 21 (1897):598ff). He spent the years ca. 280 to his death ca. 260 as Gonatas's governor in Greece, with his seat at Korinth. He apparently was the author of a compilation of Athenian decrees, indicating again the quality of his education and that he shared his half-brother's literary interests (see *FGrH,* no. 342).

Further reading. F. Jacoby, *RE* s.v., no. 1; P. Schoch, *RE* s.v., no. 1; *FGrH,* no. 342; Tarn, *Antigonos Gonatas,* via index.

61. LEONIDAS, Macedonian

Sources. Curtius VII 2,35 (cf. Diodoros XVII 80,4; Justin XII 5,8); Polyainos IV 6,6; Diodoros XX 19,4; and cf. *IG* XI.4 161b, line 77.

Career. Polyainos records (IV 6,6) that in winter 320/19, near Kappadokia, 3,000 Macedonian infantry rebelled against Antigonos under the leadership of Olkias (no. 83 below), seized certain strong hills in Lykaonia and began to ravage Lykaonia and Phrygia. Fearing that this would provide an opportunity for his enemy Alketas, Antigonos sent one of his generals, Leonidas, to approach these rebels as if himself joining the rebellion. Gaining the confidence of the rebels, Leonidas led them down into a plain where Antigonos was able to surround them with cavalry and force them to surrender. He then put Leonidas in charge of them and ordered him to lead them back to Macedon. This Leonidas, then, was evidently a Macedonian and a senior officer in Antigonos's force, who must have seen service under Alexander. Berve (below) plausibly identifies him with the Leonidas, a friend of Parmenion, who was placed in command of a regiment of malcontents by Alexander after the execution of Philotas and Parmenion (Curt. VII 2,35). He never appears again under Antigonos, but it is possible the Leonidas who commanded Ptolemy's expeditionary force against Kilikia Trachea in 310 (Diod. XX 19,4) could be the same man, having gone to Ptolemy from Macedon. If so, Leonidas evidently had a mercurial career. At any rate, it seems likely the Leonidas who dedicated a wreath at Delos in the Diadoch period was this man (*IG* XI.4 161b, line 77).

Further reading. Stähelin, *RE* s.v., nos. 5 and 6; Berve, no. 470.

62. LYKISKOS, son of T——

Sources. *IG* II[2] 471; *SEG,* 16, no. 60 (= *Hesperia* 7 [1938]:303–5, no. 27, and *ABSA* 51 [1956]:6–8, no. 9).

Career. Two Athenian inscriptions attest to a certain Lykiskos, who seems to have been an officer of the kings Antigonos and Demetrios ca. 306–301. The first (*IG* II[2] 471) is from the archonship of Koroibos (306/5), and was proposed by the noted pro-Antigonid politician Stratokles to honor the *oikeioi* of Lykiskos (friends? relatives?) for the goodwill they had shown to the Athenians while at the court of Antigonos and Demetrios and, more important, for fighting along with the Athenian people, doubtless against Kassandros. The second inscription (*SEG,* 16, no. 60) is very fragmentary and has been heavily restored, partly on the basis of the first inscription, but it evidently records honors for Lykiskos himself, first for having aided refugees from a sea battle (that against Kleitos in the Hellespont during the Lamian War, most probably), and, more immediately, for some sort of help or goodwill in, it seems, 320/19 (see Stroud, below). Not enough remains of either inscription to determine the exact nature of Lykiskos's service under the Antigonids, and nothing more is known of him.

Further reading. R. S. Stroud, *Hesperia* 40 (1971):174, no. 25.

63. LYKON

Sources. Diodoros XIX 73,6.

Career. Lykon was an officer sent out by Antigonos in 312 with a fleet to aid the city of Kallatis on the Black Sea in its struggle for freedom against Lysimachos. Lykon's fleet was to have been aided by a land force under Pausanias (no. 87 below), but this was intercepted and destroyed by Lysimachos. The ultimate fate, success or failure, of Lykon and his fleet is not recorded (for a possible further testimony to this expedition, see Naukasamas, no. 133 below).

Further reading. Hauben, *Vlootbevelhebberschap,* pp. 56–59.

64. LYSANIAS, Macedonian?

Sources. Diodoros XIX 29,2, and cf. Arrian *Anab.* I 2,1

Career. A cavalry commander under Antigonos in the war against Eumenes, Lysanias is mentioned specifically at the battle of Paraitakene (316) as being in charge of 400 lancers (*xustophoroi*) who were drawn up with the cavalry on the left wing under the overall command of Peithon, satrap of Media. It was a fairly important command, of the sort one might expect to be entrusted to a senior Macedonian officer (though not one of the first rank). Perhaps, then, one might identify this man with the Lysanias who is mentioned once under Alexander (Arrian *Anab.* I 2,1) as having been entrusted, together with a certain Philotas, with the task of escorting the booty of Alexander's Thracian campaign (335) to the coast to be sold, though this identification is at best only a possibility.

Further reading. Berve, no. 479.

65. MACHAON

Sources. Blümel, *I. Iasos,* 1, no. 2; cf. Diodoros XIX 75,5.

Career. Machaon was one of three officers named in the above inscription, stationed at Iasos by Antigonos's nephew and general Polemaios ca. 312–309, and thus an Antigonid officer in that period. See further Hieron, no. 50 above; Sopolis, no. 108 below.

Further reading. Pugliese Carratelli, *ASAA*, n. s., 29/30 (1967/68):437–45, no. 1; J. and L. Robert, "Bull. ép.," 1971, no. 620; Garlan, *ZPE* 18 (1975):193–98; Bagnall, *Ptolemaic Administration*, pp. 89–91.

66. MANTIAS

Sources. Diodoros XX 98,4–9.

Career. A trusted officer in Demetrios's army at Rhodes in 305/4, Mantias was selected along with Alkimos of Epeiros (no. 8 above) to command a picked body of 1,500 soldiers in a special night attack on the city. They were to penetrate through a gap in the city wall deep into Rhodes and create a diversion enabling a general assault by Demetrios to capture the city; but the attempt failed, and Mantias and Alkimos were killed while trying to lead their men back out of Rhodes.

Further reading. U. Kahrstedt and P. Schoch, *RE* s.v., nos. 2 and 3.

67. MARSYAS, son of Periandros, Macedonian from Pella

Sources. Diodoros XX 50,4; Plutarch *Mor.* 182c; Suda s.v. Marsyas Periandrou Pellaios; and cf. *FGrH*, no. 135.

Career. Marsyas is described by Plutarch and the Suda as the brother of Antigonos; since the two men had different fathers, this must mean they were sons of the same mother by separate marriages. The Suda also informs us that Marsyas was a *syntrophos* (childhood companion) of Alexander the Great (born 356), which indicates that Marsyas was more than twenty years younger than his half-brother Antigonos (born ca. 382). The chief claim of Marsyas to the attention of posterity was as a historian of Macedon. He apparently wrote a history of Macedon from the earliest times to 330 B.C. in ten books, the bulk of which (probably books 3–7—see Heckel, below) dealt with the reign of Philip II, Antigonos's exact contemporary (see *FGrH*, no. 135 for Marsyas's historical fragments).

Besides being a historian, Marsyas evidently had some kind of political and military career. As a childhood friend of Alexander, he doubtless accompanied him on the Anabasis, at least until 330 (the return from Egypt) when his history seems to have broken off. Heckel (below) conjectures that from 330 on Marsyas remained with his half-brother, then satrap of Phrygia. In 306 Marsyas appears as a naval officer under his nephew Demetrios at the battle of Salamis, in joint command of the center of Demetrios's fleet (Diod. XX 50,4). Plutarch preserves an anecdote from the time when Antigonos was king (306–301) indicating that Marsyas then resided at his brother's court: he was involved in a lawsuit, which Antigonos insisted upon conducting in public so that any appearance of favoritism could be avoided (Plut. *Mor.* 182c). Nothing else is reported of Marsyas, and it is not clear when he died or when he wrote his history. If Diodoros's reference to him as a historian when mentioning his participation in the battle of Salamis is derived from Hieronymos of Kardia, it would follow that Marsyas wrote before Hieronymos, whose rough contemporary he was.

Further reading. R. Laqueur, *RE* s.v., no. 8; Berve, no. 489; Heckel, *Hermes* 108 (1980):444–62; Hornblower, *Hieronymus,* p. 130; Hauben, *Vlootbevelhebberschap,* pp. 59–60, 119.

68. MEDEIOS, son of Oxythemis, of Larissa

Sources. Arrian *Ind.* 18,3; *Anab.* VII 24,4–25,3; 27,2; *Met' Alex.* 24,6; Plutarch *Alex.* 75; *Demetrios* 19; *Mor.* 65c; Diodoros XVII 117,1; XIX 69,3; 75,3–8; 77,2–5; XX 50,3; Justin XII 13,7; Nikoboule *apud* Athenaios X 434c; Ps.-Kallisthenes III 31,4–9; *Epitome Mettensis* (ed. Thomas) 97; *IG* II^2 498 (= *Syll.* no. 342); C. Habicht, *Arch. Mak.* 1 (1970): 265–69; Strabo XI 530.

Career. Medeios was from an ancient noble family of Larissa in Thessaly, possibly a branch of the Aleuadai; his grandfather had been dynast in Larissa in 395 (Diod. XIV 82). Though Medeios is not mentioned as being with Alexander until 326 in India (Arrian *Ind.* 18,3), it is likely that he accompanied Alexander throughout the expedition, perhaps at first as an officer in the Thessalian cavalry contingent. In India he was one of the trierarchs of the Indus river fleet, and he subsequently rose to high favor with Alexander, becoming one of the *hetairoi*. He was accused of being an arch-flatterer (Plut. *Mor.* 65c) and figures prominently in the accounts of Alexander's last days. Medeios was host at the great banquet at which Alexander first fell ill (Arrian *Anab.* 24,4–25,1; Diod. XVII 117,1; Plut. *Alex.* 75; Athen. X 434c; Justin XII 13,7), and he was subsequently accused of complicity in the reputed Antipatrid plot to poison Alexander (Ps.-Kall. III 31,4–9; *Epit. Met.* 97). After the death of Alexander, Medeios served under Perdikkas, being sent by the latter as commander of the mercenaries on the expedition to Cyprus in 320 under the overall command of Aristonous (Arrian *Met' Alex.* 24,6).

Later Medeios entered the service of Antigonos, perhaps as a result of capture in Cyprus. He first appears as an officer of Antigonos in late 313, when he was in charge of a fleet summoned by Antigonos from Phoenicia to Karia, and on the way met and routed some ships of Kassandros's (Diod. XIX 69,3). In the next year he was Antigonos's main admiral in the Aegean, involved in the capture of Miletos and sailing to and fro between Asia Minor and Greece in connection with the campaigns of Telesphoros and Polemaios in Greece, and of Antigonos himself at the Hellespont (Diod. XIX 75,3–4; 75,7–8; 77, 2–5.

An Athenian inscription of 303/2 (*IG* II² 498: archonship of Leostratos) honors Medeios, recording that he had in some way benefited the Athenians while with King Antigonos in earlier times (*πρότερόν τε*: lines 6–9), which perhaps indicates that he was at Antigonos's court in 307/6, and helped the Athenian embassy that came to Antigonos then (Diod. XX 46,4). In 306 he was again active as an admiral, this time under the supreme command of Demetrios at the battle of Salamis; he commanded the front rank of the left wing of Demetrios's fleet, where Demetrios himself was also stationed (Diod. XX 50,3). Indeed, it is plausibly conjectured by Hauben (below) that Medeios was Antigonos's chief admiral throughout the period 313–304. He accompanied Antigonos and Demetrios on their abortive expedition against Egypt later in 306 (Plut. *Dem.* 19), and in 304 was sent by Antigonos with Demetrios to liberate Greece, as the Athenian decree honoring him tells us (*IG* II² 498, lines 10–end). There survives also an inscription from Gonnoi in Thessaly honoring Medeios, probably from the years 294–87, when Demetrios was king of Macedon, which would indicate that Medeios remained loyal to Demetrios after Ipsos (Habicht, *Arch. Mak.*, 1:265–69). There is, finally, a reference to a book by Medeios of a historical or geographical nature (Strabo XI 530, on the origin of the name "Armenia"), which indicates that Medeios shared the literary interests of other members of Antigonos's court such as Hieronymos and Marsyas.

Further reading. F. Geyer, *RE* s.v. Medios, no. 2; Berve, no. 521; *FGrH*, no. 129; Hornblower, *Hieronymus*, pp. 126–30; Hauben, *Vlootbevelhebberschap*, pp. 60–69, 110–17, 127.

69. MEDON, son of ——ras

Sources. Matthaiou, *Horos* 4 (1986):19–23.

Career. A recently published Athenian inscription from 304/3 (archonship of Pherekles) preserves a decree honoring Medon for aiding the safety of Athens and freedom of the Greeks while serving as a general under "the kings" (i.e., Antigonos and Demetrios), and specifically records that he was sent by "the king" (i.e., Demetrios) to report on the capture of the Attic frontier forts from Kassandros and Pleistarchos (lines 18–22; cf. Plut. *Demetrios* 23,1–3). The inscription breaks off at this point, so it is not known what honors were accorded Medon. Lines 10–14 state that Medon's father (Themistagoras? Pleistagoras?) also benefited Athens, but whether or not as an Antigonid official is unclear.

Further reading. None.

70. MELESIPPOS, son of Bakkhios, Boiotian from Plataia

Sources. I. Ephesos, 6, no. 2003.

Career. Melesippos was honored with citizenship by the Ephesians, having proved himself a public benefactor while at the court of Queen Phila, Demetrios's wife. This was probably ca. 306–301, when Phila had her court in Asia Minor; and Melesippos would, like Demarchos (no. 28 above), have been in Antigonid employ assigned to Phila's service.

Further reading. Robert, *Hellenica,* 2:17 n. 1.

71. MENANDROS, son of Charikles (?), Macedonian

Sources. Arrian *Anab.* III 6,7–8; IV 13,7; VII 23,1; 24,1; Curtius VI 6,35; X 10,2; Arrian *Met' Alex.* 1,6; 1,26; 25,2; Diodoros XVIII 3,1; 59,1–2; Plutarch *Eum.* 9; Justin XIII 4,15; Athenaios VI 245a; Ps.-Kallisthenes III 31,8; *Epitome Mettensis* (ed. Thomas) 97–98; Pliny *NH* XXXV 93; *Syll.,* no. 302.

Career. Menandros was one of the most senior officers and Companions in Alexander's army at the crossing into Asia in 334, commanding the 5,000 mercenary troops in the expeditionary force. This command he held until 331, when he was sent from Phoenicia to take over as satrap of Lydia (Arrian *Anab.* III 6,7–8), and it was doubtless while he was satrap of Lydia that he had his portrait painted by Apelles (Pliny *NH* XXXV 93). He remained satrap of Lydia for the rest of Alexander's reign (cf. *Syll.,* no. 302, which is dated by the eleventh year of Alexander and the satrapy of Menandros); during this time he despatched reinforcements to Alexander (Curt. VI 6,35), and in 323 he led a further body of reinforcements to Alexander in Babylon (Arrian *Anab.* VII 23,1; 24,1). He was in Babylon at the time of Alexander's death, and is reputed to have been present at Alexander's last banquet (Ps.-Kall. III 31,8; *Epit. Met.* 97–98). The Charikles who helped to disclose to Alexander the Pages' conspiracy, was the son of a Menandros (Arrian *Anab.* IV 13,7). If this was our Menandros, by Greek custom his father's name too may have been Charikles.

After the death of Alexander, Menandros was confirmed as satrap of Lydia by the conference of Babylon (Arrian *Met' Alex.* 1,6; Diod. XVIII 3,1; Curt. X 10,2; Just. XIII 4,15). He appears to have become disillusioned with Perdikkas, perhaps as a result of friendship with Antigonos, for when Antigonos returned from his flight to Europe and landed in Asia Minor with a small force in 320, Menandros promptly sided with him and warned him of Eumenes' presence in Sardis intriguing with Alexander's sister Kleopatra (Arrian *Met' Alex.* 1,26; 25,2). Nevertheless, he was not continued as satrap of Lydia at the Triparadeisos conference, being replaced by Kleitos (Berve wrongly assumes that he died). Instead, he remained in the entourage of Antigonos, becoming one of his most trusted officers. At the battle of Orkynia against Eumenes in 319, Menandros commanded Antigonos's rearguard and baggage, and was nearly surprised by Eumenes' defeated troops, who eluded Antigonos and doubled back after their retreat (Plut. *Eum.* 9).

In 318, after Eumenes had tricked his way out of the siege of Nora and was gathering new forces in Kappadokia, Menandros was sent with an army to prevent a revival of Eumenes' power there and to capture him if possible. As it happened, Eumenes had warning of Menandros's approach and moved away to Kilikia. Menandros arrived three days too late and, after pursuing the laggards among Eumenes' supporters, returned to Kappadokia (Diod. XVIII 59,1–2). Evidently Menandros had been made general over Kappadokia by Antigonos, for he seems to have remained there while Antigonos himself pursued Eumenes eastwards. When Antigonos returned from the east in 315, he found Kappadokia under attack by Kassandros's general Asklepiodoros, and sent his nephew Polemaios to reestablish order there; apparently Menandros had meanwhile died, perhaps in 317 or 316, for nothing is ever heard of him again.

Further reading. F. Geyer, *RE* s.v., no. 5; Berve, no. 501.

72. MITHRIDATES (of Kios), son of Ariobarzanes, Persian

Sources. Diodoros XVI 90,2; XX 111,4.

Career. This man is commonly known as Mithridates II of Kios, son of Ariobarzanes of Kios. The family apparently ruled a small principality on the cost of the Sea of Marmara around Kios and Myrlea, to which Mithridates succeeded on his father's death in 337 (Diod. XVI 90,2). Presumably they were descendants of the Ariobarzanes who was satrap of Hellespontine Phrygia from ca. 387 until his death ca. 362, for we hear that they were of the highest Persian nobility, from one of the seven great families (see Herodotos III 84;

Diod. XIX 40,2 referring to the nephew of the present Mithridates, no. 73 below). Mithridates ruled the principality for thirty-five years from 337 (Diod. XVI 90,2; XX 111,4); there is no evidence linking him to Alexander, either for or against; in 316 his nephew was in Eumenes' army at Gabiene (Diod. XIX 40,2). During Antigonos's rule over Asia Minor, 315–302, Mithridates evidently recognized Antigonos's suzerainty, for his nephew was at Antigonos's court (Plut. *Demetrios* 4), and he is himself described as "subject to Antigonos" (ὑπήκοος ὢν Ἀντιγόνωι: Diod. XX 111,4). However, when Lysimachos invaded Asia Minor in 302 Mithridates was suspected by Antigonos of contemplating treachery and executed (Diod. XX 111,4).

Further reading. F. Geyer, *RE* s.v., no. 6; Hornblower, *Hieronymus*, pp. 243–45.

73. MITHRIDATES (Ktistes), son of Ariobarzanes, Persian

Sources. Diodoros XIX 40,2; XX 111,4; Plutarch *Demetrios* 4; Appian *Mithridatika* 9; Trogus *Prologues* 17; Polyainos VII 29,2; Plutarch *Mor*. 183a; [Loukianos] *Makrobioi* 13; Memnon in *FGrH*, no. 434 Fs 7,2; 9,4; Apollonios in *FGrH*, no. 740 F 14; Strabo XII 562.

Career. Nephew of Mithridates of Kios, this Mithridates is commonly called Mithridates Ktistes (Founder) from the fact that he founded the kingdom of Pontos. He is described by Plutarch (*Dem*. 4) as being a coeval of Demetrios (ἑταῖρος καθ' ἡλικίαν), but this is probably a slight exaggeration: he died in 266 (Diod. XX 111,4: he ruled thirty-six years after his uncle died in 302) at the age of 84 ([Louk.] *Makrob*. 13 = *FGrH*, no. 154 F 7 Hieronymos), and was thus born about 349 and some eleven years older than Demetrios. Consonant with this is the prominent mention of him among the selected cavalry about Eumenes at the battle of Gabiene in 316 (Diod. XIX 40,2), when he would have been 33–34 years old. He is described by Diodoros as "remarkable for his courage and trained as a soldier from childhood." After the battle, he must have been among the captives who were persuaded to take service under Antigonos.

It is at Antigonos's court, and as a close friend of Demetrios, that he is attested in 302. His uncle was suspected of treason and executed, and he himself only escaped from the same fate due to a timely warning from Demetrios to flee for his life (Plut. *Dem*. 4; *Mor*. 183a; Appian *Mith*. 9; [Louk.] *Makrob*. 13). The anecdote recorded in this context by Plutarch (twice) and by Appian, that it was as a result of a dream in which he sowed a field with gold and Mithridates harvested it that Antigonos decided to kill Mithridates, is doubtless a later embroidery based on the fact that in the turmoil in Asia Minor after Antigonos's death in 301, Mithridates was able to lay the foundations of a powerful kingdom in northern Kappadokia, so that he did in a sense reap where Antigonos had sown.

When Mithridates fled from Antigonos in 302, he found refuge in the fortress of Kimiata in the Olgassys mountains in northern Kappadokia (Strabo XIX 562; Appian *Mith.* 9; and cf. Polyainos VII 29,2) from which he extended his power over the surrounding province of Kimiatene and eventually all of northern Kappadokia, aided by "the embarrassment of the Macedonian power," as Appian puts it (*Mith.* 9: ἐν τῆιδε τῆι Μακεδόνων ἀσχολίαι), consequent upon the death of Antigonos and the rivalry between Lysimachos, Demetrios, and Seleukos in Asia Minor. In 281 Seleukos made an effort to subdue Mithridates, which he was able to overcome with the aid of Herakleia, Byzantion, and Chalkedon (Trogus *Prol.* 17; Memnon in *FGrH,* no. 434 F 7,2). Shortly after the death of Seleukos in late 281, Mithridates' son Ariobarzanes secured the important city of Amastris on the coast (Memnon in *FGrH,* no. 434 F 9,4); and it seems that Mithridates weathered a later attack by Ptolemy with the aid of Galatian mercenaries (Apollonios in *FGrH,* no. 740 F 14).

Further reading. F. Geyer, *RE* s.v., no. 7; Hornblower, *Hieronymus,* via index and esp. pp. 123, 243–45; E. Olshausen, *RE* suppl. 15 s.v. Pontos.

74. MNESIMACHOS

Sources. Buckler and Robinson, *Sardis VII,* no. 1.

Career. An inscription from the temple of Artemis at Sardis records the granting of a large estate in the Lydian plain to Mnesimachos by Antigonos, evidently towards the end of the fourth century (see Debord, below). Mnesimachos had taken out a loan of 1,325 gold pieces from the temple wardens and was unable to pay it back, so he handed over the estate instead, which consisted of several villages in different districts and a few *klēroi* (lots of the sort given to soldier-settlers) besides. Evidently, then, Mnesimachos was a person high in Antigonos's favor, and he must presumably have been a high-ranking officer or official under Antigonos. A clue to his provenance may be provided by the Eretrian inscription *IG* XII.9 208 (from the beginning of the third century) honoring a certain Apellas, son of Mnesimachos, from Klazomenai in Asia Minor. However, as the name Mnesimachos is not especially uncommon, it is no more than a possibility that Apellas of Klazomenai should be the son of this Mnesimachos.

Further reading: Buckler and Robinson, *AJA* 16 (1912):22–82; Debord, *Aspects,* app. 5, pp. 244–51; Austin, *Hellenistic World,* no. 181.

75. MOSCHION, son of Moirichos, of Thera

Sources. Diodoros XIX 57,4 and cf. 58,5; Segrè, *TC,* no. 8.

Career. Moschion was sent by Antigonos as ambassador to Rhodes in 314 together with Idomeneus (no. 56 above) to negotiate an agreement enabling Antigonos to build warships there (Diod. XIX 57,4 and 58,5), in which they were successful. A late fourth century inscription from Kalymna (Segrè, *TC,* no. 8) records honors granted to one Moschion, son of Moirichos of Thera, for his benevolent attitude towards Kalymnian troops stationed under him at Pogla (the inscription reads Mogla, presumably a scribal error) a town in the Kabalia district on the frontier between Lydia and Pisidia. It is conjectured by Segrè, surely rightly, that this is the same man, who is thus revealed as a military as well as diplomatic officer of Antigonos. It is characteristic of Antigonos's tact that he should have sent as ambassador to the island of Rhodes an island Greek from Thera in the Cyclades, and placed the same man in charge of allied troops from the island of Kalymna.

Further reading. J. H. Kroll, *RE* s.v., no. 2; Olshausen, *Prosopographie,* no. 71; Seibert, *Ptolemaios I,* pp. 141, 161, 227.

76. MUS, son of Proteas, from Eresos

Sources. IG VII 4.

Career. A Megarian inscription from the years 307–300 (see no. 140 below for the nature and date of this and associated inscriptions) honors Mus with proxeny for his goodwill towards the Megarians. The first line reads ———ς διατρίβων, which is taken by the editor (Dittenberger) to be an error on the part of the stone-cutter, and seems likely to be the remainder of a phrase such as [παρὰ Δαμάτριον τὸμ βασιλέ]ạ διατρίβων, making Mus (like Philon and Kleon of *IG* VII 5 and 6 from the same year) an officer in the army of Demetrios in 304–302. The phrase was apparently omitted by the cutter, and hence added later superlinearly.

Further reading. Urban, *Wachstum and Krise des Achaiischen Bundes,* pp. 66–70.

77. NEARCHOS, son of Androtimos, from Lato on Crete

Sources. Arrian *Anab.* III 6,5–6; IV 7,2; 30,5–6; VI 2,3; 5,4; 5,5; 19,5; VII 4,6; 5,6; 19,3; 25,4; *Ind.* 18,3 and 17,6–42,10 passim; Curtius

IX 10,3; X 1,10–16; 6,10–12; Plutarch *Alex.* 10; 66; 73; 75–76; Diodoros XVII 104,3; 112,3–4; XIX 19,4–5; 69,1; Plutarch *Eum.* 2 and 18; Justin XIII 4,14–15; Ps.-Kallisthenes III 31,8; *Epitome Mettensis* (ed. Thomas) 97; Strabo XV 2,4 et al.; Suda s.v. Nearchos; Polyainos V 35; *Syll.*, no. 266; and cf. *FGrH*, no. 133.

Career. Though by birth a Cretan from Lato, Nearchos's home was Amphipolis on the border of Macedon (Arrian *Ind.* 18,3; *Syll.*, no. 266); it is thought that his father probably moved to Macedon fairly early in the reign of Philip II. Nearchos hence grew up in Macedon, and was a boyhood friend of Alexander (Arrian *Anab.* III 6,5–6; Plut. *Alex* 10), even spending some time in exile for excessive loyalty to Alexander when the latter was at odds with his father. It was apparently shortly after his return from exile that he was honored by Delphi (*Syll.*, no. 266). He accompanied Alexander on the Anabasis until 333, when he was placed over the satrapy of Lykia and Pamphylia (Arrian *Anab.* III 6,5–6; cf. id. I 24,4; Justin XIII 4,14–15). He did not remain satrap for long, however, for in 329 he led a body of mercenary troops to reinforce Alexander at Zariaspa (Arrian IV 7,2), and his satrapy apparently passed under the control of Antigonos. Back with Alexander, he was appointed chiliarch of one of the *taxeis* (1,000 strong) of the Hypaspists (which indicates how much he was thought of as Macedonian), though on occasion used as a commander of other troops, for example, the Agrianian light infantry at Dyrta in 327/26 (Arrian IV 30,5–6). He became really prominent in Alexander's force in India, when he was appointed admiral of the fleet that sailed down the Indus, and later of the expedition that sailed from the Indus to the Euphrates (see Arrian *Ind.* 17,6–42,10 passim).

Nearchos was highly successful as admiral, which led to his being appointed admiral for the expedition to Arabia that Alexander was planning in his last days (Arrian *Anab.* VII 25,4). Nearchos was much in Alexander's company at Babylon: he is reported to have passed on the Chaldaians' warning to Alexander not to enter Babylon (Plut. *Alex.* 73; Diod. XVII 112,3–4); he entertained Alexander with stories of his experiences in the Indian Ocean (Plut. *Alex.* 76); and he was given a grand farewell banquet by Alexander (Plut. *Alex.* 75). In short, he was highly esteemed and trusted by the king in every way; in Susa he had been specially crowned by the king for valor (Arrian *Anab.* VII 5,6; *Ind.* 42,9), and at the great interracial marriage ceremony organized by Alexander, Nearchos was given as his bride the daughter of Alexander's reputed concubine Barsine (Arrian *Anab.* VII 4,6). It is ironic, therefore, that Nearchos should be among those at

Alexander's last banquet accused in the later romantic tradition of complicity in the plot to poison the king (Ps.-Kall. III 31,8; *Epit. Met.* 97).

After Alexander's death, Nearchos participated in the conferences in Babylon to decide the fate of the empire, reputedly championing the claims of his brother-in-law Herakles, son of Barsine, to be considered Alexander's legitimate successor (Curt. X 6,10–12). He was not granted a satrapy either at the division of Babylon or at that of Triparadeisos. He attached himself to Antigonos, and in 317/16 he served under Antigonos on the latter's campaign against Eumenes in the east. When Antigonos forced his way through the mountainous territory of the Kossaians, Nearchos was sent ahead with a body of light troops to seize the passes in advance, an important and responsible task (Diod. XIX 19,4–5). After the capture of Eumenes at Gabiene, it was Nearchos who pleaded, along with Demetrios, for the life of Eumenes, whom most of Antigonos's officers and advisers wished to execute (Plut. *Eum.* 18). The last mention of Nearchos in the sources is of his appointment by Antigonos in 313–312 as one of the four advisers of his son Demetrios when the latter was left in charge of Syria by his father (Diod. XIX 69,1). As such Nearchos must have been present at the battle of Gaza, but his presence is not specifically attested.

A story in Polyainos (V 35) of how Nearchos captured Telmessos, since it appears to belong to the Diadoch period (Nearchos's opponent was an old friend named Antipatrides—Berve, no. 92), may record another accomplishment of Nearchos in Antigonos's service, possibly connected with the campaign against Alketas and Attalos in Pisidia in 319 (see Diod. XVIII 44,1–46,7). Attalos had earlier operated with a fleet, near the Lykian and Karian coast (Arrian *Met' Alex.* 1,39), and might then have installed Antipatrides in Telmessos. The date of Nearchos's literary activity (writing the *Anaplous,* the account of his voyage in the Indian Ocean and Persian Gulf) is not precisely known, but should perhaps fall after 312, given his busy military activity before that date. It appears to have been written to correct Onesikritos's account of the same event, in which Onesikritos falsely claimed to have been admiral of the expedition (Ones. in *FGrH,* no. 134 F 27; Jacoby, *FGrH,* vol. 2 D, p. 446, argues that Nearchos wrote to refute Onesikritos).

Further reading. H. Berve, *RE,* s.v., no. 3; W. Capelle, *RE* s.v., no. 3; Berve, no. 544; Jacoby, *FGrH,* no. 133; Pearson, *Lost Histories,* pp. 112ff.; Hornblower, *Hieronymus,* via index and esp. p. 124.

78. NEON

Sources. Diodoros XX 52,4.

Career. Neon was an officer in Demetrios's fleet at the battle of Cyprian Salamis in 306. He was sent out after the battle to pick up survivors from among the wreckage, together with Bourichos (no. 26 above).

Further reading. P. Schoch, *RE* s.v., no. 4; Hauben, *Vlootbevelhebberschap,* pp. 114–15.

79. NIKANOR, Macedonian

Sources. Arrian *Met' Alex.* 1,37; Diodoros XVIII 39,6; XIX 92,1–5; 100,3; Plutarch *Eum.* 17,2; Appian *Mith.* 8; *Syr.* 55 and 57.

Career. At the conference of Triparadeisos in 320, Nikanor was appointed satrap of Kappadokia in the place of Eumenes (Arrian *Met' Alex.* 1,37; Diod. XVIII 39,6; Appian *Mith.* 8). Hence he was presumably a high-ranking Macedonian and must have had some sort of career under Alexander, but it seems impossible to equate him with any of the known men of this name under Alexander, for they were almost all either dead or otherwise accounted for by 320, unless perchance the leader of Alexander's fleet in the Aegean in 334 was this man (see Berve, no. 555). At any rate, upon appointment to the satrapy of Kappadokia, he must have attached himself to Antigonos, for Eumenes was in Kappadokia with a large and victorious army which it was Antigonos's task to fight. Despite Antigonos's victory over Eumenes at Orkynia, however, he did not install Nikanor in Kappadokia, preferring to send Menandros there as general (Diod. XVIII 59,1–2; cf. Menandros, no. 71 above). Nikanor remained with Antigonos as one of his generals, and in 316, after the battle of Gabiene, he was sent to treat with the Argyraspids and receive from them the captive Eumenes (Plut. *Eum.* 17,2).

If Nikanor was disappointed at not receiving the satrapy of Kappadokia, he was amply indemnified by Antigonos, for he received the post of general over Media and the upper satrapies, becoming in effect Antigonos's viceroy over the eastern part of the empire (Diod. XIX 92,1–5; 100,3). He was probably appointed in late 315, after Antigonos's original disposition for Media and the east had proved unsuccessful (see Hippostratos, no. 54 above), but it is only in 311 that he is explicitly attested in this post, when Seleukos crossed the Euphrates and seized Babylonia (Diod. XIX 85,1–2). Nikanor, loyal to Antigonos, gathered from Media and Persia an army of 10,000 foot and 7,000 horse and set out to deal with Seleukos. He was ambushed by Seleukos in a surprise night attack near the Tigris, however, and decisively beaten, fleeing back to Media with a handful of followers (Diod. XIX 92,1–5). He tried to organize new forces and sent a message to Antigonos reporting on Seleukos's successes (Diod. XIX 100,3), but Seleukos invaded Media, brought Nikanor to battle, and killed him before aid from Antigonos could arrive (Appian *Syr.* 55 and 57, writing Nika*t*or). According to Isidore of Charax (in *GGM,* 1:248), the Greco-Macedonian colony at Dura (i.e., Dura-Europos) was originally founded by a Nikanor, but this was probably a different man, an officer of Seleukos, as Dura seems to have been a Seleukid foundation (see Jones, below).

Further reading. H. Berve, *RE* s.v., no. 13 and no. 7; Bengtson, *Strategie,* pp. 188ff.; Schober, *Gesch. Babyloniens,* pp. 89–90, 97–103; Jones, *Cities,* pp. 216–17.

80. NIKANOR II

Sources. Polyainos IV 7,4.

Career. Shortly after the battle of Ipsos in 301, Demetrios, who had escaped to Ephesos (Plut. *Dem.* 30), sailed to Kilikia to collect his mother, children, and much treasure, leaving an officer named Diodoros (no. 30 above) in charge of Ephesos. Soon, however, news reached him of negotiations going on for Diodoros to betray Ephesos to Lysimachos, so he sailed back with a few ships, placing them under the command of an officer named Nikanor and hiding his own persence. When Nikanor had safely sailed into Ephesos, Demetrios suddenly revealed himself to his men stationed there and had Diodoros arrested. Since Nikanor was a trusted officer of Demetrios immediately after the battle of Ipsos, he must have been in Antigonid employ already long before the battle and have joined Antigonid service during Antigonos's lifetime.

Further reading. P. Schoch, *RE* s.v., no. 14.

81. NIKODEMOS, son of Nikarchides, of Messene

Sources. Plutarch *Demosthenes* 13,4; Ecole Française d'Athènes, *Fouilles de Delphes,* 3.4, no. 7 (= *Syll.,* no. 325).

Career. Plutarch adduces Nikodemos as an example of a man who is inconstant and out for gain, explaining that he first served Kassandros but later went over to Demetrios Poliorketes, with the justification that it always pays to obey the powerful. His service with Demetrios should be placed in 303/2, when Demetrios was busy liberating Greece from Kassandros by Antigonos's order. Around this time Nikodemos was also granted proxeny and other honors by the people of Delphi.

Further reading. None.

82. NIKOMEDES, son of Aristandros, of Kos

Sources. Herzog, *RFIC*, n.s., 20 (1942):12–20; Habicht, *AM* 72 (1957):167–71, no. 3; Dunst, *Klio* 37 (1959):63–68; Paton and Hicks, *Inscr. of Cos*, pp. 32–36, nos. 17–19; pp. 184–85, nos. 221, 227; G. Pugliese Carratelli, *PP* 33 (1978):156–57.

Career. An inscription from Kos containing a complete dossier of decrees from Greek cities around the Aegean honoring Nikomedes proves that he was an important official at Antigonos's court, apparently with primarily diplomatic duties. Only a few parts of the inscription, which is very fragmentary, have been published to date, recording decrees in his honor from Athens (Herzog, pp. 12–13), Ephesos (Paton and Hicks, no. 18), Samos (Habicht), Chios (Dunst), Klazomenai (Pugliese Carratelli), and probably Erythrai (Herzog, p. 18). In addition, fragments of decrees from Miletos, Gryne, Phokaia, Antandros, Hamaxitos, and the Athenian colony on Lemnos are recorded (Herzog, p. 12). There are also extant two other inscriptions from Kos, one from the base of a statue of Nikomedes (Paton and Hicks, no. 221), and one from the funerary stele of his mother, Olympias (Paton and Hicks, no. 227). The Erythraian (?) decree honors Nikomedes' brother Kleumachos as well as Nikomedes.

From all of this, a picture can be formed of a man high in Antigonid service and very well respected in his home city of Kos. The main inscription was inscribed on a monument honoring Nikomedes in the Asklepieion of Kos, recording all of the many honors accorded him by Greek cities. The Samian decree records specifically that Nikomedes had helped a Samian embassy to Antigonos (lines 11–12), and apparently dates from well before 306, perhaps ca. 312–310 (see Habicht, pp. 171, 262–66). The Athenian decree, which appears to date from ca. 303/2 (Herzog, p. 12), records that Nikomedes was a member of Demetrios's expedition to liberate Greece in 304–302 (lines 4–6). Some of the other decrees mention Nikomedes' aid to embassies and/or private citizens visiting Antigonos's court (Herzog, p. 12), from which it seems Nikomedes' duties involved vetting embassies or individuals who sought access to Antigonos and arranging audiences.

Further reading. J. and L. Robert, "Bull. ép.," 1948, no. 181;

Sherwin-White, *Ancient Cos,* pp. 86–88, 122 n. 217; Osborne, *Naturalisation in Athens,* no. D 51.

83. OLKIAS (or HOLKIAS), Illyrian (?)

Sources. Ps.-Kallisthenes III 31,8–9; 32,8; 33,1–25; *Epitome Mettensis* (ed. Thomas) 97–98; 103; 106; 109–23; Polyainos IV 6,6.

Career. Olkias, unknown to the regular sources on Alexander, is extraordinarily prominent in the romantic accounts of Alexander's last days. He is recorded (Ps.-Kall. III 31,8–9; *Epit. Met.* 97–98) to have been one of the twenty high-ranking officers who attended the banquet Medeios of Larissa (no. 68 above) gave for Alexander, and one of the six of these who were innocent of the alleged plot to murder Alexander (with Perdikkas, Eumenes, Ptolemy, Lysimachos, and Asandros). Subsequently, he was entrusted by the dying Alexander with his last will and testament (Ps.-Kall. III 33,1; *Epit. Met.* 106), with orders to send a copy to Rhodes (*Epit. Met.* 109). He is placed on a level with Ptolemy and Perdikkas as one of the three great men who stood around the bed of the dying king (Ps.-Kall., Armenian version, p. 105, 10–26, Raabe ed.). He read out the will of Alexander after his death (*Epit. Met.* 114), and the will ordered that Olkias's sister Kleodike be married to Leonnatos, a relative of Alexander, and that Olkias himself be appointed king of Illyria (Ps.-Kall. III 33,12; 33,23; *Epit. Met.* 116; 122.)

Given these clearly fictitious details of Olkias's importance during Alexander's last days, one would suppose him a wholly fictitious character were it not for the fact that Polyainos (IV 6,6) records his existence in a fashion that can scarcely be doubted. In the winter of 320/19, when Antigonos was encamped with an army near Kappadokia, preparatory to undertaking operations against the armies of Alketas and Eumenes, 3,000 Macedonian soldiers rebelled against him, the leader of the rebellion being Olkias. Antigonos succeeded in quashing the rebellion and capturing Olkias, with the aid of an officer named Leonidas (no. 61 above). This story tells us that by 320 Olkias was an officer in Antigonos's army, and was discontented. Antigonos's army in 320/19 was in large part made up of the army that Perdikkas had commanded in Egypt (Arrian *Met' Alex.* 1,38), these 3,000 men and Olkias no doubt among them. Merkelbach (below) argues that the extraordinary prominence of Olkias in the accounts of Alexander's last days can be explained by conjecturing a pamphlet written by Olkias as the source of those accounts. A feature of these accounts is the slander of poisoning Alexander directed at prominent enemies of Perdikkas such as Antipatros, Peithon, Meleagros, Philotas, and Menandros, while Eumenes, Perdikkas, Olkias, Lysimachos, Ptolemy, and Asandros are exculpated.

Olkias, then, was a middle-ranking officer in the Macedonian army and a supporter of Perdikkas after Alexander's death. He passed into the service of Antigonos in 320, but early in 319 raised a rebellion to help Alketas, Perdikkas's brother and Antigonos's enemy (so Polyainos IV 6,6). After his capture by Antigonos, he is not heard of again, but he probably lived on for some time, for the accounts of Alexander's last days based on his putative pamphlet show knowledge of Onesikritos's history, chiding him for not naming the plotters against Alexander (*Epit. Met.* 97), and of other events of the Diadoch period (see Merkelbach's in-depth treatment). Perhaps, given Olkias's "appointment" as king of Illyria, he actually was an Illyrian.

Further reading. J. H. Kroll, *RE* suppl. 3 s.v. Holkias; Berve, no. 580; Merkelbach, *Quellen des griechischen Alexanderromans,* pp. 164–93, esp. 171–73; also pp. 253–83 for texts of the relevant portions of the *Epitome Mettensis* and Ps.-Kallisthenes.

84. ONOMARCHOS

Sources. Plutarch *Eum.* 18,4: Nepos *Eum.* 11,3–4.

Career. When Antigonos captured Eumenes in 316 after the battle of Gabiene, he was for some time undecided what to do with him, and kept him meanwhile under heavy guard. Onomarchos is recorded as the captain of this guard in a story, preserved in essentially the same form by both Plutarch and Nepos, of a sharp verbal exchange between Eumenes and his guard. Hence Onomarchos would have been a fairly low-ranking officer, but one considered reliable.

Further reading. None.

85. ORONTOBATES of Media

Sources. Diodoros XIX 46,5–47,2.

Career. After the defeat of Eumenes in the winter of 316/15, Antigonos had the ambitious satrap of Media, Peithon, son of Krateuas, executed on suspicion of treason, and replaced him as satrap by Orontobates the Mede, one of two native satraps appointed by Antigonos in this area (cf. Aspeisas, no. 21 above). It is not clear how long Orontobates remained satrap. In 311 Nikanor (no. 79 above) is called satrap of Media by Appian (*Syr.* 55), but this could be an error, for Nikanor was certainly general over the upper satrapies stationed in Media, and need not have been satrap of Media as well (see Diod.

XIX 92,1, calling Nikanor "general in Media," and 100,3, "general of Media and the upper satrapies").

Further reading. Schober, *Gesch. Babyloniens*, pp. 85, 89–90.

86. OXYTHEMIS, son of Hippostratos, of Larissa

Sources. Demochares *apud* Athenaios VI 253a; Phylarchos *apud* Athenaios XIV 614f; Heraklides Lembos *apud* Athenaios XIII 578b; Diodoros XXI 15; 16,5; *IG* II^2 558 (= *Syll.*, no. 343).

Career. Oxythemis, probably from the dynastic family of the Aleuadai of Larissa, was the nephew of Medeios of Larissa (no. 68 above) and the son of a Hippostratos (*Syll.*, no. 343), most probably the man appointed general of the upper satrapies by Antigonos in 315 (no. 54 above). As his father and uncle were thus both prominent officers of Antigonos, it is no surprise to find Oxythemis too serving in Antigonid employ. He was an officer in Demetrios's army in Greece 304–302, being honored with citizenship by the Athenians in 303/2 (*Syll.*, no. 343; archonship of Leostratos). According to Demochares, some Athenians went so far as to grant him heroic honors (Athen. VI 253a). An anecdote of Phylarchos's (Athen. XIV 614f) places Oxythemis at Demetrios's court as king of Macedon in 294–287 (it concerns the rivalry between Demetrios and Lysimachos at that time). That Oxythemis remained with Demetrios after Ipsos is also shown by Diodoros XXI 15 and 16,5 recording that Demetrios sent Oxythemis as his ambassador to Agathokles of Syracuse in 289. He survived Demetrios (d. 283), but was executed by Antigonos Gonatas in a dispute over Demo, Antigonos's concubine and the mother of his son Halkyoneus (Athen. XIII 578a–b).

Further reading. T. Lenschau, *RE* s.v.; Olshausen, *Prosopographie*, no. 77; Habicht, *Gottmenschentum*, pp. 55–58; Robert, *Hellenica*, 2:19, 29; Wehrli, *Antigone et Démétrios*, pp. 124–25; Osborne, *Naturalisation in Athens*, no. D 47.

87. PAUSANIAS

Sources. Diodoros XIX 73,6–10.

Career. Pausanias was sent by Antigonos into Thrace in 313/12 with a body of troops "not few in number" (Diod. XIX 73,6) to the relief of Kallatis on the Black Sea, under siege by Lysimachos. However, Lysimachos had warning of Pausanias's approach and, leaving Kallatis, set an ambush for him. Pausanias's force was taken by surprise and destroyed, and Pausanias himself was captured and killed. Since he was entrusted with an independent command over a substantial body of troops, he must have ranked fairly high in Antigonos's service before his death.

Further reading. T. Lenschau, *RE* s.v., no. 8.

88. PEITHON, son of Agenor, Macedonian

Sources. Arrian *Anab.* VI 15,4; 17,1–4; 20,1; Curtius IX 8,16; Arrian *Met' Alex.* 1,36; Dexippos in *FGrH,* no. 100 F 8,5; Diodoros XVIII 3,2; 39,6; XIX 56,4; 69,1; 80,1; 82,1; 85,2; Justin XIII 4,21.

Career. Peithon, son of Agenor, was a senior officer in the army of Alexander the Great, first mentioned in 326/25, when he was appointed satrap of the lower Indus valley in India (Arrian *Anab.* VI 15,4). The importance of this post indicates that he must already have held high offices before and been with Alexander for some time, perhaps even from the first crossing into Asia. As satrap he was charged with an independent command against the rebellious Indian king Mousikanos, which he completed successfully, bringing Mousikanos captive to Alexander's camp (Arrian *Anab.* VI 17,1–2; Curtius IX 8,16). He was then sent with troops to settle affairs on the left bank of the Indus and see to the colonizing of the towns being built there (Arrian *Anab.* VI 17,4). He joined Alexander again at Patala (Arrian *Anab.* VI 20,1).

This is all that is recorded of his career under Alexander, but it shows him as an able and trusted general. Before Alexander's death he seems to have been moved to the satrapy between the Hindu Kush and the upper Indus, of which region he was confirmed as a satrap at Babylon (Dex. F 8,5; Diod. XVIII 3,2), perhaps still with oversight of the colonies along the lower Indus (Justin XIII 4,21). At the conference of Triparadeisos he was again confirmed in his satrapy (Arrian *Met' Alex.* 1,36; Diod. XVIII 39,6), but during the next few years it seems the rise of Indian nationalism made his position untenable, and he was forced to evacuate India (see Schober, below, for full details).

At any rate, Peithon left India and returned to the west to meet and join Antigonos in 315. Such an able and experienced commander was evidently a welcome addition to the circle of Antigonos's officers and friends, and Peithon was promptly appointed to succeed the fugitive Seleukos as satrap of Babylonia (Diod. XIX 56,4). Oddly, no satrap of northern Mesopotamia is known in this period since the deposing in 315 of Blitor (no. 24 above). Perhaps Mesopotamia was added to Peithon's satrapy of Babylonia, for in 313–312 Peithon was co-commander with Demetrios of the Antigonid forces in Syria. To come from Babylonia to Syria, one had to pass through Mesopotamia along the Euphrates valley, and it seems logical to suppose that Peithon came to Syria as commander of forces raised in Babylonia and Mesopotamia to strengthen Syria against possible attack by Ptolemy. This hypothesis explains the lack of mention of any satrap of Mesopotamia in these years, and the ease with which Seleukos seized Babylonia and Mesopotamia after the battle of Gaza, where Peithon died.

However that may be, Peithon was appointed co-commander with Demetrios in Syria in 313 (Diod. XIX 69,1); he was left in charge of the army by Demetrios when the latter rushed to oppose Ptolemy in Kilikia in early 312 (Diod. XIX 80,1); and he was in joint command with Demetrios at the battle of Gaza in late 312 (Diod. XIX 82,1), being stationed with him on the left wing. He died in this battle, the most distinguished of Demetrios's losses that day (Diod. XIX 85,2); perhaps he fell fighting a rear-guard action while Demetrios sought to rally the fleeing Antigonid forces (cf. Diod. XIX 84,5–85,5).

Further reading. H. Berve, *RE* s.v., no. 2; Berve, no. 619; Schober, *Gesch. Babyloniens,* pp. 15–26, 88, 91–96, 158–60.

89. PERILAOS

Sources. Diodoros XIX 64,5–8; cf. Plutarch *Mor.* 179f; Curtius X 8,15.

Career. Perilaos was a general in Antigonos's service who in 313 commanded a small army marching along the coast from Lykia to Kilikia, presumably intending to join Antigonos in Syria, accompanied by a fleet under Theodotos (no. 113 below). A Ptolemaic fleet was then cruising off Pamphylia and, getting wind of Perilaos's and Theodotos's movements, sailed to Aphrodisias in Kilikia to set up an ambush for the unwary Antigonid forces. The ambush succeeded, and Perilaos was captured and carried off to Egypt, but was quickly ransomed by Antigonos.

It is possible that the Perilaos or Perillos attested as a Macedonian *hetairos* of Alexander in an anecdote by Plutarch (*Mor.* 179f) and the Perilaos who mediated between the cavalry and the infantry during the dispute at Babylon after Alexander's death could be the same man. As holder of an independent command under Antigonos, Perilaos was clearly a man of some standing, so that it is to be expected he would already have had a career under Alexander.

Further reading. H. Berve, *RE* s.v. Perillos; Berve, no. 630.

90. PEUKESTAS, son of Alexandros, Macedonian

Sources. Arrian *Anab*. VI 9,3–10,4; 28,3–4; 30,2–3; VII 5,4; 6,3; 23,1–3; 24,1; 26,2; *Ind*. 18,6; 19,8; *Met' Alex*. 1,35; Curtius IX 5,14–18; Diodoros XVII 99,4; 110,2; XVIII 3,3; 39,6; XIX 14,2; 15,1; 17,4–18,1; 21,1–24,6; 28,3; 37,6–38,1; 42,4–43,5; 48,5; 56,1; Plutarch *Alex*. 41; 42; 63; *Eum*. 13,4; 14,3; 15,4; 16,5; Phylarchos *apud* Athenaios XIV 614f; Ps.-Kallisthenes III 4; 31; 33,22; Justin XIII 4,23; Polyainos IV 6,13; 8,3; Robert, *Coll. Froehner*, no. 52, line 13, and pp. 70–71 n. 1; *IG* XI.4 161b, lines 55, 81; 162b, line 43.

Career. First mentioned in our sources as Alexander's shield-bearer and a member of the Hypaspists (Arrian *Anab*. VI 9,3; Diod. XVII 99,4) at the city of the Mallians in India in 325, when he saved Alexander's life, Peukestas must have been a member of the expeditionary force for some time already, most likely from the beginning of the expedition. As a result of his heroism in India, Peukestas was appointed to Alexander's staff as a *sōmatophylax* (Arrian *Anab*. VI 28,3), granted the position of satrap of Persis (Arrian *Anab*. VI 28,4), and in 324 publicly crowned with gold at Susa (Arrian *Anab*. VII 5,4). Peukestas was a very popular satrap in Persia owing to his use of Persian dress and the Persian language (Arrian *Anab*. VII 6,3), though this caused many Macedonians to regard him askance. In 323 he brought new Persian and Kossaian troops to Alexander in Babylon (Arrian *Anab*. VII 23,1–3; 24,1; Diod. XVII 110,2), and was in Babylon during Alexander's illness and death. He attended the famous banquet of Medeios at which Alexander fell ill (Ps.-Kall. III 31,8), and was one of those who sought the advice of the deity "Serapis" in Babylon concerning the king's health (Arrian *Anab*. VII 26,2).

After Alexander's death Peukestas was confirmed as satrap of Persis at the Babylon conference (Diod. XVIII 3,3; Justin XIII 4,23), and again at the Triparadeisos conference in 320 (Arrian *Met' Alex* 1,35; Diod. XVIII 39,6). When Peithon, son of Krateuas, attempted to assert his authority over all of the upper satrapies, the resistance was largely led and organized by Peukestas, and he was the commander of the combined army which defeated Peithon ca. 317 (Diod. XIX 14,1–2). Upon Eumenes' arrival in the trans-Tigris region in 316, this army of the upper satrapies joined him in his war against Antigonos, and Peukestas became Eumenes's rival for the overall command (Diod. XIX 14,5–15,4; Plut. *Eum*. 13,4). To bolster his claim to primacy, he brought up reinforcements from Persia (Diod. XIX 17,4–18,1), and entertained the entire army magnificently in

Persia in the summer of 316 (Diod. XIX 21,1–24,6). Eumenes had to forge a letter telling of major successes by his backers in Macedon to remain leader (Diod. XIX 23,1–3; Plut. *Eum.* 14,3; Polyain. IV 8,3).

Peukestas was present at the great battle of Paraitakene in 316 (Diod. XIX 28,3), and in the winter of 316/15 seems to have virtually reached the position of co-commander with Eumenes (Diod. XIX 37,6–38,1; Plut. *Eum.* 15,4). However, at the winter battle of Gabiene, in which Peukestas was stationed with Eumenes on the left, his retreat in the face of Antigonos's vigorous cavalry attack was blamed for the army's defeat (Diod. XIX 42,4–43,5; Plut. *Eum.* 16,5), and in the battle's aftermath he surrendered himself and his Persian troops to Antigonos (Polyain. IV 6,13). Antigonos refused to perpetuate his authority in Persia because of his great influence there (Diod. XIX 48,5) and carried him back to the west with promises of suitable employment.

Traces of such employment are apparently preserved by an inscription from Theangela in Karia, which mentions a treaty made by Peukestas with Theangela (Robert, *Coll. Froehner,* no. 52, line 13, and pp. 70–71 n. 1). Combination of this inscription with a corrupt passage in MS F of Diodoros XIX 75,4–5 makes it probable that Peukestas was sent to Theangela and the Halikarnassos Peninsula as part of Antigonos's Karian campaign at the beginning of 312 (see Billows, below). At some time during the years 307–286, Peukestas probably accompanied Demetrios on a campaign in the Aegean, as he is recorded as the giver of a dedication in two inventory lists at Delos (*IG* XI.4 161b, lines 55, 81; 162b, line 43), along with Demetrios and other persons of the period. Peukestas evidently stayed with Demetrios after Ipsos, for an anecdote recorded by Phylarchos (Athen. XIV 614f) attests his presence at Demetrios's Macedonian court ca. 294–87 (see Berve, below).

Further reading. H. Berve, *RE* s.v., no. 1; Berve, no. 634; Schober, *Gesch. Babyloniens,* via index; Hornblower, *Hieronymus,* via index; Billows, "Anatolian Dynasts," at n. 38.

91. PHILETAIROS, son of Attalos, from Tieion in Paphlagonia

Sources. Strabo XIII 543; XII 623–24; Pausanias I 8,1; 10,4; Appian *Syr.* 63; [Loukianos] *Makrobioi* 12; Karystios *apud* Athenaios XIII 577b; H. Hepding *AM* 35 (1910):437–38.

Career. Though the father of Philetairos bore the good Greek name Attalos, he came from Paphlagonia, and Philetairos's mother, Boa, was certainly a native Paphlagonian (Athen. XIII 577b; *AM* 35

[1910]:437–38). Philetairos was of at least half non-Greek stock, then; since he died in 263/62 (as can be deduced from Strabo XIII 624 and Polybios XVIII 41,8) at the age of eighty ([Louk.] *Makrob.* 12), he was presumably born ca. 343/42. He first enters history as an officer serving with Antigonos's general Dokimos in 302 (Paus. I 8,1), though he had doubtless been in Antigonos's service some time before that year, when he would already have been forty years old (cf. Hansen, below, for this supposition). It is ironic, then, that he should only be mentioned as an Antigonid officer at the time when, along with his superior Dokimos (no. 35 above), he deserted Antigonos for Lysimachos.

Philetairos is, of course, far better known for his career as dynast of Pergamon than as an officer of Antigonos's. He was, according to Strabo (XII 543), a eunuch as a result of a childhood accident in his home town of Tieion. Lysimachos appointed him to the guardianship of his treasury (9,000 talents) at Pergamon (Strabo XIII 623; Paus. I 8,1), the sort of post traditionally reserved for eunuchs. This treasure he guarded faithfully for some time, until the growing influence of Lysimachos's young wife, Arsinoe, in the 280s led to the murder of Lysimachos's son Agathokles, and made Philetairos fearful for his own safety (Paus. I 10,4). He went over to Seleukos, and after Seleukos's death he made himself pleasing to Seleukos's son Antiochos by purchasing the dead king's corpse from his slayer, Ptolemy Keraunos, decently cremating it, and forwarding the remains to Antiochos with all honors (Appian *Syr.* 63). Thus he purchased himself virtual independence in his stronghold of Pergamon for the next twenty years, gradually waxing stronger (Strabo XIII 623–24), and subsequently passed on his lordship to his nephew Eumenes. A full account of Philetairos's career as lord of Pergamon can be found in the works listed below.

Further reading. W. Hoffmann, *RE* s.v., no. 1; Hansen, *Attalids of Pergamon,* pp. 14–21, 26–30, 36–38, and passim via index; Allen, *Attalid Kingdom.*

92. PHILIPPOS, son of Antigonos, Macedonian

Sources. Diodoros XX 19,5; 73,1; Plutarch *Demetrios* 2,1–2; 23,4; *Mor.* 182b; Cicero *De off.* II 48; Frontinus *Strat.* IV 1,10; *OGIS,* no. 6, line 30.

Career. Philippos was the second son of Antigonos Monophthalmos and Stratonike; named after his paternal grandfather, he was only a few years younger than his brother Demetrios (Plut. *Dem.* 2,1–2), who was born in 336. Philippos, therefore, must certainly have been born before 330. It has been suggested (e.g., by Berve and Treves, below) that Philippos may have been born in Kelainai while his father was satrap there, presumably about 332 or 331. However, since he was considered old enough to conduct an important military campaign in 310/9, his birth should be placed as early as possible, and I suggest therefore that he was born in 334, his mother being pregnant with him when Antigonos crossed to Asia with Alexander in that year. However that may be, Philippos was probably brought up at his father's satrapial court in Kelainai in greater Phrygia, and he seems to have been brought up fairly strictly. Cicero (*De off.* II 48) records that there were extant in his day letters of advice from Antigonos to Philippos ("Exstant epistulae . . . Antigoni ad Philippum filium"). While it is likely that these letters, which are mentioned along with similar letters from Philip to Alexander and from Antipatros to Kassandros, were pseudepigraphous, their existence nevertheless attests to the care with which Antigonos is thought to have raised Philippos.

Two anecdotes preserved by Plutarch further illustrate this, both dealing with the period when Philippos was an adolescent receiving his military training under his father's command. In one, Antigonos is said to have heard while on campaign that Philippos had been billeted in the house of a widow with three nubile daughters and, worried about his son's morals, ordered the quartermaster to find him other quarters (Plut. *Dem.* 23,4; *Mor.* 182b [= *Apophth. Ant.* 5]; Frontinus *Strat.* IV 1,10). The other records that Philippos on some occasion asked when they would be breaking camp and Antigonos retorted that he would learn it from the signal like everyone else (Plut. *Mor.* 182b [= *Apophth. Ant.* 4]; repeated at *Mor.* 506c and at *Dem.* 28,5 where, however, it refers to Demetrios).

It is at least clear from these anecdotes that Antigonos took Philippos with him on some of his campaigns, presumably in 314–311 after returning from his eastern *anabasis*. In late 311, after the conclusion of the Peace of the Dynasts, Philippos was honored together with his brother Demetrios by the people of Skepsis, being awarded a "crown" of 50 drachmas when they decreed divine honors to Antigonos for his services to the cause of Greek freedom (*OGIS*, no. 6, at line 30). In the next year, when Ptolemy sent a force to raid the coast of Kilikia and Antigonos's governor in the Hellespontine region, Phoinix, rebelled at the instigation of Polemaios, Antigonos sent Demetrios to deal with the trouble in Kilikia and despatched

Philippos with an army to fight Phoinix and recover the Hellespontine region (Diod. XX 19,5).

The course and outcome of Philippos's campaign are nowhere recorded, but it is certain that he was successful, for Antigonos founded three cities and a military post in the Hellespontine region in the years between 310 and 307, which shows that he had recovered control there. The campaign of Philippos was probably recounted by Hieronymos of Kardia apropos of Philippos's death in 306 and burial at Antigoneia-on-the-Orontes, for when Diodoros reports Philippos's death (XX 73,1) he accidentally calls him Phoinix, a mistake most likely due to the fact that his source (here most probably Hieronymos) mentioned the campaign against Phoinix at this juncture. Philippos's premature death in 306, then, aged about 26–28, was a severe blow to Antigonos, who thus lost not merely a son, but a general who might have been of the greatest value to him in his last campaigns of the next few years.

Further reading. P. Treves, *RE* s.v., no. 14; Berve, no. 776.

93. PHILIPPOS (son of Balakros ?), Macedonian

Sources. Diodoros XIX 69,1; XX 107,5; *IG* II^2 561; and cf. Diodoros XIX 40,4; 42,7; *PSI,* no. 1284, col. iii, lines 14–15; also Diodoros XVII 57,3; Curtius IV 13,28.

Career. In 313/12, when Antigonos left Demetrios in command of Syria, he left with him four advisers, all senior men who had seen extensive service under Alexander the Great; Philippos was one of these men (Diod. XIX 69,1). It is thought (e.g., by Hornblower, below) that the Philippos who in 302 saved Sardis for Antigonos when the place was under attack by Lysimachos's general Prepelaos was the same man (Diod. XX 107,5). This is made more plausible by *IG* II^2 561, an Athenian decree honoring Philippos and Iolaos who were formerly officers of Alexander and subsequently served with Antigonos. As Antigonos is unlikely to have had two senior officers named Philippos who had both formerly served with Alexander, it seems best to suppose that this is one and the same man. He was, then, still alive in about 307 (the date Athens went over to Antigonos) and so could easily still have been alive in 302. The idea suggested by Habicht, Burstein, and Heckel (see below) that the Alexander mentioned in *IG* II^2 561 was Alexandros IV, not Alexander the Great, should be rejected (see Iolaos, no. 57 above).

The question arises whether it is possible to identify the service under Alexander of this Philippos, who was clearly one of Antigonos's most important subordinates. There were a considerable number of men named Philippos in Alexander's army, of whom five (Berve nos. 778, 779, 780, 783, 784) come into serious contention as being of appropriate rank and potentially still alive after 323. Fortunately *IG* II² 561 offers some help. Philippos had been a *sōmatophylax* of Alexander, that is most probably an officer in the royal squadron of the Hypaspists, Alexander's personal *sōmatophylakes* (bodyguards, cf. Arrian *Anab.* III 17,2; IV 3,2; 30,3); furthermore, there is after the name Philippos in line 5 a trace of the next letter, which must have formed part of the letter Β,Γ,Ε,Π, or Ρ (*contra* Heckel, below, but I have now confirmed this reading by personal inspection of the stone). Hence it should be understood as the first part of the man's patronymic (rather than of the word *καὶ*, as Burstein implicitly suggests), which must have started with one of those letters. Only one officer under Alexander fits the bill: Philippos, son of Balakros, who according to Diodoros and Curtius (Diod. XVII 57,3; Curt. IV 13,28) commanded the phalanx battalion of Amyntas at the battle of Gaugamela, Amyntas being absent on a recruiting mission in Macedon (see further Bosworth, below). This man (no. 778 in Berve) must then have been Antigonos's officer.

A further point arises from the consideration that this Philippos is not mentioned in Antigonos's service until 313. In 316, at the battle of Gabiene, a certain Philippos was in command of Eumenes' right wing (Diod. XIX 40,4). This man would probably, if he survived the battle, have fallen into the hands of Antigonos like his chief and his comrades Hieronymos and Mithridates (nos. 51 and 73 above). Like these men, too, he may have entered Antigonos's service and could, in short, have been the very same Philippos as Antigonos's trusted officer in 313–302 (cf. Hornblower, below). That this Philippos was a senior commander is shown by his role at Gabiene; he is further recorded (*PSI,* no. 1284, col. iii, lines 14–15) to have been with Eumenes already in 320, when he seems to have been involved in negotiations concerning the surrender of Krateros's defeated phalanx to Eumenes. Presumably, then, he was an officer in the army given to Eumenes by Perdikkas to fight Krateros and Antipatros. Such an officer must, again, clearly have already made a career under Alexander, so that the whole series of identifications fits together very plausibly, if not (in the present state of the evidence) altogether compellingly.

Further reading. P. Schoch, *RE* s.v. Philippos, nos. 16, 17, 18; Berve, no. 778; Hornblower, *Hieronymus,* pp. 123–24; Habicht,

Akten des VI Intern. Kong. Epig., p. 374 n. 35; Burstein, *ZPE* 24 (1977):223–25; Heckel, *ZPE* 40 (1980):249–50; id., *ZPE* 44 (1981):75–77; Wirth, *Klio* 46 (1965):283–88; Bosworth, *Commentary*, 1:300–301.

94. PHILON, son of Kleon, of Erythrai

Sources. *IG* VII 6.

Career. Philon, like his brother Kleon (no. 59 above), was an officer of King Demetrios honored by the Megarians with proxeny. The royal title of Demetrios dates the inscription after 306, so that one must assume that the occasion for it fell during 304–302, when Philon would have been a member of Demetrios's expedition to free Greece. See further no. 140 below on the date and nature of this and associated inscriptions.

Further reading. Urban, *Wachstum und Krise des Achaiischen Bundes*, pp. 66–70.

95. PHILOTAS, Macedonian

Sources. Arrian *Met' Alex.* 1,5; 24,2; Curtius X 10,2; Dexippos in *FGrH*, no. 100 F 8,2; Diodoros XVIII 3,1; 62,4–63,5; Justin XIII 4,12; Ps.-Kallisthenes III 31,8.

Career. At the conference of Babylon after Alexander's death in 323, a certain Philotas was appointed satrap of Kilikia (Arrian *Met' Alex.* 1,5; Curt. X 10,2; Dex. F 8,2; Diod. XVIII 3,1; Just. XIII 4,12). As the satrap appointed in 333 by Alexander had died while Alexander was still alive (Diod. XVIII 22,1), it is conjectured that Philotas was actually named to the satrapy by Alexander, and only confirmed by the conference after the king's death (see Julien, below). It is highly probable that the Philotas named as having participated in Medeios's famous banquet in Babylon was this man (Ps.-Kall. III 31,8). Philotas's incumbency as satrap of Kilikia did not last long, however, for in 320 Perdikkas replaced him with one Philoxenos, considering Philotas to be too friendly to Krateros (Arrian *Met' Alex.* 24,2). No doubt Philotas then took himself off to join the camp of those for the sake of whose friendship he lost his satrapy, who of course included Antigonos. Hence, when we find Antigonos in 318 sending a prominent Macedonian officer named Philotas, with an escort of thirty other Macedonians, to Eumenes' camp in Kilikia in order to persuade the Argyraspids to abandon Eumenes, it is natural to suppose that this was the same man. Though Philotas had an initial success in managing to bribe Teutamos, one of the two Argyraspid commanders, and created a strong impression by reading out to the Argyraspids a letter from Antigonos, Eumenes was ultimately able to prevent Philotas's success, aided by Antigenes, the other commander of the Argyraspids (Diod. XVIII 62,4–63,5). Of Philotas's subsequent fate nothing is known.

Further reading. H. Berve, *RE* s.v., nos. 7 and 8; P. Schoch, *RE* s.v., no. 10; Berve, no. 804; Julien, *Verwaltung der Satrapien,* p. 20.

96. PHOINIX of Tenedos (?)

Sources. Diodoros XVIII 40,2–4; XX 19,2–5; Plutarch *Eum.* 7.

Career. Phoinix of Tenedos was an officer in the army of Eumenes in 320, when he commanded the cavalry on the left wing of Eumenes' battle line against Krateros, together with Eumenes' brother-in-law Pharnabazos (Plut. *Eum.* 7). Early in 319 he was given a force of 4,000 infantry and 1,000 cavalry to deal with Eumenes' officer Perdikkas, who had rebelled together with his troops, 3,500 in number. This Phoinix dealt with highly successfully, capturing the entire rebel force without a blow by a surprise night attack, and handing them over to Eumenes (Diod. XVIII 40,2–4). He presumably remained with Eumenes thereafter though he is not mentioned again, and it has been conjectured (see Hornblower, below) that he (like Hieronymos and Mithridates, nos. 51 and 73 above) joined Antigonos after Eumenes' death. For in 310 we hear of a Phoinix who was in charge of Hellespontine Phrygia as the representative of Antigonos's nephew Polemaios (Diod. XX 19,2). Phoinix was at this time one of Polemaios's most trusted friends, and when Polemaios rebelled against Antigonos, he sent troops to Phoinix and instructed him to garrison Hellespontine Phrygia against Antigonos, who sent his young son Philippos with an army to deal with the situation (Diod. XX 19,5). The outcome of the fighting between Phoinix and Philippos is not recorded (but see Philippos, no. 92 above).

Further reading. W. Hoffmann, *RE* s.v., nos. 8 and 9; P. Schoch, *RE* s.v., no. 10; Hornblower, *Hieronymus,* p. 130 n. 105.

97. PHOINIX

Sources. Diodoros XX 107,5.

Career. When Lysimachos and Prepelaos invaded Asia Minor in 302, Prepelaos was sent by Lysimachos to try to conquer Ionia and Lydia. In Lydia a general of Antigonos stationed there named Phoinix went over to Prepelaos, handing over to him Sardis itself, except the acropolis, which was saved for Antigonos by his friend Philippos (no.

93 above). There is no good reason to suppose that this Phoinix was the same as the friend of Polemaios who had rebelled against Antigonos in 310 (Phoinix of Tenedos, no. 96 above); rather one would imagine that Antigonos would not have put a man who had already proved unfaithful to him once in a position to do further harm.

Further reading. W. Hoffmann, *RE* s.v., no. 9.

98. PLEISTIAS of Kos

Sources. Diodoros XX 50,4.

Career. Pleistias was a naval officer in Antigonid service, specifically recorded as having been with Demetrios at the naval battle of Salamis in Cyprus. He was the chief pilot of Demetrios's fleet on this campaign (perhaps in effect second-in-command of the fleet; see Hauben, below), and was placed in command of Demetrios's right wing in the battle, together with Hegesippos of Halikarnassos (no. 46 above).

Further reading. T. Lenschau, *RE* s.v.; Hauben, *Vlootbevelhebberschap,* pp. 78, 117–19.

99. POLEMAIOS I, son of Philippos, Macedonian

Sources. Arrian *Anab.* I 14,6; 15,1; 23,6; II 5,7; Curtius III 7,4; Diodoros XIX 68,5; Blümel, *I. Iasos,* 1, no. 2; cf. *Syll.,* no. 332.

Career. An inscription from Iasos in Karia (*I. Iasos,* no. 2) reveals that the father of Antigonos's nephew Polemaios was likewise named Polemaios (see line 10). Diodoros records (XIX 68,5) that the father of the younger Polemaios died in late 313. The question arises whether this elder Polemaios was the brother or brother-in-law of Antigonos. Since the name of the younger Polemaios (no. 100 below) is invariably given as *Ptolemaios* in our literary sources, the appearance in Arrian's *Anabasis* (I 14,6; 15,1) of an officer of Alexander's named Ptolemaios, son of Philippos, enables us to answer with considerable confidence: in all probability Antigonos son of Philippos and P(t)olemaios son of Philippos were brothers. This has already been suggested by Beloch (*GG,* 3.2: 90) and is now confirmed by the Iasos inscription. Arrian records that P(t)olemaios led a *taxis* of the *hypaspistai* and an *ilē* of the Companion cavalry across the river Granikos together with the Paionian cavalry and *prodromoi* under Amyntas Arrhabaiou; these engaged the Persians on the opposite bank and paved the way for Alexander to charge across with the main body of the Companion cavalry (cf. Berve, no. 671, and Volkmann, below). P(t)olemaios presumably saw further service under Alexander, but due to Arrian's habit of only occasionally identifying officers by their patronymics (usually the first time they are mentioned), we cannot say for certain what this was. However, as Berve points out, the only possible identifications are with the Ptolemaios who was a *sōmatophylax* and died at Halikarnassos in 334 (Berve, no. 672), or the Ptolemaios who was left behind by Alexander as *stratēgos* of Karia with 3,000 mercenaries at the end of 334 (Berve, no. 674). But since P(t)olemaios Philippou is now known to have died in 313, only the latter identification remains possible.

Most likely, then, Polemaios Philippou was appointed *stratēgos* of Karia by Alexander (Arrian *Anab.* I 23,6), with the task of completing the siege of Halikarnassos, which was held by a Persian garrison under Orontobates. He was eventually successful in this; and in following up his victory he captured Myndos, Kaunos, Thera, Kallipolis, Kos, and Triopion, all during the year 333, thus pacifying Karia (Arrian *Anab.* II 5,7; Curtius III 7,4). Nothing more is heard of Polemaios, and at the end of Alexander's life a certain Philoxenos was satrap of Karia (see Berve, no. 794). Whether Polemaios was then still in Karia is not known. Surprising is the fact that between 323 and his death in 313 he is never mentioned serving his brother Antigonos, though his son Polemaios the younger was one of Antigonos's most important helpers. Perhaps Polemaios the elder was incapacitated at this time and lived in retirement. That he nevertheless dwelt in his brother's territory is clear from the fact that in 313 the younger Polemaios was able to travel from his winter quarters in Karia to attend to his father's funeral and return in time to scotch an attempt to ambush his army in his absence (see for details Polemaios II, below). Perhaps, indeed, Polemaios I was in Karia when he died, aiding his son with advice based on knowledge of the region. At any rate, he must surely from time to time have formed part of his brother Antigonos's *synedrion* during the years 323–313. It seems, finally, that he at some time (in 334 perhaps—see Plut. *Alex.* 15,3–6) received an estate at Spartolos in Bottiaia from Alexander (*Syll.*, no. 332, lines 15–27), if one is right in identifying the Ptolemaios, son of Ptolemaios, who sold this estate to Perdikkas Koinou as Antigonos's nephew (see Polemaios II below).

Further reading. H. Volkmann, *RE* s.v. Ptolemaios, nos. 4 and 10; Berve, nos. 671 and 674; Pugliese Carratelli, *ASAA* 29/30 (1967/68):437–45, no. 1; Garlan, *ZPE* 18 (1975):193–98.

100. POLEMAIOS II, son of Polemaios I, Macedonian

Sources. Diodoros XIX 57,4; 60,2–4; 62,5; 68,5–7; 75,5; 77,1–5; 78,2–5; 87,1–3; XX 19,2; 27,3; Plutarch *Eum.* 10; Memnon in *FGrH*, no. 434 F 4,6; *IG* II[2] 469 (= *Syll.*, no. 328); *OGIS*, no. 5, line 9; Blümel, *I. Iasos*, 1, no. 2; cf. Arrian *Met' Alex.* 1,38; *Syll.*, no. 332.

Career. Polemaios was a nephew of Antigonos (see, e.g., Plut. *Eum.* 10; Diod. XX 27,3; Memnon F 4,6) and was his uncle's right-hand man in the years 314–310. In the literary sources he is always named *Ptolemaios*, as also in *OGIS*, no. 5, line 9; though in *IG* II[2] 469, line 4 and in *I. Iasos*, no. 2 his name is given as Polemaios. The difference probably has no real significance, but the form Polemaios is convenient as distinguishing this man from others named Ptolemaios, and hence is used here. The inscription from Iasos has established that Polemaios's father was likewise named Polemaios (see line 10), thus disposing of the hypothesis that Polemaios was the son of Antigonos's older brother Demetrios (see, e.g., Lenschau, below). This hypothesis was in any case impossible, as Demetrios clearly died at the latest shortly after 338 (see Plut. *Dem.* 2), whereas Polemaios's father died in 313 (Diod. XIX 68,5; see further no. 99 above).

Polemaios II is first certainly attested in our sources in 319, when Antigonos sought to parley with Eumenes, whom he was besieging at Nora. Eumenes agreed to come out when Antigonos sent in his nephew Polemaios as a hostage (Plut. *Eum.* 10). From this, and from the importance of the commands entrusted to him in 314–310, it is clear that Polemaios was already an adult in 319, probably in his late twenties at least. Hence one should concur with Berve (no. 643) that Polemaios would have already started his military career under Alexander. One Ptolemaios, son of Ptolemaios, is named by Arrian (*Met' Alex.* 1,38) as one of the *sōmatophylakes* of King Philippos Arrhidaios appointed by Antipatros in 320. The other three men appointed were all relatives of prominent Diadochoi: Autodikos, son of Agathokles, was a brother of Lysimachos; Amyntas, son of Alexandros, was a brother of Peukestas; Alexandros was the son of Polyperchon. It makes sense to suppose that Ptolemaios, son of Ptolemaios, the fourth *sōmatophylax*, was none other than Antigonos's nephew, Antipatros's appointments being a political move to honor the relatives of the men appointed.

In 315 Antigonos returned from his long war against Eumenes in the east, on which Polemaios had presumably accompanied him. He found the other three dynasts (Ptolemy, Lysimachos, and Kassandros) had formed an alliance against him, and that an army of Kassandros under his general Asklepiodoros was in Kappadokia, besieging Amisos. In 314, accordingly, Antigonos sent Polemaios into Asia Minor with an army to reestablish control over Kappadokia, eject Asklepiodoros, settle affairs along the Black Sea littoral, and take up a position on the Hellespont to guard against further enemy invasions of Asia Minor (Diod. XIX 57,4). In these tasks Polemaios was successful, traversing Kappadokia in time to relieve the siege of Amisos and send Asklepiodoros packing, marching along the Black Sea coast to the Propontis, where he saved the cities of Chalkedon and Astakos from siege by Zipoites of Bithynia and forced Zipoites to recognize Antigonos's suzerainty (Diod. XIX 60,2–3), and along the way making an alliance with the tyrant Dionysios of Herakleia, cemented by marrying the tyrant's daughter (Memnon F 4,6). Polemaios was at this time, it seems, made general in charge of the Hellespontine region by Antigonos (*στρατηγὸς τῶν περὶ τὸν Ἑλλήσποντον*: Memnon F 4,6).

Later in this same year of 314, Polemaios was called south into Lydia and Ionia by Antigonos to protect the coastal cities against raids by a Ptolemaic fleet under Seleukos. He arrived just in time to disrupt Seleukos's attempt to capture Erythrai (Diod. XIX 60,4), and no doubt began to pressure the satrap Asandros of Karia, who had joined the coalition against Antigonos (Diod. XIX 62,2); Polemaios must have established his troops in winter quarters near Karia. In the following year, Polemaios evidently began to campaign against Asandros, who received aid from Ptolemy to help fight him (Diod. XIX 62,5). At the end of the year 313 Polemaios's father died, and while he was away attending to the funeral, Asandros brought reinforcements from Macedon into Karia under Kassandros's general Prepelaos. The two decided to attack Polemaios's troops in their general's absence and while they were scattered around northern Karia in winter quarters, sending out Eupolemos to Kaprima with 8,000 foot and 200 horse. Polemaios got wind of this move in time, however, and managed to gather a large force and ambush Eupolemos, capturing the entire force (Diod. XIX 68,5–7).

That same winter Antigonos crossed from Syria into Phrygia, intending to deal with Karia in person, and in the early months of 312 he led a three-pronged assault that succeeded in reducing all of Karia. Dokimos and Medeios (nos. 35 and 68 above) led a combined land and sea attack on Miletos in the north, Polemaios seized Iasos in the central coastal region, while Antigonos led a drive through the interior from Tralleis in the north to Kaunos in the south (Diod. XIX

75,3–5). Having captured Iasos, Polemaios left some mercenary troops in command of certain heights near Iasos, to secure Antigonos's control of the area (see *I. Iasos,* no. 2, and cf. Pugliese Carratelli, below).

In midsummer 312 Polemaios was despatched with a force of 5,000 infantry and 500 cavalry to Greece, together with a large fleet under Medeios (Diod. XIX 77,2), with the title of general in charge of affairs in Greece (*στρατηγὸς τῶν κατὰ τὴν* Ἑλλάδα *πραγμάτων*: Diod. XIX 87,3). He landed at the Boiotian harbor of Bathys, received from the Boiotians an allied contingent of 2,200 foot and 1,300 horse, and fortified Salganeus opposite Chalkis in Euboia, forcing Kassandros to give up the siege of the pro-Antigonid town of Oreos (Diod. XIX 77,4–5). When Antigonos made a diversionary march to the Hellespont as if to cross over into Europe, Kassandros hurriedly abandoned central Greece and rushed back to Macedon (Diod. XIX 77,5–6). In the absence of Kassandros, Polemaios was able to capture all of Euboia, Boiotia, Phokis, and Lokris for Antigonos, and even forced Athens to open negotiations with Antigonos (Diod. XIX 78,2–5). To prove Antigonos's goodwill, Polemaios refrained from garrisoning the cities, even the key one of Chalkis (Diod. XIX 78,2), though he did subsequently establish a guard post at the Euripos (under an officer named —otimos: no. 125 below, and see *Syll.*, no. 328).

In 311 Antigonos's other nephew Telesphoros (no. 111 below), who was stationed in the Peloponnesos, rebelled in anger at seeing his cousin Polemaios placed over himself, occupying Kyllene and ravaging Elis. Polemaios, however, quickly intervened and restored the situation (Diod. XIX 87,1–3). About the same time Polemaios opened negotiations with Kassandros with a view to arranging a truce, and apparently reached an agreement on the basis of which he sent Aristodemos (no. 16 above) to Antigonos to ratify the peace, while Kassandros sent Prepelaos as his representative (*OGIS,* no. 5, and cf. Gullath, below). By this peace Kassandros, though named *stratēgos* of Europe, effectively ceded Greece south of Thermopylai, where Polemaios remained as Antigonos's general in charge, while also governing Hellespontine Phrygia through his friend Phoinix (Diod. XX 19,2).

In view of the importance of the offices and commands thus entrusted to Polemaios, it comes as a great surprise to find him in 310 rebelling against his uncle, claiming that he was insufficiently honored (Diod. XX 19,2). He at first made an agreement with Kassandros (a συμμαχίαν according to Diod. XX 19,2); but in 309 changed his mind and opened negotiations with Ptolemy, who was then operating off the coast of Karia and making noises about "liberating" the Greeks. A meeting was arranged between the two dynasts at Kos, to which Polemaios sailed with a considerable force. Ptolemy received him graciously at first, but then arrested him, forced him to commit suicide, and incorporated his troops in his own forces (Diod. XX 27,3). The cause of this foolish and ultimately fatal rebellion by Polemaios has been linked to various politico-military factors of this time by Lenschau (see below); more probably the cause was simple jealousy of Antigonos's son and heir Demetrios, whose increasing employment on important missions by Antigonos in 312–310 threatened to end Polemaios's favored position as Antigonos's right-hand man. In conclusion, I note another inscription (*Syll.*, no. 332), which records Kassandros's ratification as king (i.e., after 305) of an earlier sale of lands in Macedon by one Ptolemaios, son of Ptolemaios, to Perdikkas, son of Koinos. This could refer to Polemaios, taking the opportunity of the peace in 311/10 to sell for hard cash ancestral lands in Macedon of which he was unlikely ever again to be able to enjoy the fruits.

Further reading. T. Lenschau, *RE* s.v. Polemaios; H. Volkmann, *RE* s.v. Ptolemaios, no. 11; Gullath, *Gesch. Boiotiens,* pp. 107–9, 153–75; Bakhuizen, *Salganeus,* pp. 103ff.; Picard, *Chalcis,* pp. 225–61; Pugliese Carratelli, *ASAA* 29/30 (1967/68): 437–45, no. 1; Garlan, *ZPE* 18 (1975):193–98.

101. POLYARCHOS

Sources. Diodoros XIX 91,3.

Career. Polyarchos was an officer in command of a district in Babylonia under Antigonos's satrap Peithon, son of Agenor, ca. 315–311, as we learn from his occupation of that post in 311 when Seleukos reentered Babylonia. Since Polyarchos, with his roughly 1,000 soldiers, promptly betrayed Antigonos's cause and went over to Seleukos, it seems possible that he had already been stationed in Babylonia under Seleukos.

Further reading. Lenschau, *RE* s.v., no. 1.

102. POLYKLEITOS of Athens

Sources. *IG* II² 1492b.

Career. An Athenian inscription bearing the records of the treasurers of Athena for the year 306/5 (archon Koroibos) mentions the disbursal of funds to two officers, Polykleitos the Athenian and Heraklei(des?) of Erythrai (no. 48 above). To judge from the use of the ethnic *Athēnaios* for Polykleitos (normally never added to the names of Athenians in Attic inscriptions: a citizen would be identified by his demotic, as are other Athenians in this very inscription), and from the fact that Polykleitos's colleague was a foreigner, it would seem that the two were not officials of the Athenian state. The money came from a gift of 140 talents donated by Antigonos (lines 97–103), and was evidently intended and used for military purposes (the money is disbursed to P. and H. and "the generals"), so it seems probable that Polykleitos and Heraklei(des?) were officers in Antigonid employ left behind with a body of troops by Demetrios to help defend Athens against Kassandros.

Further reading. None.

103. PYRRHOS, son of Aiakides, of Epeiros

Sources. Plutarch *Demetrios* 25; 31; *Pyrrhos* 4.

Career. Pyrrhos, the famous king of Epeiros, in his youth served for a time under Antigonos and Demetrios. His sister Deidameia married Demetrios in 303 (Plut. *Dem.* 25), and when Pyrrhos himself was expelled from his kingdom by Kassandros in 302, he naturally sought refuge with his brother-in-law Demetrios, Kassandros's enemy. He traveled with Demetrios to Asia and fought as an officer in the cavalry under Antigonos and Demetrios at the battle of Ipsos (Plut. *Pyrr.* 4). He remained with Demetrios after Ipsos, being placed over certain cities in Greece for a while ca. 300–298 (Plut. *Dem.* 31), and was subsequently sent by Demetrios as a hostage to Ptolemy in Egypt (Plut. *Pyrr.* 4), thereafter passing out of the Antigonid orbit; he subsequently became a bitter enemy of Demetrios and his son Antigonos Gonatas, fighting against whom he finally was killed at Argos in 272. A full account of the life of Pyrrhos would be out of place here: see the works listed below.

Further reading. P. Kienast, *RE* s.v., no. 13; Tarn, *Antigonos Gonatas,* via index; Bengtson, *Herrschergestalten,* pp. 91–109; Lévêque, *Pyrrhos;* P. Garoufalias, *Pyrrhos King of Epirus* (London, 1979).

104. PYTHEOS, Lydian (?)

Sources. Buckler and Robinson, *Sardis VII,* no. 1.

Career. Pytheos is named in the famous Mnesimachos inscription from the temple of Artemis at Sardis, as a chiliarch in charge of an administrative region of the plain of Sardis, including the village of Tobalmoura. In addition he is named as co-owner (together with Adrastos, no. 2 above) of a farmstead at Tobalmoura. It is not certain what his precise duties as chiliarch would have been, but the term suggests a military command, and the chiliarchies were evidently (as the inscription tells us, lines 4–12) tax-gathering units, among other things no doubt. Most probably, then, the duties of the chiliarch were those of fully responsible local governor—military, administrative, and fiscal. The name "Pytheos" suggests Lydian origins (see Buckler and Robinson, below), and another chiliarch mentioned in this inscription (Sagarios, son of Koreis, no. 105 below) was certainly Lydian, so it seems Antigonos to some extent used natives as local governors.

Further reading. Buckler and Robinson, *AJA* 16 (1912):12–82, esp. pp. 38–39; Debord, *Aspects,* app. 5, pp. 244–51.

105. SAGARIOS, son of Koreis, Lydian

Sources. Buckler and Robinson, *Sardis VII,* no. 1.

Career. The inscription recording the contract between Mnesimachos (no. 74 above) and the temple of Artemis at Sardis mentions Sagarios as a chiliarch in charge of a district in Lydia, apparently near Attoudda (lines 9–11). The name "Sagarios" derives from the river in Asia Minor (the Sangarios in Bithynia); the suggestion of "native" status that this implies is confirmed by the fact that Sagarios is given, not a patronymic, but a matronymic (son of Koreis) according to Lydian custom (cf. Buckler and Robinson, below). As chiliarch it seems that Sagarios combined military duties (as the term itself implies) with administrative functions (including the overseeing of tax-collecting, lines 4–12; cf. Pytheos, no. 104 above).

Further reading. Buckler and Robinson, *AJA* 16 (1912):12–82, esp. pp. 35–36, 39–40; Debord, *Aspects,* app. 5, pp. 244–51.

106. SIBYRTIOS, Macedonian (?)

Sources. Arrian *Anab.* V 6,2; VI 27,1; *Met' Alex.* 1,36; Curtius IX 10,20; Dexippos in *FGrH,* no. 100 F 8,6; Diodoros XVIII 3,3; XIX 14,6; 23,4; 27,4; 48,3; Justin XIII 4,22; Plutarch *Eum.* 19; Polyainos IV 6,15.

Career. Sibyrtios was a high-ranking officer of Alexander the Great's, first mentioned in 325, but presumably already with Alexander for some time before that date. In that year he was appointed to be satrap of Karmania, but did not remain there for long, being moved almost at once to Gedrosia (Arrian *Anab.* VI 27,1). Arachosia was added to Sibyrtios's satrapy when its former satrap, Menon, died (Curt. IX 10,20), and he was confirmed as satrap of Arachosia/ Gedrosia by the conference of Babylon after Alexander's death (Dex. F 8,6; Diod. XVIII 3,3; Just. XIII 4,22), and reconfirmed at Triparadeisos in 320 (Arrian *Met' Alex.* 1,36). He presumably took part in the campaign of the upper satraps against Peithon, son of Krateuas (cf. Peukestas, no. 90 above), for in 316 he was with the combined army of the upper satraps under Peukestas's leadership that met and joined Eumenes in Susiane. Sibyrtios's detachment in this army was 1,000 foot and 610 horse (Diod. XIX 14,6).

As a member of this force joined to Eumenes, Sibyrtios took part in the war against Antigonos, but not very wholeheartedly. He was a close friend of Peukestas's and was evidently discontented with Eumenes' leadership. In the autumn of 316, to assert his authority, Eumenes chose to make an example of Sibyrtios, despatching forces to occupy Arachosia, impounding Sibyrtios's baggage, and summoning him to trial. Sibyrtios fled and managed to make good his escape (Diod. XIX 23,4), and command of his troops was handed over to Kephalon (Diod. XIX 27,4). As a result, Sibyrtios naturally became well-disposed towards Antigonos, who, after his final victory over Eumenes in early 315, reappointed Sibyrtios satrap of Arachosia, giving him in addition 1,000 of the Argyraspids as garrison troops, with orders to wear them down with frontier fighting so that they could cause no more trouble (Polyainos IV 6,15; Diod. XIX 48,3; Plut. *Eum.* 19). Sibyrtios remained satrap during Antigonos's rule, and when Seleukos made himself lord over the eastern satrapies, he seems to have made friends with Sibyrtios too, for we hear that Sibyrtios remained satrap of Arachosia and played host to Seleukos's ambassador to India, Megasthenes (Arrian *Anab.* V 6,2). Berve and Geyer (below) conjecture that he was a Macedonian, though there does not seem to be any clear evidence for this.

Further reading. F. Geyer, *RE* s.v., no. 1; Berve, no. 703; Schober, *Gesch. Babyloniens,* via index; Julien, *Verwaltung der Satrapien,* pp. 32, 39, 41.

107. SOLON, son of Straton, of Bargylia

Sources. IG II^2 496 + 507 (= *Syll.*, no. 347).

Career. Solon, from the small town of Bargylia near Iasos in Karia, was honored by the Athenians with citizenship in 303/2 (archon Leostratos) on the motion of the pro-Antigonid Stratokles. As officer of Demetrios on the Greek expedition of 304–302, he is recorded (lines 5–6) to have done his best to advance the causes of the Athenian people and of the kings (i.e., Antigonos and Demetrios).

Further reading. P. Schoch, *RE* s.v., no. 2; Osborne, *Naturalisation in Athens,* no. D 61.

108. SOPOLIS

Sources. Blümel, *I. Iasos,* 1, no. 2; cf. Diodoros XX 27,1–3.

Career. Sopolis was one of three officers named in the above inscription, which records a treaty between these officers, the people of Iasos, and Ptolemy about 309/8, when Ptolemy campaigned along the coast of Lykia and Karia (Diod. XX 27,1–3). These officers and their troops were stationed in the area of Iasos by Polemaios, Antigonos's nephew and general, who had captured Iasos on behalf of Antigonos in 312 (Diod. XIX 65,5). Hence Sopolis and his colleagues were in Antigonid service between ca. 312 and 309/8 (see further Hieron, no. 50 above).

Further reading. Pugliese Carratelli, *ASAA* 29/30 (1967/68):437–45, no. 1; J. and L. Robert, "Bull ép.," 1971, no. 620; Garlan, *ZPE* 18 (1975):193–98; Bagnall, *Ptolemaic Administration,* pp. 89–91.

109. SOSTRATOS, son of Ste(phanos?)

Sources. Keil, *JÖAI* 16 (1913):236, 243, no. IIIb (= *I. Ephesos,* 5, no. 1440).

Career. An Ephesian decree awarded Sostratos citizenship for services to the Ephesians while he was an officer of King Demetrios stationed on Samos. The decree dates from between 306 and 295, so it is likely that Sostratos, who was evidently in charge of Antigonid troops on Samos, was already in Antigonid service during the lifetime of Antigonos.

Further reading. None.

110. SOTIMOS, son of Dositheos, of Kyrene

Sources. Koumanoudes, *Horos* 4 (1986):11–18

Career. A recently published Athenian decree from 304/3 (archon Pherekles) honored Sotimos at the request of King Demetrios as a *philos* of the king and benefactor of the Athenians, having fought on behalf of their freedom and democracy, as well as promoting the affairs of "the kings" (i.e., Antigonos and Demetrios). Sotimos was thus an aide of Demetrios during his expedition to Greece in 304–302. The decree, granting Sotimos a gold crown and citizenship, was proposed by the well-known pro-Antigonid politician Stratokles on the same day as the similar decrees for nos. 23 and 40 above.

Further reading. None.

111. TELESPHOROS, Macedonian

Sources. Diodoros XIX 74,1–2; 75,7; 87,1–3; Diogenes Laertios V 79.

Career. Although it is nowhere explicitly stated, Telesphoros was evidently a nephew of Antigonos. This follows from a story recorded by Diogenes Laertios (V 79) concerning the comic poet Menander: after Demetrios Poliorketes had expelled Kassandros's *epimelētēs* Demetrios of Phaleron from Athens in 307, Menander was attacked by the democrats as having been a close friend of Demetrios of Phaleron, but Demetrios's cousin (*anepsios*) Telesphoros begged him off. Now clearly the Demetrios whose cousin Telesphoros was was not Demetrios of Phaleron (whose friendship was so dangerous), but Demetrios Poliorketes, the liberator of Athens, whose influence at this time would easily have sufficed to save Menander from trial.

Telesphoros first enters history in early 312, when he was sent with a fleet of fifty ships and an infantry force to aid Aristodemos (no. 16 above) in liberating the Greeks. Telesphoros sailed to the Peloponnesos and rapidly succeeded in expelling the garrisons of Polyperchon and Alexandros from all of the cities except Korinth and Sikyon (Diod. XIX 74,1–2). In the summer of 312 he left the Peloponnesos with a force of twenty ships and 1,000 soldiers to try to raise Kassandros's siege of Oreos in Euboia (Diod. XIX 75,7). This proved beyond his power, and Antigonos despatched Polemaios to be general over all Greek affairs with a much larger force. Telesphoros returned to the Peloponnesos and, enraged at his subordination, decided in early 311 to rebel. He sold his ships, enlisted mercenaries, and seized Elis under pretense of friendship. Fortifying the citadel and plundering Olympia, he began to enroll more mercenaries and garrisoned Kyllene. However, Polemaios quickly entered the Peloponnesos, retook Elis, and restored the situation, and reasoned with Telesphoros, persuading him to give up his schemes and remove his garrison from Kyllene (Diod. XIX 87,1–3).

These events, narrated in such detail by Diodoros, suggest that Polemaios (likewise a nephew of Antigonos, see no. 100 above) and Telesphoros were not brothers: Diodoros would hardly have omitted so interesting a fact. He cannot have been a son of Antigonos's older brother Demetrios, for that man had married Stratonike before Antigonos did so, and by her Telesphoros would have been the half-brother rather than cousin of Demetrios Poliorketes. Telesphoros must thus have been the son of an unknown third sibling of Antigonos. That Telesphoros's break with Antigonos was only temporary can be seen from his presence at Athens and influence with

Demetrios in 307/6 (Diog. Laert. V 79). No doubt he was a member of Demetrios's staff. Berve (below) is wrong to suggest that the Telesphoros who was later an officer of Lysimachos (Athen. XIV 616c; Plut. *Mor.* 606b) was the same man, for Seneca (*De Ira* III 17,2–4) informs us that this Telesphoros was a Rhodian; and in any case, we have seen that Telesphoros was reconciled with his uncle Antigonos and cousin Demetrios.

Further reading. H. Berve, *RE* s.v., no. 1; Bengtson, *Strategie,* 1:149–53; Hauben, *Vlootbevelhebberschap,* pp. 93–98.

112. THEMISON of Samos

Sources. Diodoros XIX 62,7; XX 50,4.

Career. Themison was a naval officer in the service of Antigonos between the years 314 and 306 at least. In 314 he brought to Antigonos at Tyre a squadron of forty ships from the Hellespontine region (Diod. XIX 62,7), possibly from the fleet with which Antigonos had fought Kleitos in the Hellespont in 317 (Diod. XVIII 72,2–73,1), so that Themison may already have been with Antigonos as early as that year. At any rate, we next hear of Themison at the sea battle of Cyprian Salamis in 306, when he was placed by Demetrios in command of the lighter ships stationed in the center of the battle line, together with Demetrios's uncle Marsyas of Pella (no. 67 above).

Further reading. F. Schachermeyr, *RE* s.v., no. 5; Hauben, *Vlootbevelhebberschap,* pp. 99–100.

113. THEODOTOS

Sources. Diodoros XIX 64,5–7.

Career. Theodotos was a naval commander in Antigonos's service, who in 314 was sailing with a squadron of ships built for Antigonos in Rhodes (cf. Diod. XIX 58,5) and manned by Karians. He was escorted along the Lykian coast by the general Perilaos (no. 89 above), but in Kilikia near Aphrodisias both fell into an ambush laid for them by the Ptolemaic admiral Polykleitos. The land ambush was sprung first, and when Theodotos sent his crews to the aid of Perilaos, Polykleitos's ships came up and attacked Theodotos in the rear. After some hard fighting the Antigonid forces were defeated and captured, including Theodotos, who, however, died of wounds a few days later.

Further reading. F. Geyer, *RE* s.v., no. 8; Hauben, *Vlootbevelhebberschap,* p. 100.

114. THEOKRITOS of Chios

Sources. Strabo XIV 645; Suda s.v. Theokritos Chios Rhetor; Plutarch *Mor.* 11a–c; 534b; 603c; 633c; Athenaios I 21c; XII 540a; Stobaeus *Sermon* XXXXVI 217; CXXIII 617; Diogenes Laertios V 11; Macrobius *Satires* VII,3; Theopompos in *FGrH,* no. 115 F 252.

Career. Theokritos of Chios was a famous rhetor (the Suda) and sophist (Strabo XIV 645), and a contemporary and political opponent of the famous historian Theopompos. He was apparently of fairly humble origins, but became immensely wealthy as a result of his fame (Theop. F 252). His reputation today rests on a number of witty sayings attributed to him (usually bitingly sarcastic), apparently drawn from a book written after his death by his friend and countryman Bryon (Diog. L. V 11, and cf. Laqueur, below). According to the Suda he also wrote a history of Libya. As a pupil of the Isokratean Metrodoros (the Suda) he would have been somewhat younger than Theopompos, who was a pupil of Isokrates himself. He was apparently opposed to the Macedonian expansionism of Philip II and Alexander: there are preserved a number of nasty sayings aimed at Alexander (Plut. *Mor.* 11a; Athen. XII 540a), at Aristotle during his stay in Macedon (Diog. L. V 79; Plut. *Mor.* 603c), and at Alexander's court rhetorician and historian Anaximenes of Lampsakos (Stob. *Serm.* XXXXVI 217; Athen. I 21c).

After the death of Alexander, it seems that Theokritos was reconciled to Macedonian power, for he turns up at the court of Antigonos. However, he had not lost his sharp tongue, which got him into trouble with Antigonos. Plutarch tells us (*Mor.* 11b–c) that Antigonos once sent Eutropion (no. 42 above) to invite Theokritos for dinner and conversation, but that Theokritos rejected the invitation with an insult both to Eutropion (whom he accused of being a butcher) and to Antigonos (calling him the "Cyclops"). When this was reported to Antigonos, he had Theokritos arrested for execution. A last-ditch attempt by Theokritos's friends to save him was foiled when Theokritos, informed that he might successfully plead for mercy before the king's eyes, retorted that this would be impossible (again playing on Antigonos's loss of one eye). Thus even though Antigonos was as a rule ready to laugh at his deformity (as Plutarch tells us, *Mor.* 633c), on this occasion Theokritos had gone too far and was executed.

Further reading. R. Laqueur, *RE* s.v., no. 2; C. and T. Müller, *FHG,* 2:86–87.

115. THEOTIMIDES, son of Theophilos, Macedonian

Sources. Schede, *AM* 44 (1919):11–12, no. 5m (= *SEG*, 1, no. 351).

Career. A very well preserved inscription from Samos dating from before 306 (it mentions Antigonos without the royal title) tells us that Theotimides had proved himself a friend and benefactor of the Samians during their exile (i.e., before 322 B.C.), when he was stationed with Antigonos (lines 4–6), and continued to be well-disposed towards them after their return from exile, for which he was granted citizenship and other honors. Since Theotimides was already with Antigonos before the Samians returned from their exile in 322, he must have been a member of Antigonos's staff as satrap of Phrygia, and would presumably have been one of those friends with whom Antigonos fled from Asia Minor in 321 (Diod. XVIII 23,3–4: *μετὰ τῶν ἰδίων φίλων*). Theotimides is thus the only certainly identified friend and officer of Antigonos before 323, though a strong case can be made for placing Aristodemos and Boiotos (nos. 16 and 25 above) in that category also.

Further reading. None.

116. THORAX of Larissa

Sources. Plutarch *Demetrios* 29,5.

Career. Thorax of Larissa is recorded to have been a personal friend of Antigonos, being in his entourage at the battle of Ipsos and remaining with him to the end, even guarding his dead body when all his other friends and guards had fled. He is likely, as friend of a monarch, to have been of aristocratic birth, and it is interesting therefore to note the existence of another Thorax of Larissa (E. Bernert, *RE* s.v., no. 5) who was *tagos* (federal commander) of Thessaly during the Persian Wars (Herod. VII 6; IX 1; IX 58; Pindar *Pyth*. X, line 64). This man was head of the family of the Aleuadai, which suggests that Antigonos's friend Thorax may have been an Aleuad, and a relative of Antigonos's other Larissan friends Hippostratos, Medeios, and Oxythemis (nos. 54, 68, and 86 above), who also seem to have been Aleuadai. Appian (*Syr*. 64) refers to a certain Thorax of Pharsalos as a loyal officer of Lysimachos, who stayed by his body after he died at the battle of Kurupedion in 281. This is obviously a doublet of Plutarch's story, which should be preferred, for we find elsewhere a different story about Lysimachos's corpse, involving his favorite dog and his son Alexandros (see Marasco, below).

Further reading. F. Geyer, *RE* s.v., no. 7; Marasco, *Appiano,* pp. 134–39.

117. TIMOKLES

Sources. Diodoros XX 97,5–6.

Career. Timokles is mentioned by Diodoros as a pirate chieftain employed by Demetrios at the siege of Rhodes in 305/4. He operated with three ships along the Karian coast, helping the blockade of Rhodes, but was surprised and captured by a Rhodian squadron under the nauarch Amyntas.

Further reading. K. Ziegler, *RE* s.v., no. 2; Hauben, *Vlootbevelhebberschap,* p. 106; Ormerod, *Piracy in the Ancient World,* p. 123.

118. XENOPEITHES

Sources. Diodoros XIX 16,1.

Career. In 319 at the battle fought in the Pisidian *aulon* (Diod. XVIII 44,1–45,3; Polyainos IV 6,7) Antigonos captured the Perdikkan leaders Attalos, Dokimos, Polemon, Antipatros, Philotas, and three others. He imprisoned them in a fortress near the Phrygian border, placing a guard of 400 men over them, of which Xenopeithes was the captain. In 317 or 316 the prisoners managed to take Xenopeithes by surprise and capture him, whereupon they threw him from the wall at the point where the cliff was one stade (ca. 600 ft.) high, presumably to his death.

Further reading. None.

119. XENOPHILOS

Sources. Curtius V 2,16 (but cf. Arrian *Anab.* III 16,9); Diodoros XIX 17,3; 18,1; 48,6–7; Chares *apud* Athenaios XII 514e–f (= *FGrH,* no. 125 F 2); Amyntas in *FGrH,* no. 122 F 6.

Career. Xenophilos was appointed captain of the acropolis of Susa and the treasure stored there by Alexander either in 331 (so Curtius V 2,6) or later (see Berve and Habicht, below). At any rate, he was in command of the fort at Susa in 316 when Eumenes arrived there with letters of authority from Polyperchon and Olympias. Eumenes ordered Xenophilos to guard the treasure (15,000 talents and much other gold and finery: Diod. XIX 48,7; Athen. XII 514e–f; Amyntas F 6) and to refuse all orders, or even offers of parley, from Antigonos. Thus when Antigonos arrived at Susa he found the treasury strongly held against him, and could only leave Seleukos behind in charge of

Susiane with orders to besiege Xenophilos (Diod. XIX 17,3; 18,1). After Antigonos's victory over Eumenes, however, Xenophilos quickly came to terms with Seleukos, though without surrendering the fort. Seleukos sent him to Antigonos, whom he met at the Pasitigris river in early 315. Antigonos received him honorably and enrolled him among his *philoi* (i.e., personal staff) and thus gained control of the Susa treasury (Diod. XIX 48,6–7). Xenophilos presumably remained thenceforth in Antigonos's service.

Further reading. C. Habicht, *RE* s.v., no. 3; Berve, no. 578.

120. ZENODOTOS, son of Baukideus, from Halikarnassos

Sources: Michel, *RIG,* no. 452; Wilhelm, *"Att. Urk.",* pt. 1, pp. 37–44; and cf. Plutarch *Demetrios* 25.

Career. Two inscriptions, one from Halikarnassos (Michel, *RIG,* no. 452) and one from Troizen (Cyriacus of Ancona *apud* Wilhelm, above), record praise accorded to Zenodotos. The latter praises his goodwill, confirms earlier honors awarded him, and grants some further honors. The former mentions that the Troizenians had written praising Zenodotos for helping to liberate Troizen from a (foreign) garrison. The inscription is early Hellenistic and there is no difficulty in identifying the occasion (with Hicks, below, and Wilhelm, above) as Demetrios's campaign to expel Kassandros's garrisons in the Peloponnesos in 303 (see Plut. *Dem*. 25). Oddly, Wilhelm claims (p. 43) that Zenodotos must have been an exiled Troizenian living in Halikarnassos, citing line 8 of the Halikarnassian inscription, which reads:

> *ἀξίως τῆς τε πατρίδος καὶ τῆς / οἰκειότητος καὶ εὐνοίας τῆς ὑπαρχούσης / τῆι πόλει πρὸς Τροζηνίους*.
>
> (lines 7–9)

I see no evidence of Troizenian nationality for Zenodotos here: on the contrary, Zenodotos is described as having acted worthily of his fatherland and its ancient friendship and goodwill towards the Troizenians, which clearly shows that Zenodotos was a Halikarnassian, not a Troizenian. He was evidently an officer in Demetrios's army, and perhaps was sent out with a special detachment to see to the expulsion of Kassandros's garrison at Troizen.

Further reading. E. L. Hicks, *JHS* 2 (1881):98–101.

121. ZIPOITES, son of Bas, Bithynian

Sources. Diodoros XIX 60,3; Memnon in *FGrH,* no. 434 F 6,1–3;

F 9,1–2; F 12,4–6; Arrian *Bithynika* F 63 (Roos ed.); Plutarch *Mor.* 302e; Pausanias V 12,7; Steph. Byz. s.v. Zipoition.

Career. Zipoites was the son of the Bithynian dynast Bas, who established the independence of Bithynia by defeating Alexander's satrap of Hellespontine Phrygia, Kalas (Memnon F 12,4). He succeeded to his father's power in 328 or 327 and ruled Bithynia for forty-eight years until his death at the age of seventy-six about 280 B.C. (Memnon F 12,5, and cf. Habicht, below). The earliest activity recorded of him is in 314, when he besieged the Greek cities of Astakos and Chalkedon; these held the best harbors on the peninsula between the Sea of Marmara and the Black Sea to west and east and the river Sangarios to the south, which comprised Bithynia at that time (see Vitucci, below). However, Zipoites was prevented from capturing these cities by the arrival with a large army of Antigonos Monophthalmos's nephew Polemaios, who guaranteed the autonomy of these two Greek cities and enrolled them as allies of Antigonos, and who also obliged Zipoites to make an alliance with Antigonos and to hand over hostages (Diod. XIX 60,3). Vitucci and Habicht argue that Zipoites did not thereby recognize Antigonos's suzerainty, though this is open to doubt (see for the opposite view, e.g., E. Meyer, *RE* s.v. Bithynia, col. 515). At any rate, Zipoites never subsequently gave Antigonos any trouble, but remained a loyal ally until Antigonos's death.

After the dissolution of the empire of Antigonos due to the battle of Ipsos, Zipoites quickly began to revive his ambitions and reassert his independence of action. He campaigned successfully against Chalkedon and seems to have captured Astakos (Plut. *Mor.* 302e; Paus. V 12,7; and cf. Habicht, below). Though he came under heavy pressure from Lysimachos, he warded off the attacks of the latter's generals, killing one and driving the other out of Bithynia (Memnon F 12,5). It may have been as a result of these successes that Zipoites assumed the royal title, which he apparently did in 297 (see Habicht), and founded the city of Zipoition (Memnon F 12,5; Steph. Byz. s.v. Zipoition). He is even recorded to have defeated Lysimachos himself (Memnon F 12, ·), perhaps a reference to participation on the side of Seleukos at the battle of Kurupedion in 281 (see the arguments of Habicht for this). After this battle he attacked Herakleia Pontika, which had aided Lysimachos against him, and fought successfully against this city despite the diplomatic intervention of Seleukos (Memnon F 6,1–3). After the death of Seleukos, the Herakleotes persuaded Antiochos's general Hermogenes to invade Bithynia in 280, but Zipoites ambushed his army and destroyed it (Memnon F 9,1–2). He apparently died in that year, and was succeeded by his oldest son, Nikomedes I (Memnon F 9,3; 12,6; Arrian F 63). The successful assertiveness of Zipoites against Lysimachos, Seleukos, and Antiochos forms a marked contrast to his quiescence under Antigonos's rule, testifying to Antigonos's power and, perhaps, his conciliatory policy.

Further reading. C. Habicht, *RE* s.v., no. 1; Berve, no. 338; Vitucci, *Il regno di Bitinia,* pp. 11–21.

122. ZOES

Sources. SEG, 16, no. 59 (= *Hesperia* 2 (1933):402–3, no. 19).

Career. Zoes was honored with citizenship by the Athenians, according to a very fragmentary inscription which can be dated no more precisely than 307–301. Mention in lines 2–3 of "the kings" (i.e., Antigonos and Demetrios) shows that Zoes was an officer or official in Antigonid employ, who must have made himself useful to Athens in connection with one of Demetrios's campaigns, either in 307–6 or 304–2.

Further reading. Osborne, *Naturalisation in Athens,* no. D. 66.

123. ZOILOS, son of Kelainos, of Boiotia

Sources. IG VII 1 (= *Syll.,* no. 331).

Career. Zoilos was one of those officers in the army of Demetrios ca. 307–301 who were honored with citizenship by the Megarians (cf. no. 140 below for the nature and date of this and related inscriptions). This is the most detailed of the Megarian decrees, recording that Zoilos was in command of a body of troops stationed in Megarian territory at Aigosthenai, and that he was awarded a gold crown for his services there as well as citizenship.

Further reading. Urban, *Wachstum und Krise des Achaiischen Bundes,* pp. 66–70.

124. ZOILOS of Cyprus

Sources. Plutarch *Demetrios* 21,5.

Career. Plutarch records that Zoilos of Cyprus was an engineer in Demetrios's employ during the siege of Rhodes in 305/4. Specifically we learn that Zoilos manufactured two suits of special iron armor, which tests showed to be proof against even heavy catapult bolts. The two iron corselets were worn in the fighting at Rhodes by Demetrios himself and by one of his strongest and bravest officers, a man named Alkimos of Epieros (no. 8 above).

Further reading. K. Ziegler, *RE* s.v., no. 3; Marsden, *Greek and Roman Artillery,* 1:96–97; Wehrli, *Antigone et Démétrios,* pp. 204, 208.

125.——OTIMOS

Sources. IG II² 469 (= *Syll.,* no. 328).

Career. A decree proposed by the pro-Antigonid Athenian politician Stratokles honored —otimos about 306/5 for his aid to the Athenians in the fighting against Kassandros. It records in lines 3–8 that —otimos was an officer in Antigonid employ serving under Antigonos's nephew Polemaios, and placed by him in command of a guard post at the Euripos near Chalkis about 312/11. When Polemaios rebelled against Antigonos and was subsequently killed by Ptolemy, —otimos remained loyal to Antigonos, and handed over his guard post to the Chalkidians to complete their liberation. He must have joined Demetrios when the latter arrived in Greece in 307, and have been left behind with a force to aid the Athenians against Kassandros when Demetrios sailed to Cyprus (cf. Heraklei[des?] and Polykleitos, nos. 48 and 102 above).

Further reading. Gullath, *Gesch. Boiotiens,* pp. 160–61 n. 4; Picard, *Chalcis, p.* 259.

126. ——OS, son of Kalleas, from Arkadia

Sources. Schede, *AM* 44 (1919):4–19, no. V o.

Career. This man from Arkadia was an officer or official of Antigonos who in some way helped the Samians and was honored for this. The inscription recording this cannot be dated more closely than 315–301, nor is anyone known with whom this person could be identified.

Further reading. None.

127. ———, son of Menelaos, from Macedon

Sources. IG II² 559 + 568, with addenda.

Career. The son of Menelaos was an officer of Antigonos of fairly long standing, who in 304–302 accompanied Demetrios to Greece and fought for the liberty and democracy of Athens and the Greeks, for which the Athenians honored him (above). An anecdote of Phylarchos preserved by Athenaios (XIV 614 f) records the presence of a Menelaos at Demetrios's court, apparently in Macedon ca. 294–287. This would probably be the son, rather than the father, of the honorand of the Athenian decree. Kirchner (the editor of *IG* II[2]) tentatively suggests that the honorand might be identified with the Philippos, son of Menelaos, who served under Alexander as commander of allied and mercenary cavalry from 334 to 329 (Arrian *Anab.* I 14,3; III 11,10; 25,4), but this remains highly uncertain in view of the fact that this Philippos is never mentioned after 329, while in the same year a certain Karanos replaced him as cavalry commander (Arrian *Anab.* III 28,3; IV 3,7). Philippos may have died in one of the skirmishes in Sogdia, and in view of this one cannot with any confidence identify further Antigonos's officer (*contra* J. and L. Robert, below, who identify him with Philippos, no. 93 above).

Further reading. Wilhelm, *AM* 36 (1914):281; J. and L. Robert, "Bull. ép.," 1982, no. 156.

128. ———, son of ——arios

Sources. Buckler and Robinson, *Sardis VII,* no. 1.

Career. The well-known Mnesimachos inscription from the temple of Artemis at Sardis mentions ——— son of ——arios as chiliarch of a region in Lydia under Antigonos (lines 7–8). For further details, see Pytheos and Sagarios, nos. 104 and 105 above.

Further reading. Buckler and Robinson, *AJA* 16 (1912):12–82; Debord, *Aspects,* app. 5, 244–51.

INCERTI ET ANONYMI

Possible Antigonid Officers

129. ABDALONYMOS of Sidon

Sources. Curtius IV 1,19–21; Justin XI 10,8–9; Diodoros XVII 47; Graeve, *Alexandersarkophag,* pp. 123–25; cf. Diodoros XIX 58,1–3.

Career. Abdalonymos was plucked from obscurity by Alexander in 333 and made king of Sidon, of whose royal family he was a member (Curtius IV 1,19–21; Justin XI 10,8–9; Diod. XVII 47, erroneously giving Tyre rather than Sidon). He is presumed to have ruled Sidon for the next few decades, since the next ruler of Sidon we hear of is Philokles in the early third century; hence Abdalonymos is thought to be the ruler who commissioned the famous "Alexander sarcophagus" found in the royal necropolis at Sidon, which dates from the end of the fourth century B.C. (Graeve, above). We know (see Diod. XIX 58,1–3) that the ruler of Sidon was from 314 onwards a subject of Antigonos; if Abdalonymos was still alive at that time, he was thus a subordinate dynast under Antigonos. Charbonneaux (below) has argued in fact that just as Abdalonymos portrayed his original patron Alexander on his sarcophagos, so Antigonos too was portrayed in the same way.

Further reading. J. Kaerst, *RE* s.v.; Berve, no. 1; Charbonneaux, *Rev. des arts* 2 (1952):219–23.

130. ARISTONIKOS, son of Aristodemos, of Karystos

Sources. Athenaios I 19a; *IG* II² 385(b) (cf. *SEG,* 21, no. 341); *IG* XII.9 207, line 41.

Career. Athenaios records that Aristonikos of Karystos was a famous ball player (*sphairistēs*) at the court of Alexander the Great, and was subsequently granted citizenship and a statue by the Athenians, who were impressed by his virtuosity (*technē*). As it happens a very fragmentary Athenian inscription survives honoring a man named Aristonikos, son of Aristodemos, with citizenship (*IG* II² 385), in addition to a gold crown and other honors. It is suggested by Wilhelm and Dow (see below) that this man is Aristonikos of Karystos, the ethnic fitting nicely into the available space in the inscription. The same man was apparently voted cult honors in Eretria by the late 290s (*IG* XII.9 207, line 41). Osborne notes (see below) that the grant by the Athenians of the right to partake of public meals in the Prytaneion (*IG* II² 385b, line 17) must have been governed by the law of Lykourgos stating that only victorious generals, persons who had reestablished liberty for the city, those who had given their money for the state's safety, and men who had been benefactors and good advisers to the city might receive permanent *sitēsis.* Hence Osborne plausibly conjectures that Aristonikos would have gained his honors as one of Demetrios's entourage in Greece, like Oxythemis and Herodoros (nos. 86 and 49 above).

Further reading. J. Kaerst, *RE* s.v., no. 5; Berve, no. 129; Ad. Wilhelm, *Wiener Jahreshefte* 11 (1908):97ff.; S. Dow, *HSCPh* 67 (1963):78ff.; Osborne, *Naturalisation in Athens,* no. D 49.

131. HAGNOTHEMIS

Sources. Plutarch *Alex.* 77,2.

Career. Plutarch records a story current about the death of Alexander, according to which Aristotle advised Antipatros to have Alexander poisoned, and himself procured the poison for the deed, namely water collected from the river Styx at Nonakris in Arkadia, which was so potently corrosive that it could only be stored in an ass's hoof.

This obviously fictitious tale (even Plutarch records that "most authorities" reject it as pure invention) was spread by certain writers on the authority of one Hagnothemis, who claimed to have heard it from King Antigonos himself. It is unclear just where one should draw the line between fact and fiction here: Antigonos is a highly unlikely source for such a fable, but it is conceivable that Hagnothemis (if he truly existed) spent some time at Antigonos's court, whether as an officer or official, or merely as a hanger-on. This at least would have enabled him to claim to have heard the story from Antigonos with some chance of being believed. Plutarch appears to imply that he was himself not a writer, but merely the source of the story spread by certain historians.

Further reading. None.

132. KALLIKRATES

Sources. Keil, *JÖAI* 16 (1913):223 and 240 no. Ig.

Career. An Ephesian inscription honors Kallikrates for helping Ephesian ambassadors to "the king." The date of the inscription is late fourth century, evidently from the years 306–301, from the mention of a king. In a monograph on the Ptolemaic admiral Kallikrates of Samos, H. Hauben (see below) studied all mentions of persons named Kallikrates in the late fourth and early third centuries and reached the conclusion that the Kallikrates of this inscription is probably a separate individual, most likely in the service of Antigonos Monophthalmos. In that case we should understand him to be an official at Antigonos's court ca. 306–301, with duties that were at least in part diplomatic.

Further reading. Hauben, *Callicrates of Samos,* pp. 16–21.

133. NAUKASAMAS, Phoenician (?)

Sources. Stefan, *Epigraphica,* 25ff.; and cf. Diodoros XIX 73,1–10; XX 25,1.

Career. In 313 the city of Kallatis on the Black Sea revolted against Lysimachos, and Antigonos sent a fleet early in 312 to its aid (Diod. XIX 73,1–10, and cf. XX 25,1) under the command of one Lykon (see above no. 63). A fourth-century Attic funerary cup found at Kallatis bears a late-fourth-century inscription reading: "the *syssitoi* of Timonax [dedicated me] to Naukasamas." A *syssition* was characteristically an association of mess-mates of a military nature (most famously in Sparta and Crete), though it might have a religious purpose. In this case it is plausibly conjectured that the *syssitoi* were the soldiers in the company of the officer Timonax, fighting against

Lysimachos. For Naukasamas is a Levantine name (Naukosmas) with a Semitic root (Kasem, Kosam), and one presumes that Naukasamas was in fact a Phoenician serving in Antigonos's fleet under Lykon, honored by the Kallantian *syssitoi* for having given his life in defense of their country. Certainly much of Antigonos's navy was built and manned by Phoenicians (cf., e.g., Diod. XIX 58,1–5).

Further reading. J. and L. Robert, "Bull. ép.," 1978, no. 322; Hornblower, *Hieronymus,* pp. 117–18.

134. NEAIOS

Sources. IG II[2] 553.

Career. Neaios was honored by the Athenians with citizenship for his help in a campaign around Eleusis. The decree is usually dated to 304/3, at the end of the Four Years' War against Kassandros, on epigraphical and historical grounds (see Osborne, below). It is natural to entertain the notion that as a foreigner fighting for Athens against Kassandros at this time, Neaios may have been connected with Demetrios, and Osborne argues plausibly that this was the case. He draws support for this conjecture from the fact Neaios's name has been defaced in a clumsy attempt at erasure in all places where it occurs; this has been done also to the Antigonid officer Herodoros (no. 49 above), and Osborne plausibly suggests this may have been done by opponents of Demetrios at Athens after 287, when Athens rebelled against Demetrios.

Further reading. Osborne, *Naturalisation in Athens,* no. D 44.

135. PEITHAGORAS of Amphipolis

Sources. Arrian *Anab.* VII 18,1–5 (= Aristoboulos in *FGrH,* no. 139 F 54); Plutarch *Alex.* 73; Appian *BC* II 152.

Career. Information deriving ultimately from the Alexander historian Aristoboulos of Kassandreia (see Arrian *Anab.* VII 18,1–5) records that Peithagoras was the brother of Alexander the Great's officer Apollodoros of Amphipolis (for this man see Berve, no. 101), and was a priest and seer who prophesied from the intestines of sacrificial victims. Arrian records that he prophesied the death of Hephaistion (*Anab.* VII 18,2), and he is also reported by Arrian (*Anab.* VII 18,3–4), Plutarch (*Alex.* 73), and Appian (*BC* II 152) to have prophesied the death of Alexander, in both cases on grounds of animals sacrificed in their behalf being without lobes to their livers. He is further reported to have made the same prophecy (of imminent death) based upon the same portent to Perdikkas and Antigonos. Aristoboulos claimed to have heard all of this from Peithagoras's own lips (Arrian *Anab.* VII 18,5). We are not, of course, required to believe Peithagoras's own claims of his talents as a prophet, but it is at least possible on the basis of this story that he spent some time as a priest in the service of Antigonos. The possibility deserves to be recorded, but without some definite corroborating evidence, the theory cannot be regarded as very probable; Antigonos is reported by Diodoros (XIX 55,8) to have been generally scornful of prophecies and suchlike superstitions.

Further reading. H. Berve, *RE* s.v., no. 2; Berve, no. 618.

136. STASANOR of Soloi on Cyprus

Sources. Arrian *Anab.* III 29,5; IV 7,1; 18,1–3; VI 27,3–6; 29,1; *Met' Alex.* 1,36; Curtius VIII 3,17; Diodoros XVII 81,3; XVIII 3,3; 39,6; XIX 48,1; Strabo XIV 683; Justin XIII 4,23; XLI 4,1; Dexippos *FGrH,* no. 100 F 8,6; Porphyrios *De abst.* IV 21.

Career. Though Stasanor's patronymic is nowhere preserved, the fact that he was from Soloi and played a prominent role under Alexander the Great and in the Diadoch period has led some scholars to suggest he may have come from the dynastic house of Cyprian Soloi, being the son of Pasikrates and brother of this man's son and successor Nikokles (see e.g., Honigmann, below). He was a *hetairos* of Alexander (Strabo XIV 683) and first appears in the sources in 329, when he was sent by Alexander to capture and replace the rebellious satrap of Areia, Arsakes (Arrian *Anab.* III 29,5; IV 7,1; Diod. XVII 81,3). The next year he rejoined Alexander at Nautaka to report the successful carrying out of further orders, and was sent back to take over Drangiane in addition to Areia (Arrian *Anab.* IV 18,1–3; Curtius VIII 3,17). When Alexander reached Karmania on his return from India, Stasanor brought him reinforcements of horses and camels; he was then sent back to his satrapy (Arrian *Anab.* VI 27,3–6; 29,1). When Alexander died, the conference at Babylon confirmed Stasanor as satrap of Areia/Drangiane (Diod. XVIII 3,3; Justin XIII 4,23; Dexippos in *FGrH,* no. 100 F 8,6), but three years later at the conference of Triparadeisos in 320 he was moved to become satrap of Baktria and Sogdia (Arrian *Met' Alex.* 1,36; Diod. XVIII 39,6; Justin XIII 4,23).

Peithon's attempt to take over the upper satrapies in 318/17 was resisted by Stasanor along with the other upper satraps, though he did not participate in person, but placed the contingent from his satrapy under his compatriot Stasandros (Diod. XIX 14,7). Thus Stasanor was also absent from Eumenes' war against Antigonos, though his troops took part against Antigonos under Stasandros. After Eumenes' death Antigonos decided to leave Stasanor in charge of his satrapy, since he could not be dislodged without military intervention (Diod. XIX 48,1). No doubt Stasanor offered in return at least token submission and tribute, though this is undocumented (but see Diod. XIX 56,5 and 61,4, which seem to indicate that all of the inner Asian satrapies acknowledged Antigonos's authority in 315/14). Subsequently Stasanor apparently lost his popularity in Baktria (Porphyrios *De abst.* IV 21), and perhaps seized control over Parthia in addition to Baktria/Sogdia (Justin XLI 4,1), but was doubtless ejected from his satrapies during the *anabasis* of Seleukos in 308–303 (see Appian *Syr.* 55 for Seleukos's conquest of Baktria and Sogdia).

Further reading. E. Honigmann, *RE* s.v.; Berve, no. 719.

137. TLEPOLEMOS, son of Pythophanes, Macedonian

Sources. Arrian *Anab.* III 22,1; VI 27,1; *Ind.* 36; *Met' Alex.* 1,35; Diodoros XVIII 3,3; 39,6; XIX 14,6; 27,3; 48,1; Justin XIII 4,23.

Career. Tlepolemos was one of the *hetairoi* of Alexander the Great and was made *episkopos* over Parthia and Hyrkania by Alexander in 330 (Arrian *Anab.* III 22,1). This post he appears to have held until 325, when he was transferred to become satrap of Karmania (Arrian *Anab.* VI 27,1; *Ind.* 36,8), and after Alexander's death he was confirmed in this satrapy by the conference of Triparadeisos in 320 (Arrian *Met' Alex.* 1,35; Diod. XVIII 39,6; Justin XIII 4,23). He took part with the other satraps of inner Asia in the campaign against Peithon in 318/17 and at the beginning of 316 was with the army of the upper satrapies which joined Eumenes of Kardia in Susiane (Diod. XIX 14,6—where the MSS read *Polemon* in error for *Tlepolemos*). He fought with Eumenes against Antigonos at the battle of Paraitakene (Diod. XIX 27,3), and without doubt also at the battle of Gabiene, escaping after Eumenes' defeat and returning to his satrapy. Nevertheless Antigonos confirmed Tlepolemos as satrap of Karmania, on the grounds that he was popular in his satrapy and it would hence require military action to dislodge him (Diod. XIX 48,1). Probably Tlepolemos had sent friendly messages to Antigonos, promising obedience and tribute in order to avoid being replaced, though this is not specifically attested. However, Diodoros XIX 56,5 and XIX 61,4 seem to imply that all the upper satraps were at this time (315–311) subservient to Antigonos.

Further reading. H. Berve, *RE* s.v., no. 5; Berve, no. 757.

138. Men honored by EPIDAUROS

There are a number of honorific decrees from Epidauros dating from the late fourth or early third centuries which may refer to officers of Antigonos or Demetrios. None gives any information as to the reasons for or historical circumstances of the awarding of honors, but in the case of one of these inscriptions (*IG* IV^2. 1 58), the reason can be securely conjectured from the fact that the person in question (Alkaios, no. 7 above) is known from a contemporary Athenian decree to have been serving in Greece under Demetrios in 304–302. Hence it seems likely that others similarly honored by Epidauros at this time would have been Antigonid officers. One should note in the first place that the stone *IG* IV^2. 1 58 recorded honors for two men. The name of the first is lost, but doubtless he was, like Alkaios, an Antigonid officer. Also worthy of consideration here are *IG* IV^2. 1 49, 51 and 53, honoring Hegesistratos Hekataiou of Kardia, Theophantos Lamprou of Lampsakos, and ———, son of Onasimenes, from Cyprian Soloi, respectively. Since these three men are all of eastern Aegean provenience, they are plausible candidates to be identified as Antigonid officers.

Further reading. None.

139. Men honored by ERETRIA

There are a number of Eretrian honorific inscriptions of the late fourth/early third centuries that are not specific in describing the reasons for honoring the persons concerned, some of whom may have had a connection with Antigonos and Demetrios, or other Macedonian dynasts. In particular, there are a number of decrees honoring Macedonians and Asiatic Greeks: *IG* XII.9 197 (Myllenas and Taurion of Macedon), 200 (———, son of Hegesipolis of Macedon), 205 and 206 (Apollodoros and his son Anaxidotos from Macedon), 208 (Apellas, son of Mnesimachos of Klazomenai), and 216 (Antiochos of Lampsakos). The great number of honorific decrees for Antigonid officers put out at this time, not all of them specifically referring to Antigonos or Demetrios (cf., e.g., Alkaios, no. 7 above), make it likely that at least one or two of the above men were in Antigonid employ.

Further reading. None.

140. Men honored by MEGARA

There exists a substantial "dossier" of early Hellenistic honorific decrees from Megara (*IG* VII 1–14 and 3473; *ABSA* 19 (1912–13):82–85, nos. 1–3: eighteen in all), of which four are definitely concerned with Antigonid officers (see nos. 59, 76, 94, and 123 above). It is likely, in fact, that many (if not all) of the other decrees in this "dossier" are for Antigonid officers, though they do not explicitly mention either Antigonos or Demetrios by name. All of these eighteen decrees are from a seven-year period, as we can tell from the Megarian magistrates named in the superscripts, presumably the years 307–300 (for the date, see Urban, below); and of the nineteen men mentioned in them (*IG* VII 10 honors two men) no less than seven are from Asia Minor (three from Halikarnassos, two from Erythrai, and one each from Iasos and Eresos on Lesbos). This unusually high percentage of Asiatics surely points to the Antigonid army operating in Greece, and it comes as no surprise that three of the four men who were certainly officers of Demetrios (Kleon and Philon of Erythrai, and Mus of Eresos) were Asiatics.

Further reading. Urban, *Wachstum und Krise des Achaiischen Bundes,* pp. 66–70.

Anonymous Antigonid Officers

141. *Source.* Schede, *AM* 44 (1919):4–19, no. 5g, recording that an ex-officer of Alexander, currently serving with the kings Antigonos and Demetrios (and hence dating to 306–301) was honored by the Samians.

142. *Source.* Habicht, *AM* 72 (1957):178, no. 13, records that this man was an aide of Demetrios honored by the Samians along with no. 143 below.

143. *Source.* Habicht, *AM* 72 (1957):178, no. 13, records that an officer of Demetrios was honored by the Samians along with no. 142 above.

144. *Source.* *IG* II[2] 538 (and cf. Wilhelm, *AM* 39 [1914]:269; Osborne, *Naturalisation in Athens,* no. D 59), records Athenian citizenship awarded to an officer or aide of Demetrios ca. 307–303.

145. *Source.* *IG* II[2] 550 records the presence on Lemnos of an officer of Antigonos, of whose name only a few letters survive (——*ονος τοῦ παρ' Ἀντιγόνου*). It is impossible to say whether this ——on is or is not a known Antigonid officer (e.g., nos. 59 or 107 above).

146. *Source.* *IG* II[2] 560 records that this man was an officer of the kings (Antigonos and Demetrios) and was honored by the Athenians together with Dionysios (no. 31 above) ca. 306–302.

147. *Source.* *IG* II[2] 562 (and cf. *Hesperia* 9 [1940]:342, dating it to 302/1) records that an official of the kings (Antigonos and Demetrios) was honored as a public benefactor by the Athenians.

148. *Source. Hesperia* 7 (1938):301, no. 25, a tiny fragment of what appears to have been an honorary decree for an official of "the kings" (line 5), that is, Antigonos and Demetrios, dating hence from 306–301.

149. *Source. Hesperia* 10 (1941):55–56, no. 19 (and cf. Osborne, *Naturalisation in Athens,* no. D 63), records the grant of citizenship to a man who had fought for the safety of Athens and the other Greeks ca. 303–301 (lines 5–7), hence presumably an officer in Demetrios's army.

Maps

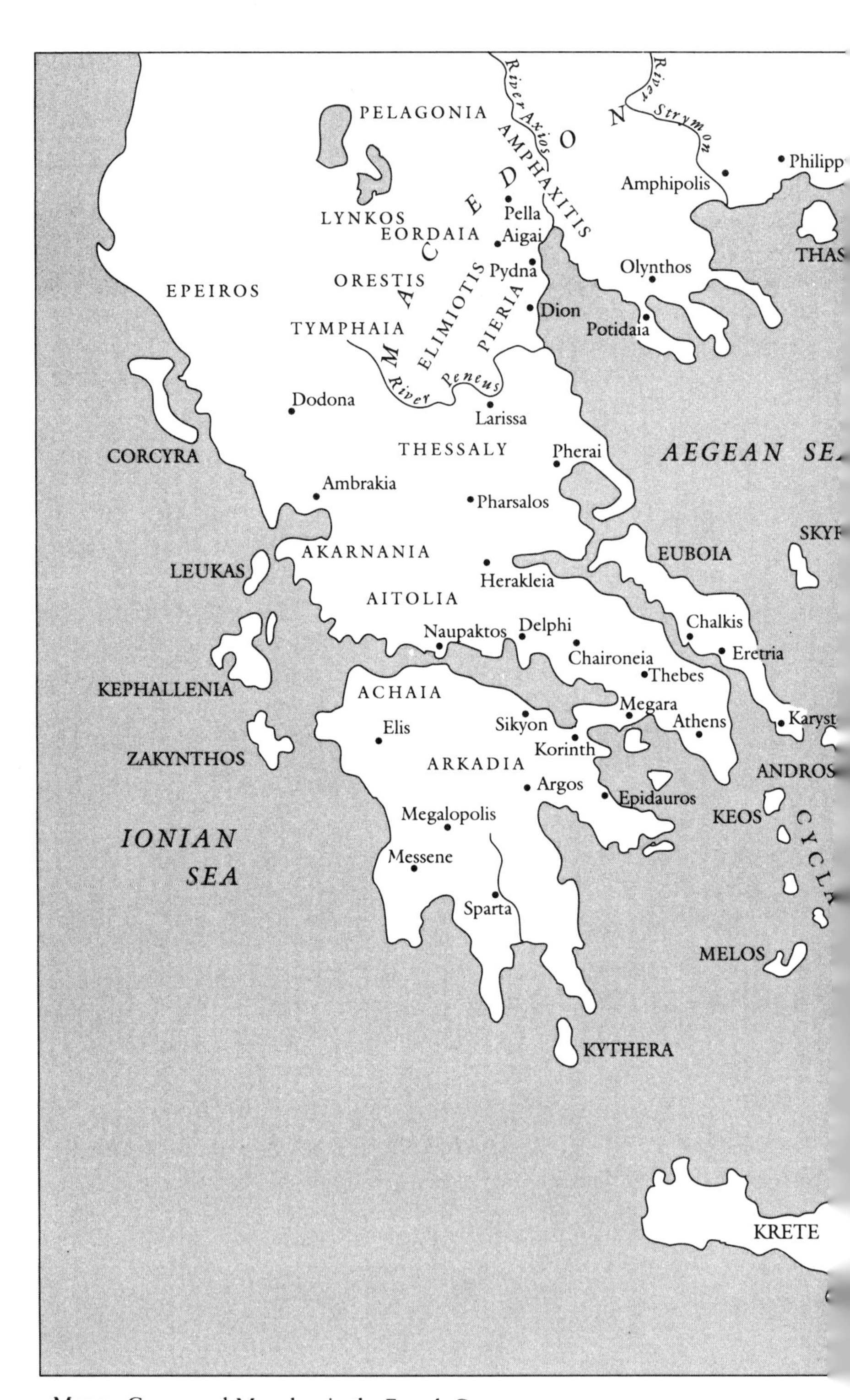

Map 1. Greece and Macedon in the Fourth Century B.C.

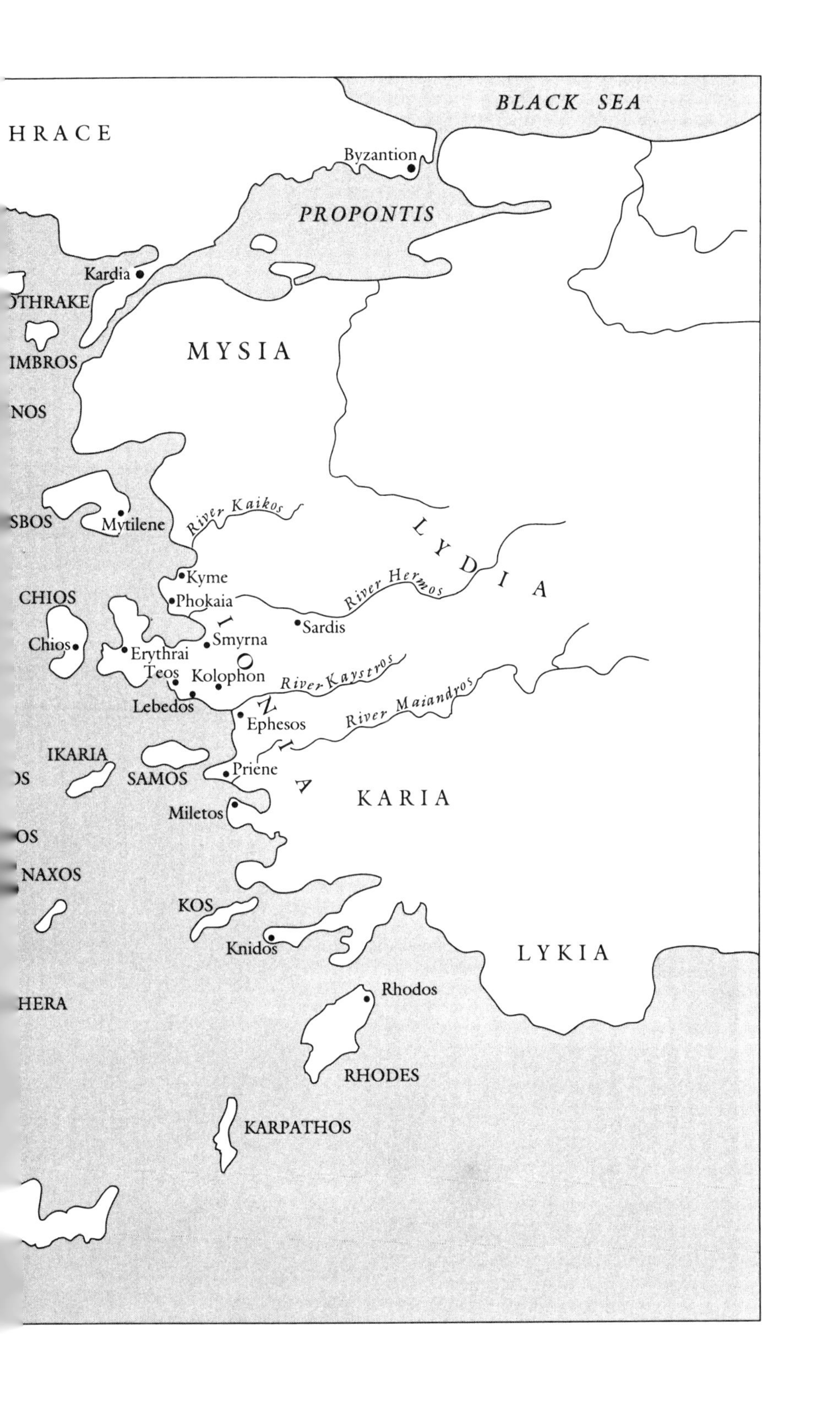
BLACK SEA
HRACE
Byzantion
PROPONTIS
Kardia
THRAKE
MYSIA
IMBROS
NOS
SBOS
Mytilene
River Kaikos
LYDIA
Kyme
Phokaia
CHIOS
River Hermos
Sardis
Smyrna
Chios
Erythrai
IONIA
Teos
Kolophon
River Kaystros
Lebedos
Ephesos
River Maiandros
IKARIA
SAMOS
Priene
KARIA
Miletos
OS
NAXOS
KOS
Knidos
LYKIA
Rhodos
HERA
RHODES
KARPATHOS

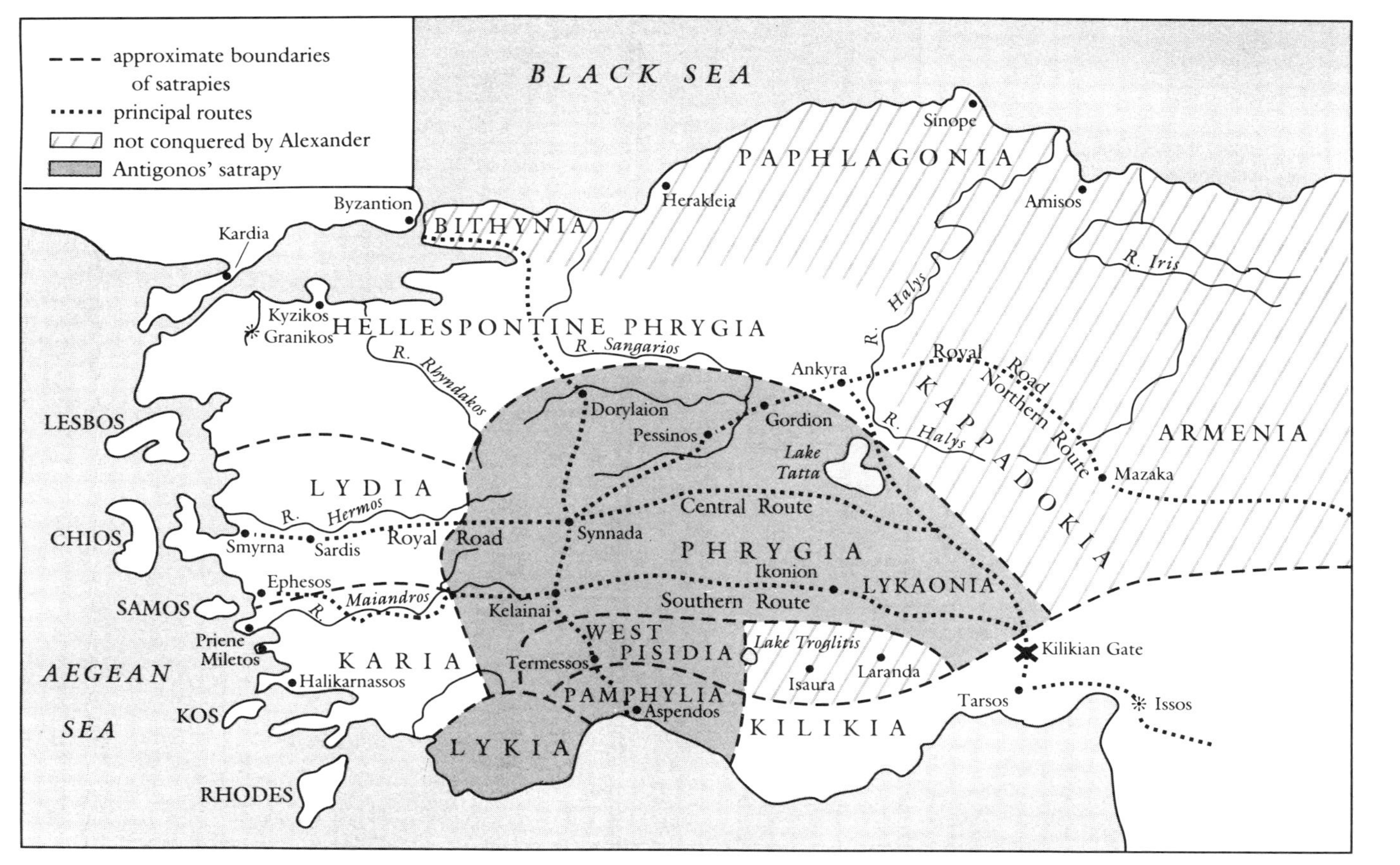

Map 2. Asia Minor under Alexander

Map 3. The Ancient Near East in the Time of Antigonos

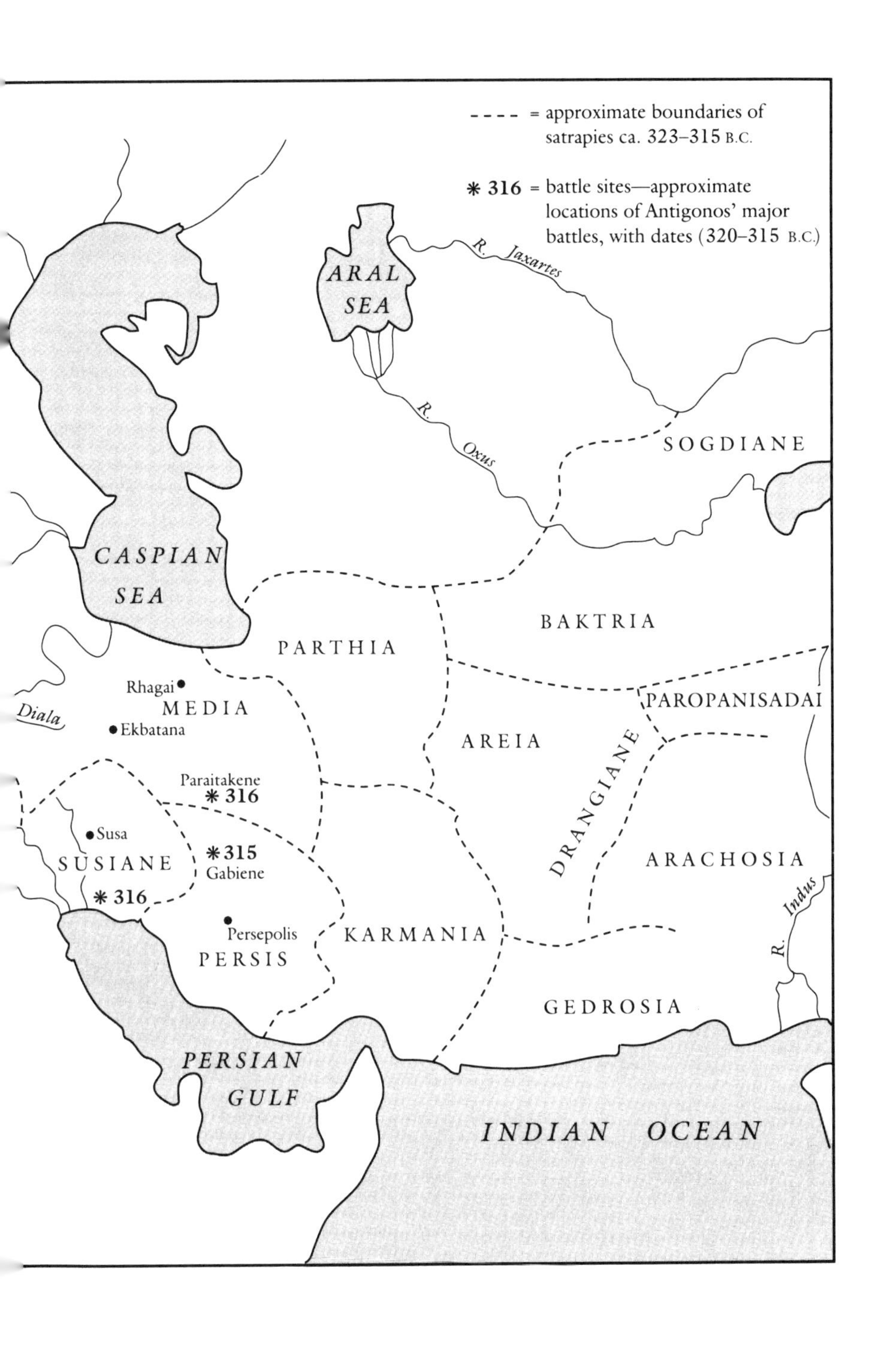

- - - - = approximate boundaries of satrapies ca. 323–315 B.C.
✱ 316 = battle sites—approximate locations of Antigonos' major battles, with dates (320–315 B.C.)
ARAL SEA
R. Jaxartes
R. Oxus
SOGDIANE
CASPIAN SEA
BAKTRIA
PARTHIA
PAROPANISADAI
Rhagai
MEDIA
Diala
Ekbatana
AREIA
DRANGIANE
Paraitakene
✱ 316
Susa
✱ 315
Gabiene
SUSIANE
ARACHOSIA
R. Indus
✱ 316
Persepolis
KARMANIA
PERSIS
GEDROSIA
PERSIAN GULF
INDIAN OCEAN

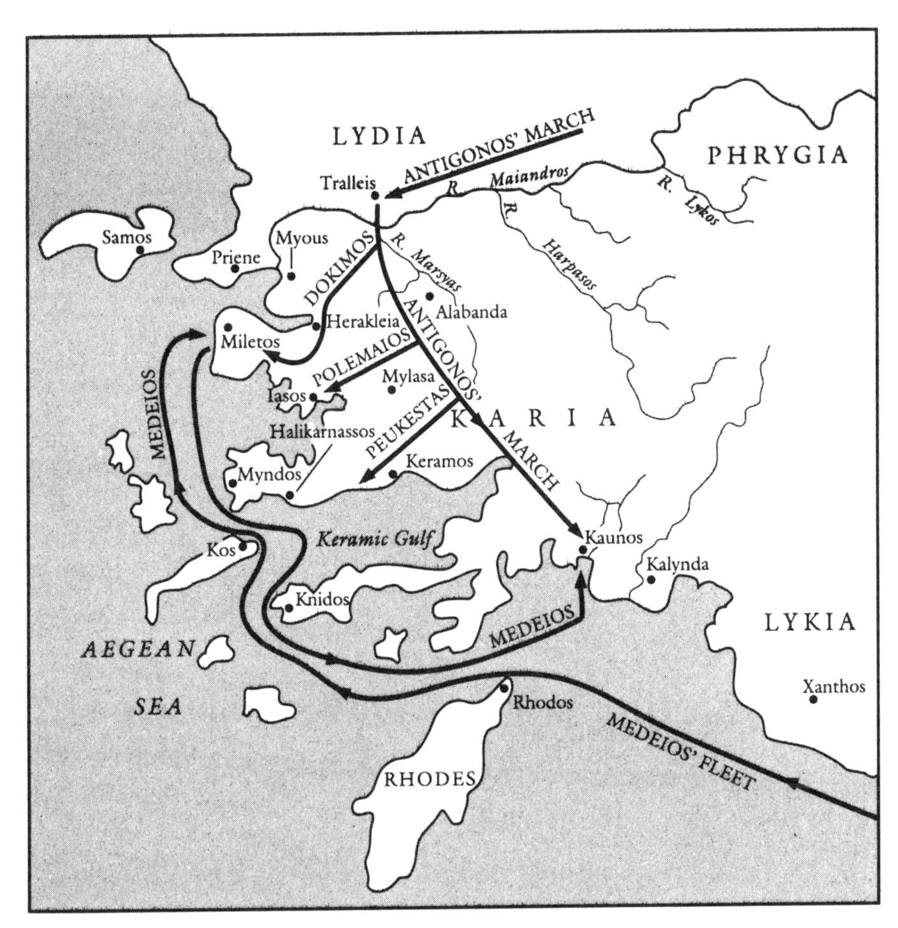

Map 4. Antigonos's Karian Campaign in 312 B.C.

Map 5. Antigonos's Realm and Sphere of Influence ca. 303 B.C.

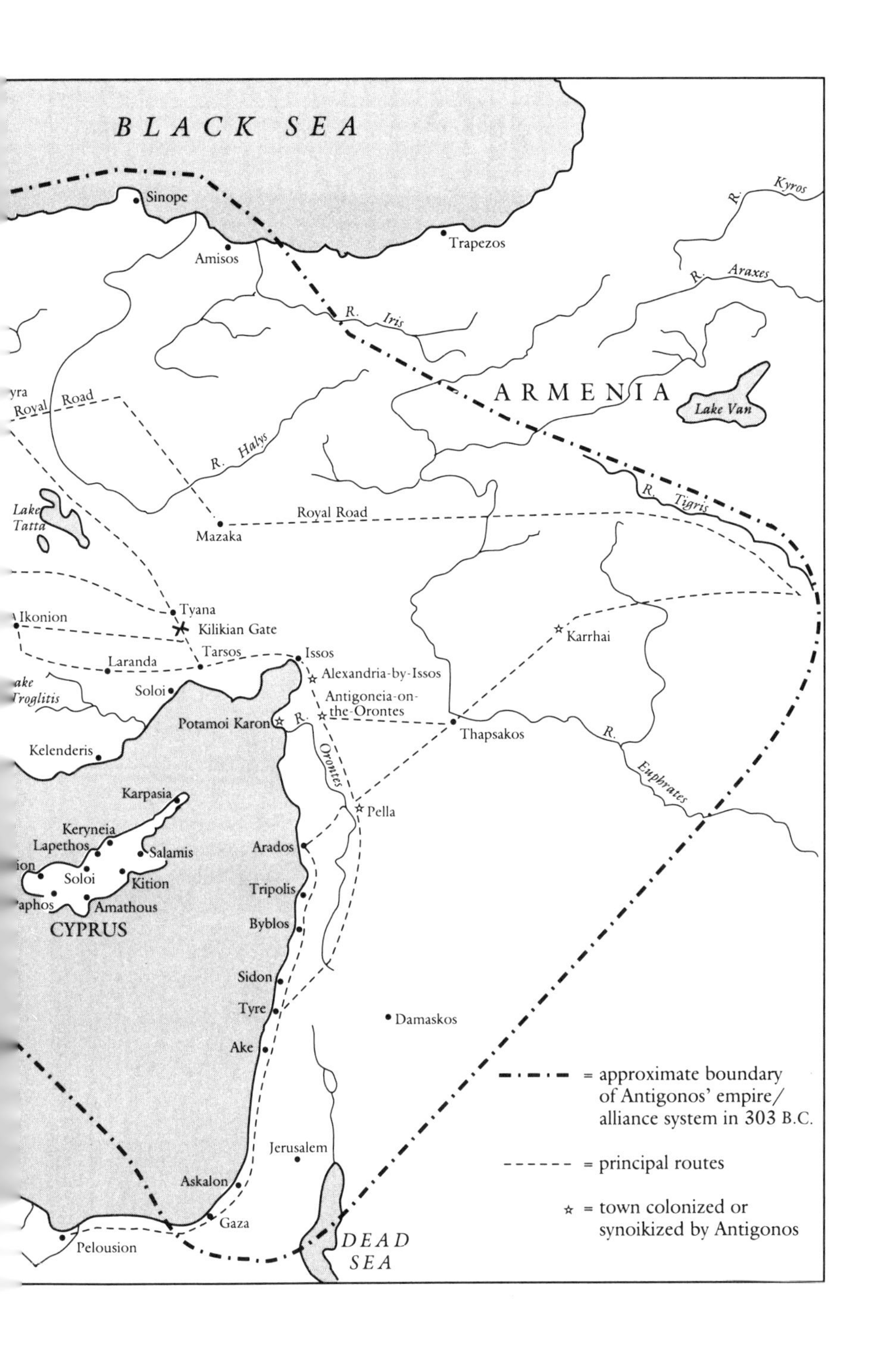
BLACK SEA
Sinope
Amisos
Trapezos
R. Kyros
R. Araxes
R. Iris
ARMENIA
Lake Van
Royal Road
R. Halys
R. Tigris
Lake Tatta
Royal Road
Mazaka
Tyana
Ikonion
Kilikian Gate
Karrhai
Tarsos
Issos
Laranda
Alexandria-by-Issos
Soloi
Antigoneia-on-the-Orontes
Potamoi Karon
R. Orontes
Thapsakos
R. Euphrates
Kelenderis
Karpasia
Pella
Keryneia
Lapethos
Salamis
Arados
Soloi
Kition
Tripolis
Amathous
CYPRUS
Byblos
Sidon
Tyre
Damaskos
Ake
= approximate boundary of Antigonos' empire/ alliance system in 303 B.C.
Jerusalem
= principal routes
Askalon
= town colonized or synoikized by Antigonos
Gaza
DEAD SEA
Pelousion

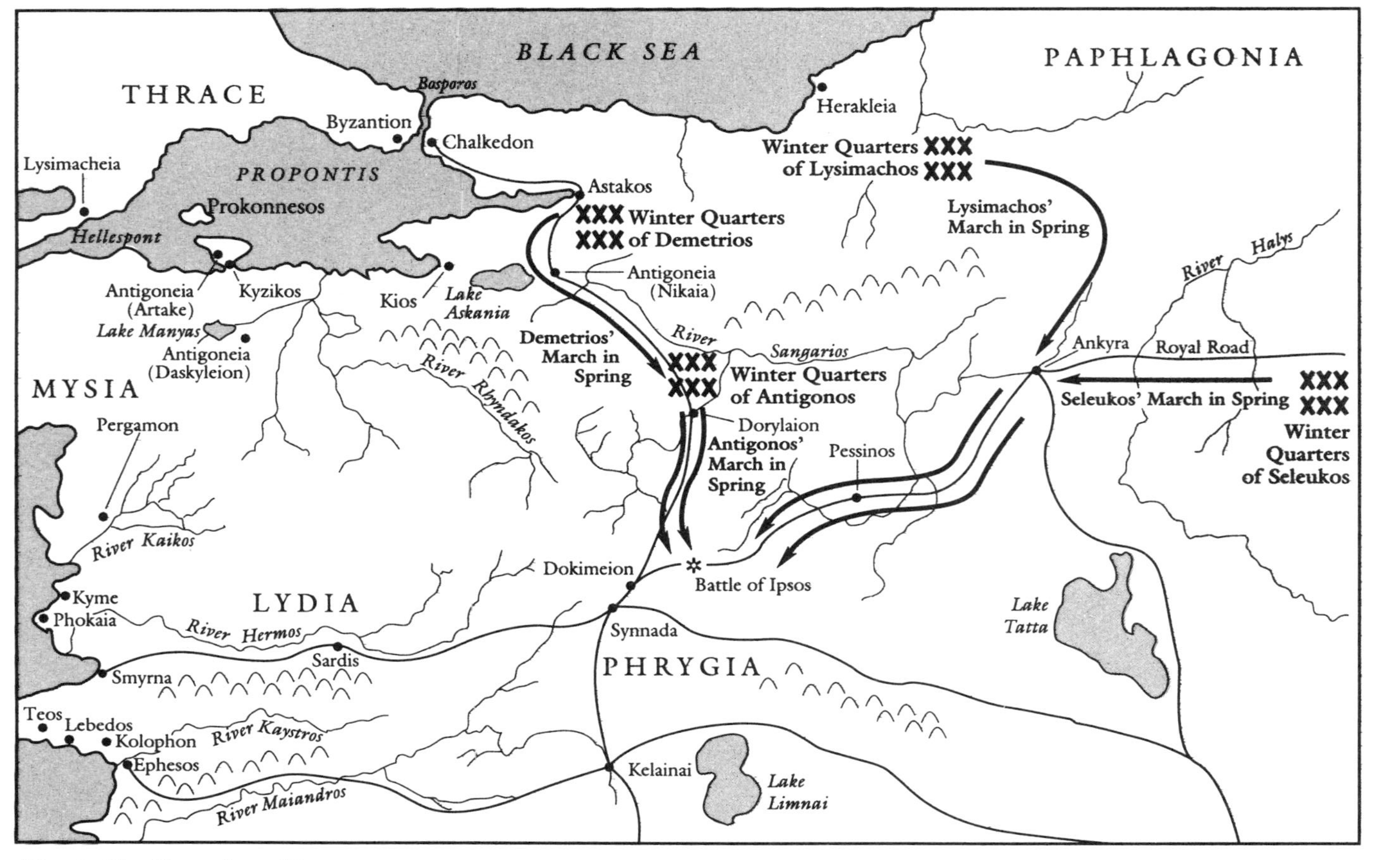

Map 6. The Campaign of Ipsos, 301 B.C.

List of Sources Mentioning or Relevant to Antigonos

1. LITERARY SOURCES

Aelian *Varia historia* IX 36; XII 16; 43; XIV 47a; and cf. II 20.
Appian *Syriaka* 52–64.
———. *Mithridatika* 8–9.
[Aristotle] *Oikonomika* II 1.
Arrian *Anabasis* I 29,3; VII 18,5.
———. *Ta Met' Alexandron*, ed. Roos, passim.
Athenaios *Deipnosophistai* VI 254a; X 415a; XIII 578a–b; XV 697a.
Cicero *De officiis* II 48.
Cornelius Nepos *Eumenes*, passim.
Curtius Rufus *Historia Alexandri Magni* IV 1, 34–35; 5,13; X 10,2.
Dexippos in *FGrH*, no. 100, passim.
Diodoros *Bibliotheke historike* XVIII–XX, passim; XXI 1–4.
Diogenes Laertios II 115; 140; V 77 and 79.
Frontinus *Strategemata* IV 1,10.
Heidelberg Epitome in *FGrH*, no. 155, passim.
Jacoby, *FGrH*, nos. 73; 75; 76; 100; 154; 155; 239b; 260; 328; 432; 434.
Josephus *Jewish Antiquities* XII 2.
———. *Contra Apionem* I 185; 213–14.
Justin *Epitome hist. phil.* XIII–XVI, passim.
[Loukianos] *Makrobioi* 11.
Malalas, p. 201 (Bonn ed.).
Memnon in *FGrH*, no. 434 F 4,6–9.
Pausanias *Periegesis* I 6,4–7; 8,1; 9,7; 12,1; 16,1; 25,6; VI 11,1; 15,7; X 10,2.
Photios *Myriobiblion* (see above Arrian, Dexippos, Memnon).
Pliny *Naturalis historia* XII 56; XIII 73; XXXV 90, 96, and 106.

Plutarch *Alexander* 70,4–5; 77,3–4.
———. *Demetrios* 1–30, passim.
———. *Demosthenes* 13,4.
———. *Eumenes*, passim.
———. *Pelopidas* 1,1–2.
———. *Phokion* 29,1; 30,5.
———. *Pyrrhos* 1–4.
———. *Romulus* 17,3.
———. *Sertorius* 1,4.
———. *Moralia* 11b–c; 182a–183a (= *Apophthegmata Antigonou*); 337a; 457e; 506d; 633c; 791e; 850d.
Polyainos *Stratagemata* IV 6,2; 6,4–16; 6,19; 7,2–3; 7,6–8; 8,2–5; 9,1; 12,1; V 35; VII 29,2; VIII 58 and 60.
Polybios V 10,10; XVIII 3,5; XXVIII 20,7.
Porphyrius in *FGrH*, no. 260 F 3,5; F 41 and 42.
Seneca *De ira* III 22,2–3.
———. *De constantia sapientis* V 6–7.
Stephanos of Byzantion s.v. Antigoneia.
Strabo *Geography* XII 565; XIII 593; 597; 607; XIV 646; 672; 657; XVI 750.
Suda s.v. Anaxippos; Demetrios Antigonou; Eumenes; Marsyas Periandrou; Paraloi.
Theophrastos *Hist. plant.* IV 8,4; IX 4,8.
Trogus Pompeius *Prologues* XIV; XV.

2. EPIGRAPHIC SOURCES

[Many of the following inscriptions have been published and discussed several times; I list only one publication of each, which seems to me the most useful and/or accessible.]

Blümel, *I. Iasos,* 1, nos. 2 and 32.
Buckler and Robinson, *Sardis VII,* no. 1.
Buschor, *Miscellanea Acad. Berol.* 2 (1950):25–30.
Dunst, *Klio* 37 (1959):63–68.
Engelmann and Merkelbach, *I. Erythrai und Klazomenai,* nos. 30 and 31.
Engelmann, Knibbe, and Merkelbach, *I. Ephesos,* 5, nos. 1448, 1450 and 1451; 6, no. 2003.
Habicht, *AM* 72 (1957):152–274, nos. 3, 4, 13, 19, 20, 21, and 22.
Herzog, *RFIC*, n.s., 20 (1942):12.
Hesperia 7 (1938):301, no. 25; 10 (1941):55–56, no. 19; 15 (1946):150–51, no. 10; 37 (1968):381–84.
Hiller von Gaertringen, *I. Priene,* nos. 2, 37, 40.
IG II^2 450, 459, 466, 469, 471, 486, 491, 492, 495, 496 + 507, 498, 525 + 675, 538, 550, 553, 555, 558, 559 + 568, 560, 561, 562, 563 + 485 + 621, 569, 646, 657, 682, 773, 1129, 1492b.

IG III^2 3424.
IG IV^2.1 58 and 68.
IG VII 1, 4, 5, 6.
IG XI.2 146a, 154a.
IG XI.4 514, 556, 1036.
IG XII.5 444 (= Marmor Parium)
IG XII.9 192, 198, 199, 207, 210, 212.
IG XII, suppl. 168.
Keil, *JÖAI* 16 (1913):231–44, nos. Ig, IIn, IIp, IIIb.
Knibbe and Iplikçioglu, *JÖAI* 53 (1982):130–32, no. 5.
Koumanoudes, *Horos* 4 (1986):11–18
Matthaiou, *Horos* 4 (1986):19–23
Meritt, *AJPh* 56 (1935):361.
Michel, *RIG*, no. 452.
Moretti, *ISE*, nos. 7, 9, 39, 72, 73.
OGIS, nos. 5, 6, 7, 8, 9.
Rehm, *Milet*, 1, no. 123.
Robert, *Coll. Froehner*, no. 52.
Schede, *AM* 44 (1919):4–19, nos. 5g; 50.
Schmitt, *Staatsverträge*, 3, no. 445.
SEG, 1, nos. 351, 354, 355, 356, 358, 360, 362.
SEG, 14, no. 60; 16, nos. 58, 59; 28, nos. 696, 697.
Segrè, *RPAA* 17 (1941):30–34.
———. *Tituli Calymnii*, no. 8.
Syll., nos. 330, 332, 333, 337, 344, 349, 350, 351, 352, 487.
Wilhelm, "Att. Urk.", pt. 1, pp. 37–44.
Woodhead, in *Edson Studies*, ed. Dell, pp. 357–67.

3. PAPYRI AND CUNEIFORM SOURCES

P. Berol., no. 11632.
P. Köln, no. 287.
P. Oxy. I, no. 12.
PSI, no. 1284.
Noret, *AC* 52 (1983):235–42.
Grayson, *Assyrian and Babylonian Chronicles*, no. 10 (= Bab. Chron.).
Kugler, *Orientalia*, n.s., 2 (1933):97–116 (BM 32154).
Sachs and Wiseman, *Iraq* 16 (1954):202–12.

Bibliography

RE articles not included.

Adams, W. L.
1975 "Cassander: The Policy of Coalition." Diss., University of Virginia.

———.
1979 "Cassander and the Crossing of the Hellespont, Diodorus 17, 17, 4." *AncW* 2, no. 4:111–15.

Adcock, F. E.
1957 *The Greek and Macedonian Art of War.* Berkeley.

Allen, R. E.
1983 *The Attalid Kingdom: A Constitutional History.* Oxford.

Anson, E. M.
1975 "Eumenes of Cardia." Diss., University of Virginia.

———.
1981 "Alexander's Hypaspists and the Argyraspids." *Historia* 30:117–20.

Atkinson, J. E.
1980 *A Commentary on Q. Curtius Rufus "Historiae Alexandri Magni" Bks. 3 and 4.* Amsterdam.

Atkinson, K. M. T.
1972 "A Hellenistic Land Conveyance." *Historia* 21:45–74.

Aucello, E.
1957 "La politica dei diadochi e l'ultimatum del 314 a. C." *RFIC*, n.s., 35:382–404.

Austin, M. M.
1981 *The Hellenistic World from Alexander to the Roman Conquest.* Cambridge. (*Hellenistic World*)

Avi-Yonah, M.
1978 *Hellenism and the East.* Jerusalem.

Aymard, A.
1967 *Etudes d'histoire ancienne.* Paris.

Badian, E.
1958 "Alexander the Great and the Unity of Mankind." *Historia* 7:425–44.

———.
1958 "The Eunuch Bagoas: A Study in Method." *CQ*, n.s., 8:144–57.

———.
1960 "The Death of Parmenio." *TAPhA* 91:324–38.

———.
1960 "The First Flight of Harpalus." *Historia* 9:245–46.

———.
1961 "Harpalus." *JHS* 81:16–43.

———.
1962 "Alexander and the Loneliness of Power." *AUMLA* 17:80–91.

———.
1962 "The Struggle for the Succession to Alexander the Great." *Gnomon* 34:381–87.

———.
1963 "The Death of Philip II." *Phoenix* 17:244–50.

———.
1964 *Studies in Greek and Roman History.* Oxford.

———.
1965 "The Administration of the Empire." *G & R* 12:165–82.

———.
1966 "Alexander the Great and the Greeks of Asia." In *Ancient Society and Institutions: Studies Presented to Victor Ehrenberg,* pp. 37–69. Oxford.

———.
1967 "A King's Notebooks." *HSCPh* 72:183–204.

———.
1977 "The Battle of the Granikos: A New Look." *Arch. Mak.* 2 (Thessaloniki):271–93.

———.
1981 "The Deification of Alexander the Great." In *Ancient Macedonian Studies in Honor of Charles F. Edson,* edited by H. J. Dell, pp. 27–71. Thessaloniki.

Badian, E., and T. R. Martin
1985 "Athenians, Other Allies, and the Hellenes in the Athenian Honorary Decree for Adeimantos of Lampsakos." *ZPE* 61:167–72.

Bagnall, R. S.
1976 *The Administration of the Ptolemaic Possessions outside Egypt.* Leiden. (*Ptolemaic Administration*)

Bakhuizen, S. C.
1970 *Salganeus and the Fortification on Its Mountains*. Groningen. (*Salganeus*)
Bar-Kochva, B.
1976 *The Seleucid Army*. Cambridge.
Barron, J.
1962 "The Tyranny of Duris of Samos." *CR* 12:189–92.
Bartoletti, V.
1951 "Frammento di storia dei diadochi (Arriano?)." In *PSI*, vol. 12, no. 1284. Florence.
Bauer, G.
1924 *Die Heidelberger Epitome: Eine Quelle zur Diadochengeschichte*. Diss., Leipzig.
Bellinger, A. R.
1964 *Essays on the Coinage of Alexander the Great*. New York.
Beloch, K. J.
1922–27 *Griechische Geschichte*. 4 vols. 2d ed. Strassburg, Berlin, Leipzig. (*GG*)
Bengtson, H.
1964 *Die Strategie in der hellenistischen Zeit*. 2 vols. 2d ed. Munich. (*Strategie*)
———.
1975 *Herrschergestalten des Hellenismus*. Munich.
Berthold, R. M.
1984 *Rhodes in the Hellenistic Age*. Ithaca, N.Y. (*Rhodes*)
Berve, H.
1926 *Das Alexanderreich auf prosopographischer Grundlage*. 2 vols. Munich. (Berve)
Bevan, E. R.
1902 *The House of Seleucus*. 2 vols. London.
Bickerman, E. J.
1966 "The Seleucids and the Achaemenids". In *Atti del convegno sul tema: La Persia e il mondo greco-romano, Acc. Lincei* 363:87–117.
———.
1968 *Chronology of the Ancient World*. Ithaca, N.Y.
Bikerman, E. J.
1934 "Alexandre le Grand et les villes d'Asie." *REG* 47:346–74.
———.
1938 *Institutions des Séleucides*. Paris.
———.
1939 "La Cité grecque dans les monarchies hellénistiques." *RPh*, 3d ser., 13:335–49.
Billows, R. A.
1989 "Anatolian Dynasts: The Case of the Macedonian Eupolemos in Karia." *CA* 8, no. 2: forthcoming.

Blümel, W.
1985 *Die Inschriften von Iasos*. Vol. 1. Bonn. (*I. Iasos*)
Bon, A., R. Carpenter, and A. W. Parsons
1936 *Corinth 3.2: The Defenses of Acrocorinth and the Lower Town*. Cambridge, Mass.
Bosworth, A. B.
1971 "The Death of Alexander the Great: Rumour and Propaganda." *CQ*, n.s., 21:112–36.
———.
1971 "Philip II and Upper Macedonia." *CQ*, n.s., 21:93–105.
———.
1973 "ASTHETAIROI." *CQ*, n.s., 23:245–53.
———.
1975 "Arrian and the Alexander Vulgate." *Entretiens Hardt* 22:1–33.
———.
1980 "Alexander and the Iranians." *JHS* 100:1–21.
———.
1980 *A Historical Commentary on Arrian's History of Alexander*. Vol. 1. Oxford. (*Historical Commentary*)
Bottin, C.
1928 "Les Sources de Diodore de Sicile pour l'histoire de Pyrrhus, des successeurs d'Alexandre et d'Agathocle (livres 18 à 22)." *RBPh* 7:1306–27.
Bowersock, G.
1983 *Roman Arabia*. Cambridge, Mass.
Braunert, H.
1968 "Staatstheorie und Staatsrecht im Hellenismus." *Saeculum* 19:47–66.
Briant, P.
1973 *Antigone le Borgne*. Paris.
———.
1982 *Rois, tributs et paysans*. Besançon.
Broughton, T. R. S.
1959 "Roman Asia Minor." In *An Economic Survey of Ancient Rome*, edited by Tenney Frank, vol. 4, pt. 4. Patterson, N.J.
Brown, T. S.
1947 "Hieronymus of Cardia." *AHR* 53:684–96.
———.
1949 *Onesicritus: a Study in Hellenistic Historiography*. Berkeley.
Browing, I.
1982 *Petra*. London.
Brunt, P. A.
1962 "Persian Accounts of Alexander's Campaign." *CQ*, n.s., 12: 141–55.

———.
1963 "Alexander's Macedonian Cavalry." *JHS* 83:27–46.

———.
1965 "The Aims of Alexander." *G & R* 12:202–15.

Buckler, W. H., and D. M. Robinson
1912 "Greek Inscriptions from Sardis." *AJA* 16:12–82.

———.
1932 *Sardis VII: Greek and Latin Inscriptions. Part 1: Seasons 1910–1914.* Leiden. (*Sardis VII*)

Buraselis, K.
1982 *Das hellenistische Makedonien und die Ägäis.* Munich. (*Das hellenistische Makedonien*)

Burn, A. R.
1957 "Notes on Alexander's Campaigns, 332–330." *JHS* 72:81–91.

———.
1965 "The Generalship of Alexander." *G & R* 12: 140–54.

Burstein, S. M.
1976 *Outpost of Hellenism: The Emergence of Heraclea on the Black Sea.* Berkeley.

———.
1977 "IG II^2 561 and the Court of Alexander IV." *ZPE* 24: 223–25.

Buschor, E.
1950 "Eine samische Ehrenurkunde." *Misc. Acad. Berol.* 2: 25–30.

Cary, M.
1951 *A History of the Greek World from 323–146* B.C. 2d ed. London.

Cavaignac, E.
1926 "Le Debut de l'ère des Séleucides (311)." *RAss* 23:5–11.

Cawkwell, G. L.
1978 *Philip of Macedon.* London.

Charbonneaux, J.
1952 "Antigone le Borgne et Démétrios Poliorcète sont-ils figurés sur le sarcophage d'Alexandre?" *Rev. des arts* 2:219–23.

Cloché, P.
1948 "Remarques sur la politique d'Antigone le Borgne a l'égard des cités grecques." *AC* 17:101–18.

———.
1949 "Remarques sur les étapes de l'ambition d'Antigone Ier jusqu'en 316 av. J.-C." In *Mélanges d'archéologie et d'histoire offerts à Charles Picard,* vol. 1, pp. 187–95. Paris.

———.
1957 "La Coalition de 315–311 av. J.-C. contre Antigone le Borgne." *CRAI*:130–39.

———.
1959 *La Dislocation d'un empire: Les Premiers Successeurs d'Alexandre le Grand.* Paris.

Cohen, G. M.
1978 *The Seleucid Colonies* (= *Historia*-Einzelschr. 30). Wiesbaden.
Costanzi, V.
1916 "La pace fra Antigono e i dinasti coalizzati contro di lui." *AUT*, n.s., 1, no. 4:1–20.
Daux, G.
1936 *Delphes au 2e et au 1er siècles*. Paris. (*Delphes*)
David, E.
1981 *Sparta between Empire and Revolution (404–243 B.C.)*. New York.
Debord, P.
1972 "L'Esclavage sacré: Etat de la question." In *Actes du colloque 1971 sur l'esclavage*, pp. 135–50. Paris.
———.
1982 *Aspects sociaux et économiques de la vie réligieuse dans l'Anatolie gréco-romaine*. Leiden. (*Aspects*)
Dell, H. J., ed.
1981 *Ancient Macedonian Studies in Honor of Charles F. Edson*. Thessaloniki. (*Edson Studies*)
Devine, A. M.
1984 "Diodorus' Account of the Battle of Gaza." *AClass* 27:31–40.
———.
1985 "Diodorus' Account of the Battle of Gabiene." *AncW* 12, nos. 3/4:87–96.
———.
1985 "Diodorus' Account of the Battle of Paraitacene." *AncW* 12, nos. 3/4:75–86.
Dimitrakos, G. S.
1937 *Demetrios Poliorketes und Athen*. Diss., Hamburg.
Dittenberger, W.
1903–5 *Orientis Graeci inscriptiones selectae*. 2 vols. Leipzig. (*OGIS*)
———.
1915 *Sylloge inscriptionum Graecarum*. Vol. 1. 3d ed. Leipzig. (*Syll.*)
Downey, G.
1961 *A History of Antioch in Syria from Seleucus to the Arab Conquest*. Princeton.
———.
1963 *Ancient Antioch*. Princeton.
Droysen, J. G.
1952 *Geschichte des Hellenismus*. 3 vols. 3d ed. Reprint, Basel.
Dunst, G.
1959 "Ein neues chiisches Dekret aus Kos." *Klio* 37:63–68.
Ecole française d'Athènes
1902–87 *Fouilles de Delphes*. Paris.

Edson, C. F.
1934 "The Antigonids, Heracles and Beroea." *HSCPh* 45:213–46.
———.
1934 "The Personal Appearance of Antigonus Gonatas." *CPh* 29:254–55.
———.
1970 "Early Macedonia." *Arch. Mak.* 1 (Thessaloniki):17–44.
Ehrenberg, V.
1938 *Alexander and the Greeks.* Oxford.
———.
1969 *The Greek State.* 2d ed. Oxford.
Elkeles, G.
1941 *Demetrios der Städtebelagerer.* Diss., Breslau.
Ellis, J. R.
1969 "Population Transplants by Philip II." *Makedonika* 9:9–17.
———.
1970 "The Security of the Macedonian Throne under Philip II." *Arch. Mak.* 1 (Thessaloniki):68–75.
———.
1971 "Amyntas Perdikka, Philip II and Alexander the Great." *JHS* 91:15–24.
———.
1976 *Philip II and Macedonian Imperialism.* London.
———.
1977 "The Dynamics of 4th Century Macedonian Imperialism." *Arch. Mak.* 2 (Thessaloniki): 103–14.
———.
1981 "The Assassination of Philip II." In *Ancient Macedonian Studies in Honor of Charles F. Edson,* edited by H. J. Dell, pp. 99–137. Thessaloniki.
Engel, R.
1971 "Anmerkungen zur Schlacht bei Orkynia." *MH* 28:227–31.
———.
1972 "Die Überlieferung der Schlacht bei Kretopolis." *Historia* 21:501–7.
———.
1973 "Polyains Stratagem IV 6,8 zur Seeschlacht am Hellespont." *Klio* 55:141–45.
———.
1977 *Untersuchungen zum Machtaufstieg des Antigonos I. Monophthalmos.* Kallmünz (FRG). (*Untersuchungen*)
Engelmann, H.
1976 *Die Inschriften von Kyme.* Bonn. (*I.Kyme*)

Engelmann, H., D. Knibbe, and R. Merkelbach.
1979–84 *Die Inschriften von Ephesos*. 8 vols. Bonn. (*I. Ephesos*)
Engelmann, H., and R. Merkelbach.
1972–74 *Die Inschriften von Erythrai und Klazomenai*. Bonn. (*I. Erythrai und Klazomenai*)
Engels, D. W.
1978 *Alexander the Great and the Logistics of the Macedonian Army*. Berkeley.
Ensslin, W.
1925 "Die Gewaltenteilung im Reichsregiment nach Alexanders Tod." *RhM* 74:293–307.
Errington, R. M.
1969 "Bias in Ptolemy's History of Alexander." *CQ*, n.s., 19:233–42.
———.
1970 "From Babylon to Triparadeisos, 323–320 B.C." *JHS* 90:49–77.
———.
1974 "Macedonian 'Royal Style' and Its Historical Significance." *JHS* 94:20–37.
———.
1977 "Diodorus Siculus and the Chronology of the Early Diadochoi, 320–311 B.C." *Hermes* 105:478–504.
———.
1978 "The Nature of the Macedonian State under the Monarchy." *Chiron* 8:77–133.
———.
1983 "The Historiographical Origins of Macedonian Staatsrecht." *Arch. Mak.* 3 (Thessaloniki):89–101.
———.
1986 *Geschichte Makedoniens*. Munich.
Fellmann, W.
1930 *Antigonos Gonatas, König der Makedonier, und die griechischen Staaten*. Diss., Würzburg.
Ferguson, W. W.
1911 *Hellenistic Athens*. London.
Fontana, M. J.
1960 *Le lotte per la successione di Alessandro Magno dal 323 al 315*. Palermo. (*Le lotte*)
Fortina, M.
1965 *Cassandro, re di Macedonia*. Turin.
Francisci, P. de.
1947–48 *Arcana imperii*. 4 vols. Milan.
Frye, R.
1984 *A History of Ancient Iran*. Munich.

Funck, B.
1971 "Die Babylonische Chronik Smith (BM 34660 und BM 36313) als Quelle des Diadochenkampfes." In *Beiträge zur Geschichte, Kultur und Religion des alten Orients, in memoriam E. Unger*, pp. 217–40. Baden-Baden.

Furlani, G., and A. Momigliano.
1932 "La cronaca babilonese sui Diadochi." *RFIC*, n.s., 10:462–84.

Garlan, Y.
1975 "Alliance entre les Iasiens et Ptolemée Ier." *ZPE* 18:193–98.

Garstang, J.
1943 "Hittite Military Roads in Asia Minor." *AJA* 47:35–62.

Geagan, D. J.
1968 "Inscriptions from Nemea." *Hesperia* 37:381–84.

Gesche, H.
1974 "Nikokles von Paphos und Nikokreon von Salamis." *Chiron* 4:103–25.

Geyer, F.
1925 *Alexander der Grosse und die Diadochen*. Leipzig.

———.
1930 "Euboia in den Wirren der Diadochenzeit." *Philologus* 85:175–91.

———.
1930 *Makedonien bis zur Thronbesteigung Philipps II*. Munich and Berlin.

Gomme, A. W.
1967 *Essays in Greek History and Literature*. Freeport, N.Y.

Goukowsky, P.
1975 "Antigone, Alexandre et l'assemblée macédonienne." *RPh*, 3d ser., 49:263–77.

———.
1978 *Essai sur les origines du mythe d'Alexandre*. Nancy. (*Essai*)

———.
1981 "Un Aspect de l'administration d'Alexandre dans les hautes satrapies." In *La Géographie administrative et politique d'Alexandre à Mahomet: Actes du colloque de Strasbourg, 14–16 juin 1979*, edited by T. Fahd, pp. 7–17. Leiden.

Graeve, V. von.
1970 *Der Alexandersarkophag und seine Werkstatt*. Berlin. (*Alexandersarkophag*)

Granier, F.
1931 *Die Makedonische Heeresversammlung: Ein Beitrag zum antiken Staatsrecht* (= Münchner Beiträge 13). Munich.

Grayson, A. K.
1975 *Assyrian and Babylonian Chronicles*. Vol. 5 of *Texts from Cuneiform Sources*. New York. (Bab. Chron.)

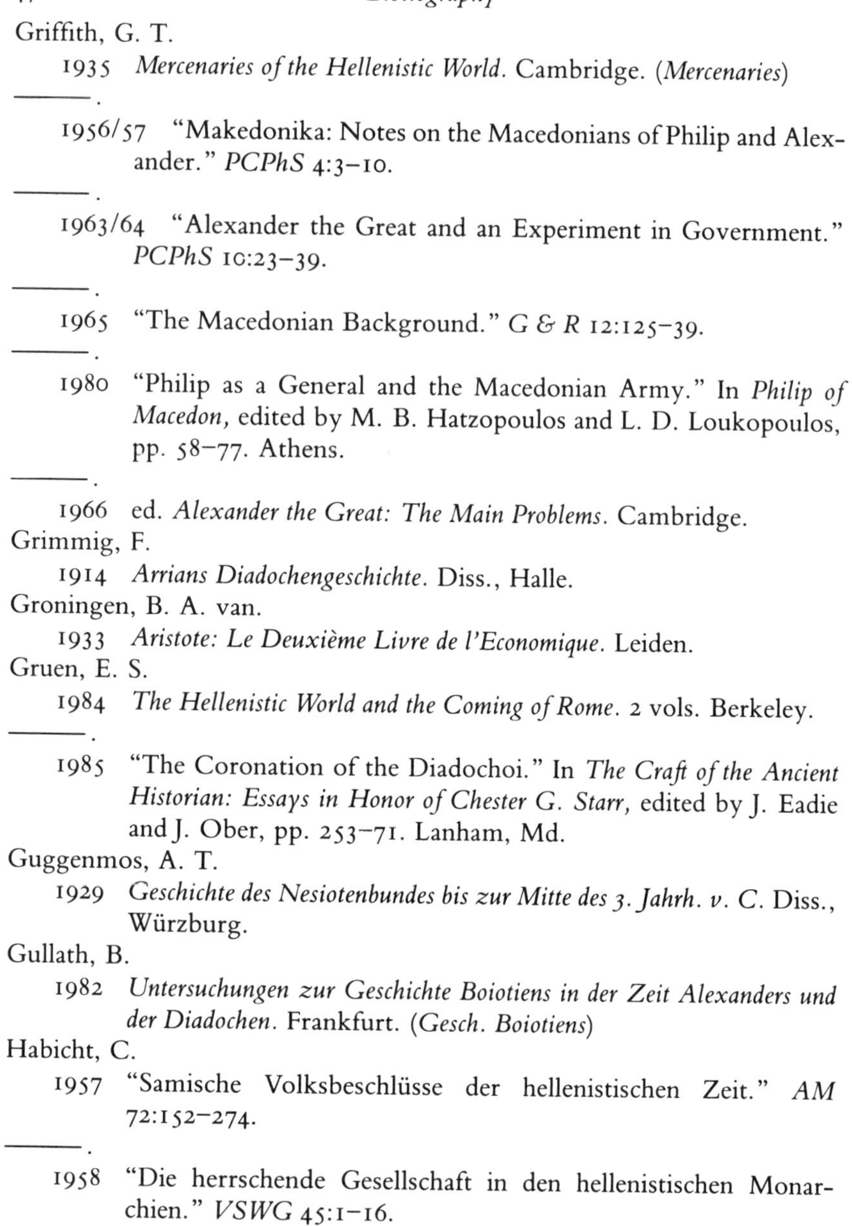

Griffith, G. T.

1935 *Mercenaries of the Hellenistic World.* Cambridge. (*Mercenaries*)

———.

1956/57 "Makedonika: Notes on the Macedonians of Philip and Alexander." *PCPhS* 4:3–10.

———.

1963/64 "Alexander the Great and an Experiment in Government." *PCPhS* 10:23–39.

———.

1965 "The Macedonian Background." *G & R* 12:125–39.

———.

1980 "Philip as a General and the Macedonian Army." In *Philip of Macedon,* edited by M. B. Hatzopoulos and L. D. Loukopoulos, pp. 58–77. Athens.

———.

1966 ed. *Alexander the Great: The Main Problems.* Cambridge.

Grimmig, F.

1914 *Arrians Diadochengeschichte.* Diss., Halle.

Groningen, B. A. van.

1933 *Aristote: Le Deuxième Livre de l'Economique.* Leiden.

Gruen, E. S.

1984 *The Hellenistic World and the Coming of Rome.* 2 vols. Berkeley.

———.

1985 "The Coronation of the Diadochoi." In *The Craft of the Ancient Historian: Essays in Honor of Chester G. Starr,* edited by J. Eadie and J. Ober, pp. 253–71. Lanham, Md.

Guggenmos, A. T.

1929 *Geschichte des Nesiotenbundes bis zur Mitte des 3. Jahrh. v. C.* Diss., Würzburg.

Gullath, B.

1982 *Untersuchungen zur Geschichte Boiotiens in der Zeit Alexanders und der Diadochen.* Frankfurt. (*Gesch. Boiotiens*)

Habicht, C.

1957 "Samische Volksbeschlüsse der hellenistischen Zeit." *AM* 72:152–274.

———.

1958 "Die herrschende Gesellschaft in den hellenistischen Monarchien." *VSWG* 45:1–16.

———.

1970 *Gottmenschentum und griechische Städte* (= Zetemata 14). 2d ed. Munich.

———.

1973 "Literarische und epigraphische Überlieferung zur Geschichte

Alexanders und seiner ersten Nachfolger." In *Akten des VI. Intern. Kongr. für griech. und latein. Epigraphik,* pp. 367–77. Munich.

———.

1977 "Athenisches Ehrendekret vom Jahre des Koroibos (306/5) für einen königlichen Offizier." *AJAH* 2, no. 1:37–39.

———.

1979 *Untersuchungen zur politischen Geschichte Athens im 3. Jahrh. v. C.* (= Vestigia 30). Munich. (*Untersuchungen*)

———.

1982 *Studien zur Geschichte Athens in hellenistischer Zeit* (= Hypomnemata 73). Göttingen. (*Gesch. Athens*)

———.

1986 *Pausanias' Guide to Ancient Greece.* Berkeley. (*Pausanias*)

Hadas, M.

1959 *Hellenistic Culture: Fusion and Diffusion.* New York.

Hadley, R. A.

1969 "Hieronymus of Cardia and Early Seleucid Mythology." *Historia* 18:142–52.

Hafner, G.

1980 "Lanassa." *RdA* 4:17–25.

Hamilton, J. R.

1969 *Plutarch "Alexander": A Commentary.* Oxford.

Hammond, N. G. L.

1978 "A Cavalry Unit in the Army of Antigonos Monophthalmos: Asthippoi." *CQ*, n.s., 28:128–35.

———.

1980 "The Battle of the Granicus River." *JHS* 100:73–88.

———.

1984 "Alexander's Veterans after his Death." *GRBS* 25:51–61.

Hammond, N. G. L., and G. T. Griffith.

1972–79 *A History of Macedonia.* 2 vols. Oxford.

Hampl, F.

1934 *Der König der Makedonen.* Weida (now GDR).

Hansen, E. V.

1971 *The Attalids of Pergamum.* 2d ed. Ithaca, N.Y.

Hauben, H.

1970 *Callicrates of Samos: A Contribution to the Study of the Ptolemaic Admiralty* (= Studia Hellenistica 18). Leuven. (*Callicrates*)

———.

1973 "On the Chronology of the Years 313–311 B.C." *AJPh* 94:256–67.

———.

1974 "An Athenian Naval Victory in 321 B.C." *ZPE* 13:61–64.

———.
1974 "A Royal Toast in 302 B.C." *AncSoc* 5:105–19.

———.
1975 *Het vlootbevelhebberschap in de vroege Diadochen tijd (323–301 v. C.): Een prosopographisch en institutioneel onderzoek*. Brussels. (*Vlootbevelhebberschap*)

———.
1975/76 "Antigonos' Invasion Plan for his Attack on Egypt in 306 B.C." *OLP* 6/7:267–71.

———.
1976 "Fleet Strength at the Battle of Salamis (306 B.C.)." *Chiron* 6:1–5.

———.
1977 "The First War of the Successors (321 B.C.): Chronological and Historical Problems." *AncSoc* 8:85–120.

———.
1977 "Rhodes, Alexander and the Diadochi from 323/2 to 304 B.C." *Historia* 26:307–39.

———.
1978 "The Ships of the Pydnaians: Remarks on Kassandros' Naval situation in 314/13 B.C." *AncSoc* 9:47–54.

Heckel, W.
1978 "The *Somatophylakes* of Alexander the Great: Some Thoughts." *Historia* 27:224–28.

———.
1980 "IG II^2 561 and the Status of Alexander IV." *ZPE* 40:249–50.

———.
1980 "Kelbanos, Kebalos or Kephalon?" *BN* 15:43–45.

———.
1980 "Marsyas of Pella, Historian of Macedon." *Hermes* 108:444–62.

———.
1981 "Honours for Philip and Iolaos (IG II^2 561)." *ZPE* 44:75–77.

———.
1982 "The Early Career of Lysimachos." *Klio* 64:373–81.

Heichelheim, F.
1959 "Roman Syria." In *An Economic Survey of Ancient Rome,* edited by Tenney Frank, vol.4, pt. 2. Patterson, N.J.

Heisserer, A. J.
1980 *Alexander the Great and the Greeks: The Epigraphic Evidence*. Norman, Okla.

Herman, G.
1980/81 "The 'Friends' of the Early Hellenistic Rulers: Servants or Officials?" *Talanta* 12/13:103–49.

Herzog, R.
1942 "Symbolae Calymniae et Coae." *RFIC*, n.s., 20:1–20.

Heuss, A.

1938 "Antigonos Monophthalmos und die griechische Städte." *Hermes* 73:133–94.

———.

1937 *Stadt und Herrscher der Hellenismus in ihrer Staats- und Völkerrechtlichen Beziehungen* (= *Klio,* suppl. 39). Leipzig.

Hiller von Gaertringen, F.

1906 *Die Inschriften von Priene.* Berlin. (*I. Priene*)

———.

1918 "Aus der Belagerung von Rhodos 304 v. Chr." *SDAW:* 752–62.

Hoffmann, O.

1906 *Die Makedonen: Ihre Sprache und ihr Volkstum.* Göttingen. (*Die Makedonen*)

Holleaux, M.

1938–57 *Etudes d'épigraphie et d'histoire grecques.* Edited by L. Robert. 6 vols. Paris.

Hölscher, T.

1973 *Griechische Historienbilder des 5. und 4. Jahrhunderts v. Chr.* Würzburg.

Honigmann, E.

1935 "Sur quelques évêchés d'Asie Mineure." *Byzantion* 10:647–51.

Hornblower, J.

1981 *Hieronymus of Cardia.* Oxford.

Hünerwadel, W.

1900 *Forschungen zur Geschichte des Königs Lysimachos von Thrakien.* Diss., Zurich.

Instinski, H. U.

1949 *Alexander der Grosse am Hellespont.* Munich.

Jacoby, F.

1923–58 *Die Fragmente der griechischen Historiker.* Berlin and Leiden. (*FGrH*)

———.

1949 *Atthis: The Local Chronicles of Ancient Athens.* Oxford.

Jones, A. H. M.

1940 *The Greek City from Alexander to Justinian.* Oxford. (*Greek City*)

———.

1971 *Cities of the Eastern Roman Provinces.* 2d ed. Oxford. (*Cities*)

Jordan, D. M.

1980 "Two Inscribed Lead Tablets from a Well in the Athenian Kerameikos." *AM* 95:225–39.

Jouguet, P.

1932 *Macedonian Imperialism and the Hellenisation of the East.* New York. (*Macedonian Imperialism*)

Judeich, W.
1908 "Die Schlacht am Granikos." *Klio* 8:372–97.

Julien, P.
1914 *Zur Verwaltung der Satrapien unter Alexander dem Grossen*. Diss., Jena. (*Verwaltung der Satrapien*)

Kaerst, J.
1926–27 *Geschichte des Hellenismus*. 2 vols. Leipzig.

Kallenberg, H.
1877–78 "Die Quellen für die Nachrichten der alten Historiker über die Diadochenkämpfe bis zum Tode des Eumenes und der Olympias." *Philologus* 36:305–27, 488–528, 637–70; 37:193–227.

Kalleris, J. N.
1954–76 *Les Anciens Macédoniens*. 2 vols. Athens.

Kanatsulis, D.
1968 "Antipatros als Feldherr und Staatsmann nach dem Tode Alexanders des Grossen." *Makedonika* 8:123–84.

Kebric, R. B.
1977 *In the Shadow of Macedon: Duris of Samos* (= *Historia*-Einzelschr. 29). Wiesbaden.

Keil, J.
1913 "Ephesische Bürgerrechts- und Proxeniedekrete aus dem vierten und dritten jahrhdt. v. Ch." *JÖAI* 16:231–48.

Kertesz, I.
1978 "Bemerkungen zum Kult des Demetrios Poliorketes." *Oikumene* 11:163–75.

Kienast, D.
1971 *Philipp II. von Makedonien und das Reich der Achaimeniden*. Munich.

Kiepert, H.
1902 *Atlas antiquus: Zwölf Karten zur alten geschichte*. 12th ed. Berlin.

Knibbe, D., and B. Iplikçioglu
1982 "Neue Inschriften aus Ephesos." *JÖAI* 53:87–150.

Koehler, U.
1898 "Das Asiatische Reich des Antigonos." *SDAW*, pp. 824–43.

König, W.
1913 *Der Bund der Nesioten*. Diss., Halle.

Koumanoudes, S.
1986 "Sotimos Dositheou Kyrenaios" *Horos* 4:11–18.

Kreissig, H.
1978 *Wirtschaft und Gesellschaft im Seleukidenreich*. Berlin.

Kromayer, J., and E. Kahnes
1931 "Drei Diadochenschlachten." In *Antike Schlachtfelder*, edited by J. Kromayer and G. Veith, vol. 4. Berlin.

Kugler, F. X.
1933 "Drei babylonische Planetentafeln der Seleukidenzeit." *Orientalia,* n.s., 2:97–116.

Larsen, J. O. A.
1925–26 "Representative Government in the Pan-Hellenic Leagues." *CPh* 20:313–29; 21:52–71.
1955 *Representative Government in Greek and Roman History.* Berkeley.

Launey, M.
1949–50 *Recherches sur les armées hellénistiques* (= *BEFAR* 169). 2 vols. Paris. (*Recherches*)

Lazzarini, L.
1983 "L'inizio della monetazione di Assos e una nuova ipotesi su Aioleis (Troade)." *RIN* 85:3–15.

Lévêque, P.
1957 *Pyrrhos* (= *BEFAR* 185). Paris.

———.
1968 "La Guerre a l'époque hellénistique." In *Problèmes de la guerre en Grèce ancienne,* edited by J.-P. Vernant, pp. 261–87. Paris.

Lock, R. C.
1977 "The Macedonian Army Assembly in the Time of Alexander the Great." *CPh* 72:92–107.

———.
1977 "The Origins of the Argyraspids." *Historia* 26:373–78.

Macurdy, G. H.
1932 *Hellenistic Queens: A Study of Woman Power in Macedonia, Seleucid Syria, and Ptolemaic Egypt.* Baltimore.

Magie, D. M.
1950 *Roman Rule in Asia Minor.* 2 vols. Princeton.

Manni, E.
1949 "Tre note di cronologia ellenistica." *RAL* 4:53–85.

———.
1952 *Demetrio Poliorcete.* Rome.

Marasco, G.
1982 *Appiano e la storia dei Seleucidi fino all'ascesa al trono di Antioco III.* Florence. (*Appiano*)

Marsden, E. W.
1964 *The Campaign of Gaugamela.* Liverpool.

———.
1969–71 *Greek and Roman Artillery.* 2 vols. Oxford.

Mastrocinque, A.
1976/77 "L'eleutheria e le città ellenistiche." *AIV* 135:1–23.

———.
1979 *La Caria e la Ionia meridionale in epoca ellenistica,* 323–188 *a.c.* Rome. (*La Caria*)

Matthaiou, A. P.
1986 "An Athenian Decree of 304/3 B.C." *Horos* 4:19–23.
Mehl, A.
1980/81 "Doriktetos Chora." *AncSoc* 11/12:173–212.
———.
1986 *Seleukos Nikator und sein Reich*. Vol. 1 (= Studia Hellenistica 28). Leuven.
Melber, J.
1885 "Über die Quellen und den Wert der Strategemensammlung Polyäns." *JClPh*, suppl. 14:419–688.
Meritt, B. D.
1935 "Inscriptions of Colophon." *AJPh* 56:358–97.
Merkelbach, R.
1977 *Die Quellen des Griechischen Alexanderromans* (= Zetemata 9). 2d ed. Munich.
Merker, I. L.
1970 "The Ptolemaic Officials and the League of the Islanders." *Historia* 19:141–60.
———.
1974 "Demetrios Poliorketes and Tyre." *AncSoc* 5:119–26.
Meyer, E.
1925 *Die Grenzen der hellenistischen Staaten in Kleinasien*. Zurich and Leipzig.
Michel, C.
1900 *Recueil d'inscriptions grecques*. Brussels. (*RIG*)
Milns, R. D.
1967 "Philip II and the Hypaspists." *Historia* 16:509–12.
———.
1971 "The Hypaspists of Alexander III." *Historia* 20:186–95.
———.
1975 "The Army of Alexander the Great." *Entretiens Hardt* 22:87–129.
———.
1981 "Asthippoi Again." *CQ*, n.s., 31:347–54.
Momigliano, A.
1930 "La pace del 311." *SIFC*, n.s., 8:83–86.
Moretti, L.
1967–75 *Iscrizione storiche ellenistiche*. Vols. 1 and 2. Florence. (*ISE*)
Moser, E.
1914 *Untersuchungen über die Politik Ptolemaios' I in Griechenland*. Diss., Leipzig. (*Politik Ptolemaios' I*)
Müller, C., and T. Müller
1841–53 *Fragmenta historicorum Graecorum*. 4 vols. Paris. (*FHG*)

Müller, O.
1973 *Antigonos Monophthalmos und das "Jahr der Könige."* Bonn. (*Antigonos Monophthalmos*)

Musti, D.
1966 "Lo stato dei Seleucidi." *SCO* 15:61–197.

———.
1984 "Syria and the East." In *CAH*, vol. 7, pt. 1, pp. 175–220. 2d ed. Cambridge.

Neppi Modona, A.
1932 "Studi diadochei." *Athenaeum* 10:22–36.

Nikolitsis, N. T.
1973 *The Battle of the Granicus: A Source-Critical Study*. Stockholm.

Noret, J.
1983 "Un Fragment du dixième livre de la *Succession d'Alexandre* par Arrien retrouvé dans un palimpseste de Gothenbourg." *AC* 52:235–42.

Olmstead, A. T.
1937 "Cuneiform Texts and Hellenistic Chronology." *CPh* 32:1–14.

———.
1948 *History of the Persian Empire*. Chicago.

Olshausen, E.
1974 *Prosopographie der Hellenistischen Königsgesandten, Teil I: Von Triparadeisos bis Pydna* (= Studia Hellenistica 19). Leuven. (*Prosopographie*)

Ormerod, A.
1924 *Piracy in the Ancient World*. Liverpool.

Orth, W.
1977 *Königliche Machtanspruch und städtische Freiheit* (= Münchner Beiträge 71). Munich. (*Königliche Machtanspruch*)

Osborne, M. J.
1981 *Naturalisation in Athens*. 2 vols. Brussels.

Ostwald, M.
1982 *Autonomia: Its Genesis and Early History* (= American Classical Studies 11). Chico, Calif.

Palm, J.
1955 *Über Sprache und Stil des Diodoros von Sizilien*. Lund.

Pandermalis, D.
1984 *Dion*. Thessaloniki.

Parke, H. W.
1933 *Greek Mercenary Soldiers from the Earliest Times to the Battle of Ipsos*. Oxford. (*Greek Mercenary Soldiers*)

Parker, R. A., and W. H. Dubberstein
1956 *Babylonian Chronology, 626* B.C.–A.D. *75*. Providence.

Paton, W. R., and E. L. Hicks
1891 *The Inscriptions of Cos*. Oxford.

Pearson, L.
1954 "The Diary and Letters of Alexander the Great." *Historia* 3:429–55.

———.
1960 *The Lost Histories of Alexander the Great*. New York. (*Lost Histories*)

Picard, O.
1979 *Chalcis et la confédération eubéenne: Etude de numismatique et d'histoire* (= *BEFAR* 234). Paris. (*Chalcis*)

Poole, R. S.
1923–69 *A Catalogue of Greek Coins in the British Musem*. 29 vols. London. (*BMC*)

Possenti, G. B.
1901 *Il re Lisimaco di Tracia*. Turin.

Préaux, C.
1954 "Sur l'origine des monopoles lagides." *CE* 29:312–37.

Pritchett, W. K.
1937 "A Decree of the Year of Koroibos." *AJPh* 58:329–33.

Pugliese Carratelli, G.
1967/68 "Supplemento epigrafico di Iasos." *ASAA*, n.s., 29/30:437–45.

Raaflaub, K.
1981 "Zum Freiheitsbegriff der Griechen." In *Soziale Typenbegriffe im Alten Griechenland,* edited by E. Welskopf, vol. 4, pp. 180–405. Berlin.

Ramsay, Sir W. M.
1920 "Military Operations on the North Front of Mount Taurus, III: The Imprisonment and Escape of Dokimos (Diod. XIX 16)." *JHS* 40:107–12.

———.
1923 "Military Operations on the North Front of Mount Taurus, IV: The Campaigns of 320 and 319 B.C." *JHS* 43:1–10.

Rehm, A., and G. Kawerau
1914 "Das Delphinion von Milet." In *Milet: Ergebnisse der Ausgrabungen und Untersuchungen seit dem Jahre 1899*, edited by Th. Wiegand, vol. 1, pt. 3. Berlin. (*Milet*)

Reinach, Th.
1890 *Mithridates Eupator, roi du Pont*. Paris.

Reuss, F.
1876 *Hieronymos von Kardia*. Berlin.

Ritter, H.
1965 *Diadem und Königsherrschaft* (= Vestigia 7). Munich.

Robert, J., and L. Robert
"Bulletin épigraphique," Published annually in *Revue des études grecques*. ("Bull. ép.")

Robert, L.
1936 *Collection Froehner I: Inscriptions grecques*. Paris.

———.
1936 "Etudes d'épigraphie grecque." *RPh*, 3d ser., 10:113–70.

———.
1940–65 *Hellenica*. 13 vols. Paris.

———.
1951 *Etudes de numismatique grecque*. Paris.

———.
1973 "Les Juges étrangers dans la cité grecque." In *Xenion: Festschrift für Pan. J. Zepos*, vol. 1, pp. 765–82. Athens.

Robinson, E. S. G.
1921 "Aspeisas: Satrap of Susiana." *NC*, 5th ser., 1:37–38.

Roos, A. G.
1968 *Flavii Arriani quae exstant omnia*. 2 vols. 2d ed., with additions by G. Wirth. Leipzig.

Rosen, K.
1967 "Political Documents in Hieronymus of Cardia (323–302 B.C.)." *AClass* 10:41–94.

———.
1967 "Die Reichsordnung von Babylon (323 v. Ch.)" *AClass* 10:95–110.

———.
1968 "Die Bundnisformen der Diadochen und der Zerfall des Alexanderreiches." *AClass* 11:182–210.

Rostovtzeff, M.
1910 *Studien zur Geschichte des römischen Kolonates*. Leipzig and Berlin.

———.
1941 *The Social and Economic History of the Hellenistic World*. 3 vols. Oxford. (*SEHHW*)

Ryder, T.
1965 *Koine eirene*. Oxford.

Sachs, A. J., and D. O. Wiseman
1954 "A Babylonian King-List of the Hellenistic Period." *Iraq* 16:202–12.

Sacks, K. S.
1982 "The Lesser Prooemia of Diodorus Siculus." *Hermes* 110:434–43.

Saitta, G.
1955 "Lisimaco di Tracia." *Kokalos* 1:62–153.

Schachermeyr, F.
1925 "Zu Geschichte und Staatsrecht der frühen Diadochenzeit." *Klio* 19:435–61.

———.
1970 *Alexander in Babylon und die Reichsordnung nach seinem Tode.* Vienna. (*Alexander in Babylon*)

Schede, M.
1919 "Aus dem Heraion von Samos." *AM* 44:1–46.

Schmidt, P.
1875 *De expeditionibus a Demetrio Poliorcete in Graeciam susceptis.* Pyritz (now Pyrzyce, Poland). (*Dem. Pol. in Graeciam*)

Schmitt, H. H.
1969 *Die Staatsverträge des Altertums.* Vol. 3. Munich. (*Staatsverträge*)

Schmitthenner, W.
1968 "Über eine Formveränderung der Monarchie seit Alexander d. Gr." *Saeculum* 19:31–46.

Schober, L.
1981 *Untersuchungen zur Geschichte Babyloniens und der Oberen Satrapien von 323–303 v. Chr.* Frankfurt. (*Gesch. Bqbyloniens*)

Schubert, R.
1877/78 "Die Quellen Plutarchs in dem Lebensbeschreibungen des Eumenes, Demetrios und Pyrrhos." *JClPh*, suppl. 9:647–837.

———.
1914 *Die Quellen zu Geschichte der Diadochenzeit.* Leipzig.

Schur, W.
1934 "Das Alexanderreich nach Alexander." *RhM* 83:129–56.

Schwahn, W.
1930 "Heeresmatrikel und Landfriede Philipps von Makedonien." *Klio*, suppl. 21:1–63.

———.
1930–31 "Die Nachfolge Alexanders des Grossen." *Klio* 23:211–38; 24:306–32.

———.
1931 "Diyllos." *Philologus* 86:145–68.

Scott, K.
1928 "The Deification of Demetrios Poliorketes." *AJPh* 49:137–66, 217–39.

Scullard, H. H.
1974 *The Elephant in the Greek and Roman World.* London.

Segrè, M.
1941 "Documenti di storia ellenistica." *RPAA* 17:30–34.

———.
1952 *Tituli Calymnii* (= *ASAA*, n.s., 6/7 [1944/45]). Bergamo. (*TC*)

Seibert, J.
1967 *Historische Beiträge zu den dynastische Verbindungen in hellenistischer Zeit* (= *Historia*-Einzelschr. 10). Wiesbaden. (*Dynastische Verbindungen*)
———.
1969 *Untersuchungen zur Geschichte Ptolemaios' I* (= Münchner Beiträge 56). Munich. (*Ptolemaios I*)
———.
1972 *Alexander der Grosse*. Darmstadt.
———.
1983 *Das Zeitalter der Diadochen*. Darmstadt. (*Diadochen*)
Shear, T. L., Jr.
1978 *Kallias of Sphettos and the Revolt of Athens in 286 B.C.* (= *Hesperia*, suppl. 17). Princeton. (*Kallias of Sphettos*)
Sherk, R. K.
1969 *Roman Documents from the Greek East*. Baltimore.
Sherwin-White, S. M.
1978 *Ancient Cos* (= Hypomnemata 51). Göttingen.
Shipley, D. G.
1987 *A History of Samos, 800–188 B.C.* Oxford.
Simpson, R. H.
1955 "Polemaios' Invasion of Attica in 313." *Mnemosyne*, 4th ser., 8:34–37.
———.
1957 "Antigonus, Polyperchon and the Macedonian Regency." *Historia* 6:371–73.
———.
1957 "A Note on Cyinda." *Historia* 6:503–4.
———.
1957 "A Possible Case of Misrepresentation in Diodorus XIX." *Historia* 6:504–5.
———.
1958 "Aetolian Policy in the Late Fourth Century BC." *AC* 27:357–62.
———.
1959 "Abbreviation of Hieronymus of Cardia in Diodorus." *AJPh* 80:370–79.
———.
1959 "Antigonus the One-Eyed and the Greeks." *Historia* 8:385–409.
Sinclair, R. K.
1963 "Diodorus Siculus and the Writing of History." *PACA* 6:36–45.
Smith, L. C.
1961 "The Chronology of Books XVIII–XX of Diodorus Siculus." *AJPh* 82:283–90.

Smith, R. R. R.
1988 *Hellenistic Royal Portraits*. Oxford.

Smith, S.
1924 *Babylonian Historical Texts relating to the Capture and Downfall of Babylon*. London.

———.
1925 "The Chronology of Philip Arrhidaeus, Antigonus and Alexander IV." *RAss* 22:179–97.

———.
1928 "The Deaths of Alexander the Great and Philip Arrihidaeus." *Journ. Royal Asiat. Soc.*: 618–21.

Stadter, P. A.
1980 *Arrian of Nicomedia*. Chapel Hill, N.C.

Stagakis, G. S.
1962 "Institutional Aspects of the Hetairos Relation." Diss., University of Wisconsin.

———.
1970 "Observations on the *Hetairoi* of Alexander the Great." *Arch. Mak.* 1 (Thessaloniki): 86–102.

Stefan, A.
1977 "Graffite callatien du 4e siècle av. n. ère." In *Epigraphica: Travaux dediés au 7e congres d'épigraphie grecque et latine,* edited by D. M. Pippidi and E. Popescu, pp. 25–30. Bucharest. (*Epigraphica*)

Stroud, R. S.
1984 "An Argive Decree from Nemea concerning Aspendos." *Hesperia* 53:193–216.

Sweet, H.
1951 "Sources of Plutarch's Demetrius." *CW* 44:177–78.

Tarn, W. W.
1913 *Antigonos Gonatas*. Oxford.

———.
1921 "Herakles, Son of Barsine." *JHS* 41:18–28.

———.
1926 "The Proposed New Date for Ipsus." *CR* 40:13–15.

———.
1930 *Hellenistic Military and Naval Developments*. Cambridge. (*HMND*)

———.
1933 *Cambridge Ancient History*, vol. 6, chaps. 14 and 15, pp. 438–504. Cambridge.

———.
1940 "Two Notes on Seleucid History: 1. Seleucus' 500 Elephants." *JHS* 60:84–89.

———.
1948 *Alexander the Great.* 2 vols. Cambridge.

Tod, M. N.
1948 *Greek Historical Inscriptions.* 2 vols. 2d ed. Oxford. (*GHI*)

Toynbee, A. J.
1969 "If Ochus and Philip Had Lived On." In *Some Problems of Greek History,* pt. 4, chap. 2. Oxford.

Tréheux, J.
1949 "Les Dernières années de Délos sous le protectorat des Amphictions." In *Mélanges d'archéologie et d'histoire offerts à Charles Picard,* vol. 2, pp. 1008–32. Paris.

Tscherikower, V.
1926 *Die hellenistischen Städtegründungen von Alexander dem Grossen bis auf die Römerzeit* (= *Philologus,* suppl. 19). Leipzig. (*Städtegründungen*)

Urban, R.
1979 *Wachstum und Krise des Achaiischen Bundes* (= *Historia*-Einzelschr. 35). Wiesbaden.

Vezin, A.
1907 *Eumenes von Kardia: Ein Beitrag zur Geschichte der Diadochenzeit.* Diss., Münster.

Vitucci, G.
1953 *Il regno di Bitinia.* Rome.

———.
1963 "Il compromesso di Babilonia e la 'prostasia' di Cratero." In *Miscellanea di studi alessandrini in memoria di A. Rostagni,* pp. 63–67. Turin.

Walbank, F. W.
1981 *The Hellenistic World.* London.

———.
1984 "Monarchies and Monarchic Ideas." In *CAH,* vol. 7, pt. 1, chap. 3, pp. 62–100. 2d ed. Cambridge.

Wehrli, C.
1964 "Phila, fille d'Antipater et épouse de Démétrios roi des Macédoniens." *Historia* 13:140–46.

———.
1968 *Antigone et Démétrios.* Geneva.

Weiskopf, M.
1982 "Achaemenid Systems for Governing Anatolia." Diss., University of California, Berkeley.

Welles, C. B.
1934 *Royal Correspondence in the Hellenistic Period.* New Haven. (*RC*)

———.

1963 "The Reliability of Ptolemy as an Historian." In *Miscellanea di studi alessandrini in memoria di A. Rostagni*, pp. 101–16. Turin.

Westermann, W. L.

1921 "Land Registers of Western Asia under the Seleucids." *CPh* 16:12–19.

Westlake, H. D.

1969 "Eumenes of Cardia." In *Essays on the Greek Historians and Greek History*, pp. 313–30. New York.

Wilcken, U.

1967 *Alexander the Great*. Trans. G. C. Richards. New York.

Wilhelm, A.

1937 "Ein Gedicht zu Ehren der Könige Antigonos und Demetrios (*IG* II/III 3424)." *AE*, pp. 203–07.

———.

1943 "Beschluss zu Ehren des Demetrios *ho megas*." *Wiener Jahreshefte* 35:157–63.

———.

1974 "Attische Urkunden, I–V." In *Akademieschriften zur griechischen Inschriftenkunde*, vol. 1. Leipzig. ("Att. Urk.")

Will, Ed.

1979–82 *Histoire politique du monde hellénistique*. 2 vols. 2d ed. Nancy. (*Histoire politique*)

———.

1984 "The Succession to Alexander." In *CAH*, vol. 7, pt. 1, chap. 2, pp. 23–61. 2d ed. Cambridge.

Williams, J. M.

1984 "A Note on Athenian Chronology, 319–317." *Hermes* 112:300–5.

Wirth, G.

1965 "Zur Grossen Schlacht des Eumenes 321 (*PSI* 1284)." *Klio* 46:283–88.

———.

1985 *Geschichte Makedoniens I: Philipp II*. Stuttgart.

Woodhead, A. G.

1981 "Athens and Demetrios Poliorketes at the End of the Fourth century B.C." In *Ancient Macedonian Studies in Honor of Charles F. Edson*, edited by H. J. Dell, pp. 357–67. Thessaloniki.

Zancan, P.

1934 *Il monarcato ellenistico nei suoi elementi federativi*. Padua.

Name Index

Place Index

Subject Index